MW00654817

汉语近义词典

A Dictionary of Chinese Synonyms

编委会

主　　编　Editor in Chief

王　还　Wang Huan

副 主 编　Deputy Editor in Chief

许德楠　Xu Denan

张　维　Zhang Wei

参编人员　Senior Editors

王　还　Wang Huan

许德楠　Xu Denan

张　维　Zhang Wei

刘京玉　Liu Jingyu

正文英译　Translators for Mainbody

王　还　Wang Huan

何昕晖　He Xinhui

例句英译　Translators for Example Sentences

于培文　Yu Peiwen

国　荣　Guo Rong

CHINESE REFERENCE SERIES FOR FOREIGNERS

外国人学汉语工具书

汉英双解

汉语近义词典

A Dictionary of Chinese Synonyms

with English Translation

王　还　主编

许德楠　张　维　副主编

(京) 新登字 157 号

图书在版编目 (CIP) 数据

汉语近义词典：汉英双解 / 王还主编.
—北京：北京语言大学出版社，2005
(外国人学汉语工具书)
ISBN 7-5619-1413-X

I. 汉 …
II. 王 …
III. 汉语—同义词—双解词典—汉 · 英
IV. H136. 2-62

中国版本图书馆 CIP 数据核字 (2005) 第 022753 号

书　　名：汉语近义词典
责任印制：汪学发

出版发行：北京语言大学出版社
社　　址：北京市海淀区学院路 15 号　邮政编码：100083
网　　址：http://www.blcup.com
电　　话：发行部　82303648/3591/3651
　　　　　编辑部　82303647
　　　　　读者服务部　82303653/3908
印　　刷：北京鑫丰华彩印有限公司
经　　销：全国新华书店

版　　次：2005 年 6 月第 1 版　2005 年 6 月第 1 次印刷
开　　本：850 毫米×1168 毫米　1/32　印张：16.875
字　　数：496 千字　印数：1-5000
书　　号：ISBN 7-5619-1413-X/H·05024
定　　价：48.00 元

总 目
Contents

前　言

本词典是供外国留学生使用的汉语学习词典；也可供对外汉语教师作为教学参考书。

本词典从对外汉语教学的需要出发，主要根据《汉语水平词汇与汉字等级大纲》8822 个常用词，选定了 420 组近义词。在分辨各组近义词的用法异同时，本词典力求做到在词义、用法、搭配等方面描述清楚，在描述中辨析。并从近义词的各组排列上，多方面予以比较，如分别辨析了“假如、如果、要是”、“如、如果”、“若、如果”，以求全面。为了使外国留学生更好地理解，注释部分和例句均有英文翻译。

本词典由北京语言大学著名教授王还主编。参编人员的分工如下：许德楠（300 条）、张维（近 90 条）写了大部分词条，刘京玉写了部分词条。定稿由张、许二人完成。最后由王还审阅。王还为注释加了英语译文，于培文等为例句加了英语译文。何昕晖做了注释部分英语译文的校对及若干补充工作。徐桂莲、赵淑梅做了电脑录入工作。

本词典的不足之处，敬请读者不吝指正。

Preface

This dictionary is compiled for the foreigners who have mastered a certain amount of the Chinese language. It can also be used as a reference for those teaching Chinese as a foreign language as well as Chinese teachers and students in college, primary schools and middle schools.

In order to meet the needs of teaching Chinese as a foreign language, we selected 420 groups of synonyms from the 8822 commonly-used words of *The Outline of Grade of Chinese Words and Characters for HSK* (*the Chinese Abbreviation for Chinese Proficiency Test*). In differentiating the different words in each group, we did our best to distinguish them in meaning, usage collocation, etc. To help foreign learners have better comprehension, all the notes and examples have English translation respectively.

Wang Huan is the editor-in-chief of this dictionary. Those who took part in the editorial work include: Xu Denan, who wrote about 300 entries; and Zhang Wei, who wrote about 90 entries; Liu Jingyu, who wrote some of the entries. Xu and Zhang finalized the manuscript while Wang Huan went over the whole manuscript and did the English translation. Yu Peiwen, Guo Rong did the English translation of the examples. He Xinhui proofread all the translation of explanations and did some necessary complementary work. Xu Guilian and Zhao Shumei did the computer input.

We hope that users will point out and correct the mistakes found in this dictionary.

凡 例

一、词条顺序,按各组近义词的第一个字的汉语拼音字母顺序。

二、正文前有“词语检索表”和“近义词检索表”两个索引。

三、词头、注释及例句部分均有英语译文。

四、各组近义词,标注词性:(名)表示名词,(动)表示动词,(形)表示形容词,(介)表示介词,其他类推。

五、词头均有汉语拼音方案注音。凡是词的,注音连写;是短语的,注音分写。

六、正文中符号用法说明:Ⓔ 代表英文释义;◪ 代表辨析;▶ 代表参见。

Guide to the Using of the Dictionary

1. The entries are arranged in the alphabetical order of the first word of each group of synonyms.
2. At the beginning of the dictionary are two indexes: Guide to Entries, Guide to Synonyms.
3. All the entries, notes and examples have English translation.
4. All the parts of speech of the synonyms are marked: nouns(n.) are marked with(名); verbs(v.) are marked with(动); adjectives(adj.) are marked with(形); prepositions(prep.) are marked with(介), and so on.
5. The words of the entries are marked with the phonetic symbols according to Phonetic System of the Chinese Language. That of a word is in connected form, and that of a structure, in separate form.
6. Symbols: English definitions are marked with Ⓔ; synonym discrimination and analysis are marked with ◪; see (used in notes) are marked with ▶.

词语检索表
Guide to Entries

E

F

G

H

J

K

L

R

S

Z

近义词检索表
Guide to Synonyms

A

B

C

D

E

F

G

H

J

K

L

M

N

O

P

Q

R

S

T

W

Z

A

哀悼 悼念 追悼

（动） （动） （动）

āidào dàoniàn zhuīdào

Ⓔ grieve over sb.'s death/ grieve over sb.'s death/ grieve over sb.'s death

◪ 这三个动词都表示对死者的怀念。"哀悼"和"悼念"更常用，可做"表示"的宾语，下面三句两个词可互换 ◇ The three verbs all mean "to think of the dead". 哀悼 and 悼念 are used more frequently and can be used exchangeably as the object of 表示：

①大家对张先生的逝世表示**哀悼**（/**悼念**）。Everybody shows deep grief over the death of Mr. Zhang.

② 母亲逝世了，儿女们都在沉痛地**悼念**（/**哀悼**）她。The mother passed away and all the children are grieving deeply for her.

③ 他在悼词中表示了对亡友的**哀悼**（/**悼念**）之情。In the memorial speech, he expressed great condolences over his deceased friend.

"追悼"更为正式，常说"追悼会" ◇ 追悼 is more formal and 追悼会, meaning memorial meeting, is commonly used.

④ 孙先生病逝，学校为他举行了**追悼会**。After Mr. Sun died of illness, the school held a memorial meeting in honor of him.

⑤ 在**追悼会**上，朋友们表示了对死者的哀思。At the memorial meeting, friends expressed their deep grief over the deceased.

在较正式的场合，三个词可通用 ◇ At a formal occasion any of the three can be used：

⑥ 在**追悼**（/**哀悼**/**悼念**）死难烈士之际，大家都表示要继承死者未竟的事业。At the moment of mourning over the martyrs, all of the people present voiced their strong will of carrying on the unaccomplished cause.

爱 喜欢

（动） （动）

ài xǐhuan

Ⓔ to love/to like

◪ **1**. 两词都可表示对人或集体有深厚感情，包括爱情、友情、亲情等。在日常生活中,用“喜欢”多一些,如:“她喜欢孩子”,而在爱情方面,用“爱”要比用“喜欢”表示的程度深一些,如:“他爱上了一个姑娘” ◇ Both words mean" to cherish a strong feeling of fondness such as love between lovers, friends, relatives". In daily life,喜欢 is used more often,e. g. 她喜欢孩子. However, when love is concerned,爱 is more often used to indicate the deep degree, e. g. 他爱上了一个姑娘.

表示对国家、群体的感情,多用“爱”,如:“爱祖国”、“爱厂如家”。有时也用“喜欢”(较随便的说法),如:“同学们,我真喜欢你们” ◇ To express one's feelings for one's country or a group 爱 is preferable, e. g. 爱祖国,爱厂如家. Sometimes 喜欢 may also be used (in a more casual way), e. g. 同学们,我真喜欢你们.

“爱”可以做主语、宾语,“喜欢”不行 ◇ 爱 can be used as the subject or object of a sentence, but 喜欢 cannot:

① 他对妻子的**爱**很真挚。His love for his wife is very sincere.

② 他不知道怎样表达自己的**爱**。He is not sure how to express his love.

2. 两词也可表示对事物有好感 The two words can also be used to show one's favorable opinion for sth.:

① 他**爱**(/**喜欢**)小动物。He loves/likes little animals.

② 她**爱**(/**喜欢**)花。She loves/likes flowers.

③ 我不**爱**(/**喜欢**)唱歌。I do not love/like singing.

3.“爱”表示爱护、珍惜、吝惜,“喜欢”一般不可以。如:“爱书”、“爱财如命” ◇ 爱 also means" to treasure, to cherish", e. g. 爱书,爱财如命, but 喜欢 has no such meaning usually.

4.“爱”可以表示时常发生(某种行为或状况)。“喜欢”不行 ◇ 爱 can be used to indicate recurring of an action, but 喜欢 has no such usage:

① 他冬天**爱**感冒。He is apt to catch cold in winter.

② 那姑娘真**爱**笑。There is always a smile on the girl's face.

③ 铁**爱**生锈。Iron rusts easily.

5. 两个词还可以表示动植物具有某种习性 ◇ The two words also imply an inclination of an animal or a plant:

① 这种花**爱**(/**喜欢**)阴凉。This kind of flower is fond of the shade.

② 老鼠**爱**(/**喜欢**)打洞。The mouse is always ready to dig holes.

A

6. 口语中的"你爱(/喜欢)去哪就去哪儿","爱"或"喜欢"表示愿意。但浓缩为"爱谁谁吧"、"爱哪儿哪儿吧"等(表示"谁都可以、哪儿都可以"等),不用"喜欢" ◇ In the very colloquial expression:你爱(/喜欢)去哪就去哪儿,爱 or 喜欢 means "to be willing". This expression can be condensed into 爱谁谁吧,爱哪儿哪儿吧 meaning "whoever will do" and "wherever will do". Here 喜欢 cannot be replaced by 爱.

另外,由于音节等原因,"爱不释手"、"爱屋及乌"等也不用"喜欢" ◇ Moreover, because of syllabic or some other reasons, 喜欢 is not used in idiomatic phrases such as 爱不释手,爱屋及乌 etc.

▶ [爱好 àihào —喜欢 xǐhuan]
[爱情 àiqíng —爱 ài]
[好 hào—爱 ài]
[喜欢 xǐhuan—喜爱 xǐ'ài]

爱戴 (动) àidài　拥护 (动) yōnghù　敬爱 (动) jìng'ài

Ⓔ love and esteem/
support/
respect and love

1. "爱戴"表示尊敬、热爱和拥护。常用于群众对上级或个体对群众。可做"受到"等的宾语 ◇ 爱戴 means "respect", "love" or "support shown by the people towards the leader or the individual towards the crowd". It can be the object of 受到:

① 老百姓**爱戴**自己的领袖。People venerate their leaders.

② 这位人民代表热心为人民服务,受到选民的**爱戴**。The representative has won the love and esteem of the constituency because of his whole-hearted serving people.

③ 得奖的演员表示:受到观众的**爱戴**,心情十分激动。The awarded actors indicated that they were very excited about audience's love and support.

例③也可换用"拥护" ◇ In example ③爱戴 can be replaced by 拥护.

2. "拥护"用法基本与"爱戴"相同,常用于群众对领导机构或领导人 ◇ The usage of 拥护 is basically the same as that of 爱戴. It is usually used to express the support of the people to their leader or leading organization.

① 大家都**拥护**老张继续当厂长。People all endorse Lao Zhang to continue to be the factory director.

② 人民**拥护**人民政府。People support the leadership of government for the people.

③ 领导干部要是不为人民服务，就得不到人民的**拥护**。The leaders cannot get the support of people if they do not serve people.

3. "敬爱"表示敬重、热爱，可用于下对上，也可用于地位平等的人们之间 ◇ 敬爱 means "respect and love". It can be used by a person or masses towards the leader or between people of equal status.

① 老校长已经在本校工作了四十年，大家都很**敬爱**他。The old schoolmaster has been working for the school for forty years, and is widely loved and respected.

② **敬爱**的老师，毕业班的同学感谢你们！ Dear teachers, the graduates are grateful to you.

③ **敬爱**的朋友，你对我的帮助我永远不会忘记。Dear friends, I'll treasure your help forever.

爱好 (动、名) àihào　喜欢 (动) xǐhuan

Ⓔ be fond of/like

1. "爱好"(动)表示对事物有好感，乐于参与，和"喜欢"有共同点，但较"喜欢"书面化一些。可用于具体事物 ◇ 爱好(v.) means "to be well disposed towards" or "to love to participate". It is very similar to 喜欢 but more formal. Both can be applied to concrete things:

① 她**爱好**(/**喜欢**)织毛衣。She is fond of knitting sweaters.

② 小李特别**爱好**(/**喜欢**)甜食。Xiao Li is very fond of sweets.

"爱好"(动)还可用于抽象事物，特别是有重大意义的，如"爱好和平"、"爱好正义"等，"喜欢"不可以这样用。"爱好科学"等则可用"喜欢" ◇ 爱好(v.) can also be applied to abstract things, especially those of great importance such as peace and justice. 喜欢 cannot be used with these words, but can be used in 爱好科学, etc.

爱好(动)不用于人，这是与"喜欢"不同的 ◇ 爱好(v.) can never be applied to human beings, which is different from 喜欢.

2. "爱好"(名)表示对某事物的浓厚兴趣，而"喜欢"没有这个用法 ◇ 爱好(n.) sometimes means "a great interest in something", but 喜欢 never has such a meaning:

① 养花是他的业余**爱好**。Growing flowers is his hobby.

② 下棋是我的一点儿**爱好**，谈不上专业。I'm only fond of pla-

A

ying chess in my spare time, but not a professional.

▶[爱 ài —喜欢 xǐhuan]
[喜欢 xǐhuan—喜爱 xǐ'ài]

爱护 保护

(动) (动)
àihù bǎohù

Ⓔ cherish, take good care of/protect

1. "爱护"表示爱惜,使不受损害,可用于物或人,重点在爱惜 ◇ 爱护 means "to cherish or to hold dear (a person or thing) from harm with the stress on holding dear":

① 游人对这些古迹都很**爱护**。Visitors all cherish these historical sites.

② 电话亭的电话用一段时间就坏了,有些人怎么这样不**爱护**公物呢? The telephones in the booth are often broken after a short time. How could people be so careless with the public property?

③ 孩子好像幼苗,社会对他们应该倍加**爱护**。The children are like seedlings, and the society should take good care of them.

2. "保护"表示照顾护卫,也可用于人或物,重点在使不受损害、破坏 ◇ 保护 means "to protect (a person or thing) with the stress on keeping safe from harm":

① 在森林公园中,这些工作人员负责**保护**游人的安全。In the forest park, these staff are responsible for the visitors' safety.

② 工厂十分注意工人的劳动**保护**问题。The factory has attached great concern to the workers' labour safety.

③ 案发后**保护**现场,有利于侦破案件。To keep intact the scene of a crime or accident is helpful for the investigation.

有时两个词可互换,但侧重点仍有不同 ◇ Sometimes the two words are interchangeable, but the stress is yet not the same:

④ 这片草地应该注意**爱护**(/**保护**)。The lawn should be taken more care of.

▶[保护 bǎohù—维护 wéihù]

爱情 爱

(名) (动)
àiqíng ài

Ⓔ love/love

"爱情"是名词,指男女之间相爱的感情,如"产生爱情"、"甜蜜的爱情"等,例如 ◇ 爱情 is a noun meaning the love between a man and a woman, e.g. 产生爱

A

情，甜蜜的爱情，etc. Some other examples are：

① 我们不赞成没有**爱情**的婚姻。We are against the marriage without love.

② 他俩有了**爱情**关系。They fell in love with each other.

“爱”是动词，用法较多。“爱”做主语、宾语，往往与“爱情”的意思接近。例①可换用“爱”。“爱情”多与非单音节词语搭配，如“爱情故事”、“爱情关系”（例②）。下例“爱情”与“爱”也可互换 ◇ 爱 is a verb, with several meanings. 爱 as the subject or object of a sentence is often the same as 爱情. In example ①, 爱情 can be replaced by 爱. 爱情 mostly goes with polysyllabic words, e. g. 爱情故事，爱情关系（example ②）. 爱情 and 爱 in the following example are also interchangeable：

③ 他们的**爱情**（/**爱**）是真诚的。The love between them is sincere.

有时，“爱”与“爱情”的语义深度不同 ◇ Sometimes the semantic depth of 爱 and 爱情 is different.

④ 这只是一时的**爱**，不是真正的**爱情**。This is only a moment's impulse, not the real love.

至于“爱”的主要用法（做谓语），与“爱情”是不同的 ◇ The main usage of 爱（as the predicate of a sentence）is different from that of 爱情.

▶［爱 ài—喜欢 xǐhuan］
［好 hào—爱 ài］

安定 稳定

（形、动） （形、动）
āndìng wěndìng

Ⓔ peaceful, to calm down/ stable, to stabilize

◪ **1**.“安定”（形）表示情绪、生活、社会、秩序等正常、平静 ◇ 安定（adj.）means（mood, life, society, order, etc.）" be normal and peaceful"：

① 在毕业考试之前，她的情绪有点儿不**安定**。Before the graduation examination, she is a little nervous.

② 吃了药，病人比较**安定**了。After taking medicine, the patient calmed down.

③ 老人半生颠沛流离，晚年终于过上了**安定**的日子。The old man could finally live a peaceful life after a half life's wondering about in a desperate plight.

④ 多年来，这里社会**安定**，秩序井然。The society here has been stable and orderly for many years.

“安定”（动）表示使安定，可带宾语 ◇ 安定（v.）means" to make something normal and peaceful" and usually takes an object:

⑤ 校长的讲话**安定**了毕业生的情绪。The speech of the president reassured the graduates.

⑥ 洪水到来,干部们一方面带领大家救灾,一方面做了大量思想工作安定人心。Faced with floods, the leaders have led the people to fight against the disaster on the one hand, and done a lot of ideological work to reassure them on the other hand.

2.“稳定”(动)也可表示情绪、生活、社会、秩序等正常平静,与“安定”相似,以上“安定”的例①~④都可以换用“稳定”。但“安定”侧重于内向、内心,“稳定”侧重于外部表现 ◇ 稳定(v.) is similar to 安定. In the above examples ①~④安定 can be replaced with 稳定, but 安定 stresses the inner condition, while 稳定 stresses the outward expression.

另外,“稳定”(形)还表示水位、价值、病情、物价、疗效等的平衡 ◇ Besides, 稳定 (adj.) also means the stability of water level, value, illness, price, curative effect, etc.:

① 洪峰过去了,水位趋于**稳定**。The flood peak has passed and the water level has gradually become stable.

② 今年本市的物价**稳定**。Prices in this city remain stable this year.

③ 她的血压一直很**稳定**。Her blood pressure has been stable all the time.

④ 最近老人的病情比较**稳定**。Recently the condition of the old man's illness is comparatively stable.

“安定”没有这些用法 ◇ 安定 cannot be used in such ways.

“稳定”(动)表示使稳定,可带宾语。“安定”(动)的例⑤⑥也可换用“稳定” ◇ 稳定(v.) means "to be stable" or "to stabilize" and can take an object. In examples ⑤ and ⑥ 安定 can be replaced with 稳定.

⑤ 我们要**稳定**教师队伍。We must stabilize the teaching staff.

⑥ 为了**稳定**物价,采取了一些措施。In order to stabilize the prices, some measures have been taken.

安静 清静

(形) (形)

ānjìng qīngjìng

Ⓔ quiet, peaceful/
quiet, secluded

1. 这两个词都表示环境中没

有嘈杂的声音、没有干扰等 ◇ Both words mean " an absence of noise or disturbance":

① 他想找个**安静**(/**清静**)的地方写作。He wants to look for a quiet place to write.

② 这个地方在闹市区,太不**安静**(/**清静**)了。Located in the downtown, the place is too noisy.

也可指无打扰的(生活) They can also mean "a quiet life":

③ 老人**清静**(/**安静**)日子过惯了,客人太多他嫌吵。The old man is used to the quiet and peaceful life, and would be annoyed if there are many guests.

④ 她喜欢一个人**安安静静**(/**清清静静**)地生活。She likes to live a peaceful life all by herself.

2. "安静"可以指人的性格喜静不喜动等;"清静"没有这个意思 ◇ 安静 can also mean" a quiet disposition", while 清静 cannot:

① 这孩子很**安静**,半天听不见他说一句话。The child is very quiet. You cannot hear him say even one sentence for half a day.

② 她想找个性情**安静**的人做伴侣。She wants to find a quiet person as her companion.

3. "安静"还可以指睡得平静、安稳;"清静"不能 ◇ 安静 can also be applied to a quiet slumber, but 清静 cannot:

① 老人睡得很**安静**。The old man is sleeping soundly.

② 那孩子睡得一点儿也不**安静**,被子都掀开了。The kid is by no means sleeping soundly. Even the quilt has been kicked away.

这两个词都可以重叠(AABB/ABAB)。如1的例④。再如 ◇ Both words can be reduplicated (AABB/ABAB) as in example ④, point 1 and the following example:

③ 别吵了,让我们**安静安静**(/**清静清静**)吧! Don't make any noise! Please give us some quiet time.

安排 (动) ānpái　安置 (动) ānzhì

Ⓔ set or arrange (the staff)/ set or arrange (the staff)

1. 这两个词都有恰当地处理人员的意思,"安排"侧重于有先后秩序、轻重缓急,"安置"侧重于有着落 ◇ Both words mean" to set or arrange the staff properly". 安排 stresses the order of importance and urgency, while 安置 stresses whereabouts:

① 领导**安排**小王做资料工作。The leader assigns Xiao Wang to do the job of sorting out the data.

② 这些复员军人的**安置**工作已经完成。The arrangements of the demobilized soldiers have been completed.

有时两个词可以兼容 ◇ Sometimes the two are interchangeable:

③ 请你**安排**(/**安置**)一下他们的工作。Would you please make an arrangement of their job?

但词意仍有些侧重。如不强调着落,一般仍用"安排" ◇ However, there is a nuance in stress. If whereabouts is not stressed, 安排 is usually used.

2. 两个词还有合理地处理事物的意思,这时多用"安排";少数情况下可用"安置",多与人事有关 ◇ Both words mean "to handle or deal with something reasonably";in this case, 安排 is usually preferable; 安置 can be used in some cases, mostly concerning personnel matters:

① 父亲母亲正在帮助她**安排**婚事。Father and mother are helping her arrange her marriage ceremony.

② 明天的活动都**安排**好了吗? Is everything arranged properly for tomorrow's activities?

③ 移民的住处已经**安置**好了。The lodging of the immigrants has been properly settled.

以上例③可换用"安排"。用"安置"仍强调落实 ◇ In example ③ 安排 can be used instead. If 安置 is used, the stress is on putting into effect.

3. "安排"还有规划、改造的意思;"安置"没有这个意思 ◇ 安排 also means to make a long-term program or reform; 安置 does not mean that:

① 公司正在**安排**厂房的改建问题。The company is planning the rebuilding of the factory workshop.

② 区里已经对明年的绿化工作做了**安排**。The District has arranged the greening work of the next year.

4. "安置"有放置好东西的意思,"安排"没有这个意思 ◇ 安置 sometimes means " to lay up things";安排 does not mean that:

① 那批货物已经**安置**好了。The goods have been properly arranged.

② 请**安置**一下行李,然后去用餐。Please put the luggage in the right place and then go and have something to eat.

例①如换用"安排",就没有放置的意思,而是安排出路或销售渠

道等 ◇ If 安排 is used instead in example ①, it will not mean "to lay up", but "to find a sales market".

下面的情况比较特殊 ◇ The following usage is rather different:

③ 我把他**安排**(/**安置**)在老张的左右。I assigned him to be in close attendance on Lao Zhang.

既可指一般的人事处理,也可指把自己的人放在必要的地方。这时用"安排"或"安置"都是可以的 ◇ Both 安排 and 安置 can be used to mean "transfer of personnel, or placing one's trusted follower in a post".

两个词还可以做四字语中的中心语,如 ◇ These two words can make up many four-character phrases, for example:

人事安排 personnel arrangement
住宿安排 accommodation arrangement
人员安置 personnel allocation
移民安置 immigrant settlement

安全 (形、名) ānquán　稳妥 (形) wěntuǒ

Ⓔ no danger or mishap/ no danger or mishap

◪ 这两个词都有无危险、无意外的意思。"安全"一般涉及较大的事,"稳妥"涉及的是较具体的事。同时,前者侧重于客观上不出事故,后者侧重于主观上无纰漏,有时还可表示人的性格倾向等 ◇ Both words mean "no danger or mishap". 安全 concerns with more important business, while 稳妥 is applied to concrete affairs. The former stresses no mishap objectively and the latter stresses not making a slip subjectively. 稳妥 may also describe a person's disposition.

1. 安全

① 工地上的劳动保护措施很到位,基本上做到了**安全**生产。The working safeguard on the construction site is quite good, basically up to the standards of safe production.

② 大会期间,警方全力出动,以保证与会人士的**安全**。During the conference, the policeman went all out to ensure the security of the participants.

③ 母亲已经**安全**到达广州。Mother has arrived in Guang-Zhou safely.

④ 开车要注意交通**安全**。Be careful when you drive./When driving, pay attention to the traffic./Drive safely.

例②④"安全"是名词 ◇ In examples ② and ④, 安全 is a noun.

2. 稳妥

①这件事情要处理得**稳妥**些，使各方都没意见。The matter should be handled soundly so that each party will be satisfied with it.

② 为了**稳妥**，他寄的是挂号信。He had the letter registered for safety.

③ 小王办事**稳妥**，让他负责这项工作，大家都放心。Xiao Wang is reliable. If he is trusted to be in charge of the work, everyone would be at ease.

有时两个词可以互换，但侧重点有所不同 ◇ Sometimes the two words are interchangeable, yet with different stresses：

④ 让十三岁的孩子一个人出远门，是不**安全**（/**稳妥**）的。It is unsafe for a thirteen-year-old child to go on a long journey alone.

⑤ 为了**安全**（/**稳妥**）起见，门上加了两把锁。Two locks have been put on the door for the sake of safety.

安装 装配

（动） （动）

ānzhuāng zhuāngpèi

Ⓔ install/assemble

◪ "安装"是把机器、器材、设备等固定在合适的位置上；"装配"则是把零件、部件组装成整机 ◇ 安装 means "to install" and 装配 means "to assemble".

下面三句用"安装"，不能用"装配" ◇ In the following three sentences, 安装 is used and cannot be replaced by 装配：

① 他家新买的空调，已经**安装**好了。His newly-bought air-conditioner has been installed.

② 这个商厦**安装**了报警器。The warning system has been installed in the shopping center.

③ 新房子刚建成，还没有**安装**门铃。The bell has not been installed, for the house has just been completed.

下面两句，只能用"装配" ◇ In the two sentences below, only 装配 can be used：

④ 工人们已经把这些零部件**装配**到机器上了。The workers have fit these spare parts to the machine.

⑤ 他在这家工厂的**装配**车间工作。He works in the assembling workshop of this factory.

但一些较复杂、大型的装置，既有安装也有装配的问题，两个词有时可换用 ◇ But when talking about complicated equipment of a large scale which involves both installment and assembling, the two are interchangeable sometimes：

⑥ 发电机组还没有**安装**（/**装配**）

A

好。The generating set hasn't been assembled/installed.

⑦ 这些机器设备正在**安装**(/**装配**)中。The equipment is being assembled/installed.

按　按照　依照

(介、动)　(介)　(介)

àn　ànzhào　yīzhào

Ⓔ according to/
according to/
according to

◥ 这三个词都是介词。其中"按"还是动词,表示用手或手指压("按电铃")、抑制("按不住心头的怒火")、加按语("编者按")等,这些与介词意义相差较远,这里不谈。现在主要谈三个介词的异同 ◇ These three words are all prepositions. Among them 按 is also used as a verb, meaning "to press with a hand or a finger" (e. g. to press the electric bell), "to restrain" (e. g. can't restrain one's anger)," according to the note" (e. g. editor's note) etc. , all of which have little to do with the connotation of 按 as a preposition. Here we only discuss the meaning of the three as prepositions.

三个介词都表示以某一事物作为言论行为的凭借、根据。有时可以互换 ◇ All the three mean "to take something as evidence or basis", and sometimes are interchangeable.

① **按**(/**按照**/**依照**)经理的指示,这事应该这样办。According to the instruction from the manager, the matter should be handled this way.

② 他没有**按**(/**按照**/**依照**)规定纳税,被罚了款。He is fined because he didn't pay taxes according to the requirements.

以上两句,虽可互换,"按"和"按照"侧重凭某条件(办事),"依照"侧重有根据,更为正式和书面化 ◇ Although the three words are interchangeable in the two examples, 按 and 按照 stress doing something under certain condition while 依照 stresses that an action is not groundless and the statement is more formal and literary.

下面这种口语中表示一般凭借条件的,一般用"按",有时可用"按照" ◇ In the following more colloquial speech, 按 is usually used to mean " under certain condition". 按照 can also be used in some cases:

③ 请**按**次序上车。Please get on the bus in turn.

④ **按**(/**按照**)我的意见,我们应该明天早上出发。In my opinion, we should set off tomorrow morning.

“按”还常说“按着”、“按……说”、“按……讲”◇按 is often replaced by 按着，按……说，按……讲：

⑤ 他**按着**(/**按照**)名片上的地址，找到了张先生的家。He found Mr. Zhang's house by the address on the visiting card.

⑥ **按**道理说，今天应该我们宴请你们。Of course, we should have held a banquet in honor of you.

“按”还可加人称代词再加“说”或“讲”◇A personal pronoun can be inserted before 说 or 讲：

⑦ **按我说**，应该给他报酬。In my view, he should be paid.

⑧ 张先生，**按你这么讲**，我们都错了。Mr. Zhang, in your opinion, we are all wrong.

“按”可以与单音节词搭配，如“按日计算”、“按月发给”、“按人分配”、“按质论价”等，“按照”、“依照”不可以◇按 can be used with monosyllabic words but 按照 and 依照 cannot, e. g. 按日计算(Counting daily)，按月发给(paying monthly)，按人分配(distributing according to the number of people)，按质论价(fixing the price according to quality)，etc.

“依照”由于强调根据性，有照办的意思，下面涉及法律的句子一般用“依照”◇Since 依照 stresses act in accordance with rules and regulations, it is usually used in sentences relating to law, as follows：

⑨ **依照**交通法规第五条，这种行为应该处以罚款。According to the Fifth Clause of the Traffic Regulations, this act should be fined.

⑩ 这件事必须**依照**法律规定予以解决。This matter should be solved according to the law.

暗暗（副）ànàn　偷偷（副）tōutōu

Ⓔ stealthily/stealthily

◪ 这两个词都是副词，经常修饰动词，都可以加“地”◇Both words are adverbs qualifying verbs and can take 地 after them.

1.“偷偷”的意思是背着他人，不使人觉察，侧重于具体行为。可以用于贬义或非贬义◇偷偷 means "stealthily", with the stress on specific behaviour with or without a derogatory sense. e. g.：

① 他**偷偷**地把东西卖了。He has sold it stealthily.

② 他背着父母**偷偷**地离开了家。He left home secretly with his parents unaware.

2.“暗暗”也有不使人觉察的意思，多指心理状态，不表现在语

A

言或行动上 ◇ 暗暗 also means "stealthily", with the stress on one's psychology rather than on actual words or behaviour.

① 他**暗暗**下了决心，一定要学好汉语。He inwardly made up his mind to learn Chinese well.

② 看到那家伙受到报复，他**暗暗**在心里发笑。He laughed up his sleeve at the fellow's being revenged.

但当行为的过程较长，处于具体或抽象的模糊状态时，"偷偷"、"暗暗"有时都可以用 ◇ When the actual action lasts rather long and is hard to tell whether it is concrete or abstract, either 偷偷 or 暗暗 can be used:

③ 她早就**暗暗**（/**偷偷**）地把信息资料转移出去了。She has transferred the information out secretively at an earlier date.

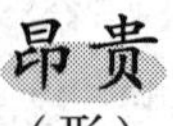

（形）

ánggui

（形）

guì

Ⓔ expensive, costly/
expensive, costly

◪ 这两个形容词都可表示价格、价值高。前者较书面化，并可用于抽象意义，后者较口语化 ◇ Both adjectives mean "high price or high value". The former is more literary and can be used in an abstract sense, whereas the latter is more colloquial:

1. 用于一般商品时，因为"昂贵"是双音节词，可直接与"价格"等搭配，"贵"则常加"很"等 ◇ When applied to merchandise, 昂贵, being a disyllabic word, can collocate with 价格 while 贵 usually takes 很:

① 这种毛皮价格**昂贵**。This kind of fur is very expensive.

② 这种毛皮价格很**贵**。This kind of fur is dear/costly.

注意：在"比"字句中，不能出现"很" ◇ Note: In a sentence with the word 比, 很 cannot be used:

③ 这种牌子的商品比那种**昂贵**（/**贵**）得多。This brand of merchandise is much more expensive/costly than that one.

"昂贵"常用于贵重物品，如"昂贵的首饰"、"那幅画十分昂贵"等。"贵"则可用于多种物品 ◇ 昂贵 is often applied to valuables, e. g. 昂贵的首饰(expensive jewellery), 那幅画十分昂贵(The painting is costly) etc., while 贵 is applied to all sorts of things.

2. 用于抽象意义时，常用"昂贵" ◇ 昂贵 is usually used in an abstract meaning:

④ 探索适合本国经济发展的道路，我们付出了**昂贵**的代价。

We are at such a cost in exploring the ways suitable for the economic development of our country.

3. “贵”还有其他一些义项，如表示可贵：“人贵有自知之明。”表示值得提倡和重视：“学习外语，贵在坚持。”用于敬辞：“您贵姓？”“我曾到过贵国。” ◇ 贵 also has several other meanings and usages, e. g. " to be commendable" : It is a good thing for one to be able to have a proper appraisal of oneself; " to be highly valued" : To learn a foreign language, perseverance is important; " to be used as a term of respect" : May I ask your honourable name, please? I've been to your honourable country.

B

B

拔 抽 拉

(动) (动) (动)
bá chōu lā

Ⓔ pull up/
pull out (from in between)/
pull, draw

◪ 这三个动词都有向外或向某一方向取物的意思 ◇ These three verbs all mean "to pull sth. out or toward a certain direction".

1. 拔

表示使物从固定处或隐藏处取出,有时需一定力度 ◇ 拔 means "to pull up sth. fixed or hidden, usually with force":

① 她正在后院**拔**草。She is weeding in the back yard.

② 强盗从腰间**拔**出刀来威胁他。The robber drew his sword from behind his waist and threatened him.

③ 用钳子把墙上的钉子**拔**下来。Please pull out the nails in the wall with the plier.

2. 抽

表示从固定处或较密集的同类物或排列物中取出 ◇ 抽 means "to pull out something from a pack":

① 他从书架上的一排书中**抽**出一本。He took out one from the books on the shelf.

② 老王从信封中**抽**出信,仔细地看了起来。Lao Wang took out the letter from the envelope and began to read carefully.

③ 他运气不错,**抽**了个二等奖。He luckily drew a second prize.

④ 口试的先后次序由**抽**签决定。The turns for oral test will be decided by lots.

"拔"和"抽"有时可互换,如1"拔"的例②,也可换用"抽"。再如 ◇ 拔 and 抽 are sometimes interchangeable as in example ② of entry 1 拔, 抽 can replace 拔, also in the following example:

⑤ 运动员**抽**(/**拔**)出一支箭,搭在弓上。The athlete drew an arrow and put it over the bow.

"抽"有时可表示抽象意义的选取 ◇ 抽 also mean "to select in an abstract sense":

⑥ 从我们组**抽**出两个人,支援他们。Two persons of our team will be assigned to help them.

3. 拉

表示用力使事物或人向自己方

向(或随同自身)移动 ◇ 拉 means "to pull something or somebody towards or with oneself":

① 他**拉**开抽屉,拿出一些钱。He drew the drawer and took out some money.

② 台子太高了,小王爬不上去,大家一起使劲把他**拉**了上去。The platform was too high for Xiao Wang to get on, and we worked in concert to drag him onto it.

③ 他从屋角**拉**过一把椅子来。He pulled over a chair from the corner of the room.

例③也可用"抽",但意思有所不同 ◇ 抽 can also be used in example ③, but with a little difference:

④ 他从屋角(几把椅子中)**抽**过一把椅子来。He pulled over one of the chairs from the corner of the room.

三个词还有许多不同的义项,如"拔毒"(吸出毒来)、"抽烟"(吸进或呼出烟)、"拉车"(拉动车辆)、"拉小提琴"(牵动琴弦)等,彼此无共同点 ◇ Each of the three words also has different meanings, e.g. 拔毒 (draw out pus), 抽烟 (inhale or puff out), 拉车 (pull a cart), 拉小提琴 (pluck the strings of a musical instrument), etc.

爸爸 (名) bàba　　父亲 (名) fùqin

Ⓔ papa, father/father

两个词都指有子女的男子。前者口语化,后者较书面化和正式 ◇ Both words mean "a man with a child or children". The former is colloquial and the latter is literary and formal.

"爸爸"常用于称呼 ◇ 爸爸 is usually used as a form of address:

① **爸爸**,我五点钟放学,您来接我吧。Dad, could you pick me up when school is over at five?

"父亲"因较正式,一般不用于称呼。但在很正统的家庭或书信中也可用于称呼 ◇ 父亲 is more formal and so not used in address but can be so used in letters or a very traditional family:

② 父亲:见信如面。近来您身体还好吧? Dear Father: Reading the letter as if you were seeing me. I hope everything goes well with your health.

用于非直接称呼外,两个词都可以,但语体色彩不同 ◇ When referring to father, either can be used, but with different stylistic value:

③ 这是我**爸爸**(/**父亲**)。This is my dad/father.

④ 这家三口人：**爸爸**(/**父亲**)、妈妈(/母亲)，还有孩子。There are three members in the family: dad/father, mum/mother and the child.

另外，说别人的家长时，用"父亲"较为尊敬 ◇ When referring to another person's father, 父亲 shows more respect:

⑤ 你**父亲**在哪儿工作？Where does your father work?

⑥ 他**父亲**是我们学校的著名教授。His father is a famous professor in our college.

用"爸爸"也可以，较为随便 ◇ 爸爸 can also be used but sounds more casual.

白 (副) bái　　**白白** (副) báibái

Ⓔ in vain; for nothing/ in vain; for nothing

◥ 这里辨析作为副词的"白"和"白白"的异同 ◇ Following is the differentiation between adverbs 白 and 白白.

A. "白"有三个义项，一般与单音节动词搭配或与单音节动词+补语、助词、宾语等搭配，都不能加"地" ◇ 白 has three meanings and is generally used with monosyllabic verbs or monosyllabic verbs with auxiliary word, complement or object. 地 could not be added in any case:

1. 表示(行为、动作)没有取得应有的效果、没有达到预期的目的或没有得到应得的报酬 ◇ Indicating that an action or behaviour did not get any effect, reach any aim, or receive any due reward:

① 事情没办成，他**白**去了一趟。He failed to make the thing settled and made a fruitless trip.

② 大家没**白**受累，展览会办得很不错。The successful exhibition didn't make our efforts in vain.

③ **白**干了几天，人家也没给报酬。We worked in vain for several days. They did not pay us.

2. 表示不付代价而得到好处 ◇ Meaning "to gain benefit for nothing":

① 旅馆不会让人**白**住。The hotel would not allow guests to stay without charge.

② 他不愿意**白**吃**白**喝，所以问能为对方干些什么活儿。He was unwilling to stay in the house at the host's expenses, so he asked if there was any work he could do for the host.

③ 这束花是花店主人**白**送的，不

要钱。The bouquet of flowers given by the florist was free of charge.

3. 表示(做坏事)而不受惩罚或处置 ◇ Indicating the sense " to do a bad thing without being punished" :

① 他打了人就**白**打了吗? 不行,一定要告他! Can he batter others without being punished? Definitely not. He should be accused.

② 谁也不能**白**拿公家的东西。Nobody can take public property home without pay.

B. "白白"没有"白"2 的用法,而与"白"1、3 有共同点,但在音节上要求与双音节以上的多音节词语搭配。"白白"可加"地" ◇ 白白 cannot be used as in entry 2 of 白, but it's the same as 白 used in the cases of entries 1and 3, but must be used to modify disyllabic or polysyllabic words or phrases. 白白 can take 地 after it:

1. 意思上同"白"1 ◇ The meaning is the same as that of 白 in entry 1:

① 这件事你就是告诉他,也是**白白**增加他的烦恼。Even if you tell him about, it can do nothing good but add to his worry.

② 他最后没有参加考试,**白白**交了报名费。His registration fee was in vain for he did not take the examination.

③ 因为火车误点,她在车站**白白**地耽误了两个小时。She wasted two hours in vain at the railway station because of the delayed train.

2. 意思上同"白"3 ◇ The meaning is the same as that of 白 in entry 3:

① 不能让他们**白白**砍伐国家森林而不受任何惩处。They cannot get away with felling the forest of our country.

② 怎么能**白白**地受冤枉? 得找他评评理。How could you be wronged without any reason? You must reason things out with him.

比较一下即可看出:可说"白吃",不能说"白白吃",或"白白吃了",必须说"白白吃了人家的东西"、"白白喝了人家的酒"、"白白赔上两天时间"等。"白白"后面起码是单音节动词+助词或补语+宾语等组成的短语 ◇ It is obvious that one can say 白吃, but not 白白吃, or 白白吃了. Yet one may say 白白吃了人家的东西, 白白喝了人家的酒, 白白赔上两天时间 etc. What follows 白白 must at least be a monosyllabic verb plus auxiliary word or complement plus object, etc. to form a phrase.

B

摆 搁 放

(动) (动) (动)
bǎi gē fàng

Ⓔ place, put/
place, put/
place, put

1. 这三个词都有(把东西)置于(某处)的意思。"摆"侧重于陈列、排列,"搁"在中国北方较通用、口语化,有时含"留置"的意思。"放"书面、口语都可以用 ◇ All the three words mean "to place sth. at a certain place". 摆 stresses display, 搁 is comparatively colloquial and more popular in the north of China and 放 is both colloquial and literary.

① 她把两盆花**摆**在窗前。She placed two pot flowers in front of the window.

② 架子上**摆**了一些工艺品。Some handicrafts are displayed on the shelf.

例①②用"摆"最合适,因为花盆、工艺品是排列或陈列的。但如不强调排列或陈列,用"搁"或"放"也可以 ◇ In these two examples 摆 is most appropriate because potted flowers and handicrafts are specially for display. If the sense of display is not stressed, 搁 and 放 will also do.

③ 新买的沙发**放**(/**搁**/**摆**)在哪儿? Where should we put the newly-bought sofa?

例③如强调排列,可用"摆";否则,也可用"放"或"搁" ◇ If the meaning of display in ③ is stressed, 摆 can be used, otherwise 放 or 搁 will also do.

④ 这些钱先**搁**(/**放**)在银行吧,用时再取。You can deposit the money in the bank and withdraw it when needed.

例④用"搁"较合适,因为有"留置"的意思,用"放"也可以。用"摆"不行,因为句中没有陈列、排列的意思 ◇ In example ④ 搁 will also do and is more appropriate because it means " to lay aside". 放 will also do. 摆 will not do because the sense of display is not meant in the sentence.

⑤ 鱼炸好了,先**放一放**,稍凉一些再吃。After the fish is fried, cool it for a while, and then serve it.

例⑤用"搁"也可以,更口语化。用"摆"不行,理由同例④ ◇ In example ⑤ 搁 will also do and is more colloquial. 摆 will not do, for the same reason as in example ④.

2. "搁"还有"搁置"的意思 ◇ 搁 also means "to put aside":

① 这个问题不忙,**搁**几天再说吧。The problem is not pressing now. You may put it aside for several days.

② 那个报告**搁**在他那儿好多天了。The report has been left to him for quite a few days.

例①②用"放"也可以,但用"摆"不行 ◇ In examples ① and ② 放 will also do, but 摆 will not do.

3. "搁"和"放"还有"添加"的意思 ◇ 搁 and 放 also mean "to add to", e. g.:

① 汤里要**放**(/**搁**)些胡椒。You'd better put some pepper into the soup.

②你喝咖啡**放**(/**搁**)糖不**放**(/**搁**)? What coffee would you prefer: with sugar or not?

摆动　摇摆　摇晃

(动)　(动)　(动)

bǎidòng yáobǎi yáohuàng

Ⓔ swing, sway/
swing, sway, rock/
rock, sway, shake

◣ "摆动"、"摇摆"、"摇晃"这三个动词都可表示物体来回晃动,但有所不同 ◇ The three verbs 摆动, 摇摆, 摇晃 all mean "to swing", but they are not identical.

1. 摆动

"摆动"有时比"摇晃"来回晃动的幅度略大,常用于具体的东西,可带宾语 ◇ 摆动 sometimes involves a bigger range in sway and is often applied to concrete things. It can take an object.

① 路很不平,她在车中也随着车身**摆动**起来。The road was uneven, and she rocked with the cart.

② 嫩绿色的柳枝在晨风中**摆动**。The light green willow twigs are swaying in the morning wind.

③ 她**摆动**双手,向送行的人告别。With her hand waving, she said good-bye to the seeing-off people.

例①②可换用"摇晃"或"摇摆"。"摆动"不能重叠 ◇ In examples ①② 摇晃 or 摇摆 can be used instead. 摆动 can not be reduplicated.

2. 摇摆

"摇摆"用于具体的物,也用于"立场"、"政策"等抽象事物;另外在带宾语(如"手"、"脑袋")时还含有不同意的意味 ◇ 摇摆 is applied to concrete things, and also to abstract things such as "stance", "policy", etc. When it takes an object (such as "hand", "head") it implies disagreement.

① 小狗**摇摆**着尾巴。The little dog wagged its tail.

② 姐姐向弟弟要画册,弟弟竟**摇**

B

摆着小手，说不。The sister asked her younger brother to give her the picture book, but he waved his little hands saying no.

③ 这位领导，在执行上级政策时，不是左就是右，总有些**摇摆**。When carrying out policies from above the leader was not always implementing them accurately.

以上例①可换用"摇晃"或"摆动" ◇ In example ①摇晃 or 摆动 can be used instead.

"摇摆"可重叠，但带宾语时不能重叠。例③可重叠为"……总有些摇摇摆摆" ◇ 摇摆 can be reduplicated, but cannot when it has an object. ③ can be reduplicated into ……总有些摇摇摆摆.

3. 摇晃

"摇晃"多用于具体事物，可重叠，可带宾语 ◇ 摇晃 is usually applied to concrete things; it can be reduplicated, and can take an object:

① 灯笼在风中**摇晃**着，灯光也隐隐约约的。The lantern swung and flickered in the wind.

② 小王**摇晃**着帽子向车外送行的父母说再见。Xiao Wang waved his hat to say goodbye to his parents, who were standing outside the train seeing him off.

③ 小船**摇摇晃晃**的，他有点儿晕。The boat was rocking and he felt a little sick.

"摇晃"有时指人摇动（某物），使其来回晃动，如例②，再如 ◇ 摇晃 sometimes means " to wave sth. in one's hand" , as in example ② and the following sentences:

④ 别**摇晃**桌子，我在写字呢。Don't shake the table. I'm writing.

⑤ 小树刚种上，总**摇晃**它，就会死。The tree was newly planted. It may die if you always shake it.

⑥ 这种药，服用前先要**摇晃**一下。You'd better shake the bottle of medicine before taking.

以上用法，不能用"摆动"、"摇摆"替换 ◇ In examples ④⑤ and ⑥摆动 or 摇摆 cannot replace 摇晃.

拜访 拜会

（动） （动）

bàifǎng bàihuì

Ⓔ pay a visit, call on/
pay an official call, call on

◥ 这两个词都是动词。"拜访"表示访问师友、亲朋，"拜会"表示会见、访问官场或外交界的官员。都含有正式、客气、谦敬的意思 ◇ Both words are verbs. 拜访 is used " to mean a visit to one's teachers or relatives"; while 拜会 means "a visit to an official or diplomat". Both words imply formality and respect:

① 他这次回国,**拜访**了几位大学时期的老师。He visited some of his university teachers on his return home.

② 这次来中国参展,我们想顺便**拜访**一下贵公司。We would like to visit your honorable company during the exhibition in China.

③ 中国外交部长**拜会**了该国政府首脑。The foreign minister of China paid an official call to the head of that country.

④ 新任校长到市教育局**拜会**了各位领导。The new headmaster paid an official visit to the leaders of the city bureau of education.

搬 (动) bān　　**搬运** (动) bānyùn

Ⓔ move, take away/carry, transport

"搬"、"搬运"这两个动词都表示移动物体。"搬"表示移动较大、较重的物体,但移动的距离一般较短,较口语化,常用于日常生活 ◇ Both 搬 and 搬运 mean " to move sth. ". 搬 means "to move rather big and heavy things but only for a short distance". It is colloquial and often used in daily life:

① 他俩把衣柜**搬**到东面靠墙的地方。They two moved the wardrobe to near the eastern wall.

② 椅子不够用了,你再**搬**几把来。The chairs are not sufficient. Go and carry several more chairs here.

③ 这张桌子太重,两个孩子**搬**不动。The table is too heavy for the two kids to move.

"搬运"则多指移动成批的物体,距离也较长,多使用车辆 ◇ 搬运 means " to move batches of things for a long distance and usually with a vehicle":

④ 工人把货物**搬运**到仓库。The workers carried the goods to the warehouse.

⑤ 他是火车站的**搬运**工人。He works as a porter in the railway station.

⑥ 这家**搬运**公司,工作很负责,收费也比较合理。The people in this transportation company are responsible and their charge is reasonable as well.

另外,"搬"还有迁移家庭住址和其他的比喻意义(例如把文学作品变为影视等表演形式或套用别人的

B

理论、经验、语言等),“搬运”没有这些用法 ◇ Besides,搬 also means "to move (house) and can be used metaphorically" (such as to turn a literary work into a movie, or copy indiscriminately the theory, experience and language of others, etc.). 搬运 has no such usage:

⑦ 他家**搬**到西城去了。He has moved to the western part of the city.

⑧ 他把这本小说**搬**上了银幕。He has adapted the novel into a movie.

⑨ 外国的经验我们不能照**搬**。We cannot copy the experience of other countries.

▶[搬 bān—抬 tái]

搬 (动) bān　抬 (动) tái

Ⓔ move/lift up, raise

◪“搬”、“抬”这两个动词都表示移动物体,物体多是较大或较重的。“搬”可用于一个人或几个人用手移物,“抬”多用于两个或两个以上的人移物,而且可用手或肩,移物时离开地面的高度也较大。以下例①用“搬”;例②两个词均可用;例③④因属于几个人移动物体及“抬轿子”是习惯搭配,用“抬” ◇ Both 搬 and 抬 are verbs meaning " to move sth. that is rather big and heavy". 搬 is applied to one person or several people using hands to move sth.,抬 is applied to two or more people moving sth. with hands or shoulder and when moving, the thing is rather high above the ground. In example ① below,搬 is used; in example ② either word will do; in examples ③ and ④,抬 is used since the action involves several people and 抬轿子 is idiomatic expression:

① 他**搬**了一把椅子过来。He shifted a chair over.

② 小李和小王把柜子**搬**(/**抬**)到了外屋。Xiao Wang and Xiao Li shifted the cupboard into the outer room.

③ 几个医生**抬**着担架把病人送上了救护车。Several soldiers carried the wounded on the stretcher to the ambulance.

④ 过去结婚,新娘是要用轿子**抬**到丈夫家的。On the wedding day in the past, the bribe would be carried to her husband's home in a bridal sedan chair.

“抬”还可表示手、脚、头等高举 ◇ 抬 can also mean " to raise one's head, hand, foot":

① 他**抬**起头来,看了看天上。He raised his head and looked into the sky.

B

② 请**抬**一下脚，你踩到了我了。Please lift up your foot. You step on me.

“搬”还可表示家庭的迁移及抽象意义 ◇ 搬 also means " to move one's house" and some abstract meaning.

▶[搬 bān —搬运 bānyùn]

办事　做事
bàn shì　zuò shì

Ⓔ handle affairs, work/ handle affairs, do a deed, work

1. “办事”和“做事”都是动宾词组。“办事”连用时，多表示从事公务或较大的事，如机关的名称“陕西省驻北京办事处”、“某某办事机构” ◇ Both 办事 and 做事 are verb-object phrases. 办事 is applied to an official business, e. g. in the title of an office; such as "the agency of Shaanxi Province in Beijing", "the working body of this and that", also:

① 他到北京是来**办事**的，忙得很。He came to Beijing on a business and had a lot of things to do.

② 他**办事**公道，大家都信得过他。He is fair and square in what he does. We all have confidence in him. We all trust him.

③ 他**办事**能力很强。He is competent at administrative affairs.

“办”和“事”中间插入其他成分，或分开，甚至颠倒时，所指的事可大可小 ◇ Some elements can be inserted between 办 and 事 or 办 and 事 can even be reversed to indicate the business to be important or unimportant:

④ 等**办完了事**，我们可以在这个城市游览两天。After handling all the affairs, we can enjoy ourselves for several days in the city.

⑤ 这件**事他办得**不错。He handled the affair properly/smartly.

以上都不用“做事” ◇ 做事 cannot be used in the examples above.

2. “做事”连用时有在机关、公司等从事工作的意思 ◇ 做事 can mean " to work in an organization or company":

① 他在一家公司**做事**。He worked for a company.

“做”和“事”分开用则指做具体的事 ◇ Usually 做事 can be separated to mean " to do something concrete":

② 今天**做**了不少**事**：分配的工作都完成了，还写了几封信。I did a lot of things today: I not only finished my assignments, but also wrote several letters.

B

③ 我想请你帮我**做点儿事**。I'd like you to do me a favor.

半拉　半个　一半

(数)

bàn lǎ　bàn gè　yībàn

Ⓔ half (of sth.)/
half (of sth.)/
half

◪ "半拉"、"半个"是数量词组，"一半"是数词，都有1/2的意思 ◇ 半拉 and 半个 are numeral-classifier phrases, while 一半 is a numeral. All the three mean " one half".

1. "半拉"、"半个"，指东西的一半 ◇ 半拉 and 半个 mean " one half of sth."

① 我吃不了一个苹果，**半个**(/**半拉**)就够了。An apple is too much for me and half is enough.

② 昨天吃剩下的**半个**(/**半拉**)西瓜，今天已经坏掉了。The rest half of the watermelon left yesterday has gone bad.

③ 工程还需要**半个**(/**半拉**)月左右，就可结束。It will take us about half a month to complete the project.

2. "一半"指1/2，可指具体事物，如：1中的例①②均可换成"一半"，因此，指具体的事物时，"半拉"、"半个"、"一半"可以互换。而1中的例③是指时间，可以用"半拉"、"半个"，不能用"一半" ◇ 一半 means "1/2" and can be applied to concrete things, e. g. in examples ①②一半 can be used instead. Therefore, when referring to concrete things the three are interchangeable; while in example ③, when referring to time, 半拉 and 半个 will do, but not 一半.

"一半"可指更为抽象的1/2的意义 ◇ 一半 one half that is can be applied to the more abstract :

① 这篇文章只写了**一半**。Only half of the article has been finished.

② 离目的地还有**一半**的路程。There is still a half journey to go.

以上二例，均不能用"半拉"或"半个"，但"半拉"的重叠式"半半拉拉"(bànbànlālā)常用于口语中，表示未完成的 ◇ In the two examples above, 半拉 or 半个 can't be used, but 半半拉拉 is often used in colloquial speech meaning unfinished:

③ 文章怎么写了**半半拉拉**的就放下了? Why don't you complete the rest of the article?

帮 帮忙

(动)

bāng bāng máng

Ⓔ help, assist/help, give a hand

1. "帮"有两个意思,(1)当他人从事某事务时,在精神、物质上给予支持,或实际参与一部分工作。(2)指从事体力雇佣劳动,如"帮工"、"帮短工"(这个意思与"帮忙"是完全不一样的) ◇ 帮 has two meanings: (1) to support someone materially or spiritually, or actually do a part of the work (2) when he or she doing something; to wage labor, casual labourer (which is entirely different from 帮忙).

第一个意思,"帮"常带直接宾语(指人)和间接宾语(指从事某事务) ◇ In the first usage 帮 usually takes a direct object (the person) and an indirect object (doing some business), e. g.:

① 他**帮**小王办起了公司。He helped Xiao Wang set up a company.

② 请你**帮**我抬一下这个箱子。The box is quite heavy. Would you please give me a hand?

远宾语也可以指钱物等 ◇ The indirect object can be money or something else:

③ 朋友急需一笔钱,他**帮**了他一部分。His friend was in need of money badly and he helped him with some.

2. "帮忙"在结构上是动宾关系,意思上表示具体的帮助,或表示别人有具体困难或需要劳力时给予支持 ◇ 帮忙 is a verb-object phrase, meaning "actual help, or actual support to another person who needs help":

① 他**帮**了我的**大忙**。He helped me greatly.

② 我有几封信要打印出来,请你**帮帮忙**好吗? I have several letters to be typed. Would you please do me a favor?

③ 我要出去几天,请你**帮忙**,替我照顾一下家。I'm going to be away for a few days. Would you please take care of my house?

"帮倒忙"表示帮助别人时,有意无意反而给人添了麻烦。"越帮越忙"也有类似的意思 ◇ 帮倒忙 means "when trying to help somebody, intentionally or unintentionally, one makes a lot of trouble". 越帮越忙 (the more help, the more troublesome) has a similar meaning.

"帮"与"帮忙"一般不能互换。③如用"帮"应说"我要出去几天,请你帮我照顾一下家" ◇ 帮

B

and 帮忙 are not interchangeable. In example ③, if one uses 帮, one must say: "我要出去几天,请你**帮**我照顾一下家".

包含（动）bāohán 包括（动）bāokuò

Ⓔ contain, include/ include, consist of

◪ "包含"和"包括"都有"(事物里边)含有"的意思,"包含"侧重于抽象事物,"包括"则可指具体或抽象事物 ◇ Both 包含 and 包括 mean "contain", 包含 mainly applying to abstract things, while 包括 can be applied to either abstract or concrete things.

1. "包含"所指的抽象事物,多指"意思"、"内容"等 ◇ 包含 very often takes 意思 or 内容, etc. as its object:

① 这篇文章**包含**两方面的内容。The article discusses two main aspects.

② 那个句子**包含**几层意思。The sentence contains several dimensions of meaning.

有时因抽象事物的内涵不同,也有"藏有"的意思 ◇ Sometimes 包含 means "something hidden inside":

③ 他这种做法**包含**着不可告人的目的。There are ulterior motives implied in his course of action.

2. "包括"可指具体的事物 ◇ 包括 can be applied to concrete things:

① **包括**我在内,都不赞成这种做法。All of us, including me, disapproved the way of doing it.

② 这套房子一共有100平方米,**包括**阳台。The house, including its balcony, is 100 square meters large.

也可指较抽象的事物 ◇ 包括 can also be applied to abstract things:

③ 这本书**包括**好几部分内容。The book consists of several parts.

当指抽象事物时,有时用"包含"和"包括"都可以。但仍有所侧重 ◇ When applied to abstract things, either 包含 or 包括 can be used but with different stresses:

④ 这本书**包含**(/**包括**)好几部分内容。The book contains several parts.

而当用于"藏有"意义时,则只能用"包含"(见1例③),不能用"包括" ◇ When the sense of "being hidden" is meant, only 包含 is used (see example ③ entry 1) and not 包括.

保持 维持

(动) (动)

bǎochí wéichí

Ⓔ keep, maintain/ keep, maintain, preserve

1. "保持"有使状况、局面继续不变的意思。可带各种名词性宾语,也可带双音节动词、形容词宾语 ◇ 保持 means " to keep a state or situation unchanged" and can take all sorts of nominal objects and disyllabic verbal and adjectival objects. e. g. :

① 小城的建筑,一直**保持**着明清时代的风貌。The buildings in the small town remain the styles of the Ming and Qing Dynasties.

② 他在工作中永远**保持**着积极乐观的精神。He's always positive and optimistic in his work.

③ 遇到这种尴尬的场面,他只能**保持**沉默。What he can do is keeping silent in such an awkward situation.

④ 情况紧急,我们要想办法使大家的情绪**保持**稳定。The situation is urgent, and we should try our best to keep everyone calm.

⑤ 从那以后他们俩一直**保持**着联系。From then on, they two have kept in touch till today.

"保持"有时可受名词修饰 ◇ 保持 sometimes can be modified by a noun:

⑥ 一定要注意水土**保持**。Attention must be paid to the soil and water conservation.

以上各句均不能用"维持"代替 ◇ 维持 cannot take the place of 保持 in the above examples.

2. "维持"除了有使原有状况、局面不变的意思以外,含有比较勉强的、被动的、不得不继续下去的意思(如例②③) ◇ Besides keeping sth. unchanged, 维持 also implies reluctance, passivity and something that must continue (e. g. examples ② and ③):

① 会场秩序由大会工作人员负责**维持**。The conference staff is responsible for the order in the assembly hall.

② 她的工资仅够**维持**两个人的生活。Her salary is only enough for two persons.

③ 病人情况十分危急,现在靠输液**维持**生命。The patient is critically ill, depending completely on infusion.

有时二词可互换 ◇ Sometimes the two words are interchangeable:

④ 两家公司还**保持**(/**维持**)着合作关系。They two companies still keep in touch.

但用"保持"多指正常的、不费力的关系,用"维持"常指被动的或勉强的关系 ◇ 保持 is usually applied to normal and effortless relationship, while 维持 to passive or reluctant relationship.

"维持"还有维护支持的意思,如"暗中维持"、"多方维持"等 ◇ 维持 also means safeguard and support, e.g. 暗中维持(to give secret support to),多方维持(make every effort to defend),etc.

保护 维护

(动) (动)

bǎohù wéihù

Ⓔ defend, protect/ uphold, defend

◪ 这两个动词都有采取行动使之不受损害的意思。前者更具体;后者较为正式,一般用于比较重大的抽象事物。"保护"可说"受……保护","维护"不能这样说 ◇ Both verbs mean " to take protective action or safeguard". The former is more concrete and the latter is more formal, and can be applied to more important abstract things. One can say: 受……保护(under the protection of) but 维护 cannot be used in this way.

1. 保护

① 阳光很刺眼,他戴上墨镜以便**保护**眼睛。The sunshine was so dazzling that he wore dark sunglasses to protect his eyes.

② 公民的生命、财产受到法律的**保护**。The life and property of citizens are protected by law.

③ 车祸发生后,要**保护**好现场。Don't spoil the spot when traffic accidents take place.

以上这种很具体的意义,用"保护"不用"维护" ◇ In all the above concrete cases, 保护 is used, but not 维护.

2. 维护

多用于抽象意义 ◇ 维护 is usually used in an abstract sense:

① 各国都有**维护**国际和平的义务。All nations are responsible for the maintaining of the world peace.

② 我们要**维护**法律的尊严。We should stand up for the dignity of the law.

"维护"还表示维持现有的状态,使之继续存在下去 ◇ 维护 also means "to withhold existing state", e.g.:

③ **维护**社会的正常秩序是公安部门的神圣职责。To maintain public orders is the holy responsibility of the public security departments.

有时，既具体又抽象的事物（如“权力”、“权益”、“利益”等），“保护”、“维护”均可用 ◇ Sometimes, for things that can be both abstract and concrete, either 保护 or 维护 can be used.

④ 每个公民都应**保护**（/**维护**）自己的正当权益。Every citizen should safeguard his or her own just rights and interests.

▶［爱护 àihù—保护 bǎohù］
［保障 bǎozhàng—保护 bǎohù］
［掩护 yǎnhù —保护 bǎohù］

保卫 防卫

（动） （动）

bǎowèi fángwèi

Ⓔ protect/protect, defend

◥ 这两个动词都表示保护使不受破坏、侵犯 ◇ Both verbs mean "to protect against".

1.“保卫”使用范围较广，宾语可以是较具体的事物，也可以是抽象的事物 ◇ 保卫 has more usages than 防卫. Its object can be a concrete thing as well as an abstract thing, e. g. :

① 抗洪军民努力**保卫**着大坝的安全。The flood-combating soldiers and civilians made every effort to protect the dam.

② 公安干警的职责就是**保卫**人民的生命财产安全。The public security officers are responsible for the security of people's life and property.

③ 我们要**保卫**世界和平。We should safeguard the world peace.

以上各句都不能用“防卫” ◇ 防卫 cannot be used in any of the above examples.

2.“防卫”使用范围较窄，除了保护以外，还有防御的意思 ◇ 防卫 has a more limited usage. Besides "protection" it also means "defense":

① 军队是一个国家的**防卫**力量。Millitary forces exercise the defense function of a state.

② 受到坏人的袭击，他进行了反击，这是正当**防卫**。When attacked, he stroke back. This is legitimate defence.

例①②不能用“保卫” ◇ 保卫 cannot be used in examples ① and ②.

保障 保护

（动、名） （动）

bǎozhàng bǎohù

Ⓔ safeguard/protect

◥ “保障”（名）是指起保障作用的事物，如“社会保障”等，与“保护”（动）不可能混淆。所以，这

B

里只分析“保障”(动)跟“保护”(动)的异同 ◇ 保障 as a noun means " the thing which is the safeguard", e. g. 社会保障(social security) and so cannot be confused with 保护, a verb; therefore in what follows only the similarity and difference between 保障 used as a verb and 保护 are analyzed.

“保护”(动)的意思是对人或事物照顾维护,使不受伤害或保持完好。而“保障”(动)的意思是维护权利、财产、人身安全等使不受侵害,多指法律、政策等 ◇ 保护 as a verb means " to protect a person or thing against harm". 保障 as a verb means " to safeguard somebody's right, property, safety, etc. ", and is usually applied to law and policy.

1. 保护(动)

① 使用电脑时,要注意**保护**眼睛。Take good care of your eyes while using a computer.

② 对公园里的花木,一定要**保护**好,不要践踏和攀折。Please cherish flowers and trees in the park and keep them off.

“受保护”、“得到保护”等中的“保护”仍为动词,如 ◇ 保护 is still a verb in 受保护, 得到保护, etc. , e. g. :

③ 他虽是孤儿,但受到监护人(亲戚)无微不至的照顾和**保护**。Though he was an orphan, he was taken the greatest care of and under very good protection of his guardian (or relatives).

④ 这种行为不受法律的**保护**。This conduct is beyond the protection of the law.

以上都不能用“保障” ◇ In examples ③ and ④ 保障 cannot be used.

2. 保障(动)

① 这项法律是**保障**妇女的社会权利的。This section of the law is to safeguard the women's social rights.

② 签署了用工合同,就可以**保障**劳动者的合法权益。The workers' just rights and interests can be guaranteed if the work contract is signed.

“受保障”、“有保障”等,“保障”仍为动词 ◇ In 受保障, 有保障 etc. , 保障 is still a verb.

当“保护”用于较重要事物时,也会涉及法律、政策等内容,这时与“保障”可通用,如 ◇ When 保护 is applied to serious business, for instance, something related to law, policy, etc. and can be used interchangeably with 保障, e. g. :

③ 这项法令的出台有利于**保障**(/**保护**)妇女和儿童的权益。The issue of this decree is good for the protection of rights and interests of women and children.

有时“保障”和“保护”虽可通用，二者仍有细微差别 ◇ Still, there is slight difference between the two, e. g. :

④ 法律**保障**公民的合法权益。(侧重于抽象事物)The law can protect the just rights and interests of citizens. (emphasizing abstract thing)

⑤ 许多国家都颁布了**保护**野生动物的法律。(侧重于具体事物) Many countries have enacted laws for wildlife conservation. (emphasizing concrete thing)

▶ [爱护 àihù—保护 bǎohù]
[保护 bǎohù—维护 wéihù]
[掩护 yǎnhù—保护 bǎohù]

报 (名) bào　　报纸 (名) bàozhǐ

Ⓔ newspaper/newspaper

◣ 这两个词都指刊载消息、信息的定期出版物(多为日刊)，“报”可以作为这种刊物名称的中心语，如:《大公报》、《文汇报》、《体育报》，也常说“日报、周报、晚报”等(如《人民日报》、《北京周报》)。“报纸”不作为这种名称 ◇ Both words mean "newspaper" (mostly daily paper). 报 is usually used as the main word in the names of such publication, e. g. 《大公报》(*Takungpao*),《文汇报》(*Wenhui Bao*),《体育报》(*Sports*), or 日报 (daily),周报 (weekly),晚报 (evening paper), etc. (e. g. 《人民日报》*People's Daily*,《北京周报》*Beijing Review*). 报纸 is never used in the names of newspapers.

两个词都可以表示上述刊物的实体 ◇ Both words can refer to the actual publications, e. g. :

① 他正在看**报**。He is reading a newspaper.

② 我买了两份**报纸**。I bought two newspapers.

上面二例中，“报”和“报纸”一般可互换。但在习惯上，单音节 + 单音节、双音节 + 双音节比较常见 ◇ In the two examples above, 报 and 报纸 are interchangeable, but usually in the mode of monosyllabic + monosyllabic or disyllabic + disyllabic. e. g. :

办报 running a newspaper
买报 buying a newspaper
看报 reading a newspaper
卖报 selling a newspaper
创办报纸(他创办了一份报纸) running a newspaper (He ran a newspaper.)

B

编辑报纸 editing a newspaper

另外,“报纸”可指看过的或过期的、可以利用来包东西的纸张 ◇ 报纸 can mean " old newspapers used as wrappers" ,e. g. :

③ 他用**报纸**把两本书包了起来。He wrapped the two books with newspapers.

④ 这些**报纸**可以卖给废品收购站。These newspapers can be sold to the salvage station.

这时也可以用“报”,但用得较少 ◇ 报 can, but rarely, replace 报纸 in such cases.

“报”还可以作为词素表示其他刊物如“学报”、“画报”、张贴物(如“海报”)等 ◇ 报 can be used as a morpheme to mean "many other publications" (such as " journal ", "pictorial"),posters (such as "playbill"), etc.

抱歉　　对不起

(形)

bàoqiàn　　duì bu qǐ

Ⓔ be sorry, feel apologetic/ be very sorry

◥“抱歉”、“对不起”这两个词语表示因做了不利于人的事,对别人有愧。前者是形容词,后者是动词词组。但“对不起”词义较具体,可带宾语,可以直接用于对别人表示道歉;“抱歉”不能带宾语。以下例①②③,两个词可通用 ◇ Both 抱歉 and 对不起 are used to apologize. 抱歉 is an adjective and 对不起 is a verb phrase. The meaning of 对不起 is very concrete and it can take an object. It can be used directly to apologize. 抱歉 cannot take an object. In examples①,②and ③the two expressions are interchangeable:

① 小张对小王说:“真**抱歉**(/**对不起**),我弄坏了你的相机。”Xiao Zhang said to Xiao Wang:“I'm sorry that I have spoiled your camera.”

② 小张说了声“**抱歉**(/**对不起**)”,小王也就算了。Xiao Zhang apologized, and Xiao Wang forgave him.

③ 他表示十分**抱歉**(/**对不起**)。He expressed his great apology.

“对不起”可直接带宾语,“抱歉”不能 ◇ 对不起 can take an object, while 抱歉 cannot:

④ 真**对不起**你,弄坏了你的东西。I'm terribly sorry for spoiling your articles.

⑤ 我从来不做**对不起**人的事。I never do things harmful to others.

“抱歉”可做状语,“对不起”不能 ◇ 抱歉 can function as an adverbial, while 对不起 cannot:

⑥ 她**抱歉**地说:是我不对。She apologized that it's her fault.

⑦ 来晚了,老李**抱歉**地向大家拱拱手。Lao Li apologized to all the people present with a cupped-hand salute.

爆发 发生

(动) (动)

bàofā fāshēng

Ⓔ erupt/happen

"发生"表示事物的产生;"爆发"则表示重大事变的突然来临及情绪、积聚力量的突然发作 ◇ 发生 means "that sth. takes place or happens";while 爆发 means "a sudden eruption of some emergency or a flare up of some accumulated force":

1. 爆发

① 1911 年,中国**爆发**了辛亥革命。Xinhai Revolution (the Chinese bourgeois democratic revolution led by Dr. Sun Yat-sen) took place in China in 1911.

② 这次火山**爆发**,事前还是有一定迹象的。There were some signs before the erupting of the volcano.

③ 她受到刺激,情绪一下子**爆发**了出来。She burst out emotionally because of the stimulation.

④ 这两个人积怨已久,终于**爆发**了一场争吵。A great deal of resentment has been incurred and finally a quarrel broke out between them.

以上例①如不强调其突然性,也可用"发生" ◇ In example ①, if suddenness is not stressed, 发生 can take the place of 爆发.

2. 发生

⑤ 你脸色苍白,**发生**了什么事情? You look pale. What's up?

⑥ 那条街上**发生**了严重的交通事故。There was a severe traffic accident in that street.

⑦ 用药之后,奇迹**发生**了,他醒过来了。After the medicine was taken, the wonder worked, and he came round.

杯 杯子

(名) (名)

bēi bēizi

Ⓔ cup/cup

这两个词都指盛液体的圆柱形器具。"杯"是半粘着词,可说"玻璃杯、酒杯、茶杯、纸杯、大杯、小杯"等等,一般不能独立使用。可临时作名量词(可重叠) ◇ Both words mean "cylindrical container". 杯 is a semiagglutinative word, which can be used as a morpheme to form words, e. g. 玻璃杯, 酒杯, 茶杯, 纸杯, 大杯, 小杯, etc., but can't be used by it-

B

self. It can also be used as a temporary measure word (can be reduplicated):

一杯酒 a cup of wine

两杯水 two glasses of water

一大杯啤酒 a big cup of beer

一小杯白酒 a small cup of wine

杯杯酒都要斟满。Pour all the cups fully, please.

"杯子"是自由词,可以独立使用 ◇ 杯子 is a free word and can be used independently, e.g.:

① 这个**杯子**很漂亮。The cup is very beautiful.

② 拿一个**杯子**来。Bring me a cup.

也可做定语 ◇ It can be an attributive too:

③ 那种**杯子**的形状很美。The shape of the cup is pretty nice.

有时可暂做量词(不能重叠) ◇ It can be a temporary measure word (can not be reduplicated):

④ 他喝了满满一**杯子**茅台酒。He drank a full glass of *Maotai* (a famous Chinese spirit).

悲哀 (形) bēi'āi　悲痛 (形) bēitòng

Ⓔ grieved, sorrowful/ grieved, sorrowful

◥ 这两个形容词都含有由于遭受不幸或不如意的事而伤心、难过的意思。遭到较大的不幸时,这两个词都可以用。如在下面的例子中,二词可以换用 ◇ Both of the adjectives mean "grieved". If the misfortune is serious, either word will do. For instance, in the following examples, the two adjectives are interchangeable:

① 母亲去世了,儿女们都十分**悲哀**(/**悲痛**)。The daughters and sons felt greatly grieved for their mother's death.

② 小王在飞机失事中遇难,朋友们都很**悲哀**(/**悲痛**)。Xiao Wang was killed in the air crash and his friends all felt grieved for his death.

如是遭到不如意的事或对某事感到失望、惋惜、感慨等,则用"悲哀" ◇ If it is some slight feeling of grief or disappointment over some unhappy things, only 悲哀 is used:

③ 看到这些失足的少年,我觉得**悲哀**。I felt sorry for these young criminals.

④ 秋天到了,遍地是黄叶,多愁善感的她感到一种莫名的**悲哀**。The fall comes, yellow leaves are everywhere, and she, a sensitive person, felt a nameless grief.

北 (名) běi　北边 (名) běibiān

Ⓔ north/north side

◥ 这两个词都是方位名词。"北边"是自由词,"北"是半粘着词 ◇ Theses two words are both nouns of locality. 北边 is a free word, while 北 is a semi-agglutinative word:

① 我家的**北边**是一片绿地。To the north of my house, there is a plot of grassland.

② **北边**那座楼是学校的办公楼。The building in the north is the administrative building of our university.

以上两句,都不能用"北" ◇ 北 cannot be used in examples ① and ②.

"北"常和别的单音节词组合使用,如"北风"、"北国"、"北上",再如 ◇ 北 is usually used together with another monosyllabic word, e. g. 北风(the north wind),北国(a northern country), 北上(go up north),and:

③ 城**北**是住宅区。The residential quarters are located in the northern part of the city.

④ 村**北**有一片小树林。There is a grove to the north of the village.

⑤ 山南的村子叫南村,山**北**的村子叫**北**村。The village to the south of the mountain is called "South Village"; while the one to the north called "North Village".

以下的句子,在介词"向"、"往"等后面,"北"和"北边"都可以做宾语 ◇ In the following examples, after prepositions like 向,往, etc., both 北 and 北边 can be used as the object:

⑥ **往(/向)北(/北边)**走五分钟,就到邮局了。Walk north about five minutes, and you will find the post office.

在动词后,只能用"北边",不能用"北"做宾语 ◇ After a verb, however, only 北边 and not 北 can be the object:

⑦ 他住**北边**,我住南边。He lives in the northern part while I live in the southern part.

⑧ 他把车停到了商场的**北边**。He parked his car to the northern part of the shopping center.

熟语性的格式多用"北" ◇ In idiomatic phrases, 北 is usually used:

走南闯北 travel widely

南来北往 be always on the move

北燕南飞 The migratory swallows fly to the south.

"朝北"是动词—宾语关系,比较

特殊，可以独立使用 ◇ 朝北 is a verb-object phrase and can be used independently：

⑨ 这间房子**朝北**。The house faces north.

“南”和“南边”、“东”和“东边”、“西”和“西边”的区别，与本条类似 ◇ The difference between 南 and 南边，东 and 东边，西 and 西边 are similar.

本（名）běn　本子（名）běnzi

Ⓔ book，notebook/book，notebook

◥ 两个词都指册子。“本”是粘着词，“本子”是自由词。“本”不能独立使用，常和其他词合用 ◇ Both words mean "notebook". 本 is an agglutinative word while 本子 is a free word. 本 cannot be used freely and usually is used with some other words，e. g.：

练习本 an exercise-book
图画本 a picture-book
日记本 a diary-book
笔记本 a note-book
户口本 a household-book
大本 a big book
小本 a small book

“本子”可以独立使用 ◇ 本子 can be used independently：

① 这个**本子**是记账用的。The notebook is for keeping accounts.

② 他买了几个**本子**。He bought several notebooks.

③ **本子**上面拉拉杂杂地写了不少东西。There are many things written ramblingly on the notebook.

以上①②③不能用“本”。但儿化（本儿 běnr）后可以 ◇ In examples ①②③，本 cannot be used，but 本儿 will do.

本来（形）běnlái　原来（形）yuánlái

Ⓔ original/original

◥ 这两个词都可表示先前已发生的，都是非谓形容词 ◇ Both mean "former" and are adjectives which function as predicate，adverbial or complement.

A. 共同点 Similarity：

1. 表示以前，起初 ◇ Meaning "former"：

① 他**本来**（/**原来**）是读法律的，后来又学了经济。He studied law first，and then he changed to economics.

② 我**本来**（/**原来**）不认识他，到这里才成了朋友。I didn't know him until I came here and made friends with him.

③ **本来**(/**原来**)用两个小时才能做完的事,他只用了一个半小时。It took him only one hour and a half to finish the matter, which was planned to be finished in two hours.

2. 表示原有的 ◇ Meaning "original":

① 洗了几次,这衣服**本来**(/**原来**)的颜色褪了不少。After several washing, the dress faded a lot.

② 她已经失去了**本来**(/**原来**)的勇气和天真。She has lost her former courage and naive.

B. 不同点 Meaning difference:

1. 表示发现一度不清楚的真实情况,用"原来"(多为状语)◇ 原来 is used to indicate the discovery of sth. unknown before:

① 他**原来**是你的男朋友呀!我还以为是你哥哥呢。He turned out to be your boyfriend. I thought he was your elder brother.

② 我说怎么这么痒呢,**原来**被蚊子叮了。I doubt why my skin itched. It turned out to be the sting of mosquito.

2. 做介宾结构的宾语,表示前后对比,用"原来" ◇ 原来 is used as the object of a preposition-object phrase, to show contrast:

① 她比**原来**瘦多了。She is thinner than she was.

② 最近物价较**原来**有所回落。The price has fallen a little recently.

3. 做定语时,表示没有经过改变的,一般用"原来" ◇ When used as an attributive, 原来 is used to mean "something not altered":

① 我们的工作不能停留在**原来**的水平上。Our work cannot remain at the same level as before.

② 他还住在**原来**的地方。He still lives in the same place.

4. 表示早该如此,理当如此,或表示某事实或道理一直如此,用"本来" ◇ 本来 is used to indicate that something ought to have been so or has been so:

① 这件事**本来**就该这么办。Of course, the matter should be handled this way.

② **本来**嘛,学习哪能不下点儿功夫呢!Certainly, learning demands efforts.

③ 生活**本来**就是丰富多彩的,它是文学艺术创作的源泉。It goes without saying that life is colorful and it is just the source of creative writing.

④ 这类问题**本来**就难处理,别着急,慢慢来。It is true that this kind of problem is difficult to be dealt with, so take it easy.

还有些习惯搭配如:"原来如此"表示发现真实情况。"本来如此"表示历来就是这样。"本来面目"表示早已存在的真实面目 ◇ There are some idiomatic phrases, such as 原来如此 indicating the discovery of a real situation. 本来如此 means "that it has been so all along". 本来面目 means "the original true colours".

本领 本事 能力

(名) (名) (名)

běnlǐng běnshi nénglì

Ⓔ skill, ability/
skill, ability/
capability, ability

◥ 这三个词都表示能胜任某事的知识、技能、条件等。常与"有"或"没有"搭配。有时三个词可互换 ◇ The three words all mean "skill and ability" and are usually the object of 有 or 没有. Sometimes the three are interchangeable:

① 他这个人很有**本事**(/**能力**/**本领**),公司里处处离不开他。He is so capable that he is indispensable in the company.

② 老李没什么**本事**(/**能力**/**本领**),但是人很可靠。Lao Li is not an able man, but he is reliable.

"本领"和"本事"常说"本领大"、"本事大",而"能力"常说"能力强"、"能力弱"、"能力不够"等。同时,"能力"侧重于知识技能等,"本事"、"本领"有时侧重于做事的诀窍、门路等 ◇ When referring to 本领 and 本事, we usually say 本领大 or 本事大 (very capable), but 能力强, 能力弱 (uncapable), 能力不够 (unable) are used instead. Besides, 能力 stresses knowledge and skill, while 本事 and 本领 stress secret of success or knack, e. g.:

③ 由于**能力**不够,他没有按时完成这个项目。Due to his incompetence, he didn't finish the project in time.

④ 他的**本事**真大,用那么少的钱能干这么大的事。He was so great that he could make use of the limited money to complete the costly work.

⑤ 我是个手艺人,凭**本事**吃饭。I am a craftsman, living on my crafts.

例③只能用"能力"。例④是指门路等,例⑤是指技术等,多用"本事",用"本领"也可以 ◇ Only 能力 can be used in example ③. 本事 in example ④ indicates special influence or personal advantage; in example ⑤ 本事 is used to mean "skill or tech-

nigue",本领 will also do.
“本领”还指技艺、技术、武功等,如“使出看家本领”、“本领高强”等。这个意义也可用“本事”,但不宜用“能力” ◇ 本领 also means " artistry, skill, martial arts", etc., e. g. 使出看家本领(use all one's resources),本领高强(excel in ability),etc. 本事 can also be used, but not 能力.

本人 (代) běnrén　　本身 (代) běnshēn

Ⓔ oneself, in person/ oneself, itself

“本人”,“本身”都有强调自身的意思 ◇ Both of 本人 and 本身 have the connotatian of stressing oneself.

1.“本人”指人,可以单用,表示自指,意思较郑重,但也可以较诙谐 ◇ 本人, with a referrence of oneself indicates human being. When used by itself, it is very formal, but may also be used humorously.

① **本人**奉上级委派,来调查这件事情。(郑重) I was assigned to investigate the matter. (solemn)

② 你多喝几杯吧,**本人**舍命陪君子。(诙谐) Help yourself to more glasses of wine. I will throw in my lot with you. (humorous)

“本人”还常用于复指前面提到的自己或他人,常说“我本人”、“他本人”等 ◇ 本人 is often used to refer to the above mentioned oneself or someone else, such as 我本人(myself), 他本人(himself), etc.

③ 我虽然是局长,但这事关系重大,我**本人**说了不算数。Though I am the office head, I cannot decide it by myself, for it matters so much.

④ 他的想法,还是由他**本人**来说吧! His idea should be expressed by himself.

2.“本身”不限于指人,强调人或事物自身,多复指上文提到的事物或人;有时含有前后文对比的意味 ◇ 本身 is not limited to a person, but stressing the person himself or the thing itself. It is mainly used to refer to the thing or persons mentioned previously, sometimes indicating a contrast:

① 这个机器**本身**没有毛病,问题出在操作上。(指物) (referring to things) There is nothing wrong with the machine. The problem is in operation.

② 这个学术团体的规模虽然不大,但**本身**有很强的实力。

B

(指团体)(referring to a working body) Though the size of the academic society is not big, it is powerful by nature.

③ 他虽然现在是研究所的行政负责人,但**本身**是搞技术的,是内行。(指人)(referring to a person) As an administrative head of the institute now, he was a technician originally, and he is expert.

④ 要提高教学质量,培养优秀人才,首先要注意提高教师队伍**本身**的素质。(指人) To improve teaching quality and train competent teachers, we should improve the quality of teachers first. (referring to a group persons)

⑤ 方法比事情**本身**更重要。(指事) The handling ways are more important than the matter itself. (referring to things)

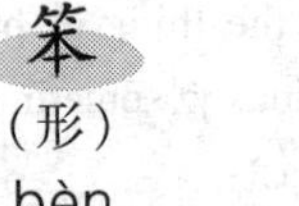

笨 (形) bèn　蠢 (形) chǔn

Ⓔ stupid, foolish/stupid, foolish

"笨"和"蠢"都是形容词,表示不聪明,两个词一般可换用 ◇ Both 笨 and 蠢 are adjectives meaning not clever. The two words are interchangeable usually:

① 我真**笨**(/**蠢**),这么简单的账都算错了。I was so stupid that I made a mistake in such a simple accounting.

② 那家伙是个**笨**(/**蠢**)人,做事不动脑子。The chap is stupid for he does not use his head.

③ 这是个**笨**办法,但比较保险。The method is stupid, but it is safe.

但例③"笨办法"表示较费力而比较可靠的办法,一般不说"蠢办法"。表示不灵巧,常说"笨手笨脚"、"嘴笨"或"发笨"、"发蠢" ◇ 笨办法 in example ③ means " a strenuous but reliable method"; but one does not say 蠢办法 (clumsy) usually. 笨手笨脚 (intakative), 嘴笨 (not good at expressing), 发笨 (be awkward), 发蠢 (be awkward) are often used to mean not dexterous:

④ 他干起活儿来**笨手笨脚**的。He seems to be all thumbs at work.

⑤ 老王肚子里有学问,只是**嘴**有点儿**笨**,不善于表达。Lao Wang is knowledgeable, but he is not good at expressing himself.

⑥ 她怀了孩子,身子有点儿**发笨**(/**蠢**)。She is expecting a child, so she is a little bit awkward in action.

表示笨重,两个词可换用 ◇ To

mean " clumsiness " ,the two words are interchangeable:

⑦ 这些家具又**笨**(/**蠢**)又大,摆在小房间里不合适。These furniture is large and heavy, not suitable for small rooms.

⑧ 这种鞋结实是结实,可是样子显得太**蠢**(/**笨**)了。The pair of shoes is strong,but they look clumsy.

比 (动、介) bǐ　比较 (动、副) bǐjiào

Ⓔ compare;contrast/ compare;contrast

A. 作为动词,"比"和"比较"都表示辨别两种(或两种以上)事物(多为同类事物)的异同或高下,但"比"可用于具体或抽象事物,而"比较"多用于抽象事物 ◇ As a verb,比 or 比较 means " to compare two or more things (usually of the same kind) in quality or quantity". 比 is applied to concrete as well as abstract things, while 比较 is mostly applied to abstract things:

① 你们俩**比一比**,看谁高一点儿。You two stand back to back. Let's see who's taller.

② 两种布放在一起一**比**,就看出颜色的不同了。It is easy to distinguish the colors of the two kinds of cloth if we put them together.

③ 我想**比较**一下两个公司的产品和价格,然后再做决定。Firstly,I would like to compare the products and prices of the two companies,and then I can make a decision.

④ 经过**比较**,我们认为这个方案更实际些。After comparison, we reached an agreement that this plan was the most practical.

"比"还有"可以互相对比"的意思,"比较"没有这样的意思 ◇ 比 also means " comparable with" , while 比较 does not have such a meaning:

⑤ 做买卖不**比**读书,也不**比**种田,光有勤快是不行的。Doing business is unlike learning or farming,for what it requires is beyond diligence.

⑥ 上台讲话不**比**随便发言,难免有些紧张。Delivering a speech before class is not as casual as chatting. It is natural to be nervous.

"比"还有"较量"、"攀比"等意思,"比较"没有这个意思 ◇ 比 also means " to contest,to cite the cases of others in support of one's own claim" ; 比较 has no such meaning:

⑦ 打乒乓球,别和他**比**,你是业余的,他是专业的。Don't compete with him in playing table tennis. You are an amateur and he is professional.

⑧ 不**比**阔气**比**健康,已成为当今新时尚。Comparing health instead of wealth is a new current fashion.

B. 介词"比"与后面的名词、代词组成介词结构,放在形容词(谓语或状语等)前面。"比较"不可以 ◇ 比, forming a prepositional phrase with its following noun or pronoun, can be placed before an adjective (a predicate or an adverbial), while 比较 has no such usage:

1. 两种不同的事物相比较 ◇ Indicating comparison between two different persons or things, e. g. :

① 她**比**她妹妹高一些。She is taller than her younger sister.

② 我**比**小王早到一个小时。I came one hour earlier than Xiao Wang.

2. 同一事物在不同的时间内相比较 ◇ Indicating comparison of one thing at different times:

③ 这条街**比**以前热闹多了。The street is more busting than it was before.

④ 这几天的天气**比**前些日子好多了。The weather is much better these days.

C. "比较"(副)表示相比起来有一定程度,但不是很高。这时不能用"比" ◇ 比较, as an adverb. indicating the meaning of " comparatively, to a certain degree, but not very high":

① 这里的交通**比较**方便。The traffic here is convenient.

② 这种技术**比较**容易掌握。It is easier to master the technology.

③ 她的汉语在班里是**比较**好的。Her Chinese is quite good in her class.

④ 我想找一间**比较**大的房子。I want to look for a bigger room.

▶[比 bǐ—比赛 bǐsài]
[较 jiào—比 bǐ]

比 (动) bǐ　　比赛 (动) bǐsài

◪ "比"和"比赛"都是动词("比"也是介词,参见"比、比较")。"比"用得较宽,既表示一般的比较、相比,也可表示通过比较能力或水准的高低来分出高下,但不用于正式竞赛。而"比赛"用得较窄,只表示生活、生产或体育项目的比试高低,或竞赛 ◇ 比 and 比赛 are both verbs (比 is also a preposition, see

比,比较). 比 has a wider usage. It means "compare as well as contest, but it is not used at a formal competition". 比赛 has a narrower usage and is used at formal competitions of sports or manufacturing production. e. g.:

① 你们俩站在一起**比**一下,看谁高。You two stand back and back, and see who is taller.

这个句子不能用“比赛”。因为这是一般的比较,没有竞赛或比试的意味。再如下面的一句有互相对比或较量的意思,也不用“比赛” ◇ 比赛 cannot be used in example ① because it is just an ordinary comparison; neither can it be used in the following sentence to mean "a contrast":

② 上台唱歌不**比**自己随便唱,难免有点儿怯场。Singing at the stage is not like singing to oneself, so it is natural to be a little bit nervous.

又如 ◇ Another example:

③ 咱们俩**比一比**,看谁啤酒喝得多。Let's compete to see who can drink more beer.

例③也可用“比赛”,因为这里已经有比试的意味 ◇ 比赛 can also be used in example ③ because there is a flavour of contest.

④ 两组大学生正在**比赛**制作机器人。The two teams of college students are competing to make robots.

例④不能用“比”,因为这是正式的竞赛。除非淡化正式竞赛的意思,可说“咱们比一比,看哪个组做得好” ◇ 比 cannot be used in example ④ because it is a formal competition. If one wants to diminish the meaning of formal competition, one can say 咱们比一比,看哪个组做得好。

另外,“比赛”可做主语、宾语,“比”不行 ◇ Moreover, 比赛 can be used as the subject or object of a sentence, while 比 cannot:

⑤ 昨天的足球**比赛**,甲队胜了。Group A won yesterday's football match.

⑥ 你看那场**比赛**了吗? Did you watch the match?

▶[比 bǐ—比较 bǐjiào]
[较 jiào—比 bǐ]

必 必定 一定

必	必定	一定
(副)	(副)	(形、副)
bì	bìdìng	yīdìng

Ⓔ be bound to, be sure to/
be bound to, be sure to/
fixed, definite, be sure to, bound to

A. “必”,在意思上与“必定”相同,但有书面语意味。因为“必”是单音节的,不直接修饰双音节动词,只修饰单音节动词(如“必胜”、“必败”或“必有

B

……"、"必是……")、单音节助动词(如"必能"、"必会")、单音节介词(如"必被……")、单音节副词(如"必将") ◇ 必 has the same meaning as 必定 but with a literary flavor. Since 必 is monosyllabic, it does not qualify disyllabic verbs but only monosyllabic ones (e. g. 必胜, 必败 or 必有……, 必是……), monosyllabic auxiliary verbs (e. g. 必能, 必会), monosyllabic prepositions (e. g. 必被……), monosyllabic adverbs (e. g. 必将).

1. 同"必定"1，表示极有把握的估计 ◇ The usage is the same as 必定 1, meaning "sure estimate":

① 这两支球队**必**有一场大战。There must be a wonderful game between the two ball teams.

② 他们队**必**能取得胜利。Their team is likely to win.

③ 谎言**必**会被事实推翻。The facts will certainly expose lies in the end.

④ 新的工作方案实施后，**必**将产生良好的效果。The implementation of the new plan will surely have a good effect.

2. 同"必定"2，表示必要或必然 ◇ The usage is the same as 必定 2, meaning "be sure to, inevitable":

① 他这么早来找你，**必**有急事。There must be something pressing, otherwise he would not come to see you so early.

② 三人行**必**有我师。Two heads are better than one.

③ 这些参考书都是我写论文时**必**读的。These reference books are required for my paper writing.

3. 同"必定"3，表示意愿的坚决 ◇ The usage is the same as 必定 3, meaning "resolute and firm":

① 下次还出现这种情况，我**必**不原谅。I cannot forgive you if it happens again.

② 每天晚上七点，他**必**去图书馆。He surely goes to the library at seven every night.

四字短语也可用"必"，如"必成大器"、"必有大用"等，"必"和"必是"一样，没有直接的否定形式("不必"有别的意思) ◇ 必 is also used in four-character phrases, e. g. 必成大器 (will surely become a man of great talent), 必有大用 (must be of great use), etc. 必, the same as 必是, has no negative form. (不必 has a different meaning)

B. "必定"，常修饰动词或助动词 ◇ 必定 usually qualifies verbs or auxiliary verbs.

1. 表示极有把握的估计 ◇ Indicating sure estimating:

① 他这样做,**必定**有他的理由。He must have his own reason to do so.

② 这种股票**必定**会涨的。The stock would certainly be rising.

③ 打雷以后**必定**会下大雨。It is very likely to rain after the thunder.

2. 表示必要或必然 ◇ Indicating the meaning of inevitable,essential:

① 从这里到对岸**必定**得坐船。It is sure that you will take a boat to cross the river.

② 你这样粗心大意**必定**会出错。It is sure that you will make mistakes if you are so careless.

③ 正义**必定**战胜邪恶。The just will surely win over the evil.

3. 表示意志、意愿的坚决,多用于第一人称 ◇ Indicating the sense of being firm,resolute,mostly used in the first person:

明天不管多么忙,我**必定**亲自去机场接他。I will surely go to the airport to pick him up whatever busy I am tomorrow.

"必定"没有否定形式,绝不能说"不必定"或"没有必定"。但可用"未必"表示否定。如 ◇ 必定 has no negative form,so one cannot say 不必定 or 没有必定. Yet we can use 未必 to show the negative meaning. e. g. :

① 他**未必**会来接我。He does not necessarily come to pick me up.

② 早睡早起身体**未必**好。Early to bed and early to rise does not necessarily do good to your health.

以上有的例句(如 B 1 ①)也可用"必" ◇ In some of the examples above (e. g. B 1 ①)必 can be used instead.

以上的"必定"1、2 都可以换用"一定",但"一定"的语气略轻(详见下文"一定") ◇ All the explanations of 必定 in points 1,2 above can be applied to 一定,but 一定 sounds less resolute (see 一定 below).

C. "一定",与"必定"、"必"不同的是:"一定"是形容词和副词 ◇ 一定 is different from 必定 and 必 in that it is an adjective and adverb.

a. 作为形容词,"一定"经常做定语,表示 ◇ As an adjective,一定 usually functions as an attributive,meaning:

1. 相当程度的,不太高的 ◇ A certain, limited degree, which is not very high:

① 她的演奏具有**一定**的水平。Her performance has reached a fairly high level.

② 投资这个项目有**一定**的风险。Investing on this project has certain risk.

B

2. 必然的（常用于否定式）◇ Necessary (usually in the negative form):

① 这两件事没有**一定**的联系。There is no certain connection between the two matters.

② 见识、成就与身材、相貌没有**一定**的关系。There is no certain connection among the horizon, achievements, height and looks of a person.

3. 规定的，确定的 ◇ Fixed, definite:

① 自然万物按**一定**的规律不停地循环运动着。All things in the world go continuously by their certain laws.

② 车辆没有**一定**的停放地点不行。There must be a certain parking lot for vehicles.

4. 特定的 ◇ Specific:

① 气温降到**一定**程度，空气中的水蒸气就会变成雪。When temperature drops to a certain degree, the steam in the air will turn into snow.

② 量积累到**一定**水平就会有质的变化。Quantitive accumulation to certain degree will bring on quatitive changes.

总之，作为形容词的"一定"，完全没有"必"、"必定"的意思 ◇ To be short, as an adjective, 一定 does not have the meaning of certainty at all.

b. 作为副词的"一定"，只能作状语 ◇ As an adverb, 一定 can only function as an adverbial:

1. 表示有把握的推断 ◇ Indicating sure estimation:

① 跑了一天，他**一定**累了。He must be tired after a day's being on the move.

② 这件礼物，相信你**一定**会喜欢。I am sure you will like the gift.

"必"、"必定"表示极有把握的估计，意思上较这种"一定"为重，上面两例可以换用"必定"，语气较重，而"必"是单音节，不宜用于这两个句子 ◇ 必 and 必定 indicate a very sure estimation and are more forceful than 一定 in meaning. In the two examples above, 必定 can be used instead and will be more forceful. 必 is monosyllabic and does not fit in here.

2. 表示坚定的决心和意愿 ◇ Indicating a strong resolution:

① 如果他**一定**不肯参加，不要勉强他。If he refused to take part in, don't force him to.

② 我说不让他送我，可他**一定**要送。He insisted on seeing me off though I protected again and again.

3. 表示必然 ◇ Indicating inevitability:

① 粗心**一定**出错。It is sure that carelessness will lead to mistakes.

② 这种花，水浇多了**一定**会死。The flower is very likely to die if watered too much.

4. 加强表示必须、愿望等的语气 ◇ Indicating a more forceful tone of necessity:

① 学生在课堂上**一定**要遵守纪律。Students should follow disciplines in class.

② 分别时，他**一定**要送我一件礼物。He insisted on giving me a present when he parted with me.

例①是"必须"的意思，如换用"必定"，口气显得更重，例②表示愿望，又不是第一人称，不宜用"必定" ◇ In example ①一定 means 必须. If 必定 is used instead, it sounds more forceful. The example ② indicates a wish and is not in the first person, so 必定 is not suitable.

5. "不一定"有两种意思 ◇ 不一定 has two meanings:

表示"可以不"（不是非这样不可）◇ Indicating the sense of not necessarily so:

① 这东西不急用，我**不一定**买。I will not necessarily buy it for it is not badly needed now.

② 选修课**不一定**全都选，选够要求的学分就可以了。Getting the required credits is ok for you ,so you do not necessarily take all the selective courses.

表示"可能不"、"也许不" ◇ Indicating the sense of may not, probably not.

③ 真正的爱情**不一定**只有一次。The true love does not necessarily come just once.

④ 女儿**不一定**能理解父母的用心。The daughter does not necessarily know the good intention of her parents.

►［必然 bìrán—必定 bìdìng］

必然	必定
（形）	（副）
bìrán	bìdìng

"必然"和"必定"都表示确定不移，但"必然"侧重事理上确定不移，"必定"侧重主观上认为确定不移 ◇ Both 必然 and 必定 mean "definite" ,but 必然 stresses certainty in argument, while 必定 stresses " the certainty in one's subjective mind".

"必然"和"必定"词性不同，"必然"可做多种句子成分，而"必定"只充当状语。在做状语时，有时二词可通用 ◇ 必然 and 必定 have different syntactical functions. 必然 can be used as differ-

B

ent sentence elements, while 必定 can only function as an adverbial. The two words are interchangeable sometimes:

① 创业**必然**(/**必定**)要冒风险。Launching a career is very likely to take risks.

② 胜利**必然**(/**必定**)属于意志坚强的人。Success definitely belongs to those with strong will.

以上二词可互换的句子,限于指较正式或较抽象的事物 ◇ The above sentences where the two words are interchangeable are limited to more formal sentences or sentences concerning abstract things.

"必然"可做主语、宾语(表示哲理上的不依人的意志为转移的客观规律) ◇ 必然 can function as the subject or object of a sentence (indicating the objective law independent of man's will), e.g.:

③ 新事物代替旧事物,这是社会发展的**必然**。It is an objective law of social development that new things will take the place of the old ones.

④ 客观的**必然**,是不以人的意志为转移的。The objective certainty is independent of man's will.

"必然"还可做定语、谓语(加"是……的") ◇ 必然 can also function as attributive and predicate (with 是……的):

⑤ 人要衰老、死亡,这是**必然**的规律。(定语) It is natural that man will get old and die. (attributive)

⑥ 不进步就会落后,这是**必然**的。(谓语) It is certain that if you do not make progress, you will fall behind. (predicate)

"必定"常表示一般的判断或表示坚决的意愿 ◇ 必定 indicates judgment or resolute will:

⑦ 天边乌云滚滚,呆会儿**必定**会下雨。The dark clouds billows across the sky, and surely it is going to rain soon.

⑧ 一年以内,我**必定**来娶你。I will marry you within a year.

这时不用"必然" ◇ 必然 cannot be used here.

▶[必 bì—必定 bìdìng——定 yīdìng]

必须 (助动) bìxū　　必需 (动) bìxū

Ⓔ must, have to/ essential, indispensable

1. "必须"是助动词,常用在主要动词之前,表示一定要、一定应该 ◇ 必须 is an auxiliary verb used in front of the main verb, indicating the meaning of " must, ought to", e.g.:

① 通过海关时**必须**检查护照。Passport is required to show at the Customs.

② 大家**必须**团结合作，共同克服困难。All of us should hang together to defeat difficulties.

如果有状语，要放在主要动词之前、"必须"之后 ◇ If there is an adverbial, it must be placed before the main verb and after 必须：

③ 这件事你**必须**亲自跑一趟。As for the matter, you must go there in person.

④ 这个问题我们**必须**再仔细研究一下。We must study it carefully again.

"必须"和主要动词也可以共同做定语，修饰主语或宾语 ◇ 必须 and the main verb can be used together as the attributive modifying the subject or object, e. g. :

⑤ 环保是每个人都**必须**做的事。Environmental protection is what everyone should do.

⑥ 这是几个**必须**记住的数字。These numbers must be memorized/born in mind.

2."必需"是动词，意思是一定需要的，一定要具备的。常做定语 ◇ 必需 is a verb meaning indispensability and usually functions as an attributive：

① 蛋白质是人体**必需**的营养。Protein is vital to our body.

② 他每月**必需**的生活费是800元。His monthly living expenses are 800 *yuan* at least.

"必需"还可以纳入"……所必需的"框架 ◇ 必需 can make up the phrase……所必需的：

③ 米、面、油、盐是日常生活**所必需**的。Rice, flour, oil and salt are all daily necessities in life.

"必需品"已经结合成词 ◇ 必需品(necessity) is a word.

▶[得 děi—必须 bìxū]

闭 关 关闭

闭	关	关闭
(动)	(动)	(动)
bì	guān	guānbì

Ⓔ close, shut/
close, shut/
close, shut

"闭"、"关"、"关闭"这三个动词都表示合拢等，但有很多不同点 ◇ The three words 闭, 关, 关闭 all mean " close but they are quite different from each other".

1. 表示合拢 ◇ The usage of indicating close：

(1)在表示合拢时，"关"的动作范围较大，"闭"较小 ◇ 关 is applied to bigger scopes of action, while 闭 to smaller ones：

① 请把门**关**上。Please shut the door.

② 放完了东西，他**关**上了箱子。

He closed the box after putting articles in it.

B

③ 他**闭**上嘴，不说话了。He became silent.

④ 忙了大半天，在汽车里他**闭**上眼睛休息了一会儿。He closed his eyes for a rest in the car after working a long time.

以上，例①②用“关”，例③④用“闭” ◇ In examples ① and ②关 is used; in examples ③ and ④闭 is used.

“关闭”也可表示合拢，如可说“关闭大门”，但限于特定目的，含“紧密合拢”的意味 ◇ 关闭 can also indicate the meaning of "close", for instance, one can say 关闭大门(close the gate), stressing that it is tightly closed.

⑤ 怕坏人骚扰，他赶紧**关闭**了大门。He closed the gate hastily in case that someone comes to disrupt him.

⑥ 这房子无人居住，门窗都紧紧地**关闭**着。All the windows and doors of the house are closed tightly for there is nobody living in it.

(2) 由于“闭”受古代汉语的影响，有时较书面化，所以常用于成语，“关”和“关闭”一般不这样用 ◇ Since 闭 is used in classical Chinese and sounds more literary, it is often used in idioms. 关 and 关闭 cannot be so used:

⑦ 最近他在写一篇论文，**闭门谢客**，专心写作。He has been working on a paper recently. In order to be devoted to it, he has stopped receiving visitors.

⑧ **闭关锁国**是行不通的，必须实行改革开放。It is unreasonable to cut one's country from the outside world; we must carry out the reform and opening-up policy.

再如“闭门思过”、“闭门造车”等 ◇ 闭门思过(ponder over one's mistakes in seclusion), 闭门造车(act blindly) are all set phrases.

2. 表示停止、结束 ◇ 闭 also means " to stop, to come to an end".

“闭”可用于这种意义，但有固定搭配，用例较少。“关”不能这样用(但可用于“关机”，见 3)。“关闭”可用于这种意义 ◇ 闭 sometimes means " to come to an end", but it must be used in some set phrases which are rather rare. 关 has no such meaning (but can be used in 关机 (to be power off), see 3). 关闭 can have this meaning:

① 大会开了五天，昨天已经胜利**闭**会。The congress lasted for five days and concluded successfully yesterday.

② 因装修,这里的集市将**闭**市三天。The fair here will be suspended for three days because of its internal refurbishment.

③ 企业虽然**关闭**了,但职工得到了妥善的安置。Though the enterprise closed down, the workers have been arranged properly.

④ 机场因大风雪暂时**关闭**。The airport closed tentatively because of the strong wind and heavy snow.

3. 表示使机器、电器等停止运作,用"关" ◇ 关 can be used to indicate to stop a machine, an electric apparatus:

① 机器已经**关**了,今天工作结束了。The work is over today and the machine has been switched off.

② 请你临走的时候**关**一下灯,好吗? Would you please turn off the light when you leave the room?

③ 电脑**关**了吗? Is the computer turned off?

这些用法,一般不用"闭"。"关闭"在书面语中可用于这项意义,如"线路关闭"、"关闭电脑" ◇ In these usages, 闭 is not used. 关闭 can be used this way in written language, e. g. 线路关闭 (switch off the circuit), 关闭电脑 (turn off computer).

4. 表示关押或把鸟兽置于栏、笼中,一般用"关" ◇ To indicate "to put in prison or to keep animals in a pen or cage", 关 is used:

① 那家伙因贪污罪被**关**进监狱了。The man was put into prison for embezzlement.

② 小鸟**关**在笼里,从这边跳到那边。The bird was caged and it hopped here and there.

毕竟 究竟

(副) (副、名)

bìjìng jiūjìng

Ⓔ after all, in the final analysis/
after all, outcome

A. 毕竟:

"毕竟"有两个义项 ◇ 毕竟 has two meanings:

1. 指出关键之点、根本条件等,下文常退一步说出应付的代价或可理解的不足之处 ◇ pointing out the crux but what follows will usually state admittedly the price one must pay or the understandable drawback:

① 这**毕竟**是竞争,总要付出心血的。After all, it is a competition, and it is necessary for you to make efforts.

② 小王**毕竟**还年轻,考虑问题有时欠周到。After all, Xiao Wang

is young and cannot take all factors into consideration.

下文也可以是正面叙述 ◇ What follows can also be some positive view:

③ 王先生**毕竟**是位数学家,逻辑思维能力很强。Mr. Wang is a mathematician, you know, and, naturally, his logical thinking is strong.

另外,这个义项下的"毕竟",常用"考试毕竟是考试"、"竞争毕竟是竞争"、"数学毕竟是数学"等回环形式,指出关键之点 ◇ Besides, one often say 考试毕竟是考试,竞争毕竟是竞争,数学毕竟是数学, etc. to point out the crucial point:

④ 考试**毕竟**是考试,怎能当儿戏呢! After all, it is a test. How could you take it as a trifling matter?

2. 表示终于,含有来之不易、必然如此或盼望已久等意思 ◇ Meaning "after all", implying something is hard-earned, long-awaited, etc.

① 虽然费了很多口舌,但他**毕竟**明白了这个道理。In the final analysis, he has understood the principle.

② 虽然还有些冷,但**毕竟**是春天了,田野开始有了些绿色。It is still a bit cold, but it is spring and the fields are covered with green.

B. 究竟(副):

1. 表示到底,用于正反、选择、特指疑问句,含有进一步追究的语气 ◇ 究竟, as an adverb, means "after all" and can be used in all sorts of questions to show the mood of further investigation:

① 做这件事情,你**究竟**有没有信心? Frankly speaking, do you have confidence in it?

② 你**究竟**去上海还是去西安? Where are you going actually, Shanghai or Xi'an?

③ 选择了这么半天,她**究竟**想学什么专业? What major on earth does she want to study after thinking about it for a long time?

以上的"究竟"不能代以"毕竟" ◇ 究竟 in ①②③ cannot be replaced by 毕竟.

2. 基本同"毕竟"(副)1,如 ◇ The usage of 究竟 is basically the same as 毕竟(adv.) in point 1, e. g. :

① 她**究竟**(/**毕竟**)是你妹妹,你应该多关心她。Anyway, she is your sister, and you should take more care of her.

② 他**究竟**(/**毕竟**)学过几年画,有一些基本功。After all, he learned painting for several years, so he has some basic skills.

3."究竟"作为名词,表示原委或结果,常说"问(一)个究竟"、"知道个究竟" ◇ 究竟 as a noun means " outcome or what actually happened". One can say 问(一)个究竟(know sth. clearly) or 知道个究竟, for example:

事情为什么没办成,他想知道个**究竟**。He wants to know why the thing hasn't been done.

▶[到底 dàodǐ—究竟 jiūjìng]

变 变化 变成

(动) (动、名)

biàn biànhuà biànchéng

Ⓔ change, become/ change, vary, variation/ become, turn into, change into

◪ 这三个词都指事物跟原来有所不同 ◇ All three words mean " to become different".

1."变"可以不带宾语 ◇ 变 can do without an object:

① 几年没见,他的样子完全**变**了。I haven't seen him for several years, and his appearance has changed completely.

② 到了山顶,天突然**变**了。On arriving the top of the mountain, the weather changed suddenly.

"变"带宾语也是有限的,如"变样子"、"变形"、"沙漠变良田"等。如果加上补语"为"等,再带宾语则较自由 ◇ 变 can take a very limited number of objects, e. g. 变样子(change), 变形(be out of shape), 沙漠变良田(Deserts have been turned into fertile fields.), etc. If it takes a complement, such as 为, it can have an object more freely, e. g.:

③ 那片荒地已经**变**为良田。The wasteland has been turned into fertile land.

"变"一般不做主语、宾语,除非用于少数较固定格式 ◇ 变 usually does not function as the subject or object of a sentence except in some set phrases, e. g.:

④ **变**总比不**变**好。Changes are better than the rigid.

再如"万变不离其宗"、"以不变应万变"等 ◇ or 万变不离其宗(change time and again, yet stay much the same), 以不变应万变(cope with a constantly changing situation by sticking to a fixed principle or policy), etc.

"变"加上"得",再带形容词是相当自由的 ◇ 变 plus 得 can take an adjective after it freely:

⑤ 他的性格**变得**开朗多了。He becomes more open and optimistic.

⑥ 这八年,北京**变得**我都快不认识了。I cannot nearly recognize Beijing after its eight-year changing.

以上一般都不能用"变化" ◇ In these examples 变化 cannot be used mostly.

2."变化"较正式,也略微抽象。如要带宾语,必须加上"成"、"出"等 ◇ 变化 is more formal and abstract. If it takes an object it must take 成,出,etc. after it:

① 情况在不断地**变化**。Things are ever changing.

② 经过改进,这个电脑软件又**变化**出了许多新花样。After improvement, the computer software has been added many new functions.

"变化"还是名词。特别是"发生……变化"、"产生……变化"、"起……变化"等较为常见 ◇ 变化 is also a noun, especially in these common used phrases 发生……变化(changes take place),产生……变化(causing changes),起……变化(having changes):

③ 小山村几年来已经发生了很大的**变化**。In recent years, the small mountain village has changed greatly.

④ 虽然只经过短短的两天,他的态度却发生了根本的**变化**。Though only two days passed, his attitude has changed radically.

"变化"还常做四字语中的中心语,如"物理变化"、"化学变化"、"天气变化"等 ◇ 变化 is often found in phrases of four characters:物理变化(physical change),化学变化(chemical change),天气变化(weather change),etc.

但在一般的句子中,"变"和"变化"是可以互换的,如例②。除非在词义十分具体,直接带宾语的情况下,只能用"变" ◇ But in many sentences,变 and 变化 are interchangeable, as in example ②. In those sentences that the meaning of changing is very concrete and that have an object, only 变 can be used.

⑤ 风向**变**了,北风**变**南风了。The wind has changed its direction: the north wind has turned into the south wind.

3."变成"实际是动词"变"加补语"成",所以必须再带宾语 ◇ 变成 is actually formed by adding complement 成 to the verb 变,so it must take an object:

① 几年不见,她已经**变成**大姑娘了。I have not seen her for several years, and she is a big girl now.

② 发生日全食时,白天似乎瞬间**变成**了黑夜。During the process of total solar eclipse, the day turns to be dark in an instant.

表达 表示

(动) (动、名)

biǎodá biǎoshì

Ⓔ express/express, expression

1. 这两个动词都可指用语言、文字及行为传达、显示思想感情等。但"表达"较抽象(如"充分表达了爱国之情"),"表示"较具体(如"表示失望"、"表示欢迎")。"表示"有时就是"说","表达"则较间接 ◇ Both verbs can mean " to express in words or action one's thought or feeling", etc., but 表达 is more abstract e. g. 充分表达了爱国之情 (fully expressing one's patriotism), and 表示 is more concrete (e. g. 表示失望 (be disappointed), 表示欢迎 (to extend a welcome)). 表示 sometimes just means " to say", while 表达 is more indirect. e. g.:

① 这些纪念品,**表达**了毕业生对母校的感激之情。These mementoes are manifestation of graduates' gratitude to their school.

② 他点点头**表示**同意。He nodded his assent.

即使同是使用语言、文字作媒介,也有抽象、具体的不同 ◇ Even though both words can use language and written words as the medium, there can still be the difference of being abstract or concrete over what has been expressed:

③ 这本回忆录**表达**了作者对往日的无限怀念。The reminiscences conveyed the writer's boundless memories of his past.

④ 他对客户**表示**感谢。He expressed his gratitude to his clients.

但在少数情况下,两个词可换用(可以是抽象或具体,意义较为模糊的) ◇ In some rare cases, the two words are interchangeable especially when it is ambiguous whether the case is concrete or abstract:

⑤ 她的信**表达**(/**表示**)了她对对方的爱慕之情。Her letter conveyed her admiration for the man.

2. "表示"还指事物本身或凭借某种特征显示某种意义,"表达"没有这种用法 ◇ 表示 can also mean that something or some features can indicate the meaning or the sense of some other things, while 表达 has no such meaning:

① 他的沉默**表示**他对此事还有些犹豫。His silence indicated his hesitation at the matter.

② 红灯**表示**车辆禁止通行。The red traffic light stands for stop.

"表示"也是名词,与"表达"无

B

共同点 ◇ 表示 is also a noun which has nothing in common with 表达:

① 点头一般是同意的**表示**。Nods normally imply assent.

④ 送人礼物是一种友好的**表示**。To offer presents is an expression of friendship.

►[表示 biǎoshì—表明 biǎomíng]

表示 表明

(动) (动)

biǎoshì biǎomíng

Ⓔ show, express/ make known, make clear

1. "表示"是通过言行来显现思想、情感等,或凭借一定的事物来显现一定的意思,如 ◇ 表示 is to express in words or action one's thought, feeling, etc., or to show a certain intention by an event, e. g. :

① 他**表示**有兴趣参加这项活动。He showed some interest in taking part in the activity.

② 中国人用摇头**表示**不同意或不以为然等。The Chinese people usually shake their heads to express disagreement or disapproval.

③ 机械表一般用指针**表示**时间。The mechanical watch generally tells time by hands.

④ 房价看涨,**表示**房地产交易发展迅猛。The rising housing prices show the rapid development of real estate.

2. "表明"是"表示明白"的意思。以上四个例句都不能用"表明"。"表明"的宾语,可以是态度、立场、观点、身份等,其中有的与"表示"的宾语一样,但意思不一样 ◇ 表明 means to make clear. In the four examples above, 表明 cannot be used. The object of 表明 can be attitude, standpoint, opinion, status, etc. , some of which may be the same as the objects of 表示, but with a different implication, e. g. :

① 他早已**表明**了自己对处理这个问题的立场。He has made clear his stance for the problem earlier.

② 她**表明**了自己的态度:坚决反对这样做。She showed her attitude clearly, i. e. , she objected it firmly.

例①②虽可以换用"表示",但"表示"只是"说出"的意思,"表明"还有"说清楚"、"明白无误地说出"的意思 ◇ Although 表示 can be used instead in examples ① and ②, 表示 only means to tell, while 表明 means to tell clearly and explicitly.

3. "表示"的宾语可以是双音节

B

动词或其扩展 ◇ The object of 表示 can be a disyllabic verb or its expansion, e. g. :

表示同意 show one's approval
表示十分同意 show one's utter approval
表示反对 show one's disapproval
表示坚决反对 show one's resolute disapproval

"表明"不能带这样的宾语 ◇ 表明 cannot take such an object.

"表示"的宾语还可以是双音节形容词及其扩展 ◇ 表示 can also take a disyllabic adjective or its expansion as its object, e. g. :

表示高兴 show one's happiness
表示十分高兴 show one's great happiness
表示不满 show one's disatisfaction
表示强烈不满 show one's extreme disatisfaction

"表明"也不能这样用 ◇ 表明 cannot be used this way.

"表明"的宾语如果是动词性或描写性的,不能是一个双音节词,而必须是小句 ◇ If the object of 表明 is verbal or descriptive, it must not be a disyllabic word but a clause, e. g. :

① 大家一致同意,**表明**全班是团结的。The consensus of the class showed that the class was united.

② 这**表明**他的话全是谎言。This shows what he said are all lies.

③ 结局**表明**他的计划十分荒谬。The ending shows his plan is sheer absurd.

如果意思上需要,"表示"也可以带小句宾语,如 1 中的例④ ◇ When necessary, 表示 can also have a clause as its object, e. g. example ④ in point 1.

"表示"可以做主语、宾语,"表明"不可以 ◇ 表示 can be the subject or object of a sentence, while 表明 cannot, e. g. :

④ 他的这种**表示**,似乎还不可能取得大家的信任。His remarks don't seem to win others' confidence.

⑤ 他听了那番话没有什么特别的**表示**。He said nothing special at those words.

▶[表达 biǎodá—表示 biǎoshì]

别 (形) bié 别的 (形) biéde

Ⓔ other, another/other, another

这两个形容词都是非谓形容词,也叫"区别词"。意思都是除了指定的某事物以外,所剩下的

B

人或事物。“别”只修饰少数名词,如“别人”、“别称”、“别名”、“别号”等,有的已经固定成词。“别的”修饰名词等较自由,它所修饰的名词,可以是单数的也可以是多数的,但多数的较多 ◇ Both 别 and 别的 are adjectives which can only be used as attributives, not as predicates, adverbials, or complements. 别 can qualify only a few nouns, e. g. 别人, 别称, 别名, 别号 etc. Some of them have become words, and not phrases. 别的 is quite free in qualifying nouns and the nouns qualified can either be singular or plural, but mostly plural, e. g. :

① 除了这种方法,**别的**方法都不行。Except for this one, none of the methods works.

② 还有**别的**样式的衣服吗? Are there any other styles of clothes?

③ 这两件衣服除了颜色,没有**别的**不同。Except for the color, the two coats are the same.

修饰“人”时,这两个词也有差别:“别”只能修饰单音节的“人”(已经固定成词),“别的”可以是“别的朋友”、“别的同学”、“别的老师”等。有时二词可互换 ◇ When qualifying 人, there is a difference between the two words: 别 can only qualify the monosyllabic 人(别人 has become a fixed word), 别的 can be used to form phrases like 别的朋友(other friends), 别的同学 (other classmates), 别的老师 (other teachers), etc. Sometimes the two are interchangeable:

④ 除了妈妈,你家里还有**别人**(/**别的人**)吗? Besides your mother, do you have any other family members?

至于“别无选择”、“别有洞天”、“别说了”等中的“别”,是副词 ◇ 别 is an adverb in 别无选择 (without any other choice), 别有洞天(a place of unique, enchanting beauty), 别说了(don't say any more), etc.

如有数量词,“别的”可放在数量词之前或数量词之后(表示除了指定以外的一个或一些) ◇ If there is a numeral-measure word, 别的 can be placed either before or after it (to mean other or another):

⑤ 她和**别的**五个女孩子一起去旅行。She went on a trip with other five girls.

⑥ 她和五个**别的**女孩子一起去旅行。She and other five girls went on a trip.

别人 (代) biérén　　**他人** (代) tārén

Ⓔ another person, other people/

another person, other people

1. "别人"表示除了提到或指定的人 ◇ 别人 means " another person or other people", e. g. :

① 明天的联欢会只有我们单位的人参加,没有**别人**。Only the staff from our working unit will take part in the get-together tomorrow.

②——明天的联欢会,我可以带**别人**来吗? Can we take others to the get-together tomorrow?
——可以带你的爱人,**别人**不行。Only your spouse. Others won't do.

"别人"还表示当事者(自己或某人)以外的人,这个意义的"别人"有时读 biéren ◇ 别人 means "another person or other people besides oneself" sometimes, it is pronounced as "biéren":

③ 他很自负,看不起**别人**。He is very self-conceited, and looks down upon others.

④ **别人**的东西,不要随便动。Don't touch the articles without their owner's permission.

2. "他人"意思和"别人"相同,但书面色彩较浓,多用于较正式的表述、格言或四字语中 ◇ 他人 has the same meaning as 别人, but is more literary and mostly used in more formal statements, maxims or four-character phrases:

⑤ 这位老农在山上种了一大片树,不但惠及**他人**,也惠及子孙。The old farmer planted a lot of trees on the mountain, which can not only do good to others, but also to his offsprings.

⑥ 作家应该善于在平凡的事物中发现**他人**所忽略的意义。Writers should be good at discovering the significance of common things that are neglected by ordinary people.

⑦ 他总是关心**他人**,胜过关心自己。His concern for others is above for himself.

并 (副、连) bìng　并且 (连) bìngqiě

Ⓔ side by side, simultaneously/and

1. **并**(副):

(1)表示两种事或两种以上的事同时存在或进行,一般用于某些单音节动词前 ◇ 并, as an adv., expresses two or more things that exist simultaneously, mostly used before monosyllabic verbs:

① 这两种说法可以**并**存。The two expressions are both acceptable.

② 理论和实践应该**并**重。Theory and practice should be equally valued.

(2) 用在否定词前加强否定语气或反驳语气 ◇ It can be used in front of a negative word to reinforce the tone of negation or refutation:

③ 你以为他糊涂,其实他**并不**糊涂。You thought he was stupid;in fact,he is not stupid at all.

④ 这件事我**并没有**同意呀! As for this matter,I didn't agree to it at all.

⑤ 我们主张大家团结,但团结**并非**一团和气。We advocate unity,which does not mean keeping on good terms with everyone at the expense of principles.

以上都不能用"并且" ◇ 并且 cannot be used in the examples above.

2. "并"(连)和"并且"(连)有共同点 ◇ 并 (conj.) and 并且 (conj.) have something in common:

(1) 表示两种动作、状况先后或同时存在或进行(用在两个谓语或短语之间,也可用在两个助词之间) ◇ Indicating two actions or conditions happen one after another or simultaneously (used between two predicates or phrases,or between two auxiliaries):

① 他们研究**并**(/**并且**)制定了工作计划。They studied and have worked out a work plan.

② 这个项目,我们应该**并**(/**并且**)必须按时完成。The project should and must be completed on time.

③ 他 1997 年大学毕业,**并**(/**并且**)于同年出版第一本著作。He graduated from university in 1997 and published his first book in the same year.

(2) 用在后一分句,表示递进 ◇ Used in the second clause to show progression:

④ 大家提出了方案,**并**(/**并且**)指定专人负责完成。We have worked out a plan and assigned a person specially to carry it out.

⑤ 他们俩相爱,**并**(/**并且**)准备结婚。They love each other and are about to get married.

3. "并且"(连)还有以下用法 ◇ 并且 as a conjunction has two more usages:

(1) 表示更进一层,常用于描写性词语之间,有时还可用于小句之间 ◇ Meaning "besides or moreover, mostly used between descriptive words or phrases and even clauses":

① 这种商品便宜**并且**耐用。The

merchandise is cheap and enduring.

② 这座建筑宽敞适用**并且**环境幽雅。The building is spacious and suitable; what is more, the surrounding is fine.

③ 他们情绪很高**并且**每个人都做好了准备。They are in high spirits and each of them has made full preparation.

(2) 用"不但……并且"表示更进一层 ◇ 不但……并且 means "not only... but also":

④ 他**不但**健康,**并且**长寿。He was not only healthy, but lived a long life.

⑤ 她**不但**喜欢钢琴,**并且**能演奏很多曲目。She not only likes piano, but also can play many melodies.

"并"不能这样用 ◇ 并 as a conjunction cannot be so used.

▶[而且 érqiě—并且 bìngqiě]

病 (名、动) bìng　疾病 (名) jíbìng

Ⓔ illness, be ill/disease

这两个词都表示生理或心理的不健康状况。"病"(名)表示具体的病患,如"心脏病、眼病、神经病"等;"病"(动)表示患病、得病。"疾病"(名)一般是病的总称,较正式,也可用于抽象意义 ◇ Both words mean "illness". 病(n.) means "a particular disease", e. g. heart disease, ophthalmia, neuropathy etc. 病(v.) means "to be ill". 疾病(n.) is a general term for ailment, which is more formal and can be used figuratively.

① 他得了**病**,需要在家休息几天。He is ill and needs to stay at home for a few days' rest.

② 老师因**病**请假两天。The teacher asked for two days' leave because of his illness.

③ 她**病**得不轻。She is seriously ill.

以上例①是名词,例③是动词,例②的病如解释为"有病",应为动词;如解释为"病患",应为名词 ◇ In the examples above, 病 is a noun in ①, a verb in ③, in ② it can either be understood as a verb or a noun.

④ 冬季来临,要防止呼吸道**疾病**的发生。When winter comes, beware of respiratory diseases.

例④"疾病"是总称 ◇ 疾病 in example ④ is a general term.

在习惯上,也常说"一种疾病"、"某种疾病",虽不是总称,仍较正式。用于抽象意义时,可说 ◇ One can usually say 一种疾病(a kind of illness) or 某种疾病(a illness), which sounds rather formal. When it is used figuratively, one can say:

⑤ 犯罪是一种社会**疾病**。Crimes are social diseases.

但也可说"犯罪是一种社会病" ◇ Or 犯罪是一种社会病.

另外,"有病"、"得病"、"患病"、"治病"等都是习惯搭配,不用"疾病" ◇ Moreover, 有病(have illness),得病(have got illness),患病(have got illness),治病(cure the illness),etc. are all commonly used phrases,where 疾病 is not used.

波浪 浪 浪潮

(名) (名) (名)

bōlàng làng làngcháo

Ⓔ wave/wave
ripple/tide
wave

◪ "波浪"、"浪"、"浪潮"都是名词,具体用法有区别 ◇ 波浪, 浪, 浪潮 are all nouns, but they have different usages.

1. 波浪

指(江、河、湖、海等)起伏的水面 ◇ 波浪 refers to " the undulate surface of rivers, lakes and seas":

① 起风了,湖面上有了**波浪**。The wind rippled the lake.

② 虽然**波浪**很大,船还是出海了。Though the wave was rough, the ship still put out to sea.

③ 风停了,**波浪**也小多了。The wind stopped and the wave became calmer as well.

以上各例也可用"浪" ◇ In the examples above, 浪 can be used instead.

2. 浪

意思同"波浪",还可比喻与水的波浪相似的事物,如"麦浪"、"声浪"等 ◇ 浪 means the same as 波浪. It can be used metaphorically to describe similar things like 麦浪(wheat waves),声浪(sound waves),etc.

① **浪**太大,不能游泳。The wave is too rough for swimming in the sea.

② 海边上有很多人在冲**浪**。Many people are surfing in the sea.

③ 无际的麦田里麦**浪**起伏,丰收在望。In the boundless field the wheat is rippling in the wind. A good harvest is in-sight.

④ 远处传来一阵阵嘈杂的声**浪**。Hubbub of sounds is coming from the distance in waves.

例①也可用"波浪"。例②因"冲浪"是习惯搭配,例③④是比喻义,不用"波浪" ◇ In example ① 波浪 can be used instead. In example ②,however 冲浪 is an idiomatic phrase,and in ③ and ④麦浪 and

声浪 are both metaphorical usage, so 波浪 could not be used.

"一浪高过一浪"常表示比喻意义 ◇ 一浪高过一浪 is usually used metaphorically:

⑤ 科教兴国的倡议，**一浪高过一浪**。The proposal of invigorating the country with science and technology was put forward more and more urgently.

3. 浪潮

多用于抽象和比喻意义，表示社会、文化运动等 ◇ 浪潮 is mostly used in an abstract sense or metaphorically to describe social or cultural movement, etc.:

① 上个世纪80年代开始，中国掀起了改革的**浪潮**。The tide of reform began in China in the 1980s.

② 在影视界有一种新**浪潮**：大演宫廷戏。There is a new trend emerging in the film and TV circles, i. e., more and more court stories are appearing in films and TV plays.

以上两句，不用"波浪"和"浪" ◇ In examples ① and ②, neither 波浪 nor 浪 can be used.

播放 播送 播音

(动) (动)

bōfàng bōsòng bō yīn

Ⓔ broadcast/ broadcast, transmit/ broadcast

◥ "播放"可表示通过广播放送，也可表示(一般通过电视)播映影、视片等；"播送"只表示通过广播传送或放送；"播音"是动宾短语，表示通过广播播送节目。如以下二例表示广播放送时，用"播放"、"播送"都可以 ◇ 播放 can mean "to broadcast either through radio or through television", whereas 播送 only means "to broadcast through radio". 播音 is a verb-object phrase meaning "to broadcast a program". In examples ① and ② below, either will do.

① 今天北京人民广播电台将**播放(/播送)**市长讲话。Today Radio Beijing will broadcast the mayor's speech.

② 这个录音，校广播电台已经**播放(/播送)**过了。The recording has been broadcast on the school radio.

但"播送"还可表示通过广播传送具体消息，"播放"一般少用 ◇ 播送 can also mean "to broadcast a specific piece of news", but 播放 is rarely so used:

③ 新闻广播中**播送**了飞机失事的消息。The air crash has been announced through the news broadcast.

④ 现在本台**播送**大风降温警报。We now bring you the warning of strong wind and drop in temperature.

表示通过电视放映电影、电视片及节目等，则用“播放” ◇ To broadcast a film, television play or other programs by television, 播放 is usually used:

⑤ 中央电视台现在**播放**大会实况。The CCTV now will live broadcast the congress.

⑥ 这个频道经常**播放**科幻片。Science fiction films are often broadcast on this channel.

“播音”可说“播音员”、“播音室”、“播音时间”等，并可拆说 ◇ 播音 can be expanded into phrases such as 播音员(announcer), 播音室(broadcasting studio), 播音时间(broadcasting time), etc., and can be decomposed:

⑦ 这位**播音员**的嗓音真洪亮。The voice of the man announcer is really sonorous.

⑧ **播完了音**，他才去吃饭。He left for meal after the broadcast concluded.

捕 (动) bǔ　逮捕 (动) dàibǔ　捉 (动) zhuō

Ⓔ arrest, catch/
arrest/
catch, hold, grasp

◪ “捕”、“逮捕”、“捉”都是动词，但用法有区别 ◇ 捕，逮捕 and 捉 are all verbs but they have different usages.

1. 表示捉拿归案等，多用“捕”、“逮捕”；用“捉”较口语化，是非正式的。“被捕”、“捉奸”是常见搭配 ◇ To mean arrest, 捕 and 逮捕 are often used; 捉 is informal and used in colloquial language. 被捕(be arrested), 捉奸(catch adulterers in the act) are common phrases.

① 他因贪污案件**被捕**(/**逮捕**)了。He was arrested for embezzlement.

② 警方去逮**捕**(/**捕**/**捉**)嫌疑人时，已经跑掉了。The criminal had run away when the policemen went to arrest him.

③ 他在商场行窃时被当场**捉住**。He was caught on the spot when he stole in the shop.

2. 表示获取猎物，用“捉”和“捕”，前者口语中更常用 ◇ 捉 and 捕 can be used to mean "hunt for prey". The former is more colloquial.

“捕鱼”、“猫捉老鼠”等是常见搭配，例如 ◇ 捕鱼(catch fish)

and 猫捉老鼠(A cat catches a mouse.)are common phrases,e.g.:

① 湖边的百姓多以**捕鱼**为生。The residents by the lake primarily live on fishing.

② 看!猫在**捉老鼠**。Look! The cat is chasing after a rat.

③ 由于环境污染,最近这里**捉**(/**捕**)不到螃蟹了。Due to the pollution of the environment, crabs are disappearing from the area recently.

3. 表示用手握或抓,用"捉"(是文言的遗留),如"捉笔"、"捉刀"、"捉襟见肘"等 ◇ 捉 also means "to grasp with hand" (left over from classical Chinese), such as 捉笔(hold a pen), 捉刀(write an article, etc. for sb. else, ghost write), 捉襟见肘(pull together one's lapels to conceal raggedness only to expose one's elbows), etc.

① 老作家病重,双手已经不能**捉笔**为文了。The old writer is seriously ill, and he is no longer able to hold a pen writing articles.

② 最近他家经济情况不好,在开支上不免**捉襟见肘**。The financial situation of his family is not good recently, and naturally he lacks enough money to support his family.

捕捞 (动) bǔlāo　　**捞** (动) lāo

Ⓔ fish for, catch/
fish for, drag for

"捕捞"和"捞"都是动词,"捕捞"的意义较单纯,只表示从水中捕获和捞取水生动植物;"捞"的意思较多,表示从液体中取物;用不正当手段获取等。下面两句中,两个词都表示打捞鱼虾等,可以通用 ◇ Both 捕捞 and 捞 are verbs. 捕捞 simply means "to fish for and drag aquatic animals and plants"; 捞 has more complicated meaning: "to fish for, to acquire by improper means, etc". In the two examples below, both words mean "to fish for" and so are interchangeable:

① 这位渔民今天**捕捞**(/**捞**)到不少虾。The fisherman caught a lot of shrimps today.

② 由于渔业资源发生问题,最近这里**捕捞**(/**捞**)不到多少鱼了。Due to the problem of fishery source, less fish can be caught here recently.

但"捕捞"有时较书面化,如"近海捕捞"、"捕捞业""捕捞技术"等,"捞"不能这样用 ◇ However, 捕捞 is more literary, e.g. 近海

B

捕捞(in shore fishing),捕捞业(fishing),捕捞技术(fishing technology), etc., 捞 cannot be so used:

③ 这些渔民从事**近海捕捞业**。These fishermen are mainly engaged in offshore fishing.

④ 由于**捕捞技术**的提高,渔业也有很大的发展。Owing to the improvement of fishing technologies,the fishery has developed greatly.

另外,"捞"还用于其他义项 ◇ Besides,捞 has other usages:

⑤ 她的戒指不小心掉到小水沟里了,费了不少劲儿才**捞**出来。(表示从液体中取物) Due to carelessness, her ring dropped into the small drain. It took her great efforts to take it out. (to fish for sth. from liquid)

⑥ 张大妈正从油锅里把炸好的鱼**捞**出来。(同上) Grandma Zhang is taking the fried fish out of the oil wok. (ditto)

⑦ 利用职务,他这几年**捞**了不少好处。(表示用不正当手段获取)She has made a killing these years. (to acquire through unlawful means)

⑧ 这家伙当官捞钱**捞**得太厉害,被判了刑。(同上) The guy was too much to make money by abusing his official position, and was finally sentenced to the imprisonment. (ditto)

⑨ 他用行贿等非法手段,**捞**了不少政治资本。(表示比喻意义)He got quite a lot of political capital. (used figuratively)

不错 好

(形) (形)

bùcuò hǎo

Ⓔ not bad/good

1. "不错"和"好"都可表示使人满意的、优点多的 ◇ 不错 and 好 both mean " satisfactory, meritorious" :

① 今天天气**不错**(/很**好**)。(谓语)It is not bad today. (predicate)

② 这是个**不错**(/**好**)的主意。(定语)It's a good idea. (attributive)

③ 这本书写得**不错**(/**好**)。(补语)The book is fine. (complement)

以上三句,两个词基本可以互换。但"好"作谓语时常加"很"(意义已淡化),否则有比较的意味 ◇ In the three examples above,不错 and 好 are interchangeable. When used as the predicate, 好 often takes 很(with its force lost); otherwise it implies the sense of comparison.

"好极了"表示非常使人满意等,"不错"不能加"极了" ◇ 好极了 means " most satisfactory ", while 不错 can never take 极了:

④ 这个菜味道**好**极了(/**不错**)。The dish is very delicious.

2. 两个词都可表示健康、友好、亲密等 ◇ Both words can mean " healthy, friendly, intimate", etc.

① 他的身体**不错**(/很**好**)。He is in good health.

② 这两个国家关系**不错**(/很**好**)。There is a friendly relationship between the two countries.

③ 他们俩是**不错**的朋友(/**好**朋友)。They are good friends.

表示亲密、相爱时,常用"好" ◇ 好 is sometimes used to describe those who fall in love with each other:

④ 小王和张小姐**好**了。Xiao Wang fell into love with Miss Zhang.

3. 有时这两个词的词义是完全不相容的 ◇ Sometimes these two words have totally incompatible meaning:

(1)"好"做定语表示赞美、感情上的赞誉 ◇ 好 as an attributive means " praise or commend":

① "**好**孩子,别吵了!" "Dear kids, please stop quarrelling!"

② "**好**妈妈,再多给我点零花钱吧!" " Dear mummy, please give me a little more pocket money!"

③ "**好**老弟,我有话跟你说。" " My dear brother, I have something to say to you."

④ 这里的农民已经过上**好**日子了。("好日子"已成词) It's time for the farmers here to live a happy life. (好日子 is a word meaning happy life)

⑤ 这一片**好**山**好**水,就是我们的家乡! The land with beautiful landscape is our hometown.

这种"好"都是一种最高的赞美,没有程度之分,不能有"比较好、好一点儿"等,因此排斥"不错"。以上例①至⑤都不能用"不错" ◇ 好 in the five examples above means " the highest praise"; one cannot say 比较好, 好一点儿, etc. Therefore, 不错 cannot be used in either of the above examples.

(2)"还好"做谓语,可以对身体的不适(如"疼、累、热"等)表示"还可以忍受","没有大问题"等;或对事物的消极性质表示"还可以承受"等 ◇ 还好 as a predicate means " tolerable to the discomfort of the body (e.g., pain, tiredness, hotness) or the passive nature of things":

⑥ ——头疼不疼? Have you got a headache? /Is your head

still aching?

——**还好**。I am OK.

⑦ ——累了吧? Are you tired?

——**还好**。I'm OK.

⑧ ——你看我是不是太胖了? Don't you think I am too fat?

——**还好**。I don't think so.

⑨ ——这东西是不是买贵了? Don't you think the price is too expensive?

——**还好**。No, I don't.

⑩ ——外面太吵了吧? Don't you think it is too noisy outside?

——**还好**。No, it's all right.

这样的"好",也排斥"不错" ◇ Such 好 also has nothing in common with 不错.

(3)"好"还有多种义项,如表示痊愈("病好了");表示易于("好做");表示完成(补语:"写好了"、"修理好了");表示程度深(用在谓词前:"好怕"、"好厉害");表示应允("好,我同意")等。这些都不能用"不错" ◇ 好 has many other meanings, e. g., indicating the recovery from illness (病好了); something easy to be done (好做); something have been done as complement: 写好了 (have written), 修理好了 (is repaired); high degree (used before the predicate): 好怕 (be very much afraid), 好厉害 (very fierce); to agree: 好,我同意 (all right, I agree). In all these, 不错 cannot be used.

(4)"不错"有时是"不"+"错",表示正确(不做定语);"好"不能这样用 ◇ 不错 sometimes is 不 + 错 meaning correct (cannot be an attributive). 好 cannot be so used:

⑪ **不错**,这事是我干的。Yes, it is done by me.

⑫ 这个答案一点儿**不错**,完全正确。The answer is perfectly correct.

不但 (连) bùdàn　不只 (连) bùzhǐ

Ⓔ not only/not only

1. 这两个词都常用在复句的从句中,在主句中有"而且"、"还"、"也"、"并且"等呼应,表示更进一层。"不但"后肯定式、否定式都可以 ◇ Both words are often used in the subordinate clause of a complex sentence; in the main clause there is 而且, 还, 也, or 并且, etc. to correspond to mean "further more". Either a positive or a negative structure can follow 不但.

① 我们俩**不但**认识,**而且**很熟。We are not only acquaintances, but also familiar with each other.

② 你们这样吵下去,**不但**解决不了问题,**还会**把事情闹僵。Nothing would be achieved if you argue away this way. Moreover, you just worsen it.

以上例①②,也可用"不只"。"不但"略口语化一些 ◇ 不只 can also be used instead in examples ① and ②. 不但 is more colloquial.

2. 在主句中也可用"就是……也"、"连……也(都)"等,表示情况的递进达到极端的程度。两个词都可以用 ◇ In the main clause, 就是……也, 连……也(都), etc. can also be used to show the extremity of the case.

① 船驶入大海,**不但**(/**不只**)看不见陆地,**连**飞鸟都看不到了。When we sailed into the sea, the land was out of sight, so was a bird.

② 这种情况**不但**(/**不只**)在中国少有,**就是**在外国也是罕见的。This situation is not only rare in China, but also rare in other countries.

3. 有时,从句的谓词是否定式,主句中用"反而"、"反倒"、"还"等,表示某种情况没有引起应有的反应,而引起相反的反应 ◇ Sometimes, the predicate of the subordinate clause is in the negative, and there is 反而, 反倒, 还, etc. in the main clause to show that, instead of inducing due reaction, the condition brings about a contrary one:

① 我求哥哥帮忙,他**不但**不管,**反而**笑我。I turned to my elder brother. He didn't give me a hand; he made fun of me instead.

② 他忙了一辈子,退休了,**反倒**不适应清闲的生活了。He worked for most of his life, when he retired, he found it difficult to adapt himself to a leisurely life.

这种情况,以用"不但"为多。略书面化些,也可用"不只" ◇ In such cases, 不但 is often used. To be more literary, 不只 can also be used.

4. "不只……还……"等,表示数量上的递进,从句的主要谓词是"是" ◇ 不只……还……, etc. indicates the increase in quantity and the main verb of the predicate of the subordinate clause is 是:

① 来的客人**不只**是中国人,**还**有一些外国人。Not all of the guests are from China; some are from foreign countries.

② 他们家**不只**是两代人,**还**有爷爷呢。There are not just two generations, children and parents, in the family. Their grandfather also lives with them.

这时不用"不但",但严格限于数量的递进,并用主要谓词"是"。如换用别的谓词,则可用"不但" ◇ In these cases 不但 is not used, as is strictly limited to the increase in quantity and the main verb being 是. If another verb is used, 不但 will also do:

③ 来的客人**不只**(/**不但**)有中国人,**还有**外国人。Not all of the guests are from China; some of them are foreigners.

④ 他们家**不只**(/**不但**)有两代人,**还有**爷爷呢。There are not just two generations, children and parents, in their family. Their grandfather also lives with them.

或 or:

⑤ 山里**不只**(/**不但**)生活着猴子,**还**有其他小动物。The mountain is not only home to monkeys, but also to other small animals.

注意:"不只"有时不是连词,是"不"修饰"只"(副词),用于单句 ◇ Note: Sometimes 不只 is not a conjunction, but a phrase with 不 qualifying 只(adv.), used in a simple sentence:

⑥ 他**不只**有一种爱好。He has more than one hobby.

不管 不论 无论

(连) (连) (连)

bùguǎn bùlùn wúlùn

Ⓔ no matter; regardless of/ no matter; regardless of/ no matter; regardless of

这三个词,都表示在任何条件下结果不变,是用于条件关系复句的连词。其中"不管"最口语化,"无论"略书面化。句中要有表示任指的疑问代词或并列词语,后面常有"也"、"都"等呼应 ◇ The three words all indicate that the result remains unchanged under whatever condition; they are used as conjunctions in conditional complex sentences. 不管 is the most colloquial of the three. 无论 is more literary. There must be an interrogative pronoun with a general reference or juxtaposed words or phrases in the sentence, with 也, 都, etc. to go with it, e. g. :

① **不管**(/**不论**/**无论**)困难多么大,我们**也**要克服。(有表示任指的疑问代词)No matter how difficult it is, we will overcome it. (with an interrogative pronoun with a general reference)

② **不管**(/**不论**/**无论**)是谁,都得凭票入场。(同上)No matter whoever you are, you will not be admitted without tickets. (ditto)

③ **不管(/不论/无论)**下不下雨,都应该按时出发。(有并列肯定、否定形式的词语) Whether it rains or not, we will start on time. (with juxtaposed phrases)

④ **不管(/不论/无论)**是工作还是学习,她都十分努力。(有并列词语) Whether it is to work or to learn, she is industrious. (with juxtaposed phrases)

三个词可互换,但语体色彩有所不同 ◇ The three words are interchangeable but with different flavours.

在搭配上,"无论如何"是习惯搭配,而"不管怎么样"、"不论怎么样"也较常见 ◇ To see from the point of view of collocation, 无论如何 is an idiomatic phrase, and 不管怎么样 and 不论怎么样 are also common.

不过 但是 可是

(连) (连) (连)

bùguò dànshì kěshì

Ⓔ but, get, however/ but, nevertheless, however/ but, however

◥ 这三个连词都表示转折,连接分句、句子甚至段落。其中"但是"略书面化。以下三句,可互换 ◇ All the three words mean "a transition" and can be used to connect clauses, sentences, and even paragraphs. Of them, 但是 is more literary. In the sentences below, the three words are interchangeable.

① 他个子虽然不高,**不过(/但是/可是)**十分强壮。Though he is not tall, He is very strong.

② 我想买车,**不过(/但是/可是)**钱还不够。I want to buy a car, but I cannot afford it now.

③ 我们队这次打输了,**不过(/但是/可是)**不必灰心。Though we are defeated this time, don't lose heart.

后面的分句或句子如有主语,"但是"、"不过"只能用在主语之前(如例②),"可是"可用在主语前或后。有时有"虽然","却","还"等与之呼应,例如 ◇ If the following clause or sentence has a subject, 但是, 不过 can only precede it (e.g., example ②); 可是 can precede the subject or follow it. Sometimes there is 虽然, 却, 还, etc. to go with it, e.g.:

④ **虽然**很累,**可是**心里却很痛快。Though we are weary, we feel very happy.

B

⑤ 你可以休息,我**可是**还有不少事要做。You can have a rest, but I have many other things to do.

有时,"不过"等可以置于"虽然"、"尽管"等之前。"不过"等要有停顿 ◇ Sometimes,不过 can precede 虽然,尽管. There must be a pause after 不过,etc.

⑥ 你们的困难确实不少;**不过**(/**但是**/**可是**),**虽然**我想帮助你们,却是力不从心。I know you are confronted with many difficulties. Yet, regretfully, my ability falls short of my wishes.

"不过"还是副词,表示往小里说,有"只是"的意思 ◇ 不过 is also an adverb meaning "only":

⑦ 我**不过**做了我应该做的。I've just done what I should.

⑧ **不过**只用了半天,他就写完了这篇报告。He finished this report in no more than half a day.

▶ [但是 dànshì—可是 kěshì]

不是……就是……
bùshì …… jiùshì ……

不是……而是……
bùshì …… érshì ……

Ⓔ either... or... / not... but...

1. 表示二者必居其一,可以插入词、短语或小句。插入的两个成分在意义上和形式上常是具有共性的 ◇ 不是……就是…… means "either... or...". Words, phrases or clauses can be inserted. The inserted elements are often similar in meaning and structure.

① 这些天一直下雨,**不是**大雨,**就是**小雨。It has been raining all these days, either heavily or slightly.

② 周末他**不是**去歌厅唱歌,**就是**去参加舞会。On weekends, he either goes to singing house or a party.

③ **不是**你去**就是**我去,总得去一个人。Either you or I will go.

有时"二者必居其一"不是指具体人、事或行为,而是用两件事物概括一种状态 ◇ Sometimes the structure "either... or..." is not applied to actual persons, things, or actions, but two specific things that indicate a certain state. e.g.:

④ 他可真爱挑剔,**不是**嫌这个**就是**嫌那个。He is so critical that he is always complaining about this or that.

⑤ 这几天**不是**风**就是**雨,天气很不好。It has been bad all these days, either rainy or windy.

2. “不是……而是……”表示是此不是彼，也可插入各种成分。“不是”前可以有“并”等 ◇ 不是……而是，not... but, stresses the latter of two things and all sorts of elements can be inserted. 并 can be used in front of 不是：

⑥ 她要去的地方**不是**北京**而是**上海。The place she is going to visit is not Beijing but Shanghai.

⑦ 我并**不是**要你马上开始做，**而是**请你积极做好准备。I am not asking you to do it right now, but to prepare well for it.

不要紧 bù yàojǐn　没关系 méi guānxi　没什么 méi shénme　没事儿 méi shìr

Ⓔ of no importance, doesn't matter

1. 这四个词语都表示无关紧要、没有妨碍。都可用于下列二句中 ◇ The four phrases all mean" to be of no importance". In the two examples below, any of the four can be used to mean the same：

① 对不起，让你久等了。**不要紧(/没关系/没什么/没事儿)** I'm sorry to keep you waiting a long time. It's all right.

② **没关系(/不要紧/没什么/没事儿)**，一切都会好起来的。It doesn't matter, all will be OK.

从结构上看，“不要紧”可拆开，说“不大要紧”、“不怎么要紧等”，“没关系”可说“没什么关系”，“没事儿”可说“没什么事儿”，但“没什么”中间不能插入其他成分。如 ◇ To view from the structure, 不要紧 can be split into 不大要紧，不怎么要紧，没关系 can be split into 没什么关系，没事儿 into 没什么事儿，but 没什么 can't be split. e. g. :

③ 他的病**不大要紧**。His illness is not very serious.

④ 失败了也**没什么关系**，从头再来嘛。Failure doesn't matter; you can start over.

⑤ 他已经脱离危险了，**没什么事儿**了。He is OK now, for he is out of danger.

⑥ 为了帮助别人，自己累点儿**没什么**。Being tired for offering help to others is of no importance.

2. “不要紧”等还可表示表面上似乎无关紧要(后一分句有转折，指出实际上有影响) ◇ 不要紧 can be used in the subordinate clause to tell that sth. seems to be of no importance, but really does harm (stated in the main clause)：

① 这一停电**不要紧(/没什么)**，

B

冰箱里的肉全变质了。It looks all right to have a power cut, but all the meat in the refrigerator has gone bad.

② 孩子一哭**不要紧(/没事儿)**,他的文章写不下去了。The child's crying made him not be able to write on.

这时前面常有"一"。"没关系"一般不这样用 ◇ In such cases, 一 is often used in front of the verb to indicate an action to be followed by a result. 没关系 cannot be used in this way.

3. "没关系"等还可用于客气话,回答对方的"对不起" ◇ 没关系 etc. can also be used as a response to another person's apology:

① ——对不起,踩了您的脚。I am sorry for stepping on your foot.
——**没关系(/不要紧/没什么/没事儿)**。It doesn't matter.

② ——打扰你了,耽误你休息了。I am sorry for bothering you and holding you up.
——**没关系(/不要紧/没什么/没事儿)**,不客气。It doesn't matter. Don't mention it.

4. "没事儿"还可表示事情不大 ◇ 没事儿 can also be used to mean "nothing serious":

① ——出了什么问题吗? Is there anything wrong?
——**没事儿**。It's OK.

② ——他的病怎么样? How about his illness?
——**没事儿**,休息几天就会好。Nothing serious. He will be OK after a few days's rest.

(名) (名)
bùmén dānwèi

Ⓔ department, branch/unit

"部门"和"单位"这两个名词都可表示事业或企业的机构,但"单位"还可表示计算事物的标准量的名称等 ◇ Both 部门 and 单位 mean "the organization of some enterprise or business", but 单位 is also a term of a standard measurement.

1. 部门

① 他在一家企业的管理**部门**工作。He works in the managing department of an enterprise.

② 我们都在科学院,但**部门**不同。We both work in the Science Academy, but in different departments.

③ 医疗**部门**要贯彻全心全意为人民服务的精神。Medical institutions should follow the principle of serving people wholeheartedly.

以上例②③也可换用"单位"。例①的"管理部门"是习惯搭配。一般说,"部门"较"单位"大,所以两个词可以用在一个句子中,例如 ◇ In example ② and ③, 单位 can be used instead. 管理部门 in example ① is an idiomatic phrase. Generally speaking, 部门 is bigger than 单位, so the two words can be used in one sentence, e. g. :

④ 这个**部门**,一共有三个**单位**。The department consists of three sections.

2. 单位

① 附中是这所大学的附属**单位**。The affiliated middle school is attached to the university.

② 中国过去计算长度的**单位**是"丈、尺"等,现在都改用公制了。The units of length like *zhang*, *chi*, etc. were used in China in the past; but now the metric system has been adopted.

③ 公制和英制计量**单位**并不相同。The metric system is different from the English system of measures.

C

C

猜 猜测 猜想

(动) (动) (动)

cāi cāicè cāixiǎng

Ⓔ guess/
guess, conjecture/
guess, suppose

◪"猜"、"猜测"、"猜想"这三个动词都表示推测。"猜"在口语中最常用,不能做主语、宾语,不能受定语修饰。"猜测"可做主语、宾语。"猜想"除了推测的意思,还表示估计、想像,可做主语、宾语,并可用于科学推测命题 ◇ The three verbs 猜,猜测 and 猜想 all mean "conjecture". 猜 is mostly used in colloquial language; it cannot function as the subject or object and cannot be qualified by an attributive. 猜测 can function as the subject and object. 猜想, besides the meaning of "guess", also means "estimation" and can function as the subject and object; it can also be used as the topic of scientific conjecture.

"猜谜"、"猜谜语"、"猜灯谜",只能用"猜"。以下生活用语,也常用"猜" ◇ To guess a riddle, only 猜 can be used. In the following everyday speech, 猜 is usually used:

① ——你**猜**我是谁? Guess who I am.
——对不起,电话里我听不出来。Sorry, I cannot tell.

② 你们**猜猜**,这幅画值多少钱? Please guess how much the painting costs.

以下较正式的说法,三个词可互换 ◇ In the following more formal expressions, the three words are interchangeable:

③ 我**猜**(/**猜测**/**猜想**)今年的股市一定看涨。I think the stock market is likely to rise this year.

④ 人们**猜**(/**猜测**/**猜想**)不出这位明星的年龄有多大。People cannot figure out the age of the star.

但"猜测"、"猜想"可做主语、宾语,可受定语修饰 ◇ 猜测 and 猜想, however, can function as the subject and object and can be qualified by an attributive:

⑤ 这种**猜测**(/**猜想**)是没有根据的。This conjecture is baseless.

⑥ 我的话只是一种**猜测**(/**猜想**)。What I said is only guesswork.

⑦ 这完全是毫无根据的**猜测**(/**猜想**)。What I said is only guesswork.

⑧ 这只是一种科学**猜想**,需要证明。This is only a scientific assumption to be proved.

"猜测"还可做定语,如"猜测之词" ◇ 猜测 can also function as an attributive, as in 猜测之词 (words of conjeture).

财富 (名) cáifù　　财产 (名) cáichǎn

Ⓔ wealth/property

"财富"和"财产"都指较多的物质资料、钱物等。"财富"意义较抽象,可用于精神方面;"财产"意义较具体,有时也可用于比喻。以下例①②指具体钱物,用"财产"。例③既指具体钱物又带有泛指意义,两个词可通用 ◇ Both 财富 and 财产 mean "material wealth". The meaning of 财富 is more abstract, and can be applied to spiritual things. 财产 is more concrete, but can also be used metaphorically. Examples ① and ② refer to concrete things , so 财产 is used. Example ③ can refer to both specific money and thing and property with a general reference, so the two words are interchangeable here.

① 法律保护私有**财产**。Private property is under legal protection.

② 他买了一份家庭**财产**保险。He bought an insurance of family property.

③ 这位企业家,几十年来办厂、经商,已经积累了一笔相当可观的**财富**(/**财产**)。After years of running factories and engaging in business, the entrepreneur has accumulated considerable assets.

用于抽象意义时,用"财富" ◇ When used in an abstract sense, 财富 is used:

④ 唐诗是中国一笔珍贵的文化**财富**。The poetry of the Tang Dynasty is our valuable cultural heritage.

⑤ 时间是最宝贵的**财富**。Time is the most valuable wealth.

"财产"有时也可用于比喻 ◇ 财产 can also be used metaphorically:

⑥ 老人说:健康是他拥有的最有价值的**财产**。The old man said that health was his greatest wealth.

⑦ 品牌是这个公司最有价值的**财产**之一。The brand is one of the greatest assets of this company.

这种句子,有时也可用"财富",但表示的意义更抽象 ◇ In these

sentences, 财富 can also be used instead, but the meaning is even more abstract.

采用 采取 采纳

(动) (动) (动)

cǎiyòng cǎiqǔ cǎinà

Ⓔ adopt/adopt/adopt

"采用"表示(经过权衡认为恰当)加以利用,宾语从具体的"材料"到抽象的"方式"等都可以。"采取"表示根据情况选择或施行一种态度、方针等。"采纳"则表示(常为上级对下级)认为合理而接受(意见等)。"采用"和"采纳"可加"加以" ◇ 采用 means "(after weighing the pros and cons) to adopt or use a material or a style", its object can be concrete "materials" or abstract "ways", 采取 means "choose an attitude or implement a guideline, etc". 采纳 means "(the higher authorities) consider and accept (sb.'s advice, etc.)". 加以 (used before a disyllabic verb to indicate that the action is directed towards something or somebody mentioned earlier) may precede 采用 and 采纳.

① 学报主编决定**采用**那篇稿子。The journal editor-in-chief decided to accept the article.

② 这家医院**采用**了先进的医疗方法。The advanced treatment means has been employed in this hospital.

③ 他们已**采取**行动对付恐怖分子。They have taken actions to deal with those terrorists.

④ 没想到她对这件事**采取**不闻不问的态度。Surprisingly, she adopted a "none-of-my-business" attitude.

⑤ 校长已经**采纳**了这个学生的意见。The principal has accepted the proposal made by the student.

⑥ 我们的几项建议,区政府将加以**采纳**。Our proposals will be adopted by the District Government.

以上三个词不能互换 ◇ In the examples ①~⑥, the three words are not interchangeable.

另外,"采取"还可以表示取(指纹、血样等) ◇ Besides, 采取 can also mean "to sample (fingerprints, blood group, etc.)":

⑦ 警方在犯罪现场**采取**指纹,并当场进行分析、鉴定。The policemen sampled the fingerprints on the criminal spot and analyze and identify them then and there.

"采用"和"采取"只在少数情况下可以互换,如宾语是方式、手段等,意思又较抽象时 ◇ 采用

and 采取 are interchangeable only in some cases, when the object is style, measure, etc. with an abstract meaning:

⑧ 他们**采用**(/**采取**)择优录取的方式录取新生。They enrolled only the outstanding students.

⑨ 交通管理部门**采用**(/**采取**)高科技手段指挥交通。The transportation department adopted hitech to direct the traffic.

"采用"和"采纳"在少数情况下也可互换,即宾语既是被选用的恰当方法,又是被接受的建议等时 ◇ 采用 and 采纳 are also interchangeable in some cases, that is, when the object is both the adopted method and the accepted proposal:

⑩ 上级领导**采用**(/**采纳**)了这个方案。The leaders have adopted the plan.

踩 蹬 踏

(动) (动) (动)

cǎi dēng tà

Ⓔ step on/step on/step on

"踩"、"蹬"、"踏"这三个动词都可表示脚底着地或用力,但有许多细微的区别 ◇ The three verbs 踩,蹬,踏 all mean" to step on with some force" ,but there are small differences.

1. 表示脚着地或接触物体。口语中常用"踩"。"踏"较为书面化。一般不用"蹬" ◇ When expressing the meaning of " touching the gound or some other thing with the foot" . 踩 is often used in colloquial speech. 踏 is more literary. 蹬 is usually not used. e. g. :

① 刚穿的新鞋,出去遇到下雨,**踩**了两脚泥。I was caught in a heavy rain with the brand new shoes dirting mud.

② 在公共汽车上,他不小心**踩**了别人的脚。He inadvertently stepped on the foot of a passenger on the bus.

以上这种口语中表示具体意义的句子,都用"踩"。如果是意义较抽象也可用"踏"或"蹬" ◇ In the above sentences of concrete meaning in everyday speech, 踩 is used. If the meaning is more abstract, 踏 or 蹬 may also be used, e. g. :

③ 河边的草地,被人**踩**(/**踏**)出了一条小路。A path has been trodden on the grassland near the river.

④ 水泥还没凝固就被人**踩**(/**踏**)了几个脚印。The cement ground has been stepped on before it solidified.

⑤ **踩**(/**踏**/**蹬**)着别人的肩膀往

上爬,这种行径真可耻! It is really shameful to climb up/get promoted at the expense of others.

2. 表示脚、腿向下或微向前用力,一般用"蹬",较少用其他二词 ◇ To show that the foot or leg steps down or forward with force, 蹬 is usually used and not the other two words. e. g. :

① 我用力地**蹬**着自行车,很快就到了目的地。I pedaled hard and got to the destination soon.

② 过去,王大爷以**蹬**三轮为生。In the past, Grandpa Wang made a living by pedaling pedicab.

③ 她俩一边**蹬**着跑步机锻炼,一边聊天。The two girls were chatting while they were pedaling on the decline.

以上例句,在较书面化时,如例①③也可用"踏"。例②"蹬三轮"则是习惯搭配。例③偶尔也可用"踩" ◇ If the examples above are expressed more literarily, 踏 can be used in examples ① and ③. 蹬三轮 is an idiomatic phrase. In example ③ 踩 can also be used occasionally.

3. 表示用脚虚拟地或真实地踏拍子,用"踏"或"踩",常加"着",不用"蹬" ◇ To show beating time fictitiously or really, 踏 or 踩 is used, usually with 着, while 蹬 is not used. e. g. :

① 他正在专心地**踩**(/**踏**)着拍子唱歌。He is singing attentively to the tempo of the music.

② 十几位老人**踩**(/**踏**)着锣鼓点儿在扭秧歌。More than ten old people are doing the *yangko* dance to the drumbeats.

4. 表示抽象意义的"走上",用"踏",不用其他二词 ◇ To show the abstract sense of 走上(step on), 踏 is used, and neither of the other two will do:

① 毕业以后,他**踏**上了工作岗位。After graduation, he began to work.

② 勘探队完成了这里的勘探工作,又**踏**上了新的征途。After finishing the work here, the prospecting team started on another new journey.

5. 表示脚底以物体或地面为基础,以便攀升等。"踩"、"蹬"、"踏"三个词都可以用,但有习惯搭配。用"蹬"的时候,有时表示脚抬得比"踩"、"踏"要高 ◇ To express the meaning of " stepping onto sth. in order to climb", all the three words 踩, 蹬 and 踏 can be used, with different collocations. When 蹬 is used, it means " that one has to lift his foot higher than using", 踩 or 踏, e. g. :

① 书架太高,他要**踩**着小凳子才能拿到上面的书。The bookshelf is so high that he has to step onto the stool to get books.

② 他**踏**上石墩子,才上了矮墙。He stepped onto the stone block first and then climb onto the short wall.

③ 老人**蹬**着梯子上房去晒玉米。The old man got onto the roof by ladder to dry his corn.

以上的例句,三个词可以换用。但用"踩"更为口语化。例③"蹬着梯子"是习惯搭配,更为常用 ◇ In the examples above the three words can all be used, but 踩 is more colloquial. In example ③ 蹬着梯子 is an idiomatic expression which is often used.

6. 比喻贬低别人,用"踩",不用其他二词 ◇ To show the meaning of "playing down someone", 踩 is used metaphorically and not the other two words:

① 她说这话明明是夸自己,**踩**别人。Obviously, by these words, she is belittling others and showing herself off.

② 你是捧小王**踩**老李,这样对待朋友可不行啊! You are actually singing the praise of Xiao Wang and belittling Lao Li. To treat friends like this is absolutely unacceptable.

C

参观 看

(动) (动)

cānguān kàn

Ⓔ visit, look around/look at

"参观"和"看"都表示视线接触外物,但有很大的不同。"参观"是透过观察使有所得,宾语是处所,限于非单音节词,如"工厂"、"学校"、"展览会"、"摄影展"等。这处所是人工展示的。"看"除表示一般的观看(如"看看是谁来了")还表示阅读(如"看书")、诊治(如"看病")、对待(如"另眼相看")、访问等 ◇ 参观 and 看 both mean " to look at", but they are quite different from each other. 参观 means " to learn sth. by visiting" and the object must be a place (non-monosyllabic), e. g. 工厂(factory), 学校(school), 展览会(exhibition), 摄影展(picture show), etc. which must be sth. man-made. 看 means" to see or to look at" (e. g. 看看是谁来了! Look! who is coming?) and also to read (e. g. 看书), to diagnose (e. g. 看病), to treat (e. g. 另眼相看 give sb. special treatment), to visit, etc.

① 昨天我**参观**了一个画展。I visited an art show yesterday.

② **参观**这个工艺品展览的人很

多。There are many people visiting the arts crafts exhibition.

有时也可说"看画展"、"看展览"等,因此例①也可用"看"。但用"参观"较正式 ◇ Sometimes can also say 看画展,看展览, etc., therefore, in example ① 看 can replace 参观 but 参观 sounds more formal:

③ 昨天他去**看**了一位老朋友。Yesterday he went to see an old friend of his.

④ 那本书你**看**完了吗? Have you finished reading the book?

以上例③"看"表示访问、看望;例④"看"表示阅读。都不能用"参观" ◇ In example ③ 看 means "to call on"; in example ④ 看 means "to read". 参观 cannot be used in either one.

"看"也可表示观察,除例①②"画展","工艺品展览"外,对象一般是人物、地形地貌等 ◇ 看 can also mean "to observe". Besides 画展(picture show),工艺品展览(handicrafts show), the object can be persons, topography, etc.

⑤ 真**看**不透,他是个这么有心计的人。I simply didn't see him through. He was such a tricky fellow.

⑥ 工程技术人员正在**看**地形。The technical personnel of the project are surveying the topography.

例⑤⑥也不能用"参观"。因为,同样是观察,"参观"一般是边走边观察,有一个浏览过程,宾语限于处所(人为地展示出来的)。而"看"是自然形态、人为展示都可以。不能说"参观风景",因为风景是自然的,不是人为展示的处所;"看风景"则可以。只有把"参观"和"游览"放在一起,淡化了观察,加强了玩赏性,才可以说 ◇ In examples ⑤ and ⑥参观 cannot be used either. 参观 means "to walk around and observe at the same time", so there is a course of glancing, and the object must be a place (laid out specially), but 看 can be applied to either a natural place or a laid-out one. We cannot say 参观风景, because 风景 is natural. We usually say 看风景 (visiting a scence). Only when 参观 is used together with 游览, the meaning of observation is sort of diminished and so it can be applied to scenery:

⑦ 昨天客人们参观**游览**了西山风景区。Yesterday our guests visited the scenic spots around the Western Hill.

再如,"参观市容"和"看一下市容"或"参观工业开发区"和"看一下工业开发区"都是可以的。因为"市容"、"工业开发区"有人为展示的性质。而"看星空"可以,"参观星空"是不行的,因为这是自然形态 ◇ 参观市容(have a look around the city)and 看一下市容 or 参观工业开发区(visit the industrial development zone) and 看一下工业开发区 both can be said, because 市容 is laid out specially. 看星空 can be said, but 参观星空 cannot, because it is a pure natural phenomenon.

"参观"还可以做主语、宾语 ◇ 参观 can be used as the subject or the object of a sentence:

⑧ 这次**参观**很有收获。This visit is very fruitful.

⑨ 请同学们根据昨天的**参观**,写一篇观感。Dear students, please write out your impressions of the visit yesterday.

⑩ 这是机房,谢绝**参观**。This is the generator room. No visitor is allowed.

"看"在较特殊的句子中可做主语、宾语 ◇ 看 can be the subject or the object of some unusual sentences:

⑪ **看**比不**看**好,你还是实地去考察一下吧! You'd better go there and see yourself, for it is better to see than not see.

⑫ 不**看**不知道,一**看**吓一跳。You won't know if you do not see it, and you'll be startled when you actually do so.

⑬ 那些古画让**看**不让**看**? Are we allowed to see those ancient paintings?

藏 (动) cáng　　躲 (动) duǒ

Ⓔ hide/dodge

1. 藏

(1) 指人主动处于别人看不见或找不到的地方 ◇ 藏 means "to place oneself so as not to be seen":

① 孩子**藏**在门后边了。The child is hiding behind the door.

② 别**藏**了,我已经看见你了。Don't hide any more. I've found you.

(2) 使人或物处于看不见的地方 ◇ 藏 means "to keep a person or thing out of sight":

③ 他们把伤员**藏**起来,免得被敌人发现。They hide the wounded in case the enemy found them.

④ 就这么两间屋子,这东西没地方可**藏**。This can be hidden nowhere for there are only two rooms here.

⑤ 强盗们把财宝**藏**到了山洞里。The bandits hid the treasures in a cave.

这种用法不能用“躲” ◇ 躲 cannot be so used.

(3) 收存 ◇ 藏 means "to collect and store up":

⑥ 这个小图书馆**藏**书 10 万册。There is a collection of 100,000 books in this small library.

这种用法不能用“躲” ◇ 躲 cannot be so used.

2. 躲

(1) 同“藏”1,其中例①②均可换用“躲”。另如 ◇ The meaning is the same as 藏 1; in examples ① and ②, 躲 can be used instead. Other examples:

① 为了逃避债务,那个人**躲**起来了。To shirk his debt, the man has hidden away.

② 你别**躲**,**躲**到哪里我也能找到你。Don't run away. Wherever you hide, I can find you out.

(2) 指人主动避开不安全因素 ◇ Referring to people keeping oneself away from something unsafe:

③ 路上车多,你得注意**躲**车。There is a lot of traffic on the road; be careful and not to collide with them.

④ 他到一家商店**躲**雨。He came to a shop to shelter the rain.

有时“躲”只表示不愿意接近某人 ◇ Sometimes 躲 only means "to keep away from sb.":

⑤ 她不愿意理那个人,老**躲**着他。She is not willing to speak with the man, so she is always hiding from him.

以上③④⑤三句均不能用“藏” ◇ 藏 cannot be used in examples ③, ④, and ⑤.

曾 (副) céng 曾经 (副) céngjīng

Ⓔ once before/once before

◥ 这两个词都表示以前有过(一般已完成)某事或情况。“曾”较书面化 ◇ Both words indicate that sth. once happened before. 曾 is more literary than 曾经:

① 他**曾经**(/**曾**)去过一次海南岛。He has been to Hainan Island once.

② 这里**曾经**(/**曾**)是古代的战场。The place was once an ancient battlefield.

“曾”可说“不曾”、“未曾”、“何曾”、“似曾”等,“曾经”不能这样搭配 ◇ 曾 can be used in 不曾 (never before), 未曾 (never before), 何曾 (used in a rhetorical statement to mean "have not", "did not"), 似曾 (seem to be), etc. 曾经 cannot be used in these phrases:

③ 我从来**不曾**见过雪山。I have never seen a snowy mountain.

④ 他**未曾**想过这番道理。He has never thought of this argument.

⑤ 我说一不二,**何曾**说话不算数过? I stand by my words. Have you ever known that I do not?

"曾"可构成"似曾相识"等成语 ◇ 曾 can be used in idiomatic phrases such as 似曾相识(seem to have met before).

"曾经"的否定式不是"不曾经",而是"不曾"、"未曾" ◇ The negative form of 曾经 is not 不曾经, but 不曾 or 未曾.

差不多 chàbuduō (形)

差(一)点儿 chà(yī)diǎnr (副)

几乎 jīhū (副)

Ⓔ about the same, average/ almost, nearly/ almost

1. 差不多

(1)表示在程度、状态、时间、数量上是一般的或相近的;可做状语、定语、谓语等 ◇ 差不多 means "about the same in level, state, time, quantity, etc." and can be an attributive, adverbial, predicate, etc.:

① 这两间房子**差不多**大,都是40平方米左右。The areas of the two rooms are nearly the same. Both are about 40 square meters large.

② **差不多**大的成年人都可以拿得动这样的重物。The grown-ups of that age should be able to carry such heavy thing.

③ 这两件上衣的样子**差不多**。The designs of the two coats are very alike.

"差(一)点儿"、"几乎"不能这样用 ◇ 差(一)点儿 and 几乎 cannot be so used.

(2)表示接近某种程度、状态、数量等,做状语 ◇ 差不多 means "nearly", used as an adverbial:

④ 他的左眼**差不多**完全失明了。His left eye is almost blind completely.

⑤ 儿子结婚请客,他**差不多**把全村的人都请到了。He invited nearly all the villagers to celebrate his son's wedding.

⑥ 他**差不多**干了20年的记者。He has been a journalist for about 20 years.

以上例④⑤⑥也可用"几乎",但语气更强,且有书面语意味。一般生活谈话中,多用"差不多" ◇ 几乎 can also be used in examples ④, ⑤, and ⑥, but with more stress and there is a literary flavor. In everyday speech, 差不多 is mostly used:

⑦ 这个西红柿真大,**差不多**有一斤。The tomato is very big. It is about one *jīn*.

2. 差(一)点儿

(1) 表示某种不希望出现的情况,接近于出现而终于未实现,因之常有庆幸的感情色彩,很口语化 ◇ Indicating that one feels lucky because some unwished for state of affairs was not, though, nearly realized. It is very colloquial, e.g.:

① 老大妈脚下一滑,**差(一)点儿**跌倒。The old grandma slipped and nearly fell over.

② 这个棋子**差(一)点儿**被他吃掉。The piece of mine slightly escaped being taken by his.

③ 这场大病,他**差(一)点儿**丢了性命。This serious illness nearly sent him to the heaven.

值得注意的是,后面的非积极意味词语可以用否定形式,意思不变,而更为口语化,如例①可改为"差点儿没跌倒",例②可改为"差点儿没被他吃掉",例③可改为"差点儿没丢了性命" ◇ What is noteworthy is that the unwished for state of affairs can be expressed in the negative form without changing the meaning, and it is even more colloquial: example ① can be changed into 差点儿没跌倒, example ② into 差点儿没被他吃掉, example ③ into 差点儿没丢了性命.

以上三句,也可换用"几乎" ◇ The three examples above can also use 几乎 instead.

有时这种形式并不是庆幸非积极状况的终未发生,而是表示一种状况已达到极高程度(多用极端意味的词语) ◇ Sometimes this way of expression is not used to indicate the feeling of rejoicing, but some extreme cases (mostly used with words of extreme meaning):

④ 她气得**差(一)点儿**哭了出来。She was on the verge of tears because of anger.

⑤ 闻到那股味道,我**差(一)点儿**吐出来。I was on the verge of vomit at the smell.

也可用"几乎" ◇ 几乎 can also be so used.

(2) 表示希望出现的情况,几乎不能出现,而终于实现了(用否定形式) ◇ A wished-for state that seemed not to be realized has actually realized after all (used in the negative form):

⑥ 我买的那本书是最后一本,我**差(一)点儿**没买到。(买到了)The book I bought was the last one. I almost missed it. (I got it)

⑦ 这次考试,题目太多了,他**差(一)点儿**没答完。(答完了) There were too many questions in the test. He nearly failed to finish it. (He finished it)

⑧ 因为机票难订,她**差(一)点儿**没走成,幸亏最后买到了退票。(走成了)As it was hard to get a air ticket, she almost failed to leave. Fortunately, she got a returned ticket. (She left)

也可用"几乎" ◇ 几乎 can be so used too.

(3) 表示某种希望能实现的情况似乎要出现而终未出现,含有惋惜的意味(常有"就") ◇ Some state of affairs which seems to be realized but actually not. There is a flavor of regret (就 is often used):

⑨ 我**差(一)点儿**就要买到音乐会的票了,谁想到前面那个人一下子买了 15 张。(没买到) I nearly bought the ticket for the concert. Unfortunately, the person prior to me bought 15 tickets. (I did not get one)

⑩ 他**差一点儿**就得冠军了,可惜最后几秒时被别人超过了。(没得上)He nearly win the first place; however, he was exceeded in the last few seconds. (He did not win it)

也可用"几乎" ◇ 几乎 can be so used too.

以上(1)(2)(3)凡可用"几乎"换用的情况均不如用"差(一)点儿"口语化 ◇ In the examples in(1) (2) (3), all those in which 几乎 can be used instead would not be so colloquial as using 差(一)点儿.

3. 几乎

(1) 表示估量、约略 ◇ Indicating "estimation, almost, barely":

① 几年不见,他变得我**几乎**都不敢认了。I nearly could not recognize him for he changed greatly these years.

② 这个公司,博士**几乎**占了 1/3。Doctors in this working unit nearly accounts for one third.

也可换用"差不多",但语气较轻 ◇ 差不多 can also be used instead, but sounds less forceful.

(2) 同"差(一)点儿"(1)(2)(3),但不如"差(一)点儿"口语化 ◇ The usage is the same as 差(一)点儿(1)(2)(3), but not so colloquial as it:

③ 老大妈脚下一滑,**几乎**跌倒。(没跌倒) The old grandma slipped and nearly fell over. (she did not fall over)

④ 因为考题太多,他**几乎**没答完。(答完了) There are too many questions in the test. He almost failed to finish it. (He finished it)

⑤ 他**几乎**得冠军了。(没得到) He nearly won the first place. (He did not get it)

(3) 同"差不多"(2),但表示接近的程度、状态、数量必须是接近极端或夸张的水平 ◇ The us-

C

age is the same as 差不多(2),but the level,state,or quantity must be of an extreme or exaggerated nature:

⑥ 他的左眼**几乎**完全失明了。His left eye is almost blind completely.

⑦ 他的病**几乎**全好了。He almost got over.

C

长期 (形) chángqī 长久 (形) chángjiǔ 长远 (形) chángyuǎn

Ⓔ a long period of time/ a long time/ long-term;long-range

◪ 这三个词都表示长时间,但"长期"是非谓形容词,"长久"、"长远"是一般形容词 ◇ The three words all mean " a long time",but 长期 is a non-predicate adjective,while 长久 and 长远 are ordinary adjectives.

1."长期"表示长时期。常做定语、状语 ◇ 长期 means " a long period of time", and is usually used us an attributive or adverbial:

① 我想找一个**长期**的工作。I want to look for a long-term job.

② 这房子**长期**没有人住。The house has been empty for a long time.

③ 这个问题**长期**困扰着她。She has been plagued by the problem for a long time.

有时用在"是……的"格式中 ◇ Sometimes it is used in the pattern 是……的:

④ 改革的任务**是**长期**的**。The reform will take a long time.

⑤ 这项贷款**是**长期**的**。The loan is a long-term one.

2."长久"表示时间很长,有时带有主观色彩。做定语、状语、补语、谓语 ◇ 长久 means " a long time", usually with a subjective flavour. It can be used as an attributive, adverbial, complement and predicate:

① 我们的工作要有个**长久**的计划。Our work needs a long-term plan.

② 她的影子**长久**地浮现在我的脑海中。Her image has lingered in my mind for a long time.

③ 他们的关系不可能维持得很**长久**。It is impossible for their relationship to last too long.

④ 这种局面会**长久**吗? Will the situation last long?

"长期"中例①②③可用"长久"代替,但"长久"更书面化些,用得较少。"长久"中的例①可用"长期"代替 ◇ 长久 can take the place of 长期 in examples ①,②, and ③,but 长期 sounds more literary, and is not used very often. In example ① 长久 can be replaced by 长期.

"长期"、"长久"可加"以来" ◇ 长期 and 长久 can take 以来 (since) after them:

⑤ **长期**(/**长久**)以来,这里一直使用太阳能。The solar energy has been used here for a long time.

⑥ 他**长期**(/**长久**)以来,一直从事教学法的研究工作。He has been working on the research of teaching methodology for a long time.

3. "长远"指未来的时间跨度很大,距离很远。做定语、状语、补语、谓语 ◇ 长远 means " long range or long term of the future time", and is used as an attributive, adverbial, complement and predicate:

① 订计划要有**长远**打算。Decision-making should be long-term-oriented.

② 这种优良的传统要**长远**地保持下去。The good tradition should be remained forever.

③ 他考虑问题十分**长远**。His consideration is far-sighted.

④ 实现世界和平的路还很**长远**。It is a long way for the world peace to go.

例①②可用"长期"、"长久"替换。由于"长久"不强调时间、空间的跨度,所以这里例③④不能用"长久"替换 ◇ In examples ① and ② 长期 or 长久 can be used instead. Since 长久 does not stress the span of time, it cannot be used instead in examples ③ and ④.

"长远"可说"从长远……",一般做状语 ◇ 长远 can be said as 从长远……and is generally used as an adverbial:

⑤ 这事要**从长远考虑**,不能只顾眼前。This matter should be considered from a long point of view.

⑥ **从长远角度**考虑城市建设和发展问题,要特别重视生态环境保护。From a long-term point of view, city construction and development should specially value the protection of ecology and environment.

常 (副) cháng　　常常 (副) chángcháng

Ⓔ often, frequently/ often, frequently

这两个词都表示动作、行为或状态的重复出现、发生,间隔较短 ◇ Both words indicate that an action, behaviour or state occurs repeatedly with short intervals:

C

① 他**常**(/**常常**)和邻居们来往。He and his neighbors visited each other frequently.

② 老王**常**(/**常常**)到郊区去钓鱼。Lao Wang often goes to the suburb to fish.

两个词一般可以互换 ◇ The two words are mostly interchangeable.

在书面语中,如果后面是单音节词,多用"常" ◇ In written language, if it is followed by a monosyllabic word, 常 is mostly used:

③ 环境**常**随时间的变化而变化。Environment always change with the time.

④ 知足**常**乐是他长寿的秘诀之一。To be content and happy about one's life is also one of the secrets of his longevity.

否定式多用"不常" ◇ The negative form is mostly 不常:

⑤ 他最近**不常**来了。He seldom showed up recently.

⑥ 老太太一个人住,儿女**不常**回家。The old lady lives alone, and her children rarely visit her.

四字语中用"常",不用"常常",如"常来常往"、"常备不懈"等 ◇ In four character phrases, 常 is used and not 常常, e.g. 常来常往 (frequently come and go), 常备不懈 (always be on the alert), etc.

►[经常 jīngcháng—常常 chángcháng—常 cháng] [往往 wǎngwǎng—常常 chángcháng]

超过 (动) chāoguò　　超出 (动) chāochū

Ⓔ go beyond, exceed/ overstep, exceed

1. "超过"指甲事物从乙事物的后面赶到它的前边 ◇ 超过 means " A goes to the front of B from behind":

① 他开车比较慢,很多车都**超过**了他。He drove slowly so that many cars have overtaken him.

② 在比赛快要结束时,他连续**超过**了两个对手取得了小组第一的好成绩。At the end of the race, he overtook two competitors successively and became the first of the group.

也可表示(数字、成绩等)高出……之上 ◇ It also means " (number, score, etc.) to surpass":

③ 她原来在全班学习成绩是最后一名,现在已经**超过**了不少同学。At first she was the last in her class, but now she has caught up with some of her classmates.

④ 这个省的粮食产量第一次**超**

过了那个省。The grain output of this province has exceeded that province for the first time.

⑤ 该队队员的平均年龄已经**超过**20 岁。The average age of the team is more than twenty.

2.“超出”则指越出(一定的范围、标准) ◇ 超出 means "to exceed, go beyond (a certain scope or standard)":

① 实际产量已经**超出**定额了。The actual output has exceeded the quota.

② 今年的产量较去年有较大**超出**。The output of this year exceeded that of last year greatly.

③ 消费**超出**了预算。The spending exceeds the budget.

例①③可换用“超过” ◇ In examples ① and ③, 超过 can also be used instead.

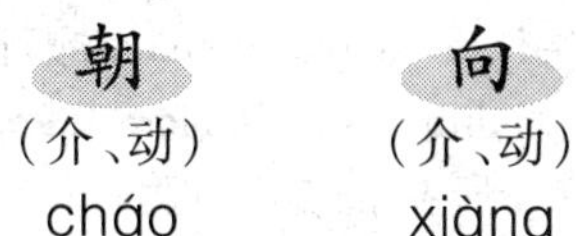

(介、动) cháo (介、动) xiàng

Ⓔ toward/face, turn towards

◥ 这两个词都表示动作的方向或对象 ◇ Both words indicate the direction or object of an action.

A. 朝(介)、**向**(介) toward, face (preposition):

1. 表示动作的方向(具体或抽象的),两个词都可以用。这时,宾语(介词的宾语)是表示方向、处所、目标等。如果带助词“着”,宾语不能是单音节的 ◇ To indicate the direction of an action (either concrete or abstract), either word can be used, and the object would be a word indicating the direction, place, target, etc. If 朝 or 向 takes the auxiliary 着 after it, the object must not be a monosyllabic word. e. g.:

① 你**朝**(/**向**)西走五分钟,就到了。Walk west five minutes, and you will find it.

② 一辆公共汽车**朝**(/**向**)车站方向开来。A bus is coming to the bus-stop.

③ 现在国际形势正**朝**(/**向**)着和平民主的方向发展。The present international situation is developing towards the direction of peace and democracy.

④ 让我们**朝**(/**向**)着光明的未来,前进! Let's march on to the bright future!

2. 表示动作的对象。“向”的宾语是人称代词或指人名词,也可以是抽象名词如“困难”、“幸福”等;“朝”的宾语一般限于人称代词或指人名词。“朝”可以带“着”;“向”不能带“着” ◇ To indicate the object of an action. The object of 向 must be a person-

C

al pronoun or noun, or an abstract noun, e. g. 困难(difficulty), 幸福(happiness) etc.; the object of 朝 is limited to personal pronoun or personal noun. 朝 can take 着 after it, but 向 cannot. e. g.:

① 他**朝**(/**向**)我点了点头。She nodded at me.

② 我们**向**当地人问路。We asked the native about the way.

③ 大家不能**向**困难低头。We should never yield to difficulties.

④ 你要发火也不应该**朝**着孩子发呀！You shouldn't have been angry with the kids!

"向"可以在一些单音节动词后做补语,"朝"不能 ◇ 向 can be the complement of some monosyllabic verbs, but not 朝:

⑤ 节日的夜晚,大家都涌**向**天安门广场。People flowed to Tian'anmen Square on the festival night.

⑥ 她把目光转**向**父亲。She turned to look at her father.

这种单音节动词是有限的,如"移"、"撤"、"指"、"奔"等 ◇ Such monosyllabic verbs are limited to words indicating movement like, 移(move), 撤(withdraw), 指(point), 奔(run), etc.

B. "朝"(动)、"向"(动)表示对着 ◇ 朝 and 向 as verbs mean "to face":

① 这间屋子**向**(/**朝**)阳。This room faces south.

② 那庙坐南**朝**北。The temple faces north.

由于习惯上的搭配,例②一般不用"向" ◇ Because of idiomatic usage, 向 is not used in example ②.

称赞 赞美

(动) (动)

chēngzàn zànměi

Ⓔ praise, eulogize/ praise, commend

◥ 这两个词都表示用语言、文字夸奖。"称赞"可用于一般的好处或优点,"赞美"用于较突出的人或事物,也更书面化 ◇ Both words mean "to sing the praise with language and written words". 称赞 can be applied to ordinary good points or advantages, while 赞美 is applied to more outstanding persons or things and is more literary. 例①②所指的是一般的人、事,宜用"称赞" ◇ Examples ① and ② are applied to ordinary people and things, so 称赞 is suitable:

① 老师**称赞**他作业做得好。The teacher praised him for his well-done homework.

② 大家都**称赞**他踏实肯干。He was acclaimed for his industriousness.

例③④所指可大可小,两个词都可使用 ◇ What examples ③ and ④ are applied to can be considered either great event or trifle, so both words can be used.

③ 这本小说受到许多人的**称赞**(/**赞美**)。The novel was widely commended.

④ 人们都**赞美**(/**称赞**)他乐于助人的精神。He was acclaimed for his being ready to help others.

例⑤则指较大的事,宜用“赞美” ◇ Example ⑤ is applied to a greater event, so 赞美 is used:

⑤ 诗人用诗歌来**赞美**生活,**赞美**祖国。Poets praise their country and life with poems.

▶[赞美 zànměi—赞扬 zànyáng]

成天 (副) chéngtiān　整天 (名) zhěngtiān

Ⓔ the whole day, all day long/ the whole day

“成天”与“整天”都有“一天到晚”的意思,但词性不同 ◇ 成天 and 整天 have the same meaning of "all day long", but they are of different parts of speech.

1. “成天”是副词,只做状语, 指每天从早到晚,有时可带“价(jie)” ◇ 成天 is an adverb and can only function as the adverbial. It means everyday, from day to night. Sometimes it takes 价(jie) after it:

① 他忙得**成天**不着家。He is so busy that he never stays at home for a moment.

② 这屋子朝阴,**成天**不见太阳。The house faces north and the sunshine cannot shine into it.

③ 她平日**成天**(价)呆在家里,很少出门。She always stays at home and rarely goes out.

2. “整天”是名词,意思只指一天内从早到晚,不指每天 ◇ 整天 is a noun meaning one whole day, but not every day:

① 我打了一**整天**桥牌。I played Bridge for a whole day.

② 一**整天**工作下来,觉得有点累。I felt a little tired after a whole day's work.

“整天”也可做状语,也可带“价”等 ,有时与“成天”意思、用法相同 ◇ 整天 can also function as the adverbial and can take 价(jie) after it; sometimes it has the same meaning and usage as 成天.

③ 那孩子**整天**玩电脑。The child played with computers all day long.

④ 他**整天**(价)游手好闲的。He is idle all day long.

C

成长 生长
（动） （动）
chéngzhǎng shēngzhǎng

Ⓔ grow up/grow

◪"成长"和"生长"这两个动词都有发育、增长的意思，在用法上有区别 ◇ The two words 成长 and 生长 both mean " to grow", but their usages are different.

1. 生长

(1)表示生物体的自然长大、成熟，具体意义多指植物，泛指意义也包括人和动物，如 ◇ Referring to the natural growing up and maturity of an organism, usually a plant, but in general human beings and animals are included, e. g. :

① 去年种的树苗**生长**得很快。The tree saplings planted last year grows quickly.

② 这里光照不够，不利于庄稼的**生长**。The sunshine here is not enough for crops to grow.

③ 人和动物的**生长**、发育，离不开环境的影响。The growth of humans and animals cannot be divorced from the influence of environment.

(2)表示人的出生和长大，有时也表示较抽象意义的人群（如"新生力量"、"后备力量"、"骨干力量"等）的产生 ◇ Indicate the birth and growth of a person, and also the people of a more abstract meaning(such as "newly emerging force", "reserve force", "backbone", etc.), e. g. :

④ 我出生在上海，**生长**在北京。I was born in Shanghai, while I was brought up in Beijing.

⑤ 在这个学术研究机构，新生力量正在**生长**，还需要多培育。The new forces in the academic research institute are developing and they need more cares.

(3)比喻经济、科学技术等的发展 ◇ Used metaphorically to indicate the development of economy, science, technology, etc. :

⑥ 在传统农业中，新技术**生长**得还不快。The new technologies in traditional agriculture are not developing rapidly enough.

⑦ 这里市场经济还在**生长**发育过程之中。Here the market economy is under development.

2. 成长

(1)表示动植物包括人的身体的长大和成熟。如"生长"和"成长"并用，前者侧重逐渐长大，后者侧重成熟 ◇ Indicating the growing and maturing of the human body. If 生长 and 成长 are used together, the former stresses growing while the latter stresses maturing:

① 这种树,**生长**期较长,幼树也较娇嫩,**成长**以后就不易受到伤害了。The growing span of the tree is long and its sapling is delicate but once it grows up, it can not damaged easily.

② 几年不见,他个子高高的,已经**成长**起来了。After a few years, He gets taller and maturer.

(2)表示人或人群的性格、素质的发展成熟 ◇ Indicating the development and maturity of a person's character and quality. e.g.:

③ 他开始工作以后,在待人处世各方面,很快**成长**起来了。After he began to work, he matured quickly in the way of getting along with people.

④ 在这所大学,年轻的师资队伍正在**成长**壮大。The young faculties in the university are becoming stronger and stronger.

出售 售 卖

(动) (动) (动)

chūshòu shòu mài

Ⓔ sell, offer for sale/sell/sell

"出售"、"售"、"卖"这三个动词都表示在交易中用物换取钱。"卖"最口语化,"出售"和"售"较书面化。由于"出售"是双音节词,在音节搭配上也有特殊性。以下口语中的句子,一般用"卖" ◇ 出售,售,卖 all mean "to sell". 卖 is the most colloquial, and the other two are more literary. Since 出售 is disyllabic, its syllabic collocation is different. In the following colloquial sentences, 卖 is used:

① 那家商店**卖**的年货又便宜又好。The special goods for the Spring Festival in that shop are cheap and fine.

② 这种电器现在**卖**什么价钱? How much is this kind of electrical appliance?

"卖"也可用于抽象意义 ◇ 卖 can be used in an abstract meaning:

③ 我是**卖**苦力的,凭力气吃饭。I am a coolie, and I live by the sweat of my brow.

④ 他不会**卖**友求荣的。He is the last person to betray his friends for personal gain.

"售"较书面化,下面例⑤宜用"售",也可用"卖",但语体色彩不同;例⑥"售票处"较正式,宜用"售" ◇ 售 is literary, and in example ⑤ it is better to use 售;卖 can also be used, but with a different style. In example ⑥售票处 is formal, so it is better to use 售:

C

⑤ 本店存货不多，**售**(/**卖**)完为止。The existing stock is not too much and will be sold out soon.

⑥ 你到**售票处**去买票吧。Please go to the booking office and buy the ticket.

"出售"更为书面化，多用于大宗商品，在音节上多与双音节词搭配。下面例⑦宜用"出售"，例⑧虽也可用"卖"，但色彩不同 ◇ 出售 is even more literary and mostly applied to big batches of merchandise. It is usually in collocation with disyllabic words. In example ⑦ below, it is better to use 出售. In example ⑧, though 卖 can also be used instead, it has a different colour.

⑦ 本店商品，一律降价**出售**。All the goods in the shop are on sale.

⑧ 这个国家以在国际市场上**出售**矿石而著名。The country is famous for exporting ores to the international market.

另外，"卖"还可表示不吝惜等，其他两个词没有这种用法 ◇ Besides, 卖 can also mean " not to spare". The other two words have no such usage.

⑨ 他干活儿真**卖**劲儿！(表示不吝惜) He spares no efforts at his work. (not to spare)

除了 (介) chúle　　除非 (连) chúfēi

Ⓔ except/
only if, only when, unless

◪ **A**. "除了"是介词，常与"外"、"以外"、"之外"、"而外"等呼应 ◇ 除了 is a preposition, often used in concert with 外, 以外, 之外, 而外, etc.

1. "除了……"表示除去个别的，强调其余的一致性，后边常有"全"、"都"等 ◇ 除了……stresses the unanimity of the rest in spite of the exception, and there is usually 全 or 都 to go with it:

① 这座房子，**除了**瓦是绿色的，其他地方**全**是朱红色。Except for the green tiles, all the other parts of the house are red.

② 他挣的那几个钱，**除了**维持最低生活之外，**全**丢到酒馆里去了。Besides the lowest life expense, he has spent all his money in the pub.

③ 这个学生**除了**数学成绩还不错以外，其他功课**都**不太好。The student is poor at all subjects except for math.

2. "除了……"后边如用否定形

式,强调前边是惟一例外 ◇ If 除了……is followed by a negative statement, it stresses the only exception:

① **除了**一个侄子,他**再没有**亲人。He has no relatives except for the only nephew.

② **除了**那双漂亮的大眼睛,她别的地方**都不**突出。She is plain except for her big eyes.

3. "除了……"有时表示在所说的之外,还有补充,后边常有"还"、"也"、"只"等 ◇ 除了…… sometimes is followed by some supplementary statement introduced by 还,也,只,etc.:

① 他在店里,**除了**售货,**也**做些零碎事情。Besides selling goods, he also does some odd jobs.

② 这孩子**除了**喜欢读书之外,**还**特别爱下棋。Besides reading, the child also likes playing chess very much.

4. "除了……就是……"、"除了……便是……"表示"不是……就是……",二者必居其一 ◇ 除了……就是……,除了……便是……means "either... or...":

① **除了**小李**就是**小王,别人不会去那个地方。Either Xiao Li or Xiao Wang, nobody else will go there.

② 母亲每天在家里,**除了**做饭,**就是**打扫卫生。My mother stays at home all the time, either do cooking or do cleaning.

③ 她晚年很少出去,每天**除了**读书**便是**画画儿。She seldom went out in her late life, either reading or drawing at home.

5. "除了……"表示这是惟一能改变下边所述的结果的条件 ◇ 除了……introduces the only condition that can change the following result:

① **除了**下雨,运动会是不会改期的。The sports meeting will not change its date unless it rains.

② **除了**你去劝说,他是听不进任何人的意见的。He listens to nobody except you.

B. "除非"是连词,指出惟一的先决条件,常跟"才"、"不"等呼应 ◇ 除非 is a conjunction introducing the only prerequisite condition, and is often used in concert with 才,不,etc.

1. "除非……才……"表示只有这样,才能产生某种结果 ◇ 除非……才……indicates the only way to produce a certain result:

① **除非**太不舒服了,他**才**去医院看病。He will not go to see a doctor until he feels very badly.

② **除非**一年有 367 天,我**才**会有

C

休息日。I have no rest time unless there are 367 days in a year.

"除非……(才)……否则(不然)……不(没有)……"表示只有这样才能有某种结果,再从反面作重复说明 ◇ 除非……(才)……否则(不然)……不(没有)……means "such is the only way leading to a certain result" and then restate it otherwise:

③ **除非**有病,他**才**请假,**否则**他是不会缺课的。He will never be absent and ask for a sick leave unless he is ill.

有时,只着重从反面说明,"才……"则被省略 ◇ Sometimes when the stress is on explaining otherwise 才……can be omitted:

④ **除非**有病,**不然**他是不会请假的。He will not ask for a sick leave unless he is ill.

2."要……除非……"指出要想取得某种结果,用"除非"引出惟一的条件。常用于格言、俗语等较固定的格式 ◇ 要……除非……points out the only way to gain a certain result which is introduced by 除非. It is often used in fixed phrases such as maxims, common sayings, etc.

① 若**要**人不知,**除非**己莫为。If you do not want people to know, you had better not do it.

② **要**他主动认错,**除非**太阳从西边出来。He is the last person to apologize for it!

3."除非……"有时和"除了……"(见 A.5)的意思相同,表示这是惟一能改变下边所述的结果的条件 ◇ 除非……sometimes means the same as 除了……(see A.5), indicating the only condition to change the result:

① **除非**下雨,运动会是不会改期的。The sports meeting will not change its date unless it rains.

② **除非**你去劝说,否则他是听不进任何人的意见的。He listens to nobody except you.

这惟一的条件可以放在结果之后 ◇ This only condition can come after the result:

③ 他怕是醒不过来了,**除非**出现奇迹。I'm afraid that he will not come awake unless a wonder works.

从总体上看,"除了"是介词,介词的宾语可以是单个的词(如 A.1 例①)也可以是句子(如 A.1 例③)等。"除非"是连词,连接两个分句,或省略了主语的动宾短语等,不可能连接单个的词。从这个角度看,虽然 B.3 的"除非"用法同 A.5 的"除了",一般仍认为"除非"是连词,"除了"是介词 ◇ On the whole, 除了 is a preposition and the object of it can be a single word (as in ① of A. 1) or a sentence (as in A. 1 ③). 除非 is a conjunction, connecting two clauses or verb-object phrases, etc. but not words. Thus, though 除非 in B. 3 has the same usage as 除了 in A. 5, it is generally considered that 除非 is a conjunction, while 除了 is a preposition.

穿 戴 带

(动) (动) (动)

chuān dài dài

Ⓔ put on, wear/
put on, wear/
bring, carry, take

这三个动词都有使物附着身体或随身的意思 ◇ The three verbs all mean to put sth. on the body.

"穿"的宾语是衣、裤、鞋、袜等，一般是套在身体某个部位的。"戴"的宾语是小装饰物以及眼镜、手表、红领巾(注意，"领带"用"打"或"系")等。"带"是携带，宾语是行李、东西、人(孩子)等 ◇ The object of 穿 is the coat, trousers, shoes, socks, etc., which is usually sth. to cover a certain part of the body. The object of 戴 is a small ornament or spectacles, watch, scarf, etc. (Note: when the object is 领带 (tie), the verb is 打 or 系). 带 is "to carry along" and the object is luggage, thing, child, etc. e. g. :

① 他今天**穿**了一身黑西装。He wears a black suit today.

② 天气冷，你出去应该**穿**大衣。It's cold. You'd better put on a coat when you go out.

③ 她**戴**了一对漂亮的耳环。She is wearing a pair of beautiful earrings.

④ 这位歌星手抱吉他，**戴**着墨镜。The singer is wearing sunglasses with a guitar in his arms.

⑤ 她**带**孩子去商店了。She went shopping with her child.

⑥ 明天出差，他晚上把要**带**的东西整理了一下。He packed his belongings this evening for he will be on a business trip tomorrow.

以上三个词是各有使用范围的。但在个别情况下，可以互换 ◇ Each of the three words has its own objects. But under certain condition, they are interchangeable, for instance:

⑦ 他臂上**戴**着黑纱，可能是为他刚去世的父亲**戴**(/**带**)孝。He wears a black armband. Probably he is in mourning for his deceased father.

"戴孝"即穿孝服(包括在袖子上

C

缠黑纱),也做“带孝” ◇ 戴孝 means to be in mourning (including wearing a black band around the sleeve). One can also say 带孝.

⑧ 他忘了**戴**表。He forgot wearing a watch.

这句与“他忘了带表”意思不同,“戴”是佩戴,“带”是携带 ◇ This sentence can also use 带表, but the meaning is different. 戴 means "to wear" while 带 means "to bring along".

⑨ 新郎新娘胸前**戴**着红花。The bride and bridegroom wore red flowers on their chest.

⑩ 他**带**着一束鲜花去医院看病人。He went to visit a patient in hospital with a bouquet of flowers.

“戴花”指在胸前或头发上别着花。如用“带”,则是携带、拿着的意思 ◇ 戴花 means "to wear flowers on the bosom or in the hair". If 带 is used, it means "to carry".

传 (动) chuán　传递 (动) chuándì　递 (动) dì

Ⓔ pass on/ transmit, deliver/ hand over

“传”、“传递”、“递”这三个动词都有传送、一方交给另一方的意思,但在义项及使用范围上有不同 ◇ The three verbs 传,传递,递 all mean "to pass on from one person to another", but they have different usages.

1. 表示转给,转交 ◇ To indicate "to pass on, to deliver":

表示这种意思时,“传”一般是经过第三者(或更多的人)转给对方;“递”一般是直接给对方,有时也可经过第三者;“传递”也是经过第三者(或更多的人)。三个词都常用补语“给”、“到”、“过来”、“过去”等 ◇ When meaning this, 传 usually means "to hand over something through a third person (or more than one) to the other"; 递 is usually "to pass on directly to the other party"; 传递 is also "through a third person" (or more than one). All the three words often take a complement 给,到,过来,过去,etc.:

① 会上,人们把意见写在一张纸上**传**给主席。(经过多人) During the meeting, people recorded their opinions on a piece of paper and passed it to the chairman. (through several people)

② 运动会开幕前,由运动员从另一城市把火炬**传递**到大会会

场，点燃圣火。（经过多人）The torch was passed on to the sports meeting arena from another city and ignited by the sportsman before the opening ceremony.(through many people)

③ 她把一杯茶**递**给我。（直接给对方）She passed to me a cup of tea. (directly to the other party)

“传球”、“击鼓传花”等，则是表示较多的人一个接一个地把物交给另一方。“递”有时是“递交”的意思，如“申请书已经递上去了”◇ 传球，击鼓传花，etc. are games in which several people pass sth. from one to another. 递 sometimes means the same as 递交(to hand over), e. g. 申请书已经递上去了(The application has been presented.).

2. 表示由上代、前代留给后代，用“传”，不用“传递”或“递”◇ To indicate "to pass on from one generation to the next", 传 is used, not 传递 or 递:

① 他家这幅宋代名画，是从爷爷那儿**传**下来的。The famous painting of the Song Dynasty was handed down from his grandfather.

② 这种牡丹栽培技术是从清朝**传**下来的。The peony cultivation technology was handed down from the Qing Dynasty.

③ 古代的优秀文化遗产，**传**给了后人，后人应该发扬光大。The cultural heritage was handed down and should be developed by the later generation.

3. 表示传授（技艺等），用“传”，不用“传递”或“递”◇ To indicate "to teach (skills, etc.)", 传 is used, and not 传递 or 递:

① 师傅把这门手艺**传**给了徒弟。The master passed on all his craftsmanship to his apprentices.

② 由于宗法观念的影响，过去他家的手艺是**传**子不传女的。Due to the influence of patriarchal clan system, the craftsmanship of his family was passed on only to boys but not girls.

4. 表示传播消息，传达消息、信息，三个词都可用，“传”用得最多，“递”限于个别习惯搭配，“传递”用得也较窄（只用在有限的范围）◇ To indicate "to spread news, or to pass on news or information", all the three words can be used. 传 is used most often; 递 is limited to some idiomatic collocations; 传递 is rarely used (only in a limited scope):

① 这个消息很快**传**开了。The news got around soon.

② 那个丑闻**传**遍了全世界。The scandal spread all over the world.

C

③ 她的丈夫对她**递**了个眼色,不让她说话。Her husband winked at her, hinting her not to say anything.

④ 你可以通过电子邮件把照片**传递**给我。You can send your photos by e-mail.

在这里,"递"习惯搭配限于"递眼色"、"递口信"、"递信儿"、"递个话儿"等 ◇ Here the idiomatic collocation of 递 is limited to 递眼色(wink at sb.), 递口信(take a message to sb.), 递信儿(take a message to sb.), 递个话儿(take a word to sb.), etc.

5. "传"还可表示传染、传召(命令别人来)、传导等,其他两个词不可以这样用 ◇ 传 can also mean "to infect, to summon (to order someone to come), to conduct, etc". The other two words have no such usages.

① 同屋的人得了感冒,也**传**给我了。My roommates got a cold and infected me as well.

② 法庭**传**证人到庭作证。The witness was called to the court for testimony.

③ 水是可以**传**电的。Water is conductive.

窗 (名) chuāng　窗户 (名) chuānghu　窗子 (名) chuāngzi

Ⓔ window/window/window

◪ 这三个词都表示屋内透光通气的装置。"窗"是粘着词,其他两个是自由词。"窗"不能独立运用,可以说"玻璃窗"、"纱窗"、"窗前"、"南窗"、"北窗"等 ◇ The three words all mean "window". 窗 is an agglutinative word, and the other two are free words. 窗 cannot be used independently. One can say 玻璃窗(glass window), 纱窗(screen window), 窗前(in front of a window), 南窗(south window), 北窗(north window) etc. e. g:

① **玻璃窗**擦得十分明亮。The glass window is brightly cleaned.

② **窗前**放着一瓶花。There is a vase of flowers in front of the window.

其他两个词可以独立运用 ◇ The other two words can be used independently:

③ 这个房间有两扇大**窗户**。There are two big windows in the room.

④ 这个**窗子**朝南,正好采光。The south window is for getting sunshine.

"窗户"和"窗子"一般可互换 ◇ 窗户 and 窗子 are usually interchangeable.

四字语中用单音节的"窗",如"窗明几净" ◇ 窗 is used in four

character phrases, e. g. 窗明几净 (with bright windows and clean tables).

用于抽象意义时,"窗"可说"服务窗"、"展示窗"等,仍不能独立运用。而"窗户"和"窗子"可说"眼睛是心灵的窗户(/窗子)"等 ◇ 窗 can be used figuratively, e. g. 服务窗(service window), 展示窗(showcase), etc. but it still can't be used by itself; 窗户 and 窗子 can, e. g. 眼睛是心灵的窗户(/窗子)(Eyes are the window of the soul.), etc.

床 床铺

(名) (名)

chuáng chuángpù

Ⓔ bed/bed

这两个词都表示供人睡觉的家具。"床"可以是复数或单数。"床铺"是总称,即一般的床和用木板搭的床,泛指各种床 ◇ Both words mean "bed". 床 can be in singular or plural number. 床铺 is a general designation, meaning "all sorts of bed":

① 屋子里有一张双人**床**。There is a double bed in the room.

② 床上铺着漂亮的**床单**。The bed is covered with a beautiful sheet.

③ 这是一家简易旅店,**床铺**家具都很简单。This is a simply-equipped hotel with simple beds and basic furniture.

两个词一般不可互换。在少数情况下,两个词都可以表示复数 ◇ The two words are not interchangeable. In some cases, they both indicate plural number.

④ 为了学生夏日午睡,学校添置了一些**床铺**(/**床**)。The school bought some beds for students' nap in summer.

次 遍

(量) (量)

cì biàn

Ⓔ time/time

这两个词都是动量词。用于反复出现的事物。"遍"同时强调从开始到结束的过程 ◇ Both are verbal measure words to indicate "the repetition of an action". 遍 also stresses the course of the action.

1. "次"可用于正式的、反复出现的大事,如"第一次全国代表大会"、"第二次国内革命战争"、"第三次旅行"等。"遍"没有以上的用法 ◇ 次 can be applied to the formal reoccurrence of major events, e. g. 第一次全国代表大会 (the First National People's Congress), 第二次国内革命战争

(the Second Revolutionary Civil War), 第三次旅行 (the third tour). 遍 cannot be so used.

C

2. "次"可说"初次"、"再次"、"前次";"遍"无此搭配方式 ◇ 次 can make up phrases, e.g. 初次 (first time), 再次 (second time), 前次 (last time), etc.; 遍 cannot make up such phrases.

3. 两个词都可受数词修饰,前面还可以加"第"、"前"、"后"、"最后"等。如"一次"、"两次"、"第三次"、"前一次"、"后一次"、"最后那次"等,以及"一遍"、"两遍"、"第三遍"、"前一遍"、"后一遍"、"最后这遍"等。但"二遍"少用,"二次"可以,如"二次进京" ◇ Both words can be qualified by a numeral preceded with 第 (used before numerals to form ordinal numbers), 前, 后, 最后, etc.: 一次, 两次, 第三次, 前一次, 后一次, 最后那次, etc., and 一遍, 两遍, 第三遍, 前一遍, 后一遍, 最后这遍, etc. 二遍 is rarely used but 二次 can be used, e.g. 二次进京 (visiting the capital again).

4. "次"用得较广较多,"遍"因表示一个从始至终的历程,一般用于"读"、"写"、"唱"、"说"、"画"等具有历程性的动作 ◇ 次 is used more often. 遍 stresses a course from beginning to end and so is applied to actions like 读, 写, 唱, 说, 画, etc. which invlove a course. e.g.

① 他来过两**次**北京。He has been to Beijing twice.

② 他从头到尾又把台词念了一**遍**。He read again his lines from the beginning to the end.

③ 他认真地打了一**遍**太极拳。He practiced *Taijiquan* earnestly.

5. 有时动作的重复性与历程性兼而有之,用"次"或"遍"均可 ◇ Some actions feature repetition as well as duration, so either 次 or 遍 can be used:

① 这首歌你再教我一**次**(/**遍**)吧。Please teach me the song again.

② 他说了一**次**(/**遍**)又一**次**(/**遍**)。He repeated it over and over again.

两个词都可以重叠 ◇ Both words can be reduplicated:

③ 一**次次**地造访,都没有见到主人。He visited the house again and again but he failed to see the host.

④ 他一**遍遍**地练习,终于掌握了动作要领。He practised again and again and finally got the snack of it.

聪明 伶俐

(形) (形)

cōngming língli

Ⓔ intelligent/clever

"聪明"、"伶俐"这两个形容词都表示脑力好、智力强 ◇ The adjectives 聪明 and 伶俐 both mean to have a good brain and to be very intelligent.

1. "聪明"一般指智力,"伶俐"兼指乖巧灵活。以下例①只能用"聪明";例②只能用"伶俐"。但两个词可连用,表示智力和应付能力都强,如例③ ◇ 聪明 means " high intelligence", while 伶俐 means "clever and nimble". In example ① only 聪明 can be used; in example② only 伶俐 can be used. But the two words can be used together to show both intelligence and the ability to cope with problems, as in example ③:

① 这孩子很**聪明**,听了一遍就会唱了。The child is so cute that he can sing a song after listening to it only once.

② 相声演员口齿要**伶俐**。The performer of cross talk is required to have a ready tongue.

③ 这个男孩**聪明伶俐**,功课又好,又会表演节目。The boy is very cute, not only good at his lessons, but also good at giving art performance.

2. "聪明"除用于人,还可用于动物等,"伶俐"一般只用于人,偶尔用于小动物 ◇ Besides human beings, 聪明 can be applied to animals. 伶俐 is only applied to human beings and occasionally to small animals:

① 这猴子真**聪明**。The monkey is so clever.

② 大家一般认为狗比猫**聪明**。It is generally believed that a dog is cleverer than a cat.

③ 马戏团里有许多**聪明**(/**伶俐**)的小动物。There are many cute animals in the circus.

从前 以前

(名) (名)

cóngqián yǐqián

Ⓔ before/before

这两个词都是时间名词,除可以做主语、宾语外,还可以做定语、状语,表示"过去的时候"、"以往的时候"。区别是:"以前"可以直接用在谓词之后(如"毕业以前"、"战争以前"、"吃饭以前"、"来以前"、"死以前"等),"从前"不能这样用。另外,"从前"在语感上比"以前"更久

远些 ◇ Both words are time nouns. Besides being subject and object, they can also be used as an attributive or adverbial to indicate past tense. The difference is that 以前 can be used immediately after a verb or a verbal phrase, while 从前 cannot. 从前 sounds a longer time ago than 以前. e. g. :

① 睡觉**以前**,他听了一会儿音乐。Before going to sleep, he listened to the music for a while.

② 你必须在会议开幕**之前**完成这份文件. You must complete the document before the opening of the meeting.

以上两句,不能用"从前" ◇ In the two examples above, 从前 cannot be used.

在下面的例句中,两个词可以互换 ◇ In the following examples, the two words are interchangeable:

③ **从前**(/**以前**)我们家在天津住过。We once lived in Tianjin.

④ 你**从前**(/**以前**)来过这里吗? Have you ever been here before?

⑤ **从前**(/**以前**)是**从前**(/**以前**),现在可不一样了。The past has passed, and things are quite different now.

⑥ 她还是**从前**(/**以前**)的她,一点儿也没变。She is the same as she was.

当后接"从来没……过"时,为避免两个"从"字同时出现,多用"以前从来没……过",不用"从前……" ◇ If there follows a clause such as 从来没……过, 以前从来没……过 is used to avoid the repetition of 从:

⑦ 我**以前**从来没听说过这个人。I have never heard this man before.

⑧ 我**以前**从来没去过那里。I have never been there before.

错 错误

(形、名) (名)

CUÒ CUÒWÙ

Ⓔ wrong; mistake, error/ mistake, error

1. 这两个词都表示不正确。"错"指较一般的不正确,较口语化。"错误"则指较大的(如言行、政治、经济等),较书面化 ◇ Both words mean "not right". 错 is applied to ordinary wrong deeds and is more colloquial. 错误 sounds more serious and literary and is applied to more serious statements or deeds such as political or economical mistakes:

(1) **错**(形)

① 他写了一个**错**字。He misspelled a word.

② 你**错**了，这里是四号楼，不是五号楼。You are wrong. This is No.4 building, not No.5.

以上二例，属于一般的小事，用"错"不用"错误" ◇ The two examples above are about ordinary things, so 错 is used.

(2)"错"常做补语如"说错"、"拿错"、"写错"、"念错"、"分析错"等。"错误"也可做补语，用在双音节动词之后，如"估计错误、理解错误" ◇ 错 is often used as a complement, e. g. 说错，拿错，写错，念错，分析错，etc. 错误 can also be used as a complement after a disyllabic verb, e. g. 估计错误(estimate wrongly)，理解错误(understand wrongly)：

③ 他拿**错**了别人的东西。He took the other one's article by mistake.

④ 对不起，我说**错**了。I am sorry for my inappropriate words.

⑤ 对于经济状况，他们估计**错误**了。They made an inaccurate evaluation about the economic situation.

(3)"错"做定语常不加"的"，如"错字"、"错话"、"错事"、"错案"。"错误"做定语，在句中有时可不加"的" ◇ As an attributive, 错 usually takes no 的, e. g. 错字(misspelt words)，错话(inappropriate wolds)，错事(misdeeds)，错案(wronged cases). 错误(mistake) as an attributive may be used in a sentence without taking 的：

错误(的)决定 wrong decision

错误(的)判断 wrong judgement

(4)"错"做谓语，如例②，再如 ◇ 错 is used as the predicate as in example ②, and:

⑥ 你这样理解，**错**了。You are wrong if you think so.

"错"后常加"了"。而"错误"做谓语时，常受双音节状语的修饰，或纳入"是……的"格式 ◇ 错 usually takes 了 after it. when 错误 used as the predicate, it is often qualified by a disyllabic adverbial, or made into the phrase 是……的：

⑦ 你的判断完全**错误**。Your judgement is completely wrong.

⑧ 这种看法是十分**错误**的。This view is a sheer mistake.

⑨ 这个答案是**错误**的。The answer is not correct.

(5) 两个词都可做状语。"错"可与单音节动词搭配，如"错判"、"错认"，与双音节动词搭配较少 ◇ Both words can be used as the adverbial. 错 can be used with a monosyllabic verb, e. g. 错判，错认，but rarely with a disyllabic verb:

⑩ 我把他**错当成**老王了。I mistook him for Lao Wang.

⑪ 他**错以为**飞机八点起飞，所以来晚了。He had thought that

the plane would take off at eight o'clock, so he was late for it.

"错误"则一般与双音节动词搭配,较为正式,一般加"地" ◇ 错误 is more formal, usually used with disyllabic verbs and followed by 地:

⑫ 他们**错误地**作出了决定。They made an incorrect decision about it.

⑬ 对这件事他们**错误地**进行了处理。They dealt with this matter incorrectly

2. 作为名词,"错误"做主语、宾语较自由 ◇ As a noun, 错误 is free to be the subject or object, e. g.:

① **错误**并不可怕,可怕的是认识不到**错误**。Error is not terrible by itself; not realizing it is terrible indeed.

② 他们很善于改正**错误**。They are good at correcting their mistakes.

名词"错"做主语、宾语可用于固定格式,如"错中错"、"错上加错"。"错"和"错误"都可做"犯"、"有"的宾语。但双音节动词更多与"错误"搭配 ◇ 错 as a noun can be used as the subject or object of a set phrase, e. g. 错中错, 错上加错. Both 错 and 错误 can be the object of 犯 and 有. Disyllabic verbs are mostly used with 错误. e. g.:

改错 correct the mistakes

改正错误 correct one's mistakes

出错 make a mistake

出现错误 mistake arises

不过单、双音节搭配不是绝对的。在语言环境清楚的时候,这两个名词,是可以互换的 ◇ But the collocation with monosyllabic or disyllabic words is not absolute. When the contexts are clear, the two words are interchangeable:

③由于疏忽大意,这个出纳员犯了一个大**错**(/**错误**)。The cashier made a great mistake because of carelessness.

D

答应 回答

（动） （动）

dāying huídá

Ⓔ to answer, respond, promise/ to reply, answer

1. "答应"表示使用简短的语言表明听见了别人的呼唤，也可表示同意、应允 ◇ 答应 means "to respond to sb.'s call with shortsentences"; it can also mean "to agree or to promise":

① 我叫了两声，没人**答应**。I called twice, but no one responded.

② 小张**答应**了小李的请求。Xiao Zhang complied with Xiao Li's request.

2. "回答"表示对提出的问题、要求等给以解释、回复，有时也可表示简单应答呼唤。例①可换用"回答"。例②不能换，如 ◇ 回答 means "to answer a question or request" and can also mean "to respond to a call". In example ①, 回答 can be used instead, but not in example ②. Another example is:

① 学生纷纷向老师提问，老师都**回答**了。The students asked the teacher questions one by one, and the teacher answered them all.

"回答"可做主语、宾语 ◇ 回答 can be used as the subject or the object of a sentence:

② 这种**回答**是令人满意的。The reply is satisfactory.

③ 对于记者的提问，他都一一做了**回答**。He has responded to all the questions put forward by the reporters.

以上三例都不能用"答应" ◇ In all the examples above, 答应 cannot be used instead.

对问题等能够作出回答或回答得好，可用"回答出来(了)"；否则，可用"回答不出来"、"没回答出来"、"回答不上来"，这时也不能用"答应" ◇ When sb. can answer a question or give a good answer, we can say 回答出来(了); otherwise, we say 回答不出来，没回答出来 or 回答不上来, and 答应 cannot be used instead. e. g.

④ 老师的问题太难，他**回答**不出来。The teacher's question was so difficult that he could not reply to it.

▶[回答 huídá—答复 dáfù]

D

打算 (动、名) dǎsuan　计划 (动、名) jìhuà

Ⓔ to intend, plan, think; plan / to plan; plan

1. 这两个词都表示事前考虑、筹划。"打算"较随便些,非正式些;"计划"郑重些、正式些。但有时从修辞上委婉的要求出发,也用"打算"表示正式的筹划。另外,"小打算"、"个人打算"等可表示纯粹从私人利益考虑的筹划 ◇ Both words mean "to consider and plan beforehand". 打算 is more colloquial and informal; 计划 is more formal. But if one wants to be tactful, one can also use 打算 for a formal plan. Moreover, 小打算 (consideration), 个人打算 (personal consideration) can be used for any plan of sheer personal advantage.

① 晚上**打算**吃什么? What would you like to eat for supper?

② 我累了,不**打算**去公园了。I am tired and I don't want to go to the park.

以上二例,因为属于小事,不用"计划" ◇ Examples ① and ② concern trifles, so 计划 is not used.

③ 学校制定了一个三年发展**计划**。The school has worked out a three-year developing plan.

④ 国家**计划**两年内拨款 50 亿元用于铁路建设。The state plans to earmark a sum of 5 billon *yuan* for railway construction in these two years.

以上二例,因为属于大事,用"计划"不用"打算" ◇ Examples ③ and ④ concern great events, so 计划 is used, not 打算.

2. 但有时大事(非法律性的)可用"计划"或"打算" ◇ Sometimes a great event (not concerning law) can be referred to by either 计划 or 打算:

① 这个企业**计划**(/**打算**)向海外发展业务。The enterprise is planning to enlarge its business to foreign countries.

"小事"两个词也都可用 ◇ Both words can be applied to trifles:

② 他们**计划**(/**打算**)下个月去旅游。They plan to go on a trip next month.

3. 两个词都是名词,如 1 例③,再如 ◇ Both words are also nouns, as in example ③ in point 1. e. g. :

① 她有一个**打算**:尽快把屋子装修一下。She has a plan that she will fit up the house as soon as possible.

② 这个假期你有什么**计划**?

What are you going to do during this holiday?

4.“计划(动)”和“打算(动)”可以重叠(ABAB) ◇ As a verb, both 计划 and 打算 can be reduplicated(ABAB):

① 大家**计划计划**,我们学校怎么样扩大招生。Please discuss how to enlarge the enrollment of our school.

② 勤俭办厂,事事都得**打算打算**。We should follow the principle of running an enterprise industriously and thriftily,and we should calculate whatever we do.

加补语时,因“计划”较郑重,加补语无限制,“打算”较随便,加补语(如“周全”、“妥当”等)受到限制 ◇ 计划 is more formal and is free in taking a complement, while 打算 is more casual and usually does not take 周全(thorough, comprehensive), 妥当 (appropriate),etc. as a complement:

③ 我们已经**计划**妥当,到时准时开工。We are fully prepared to start work on time then.

上例不用“打算”。但一般的补语(如“好”)两个词都可用 ◇ In example ③ 打算 is not used, but either word can take an ordinary complement,such as 好:

④ 聚会的方式和时间,你们**计划**(/**打算**)好了吗? Have you discussed the way and time of the party?

大半 (副、名) dàbàn　多半 (副) duōbàn

Ⓔ probably;greater part,most/probably,most likely

1. 作为副词,这两个词都有大概或有较大可能性的含义 ◇ As an adverb,both words mean "probably".

(1)表示时间上的较大可能性 To indicate "probability in time":

① 十点开会,他九点半从家里出发,现在**大半**(/**多半**)快到了。He left home at nine thirty for the meeting at ten and he must be here soon.

(2)表示数量上的较大可能性 ◇ To indicate "probability in quantity":

② 估计这个月的生产任务,**大半**(/**多半**)已经完成了。It is supposed that most of the production of this month has been done.

③ 他猜想,人**大半**(/**多半**)到齐了。He supposed that most people were present.

(3)表示情理上的较大可能性 ◇ To indicate" probability in reason or common sense":

④ 事情**多半**会成功的。It is

likely to be successful.

⑤ 这次高考,他**多半**考不上。 He is probable to fail in the college entrance examination.

以上,①②各例中两个词都可以用;③常用"多半",但书面语色彩较浓时也可以用"大半" ◇ In all the examples in ① and ② either word can be used. In the example of ③ usually 多半 is used, but when it is more literary 大半 can also be used:

⑥ 这件事情**大半**遇到了挫折。 This matter is probably faced with setbacks.

2. 作为名词"大半"表示大部分,常说"一大半";"多半"不是名词 ◇ As a noun 大半 means "the greater part" and usually one says 一大半. 多半 is not a noun.

① 来宾中**大半**是外交官。More than half of the guests are diplomats.

② 他的藏书中,**一大半**是外文书。More than half of his collection is foreign books.

③ 文章已经写了**一大半**了。He has finished more than half of his article.

大概 大约 也许

(形、名) (副) (副)

dàgài dàyuē yěxǔ

Ⓔ probably, most likely/ probably, most likely/ perhaps, probably

这三个词都可以表示很大的可能性,大致的情况等。区别是:"大概"是形容词,除了做状语,还可以做定语 ◇ All the three words mean "a great possibility or general condition". 大概 is an adjective; besides being an adverbial, it can also be an attributive, e. g.:

① 我先介绍一下**大概**的情况。 At first, I'd like to make a general introduction to it.

② 他谈了谈对那里的**大概**印象。 He told us his general impression about the place.

名词"大概"可做宾语,如 ◇ As noun sometimes it can be the object in a sentence, e. g.:

③ 对那里的工作条件先了解一个**大概**。I have general knowledge about the working conditions there.

三个词都可以做状语,都可以用于句中或句首 ◇ All three words can be the adverbial, used in the middle or the front of the sentence:

④ 这件事**大概(/大约/也许)**是我记错了。It must be my wrong memory about it.

⑤ **大概(/大约/也许)**今天他不来了。It's possible he will not come today.

例④⑤两句中，三个词可以互换 ◇ In examples ④ and ⑤, any of the three can be used.

另外，"也许"的词义偏于对情况的猜测或估计，有时表示另外的可能性，还可以单独成句 ◇ Moreover, 也许 is mostly used in conjecture or estimation, and sometimes it indicates "other possibility", and can also be used independently:

⑥ 小王**也许**二十岁，**也许**二十二岁。Xiao Wang is either twenty or twenty-two.

⑦ 这次比赛，**也许**胜，**也许**败。This match may be either successful or unsuccessful.

⑧ ——我看雨下不起来了。It seems to me it is not going to rain.

——**也许**。Maybe.

例⑧对别人的估计表示肯定。这是"大概"、"大约"两个词不具有的功能。如用"大概"、"大约"，起码应加"是" ◇ In example ⑧也许 indicates "one's agreement with the estimation of sb. else". 大概, 大约 cannot be so used. If 大概 or 大约 is used, it must be followed by 是:

⑨ ——我看雨下不起来了。It seems to me it is not going to rain.

——**大概是**。Maybe.

"大约"、"大概"还可表示估计的数字不一定精确 ◇ 大约，大概 can also mean that the estimated figure may be imprecise:

⑩ 他**大约**(/**大概**)六点到。He will arrive at about six.

⑪ 参加的人**大约**(/**大概**)有三百多。There are about over 300 participants.

"大约"并可以直接修饰"数目"、"时间"等，如 ◇ 大约 can qualify directly the words like 数目(number), 时间(time), etc. e. g.:

⑫ 这只是个**大约**的数目。This is just an approximate number.

⑬ 出发的**大约**时间是七月初。The start time is roughly at the beginning of July.

以上不能用"也许"。例⑫⑬如用"大概"一般要加"的" ◇ In examples ⑫and ⑬也许 cannot be used instead. If 大概 is used in these two examples it usually takes 的 after it.

▶[大概 dàgài—大致 dàzhì]
[恐怕 kǒngpà—也许 yěxǔ]
[可能 kěnéng—也许 yěxǔ]

大概 (形、名) dàgài　大致 (形、副) dàzhì

Ⓔ general; (idea); approximately/ general; approximately, roughly

D

1. 名词“大概”表示约略的内容或情况；常做“了解”、“知道”等的宾语，并常带有“一个”或“个” ◇ 大概 as a noun means "general idea"; it is often used as the object of verbs. like 了解 (know something), 知道 (know something), etc. and is often preceded by 一个 or 个:

① 他虽然没细问，也了解了一个**大概**。Though he didn't inquire it in detail, he got general knowledge of it.

② 关于那件事，我只知道个**大概**。I just got general knowledge of it.

“大致”没有这种用法 ◇ 大致 cannot be used in this way.

2. 形容词“大概”和“大致”表示约略、大体上，常做定语。后者较前者略多书面色彩 ◇ 大概 and 大致 as an adjective mean "general, approximate", and function as attributives. The latter is more literary than the former:

① 这故事**大概**的情节是什么？What's about the story?

② 这份计划的**大致**内容就是这样。Generally speaking, the plan is like this.

这时“大概”、“大致”可以互换，但后者的书面色彩略浓 ◇ In examples ① and ②, 大概 and 大致 are interchangeable, but 大致 is more literary.

3. 形容词“大概”也表示约略或有很大的可能性，常做状语，可在主语前或后，如在动词前，可带“地” ◇ As an adverb, 大概 means "approximately or very likely" and often functions as the adverbial. It can be placed either before or after the subject. If it precedes a verb, it can take 地:

① **大概**10点了。It's about 10 o'clock.

② 他**大概**不来了。He maybe cannot come.

③ **大概**那个人是干警卫工作的。Maybe he is a guard.

④ 他**大概**地叙述了一下工作要点。He gave a general introduction to the work essentials.

4. “大致”还表示大体上、约略地，没有“有很大可能性”的意思；常做状语，可在主语前或后，可带“地”，有时可带“上” ◇ 大致 means "roughly or approximately", and does not have the meaning of great possibility. It usually functions as the adverbial and either precedes or follows the subject. It can take 地 and sometimes 上:

① 他们一直忙了两天，工作方才**大致**就绪。The work was in order after he had been working at it for two days.

② 你把事情的来龙去脉**大致地**

谈一谈。Please tell us the sequences of the event.

③ 他能做到的，**大致上**我也能做到。I can do almost everything that he can do.

这时，3 中的例④（“大概”表示约略）和 4 中的例②（“大致”表示约略）可以互换。4 中的例①的“大致就绪”是四字短语，较为固定化，不能用“大概” ◇ In examples ④ of 3（大概 meaning not detailed）and ② of 4（大致 meaning roughly），大概 and 大致 are interchangeable. In examples ① of 4，大致就绪 is a four-character set phrase, in which 大概 cannot be used.

► [大概 dàgài—大约 dàyuē—也许 yěxǔ]

大伙儿 大家

（代） （代）
dàhuǒr dàjiā

Ⓔ all, everybody / all, everybody

◥ 这两个词都表示所有的人（一定的空间或时间内）。有时包括说话人，有时不包括。“大伙儿”更为口语化 ◇ Both words mean "all, everybody" (within a certain space or time). The speaker may or may not be included. 大伙儿 is more colloquial.

① 那时候**大家**（/**大伙儿**）都没见过欧洲人。（一定的时间）Nobody had seen a European at that time. (certain time)

② **大家**（/**大伙儿**）入座吧！（一定的空间）Let's take our seats. (certain space)

例①指历史上某个时期，例②指屋中赴宴的人。当然，时间也离不开空间范围，如例①是指中国某地，例②是在某个时候 ◇ Example ① indicates a certain time in history and example ② indicates all of the people in the room who attend the banquet. Of course, time and space cannot be separated, e. g. example ① indicates "a certain place in China" and example ② indicates "a certain space in a certain time".

③ 我来报告**大家**（/**大伙儿**）一个好消息。（不包括说话人）Allow me to tell you a piece of good news. (The speaker is not included.)

④ 咱们**大家**（/**大伙儿**）一块儿去吧。（包括说话人）Let's go together. (The speaker is included.)

“大家”可用于十分正式的场合，或正式名称，“大伙儿”因其口语化，较少在正式的场合使用 ◇ 大家 can be used at very formal occasions or in official titles. 大伙儿 is not often used at very formal occasions because it is too colloquial.

⑤ **大家**起立,唱国歌。All stand up and sing the national anthem in chorus.

⑥ 希望**大家**(/**大伙儿**)都来参加我们的"大家谈"节目。I hope all of you come to join our programme "Talks for All".

以上⑤因为是正式场合,不能用"大伙儿" ◇ Since example ⑤ indicates an official occasion,大伙儿 cannot be used.

代办 代理

(动、名) (动)

dàibàn dàilǐ

Ⓔ to do sth. for sb. ;chargé d'affaires/

to act on behalf of sb. on a responsible position

"代办"有时是名词,有其特定含义:一个国家以外交部长名义派驻另外一国的外事代表官员;或指派驻他国的使馆中,当大使、公使不在职时,在外事官员中临时委任的负责人员(叫"临时代办") ◇ 代办 sometimes is a noun and means " chargé d'affaires", such as 临时代办(chargé d'affaires ad interim).

"代理"是动词,并可与名词构成表示一定职务的词组,如:"代理部长"、"代理处长" ◇ 代理 is a verb, which can be used with a noun to form an official title, e. g. 代理部长(acting minister),代理处长(acting director).

"代办(动)"和"代理(动)"都有替别人做事的意思。"代办"除了较特殊的"邮政代办所"以外,一般指替别人做较具体的事情,如"代办托运"、"代办邮购",再如 ◇ Both 代办(v.) and 代理(v.) mean " to do sth. for sb. else". Except for 邮政代办所(postal agency),which is a rather special usage,代办 means "to do sth. concrete for sb. else",e. g. 代办托运(consign),代办邮购(undertake commission for mail-order). More examples:

① 你放心吧,在你出国期间,这件工作由我**代办**。Rest assured! I will do the job for you while you are abroad.

② 老张病了,这份公文请小李**代办**一下吧! Ask Xiao Li to deal with the document,for Lao Zhang is ill.

"代理"则一般表示替别人做较正式的事,是指受当事人委托或授权,代表当事人正式活动,如诉讼、税务、贸易等 ◇ 代理 is to do sth. officially for sb. else, that is,to be authorized to act for sb. else,such as in lawsuits, tax payment,commerce,etc.:

③ 该商店停业后,善后事宜由××律师事务所**代理**。After the

shop closed down, the xx law office was assigned to deal with its aftermath affairs.

④ 我们委托××使馆**代理**我方的签约事宜。We commissioned xx embassy to sign the contract on behalf of us.

另外,“代办”(动)的宾语是事务,“代理”(动)的宾语还可以是职务 ◇ Moreover, the object of 代办(v.) is business or work, while the object of 代理(v.) can also be the post:

⑤ 李先生委托他**代办**图书邮购手续。Mr. Li asked him to buy the books by mail for him.

⑥ 张部长病休期间,由他**代理**部长。He was in place of Minister Zhang during Zhang's illness.

带动 带领

(动) (动)

dàidòng dàilǐng

Ⓔ to take the lead/

to take the lead; to power

“带动”和“带领”都有带头进行(某事)的意思。但在用法和意义上是有差别的 ◇ 带动 and 带领 both mean "to take the lead in doing sth.", but they are different in usage and meaning.

1.“带动”指领头人或领导者通过自身的行动或树立典型,引导其他人(并把他们发动起来)投入某工作或活动 ◇ 带动 means "that the leader leads other people (and mobilizes them) to do some work or promote a certain activity":

① 以信息化**带动**工业化。We use the informatization to take the lead of industrialilzation.

② 这个城市用房改**带动**城市市房建设,居民反映良好。The city makes use of housing reform to take the lead of city construction, which is popular among the residents.

③ 树民们在他的**带动**下,也跟着种起了葡萄。Taking lead of him ,the villagers grew grapes.

2.“带动”指机器、车辆等通过动力使有关部分相应地运作起来 ◇ 带动 means "to power or spur":

① 这种旧式缝纫机是用摇把**带动**起来的。The old-fashioned sewing machine was run by a handle.

3.“带领”指领头者具体引导或指挥(人们进行某项活动) ◇ 带领 means "the leader specifically guides or directs (people in a certain activity)":

① 班长**带领**全班同学种树。The monitor headed the whole class to plant trees.

② 办喜事的车队,由一辆彩车**带**

领,按时出发了。Following a wedding float, the fleet started on time.

③ 老师**带领**着学生们去爬山。The teacher took the students to go climbing.

D

以上,1、2 中的"带动"和 3 中的"带领"是不能互换的。但有时既隐含着表示有领头人的发动和鼓励,又表示具体的引导或指挥,则"带动"和"带领"可以互换,多用在"在……的带动(/带领)下"中,但仍有所侧重,如 ◇ 带动 and 带领 in 1,2 and 3 are not interchangeable. But if one wants to hint that the leader both mobilizes and encourages and takes the lead and directs, 带动 and 带领 are interchangeable, mostly in the phrase of 在……的带动(/带领下), but with different stresses, e. g. :

④ 在校长的**带动**(/**带领**)下,师生们参加了美化校园的活动。According to the principal's advocacy, all the teachers and students took part in the activities of beautifying the campus.

▶[率领 shuàilǐng—带领 dàilǐng]

担负 (动) dānfù　负担 (动、名) fùdān

Ⓔ to bear, to shoulder/to bear, to shoulder; burden, load

1."担负"表示承担和承受,宾语多为抽象意义的"责任"、"工作"、"重任"等,也可以是较具体的"费用"等 ◇ 担负 means "to shoulder and bear", and the object is usually sth. abstract, e. g. 责任 (responsibilily), 工作 (work), 重任 (important task), etc. , but can also be the concrete words like 费用(expenses), etc. :

① 他独自一人**担负**着两个孩子的上大学费用。He supports on his own the college expenses of his two children.

② 你们毕业以后,将要在各个岗位上**担负**一定的责任。You will be responsible for your job to some extent after your graduation.

③ 她在这个公司**担负**较重要的职责。She is in an important position in this company.

2."负担"(动)较书面化,宾语也常是"责任"、"工作"、"费用"、"生活"等 ◇ 负担(v.) is more literary. Its object is also 责任(responsibility), 工作 (work), 费用 (expenses), 生活(life) etc:

① 他四十多岁时已经在政府部门**负担**重要的任务。He had been in an important position in government department in his forties.

② 这么大的责任，我可**负担**不起。I cannot take on such important responsibility.

以上，1 中的例①②③与 2 中的例①，“担负”和“负担”可互换，但“负担”书面色彩略浓。有时“负担不起”(如 2 中例②)比“担负不起”语感更为沉重些 ◇ In examples ①, ② and ③ of 1 and example ① of 2, 担负 and 负担 are interchangeable, but 负担 sounds more literary. Sometimes 负担不起(e. g. ② in 2) sounds more serious than 担负不起.

3. “负担”(名)表示所负的责任、费用，或承受的精神压力等，多指非积极的 ◇ 负担 as a noun means "responsibility, expenses, or spiritual burden, mostly non-positive":

① 他要养活全家六口人，生活**负担**不轻。It is not easy to support his family of six people.

② 辩论比赛，他是初次上阵，难免有思想**负担**。It's natural that he felt a bit nervous in his first debate competition.

③ 这笔费用，对他可是不小的**负担**。The expenses are too much for him.

④ 他心理素质不错，临场比赛时一点儿**负担**也没有。He took the match with ease for his psyquality is nice.

但是 可是

(连) dànshì　　(连) kěshi

Ⓔ but/but

◪ 这两个连词都表示转折。前面的分句常有“虽然”、“尽管”等，后面的分句有时有“却”、“仍然”、“还”、“也”等。如果转折的意思较轻，主要是补充上文，不用“虽然”等。“可是”较“但是”更口语化 ◇ Both conjunctions indicate " transition ". The preceding clause is usually headed by 虽然, 尽管, etc. and the following clause by 却, 仍然, 还, 也, etc. If the transition is not stressed, 虽然, ect. is not used. 可是 is more colloquial than 但是.

① 他的个子**虽然**不高，**但是**(/**可是**)很强壮。He is not tall, but he is robust.

② 尽管有许多困难，**但是**(/**可是**)大家还是很有信心。Though There are many difficulties, we have confidence in it.

③ 他的脸有些消瘦，**但是**(/**可是**)一双眼睛非常明亮。Though his face is a bit thin, he has bright eyes.

后面的分句如有主语，“但是”必须在主语前，“可是”可以在主语之前或之后 ◇ If the following

D

clause has a subject, 但是 must precede the subject, while 可是 may precede or follow it:

④ **虽然**他很有钱,**但是**(/**可是**)日子过得很节俭。Though he is rich, he leads a frugal life.

⑤ **虽然**他很有钱,日子**可是**过得很节俭。Though he is rich, he still leads a frugal life.

"但是"可以连接两个意思相对或相反的词语 ◇ 但是 can connect two words or phrases of opposite meanings:

⑥ 一条小胡同,狭窄**但是**干净,有半里多长。The small *Hongtong* is half *li* long, and it is narrow, but clean.

由于这种表现方法比较书面化,较少用"可是" ◇ This way of expression is more literary, so 可是 is seldom used.

注意:"可是"有时是副词"可"+"是",表示强调语气,是"确实是"、"真是"的意思,与"但是"不同 ◇ Note: Incidentally, 可是 sometimes is a phrase made up by 可 plus 是, meaning "certainly is" or "really is", which has nothing in common with 但是:

⑦ 在全市的篮球队中,这个队**可是**数一数二! Of all the basketball teams in the city, this one is the best.

⑧ 他**可是**全校的高才生! He's the best student in his school.

▶[不过 bùguò—但是 dànshì—可是 kěshì]

当 做

(动) (动)

dāng zuò

Ⓔ to become, to be/ to become, to be

"当"和"做"有许多义项。这里只分辨它们表示"担任"、"充当"意思时的异同 ◇ Both 当 and 做 have multiple meanings. Here only the meaning of "to become or to be" is analysed.

两个词都可以带表示职务、职称、身份的名词做宾语 Both words can take a noun expressing the professional title or status as the object:

① 他**当**(/**做**)了老师。He became a teacher.

② 她二十岁就**当**(/**做**)了经理。She became an manager at 20.

③ 这孩子从小就想**当**(/**做**)工程师。The child dreamed to be an engineer since his early time.

在搭配上有个别的例外,如可以说"当兵",不可以说"做兵" ◇ There are a few exceptions, e. g., one can say 当兵 but not 做兵.

而"当(/做)一名小兵"、"当(/做)了将军"、"当(/做)元帅"

等,二者都是可以用的 ◇ But in phrases 当(/做)一名小兵(to be a soldier),当(/做)了将军(to be a general),当(/做)元帅(to be a marshal),either can be used.

带补语"上"时,多用"当" ◇ When taking the complement 上,当 is mostly used:

④ 他毕业后**当上**了推销员。He worked as a salesman after his graduation.

⑤ 凭他的能力,**当不上**领导。He cannot be a leader according to his ability.

带其他补语,两个词区别不大 ◇ With other complements, either can be used with little difference:

⑥ 他**当**(/**做**)了两年经理。He worked as a manager for two years.

⑦ 这个官他有点儿**当**(/**做**)够了。He is a bit bored of being an official.

带有担任、充当、扮演等意思时,用"当",不用"做" ◇ When 当 means "to play the part of or to hold the post of",做 cannot take its place:

⑧ 在这个剧中,她**当**新娘子。She stared the bride in the play.

两个词都可重叠 ◇ Both words can be reduplicated:

⑨ 你来**当当**(/**做做**)这个科长吧! If you were the section chief!

总之,这两个词的宾语是表人名词(包括"神"、"鬼"等)。应注意的是:这种名词是某种身份,并有某种做人的责任,如"当(/做)妈妈"、"当(/做)弟弟"等,都有相关的责任 ◇ In short, the object of both verbs is a noun which indicates a person (including gods, ghosts, etc.). It is noteworthy that such a noun represents a status, along with its duty, e. g. 当(/做)妈妈(to be a mother),当(/做)弟弟(to be a brother), etc. and each has its relevant duty.

"当"(dàng)表示"作为"、"当做"时,与"做"表示"用做"时,意思也很接近 ◇ When 当 means "to be used as", it is very close to 做 in the same meaning, e. g.:

⑩ 这篇小说可以**当**(/**做**)语文教材。The novel can be used as language teaching material.

但"当"后还可带指人宾语,"做"不可以 ◇ 当 can take an object which indicates a person, while 做 cannot:

⑪ 别把我**当**客人。Don't treat me as a guest.

⑫ 我没把你**当**外人。I don't take you as a non-family.

另外,"做"不能表示"作为","当"可以 ◇ Besides, 做 cannot mean "to be regarded as", while 当 can:

⑬ 这点儿小东西,就**当**纪念品收下吧! Take the small item as a souvenir, please!

▶[干 gàn—做 zuò—搞 gǎo][作 zuò—当 dāng]

D

当前 (名) dāngqián　目前 (名) mùqián

Ⓔ present, current/present

这两个时间名词都可表示现在,但较为书面化。而且前者比后者更书面化,意义上有时含有紧迫感 ◇ Both are time nouns of the present and are rather literary. The former is even more so than the latter and usually has a sense of urgency.

① **当前**(/**目前**)的经济形势还算不错。The current economic situation is not too bad.

例①中二词可互换。这限于做定语,较书面化时。由于"当前"是从古代汉语遗留下来的,"当"原有"在"的意义,所以,"当前"可用在四字语"大敌当前"、"一事当前"等中。"目前"除了可做定语,在"到目前"、"到目前为止"、"截至目前"等词组中,可做宾语。"当前"则不能做宾语 ◇ In example ① the two words are interchangeable, but only when they are used as attributives and are literary. Since 当前 comes from classical Chinese, in which 当 means "at", 当前 is often used in four-character phrases such as 大敌当前(strong enemies), 一事当前(have something to do), etc. 目前, besides being used as an attributive, can be the object in phrases 到目前(so far), 到目前为止(up to now), 截至目前(up to now), etc. 当前 cannot be used as the object.

② 教练说:你们的对手是一支强队,**大敌当前**,可要认真对待啊! The coach said: you should take your rival team seriously, for they are very powerful.

③ **到目前为止**,这支球队是10胜3败。Up to now, the team won 10 games, and lost 3 ones.

在例②③中两词不能互换 ◇ In examples ② and ③ the two words are not interchangeable.

这两个词还可以做状语 ◇ The two words can also be used as adverbials:

④ 汛期要到了,**当前**我们要做好一切防汛准备。As the flood season is coming, we should be well prepared for it at present.

⑤ 同学们快毕业了,**目前**有什么打算? What are you going to do at your forthcoming graduation?

以上两句，同是做状语，由于例④更书面化，还有紧迫感，用“当前”为宜。而例⑤为一般叙述，用“目前”为好 ◇ In the above two examples ④ and ⑤, ④ is more literary and implies urgency, so 当前 is better. Since example ⑤ is just an ordinary remark, 目前 is more suitable.

▶ [眼前 yǎnqián—目前 mùqián]

当 认为 以为

（动） （动） （动）

dàng rènwéi yǐwéi

Ⓔ to consider, to hold/ to consider, to hold/ to consider, to hold

◪ 这三个词都表示确定看法。“认为”较正式，“以为”很一般，“当”较随便，也最口语化 ◇ The three words all mean "to ascertain one's view". 认为 is relatively formal, 以为 is most popular, while 当 is casual and most colloquial.

1. “认为”和“以为”都可以用于主观判断和实际情况的前后对比 ◇ 认为 and 以为 can both be used in the contrast between subjective judgement and actual fact:

① 我原来**认为**（/**以为**）文科好学，真学了文科才觉得很难学好。I had thought the arts were easy to learn; however, I thought it difficult after I learnt it.

② 这位农学家**认为**（/**以为**）这里的土壤条件不错。The agriculturist thought the soil here was good.

用于正面判断时多用“认为” ◇ 认为 is mostly used in positive judgement:

③ 我**认为**这是不公平的！I think it's unfair.

④ 我**认为**他的话有道理。I think what he said is sound.

但例③④如语气略为委婉，也可用“以为” ◇ In examples ③ and ④ 以为 can also be used if one wants to be more tactful.

“以为”常用在想法出现错误的时候，后面有表示转折的小句 ◇ 以为 is often used to state a mistaken understanding and is followed by a clause indicating transition:

⑤ 我**以为**他已经走了，原来他还在这儿。I had thought he had gone, but he stayed here still.

⑥ 他**以为**这是他的报纸，其实是图书馆的。He had thought the newspaper was his, but in fact, it is from the library.

2. “认为”可受副词（包括否定副词）的修饰 ◇ 认为 can be qualified by an adverb (including negative adverbs):

① 你果真**认为**是那样吗? Do you really think it is so?

② 我不**认为**是那样。I don't think so.

D

"以为"则多受单音节副词的修饰,如"真以为"、"原以为"。"以为"受否定副词的修饰是有限制的,或者在四字语中(如"不以为然"),或者是将"以"和"为"拆说(这是古代汉语的一些遗留)◇ 以为 is usually qualified by a monosyllabic adverb, e. g. 真以为(really think),原以为(had thought). It is restricted in being qualified by a negative adverb: either it is used in a four-character phrase (e. g. 不以为然), or it is split into 以…为…which is left over from classical Chinese:

③ **不以为**耻,**反以为**荣。Far from being ashamed of it, one glories in it.

④ **不以**这件不光彩的事**为**耻,**反以**此**为**荣。Instead of being ashamed of the disgraceful thing, one even is proud of it.

3. "当"最口语化;不受副词修饰 ◇ 当 is the most colloquial and never qualified by any adverb:

① 我**当**是谁呢? 原来是你。I wonder who it is. It's you!

② 屋子外面滴滴答答的,我**当**是下雨了呢! There is tittering outside. I had taken it for rain.

例①②虽可以换用"以为",但没有"当"口语化 ◇ In examples ① and ②, 以为 can replace 当, but is not so colloquial.

注意:下列受单音节副词修饰的"当"是"当做"的意思 ◇ Note: In examples ③ and ④, 当 is qualified by a monosyllabic adverb, meaning "to look on as" or "to treat as":

③ 你就**当**没有我这个弟弟好了! Don't treat me as your brother any more.

④ 口试时你只**当**没有旁听的人,大胆地说就是了! Be bold at the oral examination and suppose there is nobody but you there.

▶[认为 rènwéi—以为 yǐwéi]

到 (动) dào　赴 (动) fù

Ⓔ go to/go to

◪ "到"、"赴"这两个动词都表示去的意思,"到"多用于口语,"赴"多用于书面。以下例①②是口语,用"到";例③④"赴京"、"赴会"等是书面语,用"赴" ◇ 到 and 赴 both mean "to go to". 到 is colloquial and 赴 is literary. The examples ① and ② are colloquial and 到 is used, while ③ and ④ are literary and

赴 is used:

① 你**到**哪儿去? Where are you going?

② 他常**到**图书馆看书。He often went to the library to study.

③ 总理已经启程**赴**欧洲访问。The Premier has set out for a visit to the European countries.

④ 有关人士都**赴**会发表演说。The people concerned will go to the meeting to deliver a speech.

“赴”的用法较窄,常见用例还有“赴宴”、“赴汤蹈火”、“前赴后继”等 ◇ The usage of 赴 is limited. 赴宴,赴汤蹈火(be ready to risk one's life),前赴后继(advance fearlessly) are some commonly used idiomatic phrases.

“到”用法很宽,除了表示“去”,还表示到达、周到等,并可放在动词后做补语,表示动作达到目的或有了结果 ◇ 到 has a very wide usage. Besides "to go to", it can also mean "to arrive at, be thoughtful, etc". It can also be used after a verb as a complement to mean attaining the aim or achieving a result.

⑤ **到**下午五点,报告就可以写成了。(表示到达) The report will be finished at five p. m. (meaning to arrive at a certain time)

⑥ 来开会的人,**到**齐了吗?(表示到达) Are all the meeting participants present? (meaning to arrive at a certain place)

⑦ 招待不**到**的地方请多包涵。(表示周到) Forgive our inconsiderate treatment. (meaning to be thoughtful)

⑧ 这事办不**到**!(做补语) This can never be done! (as complement)

⑨ 昨天我在街上看**到**他了。(做补语) I saw him in the street yesterday. (as complement)

这些都不能用“赴” ◇ In all these sentences 赴 cannot be used instead.

个别的动宾短语,如“到职”、“赴职”,可以通用 ◇ There are a few verb-object phrases where 到, 赴 are interchangeable, such as 到职,赴职(arrive at one's post).

到底 (副) dàodǐ　究竟 (副) jiūjìng

Ⓔ after all/after all

这两个副词都可以用于疑问句或有疑问词的非疑问句中,表示追问,要求确定的答案。“究竟”较为书面化。但它们一般不能用于是非疑问句,而用于特指、正反及选择疑问句 ◇ Both

D

adverbs can be used in an interrogative sentence or a non-interrogative sentence with an interrogative word, to question closely for a definite answer. 究竟 is more literary. They cannot be used in a question which demands an answer of "yes" or "no" but in questions with interrogative pronouns, questions of positive and negative predicates, and questions of choice:

① 这**到底**(/**究竟**)是怎么一回事?(特指疑问句) What's up after all? (question with an interrogative pronoun)

② 他**到底**(/**究竟**)同意不同意我们的意见?(正反疑问句) Whether does he agree with me or not? (question of positive and negative predicates)

③ 你**到底**(/**究竟**)愿意还是不愿意?(选择疑问句) Whether are you willing or not? (question of choice)

④ 她要认真想想,这日子**到底**(/**究竟**)怎么过。(非疑问句) She should take it seriously about how to live. (non-interrogative sentence)

"究竟"略书面化。各句的"到底"或"究竟"都可用在主语的前或后,如例①也可说"到底(/究竟)这是怎么一回事?" ◇ 究竟 is more literary than 到底. 究竟 or 到底 can be used either before the subject or after it, e. g. in example ① can also say 到底(究竟)这是怎么一回事?

当疑问词做主语时,"到底"或"究竟"只能用在主语之前 ◇ When the interrogative word is the subject, 到底 or 究竟 can only precede the subject:

⑤ **到底**(/**究竟**)谁来了? Who has come here on earth?

⑥ **到底**(/**究竟**)什么是他的职业?是教师还是商人? What does he do on earth? A teacher or a businessman?

另外,"到底"还可表示终于、最后,"究竟"不能这样用 ◇ Besides, 到底 also means "finally, after all". 究竟 has no such meaning.

⑦ 她**到底**来了,让我等了半天。She kept me waiting for her a long time and she came at last.

注意:表示到最后、到尽头时,"到底"是动宾短语,不是词,例如 ◇ Note: When meaning "finally" or "to the end", 到底 is a verb-object phrase of 到 plus 底, and not a word, for example:

⑧ 这件疑案必须追究**到底**。The disputed case must be investigated to its end.

⑨ 总经理决心把改革进行**到底**。The Premier was determined to carry on the reforms to the end.

▶[毕竟 bìjìng—究竟 jiūjìng]

得 得到

(动) (动)

dé dédào

Ⓔ to get, to obtain/
to get, to obtain

◣这两个词都有获得的意思 ◇ Both words mean "to get".

1. 得

(1)宾语可以是分数、名次、奖项等 ◇ The object can be mark, position in a name list, prize, etc. e. g. :

① 这次考试,他**得**了90分。He got 90 marks in the examination.

② 在民歌比赛中,她**得**了大奖。She got the great award in the folksong competition.

③ 这次赛跑,我没能得第一,只**得**了第三名。I did not win the first place in the race, but only got the third place.

(2)表示计算、演算产生结果,常用于计算口诀 ◇ 得 is usually used in pithy formulas, introducing the result of calculating, e. g. :

④ 二二**得**四,二三**得**六。Two multiplies two is four; and two multiplies three is six.

⑤ 那道题的答数**得**出来没有? Have you got the result of the question?

(3)"不"+"得"表示不允许(常用于告示性语言或公文中) ◇ 不+得 means "not allowed (mostly used in an official notice or official document)":

⑥ 非经允许,**不得**入内。No admittance without permission.

⑦ 军事重地,**不得**擅入。No admittance into the military restricted area.

⑧ 方案已定,**不得**随意修改。The plan has been settled, and no change about it is permitted.

⑨ 文件要及时发出,**不得**有误。The document should be sent in time without any delay.

2. 得到

(1)宾语可以是具体的事物,也可以是抽象的 ◇ The object can be a concrete thing or sth. abstract, e. g. :

① 在这件事情上,你**得到**什么好处了? What good have you got in it?

② **得到**这个消息,他非常高兴。He is very happy at the news.

③ 工作方法已**得到**改进。The work method has been improved.

当用于具体事物时,有时可以与"得"互换 ◇ When applied to concrete things, it can sometimes be interchanged with 得:

④ 他在比赛中**得到**(/**得**)了不

少奖品。He got a lot of prizes in the matches.

(2)"得到"的否定式是"得不到"或"没得到" ◇ The negative form of 得到 is 得不到 or 没得到:

⑤ 因为**得不到**对方的支持,他十分伤心。He felt sorry for he got no support from the other party.

⑥ 他没**得到**那个职务。He did not get the position.

(3)"得到"后没有其他词语,有时可以结句,而"得"一般不能这样结句 ◇ 得到 can end a sentence,but 得 cannot. e. g. :

⑦ 好处已经**得到**。He has got the good.

⑧ 这样的便宜事怎能让他**得到**? How can you make him get such benefits?

得 (助动) děi　　必须 (助动) bìxū

Ⓔ must, have to/must, have to

1. 这两个助动词都表示一定要、一定会。"得"口语中常用,"必须"书面化一些,同时语气更强烈 ◇ Both auxilliary verbs mean "must, be bound to". 得 is very colloquial, while 必须 is more literary and forceful:

① 你发烧了,**得**(/**必须**)去医院。You have to go to hospital for you have got a fever.

② 我**得**(/**必须**)努力学习。I had to work hard.

这样的句子,两个词是可以互换的,但语体色彩是不同的。有时"必须"带有命令语气 ◇ In such sentences the two words are interchangeable,but they are of different styles. 必须 carries a commanding tone:

③ 这个任务你们**必须**在两个月内完成。You must finish the job in two months.

如果是十分口语化、相当随便的句子,多用"得"而少用"必须"(特别是北方) ◇ In very colloquial and casual speech, 得 is used more often than 必须(especially in North China), e. g. :

④ 我口渴,我**得**去喝口水。I am thirsty,and I must go to have a drink.

⑤ 这事我**得**再想想。I'd like to think about it again.

另外,这两个词还表示需要,后面可以是数量词或数量词加名词做宾语 ◇ Besides, these two words also mean "to need", and are followed by a numeral-classifier or such a compound plus a noun as the object:

⑥ 装修这套房子,**得**(/**必须**)几万块。The decoration of the

house will cost you at least thousands of *yuan*.

⑦ 这项任务**得**(/**必须**)三天时间才能完成。The task must be finished in three days.

但两个词的语体色彩还是不一样的 ◇ But they are still of different styles.

2."得"还表示猜想、预想,前面还可加"非";"必须"不能这样用 ◇ 得 can also indicate "a surmise" and be preceded by 非, 必须 cannot be so used:

① 你这么不用功,**得**拿0分! You are likely to get zero mark if you are not industrious.

② 这个球员,**得**吃红牌。The player is likely to get the red ticket.

③ 这么爱吃甜食,她将来非**得**发胖! She is likely to be fat in the future if she takes so much sweet food.

3.两个词的否定式较特殊,"得"的否定式是"不用""用不着"等,"必须"的否定式是"无须"、"不须"、"不必" ◇ The negative form of the two words is unusual. The negative form of 得 is 不用, 用不着, etc.; that of 必须 is 无须, 不须, 不必, e.g.:

① 装修这套房子**用不着**3万元。The decoration of the house will cost less than 30,000 *yuan*.

② 这项任务**不须**3天时间就能完成。It takes less than 3 days to finish the task.

▶[必须 bìxū—必需 bìxū]

D

等 等待 等候

(动) (动) (动)

děng děngdài děnghòu

Ⓔ to wait/to wait/to wait

◥ 这三个动词都表示度过所期望的人、事出现的一段时间 ◇ The three verbs all mean "to remain till sb. expected comes or sth. happens":

1."等"的宾语较具体,"等待"可用于抽象意义 ◇ The object of 等 is usually concrete, while that of 等待 can be abstract:

① 他正在**等**一个朋友。He is waiting for a friend.

② 再**等**一会儿,他就要来了。He will be here if you wait another while.

③ 这件事你得耐心**等待**时机。You have to wait for the chance patiently about it.

④ 在人生季节变换中,她似乎在**等待**着春天的来临。She seems to be waiting the coming of another life spring.

以上例①②较具体,口语化,宜用"等"。例③④是较抽象的意义,用"等待"。由于音节的关

D

系，“等”可说“等人”、“等信”、“等票”、“等车”、“等船”、“等钱(用)”及“久等”等，而“等待”不能这样用 ◇ In examples ① and ② 等 is preferred because it is concrete and colloquial. In example ③ and ④ 等待 is better because the objects are abstract things. Owing to syllabic collocation, one can say 等人(wait for someone)，等信(look forward to a letter)，等票(wait for a ticket)，等车(wait for a bus)，等船(wait for a ship)，等钱(用)(expect some money) and 久等(a long wait)，etc.，but 等待 cannot be used in such a way.

2.“等候”在所带宾语上较具体(不如“等”具体)，在语体上又较书面化，同时含有较正式的意味，所以常说“等候通知”、“等候命令”、“等候处理”、“等候任命”等 ◇ 等候 takes a more concrete object (not as concrete as 等)，is more literary in style and sounds more formal；therefore，it is often used in phrases such as 等候通知(await notices)，等候命令(await orders)，等候处理(ready to be handled)，等候任命(await appointment)，etc.，e.g.：

① 他正在**等候**正式任命。He's waiting for the official appointment.

“等候”因其可用于正式场合所以有时带有礼貌意味 ◇ Since 等候 can be used on a formal occasion，it sometimes carries a polite tone：

② 人们正在**等候**贵宾到来。The people are waiting for the coming of the distinguished guests.

上面1中例①“等”在书面语体中也可以用“等候” ◇ In example ① of 1 等 in literary style can be replaced by 等候.

从另一个角度看，“等候”多与主动性有关，而“等待”可以是被动的，所以可说“消极等待”，而不用“等候”。另外，如“等人”、“等信”、“等钱(用)”、“久等”等，均不能用“等候” ◇ Viewed from another angle，等候 sounds more active，while 等待 can be passive，so one can say 消极等待(passive wait)，while 等候 is not so used. Besides，in situations like 等人(wait for someone)，等信(expect a letter)，等钱(用)(expect some money)，久等(a long wait)，etc.，等候 cannot be used instead.

低 矮 短

(形) dī　(形) ǎi　(形) duǎn

Ⓔ low/short, low/short, brief

这三个词都指距离小。"低"和"矮"指垂直方向的距离小(是对"高"而言);"短"指平面上两端距离小(是对"长"而言)。这是它们的基本区别。在这个基础上,还有一些义项 ◇ All the three words mean "a small gap". 低 and 矮 indicate "a small perpendicular gap" (the opposite of 高); 短 indicates "a small horizontal gap (the opposite of 长)". This is their basic difference. The following are some other usages.

1. 表示人的身材小,常用"矮",很少用"低",一般不用"短" ◇ To indicate a small figure of human beings, 矮 is used. 低 is seldom used, and 短 is not used:

① 他的个子很**矮**。He is short.

② 她长得太**矮**了。She is too short.

③ 弟弟比哥哥**矮**(/**低**)一头。The little brother is a head shorter than his brother.

以上三句,只有例③两个词可以互换(口语中更多用"矮") ◇ Of the above three examples, only in example ③ the two words are interchangeable (in colloquial speech, 矮 is preferred).

但在四字语中可用"短",如"五短身材"、"身材短小" ◇ But 短 can be used in four-character phrases, e. g. 五短身材 (short in bodyand limbs), 身材短小 (of a short and small build).

2. 表示物体的高度小,一般用"矮",有时用"低" ◇ 矮 indicates "small height of things", and sometimes 低 is used instead:

① 院子周围都建了**矮**墙。There is a low wall surrounding the yard.

② 找一把**矮**(/**低**)一点儿的椅子,让孩子坐。Take a lower chair for the child.

例②这种"矮"、"低"可互换的情况是很少的。物体高度小,口语中一般用"矮"如"矮房子"、"矮桌子"、"矮凳"等。但书面语偶尔可用"低",如"远山低树" ◇ It is very rare for 矮 and 低 to be interchangeable as in example ②. Small height of things is generally expressed by 矮 in spoken language, e. g. 矮房子 (low house), 矮桌子 (low table), 矮凳 (low stool), etc. But in literary language 低 is used occasionally, e. g. 远山低树 (distant mountain and low trees).

3. 表示离地面近,用"低" ◇ 低

is used to mean " to be near the earth":

① 云层很**低**。The cloud is low.

② 飞机飞得很**低**。The plane flies very low.

③ 这风筝放得太**低**了。The kite flies too low.

与此类似的"水位",用"低" ◇ 低 is also applied to water level.

4. 抽象意义的地位等,一般用"低" ◇ 低 can be used to qualify position in an abstract sense:

① 他在那个公司里的职位不**低**。He is not in an inferior position in that company.

② 今天的股市走**低**。Today's stock prices are dropping.

③ 这种商品的销路看**低**。The goods' selling is not good.

④ 他这个人能力差,要求高,是名副其实的眼高手**低**。He is incompetent, but he is greedy. Thus he deserves the saying of that one's ability does not match his wishes.

与此类似的"物价"、"成本"、"速度"、"声音"、"能力"、"水准"等,也用"低" ◇ Price, cost, speed, sound, ability, standard, etc. can also be qualified by 低.

5. 表示等级在下,一般用"低" ◇ 低 also means "low in class":

① 妹妹比姐姐**低一**班。The little sister is one grade inferior to her sister.

② 经过评定,这种产品的等级较**低**。After evaluation, we know the quality of the product is lower.

例①在口语中也可说"矮一班" ◇ Example ① can also be turned into 矮一班 in colloquial speech.

6. "低"还有一个特殊用法:"低头"表示头部下垂 ◇ 低 has another special usage: 低头 means "to lower one's head", e. g. :

① 大家谈得很热烈,而他却**低头**不语。He looked down silently over others' heated discussion.

② 我只顾**低着头**走路,没注意对面有人走来。I walked with my head hanging and did not notice there was somebody coming to me.

7. "短"可用于物体、时间等 ◇ 短 can be applied to things, time, etc., e. g. :

① 这件上衣太**短**,我不能穿。I cannot wear the coat for it is too short.

② 他走的时间不**短**了,该回来了。He should be back for he was away for a long time.

"低"、"矮"不能这样用 ◇ 低 and 矮 cannot be so used.

"短"还是动词,有"缺少"的意思 ◇ 短 is also a verb meaning

"lack", for example:

③ 我们三个人一起做这件事，**短**了谁也不行。It won't do without anyone of us three.

的确 (副) díquè　确实 (形) quèshí

Ⓔ certainly/real, certain

"的确"和"确实"都可表示完全属实。但"的确"是副词，只能做状语。"确实"可做多种句子成分。两个词均可重叠。做状语时，一般可换用 ◇ 的确 and 确实 both mean "absolutely true". But 的确 is an adverb and can only be an adverbial. 确实 can be used as quite a few sentence elements. Both words can be reduplicated. As an adverbial, they are interchangeable:

① 他**的确**(/**确实**)说过这句话。It's true that he said it.

② 我**的的确确**(/**确确实实**)和她是中学同学。It's true that she and I are middle school classmates.

"确实"做其他成分时，不能用"的确" ◇ When 确实 functions as other sentence elements, 的确 cannot replace it:

③ 这消息不**确实**。(谓语) The news is unreliable. (predicate)

④ 请你告诉我出发的**确实**日期。(定语) Please tell me the exact start date. (attributive)

⑤ 这些数字要搞得**确确实实**的。(补语) The figures should be precise. (complement)

▶ [确实 quèshí—真实 zhēnshí—实在 shízài]

地下 (名) dìxià　地下 dì xia

Ⓔ underground, secret/ on the ground

1. "地下"(名)指地面之下；也喻指暗中活动、秘密活动的 ◇ 地下, a noun, means "underground"; figuratively it means "some secret, hidden activity":

① 这个建筑地上八层，**地下**两层。There are eight stories above the ground and two under the ground of the building.

② 战争时期他曾从事过**地下**工作。He once worked as a spy in the wartime.

③ 案发后，她转入**地下**。After the accident, her activities became secret.

以上例①是实义，例②③是比喻义 ◇ The usage in example ① is original meaning, and that of ② and ③ are figurative meaning.

D

2. “地下”（dì xia）则是名词“地”加方位词，表示地面上（也说“地上 dì shang”）◇ 地下（dì xia）is the noun 地 plus a noun of locality, meaning " on the ground (also 地上（dì shang）meaning, having the same)"：

① 眼镜掉在**地下**（/**地上**）了。The glasses fell on the floor.

② **地上**（/**地下**）是什么东西？绊了我一下。What's on the floor? I stumbled over it.

掉 落

（动） （动）

diào luò

Ⓔ fall, drop/fall, drop

◥ **1.** 表示物体从高的固定处因失去支撑而降下。两个词都可用，但“掉”更为口语化 ◇ Both 掉 and 落 mean "to fall", but 掉 is more colloquial：

① 为了这件伤心的事，她**掉**（/**落**）泪了。She wept at the sad affair.

② 因为风浪大，小船上的箱子**掉**（/**落**）在水里了。The box in the boat fell into water because of the strong wind and wave.

③ 熟透的苹果**掉**（/**落**）到地上了。The ripen apples fell to the ground.

“落”用于自然现象（例如雪、霜、尘等）的降落，这时一般不能用“掉”，但在口语中可说“掉雨点儿”◇ 落 can be applied to natural phenomena (e. g. snow, frost, rain, dust, etc.). 掉 cannot be used in such a way, but in spoken language, 掉雨点儿 can be used.

④ 一夜过后，地面上**落**了几寸深的雪。After a night, the snow on the ground was a few *cun* deep.

⑤ 草地上**落**了一层霜。The grassland is coated with frost.

⑥ 外面**落**雨了。It rained.

⑦ 雨没下起来，只**落**（/**掉**）了几个雨点儿。It did not rain heavily, but just a bit rainfall.

⑧ 屋子里长久没人住，桌上、床上**落**了一层尘土。The table and bed in the room are covered with dust for there is nobody living it.

“落”常用于（人、飞行器等）主动、安全地降下，“掉”常用于不自主地掉下 ◇ 落 often means "a voluntary, safe landing(of a person or an aircraft, etc.)", whereas 掉 often means "to fall or drop involuntarily"：

⑨ 驾驶员临危不乱，飞机终于安全**落**地。The pilot was very calm when facing the danger and he made the plane land safely at last.

⑩ 窗前**落**下几只小鸟在啄食。

There are a few birds coming to look for food in front of the window.

⑪ 那孩子不小心从椅子上**掉**下去了。The child fell off the chair carelessly.

"掉牙"、"掉头发"等是不自主的,用"掉" ◇ The fall of a tooth or hair is involuntary, so 掉 is used.

主动地使(物)下降,也用"落";被动的常用"掉" ◇ To make something to fall,落 is used;to be made to fall,掉 is often used:

⑫ 大幕**落**下,隆重的演出结束了。The curtain fell and the solemn performance was over.

⑬ 请你把遮阳伞**落**下来。Please close the parasol.

⑭ 桌布怎么**掉**在地上了? How did the tablecloth fall to the ground?

2. 表示遗失、遗漏等,用"掉",不用"落" ◇ To lose, omit, or leave out,掉 is used, not 落:

① 她不小心**掉**了钱包。She lost her purse carelessly.

② 这篇文章**掉**字太多了。There are a lot of unnecessarily-omitted words in the article.

3. 表示物价等的下降,常用"掉",有时可用"落"(可读 lào)。表示体重等的下降,常用"掉" ◇ To indicate drop in prices, etc. ,掉 is used, or sometimes 落(lào). 掉 is often used to mean "drop in weight, etc. ":

① 最近这些商品**掉**(/**落**)价了。The price of the goods has been dropping recently.

② 这种股票涨了一阵子又**掉**(/**落**)下来了。The price of the stocks dropped again after its rising.

③ 减肥减了半个月,他**掉**了几斤肉。He lost some weight after half a month's weight-losing.

4. 表示遗留在后面,两个词都可以用。但在固定词组"落榜"、"落选"等之中,只能用"落" ◇ Either word can mean " to be left behind". Yet 落榜(to fail an examination) and 落选(to fail to be chosen) are set phrases, and only 落 can be used:

① 你们俩快走啊,别**掉**(/**落**)在后边! Hurry up, you two. Don't lag behind.

② 他**落榜**了,心情很难过。He failed in the examination, and went home in low spirits.

③ 他这次**落选**,是由于选民不信任他了。That he failed in the election is because the voters did not trust him any more.

5. 表示用笔墨留下,常用"落款"、"落账"、"落笔"等 ◇ 落款(sign one's name),落账(make an entry in an account book), 落笔 (put pen to paper) all mean "to write down":

① 这幅画的**落款**是齐白石,不知是不是真的。I wonder whether the painting signed by Qi Baishi is real or fake.

② 那笔支出怎么**落账**? How to enter the expenditure in the account?

③ 由于责任重大,签字时,他迟迟不敢**落笔**。He hesitated to sign because it was of importance.

6. 表示归属,得到(伤病、下场等),用"落" ◇ 落 is used to mean"come to the end with":

① 经过一番竞争,奖状终于**落**在他的手里。After some competitions, he won the award certificate at last.

② 这个重任**落**到你肩上了,努力干吧! You are assigned to shoulder the responsibility, please work hard.

③ 战争时期,这位战士的手臂**落**了残疾。In the wartime, the soldier hurt his arm and became disabled since then.

④ 那个赌徒**落**了这种下场,是他自找的。Nobody has sympathy for the gambler's terrible end. He deserves it.

7. 表示回转、调换,用"掉" ◇ To mean "to turn, to swap", 掉 is used:

① 她把身子**掉**了过去,装作不认识他。She turned back, and pretended she did not know him.

② 车子**掉**了个方向,向南开去。The car turned and drove south.

③ 你们两个**掉**一下位置吧! Would you two swap round please!

8. 表示动作(多为"消灭"、"烧"、"改"等处置性的动词)的完成,用"掉"(做补语) ◇ 掉, as a complement, is used to mean "the completion of some action of disposal, such as 消灭 (eliminate), 烧 (burn), 改 (change), etc.:

① 这种坏习惯一定要改**掉**! The bad habit must be broken.

② 你的烟怎么还没有戒**掉**? Why not give up smoking?

③ 这些东西不能用了,处理**掉**吧! These are useless, and throw them away, please.

④ 他烧**掉**了那些旧信。He burnt those old letters.

丢失 丧失 失去

(动) (动) (动)

diūshī sàngshī shīqù

Ⓔ to lose/to lose/to lose

◪ 这三个动词都表示失掉,"丧失"、"失去"一般用于抽象事物,

"丢失"一般用于具体事物 ◇ All these three verbs mean " to lose". 丧失 and 失去 are generally applied to abstract things, while 丢失 to concrete things:

1. 丧失

① 这场大病之后,他**丧失**了部分记忆。He lost some memory after his recovery from his serious illness.

② 他在谈判中节节败退,简直**丧失**了立场。He was defeated in the negotiation with the company constantly, and he nearly lost his stand.

③ 虽然我们遇到了很大的困难,千万不能**丧失**信心。Though we are confronted with great difficulty, we cannot lose heart.

以上,都是用于抽象事物。但有时"丧失"的宾语也可指人等 ◇ In examples ①②③ 丧失 is applied to abstract things. But sometimes the object of 丧失 can be a person, etc. as well:

④ 在这次地震中,小王**丧失**了亲人。Xiao Wang lost his family in the earthquake.

2. 失去

① 这篇作品,虽然已经发表了50年,仍没有**失去**它的现实价值。The work has been published for 50 years, but its realistic value still remains.

② 这条规则过时了,已经**失去**作用。The rule is out of date and invalid now.

③ 在任何情况下,都不能**失去**理智。In any circumstance, you cannot lose your mind.

④ 老厂长去世了,我们**失去**了一位好领导。We lost a good leader after our director's death.

以上"失去"主要也用于抽象事物。还有些同类的词,如"信心"、"记忆"、"价值"、"理智"、"亲人"等,都可以做"丧失"和"失去"的宾语 ◇ In the examples above 失去 is also applied to abstract things. There are other similar words, such as 信心(confidence), 记忆 (memory), 价值 (value), 理智 (reason), 亲人 (relative), etc. , which can all be the object of 丧失 and 失去.

3. 丢失

① 我昨天不小心,**丢失**了一张信用卡。I lost a credit card carelessly yesterday.

② 因为**丢失**了贵重物品,他心里很不痛快。He was unhappy, for he lost a valuable item.

以上都是用于具体事物。但有时也可说"丢失了好传统"等 ◇ In the examples above, 丢失 is applied to concrete things, but we can also say 丢失了好传统, etc. :

③ 勤俭持家这个好传统千万不

能**丢失**。We must keep the good tradition of thrifty living.

有时还可说“丢失数字”、“丢失信息”等 ◇ We can also say 丢失数字 (lose figures), 丢失信息 (lose informatin or data), etc.:

④ 在传输过程中,**丢失**了两个重要数字。Two important figures were missing in the transmission.

冬 (名) dōng　冬天 (名) dōngtiān

Ⓔ winter/winter

◪ 这两个词都表示四季的最后一个季节。“冬”是粘着词,不能独立运用。“冬天”是自由词,可以自由运用 ◇ Both words mean "the last season of the year". 冬 is an agglutinative word, which cannot be used independently. 冬天 is a free word and can be used freely.

① 今年**一冬**没下雪。There is no snow through all the winter.

② 在这个寂静的**冬夜**,一家人围炉品茶。On the still winter night, the family sat around the oven over tea.

例①②中的“一冬”、“冬夜”,说明“冬”常与其他词语结合使用。其他还有“暖冬”、“冬去春来”等 ◇ 一冬, 冬夜 in examples ① and ② exemplify that 冬 is usually used with other words, such as 暖冬 (warm winter), 冬去春来 (spring follows winter), etc.

③ **冬天**到了。Winter is coming.

④ 这是一个寒冷的**冬天**。This is a harsh winter.

“冬天”在例③④中,是自由运用的 ◇ 冬天 in examples ③ and ④ are used independently.

除了例①,其他例句中,两个词是不可互换的 ◇ Except for example ①, the two words are not interchangeable in the other examples.

“春”和“春天”、“夏”和“夏天”、“秋”和“秋天”的区别与本条类似 The difference between 春 and 春天, 夏 and 夏天, 秋 and 秋天 is similar.

懂 (动) dǒng　懂得 (动) dǒngde

Ⓔ to understand/to understand

◪ 这两个动词都表示知道、熟悉。“懂”常做谓语,也可做补语。“懂得”只做谓语 ◇ Both verbs mean " to understand, to be familiar with". 懂 is used either as the predicate or as a complement. 懂得 can only be the predicate.

① 你**懂**广东话吗？Can you speak Cantonese?

② 他不**懂**还要装**懂**。He pretends to know his unknown.

③ 这篇外文资料我看**懂**了。I understood the foreign material.

④ 我听不**懂**他的话。I cannot understand him.

以上例①②“懂”做主要谓语，例②第二个“懂”是宾语，例③④的“懂”做补语。例①也可换用“懂得”。再如 ◇ In the above examples ① and ②，懂 is the main predicate. The second 懂 in example ② is an object. In examples ③ and ④ 懂 is the complement. 懂得 can replace 懂 in example ①. More example：

⑤ 跟他打交道，得**懂得**策略。You should know some strategies when you are in contact with him.

有时“懂得”的意思比“懂”抽象一些 ◇ Sometimes the meaning of 懂得 is more abstract than 懂，e. g.

⑥ 他**懂得**做人的道理。He knows how to be a man.

►[懂 dǒng—了解 liǎojiě —明白 míngbai]

懂 （动） dǒng **了解** （动） liǎojiě **明白** （动、形） míngbai

Ⓔ to understand/ to understand，to comprehend/ to understand

◣ 动词“懂”、“了解”、“明白”都表示知道某事物的状况或道理 ◇ The verbs 懂，了解 and 明白 all mean "to understand"，e. g.

① 你**懂**（/**了解**/**明白**）她话里的意思吗？Do you understand the underlying meaning in her words?

② 我**了解**（/**懂**/**明白**）你的希望和要求。I understand your hope and requests.

但这三个词还有区别 ◇ But they are still different from one another：

1. 懂（动）

有通晓的意思，对象可以是语言、技术等，其他两个词没有这个意思 ◇ 懂，as a verb，means "thoroughly understand"，and the object can be language，technology，etc. The other two words have no such meanings：

① 她**懂**英语。She can speak English.

② 这位先生**懂**这门技术。The man is good at the technology.

“懂”（动）还有理解的意思，对象是事物，不能是人 ◇ 懂（v.） means "to understand"，the object of which is something，and cannot be a person：

③ 我**懂**这个道理。I know it.

④ 她**懂**小王的意思。She understands what Xiao Wang means. 不能说"她懂小王" ◇ One cannot say 她懂小王.

2. 了解(动)

(1)表示知道得很清楚 ◇ 了解(v)means "to know clearly":

① 我们是同班同学,我很**了解**他。I know him well for we are classmates.

② 对这件事我只知道一部分,整个情况并不**了解**。I only know some of the matter.

③ 应该让大家**了解**事情的真相。The fact should be exposed to all.

以上用法,不能用"明白"、"懂" ◇ 明白 or 懂 cannot be used in above situations.

(2)通过打听、询问等知道某一情况 ◇ To know sth. through inquiry:

④ 他向我**了解**小赵的为人。He inquired me about Xiao Zhao.

⑤ 我先得去**了解**情况才能发表意见。First I should get an idea of it and then I will have a right to say.

⑥ 你去**了解了解**他在工作中有什么困难。Please come to know what difficulty he is confronted with in his work.

"明白"、"懂"没有这种用法 ◇ Neither 明白 nor 懂 can be used instead.

3. 明白(动、形)

(1)"明白"(动)表示知道、了解(原因、目的、道理等) ◇ 明白(v.)means "to understand, know (reason, purpose, hows and whys, etc.)":

① 学生们都**明白**这样做是不对的。All the students understand it is not right to do so.

② 他讲了半天我才**明白**。I did not understand it until he explained it for me for a long time.

③ 你现在**明白**他的目的了吧! Now you will be able to understand his purpose.

以上用法,一般均可用"了解"、"懂"替换。和"懂"一样,"明白"的宾语也不能是人,而"了解"的宾语可以是人,如(1)中的例① ◇ In the examples above, 了解 or 懂 can replace 明白 without making any difference. Like 懂, the object of 明白 cannot be a person, but the object of 了解 can be a person as in example ①in(1).

(2)"明白"(形)表示清楚、明确、容易懂 ◇ As an adjective, 明白 means "clear, definite, easy to be understood":

④ 他讲得非常**明白**。He made it very clear.

⑤ 这段话的含义**明白**得很。The meaning of the passage is very clear.

⑥ 她话里的意思已经很**明白**了。

The underlying meaning of her words is very clear.

以上用法不能用“懂”、“了解”代替 ◇ 懂 or 了解 cannot be used in the above examples.

4. “懂”和“明白”可以做结果补语等，“了解”不能 ◇ 懂 or 明白 can be used as the complement of result, while 了解 cannot:

① 这出京戏你看**懂**(/**明白**)了吗？Do you understand the Beijing Opera?

② 我听不**懂**(/**明白**)他的话。I cannot understand him.

“了解”可做主、宾语 ◇ 了解 can be used as the subject or object of a sentence, e.g.:

③ 我对这个地方的**了解**十分有限。I only have a superficial understanding about it.

④ 应对那里的情况进行**了解**。You should know something there.

“明白”、“懂”不能这样用 ◇ 明白 or 懂 cannot be used in such a way.

▶ [懂 dǒng—懂得 dǒngde]

(动)
dú

(动)
niàn

Ⓔ to read, to read aloud/ to read aloud

◪ 这两个动词有几个意义，互有分合 ◇ The two verbs are interchangeable in some cases, yet in other situations, they are used differently.

1. 表示看着文字发出声音，“读”和“念”都可以，后者更口语化些 ◇ To mean "read aloud", either 读 or 念 can be used, but the latter is more colloquial:

① 他正拿着一本中文书大声地**读**(/**念**)。He is reading Chinese aloud.

② 老太太递给孙子一封信，让他**念**(/**读**)给自己听。The old lady passed her grandson a letter and asked him to read it for her.

由于文化程度不同，“读诗班”习惯用“读”，“和尚念经”习惯用“念”(“读经”另有意义，表示阅读古代经书) ◇ Since the two words are different in terms of classical and vernacular, 读 is used in 读诗班(choir), and 念 is used in 和尚念经(of monks recite or chant scriptures)(读经 is a set phrase meaning "reading old classics").

2. 表示阅读，用“读”不用“念” ◇ To mean "read and comprehend", 读 is used and not 念:

① 最近我**读**了几本好书。I have read some good books recently.

② 这本学术著作值得一**读**。The academic work is worth reading.

③ 学习外语,要达到听、说、**读**、写四会的要求。Learning foreign languages should master four skills: listening, speaking, reading and writing.

3. 表示上学,两个词都可以,"念"更口语化些 ◇ Either can be used to mean "go to school", but 念 is more colloquial:

① 这孩子已经**念**(/**读**)小学五年级了。The child is a five-year pupil in a primary school.

② 她正在**读**(/**念**)医学。She is studying medicine.

堆 (名、量、动) duī　　堆积 (动) duījī

Ⓔ pile, to pile up/to pile up

1. 名词"堆"表示不规则体积的聚积物,如"土堆"、"砖堆"、"垃圾堆"、"瓦砾堆"等 ◇ As a noun, 堆 means "an irregular pile of sth.", e.g. 土堆(a soil pile), 砖堆(a brick pile), 垃圾堆(a rubbish pile), 瓦砾堆(a rubbles pile), etc.

2. 量词"堆"用于成堆物或成群的人等,可儿化。用于人时常含贬义(数词限于"一"、"几"等)。如"一堆垃圾"、"两堆砖头"、"成堆的问题"、"一堆人"等 ◇ 堆, as a measure word, means "a pile of sth. or a group of people" and it can take 儿 after it. When applied to people, it often has a derogatory sense (The numeral is limited to 一 or 几). e.g. 一堆垃圾(a pile of rubbish), 两堆砖头(two piles of bricks), 成堆的问题(piles of problems), 一堆人(crowds of people), etc.

3. 动词"堆"表示使分散物聚集成不规则的体积的聚积体,可带补语"成"、"到"、"满"、"在"等 ◇ As a verb, 堆 means "to pile up scattered things into an irregular heap", and it can take a complement like 成, 到, 满, 在, etc. after it. e.g.:

① 下大雪了,父亲和孩子们在院子里**堆**了一个雪人。It snowed, and the father and his children made a snowman in their yard.

② 怎么搞的,床边**堆**满了脏衣服? 快拿去洗吧! Why? The bed is covered with dirty clothes. Hurry to wash them.

也可以用于抽象意义 ◇ It can also be used in an abstract sense:

③ 这个城市管理得不好,各种问题几乎**堆**成了山。The city is in a mess, and its problems are mounting.

④ 他把各种罪名都**堆**到了别人头上。He shifted all the accusation.

4. 动词"堆积"表示使事物聚积成堆,多用于抽象义,也用于具体义。在音节上要求后面的词语以双音节为主,可形成四字语"堆积而成"、"堆积如山"等。由于"积"含有积累、积存的意思,不能再带补语"满" ◇ 堆积, as a verb, means "to pile up", and mostly used in an abstract sense, but it can also be applied to concrete things. The words used after it are usually disyllabic so as to make up a four-character phrase, e. g. 堆积而成(pile up), 堆积如山(heap up into a mound), etc. Since 积 has a sense of accumulating, it need not take the complement 满. e. g. :

① 这个企业的问题**堆积如山**。There are mountains of problems in the enterprise.

② 这篇文章内容空虚,只是**堆积**了很多好听的词汇而已。The content of the article is empty and it is full of flowery words.

"堆"与"堆积"有时可以互换 ◇ 堆 and 堆积 sometimes are interchangeable:

③ 不大一会儿,稻草就**堆**(/**堆积**)成了一座小山。The straw piled like a hill soon.

这是因为此时在音节上后面以双音节词语为主,是两个词都可以接受的;在意义上,稻草成了小山,对两个词也都适合。而例①②因音节关系,不能换用"堆"。3中的例①因"堆雪人"是习惯搭配,不能换用"堆积"。3中的例③因没有"积累"、"积存"的意思,也只能用"堆" ◇ This is because in such a situation, the words used after are disyllabic, which suits both verbs. It is also applicable to both verbs to use "hill" to describe the pile of straws. However, in examples ①②, 堆 cannot be used owing to syllabic collocation. In example ① of 3, 堆雪人 is an idiomatic phrase, and 堆积 cannot be used instead. In example ③ of 3 堆 can be used only because the only sentence does not have the meaning of accumulation.

(介) (介)

duì duìyú

Ⓔ to/to

◪ 这两个介词都用于引进动作的对象或与动作有关的事物 ◇ The two prepositions can be used to introduce the object of an action or things related to the action.

1. 有“向”或“面对”的意思,用“对”,不用“对于” ◇ To mean "to" or "face", 对 is used, and not 对于:

① 小张**对**哥哥说:“借给我点儿钱好吗?” Xiao Zhang said to his brother: Would you like to lend me some money?

② 他**对**首长行了个礼。He saluted to his senior officer.

③ 连长**对**战士下了命令。The company leader gave his soldiers orders.

2. 表示对待关系,两词都可用,如例①②;用于人与人之间的关系时,也用“对”,如例③ ◇ The two can both be used to mean "with regard to", such as examples ①②; yet to express the relationship between people, 对 can be used only, such as example ③:

① 她**对**(/**对于**)工作很认真。She is conscientious about her work.

② 他**对**(/**对于**)这个专业很感兴趣。He is very interested in this major.

③ 老师**对**学生十分关心。The teachers care about their students very much.

3. 以上各句,“对……”或“对于……”作为介宾结构,都是做状语。也可做定语 ◇ In the above examples, the preposition-object phrases of 对…… and 对于…… are both adverbials. They can also be attributives, e. g. :

① 现在我谈谈我**对**(/**对于**)这个问题的看法。Now I'd like to say something about the issue.

② 这件事唤起了我**对**(/**对于**)那个年代的回忆。This makes me recollect that time.

“对”可用在助动词或副词之后,“对于”一般不可以这样用 ◇ 对 can be placed after an auxiliary verb or adverb, but 对于 would not be used in such a way:

③ 我们会**对**你的请求作出答复。We will make a reply to your request.

④ 他没有**对**小张进行批评。He did not criticized Xiao Zhang.

“对(/对于)……”可提到主语之前 ◇ The construction 对(/对于)……can be placed in front of the subject of the sentence, e. g. :

⑤ **对**(/**对于**)学习,他没有多大兴趣。He shows little interest in his study.

⑥ **对**(/**对于**)买房子,老张十分关心。Lao Zhang cares about buying a house very much.

4. “对(/对于)……来说”表示从某人某事的角度来看 ◇ The construction 对(/对于)……来说 means " to look from the point of view of sb. or in terms of sth. ":

① **对(/对于)**你来说,这样做没有什么困难;对(/对于)我来说,就不一样了。As for you, doing so is not difficult, but as for me, things are different.

② **对(/对于)**这门课程来说,我们应该以讲授基础知识为主。The course is mainly about its ABC.

顿时 立刻

(副) (副)

dùnshí lìkè

Ⓔ at once/at once

这两个词都有马上的意思,都表示在一个动作发生时,另一个动作紧接着发生,但有几点不同 ◇ Both words mean " at once", indicating that when one action takes place, another action follows immediately; yet there are still differences between them:

1. "顿时"较书面化,"立刻"较口语化 ◇ 顿时 is more literary and 立刻 is more colloquial.

2. "顿时"具有描写性(多用于描写人或事物的情态),"立刻"一般场合都能用 ◇ 顿时 is descriptive (describing a person's mood or the state of a affair), while 立刻 can be used in any case.

3. "顿时"只用于叙述已经发生的事,"立刻"还可以表示即将发生或可能发生的事 ◇ 顿时 is only used to describe something that has happened; where as 立刻 can also be applied to something that is about to happen or may happen, e. g. :

① 他听到枪声,**顿时**惊慌失措。He got a panic at the shooting.

② 一看父亲怒容满面,她**顿时**不敢笑了。She dared not laugh as she saw her father was angry.

以上两句,是叙述已经发生的人的情态的,又较书面化,所以用"顿时" ◇ Examples ① and ② describe a person's bearing and are also more literary, so 顿时 is used.

③ 请你们在散会之后**立刻**出发。Please start as soon as the meeting is over.

④ 一旦感染了这种病毒,**立刻**就能查出来。Once you infect the disease, it can be checked immediately.

以上两句是说即将发生的事,所以用"立刻" ◇ Examples ③ and ④ describe something that is about to happen soon, so 立刻 is used:

⑤ 一到晚上九点,夜市上**立刻**(/**顿时**)热闹起来了。The night market will be busy as soon as it is after 9 p. m.

⑥ 一谈起这个话题,**立刻**(/**顿

时)出现了两种意见。When it comes to the topic, there are two views emerging about it at once.

以上两句,都是叙述已发生的事,有情态性但不强烈,所以两个词都可以用(用"顿时"略显书面化) ◇ Examples ⑤ and ⑥ describe something that has already happened, and the descriptive nature is not strong; therefore, either word can be used (顿时 is more literary).

⑦ 听到有人敲门,他**立刻**站了起来。He got to his feet immediately as he heard the knocking.

⑧ 雨一停,太阳**立刻**出来了。The sun came out from the cloud as soon as the rain stopped.

例⑦⑧这种纯客观的叙述(无情态性),则用"立刻" ◇ Examples ⑦ and ⑧ are purely objective descriptions (with no descriptive words involved); therefore, 立刻 is used.

另外,"顿时"不受否定词语的修饰,"立刻"则可以受否定词语修饰 ◇ Besides, 顿时 cannot be modified by negative words, while 立刻 can:

⑨ 对于这个突如其来的问题,他没有**立刻**表态。He said nothing about the abrupt issue.

⑩ 对于这个突如其来的问题,他不愿意**立刻**表态。He is reluctant to say anything about the abrupt issue.

▶[立刻 lìkè—立即 lìjí]
[马上 mǎshàng—立刻 lìkè]

多半 大半

(副、名) (副、名)
duōbàn dàbàn

Ⓔ probably, majority/ probably, majority

1. 副词"多半"和"大半"都有大概、有较大可能性的意思。一般不用于主语前 ◇ The adverbs 多半 and 大半 both mean "most probably", and usually do not precede the subject of a sentence:

① 他**多半**(/**大半**)是喝醉了。He was probably drunk.

② 明天**多半**(/**大半**)会晴的。It is probably going to be clear tomorrow.

③ 她完成学业,**多半**(/**大半**)是靠哥哥的资助。She finished her school mainly with her brother's help.

以上例句,两词可以互换。从使用频率来看,用"多半"较多 ◇ In the examples above, the two words are interchangeable. In terms of frequency of usage; however, 多半 is more frequently used.

2. 名词"多半"和"大半"表示大

部分。可加"一" ◇ As nouns, 多半 and 大半 mean "the greater part", and 一 can be added:

① 这本小说很吸引人,我一下子就看了**一大半(/一多半)**。The novel was appealing to me and I read much of it at one sitting.

② 来参加大会的人,**多半(/大半)**是学生。Most of the meeting participants are students.

③ 我们班的同学**多半(/大半)**是南方人。Most of the students in our class are from the south.

例②③是做状语,与1中的例①②③是一样的,但意思不同 ◇ In examples ② and ③, 多半 and 大半 are used as adverbials, the same as that in examples ①② and ③in 1, but the meaning is different.

多亏 幸亏

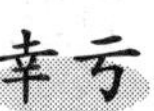

(动、副) (副)

duōkuī xìngkuī

Ⓔ thanks to, fortunately/ fortunately, luckily

1. 多亏(动)

表示由于某种有利因素,才得以避免不利情况的发生,或使事情顺利发展 ◇ As a verb, 多亏 means "that, thanks to some advantageous factors, some misfortune is avoided or something develops smoothly", e. g.:

① 事情办成,**多亏**了你。But for you, I would not have finished it.

② 我在求学过程中,**多亏**亲戚的支持。But for my relatives' help, I would not have finished my schooling.

③ 今天布置会场,**多亏**大家帮助。It was due to your help that I could set the meeting place today.

以上例句,"多亏"直接带代词宾语、动词宾语或小句宾语。因为"幸亏"是副词,所以以上例句不能用"幸亏" ◇ In the examples above, 多亏 takes a pronoun, verb or a clause as its object. Since 幸亏 is an adverb, it cannot be used instead.

2. 幸亏(副) 多亏(副):

意思同"多亏"(动),只是用法不同 ◇ As an adverb, 幸亏 has the same meaning as 多亏 used as a verb, but the usage is different:

① **多亏**遇见公正的裁判,他们队才能够出线。It was due to the fair judge that their team was able to win.

② 这孩子成绩这么好,**多亏**有老师的指导。It was due to the teachers' guide that the child was able to make so great progress.

③ **幸亏**司机经验丰富,我们才避

免了一场交通事故。It was due to the experienced driver that a traffic accident could be avoided.

④ **幸亏**我带了伞，才没被雨淋着。It was due to my umbrella that I was not caught in the rain.

以上前两句用"多亏"（副），侧重于使事情顺利发展。也可换用"幸亏"（副），则含有排除不利因素的意味（如例①可能有难以公正裁判的因素，例②可能在学习中遇到过困难）◇ In examples ① and ②，the adverb 多亏 is used with the stress on the smooth development of the thing；it can be replaced by the adverb 幸亏，but the stress will be on elimination of disadvantageous elements（such as in example ① unfair judgment and in example ② the difficulties in study may exist）.

后两句用"幸亏"（副），侧重于避免了不利情况的发生。也可换用"多亏（副）"，则语气较轻 ◇ The adverb 幸亏 is used in examples ③ and ④ with the stress on the avoidance of disadvantageous elements；it can be replaced by the adverb 多亏，but the tone is lighter.

多少 （代） duōshao　　几 （代） jǐ

Ⓔ how many，how much/ how many，how much

1. 这两个疑问代词都表示数量，常用于询问。"多少"指估计数量较大（一般超过十）；"几"指估计数量较小（一般不超过十）◇ The two interrogative pronouns are often used in inquiry of amount. 多少 is applied to a bigger estimated amount（usually more than ten）；几 is applied to a smaller amount（usually less than ten）：

① 来了**多少**人？How many people present?

② 来了**几**个人？How many people present?

例①估计数量略大，例②估计不超过十人。注意，"几"要用量词，"多少"不一定用量词。如果不知道数目大小，一般用"多少"，如"多少钱？"再如 ◇ In example ① the estimated number is bigger，while in example ② the number does not exceed ten. 几 must be followed by a measure word，but with 多少 a measure word is not compulsory. If one has no idea whether the number is big or small，it is better to use 多少，e. g. 多少钱？Another example：

③ 今天有**多少**（位）客人？How many guests are there today?

"几"可以说"十几（个）"、"几

百”、“几千”等 ◇ With 几, one can say 十几(个)(between 10 and 20),几百(several hundred),几千(several thousand),etc.

另外,“几”较书面化,在古语遗留用例中常用“几”,如“所剩无几”(口语是“剩下没有多少了”),“几番风雨”等 ◇ Moreover, 几 is more literary and often appears in the remnants of classical Chinese, e. g. 所剩无几(very little is left.),几番风雨(repeated setbacks),etc.

2.“多少”和“几”还可泛指不定的数目,用于前后对应的复句 ◇ 多少 and 几 can also be used correspondingly to indicate an indefinite number in complex sentences:

① 记住**多少**就写**多少**。Write as much as you can memorize.

② 有**多少**房间,就接待**多少**人。You can admit as many guests as your hotel can hold.

③ 你能写**几**行就写**几**行吧! Write as many lines as you can.

④ 他有**几**个(钱)就花**几**个。He spent as much money as he has.

“几”和“多少”也可以用于单句泛指数目 ◇ 几 and 多少 can also indicate an uncertain number when used in a simple sentence:

⑤ 我想买**几**本书。I want to buy a few books.

⑥ 他没**几**个朋友。/他没有**多少**朋友。He has few friends.

(“没有几……”,“没有多少……”意思是“有很少……”) ◇ (没有几…… and 没有多少…… mean " to have very little or very few")

⑦ 离开车没有**多少**时间了。There are few minutes left before the bus starts.

“多少”还可以泛指抽象意义的数量 ◇ 多少 can also be used to indicate numbers in an abstract sense, e. g. :

⑧ 他没有**多少**机会可供选择。There are few chances for him to choose.

⑨ 这件事花费了她**多少**精力啊! What efforts she has made!

“几”不能这样用 ◇ 几 cannot be used in this way.

E

E

而且 并且

(连) (连)

érqiě bìngqiě

Ⓔ and/and

◪ 这两个词都表示更进一层,可连接词、词组、分句或句子 ◇ Both words mean "in addition, besides". They can connect words, phrases, clauses or sentences:

① 这条街干净**而且**(/**并且**)安静。The street is clean and quiet.

② 这篇稿子,你应该**而且**(/**并且**)必须在一个星期内完成。Your article should and have to be finished in a week.

有时前面有"不但"、"不仅"等,则表示更进一层的意思更明显 ◇ Sometimes 不但,不仅, etc. is used in front, thus the sense of "furthermore" is clearer:

③ 那种商品不但质量好,**而且**(/**并且**)还便宜。The goods are excellent but cheap.

④ 他不仅有广博的知识,**而且**(/**并且**)还有很强的工作能力。He is not only knowledgeable, but also competent at his work.

有时有两层递进的意思时,"而且"和"并且"可用于同一句中,以免重复 ◇ When there are two levels of meaning of "additions", both 而且 and 并且 can be used in a sentence to avoid repetition:

⑤ 他不但会外语,**而且**不只一种,**并且**都很精通。He not only can speak foreign languages, but also has a good command of them.

▶[并 bìng—并且 bìngqiě]

二 两

(数) (数)

èr liǎng

Ⓔ two/two

◪ "二"和"两"都表示数目"2"。◇ 二 and 两 both mean "two".

1."二"用于读数目字 ◇ 二 is used in reading a number:

① 他家的电话是六**二**八**二二二**0**二**。His telephone number is 62822202.

② 你的门牌是一**二**五吧? Is your house number 125?

数学式子,如分数、小数中的"2",一律读"二" ◇ In mathematical formulae, 2 is pronounced 二.

2. 表示序数用“二” ◇ 二 is used in the ordinal number:

① 他是我**二**哥。He is my second brother.

② 现在是**二**月。It's February now.

3. 带量词(包括表示位数的“百、千、万、亿”等)用“两”。如“两个人”、“两间屋子”、“两万元”。但“百、千、万、亿”等也可用“二”,如“二千二百”。连续的数字,大的位数可用“两”,小的位数可用“二”,如“两万二千” ◇ When there is a measure word (including 百、千、万、亿, etc.) 两 is used, e. g. 两个人 (two persons), 两间屋子 (two rooms), 两万元 (20,000 *yuan*). But 百, 千, 万, 亿 can also used together with 二, e. g. 二千二百 (2,200). In a sequence of numbers, the bigger digits can be modifed by 两 while the small digits by 二, e. g. 两万二千 (22,000).

作为特例,在直接称呼中,“位”前可用“二”或“两” ◇ As an exception, in direct addressing, both 二 and 两 can be used to modify 位:

① **二(/两)**位吃点儿什么? What would you like to have?

② **二(/两)**位从哪儿来? Where are you from?

4. 在度量衡单位前,用“二”或“两”。如“二(/两)斤”、“二(/两)吨”、“二(/两)公里” ◇ Before the units of length, capacity and weight, either 二 or 两 can be used, e. g. 二(/两)斤 (two *jin*), 二(/两)吨 (two tons), 二(/两)公里 (two kilometers).

5. 在多音节词或四字语中,“二”表示次序或数目,如“一分为二”、“说一不二”。“两”表示“双方”,如“两全其美”、“两败俱伤”等 ◇ In polysyllabic words or four-character phrases, 二 indicates order or number, e. g. 一分为二 (one divides into two—there are two sides to everything), 说一不二 (stand by one's words); while 两 indicates two sides, e. g. 两全其美 (satisfactory to both sides), 两败俱伤 (both sides suffer, neither side gains), etc.

E

F

翻 (动) fān　　**翻译** (动、名) fānyì

Ⓔ to translate/
to translate; translation

◪ 这两个词都表示把一种语言文字用另一种语言文字表达。“翻”还有变换位置、推翻原案、数量成倍增加等意义,这里不谈 ◇ Both words mean "to put the words from one language into another". 翻 also means "to turn over, to reverse, to multiply, etc". But we are not concerned with these meanings here.

1.“翻”较“翻译”口语化,“翻译”又是名词,指做这种工作的人,“翻”不是名词 ◇ 翻 is more colloquial than 翻译. 翻译 can also be used as a noun to mean translator. 翻 is not a noun.

① 他把这篇英文小说**翻**(/**翻译**)成中文了。He has translated the English novel into Chinese.

② 稿子**翻**(/**翻译**)完了。The manuscript has been translated.

以上这种通常用法,两个词可以互换,但语体色彩略有差异。两个词的后面都可以加各种补语,如“好”、“错”、“过来”、“得……”等 ◇ In examples ① and ② the two words are interchangeable but the style is different. Both words can take complements such as 好, 错, 过来, 得……, etc. and have the same function.

③ 资料都**翻**(/**翻译**)好了。All the materials have been translated.

④ 这本书**翻**(/**翻译**)得怎么样? How do you like the translating of the book?

⑤ 我要把这本英文小说**翻**(/**翻译**)成中文。I'm going to translate the English novel into Chinese.

以下这种需要双音节词的场合,用“翻译”,不用“翻” ◇ In the following situations where a disyllabic word is needed, 翻译 is used, not 翻:

⑥ 经过**翻译**,原作的味道减色不少。There are a lot of meaning losses in the translated work.

⑦ 他是做**翻译**工作的。He works as a translator.

再如做“通过”等的宾语,也须用双音节词“翻译”,不用“翻” ◇

通过 also needs a disyllabic word as the object, so 翻译 is used, not 翻:

⑧ 他们两个人交谈,要通过小王**翻译**。Xiao Wang is their interpreter.

2. **翻译**(名) ◇ 翻译, as a noun, refers to translator, interpreter:

① 他是**翻译**。He is a translator.

② 她当过好些年**翻译**。She worked as a translator for many years.

"翻"不能这样用 ◇ 翻 cannot be used in such a way.

反 (副) fǎn　反而 (副) fǎn'ér

Ⓔ on the contrary, instead/ on the contrary, instead

这两个词表示导致相反的结果。前面叙述对立的状况,或用"不但没有"、"不再"等说明对立的情况。"反"较书面化 ◇ 反 or 反而 means "to lead to a contrary result". What precedes it states the contrary condition, with or without 不但没有 (not only…not), 不再 (no longer), etc. 反 is more literary.

① 他曾经那么有钱,由于公司破产,炒股又失利,今天**反**(/**反而**)成了穷光蛋。He was rich before, but now he becomes poor for his company's bankruptcy and his bad stocks.

② 她边听音乐边干,不但没有耽误活儿,**反而**做得更快更好。She listened to music while she was working, which did not delay her work; she worked faster and better instead.

③ 一天到晚听这种音乐,不再觉得有趣,**反**(/**反而**)有些单调了。I cannot think it interesting to listen to this kind of music all day long any more; instead it is dull.

以上例①③两个词可互换,但"反"更为书面化。例②因全句很口语化,应用"反而" ◇ In examples ① and ③ the two words are interchangeable, but 反 is more literary. Example ② is very colloquial, so 反而 ought to be used.

有时是表示在对比之下,原来是有缺点的,不正常的,竟成为可取的了 ◇ Sometimes 反 or 反而 is used by contrast to show that sth. defective or abnormal becomes desirable:

④ 让学生死读书,**反**(/**反而**)不如放任一些。We'd better give students more freedom than make them study only.

⑤ 出去旅游赶车辛苦,**反而**是在家呆着好。Going on a tour is painstaking, so you'd better stay

at home.
“反是”少见,所以例⑤应用“反而是” ◇ 反是 is rare, so in example ⑤ 反而是 is used.
注意:“反”也是形容词,表示颠倒的、方向相背的,如 ◇ Note: 反 is also an adjective meaning "reverse or opposite", e. g. :

① 这种夹克**反**着也可以穿。You can wear the jacket inside out.
② 方向**反**了,越走离目的地越远。The direction is contrary and it is further and further away from the destination.
③ 你把次序排**反**了,第四个应该在第三个的后面。You made a mistake in the turns, for the fourth should be followed by the third.

“反”还是动词,有反对、翻转、颠倒的意思 ◇ 反 is also a verb meaning "to be against or to reverse", e. g. :

④ **反**铺张**反**浪费。We are against extravagance and waste.
⑤ 教练改变了打法:**反**攻为守。The coach changed the playing way, that is, changing the attack to defense.

方法 (名) fāngfǎ　　法子 (名) fǎzi

Ⓔ method, way/way, method

1. “方法”指具体的解决问题的步骤、程序、方策等,如“学习方法”、“思想方法”、“记忆外语生词的方法”、“烹调方法”、“刷牙的方法”等。“法子”主要指一般的办事乃至生活的办法、路子,有时指一种可能性。但“好法子”等也可指较具体的办法 ◇ 方法 means "the way or method to solve a problem, the process, tactics, etc.", e. g. 学习方法 (method of study), 思想方法 (method of thinking), 记忆外语生词的方法 (method to memorize words of a foreign language), 烹调方法 (method of cooking), 刷牙的方法 (the way to brush one's teeth), etc. 法子 mainly means "the way to go about business or lead one's life", and occasionally means "a possibility". 好法子, etc., however, can also mean "a concrete method".

2. “方法”较“法子”书面色彩略浓 ◇ 方法 is more literary than 法子. e. g. :

① 学习这门课,应该找到正确的**方法**。You should find a right way to learn the course.
② 这种花很难栽培,没有必要的知识和适合的**方法**是不行的。The flower will be difficult to grow if you know little about it

and have no right planting way about it.

以上两句,"方法"都指具体步骤等 ◇ In the two examples above, 方法 means "the concrete process".

③ 我该怎么办? 请帮我想想**法子**。How can I do? Please give me some advice.

④ 邻居装修房子,他几乎没**法子**睡觉。He can hardly go to sleep for his neighbor is having their house fitted up.

⑤ 失业了,他正在想**法子**找工作。He was unemployed and he managed to look for a job.

⑥ 这孩子不爱上课,老师也没**法子**。The child hates school, and his teachers do not know how to do with him.

以上四句,指一般的办法、可能性、路子等,所以用"法子" ◇ In the four examples above, 法子 means "the ordinary way, possibility, etc".

有时既指一般的路子,也含有一定的具体方策的意思,则可以换用"法子"和"方法"(多有定语"好"等) ◇ Sometimes, when meaning "both the ordinary way and the actual process", either 法子 or 方法 can be used (usually with the attributive 好 (good), etc.):

⑦ 在农业上,用益虫杀灭害虫,是一种好**法子**(/**方法**)。It is a good way using beneficial insects to kill off pests in agriculture.

⑧ 她从邻居那里学来了一种清洁水质的好**法子**(/**方法**)。She learnt a good way of cleaning the water from her neighbor.

⑨ 学习外语,除了多听、多说、多读,没有什么好**法子**(/**方法**)。There is no good way in foreign language learning except practising listening, speaking and reading much more.

房间　屋子

(名)　(名)

fángjiān　wūzi

Ⓔ room/room

这两个词都指房内隔成的较大空间。"房间"一般用于较大的新式建筑物 ◇ Both words mean "room". 房间 usually applies to the room of a big, modern building:

① 这家旅馆一共有几十个**房间**。There are dozens of rooms in the hotel.

例①不用"屋子"(旅馆也用"客房") ◇ 屋子 is not used in example ①(客房 is also used to refer to rooms in hotels).

"屋子"一般用于人家或较小的旧

式建筑物。另外,北方用“屋子”较多,较口语化,南方较多用“房间” ◇ 屋子 usually refers to rooms of a private house or a small old-fashioned structure. Moreover, 屋子 is commonly used in the north and it is rather colloquial; the southerners usually say 房间.

② 这个四合院,有十几间**屋子**。There are more than ten rooms in the quadrangle.

例②不用“房间”,因“四合院”是典型的北方建筑 ◇ 房间 is not used in example ②, since 四合院 (compound with houses around a square courtyard) is a typical style of northern structure.

但在目前的成套居室中,两个词可以通用(只是量词有所不同) ◇ But when referring to the rooms of a suite nowadays, the two words are used interchangeably (but with different measure words):

③ 相片在我的**房间**(/**屋子**)里,你去看吧。The photo is in my room. You can go and have a look at it.

④ 她的新居,一共有四间**屋子**(/四个**房间**)。There are four rooms in her new apartment.

非常 极 十分

(副) (副) (副)

fēicháng jí shífēn

Ⓔ very, extremely/
extremely/
extremely, very

◪ 这三个副词都表示很高的程度。“十分”较“非常”略为书面化一些。“极”是单音节词,后面多带单音节形容词(如“极妙”、“极怪”、“极强”),但也可带双音节形容词,“极”也较书面化。另外,“极”可做补语 ◇ The three adverbs all indicate a very high degree. 十分 is more literary than 非常. 极 is monosyllabic and so is usually followed by a monosyllabic adjective (e. g. 极妙 wonderful, 极怪 very strange, 极强 extremely strong, etc.), but it can also precede a disyllabic word. 极 is also literary. Besides, 极 can be a complement.

① 今天的天气**非常**(/**十分**/**极**)热。It is very hot today.

例①三个词可以互换,因为这句话对文体色彩的要求比较宽泛 ◇ In example ① all the three words are interchangeable because the style of the sentence could be either literal or colloquial.

② 他的性格**极**怪。He is very eccentric.

例②由于音节的关系,宜于用“极”。如果用“非常”或“十分”,说“非常(/十分)古怪”较好。但也可说“非常(/十分)

怪”。“极”做补语可以加“了”，“非常”和“十分”不能这样用。“极”带双音节词，还可用“极其”，如“极其古怪”、“极其炎热”等 ◇ In example ② 极 is better because of syllabic collocation. If 非常 or 十分 is used, it is better to use 古怪, though 非常怪, 十分怪 are also fine. 极 plus 了 can be a complement, while 非常, 十分 cannot be so used. With a disyllabic adjective, 极其 can be used instead, e. g. 极其古怪(extremely eccentric), 极其炎热(harshly hot) etc.

③ 那里的风景美**极**了。The scenery there is very beautiful.

④ 这种电器好用**极**了。The electric appliance is very easy to use.

⑤ 今天的天气，不冷也不热，舒服**极**了。It is pleasing for it is neither cold nor hot today.

在③④⑤中只能用“极了”做补语 ◇ In examples ③, ④ and ⑤ only 极了 can be used as the complement.

书面语中可以说“非常之……”，如“非常之痛快”，“极”和“十分”不能这样用 ◇ In the literary language, 非常之……can be used in phrases like 非常之痛快. 极 and 十分 cannot used like this.

注意：“非常”还可以表示异乎寻常的、特别的，不是副词，是形容词，如“非常时期”、“非常代表大会”等 ◇ Note: 非常 can also mean " unusual, special". It's not an adverb, but an adjective, e. g. 非常时期(unusual times), 非常代表大会(nonpermanent representative conference), etc.

“十分”还可表示全部的、所有的，但是在这种用法中，它不是副词，而是词组，如“用了十分的力气”等 ◇ 十分 can also mean " the whole, all". In such a case, it is not an adverb, but a phrase, e. g. 用了十分的力气(with great efforts), etc.

▶ [极 jí—极端 jíduān—极其 jíqí]

[异常 yìcháng—非常 fēicháng]

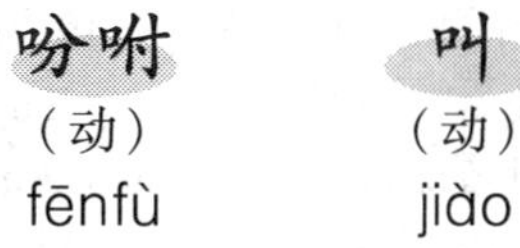

(动) (动)

fēnfù jiào

Ⓔ tell, instruct/tell, ask

这两个词都可以表示指派、要求。“吩咐”只用于上对下(长辈对晚辈、上级对下级等)，或为了表示客气而说“请(您)吩咐”。“叫”可用于各种情况，但没有客气的意思，较直率。另外，在句法上，两个词都可以用于兼语式，但“叫”只用于兼语式，“吩咐”还可单独做谓语、定语、宾语

等 ◇ Both words mean "to demand","to request". 吩咐 is used by the superior to the inferior or for the sake of courtesy:请(您)吩咐. 叫 can be used in all sorts of situations with no courtesy implied and is more straightforward. Moreover, both words are used in 兼语句 (verb-object phrase plus subject-predicate phrase with the object as the subject of the second phrase). 叫 is used only in 兼语句 while 吩咐 can also be the predicate, attributive, object, etc. of a sentence.

① 老板**吩咐**(/**叫**)她去买些办公用品。Her boss asked her to buy some office goods.

② 老师**吩咐**(/**叫**)一个学生去拿粉笔。The teacher asked a student to fetch some chalk.

以上例①②两个词可换用,但前者侧重于上对下 ◇ In examples ① and ②, the two words are interchangeable, but the former stresses the sense of superior to the inferior.

③ 我应该做什么,请您**吩咐**。Please tell me what to do.

④ 校长**吩咐**的事,记住了吗? Do you remember what the principal told you to do?

⑤ 以后你就听他的**吩咐**。You will be at his service from now on.

例③"吩咐"单独做谓语,例④"校长吩咐"做定语,例⑤"吩咐"做宾语。"叫"不能这样用 ◇ In example ③吩咐 is used as the predicate; in example ④ 校长吩咐 is the attributive; in example ⑤ 吩咐 is the object. 叫 cannot be so used.

⑥ 孩子**叫**妈妈早点儿回家。The child asked his mother to be back earlier.

例⑥是孩子要求妈妈怎么样,用"叫"虽没有客气的意思,作为旁叙是可以的。这时不能用"吩咐" ◇ In example ⑥, that the child asks his mother to do sth. 叫 does not imply courtesy but fits as narration. 吩咐 cannot be used here.

另外,"叫"还有大声喊、招呼、致使等意思。"吩咐"没有这些意思 ◇ Besides, 叫 also means "to call out loudly, to address, to cause (sb. to do sth.), etc". 吩咐 has no such meanings.

▶[喊 hǎn—叫 jiào—嚷 rǎng]
[嘱咐 zhǔfù—吩咐 fēnfù]

奋斗 斗争

(动) (动)

fèndòu dòuzhēng

Ⓔ struggle; strive/
struggle; fight

◪ 这两个词都可表示为了达到目的而竭尽全力去做,例如 ◇ Both words mean to fight hard in order to achieve one's aim, e. g. :

① 为全面建设小康社会而**奋斗**(/**斗争**)。We should work hard and strive for the coming of a well-to-do society.

② 我们要为美好的未来而**奋斗**(/**斗争**)。We should strive for our brilliant future.

但"奋斗"多表示单方面的努力 ◇ But 奋斗 often stresses one's own effort:

③ 他为文学事业**奋斗**了一生。He has worked at literature all his life.

④ 勤俭节约、艰苦**奋斗**,是我们崇高的美德。Plain living and hard working is our noble virtue.

"斗争"则表示对立的双方互相较量、冲突,如"政治斗争"、"阶级斗争"、"民族斗争"等,再如 ◇ 斗争 stresses the struggle between two opposite sides, e. g. 政治斗争(political struggle), 阶级斗争(class struggle), 民族斗争(national struggle), etc. More examples:

⑤ 正义和邪恶力量正在进行激烈的**斗争**。There is a fierce struggle between the just and the evil.

⑥ 他和恐惧**斗争**着,最后终于战胜了恐惧。He fought against his fears, and he won over them at last.

这时不能用"奋斗" ◇ 奋斗 cannot be so used in such situations.

"斗争"还可说 ◇ 斗争 can also be used in the following example:

⑦ 他常跟自己的惰性作**斗争**。He often struggles to overcome his laziness.

这也是"双方"(自己对自己的弱点)的较量,同样不能用"奋斗" ◇ This also involves "two sides" (one against one's weakness) and 奋斗 cannot be used either.

还可以说"进行斗争"(如例⑤)、"作斗争"(如例⑦),"奋斗"不能这样用 ◇ We can say 进行斗争(e. g. in example ⑤), 作斗争(e. g. in example ⑦). 奋斗 cannot be so used.

丰富 多

(形、动) fēngfù　(形、动) duō

Ⓔ abundant; enrich/ many, exceed

◪ **1**. 作为形容词,这两个词都表示数量大,但"丰富"主要表示充裕、广博,多指物产、知识、经验、节目等,"多"则常指一般事物 ◇ As adjectives, the two words mean "large quantity". However, 丰富 mainly stresses abundance and extensiveness, mostly applied to products, knowledge, experience, programs, etc., whereas 多 is usually applied to ordinary things:

① 他学识**丰富**,谈吐优雅。He is knowledgeable and talks with elegance.

② 今天来的人很**多**。There are many people present here.

以上两句,例①是说"学识广博",所以用"丰富"。例②只是说人数,所以用"多"。这两句的"丰富"和"多"是不能互换的 ◇ In the two examples above, example ① is about extensive knowledge, so 丰富 is used; example ② is about people, so 多 is used. 丰富 and 多 are not interchangeable in these two sentences.

其他如较抽象的"情节丰富"、"感情丰富"等,也不用"多" ◇ In other situations concerning abstract things such as 情节丰富 (rich and colorful plots), 感情丰富 (emotional), etc. 多 cannot be used either:

③ 她有极**丰富**的想像力。She has plenty of imagination.

即使同是说"物",较抽象的"物产"用"丰富",较具体的"粮食"、"木材"等则用"多"如 ◇ Even when applied to "things", 丰富 is used for those more abstract things like 物产 and 多 is used for those more concrete things, such as 粮食, 木材, e. g.:

④ 这里有**丰富**的矿产。The area is rich in minerals.

⑤ 粮食**多**了,就不值得珍惜了吗? Can't we treasure them if we have plenty of foods?

"丰富"有一定的褒义,"多"则是中性词。如"经验丰富"是褒义的,"经验多"是中性的。下面一句虽然说的是"知识",是仅就其数量不够而言,没有褒义,所以用"多"不用"丰富" ◇ 丰富 has a commendatory sense, while 多 is neutral. e. g. the meaning of 经验丰富 (rich experience) is commendatory, and that of 经验多 is neutral. 多 is used in the sentence below, because it means "inadequate knowledge", and 丰富 is not used:

⑥ 我天文方面的知识不**多**。I know a little about astronomy.

如果有一定的褒义,虽然说的是数量不够,也应该用"丰富" ◇ If there is a commendatory sense, even if an inadequate quantity, 丰富 should be used:

⑦ 这个学生在历史方面的知识还不够**丰富**,但基本知识还是有的。The student does not know history well, but he knows its ABC.

另外,有些固定短语,如"多才多艺","多谋善断"等,不能用"丰富" ◇ However, there are some set phrases, e. g. 多才多艺(versatile), 多谋善断(wise and resourceful), etc. where 丰富 is not used.

2. "多"可以做形容词或某些短语的补语，表示程度上相差很大，"丰富"不能这样用 ◇ 多 can function as a complement of adjectives or certain phrases to indicate a high degree; 丰富 cannot be so used:

① 经他一讲，我明白**多**了。I understand it better after his explanation.

② 他比以前懂事**多**了。He is more reasonable than he was.

"多"还可做结果补语，表示超过一定限度 ◇ 多 can also function as a complement of result to indicate an excess:

③ 他今天喝酒喝**多**了。He drank more wine than is necessary today.

④ 加水加**多**了，茶太淡了。The tea was weak for it was added to too much water.

"多"做状语，表示比较(与数量词呼应) ◇ 多 as an adverbial means more than with numbers and measure words used correspondingly:

⑤ 这个月比上个月**多**收入500元。The income of this month is five hundred *yuan* more than that of last month.

⑥ 做这些数学题，我比你**多**用了半个小时。It took me half an hour more than you to finish the math questions.

以上例句都不能用"丰富"代替 ◇ In the examples above, 丰富 cannot replace 多.

3. 动词"多"表示数量有所增加，超出原来的需要，或表示不必要 ◇ The verb 多 means "more than necessary or superfluous":

① 这里**多**了几个字，删去吧！There are a few unnecessary words here. Please leave them out.

② 我数过了，一共10枝铅笔，怎么**多**出了一枝？I have counted and there are ten pencils in all. Why is there eleven ones?

③ 这里没你的事，你**多**什么嘴？You have nothing to do with it. Why do you poke your nose into it?

4. 动词"丰富"是"使……丰富"的意思，宾语多为"经验"、"知识"、"内容"等 ◇ 丰富 as a verb means "to enrich" and the object is usually 经验(experience), 知识(knowledge), 内容(content), etc.:

① 这本书，大大**丰富**了我的知识。Reading the book enriched me.

F

② 为了**丰富**自己的课余生活，她参加了一些课外活动。She takes part in some extracurricular activities to enrich her spare time.

动词的"多"和"丰富"不能互换 ◇ As a verb，多 and 丰富 are not interchangeable.

F

否则 （连） fǒuzé　　不然 （连） bùrán

Ⓔ otherwise/otherwise

◥ 在比较这两个连词时，顺带简单提到另外两个连词"要不"和"要不然" ◇ In explaining these two conjunctions，the other two conjunctions 要不 and 要不然 will be mentioned simultaneously：

1."否则"和"不然"用于后一分句的开头，表示对前一分句作出假设的否定，并指出可能产生的结果。可加"的话" ◇ 否则 or 不然 is used at the beginning of the second clause to indicate a hypothetical negation to the preceding clause，followed by the possible result. 的话 can be added：

① 幸亏打了预防针，**否则**一定会得病。But for the vaccine，I would have been ill.

② 你必须用功，**否则**的话，成绩肯定上不去。You must work hard，or you will not catch up with the others.

③ 老师应该认真备课，**否则**怎么能教好课呢？A teacher must prepare his lessons well，or how can we expect him to teach well?

以上三句，都可换用"不然"、"要不"或"要不然"。例③"否则……?"是用反问的形式指出可能产生的结果。用"否则"或"不然"都较书面化，"要不"和"要不然"则显得口语化，加"的话"的频率更高 ◇ In the examples above，不然，要不 or 要不然 can all be used instead. In example ③ a rhetorical question is used instead to indicate the possible result. 否则 and 不然 is more literary；要不 and 要不然 is more colloquial and so more often takes 的话 after it.

2."否则"和"不然"表示选择（如果不是这种情况，就是那种情况），也用在后一分句的开头 ◇ 否则 and 不然 at the beginning of the second clause can also mean "either... or...":

① 他们经常在晚上闲谈，**否则**就一块儿听音乐。They usually either chat or listen to music together at night.

② 大家都讨厌他，见面冷冷地一点头，**否则**就装没看见走开。All of us dislike him. When we met him, we either nodded him coldly or pretended not to see him.

③ 我们开个联欢会吧,**否则**就出去玩玩。Let's either have a get-together or go out for fun.

以上三句,都可换用其他三个词。也可加"的话" ◇ In the three examples above, any of the three other words can be used, and 的话 can also be added.

夫人 (名) fūrén　太太 (名) tàitai

Ⓔ Madame; Mrs. ; Lady/ Mrs. ; Madame

这两个名词都表示对已婚女子的尊称。"夫人"是书面语,尊敬的意味更浓,一般用于社会上层。"太太"除用于尊称,有时也被丈夫用来指自己的妻子。两个词都可以用在丈夫的姓后面。"夫人"还可以用于丈夫的官称之后(如"总统夫人") ◇ Both words are respectful forms of address for a married woman. 夫人 is literary and sounds even more respectful, generally used in the high society. 太太 is sometimes used by a husband to refer to his wife when talking to other people. Both words can be used after the husband's surname. 夫人 can also be used after her husband's official title, e. g. 总统夫人.

① 今天英国教育部部长及**夫人**参观了我们学校。The minister of British Education Department and his wife visited our school today.

② 大使**夫人**代表大使参加了仪式并即席致词。The wife of the ambassador attended the ceremony and made an offhand talk on behalf of his husband.

以上二句,因为指地位较高的已婚女子,并且属于外事活动,用"夫人",不用"太太" ◇ In the two sentences above, the address is applied to a married woman with a high social status in a diplomatic activity, 夫人, and not 太太 should be used.

③ 我来介绍一下,这是我**太太**,这是李先生。Allow me to make an introduction. This is my wife, and this is Mr. Li.

这句因为属于一般的尊称,应该用"太太",不宜用"夫人"。如称一般人的妻子为"夫人",则有诙谐意味,但也不失尊敬 ◇ In this sentence above, 太太 is better than 夫人, since it is just an ordinary respectful form of address. If 夫人 is used as an address for the wife of an ordinary man, it may have a humorous flavour, but not without respect.

④ 今天怎么没带**夫人**一块出来玩呢？Why not come heve with your wife?

辅导 帮助

(动、名) (动)

fǔdǎo bāngzhù

Ⓔ coach; guidance/help

◪"辅导"有指导某人获得知识、技能等的意思，常用于老师对学生，或有关单位对所指导或服务的对象。"帮助"则可以用于知识、技能方面，也可用于其他方面 ◇ 辅导 means " to instruct sb. to obtain knowledge, skill, etc. ", and is usually applied to what a teacher does to a student, or a related unit to its target of instruction or service. 帮助 can be applied to knowledge, skill and other things as well.

① 李小刚今天上课有点儿跟不上，马老师特别在课后**辅导**了他。Li Xiaogang a bit lagged behind today in class, so Mr. Ma tutored him after class specially.

② 对于下岗职工，民政局组织了培训班，**辅导**他们再就业的有关业务知识。The Department of Civil Affairs offered a training course for the lay-off workers to train them some skills about reworking.

以上两句，因为属于老师对学生的补课，或有关单位对所服务对象进行指导，用"辅导"。例①如果不是正式补课，也可以用"帮助" ◇ In the two examples above, 辅导 is used since it means either help of a teacher to the student or a related unit to its target of service. In example ①, 帮助 can also be used, if it is not a formal instruction.

以下例句，属于一般事务，用"帮助" ◇ The following examples concern just ordinary affairs, so 帮助 is used:

③ 这道题的得数对不对？请您**帮助**我检查一下。Is the answer to the question right? Come and check it for me.

④ 哥哥**帮助**小明整理好书包。Xiao Ming's brother helped Xiao Ming packing his schoolbag.

⑤ 盲人过马路时得到了热心行人的**帮助**。The blind man got help from a pedestrian when crossing the street.

"辅导"也是名词，表示辅导课，如"今天我有辅导" ◇ 辅导 is also a noun meaning " a guidance course", e. g. 今天我有辅导(Today I will attend my tutoring class).

注意:例⑤"得到……帮助"中的"帮助"是宾语,仍为动词 ◇ Note: In example ⑤ 帮助 is the object, but is still a verb.

▶[协助 xiézhù—帮助 bāngzhù]
[援助 yuánzhù—帮助 bāngzhù]

付 给 交

(动) (动) (动)
fù gěi jiāo

Ⓔ pay/give, deliver/hand

"付"、"给"、"交"都表示使事物从一方转移到另一方 ◇ 付, 给, 交 all mean " to deliver something to somebody."

1. 付(动)

"付"表示使钱转移到另一方,而且一般是交易、商业行为,或向劳方支付报酬 ◇ 付 means" to give money to the other side in business, trade or payment for labor":

① 他到收银台去**付**款。He went to pay at the cashier's.

② **付**完了钱,我们走出餐馆。After paying the bill, we went out of the restaurant.

③ 先生,请您**付**账。Here's the bill, sir.

"付"的宾语多为"款"、"钱"、"账"以及"工资"、"报酬"等 ◇ The objects of 付 are 款(bill), 钱(money), 账(bill), 工资(wage), 报酬(reward), etc.

"付"也可用于双宾句 ◇ 付 can also be used in a sentence with double objects:

④ 我**付**你100元,不用找了。Here's 100 *yuan*. Keep the changes, please.

"付"可以用"给"做补语 ◇ 付 can take 给 as a complement:

⑤ 顾客**付**给店主500元。The customer gave the shopper five hundred *yuan*.

以上例②④可换用"给"。例⑤的"付"如换用"给",做补语的"给"应取消。都不能用"交"替换 ◇ In examples ②④付 can be replaced by 给. In example ⑤, however, if 付 is replaced by 给, the complement 给 must be omitted. All 付 here cannot be replaced by 交.

"付出"还可带表示抽象意义的宾语 ◇ 付出 can also take an object of an abstract meaning:

⑥ 为了建设这所学校,他们**付出**了辛勤的劳动和汗水。They put in a lot of work and sweat for the construction of the school.

⑦ 王先生为科学事业**付出**了毕生的精力。Mr. Wang are dedicated to the scientific cause for all his life.

2. 给(动)

(1)"给"的用法很广泛,不限于钱,也不限于交易等行为,可以是一般事物,也可以是抽象意义的"印象"、"机会"、"照顾"、"打击"、"难堪"等 ◇ The objects of the verb 给 are wide-ranging, not limited to money or trade, but can be ordinary things or abstract nouns such as 印象(impression), 机会(chance), 照顾(care), 打击(hit, strike), 难堪(embarassment), etc.:

① 爸爸**给**了他一些钱买书。His father gave him some money to buy books.

② 他**给**了钱,就走出了商店。After paying, he went out of the shop.

③ 请**给**我一杯咖啡。Please give me a cup of coffee.

④ 这件事**给**了我很深的印象。The matter impressed me deeply.

以上,例②因属于买卖交易行为,也可换用"付",但"给"更为口语化。其他三句不能用"付"。各句也不能用"交" ◇ In the above examples, example ②is about trade, so 付 can be used instead, but 给 is more colloquial. 付 cannot be used in the other three examples. 交 cannot be used in any of the four.

"给"可以做补语 ◇ 给 can be a complement, e.g.:

⑤ 我递**给**她一支笔。I passed her a pen.

⑥ 小李还(huán)**给**他两本书。Xiao Li returned him two books.

⑦ 她送**给**小王一条领带。She gave Xiao Wang a tie as a gift.

⑧ 科学院拨**给**他们专款作试验经费。The Academy of Science allocated funds to their experiment.

(2)"给"表示被、让,或做助词 ◇ 给, in the passive voice, equals to the meaning of "by":

⑨ 鱼**给**小猫偷吃了。The fish was eaten by the cat.

⑩ 花瓶**给**小弟弟打碎了。The vase was broken by my little brother.

⑪ 钱**给**他花光了。He spent all the money.

以上(2)中各例都不能用"付"、"交" ◇ In the examples in(2) above, neither 付 nor 交 can be used instead.

3. 交(动)

"交"所表示的转移行为,涉及的可以是一般事物,多为"下"对"上"(如学生对老师、纳税人对税务机关、人民对政府、劳动者对雇主等) ◇ The delivery meant by 交 can be applied to ordinary things, mostly from the inferior to the superior(such as the student to the teacher, the tax payer to the tax authority, the people to the government, the employee to the employer, etc.):

① 明天一定要把作业本子**交**老师。You must hand in your exercise-book to the teacher tomorrow.

② 她这次考试**交**了白卷。She wrote nothing in her test paper.

③ 这位店主亲自去税务所**交**了税。The shopper went to the tax office to pay his tax in person.

④ 她没有按时**交**活儿,老板不太高兴。She didn't finish her work on time, which made her boss unhappy.

除了例①可用"给",其他各句不能用"给"或"付"。但"给"有时可做"交"的补语,如例①可说"交给" ◇ With the exception of example ①, in all the examples above neither 给 nor 付 can be used. But sometimes 给 can function as the complement of 交, so in example ① 交 can be replaced by 交给.

"交"还可以表示拿出来、献出来(主动或被迫);或表示由某人去做 ◇ 交 can mean "to hand out (voluntarily or compulsively), or to hand over to somebody to be done":

⑤ 小偷被捉住了,只好**交**出赃物。The thief was caught and had to take out all the stolen items.

⑥ 这个任务就**交**给我们做吧! Let's do the job!

⑦ 父母都要出差,只好把孩子**交**奶奶带。The child was looked after by his grandmother for his parents were going on business.

"交"还表示交叉、到达(某时间)、结交等 ◇ 交 also means "to intersect, to set in (season), to make friends with, etc.":

⑧ 这两条直线**交**于一点。The two lines cross.

⑨ 节气快**交**冬至了。The winter solstice is approaching.

⑩ 他喜欢广**交**朋友。He likes making friends with variety of people.

以上不能用"付"、"给" ◇ In examples ⑧ ⑨and ⑩ neither 付 nor 给 can be used.

▶[给 gěi—为 wèi—替 tì]

妇女 妇人 女人

(名) fùnǚ　(名) fùrén　(名) nǚrén

Ⓔ woman/woman/woman

◪ 这三个名词都指女性。"女人"泛指女性,有时特指妻子(但不含

F

敬意)。"妇女"指成年女性,较正式,多为集体性称呼。"妇人"也指成年女性,词义较旧 ◇ The three words all refer to women. 女人 is a general term for women, and sometimes it refers to wife (but without respect). 妇女 means " grown women" and is rather formal, often as a collective address. 妇人 can also refer to " grown women", but is old-fashioned.

① 市里正在召开**妇女**代表大会。The women congress of the city is being held now.

② 她们在为**妇女**的正当权利进行斗争。They are working at women's righteous rights.

以上两句,应该用"妇女",因为词义较正式,而且是一个集合名词,不应该用其他两个词 ◇ In the two examples above, 妇女 is used because it is formal and is a collective noun; the other two words are not used.

③ 这是我们**女人**的事,你们男人少管。This is women's affair. Don't poke your nose into it.

④ 家里没个**女人**,不像个家,你还是找个**女人**结婚吧! A family cannot be a family without a woman. So please look for your Ms. Right to get married in a hurry.

以上例③泛指女性,用"女人"。例④用"女人"指代妻子(但缺少敬意,一般还可说"爱人"、"妻子"等) ◇ In example ③女人 is used to mean "women in general". In example ④ 女人 means " wife" (lacking in respect), where 爱人 or 妻子 can also be used.)

"妇人"词义较旧,现在已经较少使用 ◇ 妇人 is out-of-date, and rarely used.

附带说明:最常用的,还是"女"、"女的"、"女士",如:"一男一女"、"女同学"、"女博士"、"女的也可以踢足球"、"女士优先"等 ◇ Note: The most commonly used is 女,女的,女士, e. g. :一男一女 (a man and a woman), 女同学 (girl classmate), 女博士 (female doctor), 女的也可以踢足球 (Women can play football as well), 女士优先 (lady first), etc.

富有 (形、动) fùyǒu 富裕 (形) fùyù

Ⓔ rich; be rich in/well-to-do

1. "富有"(动)表示具有、大量具有,宾语是抽象意义的多音节词语 ◇ 富有 as a verb means "to have plenty of, to be rich in"; its object is usually a polysyllabic word or phrase of an abstract meaning, e. g. :

① 他在工作上**富有**进取精神。

He is aggressive at work.

② 这位作家**富有**旺盛的创作力。The writer is full of writing creativity.

③ 她**富有**同情心。She has sympathy for others.

2."富有"和"富裕"都是形容词。"富有"表示财富很多,"富裕"表示生活宽裕 ◇ Both 富有 and 富裕 are adjectives. 富有 means "rich", and 富裕 means "well-off",e. g.:

① 他的父亲是个大老板,家里非常**富有**。His family is very rich,for his father is a moneybags.

② 她的家庭十分**富有**。Her family is very rich.

③ 我家人口多,只有父亲一个人工作,生活上并不**富裕**。There are a lot of people in my family, and only my father supports it, and so we are not rich.

④ 他们的日子比以前**富裕**多了。They lead a richer life than before.

因为两个词存在着"财富很多"和只是"生活宽裕"的差别,语言环境清楚时,并不会发生混淆问题。但有时因为修辞或谦虚等原因,富有的人也会说"我家生活还算富裕",这就不只是词义问题了 ◇ Since there is a differece between these two words in the meaning of being wealthy and just well-off, there will not be any confusion when the linguistic context is clear. But sometimes because of rhetorics or modesty, a wealthy person may say:我家生活还算富裕. Then it is not a question of word meaning.

另外,"富有"还有与"贫乏"相比较的用法,一般用于抽象意义 ◇ Moreover, 富有 can be used in comparison with 贫乏, usually in an abstract meaning, e. g.:

⑤ 他常常觉得自己的物质生活虽然是**富有**的,但精神生活却是贫乏的。He often felt he was rich in material life but poor in spiritual life.

F

G

该 应该

(助动、动) (助动)

gāi yīnggāi

Ⓔ ought to, should/ ought to, should

G

1. 该(动)

(1)表示轮到,或是某人担负某种责任 ◇ Be sb.'s turn to do sth.:

① 今天**该**我值班了。It's my turn to be on duty today.

② 下学期**该**张老师给我们班上数学课了。It's Mr. Zhang's turn to teach us math next term.

③ **该**我做的事,我一定去做。I must do whatever I should do.

④ **该**谁发球? Whose turn to serve?

(2)表示欠(钱、物) ◇ Owe (money, things) to:

⑤ 我**该**你的钱,下月一定还。I am likely to repay you the money I owed next month.

⑥ 这笔钱,他**该**了我半年了。The money is owed by him for half a year.

⑦ 我**该**编辑部一篇稿子。I haven't finished a manuscript of the editorial department.

2. "该"、"应该"这两个助动词都表示应当、理所当然。"该"与单音节词结合较多,"应该"与双音节词结合较多。"该"更口语化一些 ◇ As auxiliary verbs, both 该 and 应该 mean " ought to, should". 该 is mostly used with monosyllabic words, and 应该 with disyllabic words. 该 is more colloquial:

(1)与动词一起做定语 ◇ Used with a verb as the attributive:

① **该**来的人都来了。Those are all present who should come.

② 这是他**应该**承担的责任。This is his responsibility.

以上两句,"该"与单音节的"来"结合,"应该"与双音节的"承担"结合。但这不是绝对的,例①②中这两个词也可互换 ◇ In the two examples above, 该 is used with monosyllabic 来, while 应该 with disyllabic 承担. But this is not absolute. In examples ① and ②, 该 and 应该 are interchangeable.

(2)与动词一起做谓语 ◇ Used with a verb as the predicate:

③ 客人对主人说:谢谢款待。我**该**(/**应该**)走了。The guest

said to the host: Thanks for your treat. I must go now.

④ 老天爷**该**(/**应该**)下点儿雨了! It is high time to rain.

以上两句,除了用"该"更为口语化,没有什么区别 ◇ In the two examples above, there is no difference except that 该 sounds more colloquial.

(3)纳入"是……的"框架,做谓语 ◇ Enclosed in the pattern 是……的 to function as the predicate:

⑤ 我这样做是**应该**的。It's natural that I do it this way.

⑥ 出了错误,检讨是应该的。It's natural for you to make a self-criticism after you make a mistake.

这时用"应该",不用"该" ◇ 应该 is used here, not 该.

如果与动词一起纳入"是……的",两个词都可以用 ◇ If enclosed together with the verb pattern in the 是……的, either will do, e.g.:

⑦ 你是不**该**(/**应该**)出错的! You ought not to have made the mistakes.

⑧ 这件事是**该**(/**应该**)认真对待的。You should have taken it seriously.

3."该"还是副词,表示设想、估计或感叹 ◇ 该 is also an adverb indicating estimation or exclamation, e.g.:

① 走了这么远的路,你**该**累了吧? After such a long journey, you must be tired.

② 如果他能来,大家**该**多高兴啊! How happy we will be if he can come.

▶[应 yīng—应该 yīnggāi —应当 yīngdāng]

G

改 改变

(动) (动、名)

gǎi gǎibiàn

Ⓔ change, alter/ change, alter, alteration

◪ **1**. 动词"改"、"改变"都表示人或事物、状况有了与以前不同的地方,具体、抽象均可。"改"更为口语化。在音节搭配上,"改"多与单音节词搭配,"改变"多与双音节词搭配。但这种搭配关系也不是绝对的 ◇ As a verb, 改 and 改变 both mean "to change, in either concrete or abstract way". 改 is more colloquial and mostly used with monosyllabic words, while 改变 with disyllabic words. But this is not absolute.

① 他原来叫李小明,后来**改**了名,叫李勇。His former name is Li Xiaoming, and later he changed his name to Li Yong.

② 原订的计划已经**改变**了。The

original plan has been changed.

以上两句,例①不用“改变”,例②则可换用“改”。即“改”有时搭配较灵活 ◇ In the two examples above,改变 cannot be used in example ①, but 改 can be used instead in example ②. That indicates that 改 is relatively free in collocation.

“改变”多是人为的,使事物与前不同,一般常比原来的好 ◇ 改变 are mostly artificial, that is, to make sth. different from before, usually better than before:

③ 这个城市**改变**了面貌。The city has changed.

④ 我们要**改变**工作方法。We should improve our work methods.

2.“改”还有“修改”的意思(多用于文章等) ◇ 改 also means "to correct(mostly applied to writings)":

① 老师给我**改**作文。The teacher corrected my writing.

② 这首诗有两句可以**改改**。You can make a change in the two lines of the poem.

这时不用“改变” ◇ 改变 cannot be used here.

3.“改”有把不正确的变为正确的意思 ◇ 改 has the meaning of making right:

① 你这毛病得**改一改**。You should correct the habit.

② 他已经**改**好了,还考上了大学。He has turned to be a good boy, and he is at college now.

这两句话都不用“改变” ◇ Neither can use 改变 instead.

4. 名词“改变”多做“有”、“随着”等的宾语 ◇ 改变 as a noun mostly functions as the object of 有,随着,etc.:

① 这个规划有一点儿**改变**。The plan has been made a little change.

② 随着情绪的**改变**,他和别人说话的语气也随和多了。With his mood changing, he is more easygoing when talking to others.

▶ [转变 zhuǎnbiàn—改变 gǎibiàn]

改正 (动) gǎizhèng　　纠正 (动) jiūzhèng

Ⓔ correct/

correct, put right, rectify

1. 这两个动词都可表示把不正确的变为正确的。“改正”使用较广,具体如“改正错别字”,抽象如“改正不良习惯”。“纠正”较书面化,多用于较大的事情,如思想、路线的偏差等,也可以用于具体的缺点、错误、方法等,如 ◇

Both of the two verbs mean "to put right sth. which is wrong". 改正 is used more often than 纠正. One can say 改正错别字(correct the misspelt words),改正不良习惯(correct the bad habits). 纠正 is more literary, mostly applied to more important things, e. g. deviation in thinking, line, etc. It can also be applied to concrete defects, mistakes, methods, etc. e. g. :

① 他把文章中的错字**改正**了。He has corrected the incorrect words in his article.

② 孩子大了,吮指头的习惯应该**改正**了。The child is old enough now, and he should give up the habit of sucking his thumb.

③ 社会上的不正之风,必须**纠正**。We must rectify the corrupt practices of the society.

④ 对违章驾驶,交警必须加以**纠正**,并及时作出罚款等处理。The traffic policeman should criticize violating drivers and fine them in time.

⑤ 汉语老师认真地给学生**纠正**发音。The chinese teacher corrected the students' pronunciation earnestly.

以上例①②宜用"改正";例③④⑤宜用"纠正" ◇ In the examples above, 改正 is more suitable in examples ①②and 纠正 is more suitable in examples ③④⑤.

2. 两个词前边都可加"加以"(如例④)。也说"得到改正(/纠正)","改正(/纠正)过来" ◇ Both words can be preceded by 加以(e. g. in example ④). One can also say 得到改正(/纠正),改正(/纠正)过来:

① 错误的处理已经得到**改正**(/**纠正**)。The improper disposal has been corrected.

② 老师让他把不正确的坐姿**改正**(/**纠正**)过来。The teacher asked him to correct his bad sitting posture.

③ 这种根深蒂固的坏习惯,已经很难**改正**(/**纠正**)过来了。It is difficult for him to correct his bad deep-noted habits.

对于自己多用"改正",对于别人多用"纠正",虽不是绝对的,但在同一个句子中,对自己和对他人,可分别使用"改正"和"纠正"以避免重复 ◇ Usually 改正 is applied to oneself while 纠正 to others, though this rule is not absolute. In one sentence; however, 改正 and 纠正 can be used respectively, to differentiate oneself from other people to avoid repeatition:

④ 别人的错误,容易加以**纠正**;自己的缺点,也许倒不容易**改正**。It may be easy to correct others' mistakes; while it may be difficult to correct your own ones.

►[修正 xiūzhèng—改正 gǎizhèng]

干脆 索性

（形） （副）

gāncuì suǒxìng

G

Ⓔ straightforward/resolutely

这两个词都可以表示采取直截了当甚至极端的态度或做法。当“干脆”做状语时,有时可以与“索性”互换 ◇ Both words mean "to act in a straightforward way or even going to the extreme". When 干脆 is used as adverbials, it can be replaced by 索性:

① 既然他们俩不能合作,**干脆**(/**索性**)分开做吧。Now that they cannot cooperate, you'd better separate them.

② 已经晚了,**干脆**(/**索性**)住一宿再走吧。It's too late, so you'd better stay here for the night.

这时“干脆”更为口语化一些 ◇ Here, 干脆 is more colloquial.

另外,“干脆”做状语有时有不转弯抹角的意思,“索性”不能这样用 ◇ Besides, when used as an adverbial, 干脆 sometimes means "not to mince one's words". 索性 cannot be so used.

③ **干脆**一句话:你答应不答应? Please give me a straightforward reply: yes or no?

由于“干脆”是形容词,还可以做定语、谓语、补语等,并能重叠,词义也较宽(指爽快、直截了当),“索性”则不同 ◇ Since 干脆 is an adjective, it can also function as an attributive, predicate, complement, etc. It can be reduplicated into 干干脆脆 and has a wider meaning (straightforward, point-blank). 索性 is different.

④ 她说一不二,真是个**干脆**的人。(定语) She is very firm and straightforward. (attributive)

⑤ 你做事**干脆**点儿!(谓语) You'd better be snappy! (predicate)

⑥ 他的话说得**干干脆脆**。(补语) His words are very straightforward. (complement)

干净 清洁

（形） （形）

gānjìng qīngjié

Ⓔ clean, neat/neat

1. 这两个词都可以表示无灰尘、污垢等,但“干净”口语化,而“清洁”更书面化些。“干净”可以重叠,“清洁”不能 ◇ Both words mean "free from dirt, etc". But 干净 is colloquial, while 清洁

is literary. 干净 can be reduplicated into 干干净净 while 清洁 cannot.

① 主妇很勤快,房间十分**干净**(/**清洁**)。The housewife is very diligent and keeps the room very clean.

② 经理说,大堂地面不太**干净**(/**清洁**),要再打扫一下。The manager said that the lounge floor was not clean. It needs cleaning again.

例①②中两个词可换用,但"干净"较口语化 ◇ In examples ① and ② the two words are interchangeable,but 干净 is more colloquial.

在比较正式的词语中,如"大搞清洁卫生",不用"干净"。而十分口语化的语境,以用"干净"为好 ◇ In formal phrases, e. g. 大搞清洁卫生(do a thorough cleaning),干净 is not used; while in everyday speech,干净 is better:

③ 妈妈让孩子把手洗**干净**。The mother asked her child to wash his hands clean.

"清洁"有时可带宾语,如"清洁市容",较书面化。"干净"不能这样用 ◇ 清洁 sometimes can take an object, e. g. 清洁市容, which is more literary. 干净 cannot.

2. 另外,"干净"有什么都不剩下的意思,多做补语 ◇ Besides,干净 also means "with nothing left over", and mostly functions as a complement:

① 这手巾上的红颜色能洗**干净**吗? Can the red spot in the towel be washed out?

② 爸爸让孩子把碗里的饭吃**干净**。The father asked his child to eat up the food in his bowl.

③ 人死了,什么都带不走,**干干净净**。A man cannot take anything with him after he dies.

3. "干净"还有比喻义;用于否定式时,"不干净"比喻做过坏事 ◇ 干净 also has a figurative meaning; when used in the negative,不干净 means "having committed crime previously":

① 他有前科,手上**不干净**。He committed crimes before.

另一个比喻义是做坏事时不留痕迹 ◇ Another figurative meaning is leaving no trace in doing evil:

② 他以为这次作案做得很**干净**,其实早露出马脚了。He had thought he committed the crime unnoticeably, but in fact he was exposed early.

"清洁"没有这样的意义 ◇ 清洁 has no such meanings.

干涉 干扰

(动、名) (动)

gānshè gānrǎo

Ⓔ interfere/disturb

1. "干涉"指对他人的过问、处置、制止等,多为不应有的或非正当的。小至婚姻、大至军事,都可以用"干涉" ◇ 干涉 means " to interfere with another person's business, mostly unwanted or unjustly". It can be applied to matters ranging from marriage to military affairs:

① 请不要**干涉**别人的自由。Please don't interfere in other's freedom.

② 子女的婚姻,父母不应多加**干涉**。Don't interfere in your child's marriage.

这个词较书面化,常用于"进行干涉"这样的短语(如例③) ◇ This word is literary, and one usually say 进行干涉(intervene in) (as in example ③).

有时"干涉"也可以表示出于正当目的的过问或制止 ◇ Sometimes 干涉 may mean interference or prohibition for a justified purpose:

③ 小贩在校门外叫卖,影响学生学习,校方不得不请警察出面**干涉**。The peddlers' noise disturbed the students, so the school had to turn to the police to prohibit them.

另外,"干涉"在书面语中还指干系、关系,是名词 ◇ Besides, 干涉 is also used as a noun in literary languageto mean " implication or relation":

④ 离婚之后,二人已毫无**干涉**。There was no relation between them after their divorce.

2. "干扰"指对他人正常活动的打扰(有意或无意的) ◇ 干扰 means " to disturb another person's normal activity(either intentionally or inadvertently)":

① 人家正在吃晚饭,不好贸然去**干扰**吧。They are having the supper, and there is no reason to disturb them.

② 你们家的电视声音太大,**干扰**了邻居。The loud noise of your TV set disturbed the neighbors.

③ 孩子们那么闹,他仍然读他的书,看来他是自有一套抗**干扰**的本事,能闹中求静。The children are too noisy, but he can resist it and keep on reading without disturbance.

"干扰"还特指妨碍收音机、电视机等正常接收功能的电磁振荡 ◇ 干扰 refers in particular to electromagnetic oscillation that prevents radio or television from normal reception:

④ 附近正在施工,我家电视常受**干扰**,图像不清。My TV was often disturbed by the construction nearby, so its picture was not clear.

赶紧 赶快

(副) (副)

gǎnjǐn gǎnkuài

Ⓔ hastily/quickly

◪ 两个词都表示抓紧时间加速行动,都可用于陈述(已然或未然)及祈使句 ◇ Both words mean "to speed up an action", and both can be used in a declarative (foregone or future) sentence and an imperative sentence.

① 昨天发生交通意外时,他们已经发现车子有毛病,想**赶紧**(/**赶快**)刹车,但是已经来不及了。(陈述,已然) There was no time left when they knew there was something wrong with their car. And therefore there was a traffic accident. (declarative, foregone)

② **赶快**(/**赶紧**)出发吧!时间要晚了!(祈使,未然) Please leave at once, or you'll be late. (imperative, future)

③ 如果不**赶快**(/**赶紧**)走,就赶不上飞机了。(假设,未然) If you are not in a hurry, you'll miss the plane. (hypothetical, future)

也可单用 ◇ Both can be used independently.

④ 快送他去医院,**赶快**(/**赶紧**)! Take him to the hospital immediately. Hurry up, please.

▶ [赶快 gǎnkuài—赶忙 gǎnmáng]

赶快 赶忙

(副) (副)

gǎnkuài gǎnmáng

Ⓔ quickly/hurriedly

◪ "赶快"和"赶忙"都表示加速行动,但前者可用于祈使句中,后者只能用于客观叙述,而且不能用于未发生的事情 ◇ Both 赶快 and 赶忙 mean "to hurry up", but the former can be used in the imperative, and the latter can only be used in objective narration and cannot be applied to things which have not taken place.

① 飞机快起飞了,你**赶快**登机吧! Board the plane at once, for it is taking off.

② 你**赶快**把信送给他! Please sent the letter to him as soon as possible.

以上两句都是祈使句(是未发生的事),只能用"赶快" ◇ The two examples above are in the imperative (not happened yet), and only 赶快 can be used.

③ 见老人步履艰难,他**赶快**(/**赶忙**)去搀扶。He came up to hold the old man at once when he saw him walking with difficulty.

④ 我希望孩子**赶快**毕业,好帮助我做事。I hope my child will graduate as soon as possible and help me with my business.

例③是客观叙述,而且是已经发生的事情,所以用"赶快"、"赶忙"都可以。例④虽是客观叙述,但说的是未实现的事,所以只能用"赶快" ◇ Example ③ is an objective narration of sth. that has happened, so either 赶快 or 赶忙 can be used. Though example ④ is also an objective narration, it is sth. that has not yet taken place, so only 赶快 can be used.

▶ [赶紧 gǎnjǐn—赶快 gǎnkuài]
[连忙 liánmáng—赶忙 gǎnmáng]

感到 (动) gǎndào　觉得 (动) juéde

Ⓔ feel/feel

1. 这两个词都可以表示有所感觉,多表示心理状态或生理上的感受。"觉得"更为口语化 ◇ Both words mean "to feel sth. psychologically or physiologically". 觉得 is more colloquial:

① 工作中出了错儿,老王**感到**(/**觉得**)很不安。Lao Wang felt unrest with his mistakes in his work.

② 工作了一天,他**觉得**(/**感到**)有些累。After a day's work, he felt a bit tired.

以上两句,两个词可以互换 ◇ In the two sentences above, the two words are interchangeable.

否定时多用"不觉得"、"没觉得" ◇ To show negation, 不觉得 or 没觉得 is preferred:

③ 我不**觉得**这件事有什么突然。I don't think it's abrupt.

④ 他没**觉得**别人对自己有意见。He didn't know that others were dissatisfied with him.

"感到"也可以否定,但不够口语化 ◇ 感到 can also be used in the negative, but not very colloquial:

⑤ 你不**感到**你这么办不应该吗?Don't you think you should not have done it?

⑥ 我没**感到**这样做有什么过分。I don't think it is too much doing it this way.

以上两句也可换用"觉得" ◇ 觉得 can be used instead in the two examples above.

在句法上，两个词都可以带形容词宾语（如例①②⑥），也可以带主谓结构做宾语（如③④）或动词宾语（如⑤）。另外，"感到"可以带少数几个名词做宾语，"觉得"不可以 ◇ Both verbs can take an adjective as the object (examples ① ② ⑥), or a subject-predicate construction as the object (examples ③ ④) or a verbal object (example⑤). Besides, 感到 can have several nouns as the object, but 觉得 cannot:

⑦ 他**感到**了事情的严重性。He sensed the seriousness.

⑧ 她没**感到**这项工作的压力。She didn't felt the work pressure.

2. "觉得"还有"认为"（提出主张或看法，但略委婉）的意思 ◇ 觉得 sometimes means " to think or to consider (to give one's view or make a proposition, in a tactful way)":

① 我**觉得**你还是不应该参加那个会。I think you should not have come to the meeting.

② 我们**觉得**第一个方案比第二个方案好。I think the first plan is better than the second one.

当然，在修辞上，有时用有所感觉来委婉地表示看法，如 1 中的例③⑤ ◇ To be more tactful rhetorically, sometimes one can use "feel" to present one's view as in examples ③ and ⑤ of 1.

感谢 感激

（动） gǎnxiè （动） gǎnjī

Ⓔ be grateful to/ be indebted to

1. 这两个词都表示对他人的好意、帮助，有好感或表示好感。"感激"比较含蓄、内向；"感谢"比较外在，常用言语或行动表示出来。同时"感激"的意思更深厚 ◇ Both words mean " to be grateful to other people's kindness or help". 感激 is more implicit; 感谢 is more overt usually expressed by words or actions. 感激 also has a deeper feeling.

① 我们很**感谢**（/**感激**）大家对我们的支持。We are grateful for your support.

例①中两个词都可用，但"感谢"较外露，"感激"较含蓄 ◇ In example ① either word can be used, but 感谢 is more overt while 感激 is more implicit.

2. 对一般的、具体的好意或帮助，常用"感谢"；对深情厚谊，常用"感激" ◇ 感谢 is applied to ordinary kindness or help; 感激 is applied to profound gratitude.

① 我们非常**感谢**你陪我们参观这座美丽的城市。We appreciate your accompanying in visiting the beautiful city.

② 对于父母给予我的爱,我内心十分**感激**。I am grateful to my parents for their love.

3. 有时,他人的好意或帮助是无法用言语来表达谢意的,这时候可以用"感激"带程度补语 ◇ Sometimes, when one's gratitude towards sb.'s kindness or help cannot be expressed in words, 感激 can be used with a complement of degree:

① 他无微不至的照顾,让我**感激**得热泪盈眶。I am moved to tears at their considerate cares.

② 他的热情帮助,让我**感激**得不知说什么好。I am too moved to say anything for their warm-hearted help.

"感激"可与其他词语构成四字成语,如"感激涕零"、"感激莫名"等 ◇ 感激 can form four-character set phrases, e. g. 感激涕零(shed grateful tears),感激莫名(not to know how to express one's gratitude),etc.

"感谢"可做"表示"的宾语。"感激"可做"表示"或"表达"的宾语 ◇ 感谢 can be the object of 表示;感激 can be the object of 表示 or 表达:

③ 他对主人的热情款待表示**感谢**。He expressed his gratitude to the host's cordial treat.

④ 我们无法**表达**(/**表示**)我们的**感激**(之情)。We cannot express our gratitude to you.

干 做 搞

干	做	搞
(动)	(动)	(动)
gàn	zuò	gǎo

Ⓔ do, work/do, make/do

◥ 这三个动词都有从事的意思,具体意思很多 ◇ All the three verbs mean "to do sth". and can be applied to a lot of occasions.

1. 表示制造,用"做",有时用"搞" ◇ To mean "to make", 做 is used, and sometimes 搞 can be used instead:

① 他自己动手,**做**了一个电脑。He assembled a computer by himself.

② 用这块料子,可以**做**一身西服。The cloth can be made a suit.

例①也可以用"搞",还可以说"搞出":"他自己动手,搞(出)了一个电脑。"但"做衣服"是一种习惯搭配,不用"搞" ◇ In example ① 搞 can be used instead. One can also say 搞出:他自己动手,搞(出)了一个电脑. But 搞 is never used in such idiomatic collocation as 做衣服.

2. 表示从事某种工作或活动,大的可用“干”或“搞”,一般用“做”,各有习惯搭配 ◇ To mean "to engage in certain work or activity", if it is on a large scale, 干 or 搞 is used; if it is ordinary, 做 is used. They all have customary collocations, e. g. :

干	搞	做
干事业	搞事业	(无)
干工业	搞工业	(无)
干教育	搞教育	(无)
干基建	搞基建	(无)
(无)	搞生产	(无)
干工作	搞工作	做工作
干建设	搞建设	(无)
干艺术	搞艺术	(无)
干买卖	搞买卖	做买卖
(无)	搞生意	做生意
(无)	(无)	做工
干事	(无)	做事
干活儿	(无)	做活儿

(事业 cause　工业 industry
教育 education　基建 capital
生产 production/construction
建设 construction　工作 work
艺术 art　买卖 business
生意 business　工 job
事 work　活儿 work)

3. 表示担任、充当,一般用“做” ◇ To mean to hold the post of, 做 is usually used:

做教员 be a teacher
做售货员 be a shop assistant
做厂长 be a factory director

4. 表示进行文化艺术创作,多用“做” ◇ 做 is also used to mean "cultural or artistic creation":

做文章 write articles
做节目 make programmes
做诗 write a poem
做画 draw a fainting

5. 表示设法获得,用“搞” ◇ 搞 is used to mean "to secure or to manage to get":

搞钢材 get some steel
搞粮食 get some grain
搞原材料 get raw materials
搞点儿吃的来 get something to eat
搞点儿钱花 get some money

6. 表示人与人之间关系,用“搞” ◇ 搞 is used in human relations and personnel matters:

搞关系 build a relation
搞好团结 strengthen
搞好人事关系 foster good interpersonal relations
把人际关系搞坏了 spoil interpersonal relations

有时特指男女间的婚恋关系 ◇ Sometimes 搞 refers in particular to love affairs:

搞恋爱 be in love
搞对象 be in love

7. 表示有所成就,三个词都可以

用 ◇ All three words can be used to mean"accomplishment":

干出个样子来/搞出个样子来/做出个样子来 do well

干出点儿名堂/搞出点儿名堂/做出点儿名堂 make some achievements

8. 三个词还各有一些不同用法，如“做生日”、“做寿”，“做”是“庆祝”的意思；“搞小动作”、“搞破坏”、“搞阴谋”，“搞”是“进行”的意思（含贬义）；“把……干掉”、“干”这里是“杀”的意思，等等 ◇ Each of the three also has its own usages. In phrases like 做生日（celebrate birthday），做寿（celebrate birthday/hold a birthday party），做 means to celebrate. In 搞小动作（get up to little tricks），搞破坏（do damage to），搞阴谋（plot），搞 means "to carry out（with a derogatory sense）". In the phrase 把……干掉，干 means "to kill".

9. 在口语中，“干什么”用得较多 ◇ In colloquial language，干什么（What are you up to?）is often used:

① 你在**干什么**呢？（一般询问）What are you doing now?（ordinary inquiry）

② 这种机器是**干什么**的？（询问用途）What's the use of the machine?（inquire the usage）

③ 你**干什么**这样生气？（表示不解等）Why are you so angry?（to show puzzlement）

④ 我们**干点儿什么**消遣消遣呢？（其他）Let's do something to entertain us.（other inquiry）

以上，例①②④可换用“做”；例③“干什么”实际是“为什么”（“干”不能换用“做”）；例④也可换用“搞” ◇ In examples ①②④做 can be used instead. In example ③干什么 actually means 为什么（干 cannot be replaced by 做）; in example ④ 搞 can be used instead.

“干什么”在北方口语中还常做“干吗” ◇ In northern colloquial speech 干什么 is usually replaced by 干吗.

►［当 dāng—做 zuò］
［作 zuò—做 zuò］

刚 才 刚才

（副） （副） （名）
gāng cái gāngcái

Ⓔ just/just/just now

1. “刚”和“才”都可以表示不久以前 ◇ 刚 and 才 both mean "a short time ago":

① 他**刚**（/**才**）来了十分钟就走了。He stayed here just about ten minutes and then left.

“刚才”也可表示不久以前，着眼于

不久之前的那个时间。这时三个词可以互换 ◇ 刚才 also means "just now", emphasizing the time a moment ago. In this sense the three words are interchangeable:

② 你**刚才**(/**刚**/**才**)说了一句什么? What did you said just now?

因为"刚才"是时间名词,所以它可以做定语或宾语,如"刚才的事","车祸发生在刚才"。"才"和"刚"都不能这样用 ◇ Since 刚才 is a noun, it can be used as an attributive or object, e. g. 刚才的事(something in the past/something happened just now),车祸发生在刚才(The traffic accident of a moment ago). Neither 才 nor 刚 can be so used.

2. 下面主要就"才"的用法,比较一下三个词的异同 ◇ The usage of 才 is to be discussed below, in comparison with the other two words.

(1)"才"表示时间晚或长(用在时间词语之后) ◇ 才 means "the time is late or long (used after the time word or phrase)".

① 他夜里十二点**才**到家。(已然) He didn't get home until it was 12 p. m. (past)

② 要到7月中旬才放暑假。(未然) We will enjoy our holidays until the middle of July. (future)

没有时间词语也可以,如"你才到家呀!" ◇ 才 can be used without a time word or phrase, e. g. "你才到家呀!(You just got home?)"

这时,表示已然的例①也可以用"刚",而表示未然的例②不能用"刚"。"刚"只用于已然 ◇ In example ① 刚 can be used instead, but in example ② 刚 cannot be used. 刚 can only be used for something in the past.

"刚才"不能这样用 ◇ 刚才 cannot be so used.

(2)"才"表示时间早或短(用在时间词语之前) ◇ 才 means "the time is early or short (used in front of the time word or phrase)":

③ 雨**才**下了几分钟就停了。It rained just a few minutes and then stopped.

④ 今天**才**二号,离月中还远着呢。Today is the second day of the month. And there's a few days left to the middle of the month.

"刚"也可以这样用。"刚才"不能这样用 ◇ 刚 can be used instead, while 刚才 cannot.

(3)"才"强调数量大(用在数量词语之后) ◇ 才 stresses large quantity (used after the word or phrase of quantity):

⑤ 走了3公里,**才**到达目的地。

G

After three kilometers' walk, we arrived at the destination.

⑥ 需要几十块钱,**才**能买这么一本书。The book will cost you dozens of Yuan to buy it.

"刚"和"刚才"都不能这样用 ◇ Neither 刚 nor 刚才 can be so used.

(4)"才"表示数量小(用在数量词语之前) ◇ 才 stresses small quantity(used in front of the word or phrase of quantity):

⑦ 两个人**才**弄来半桶水。They two just fetched half barrel of water.

⑧ 花了那么多钱,**才**买了这么点儿东西。It cost us a lot of money to buy such a few items.

"刚"和"刚才"不能这样用 ◇ 刚 and 刚才 cannot be so used.

(5)"才"用在复句的第一分句,表示某一动作一完成即有另一动作发生 ◇ 才 is used in the first clause of a complex sentence to show one action is immediately followed by another:

⑨ 他**才**想说就被哥哥止住了。He was stopped by his brother as he was to say.

⑩ **才**吃完药就睡下了。He went to bed as soon as he took the medicine.

可用"刚",不能用"刚才" ◇ 刚 can be used instead, but not 刚才.

(6)"才"与"必须"、"只有"、"非"等连用,强调条件是惟一的或要求很高 ◇ When 才 is used in collocation with 必须, 只有 or 非, etc. it stresses the condition is the only one or the requirement is high:

⑪ 只有这种药**才**能治他这种病。Only this drug can cure this disease.

⑫ 评语必须实事求是,**才**能对作者有益。Only the true comments will do good to the author.

不能用"刚"或"刚才" ◇ Neither 刚 nor 刚才 can be so used.

(7)"才"在复句中表示前面说的目的是惟一的 ◇ 才 is used in a complex sentence to show that the preceding statement is the only aim:

⑬ 他是为了考大学**才**努力学习的。He studies hard just for going to college.

"刚"和"刚才"不能这样用 ◇ Neither 刚 nor 刚才 can be used instead.

(8)"才"表示强调,有时有辩驳的语气,句后常用"呢" ◇ 才 indicates stress and sometimes has a refuting tone. The sentence is often ended with 呢:

⑭ 他一定不会同意,他要是同意**才**怪呢! He is unlikely to agree. I bet.

⑮ 从前她**才**不是这样呢! She was not like this before.

⑯ 我**才**懒得管呢！I'm reluctant to care about it.

"刚"和"刚才"不能这样用 ◇ Neither 刚 nor 刚才 can be used instead.

高兴 快乐

(形、动) (形)

gāoxìng kuàilè

Ⓔ delighted, be pleased to/ happy

1. 作为形容词，这两个词都表示感到愉悦。但"高兴"是从兴致方面说，多指一时之事；"快乐"是从情绪方面说，所指之事可长可短，还含有幸福、满足的意思，同时较为书面化 ◇ As an adjective, both words mean to feel happy. But 高兴 is applied to mood, mostly sth. temporary, 快乐 is applied to sentiments which may be temporary or lasting. 快乐 also implies happiness and satisfaction, and is more literary:

① 今天你能来看我，我真**高兴**。I am very glad that you are able to see me today.

② 不知道为什么，他好像有点儿不**高兴**。I don't know why he's a bit unhappy.

以上两句，都指一时之事，同时较为口语化，所以应该用"高兴" ◇ In the two examples above, it is about sth. temporary and it is colloquial, so 高兴 should be used.

③ 祝你生日**快乐**！Happy birthday to you.

④ 他虽然活了不到六十岁，但是总的来说，是**快乐**的一生。Though he died in his sixties, generally speaking, he's happy all his life.

以上两句，所指时间或短或长，但都不是一时之事，而且较为正式，含有"幸福"的意思，所以应该用"快乐" ◇ In examples ③ and ④, what referred to is not temporary and is more formal, with happiness implied, so 快乐 is used.

指小事的时候，两个词都可以用 ◇ When referring to ordinary things, either word can be used:

⑤ 今天遇到的事，都是让人不太**高兴(/快乐)**的事。What we faced today is unpleasing.

较为正式的场合，用"快乐"不用"高兴"，如"快乐教育"、"快乐晚会"、"快乐时光"等 ◇ When referring to formal occasions, 快乐 and not 高兴 is used, e. g. 快乐教育(happy education), 快乐晚会(happy party), 快乐时光(happy time), etc.

2. "高兴"还是动词，常表示乐于或坚持选择做某事(一般为具体的事) ◇ 高兴 is also a verb,

meaning to be delighted in doing sth. (usually concrete):

① 她**高兴**穿这件衣服,就穿这件吧。She like wearing this one, so put on it.

② 至于这封信,他**高兴**怎么写就怎么写吧。He can write the letter at his will.

③ ——这件事你怎么这样处理? How can you deal with it this way?
—— 我**高兴**这么办! It's none of your business.

▶[兴奋 xīngfèn—高兴 gāoxìng]

G

告 (动) gào　**告诉** (动) gàosu　**告状** gào zhuàng

Ⓔ tell, inform/
tell, let know/
go to law against sb.

1. 表示用语言表达使人了解,一般用"告诉" ◇ To let people know something by language, 告诉 is used usually:

① 我**告诉**你一个好消息。I will tell a piece of good news.

② 他把这件事**告诉**张先生了。He told it to Mr. Zhang.

③ **告诉**我,你喜欢这个电影吗? Tell me if you like the movie.

有时也可用"告",但更为口语化,而且一般限于宾语是人称代词的时候。如例①可换用"告" ◇ Sometimes 告 can be used, which is more colloquial, usually limited to cases when the object is a personal pronoun. For example, in example ①告 can replace 告诉.

在"告诉(/告)……一声"这个结构中,两个词可以换用,这时"告"的口语色彩更浓 ◇ In the phrase 告诉(/告)……一声 the two words are interchangeable, and 告 is more colloquial.

④ 你**告诉**(/**告**)他一声,8点钟开会。Please inform him of the meeting at 8.

⑤ **告诉**(/**告**)妈妈一声,我今天晚上加班。Please tell my mother that I will overwork tonight.

在表示使公众等了解的书信中,用"告……书"形式,如《告全市人民书》、《告全校师生书》。或用"敬告……"等形式 ◇ In a notice to inform the public, the formula is 告……书 (The public statement for……), e.g.《告全市人民书》(The public statement for the city),《告全校师生书》(The public statement for the school). 敬告……(Notice to……) etc. can also be used:

⑥ **敬告**各位乡亲,工程即将开工,如有不便之处,请多原谅。Notice:The project is to start, and please forgive the inconvenience the construction will bring you.

2. 表示运作的实现,用"告",限于"告一段落"等固定短语。口语中的"告吹"表示没成功,则有诙谐意味 ◇ To show the realization of an action,告 is used,but is limited to some set phrases such as 告一段落. 告吹 in colloquial language is a humorous phrase meaning failure.

① 这件事已经**告一段落**。The matter is brought to a temporary close.

② 那个工程的建设**终告成功**。The project has been completed at last.

③ 这次试验已**告失败**。The test has failed.

④ 拨款的事**告吹了**! The fund earmarking has failed.

3. 表示请求批准,用"告",但限于"告假" ◇ To apply for ratification,告 is used,but only in 告假:

① 他家里有事,向单位**告**了两天**假**。He has a family affair to handle, so he asked for two days off.

② 公司里这么忙,如果没有特殊的事谁也不许**告假**! It is very busy in the company, so nobody is permitted to ask for leave if he has nothing special.

4. 表示诉讼、控诉、检举,用"告" ◇ To mean "accuse",告 is used:

① 我**告**你妨碍公务! I will charge you with hindering public affairs.

② 他因为涉嫌贪污被人**告**了。He has been accused of suspected embezzlement.

③ 这个案子**告**下来没有? Has the case been settled?

有时可用"告状"(动 + 宾) ◇ Sometimes 告状(verb + object) is used:

④ 他因为涉嫌贪污被人**告**了一状。He was accused of suspected embezzlement.

⑤ 她向法院**告**了邻居的状。She sued her neighbor.

给以 加以 予以

(动) (动、连) (动)

gěiyǐ jiāyǐ yǔyǐ

Ⓔ give/give/give,grant

1. 动词"给以"、"加以"、"予以"带出双音节的动词(一般为并列式的)作为宾语,表示的意思就是后面的双音节动词的意思。三个词都是书面化的词,其中“予以”最书面化,“加以”次之,“给以”又次之 ◇ The verb 给以,加以 or 予以 plus a disyllabic verb as the object indicates what the disyllabic verb means. All the three words are literary, with 予以 the most literary,加以 next, and 给以 the least. e. g. :

① 无故缺课的学生,必须**给以**(/**加以**/**予以**)严肃处理。The students must be punished severely for their absence without asking for leave.

② 这个问题至关重要,应该在一星期之内**给以**(/**加以**/**予以**)解决。The problem is very important and it should be settled in a week.

③ 小王工作出色,企业决定**给以**(/**加以**/**予以**)奖励。The company decides to reward Xiao Wang for his excellent work.

以上,三个词可互换,但书面色彩的浓淡程度有所不同 ◇ In the examples above, the three words are interchangeable, but the literary flavour is different.

注意:后面的双音节动词,在意义上都带有处置性。如果没有处置性,就不能用。如不能说“给以(/加以/予以)喜欢”,因为“喜欢”是表示自然的心理状态的,没有处置性 ◇ Note: The disyllabic verb that follows must have a meaning of " disposal". Otherwise, the verb cannot be used. e. g. , one cannot say 给以(/加以/予以)喜欢,because 喜欢 means " a natural state of mind" and has no meaning of " disposal".

如果不用“给以”等,句子也是成立的,但书面色彩和正式语气就淡化了。“给以”等也不能带十分口语化的双音节动词宾语,如不能说“给以(/加以/予以)打算” ◇ All these sentences can do without 给以, etc. but if so, they would not sound as literary or formal as the former ones. Furthermore, 给以, etc. cannot take a very colloquial disyllabic verb as the object, e. g. one cannot say 给以(/加以/予以)打算.

“加以”和“予以”有时可带动宾式的双音节宾语(如“除霜”、“结账”、“判刑”等) ◇ Sometimes 加以 and 予以 can take disyllabic verb-objects(such as 除霜 defrost, 结账 check out/settle accounts, 判刑 pass a sentence on a convict, etc.):

④ 冰箱应定期**加以**(/**予以**)除霜。The refrigerator should be defrosted regularly.

2. 动词“给以”和“予以”可以带有限的名词宾语,表示“给”,也较书面化 ◇ The verbs 给以 and 予以 can take a limited number of noun-objects, meaning "to give", and is rather literary:

① 对犯了一般过失的人,应该**给以**(/**予以**)改正错误的机会。Those who make a mistake should be given a chance to correct them.

② 小王学习成绩突出,学校决定**给以**(/**予以**)一等奖学金。The school decided to award Xiao Wang the first-class scholarship for his excellent schoolwork.

3. "加以"还是连词,用在表示因果关系的复句里,表示附加的或进一步的条件或原因 ◇ 加以 is also a conjunction, used in a complex sentence of cause and effect to show an additional condition or reason:

① 他身体不好,**加以**路途遥远,所以没有来。He didn't come here for he's not feeling well and he's far away from here.

② 由于连日刮风下雨,**加以**房屋年久失修,所以漏雨很厉害。The house leaked severely for it rained continuously and it is too old and out of repair for a long time.

③ 张师傅技术娴熟,**加以**机器的性能又很好,因此他做的活儿又快又好。Master Zhang is skillful, what's more, the function of the machine is good, so he is competent at his work.

跟 (连、介、动) gēn　和 (连、介) hé

Ⓔ and, as well as/
and, as well as

1. 连词"跟"、"和"都表示平等的联合关系。"跟"更为口语化 ◇ Both 跟 and 和 are used to show connection or addition of words or sentences of the same type or importance. 跟 is more colloquial:

① 哥哥**跟**(/**和**)弟弟都来了。The brother as well as his little brother has come.

② 他买了书**跟**(/**和**)笔。He bought books and pens.

③ 这两幅画,一幅是真迹,一幅是赝品,但是真的**跟**(/**和**)假的一般人根本看不出来。One of the two paintings is real; the other fake. However, they are too alike, and it is not easy for a layman to distinguish them.

④ 这件事,对你**跟**(/**和**)对我,一样重要。It matters much to you as well as me.

以上这些句子连接一般的主语、宾语或定语、状语,两个词可互

换 ◇ In connecting the subjects, objects, attributives, or adverbials in examples above, either word can be used.

"和"可以连接有共同状语或助动词做谓语的并列动词、形容词 ◇ 和 can connect coordinate verbs or adjectives as predicate with common adverbial or auxiliary verb:

⑤ 他一定会尽快认识**和**改正自己的错误。He is likely to realize and correct his mistakes.

⑥ 她的心情有些不安**和**焦虑。She is a bit unrest and anxious

"和"也可以连接有共同宾语或补语的作谓语的并列动词、形容词 ◇ 和 can also connect coordinate verbs or adjectives as predicate with a common object or complement:

⑦ 他发现**和**改正了文章中一些不妥之处。He found and corrected the inappropriate words in the article.

⑧ 室内的家具,安排**和**布置得十分合理。The display of the furniture in the house is placed well.

由于这种句子语法较复杂,语体较正式,多用"和"不用"跟" ◇ Since the grammar of these sentences is relatively complicated and the style is formal, 和, not 跟 is usually used.

2. 介词"跟"、"和"都表示协同等。"跟"更口语化 ◇ The prepositions 跟 and 和 both indicate coordination. 跟 is more colloquial.

① 她要**跟**(/**和**)我比赛。(动作由双方进行) She wants to compete with me. (action by both sides)

② 他**跟**(/**和**)我是好朋友。(表示对待关系) He is my good friend. (treatment)

③ 小王**跟**(/**和**)老王借了点儿钱。(表示"向") Xiao Wang borrowed some money from Lao Wang. (from)

④ 这事我**跟**(/**和**)他谈。(表示"对") I will talk to him about it. (with)

⑤ 几年不见,他**跟**(/**和**)从前不一样了。(表示比较) I haven't seen him for a few years and he is different as he was. (indicate comparison)

3. "跟"还是动词,表示跟随,紧接着做;"和"不能这样用 ◇ 跟 is also a verb meaning to follow; 和 cannot be so used.

① 爸爸在前面走,儿子**跟**在后面。The son followed his father.

② 你先干,我**跟**着你。You do it first, and I will follow you.

更改 (动) gēnggǎi　更换 (动) gēnghuàn　更正 (动) gēngzhèng

Ⓔ change, alter/ change, replace/ make corrections

◥ 这三个动词都有改变的意思 All the three verbs have the meaning of "change".

1. 对语言、文字、决定、章程等的错误或不适当的内容加以改变,用"更正";重点在于用正式方式以正确的代替错误的,如 ◇ To change or alter the mistakes or improper content in language, resolutions, regulations, etc., 更正 is used, that is, to replace the mistaken content with the correct one, e. g.:

① 上期杂志中有几处错误,这期发了**更正**启事。There are a few mistakes in the last issue of the magazine and they are corrected in this issue.

② 我昨天对职工的讲话,有一个数字说错了,应该**更正**一下。I'll try to make a correction of the wrong figure in the speech I delivered to the staff yesterday.

③ 章程中的"会费"一栏,"200 元"应**更正**为"100 元",请大家注意。200 *yuan* in the "Dues" column in regulations should be changed to 100 *yuan*.

以上例①"更正启事"是常见搭配。例②如果换用"更改",就没有"用正确的代替错误"的意思了,所以不合适。例③由于没有明确说"200 元"是错误的,所以这句可以换用"更改",但侧重点也不一样。三句都不能用"更换" ◇ In example ① 更正启事 is an idiomatic collocation. In example ② if 更改 is used instead, the meaning of "using the correct one to replace the mistaken one" would be lost, so it is not suitable. In example ③ since it is not stated that 200 元 is a mistake, so 更改 can be used instead, but the stress is different. None of the three can use 更换.

2. 按时间、空间需要的不同,加以变换,用"更换";重点在表示以新换旧,以合适的代替过时的,有轮换、替换的意味 ◇ To change owing to time or space, 更换 is used, with the stress on replacing the old with the new, or replacing the suitable with the outdated. e. g.:

① 人们按季节**更换**衣服。People change their clothes according to the seasons.

G

② 这张“入场须知”，颜色都发黄了，**更换**一张吧！The Admission Notice becomes yellowish, so change it, please.

③ 我个儿高你个儿矮，咱们俩**更换**一下座位，你坐前边，好吗？I'm taller than you, so would you like to change your seat with me and take a front seat?

④ 这一届领导班子的任期已到，人员要适当**更换**。The term of the leaders is due and some of them will be changed.

⑤ 这种空气清新器需要定期**更换**过滤网。The filter of air refresher should be changed regularly.

以上不能换用其他两个词 ◇ In the examples above, neither of the other two words can be used.

3. 一般的改变，则用“更改”。“更改”的原因有各种各样的，不一定是错误，适用范围也较广 ◇ For an ordinary change, 更改 is used. The reason for 更改 can be various, not necessarily a mistake. It also has a wider application. e. g. :

① 出发的时间需要**更改**一下。The start date need to be changed.

② **更改**名字，应该到有关单位报批。You should apply the department concerned for name changing.

③ 这项计划，作了一些**更改**。Some corrections have been made to the plan.

以上不能换用其他两个词。如果例③换用“改正”，那么，必是计划中有错误 ◇ In the examples above, the other two words cannot be used. If in example ③ 改正 is used instead, it must be due to some mistakes in the plan.

更 更加 还

（副） （副） （副）

gèng gèngjiā hái

Ⓔ more/more, even more/still

1.“更”用于比较，表示程度又深一层，做状语。可修饰单音节词或多音节词语 ◇ 更 is used in comparison to indicate a further degree and functions as an adverbial. It can modify monosyllabic as well as polysyllabic words.

① 这家商店的东西比那家**更**多。（修饰谓语）The goods in this shop are much more than those in that one. (modifying the predicate)

② 风刮得**更**厉害了。（修饰补语）The wind is much stronger. (modifying the complement)

③ 我要一张**更**大点儿的桌子。（修饰定语）I need a little bigger table. (modifying the attributive)

"更加"的意思同"更",比"更"略书面化,常修饰双音节或多音节词语。例②也可换用"更加"。例③"更大点儿"不能用"更加"。"更加"可修饰双音节词+(一)些 ◇ 更加 means the same as 更, but more literary. It usually modifies polysyllabic words or phrases. 更加 can be used instead in example ②. 更大点儿 in example ③ cannot be replaced by 更加. 更加 can modify disyllabic words plus(一)些, e. g.:

④ 比较起来,他显得**更加**(/**更**)成熟些。Comparatively, he looks much more mature.

"更"和"更加"一般放在补语之前 ◇ 更 and 更加 usually precede complements:

⑤ 她的脸色变得**更**(/**更加**)难看了。Her face becomes much paler.

⑥ 他的汉语说得**更**(/**更加**)流利了。He speaks Chinese more fluently.

而"更加"可放在"变得"、"说得"等之前,这是一种书面表达法("更"不能这样用) ◇ 更加 can precede 变得, 说得, etc. This is a literary expression(更 cannot be so used):

⑦ 听了这话,她的脸色**更加**变得难看了。Her face becomes even much paler at the words.

⑧ 上了一个月的培训班,他的汉语**更加**说得流利了。He speaks Chinese even more fluently after attending a training class of a month.

2. "还"的用法很多 ◇ 还 has many usages.

(1)表示动作或状态保持不变 ◇ Indicating that an action or state remains unchanged:

① 天黑了,他**还**在那里等着。It's dark, and he's still waiting there.

② 天气**还**要再冷几天。The cold will last several another days.

(2)表示虽然有某种情况,但不受影响 ◇ Indicating that a state remains unaffected by a certain factor:

③ 他虽然年纪大了,可是动作**还**那么灵敏。Though he is old, he is still agile.

④ 他病倒了,**还**惦记着工作。Even if he fell ill, he still thought of his work.

(3)表示不应如此而仍然如此 ◇ Indicating that a state remains unchanged though it should not be so:

⑤ 你**还**睡呢,快出去看看吧! You're still in bed. Hurry up and see what's happening outside.

⑥ 这么晚了,你怎么**还**没走? Why not leave for it's so late?

G

(4)表示有所补充 ◇ Indicating supplement:

⑦ 家里有父母,**还有**两个孩子。He lives with his parents and two children.

⑧ 学习汉语,除了多听多读,**还**得多和人说。Learning Chinese should practise speaking a lot besides listening and reading a lot.

(5)表示比较 ◇ Indicating comparison:

⑨ 这个女人比男人**还**能干。The woman is more capable than a man.

⑩ 这屋**还**没有那屋暖和。The room is not as warm as that one.

⑪ 你边学习边打瞌睡,**还**不如先出去走走。You might as well go out for a walk, for you are dozing off over studying.

(6)表示过得去 ◇ Meaning sth. is not bad:

⑫ 参加那个宴会,你这身打扮**还**可以。You look nice in this dress for the feast.

⑬ 这篇报告写得**还**行。The report is nice.

注意:以上"还"的各种用法,只有(5)中的例⑨可换用"更",即表示比较(用"比字句"的肯定式)。但在意思上,"更"只表示程度加深,"还"还带有非比寻常的语气 ◇ Note: In the examples above, only in example ⑨ of(5)更 can be used instead. But 更 only means "a higher degree", while 还 implies "sth. extraordinary".

有时,一个句子先用"还"举出突出的事例,再用"更"等表示不在话下或无能为力等 ◇ Sometimes in a sentence 还 is used first to introduce a striking example, then 更 etc. is used to emphasize the impossibility, etc:

⑭ 你还觉得这篇文章难,我就**更**不行了。If you think the article is difficult, let alone me.

⑮ 小的还买不起,大的就**更**不用说了。I cannot afford to buy the small one, let alone the bigger one.

3. 1 中例①的"更",也可换用"还",因为都是比较(用"比字句"的肯定式)◇ In example ① of 1, 更 can be replaced by 还 because they both mean "comparison":

⑯ 这家商店的东西比那家**还**多。The goods in this shop are much more than those in that one.

▶[还 hái—仍 réng—仍然 réngrán]

工夫 (名) gōngfu　　**时间** (名) shíjiān

Ⓔ time/time

◥ 这两个词都指“时候”。“时间”较正式;“工夫”只用于口语,多表示时段,较少表示时点。有时可互换 ◇ Both words mean "time". 时间 is more formal. 工夫 is only used in spoken language to mean "a period of time". Sometimes the two are interchangeable:

① 只用了十天的**工夫**(/**时间**),这篇论文就写成了。It only took me ten days to finish the thesis.

② 你有**工夫**(/**时间**)参加这个晚会吗? Do you have time to go to the party?

“时间”可用于正式的表述,“工夫”不能。“时间”还可组成“时间观念”、“节约时间”、“营业时间”等搭配,“工夫”也不能 ◇ 时间 can be used in formal speech, while 工夫 cannot. 时间 can make up phrases such as 时间观念 (time concept), 节约时间 (save time), 营业时间 (business time) etc. 工夫 is not so used:

③ **时间**就是生命。Time is life.

④ 这种软件可以为您节省宝贵的**时间**。The software can save you some time.

但“工夫”可说“工夫不大”、“不大工夫”,“时间”不能 ◇ 工夫 can be used in phrases of 工夫不大 or 不大工夫 (in very short time), but 时间 cannot be so used.

⑤ 不大**工夫**,他就办完了手续。He finished his formalities in a while.

⑥ **工夫**不大他就败下阵来。He was defeated after a while.

另外,“工夫”也作“功夫”,“功夫”还指本领、造诣,乃至武功等 ◇ Moreover, 工夫 can be written as 功夫 which also means "skill, ability, and even martial arts, etc".

▶[时候 shíhou—时间 shíjiān]

姑娘 女孩子

(名)

gūniang　　nǚ háizi

Ⓔ girl/girl

◥ 这两个词语都表示年轻未婚的女子,“姑娘”可用于当面称呼,“女孩子”不可以 ◇ Both words mean "girl". 姑娘 can be used as an address, but 女孩子 cannot.

① 那个**姑娘**(/**女孩子**)穿着很入时。The girl is in fashion.

② **姑娘**(/**女孩子**)长大了,总要嫁人的。A girl is likely to get married when she is grown up.

③ **姑娘**,你要买哪种面料? What kind of cloth would you like, Madam?

以上,例①②两个词可以互换。例③是称呼对方,用“姑娘”。注意:用于当面称呼时,一般为年纪大的人称呼年龄较小的女子。略大者，多称“小姐” ◇ In examples ① and ② the two words are interchangeable. In example ③, it is an address, so only 姑娘 can be used.(Note: generally it is used by an older person to address a young girl. For a girl of older age, 小姐 is used):

另外，“姑娘”还可以表示女儿；“女孩子”偶尔也可以表示女儿 ◇ Besides, 姑娘 can mean "daughter". 女孩子 occasionally means "daughter":

④ 他家一个儿子，一个**姑娘**。He has a son and a daughter.

⑤ 她生了一个男孩子，一个**女孩子**。She has a boy and a girl.

“姑娘”多与“儿子、小子”等并称，“女孩子”多与“男孩子”并称。也可以单说 ◇ 姑娘 is often used juxtaposedly with 儿子 or 小子, while 女孩子 with 男孩子, or by itself:

⑥ 他家只生了一个**姑娘**。He has a daughter only.

“姑娘”还特指未结过婚的女子，一般加定语“大” ◇ 姑娘 sometimes means "a woman who is never married", usually preceded by 大:

⑦ 她四十多了，还是**大姑娘**。She is single though she is forty years old.

鼓励 （动、名） gǔlì　　鼓舞 （动、名） gǔwǔ

Ⓔ encourage, encouragement/inspire, inspiration

◪ 这两个词都可表示使人振作、催人奋进。先看动词用法 ◇ Both words mean "to inspire, to encourage".

1. “鼓励”(动)的施事者常是人，“鼓舞”(动)的施事者常是事件 ◇ 鼓励, as a verb, usually has a person for its subject, while the subject of 鼓舞 is usually an incident:

① 老师**鼓励**他继续努力。The teacher encouraged him to study harder.

② 母亲**鼓励**孩子勇敢地承认错误。The mother encouraged her child to admit his mistakes.

③ 比赛的胜利**鼓舞**了大家的情绪。The triumph of the match encouraged us greatly.

④ 已经取得的好成绩，大大**鼓舞**了我们。Their good achievements encouraged us greatly.

2. “鼓舞”人的事件一般是积极性的，结果也是积极的，如1中例③的“胜利”和“情绪”。“鼓励”虽以正面为主，如例①②是正面的，但有时可以是消极的 ◇ The incident that encourages a person is usually positive and the result is positive too, e. g. 胜利 and 情绪 in example ③ of 1. 鼓励, though mainly positive, as in examples ① and ②, can also be used in a negative sense:

⑤ 那不是鼓励他做坏事吗? Isn't it to encourage him to do bad deeds?

上句的"做坏事"是非正面的、消极的 ◇ 做坏事 in the example above is negative.

3. "鼓励"前面可以加"给以"、"加以","鼓舞"不能这样用，但可以说"使人鼓舞"、"令人鼓舞"等 ◇ 鼓励 can be preceded by 给以, 加以, but 鼓舞 cannot. Yet we can say 使人鼓舞(uplifting) or 令人鼓舞(encouraging), etc.:

① 对学习优异的学生，学校应该给以**鼓励**。The school cited the excellent students.

② 这消息令人**鼓舞**。The news is encouraging.

4. 名词用法:"鼓励"较具体,"鼓舞"较宽泛 ◇ The implications of 鼓励 as a noun is more concrete, while that of 鼓舞 is more general:

① 学校给予的奖品和证书，对我是一种**鼓励**。The prize and certificate awarded by the school made me encouraged.

② 抗洪的胜利，对全国人民是一个很大的**鼓舞**。The successful anti-flood is an encouragement to the whole nation.

故意 有意

(形) gùyì　　(动) yǒuyì

Ⓔ intentional/ intentional, deliberate

1. 故意

表示明知有非一般的结果，却有意识地去做。常做状语，如做谓语只能纳入"是……的"框架 ◇ 故意 means " to do sth. on purpose". It is often used as an adverbial. As predicate, it can only appear in the pattern 是……的:

① 她**故意**不理小张。She took no notice of Xiao Zhang deliberately.

② 你怎么**故意**踩人的脚? Why do you step on my foot on purpose?

③ 对不起，我这样做不是**故意**的。I'm sorry I did it inadvertently.

2. 有意

(1)有某种意愿或心思，有时只是一种打算(也可能是不能实现的) ◇ To have a certain intention, sometimes may be just a plan(which may not be realized):

① 他今年夏天**有意**去江南旅游。He intends to take a trip to the south of the Yangtze River this summer.

② 他**有意**参加那个会,可惜没有时间。He is inclined to attend the meeting, but it is really a pity that he has no time

③ 我**有意**帮助他,不知他会不会接受。I intend to help him, but I wonder whether he will accept my offer.

(2)男女之间有爱慕之情 ◇ To have feelings of love between a man and a woman:

④ 她对你有意,你难道没有感觉吗? Don't you feel that she showed love for you?

⑤ 他们俩互相**有意**,只是还没有机会表达。They love each other; however, they have no chance to express.

(3)同"故意"。以下二句两个词可互换 ◇ Same as 故意. In the two examples below, the two words are interchangeable:

⑥ 他是**有意**(/**故意**)找我的麻烦。He troubled me on purpose.

⑦ 她**有意**(/**故意**)让那个人丢丑。She made the man lose face deliberately.

但这时"有意"较"故意"的意思有些淡化,所以1中例①②不能换用"有意"。也就是说,"故意"可以用于明知会立即产生不利于对方的后果的行动,而"有意"较为隐讳,不利于对方的后果未必实现,如下例用"故意"不用"有意" If ◇ 有意 is used, it will not be as serious as 故意, so in examples ① and ② of 1 有意 cannot be used instead. In other words, 故意 is used to mean "to do sth. on purpose" knowing the immediate result will be unfavorable to the other party, while denotation of 有意 is more obscure and may not be realized, so in example ⑧ 故意 and not 有意 is used:

⑧ 在比赛时,他**故意**绊倒了对方。He made his rival stumble on purpose in the match.

▶[有意 yǒuyì—存心 cúnxīn]

怪 (形) guài 奇怪 (形) qíguài

Ⓔ strange, unusual, odd/ strange, queer

◥ 这两个形容词都表示很不寻常的、出乎意料的。由于音节的不同,"怪"有时粘着,"奇怪"多能独立运用 ◇ Both adjectives mean "unusual, extraordinary". Since they have different numbers of syllables, 怪 is sometimes agglutinative, while 奇怪 can be used independently.

1. 做定语时,"怪"常可与单音节词直接搭配,"奇怪"一般需加"的" ◇ As an attributive, 怪 is collocated with monosyllabic words, while 奇怪 needs to take the particle 的:

① 真是**怪**事,一转眼她就不见了。Strange to say, she disappeared in an instant.

② 真是**奇怪**的事,一转眼她就不见了。Strange to say, she disappeared in an instant.

③ 他对老师提了一个**怪**问题。He asked his teacher an unusual question.

④ 他对老师提了一个**奇怪**的问题。He asked his teacher an unusual question.

这说明,"怪"直接修饰某些名词,带有一定的熟语性,再如"怪人"、"怪天气"、"怪腔怪调"等 ◇ This shows that 怪 can qualify some nouns directly to form set phrases, e. g. 怪人(an eccentric), 怪天气(strange weather), 怪腔怪调(speak in a queer way), etc.

2. 做谓语时,"怪"多带程度副词,"奇怪"有时可不带 ◇ As the predicate, 怪 often takes an adverb of degree, but 奇怪 does not have to:

① 这篇文章思路很**怪**。The organization of the article is unique.

② 这篇文章思路**奇怪**。The organization of the article is unusual.

③ 今天的天气真**怪**(/**奇怪**),一会儿晴天一会儿下雨。Strange to say, it rains and clears up in turn today.

例①用"很怪",程度副词不可省,例②用"奇怪"(可不用程度副词)。都带程度副词也是可以的(如例③) ◇ In example ① 很怪 is used and the adverb of degree cannot be omitted; in example ②奇怪 is used (adverb of degree can be omitted). Both can take adverbs of degree (as in example ③).

下列例句只能用"奇怪",不能用"怪" ◇ In the following examples, only 奇怪 and not 怪 can be used:

④ **奇怪**的是,她怎么吃都不胖。Strange to say, she doesn't put on weight no matter what she eats.

⑤ 令人**奇怪**的是,她吃什么都胖。Strange to say, she puts on weight no matter what she eats.

这也说明,"奇怪"多能独立运用 ◇ This shows 奇怪 can be used independently in most cases.

"怪"加"了"也可表示出人意料 ◇ 怪 plus 了 also means "unexpected"; and 了 is necessary:

⑥ **怪**了,他说来怎么没来?

G

Why, he hasn't come, but he promised me.

“怪”也是副词,表示很、非常,与“奇怪”完全不同。“怪”还是动词,表示责怪等,更不一样了 ◇ 怪 is also an adverb, meaning "very", which is entirely different from 奇怪. 怪 is also a verb meaning "to blame", and 奇怪 does not have such an usage at all.

G

管 (动) guǎn　管理 (动) guǎnlǐ

Ⓔ be in charge; manage; run/ be in charge; manage; run

◪ 这两个动词有共同点,也有不同之处 ◇ The two verbs have meanings in common but also there are differences in between.

1. 表示保管、料理,有时两个词可互换 ◇ Both mean "to take care of". Sometimes they are interchangeable:

① 这些资料请你**管**(/**管理**)一下。Please take care of these materials.

② 小张负责**管**(/**管理**)仓库。Xiao Zhang is in charge of the warehouse.

但“管理”较正式;“管”多用于口语,可与单音节词搭配。下列二例,不能互换 ◇ But 管理 is more formal; 管 is colloquial and can be collocated with monosyllabic words. In the two examples below, the two words are not interchangeable:

③ 这个机关应该加强资金使用的计划和**管理**。The department should enhance the planning and management of the capitals.

④ 你来**管**账吧。Would you like to be in charge of the account?

例④如用“管理”,应说“管理账目” ◇ In example ④ if 管理 is used, one must say 管理账目.

2. 表示看管、操作,常用“管” ◇ To mean "to operate, manipulate", 管 is mostly used:

① 这台机器由她**管**。She is in charge of the machine.

② 张师傅**管**水泵。Master Zhang is in charge of the hydro-pump.

3. 表示管辖,用“管” ◇ 管 is used to mean "to administer or have jurisdiction over":

① 派出所归公安局**管**。The police substation is under the supervision of the public security bureau.

② 那个市**管**三个区。The city has three prefectures.

4. 表示担任或负责(职务、工作),常用“管”;较正式的可用“管理” ◇ 管 is usually used to mean " assuming the office of or holding the post of(to be more formal)",管理 can be used:

① 小张**管**文化娱乐工作。Xiao Zhang is in charge of cultural and entertainment affairs.

② 县长要**管**(/**管理**)全县的事情。The head of a county is in charge of the whole county affairs.

5.表示过问、干预、管教,用"管" ◇ To mean " to intervene, to concern oneself with, and to discipline",管 is used:

① 这是他的私事,别人**管**不着。It's his affairs and it's none of others' business.

② 她爱唱歌,你何必**管**她? Since she likes singing. Why interfere with her singing?

③ 夜晚的马路市场得**管一管**了! It's high time that the night market in the street was supervised.

6.表示照管、约束、监管,两个词都可用,但"管理"较正式 ◇ To mean "take care of, discipline, supervise", both words can be used, but 管理 is more formal:

① 张老师**管**(**管理**)教学,很有经验。Teacher Zhang has experience of teaching supervision.

② 这个部门是**管**(/**管理**)缉私事务的。The department is in charge of anti-smuggling affairs.

7.表示保证、负责供给,用"管" ◇ To mean "to guarantee, to supply",管 is used:

① 这种电器如果有问题,厂家保修**管**换。If there is something wrong with the electric appliance, the manufacturer guaranteed to repair or change it.

② 这个公司中午**管**职工一顿饭。The company provides lunch for its staff.

③ 到这家餐厅用餐,**管**你满意。You will be satisfied with the restaurant.

光	亮
(名)	(形)
guāng	liàng

Ⓔ light/bright

这两个词都与发光有关。但"光"是名词,指光波、光线。"亮"是形容词,指光线较强的 ◇ Both words concern with "light", but 光 is a noun meaning light and 亮 is an adjective meaning "bright".

1. **光**(名)

① 夜行人看到远处有**光**,就知道前面有人家了。The nightwalker knew there were households there when he saw the light in the distance.

② 这是什么**光**？是月光还是灯光？What light is it? Moonlight or lamplight?

"光"(名)有时指荣誉、光彩 ◇ 光(n.) sometimes means honour or glory.

③ 儿子出息了，他也觉得脸上有**光**。He is proud of his son's success.

④ 这几位科学家得了国际大奖，为国争了**光**。The several scientists got the reputation for our country for their international awards.

2. 亮(形)

① 房间里光线不错，显得很**亮**。The lighting of the room is nice, so it is bright.

② 灯怎么不**亮**？换个灯泡吧！Why is the light so dim? Change a bulb.

③ 这种日光灯比一般的白炽灯**亮**。The fluorescent lamp is brighter than the ordinary one.

"亮"有时还指发光 ◇ 亮 sometimes means "to shine, to give out light":

④ 漆黑的夜空**亮**了一下，是打闪了。The night flashed. It's lightening.

⑤ 手电筒不**亮**了，一定是没电了。The torch is off. It must be out of power.

或指声音强而好听 ◇ Or means "a resonant and beautiful voice":

⑥ 她嗓子真**亮**。Her voice is resonant.

⑦ 这位民歌手的歌声又脆又**亮**。The folk singer can sing resonantly.

还有明辨是非的比喻义，多用于四字语"心明眼亮"或一般的"眼睛不亮"、"眼睛很亮"等 ◇ It also has a metaphorical meaning of "making clear distinction between right and wrong", often used in four-character phrases, e.g. 心明眼亮(see and think clearly), 眼睛不亮(unsharp eyed), 眼睛很亮(sharp-eyed), etc.

▶[亮 liàng—明亮 míngliàng]

光 (副) guāng　　只 (副) zhǐ

Ⓔ only/only

◪ 这两个副词都表示限制，"光"只表示限制范围，"只"可表示限制范围或数量。"光"更为口语化 ◇ Both adverbs indicate "limitation". 光 only limits the range, while 只 can limit the range as well as the quantity. 光 is more colloquial.

1. 限制范围 ◇ To limit the range:

① 遇到困难，不能**光**(/**只**)着

急,要积极想办法。Don't be just worried when facing difficulties. You should find a way out.

② 我们**光**(/**只**)有个计划,一切都没实现呢! We only have a plan and it has not been fulfilled yet.

③ **光**(/**只**)靠你一个人不行,要靠大家。It's impossible to rely on only you, we should rely on all of us.

以上例句,两个词可互换,但"光"更为口语化。虽然是限制范围,在十分书面化的句子中,宜用"只"不用"光" ◇ In the examples above, the two words are interchangeable but 光 is more colloquial. Though the limit is on range, in very literary sentences, it is better to use 只 instead of 光:

④ **只**因缺乏管理经验,这次试验以失败告终。The test failed just because we lack experience.

⑤ 你这样说,是**只**见树木,不见森林。What you said is like seeing the trees only but not the forest.

例⑤用"只"也因为"只见树木,不见森林"是固定格式(格言) ◇ In example ⑤ 只 is used, because 只见树木,不见森林 is a set phrase(maxim).

2. 限制数量 ◇ To limit the quantity:

① 咱们**只**有三个人,三缺一,不能玩桥牌。There are only three people here, so it's impossible for us to play bridge.

② 米**只**剩几斤了,得去买。The rice is only a few *jin* left, so we have to buy some.

③ 他们俩住得很近,相隔**只**三四里。They live close to each other and there is only three *li* or four from each other.

以上例①②③只能用"只" ◇ In examples ①②③, only 只 can be used.

"光"即便是在数量词语之前,也不是限制数量,而是表示除此以外没有别的,或不把别的计算在内 ◇ Even if used in front of a word or phrase of quantity, 光 does not limit the quantity but means "there is nothing besides this, or nothing else is included":

④ **光**他一个人着急,又有什么用呢? It's no use that only he is worried.

⑤ **光**最近两年,他就发表了10篇文章。He has published 10 articles just in the past two years.

以上例④可换用"只有他……",例⑤可换用"只",但不如用"光"口语化 ◇ In example ④ 光 can be replaced by 只有他……;

G

whereas in example ⑤ 光 can be replaced by 只,but 只 is not as colloquial as 光.

光彩 光荣

(名、形) (名、形)

guāngcǎi guāngróng

Ⓔ luster;brilliant/ glory,honour;glorious

G

1. 表示悦目的色泽,用"光彩"(名)。习惯搭配短语有"光彩夺目"、"光彩照人"等("光彩照人"还可用于业绩等) ◇ To mean "beautiful colour",光彩(noun) is used. Idiomatic phrases are 光彩夺目(be bright-colored and dazzling),光彩照人(shine with brilliance),etc. (光彩照人 can also be applied to achievements):

① 在灯光下面,展出的产品都闪着夺目的**光彩**。In the light,all the items on display are glittering.

② 由于保存不好,这几件首饰已经失去了昔日的**光彩**。The jewels have lost their luster because of ill-keeping.

③ 这款新型汽车**光彩**夺目,引人注意。The car is glittering and attractive.

④ 这些歌星,个个打扮得**光彩**照人! These singers were dressed elegantly.

2. 表示荣誉、较大的事情常用"光荣"(名),较具体的事情也可用"光彩"(名词,常和"脸上"搭配) ◇ To mean "honour",光荣 is used for big events;for more concrete things,光彩 can also be used (often in collocation with 脸上):

① 小李得了数学大奖,这是她的**光荣**,也是学校的**光荣**。Xiao Li won the big prize of math, which is her glory as well as her school's.

② **光荣**归于祖国。Glory is attributed to our motherland.

③ 企业赚了钱,推销人员脸上也觉得有**光彩**。The salesman takes pride in his company's profits.

④ 学生犯了错误,张老师也觉得脸上没有**光彩**。Mr. Zhang felt ashamed of his student's mistakes.

3. 表示值得称道、尊敬的,较具体的事情或感觉用"光彩"(形),可做谓语、定语 ◇ To mean "praiseworthy, respectable",光彩(adj.) can be used for concrete things or feelings as predicate and attributive.

① 小张上了名牌大学,父母觉得脸上很**光彩**。Xiao Zhang's parents felt glorious at his being admitted by a famous university.

② 女朋友被人欺负,他却不敢吱声,真不**光彩**! How shameful he is! For when his girlfriend was bullied, he dared not to give her a hand at that time.

③ 小学生拾金不昧,这是**光彩**的事。It's honored that a pupil returns what he finds.

较大的事情或较抽象的感觉可用"光荣"(形),而且可做状语(例⑤⑥) ◇ For bigger events or abstract feelings, 光荣 (adj.) can be used and can also function as adverbials (e. g. in examples ⑤⑥):

④ 为人民立了大功,这几位公务员觉得非常**光荣**。The several civil servants felt proud of their merits for the people.

⑤ 在从事教育工作满三十年的时候,他**光荣**地获得了学校的奖励。He was prized by his school where he had been teaching for 30 years.

⑥ 老刘是在抗洪前线**光荣**牺牲的。It was in the antiflood front that Lao Liu lost his life.

⑦ 村子里给军属老李送来了"**光荣**之家"的匾额。The village presented the Lis a frame with " Glorious Family ", for their child is serving in the army.

换一个角度看,"光彩"(形)侧重于外部观感,而"光荣"侧重于全面表现 ◇ Looked at from another angle, 光彩 (adj.) stresses external impressions, while 光荣 stresses the overall manifestation.

有时,大事或小事的分别较模糊,外部观感或内心自豪感也分不大清时,两个词可换用,如 ◇ Sometimes, when the distinction between a big event and a trifle is not clear, nor is it clear-cut between the external impression and the overall manifestation, the two words are interchangeable. e. g.:

⑧ 见义勇为,这是**光彩**(/**光荣**)的事,值得赞扬。It's glorious that you do bravely what is righteous.

逛 游 游览

(动) (动) (动)

guàng yóu yóulǎn

Ⓔ stroll/
rove around/
go sightseeing; tour

这三个词都表示从容地边走边看。"逛"多用于口语,"游览"较书面化,"游"的语体色彩较为一般 ◇ All three words mean "to go sightseeing". 逛 is colloquial, 游览 is literary, and 游 is rather general.

"逛"常说"逛大街"、"逛商店"、"逛公园",甚至可说"到处逛逛”。“游”常说“游园”。“游览”多与成双词语搭配：“游览名胜”、“游览名山大川”。由于习惯搭配不同，所以完全互换的可能性不多。下列例句不可互换 ◇ With 逛, we usually say 逛大街(take a stroll in the street), 逛商店(go window-shopping), 逛公园(go to a park), 到处逛逛(stroll around); with 游, we usually say 游园(visit a garden). 游览(go sightseeing) is mostly used with disyllabic words, e. g. 游览名胜(visit places of interests/visit well-known scenic spots), 游览名山大川(visit famous mountains and great rivers). Since the three words have different customary collocations, there is little chance of interchange. In the following examples the three verbs are not interchangeable:

① 她非常喜欢**逛**商店。She likes window-shopping very much.

② **游**了一天西湖，有点儿累了。I'm a bit tired after a day's visiting the West Lake.

③ 旅游团今天**游览**市容。The travel group is going to visit the city today.

总的来说，“逛”侧重于人工景点、商店等；“游”侧重于自然风景；“游览”侧重于名胜古迹，另外，“游”还有游泳的意思 ◇ Generally, the objects of 逛 are often artificial landscape, stores, etc, while 游 emphasizes natural landscape; and 游览 emphasizes places of historical interest and scenic beauty. Besides, 游 also means "to swim":

④ 他一口气**游**到了对岸。He swam to the other side of the river without a break.

国 (名) guó　　国家 (名) guójiā

Ⓔ country, nation/ country, nation

“国”是半粘着词和准量词，“国家”是自由词。“国家”可以独立运用 ◇ 国 is a quasi-agglutinative word and para-measure word. 国家 is a free word and can be used independently:

① **国家**为了振兴科学和教育，投入了相当多的资金。To invigorate the science and education, the country has invested much in them.

② 我们必须维护**国家**的尊严。We must safeguard our country's dignity.

这里都不能用“国” ◇ 国 cannot be used instead in examples ①②.

“国”用于国名，如“中华人民共和国”、“美国”、“日本国”等。另外，前面加数词，可说“一国两制”、“两国建立了外交关系”等

◇ 国 is used in the name of a nation, e. g. 中华人民共和国, 美国, 日本国, etc. A numeral can be used in front of it without a measure word, e. g. 一国两制(one country, two systems)、两国建立了外交关系(The two countries have established diplomatic relationship), etc.

加方位词,可说"国外"、"国内"等。前面加指代词,可说"我国"、"各国"、"你是哪国人"等。前面加动词,可说"出国"、"回国"、"复国"、"亡国"、"(科教)兴国"等,没有这些条件,"国"不能独立运用 ◇ A noun of locality can be added to 国, e. g. 国外(abroad), 国内(home), etc. It can be preceded with a demonstrative pronoun or personal pronoun, e. g. 我国(our country), 各国(all countries), 你是哪国人(Where are you from?), etc. What's more, it can be preceded with a verb, e. g. 出国(go abroad), 回国(return to one's country), 复国(restore the ruling), 亡国(doom of a country), (科教)兴国(in vigorate a country by science and technologies), etc. Otherwise, 国 cannot be used independently.

果实 (名) guǒshí　　成果 (名) chéngguǒ

Ⓔ fruit/achievement, fruit

"果实"可以表示植物体的一部分 ◇ 果实 may mean "a part of a plant, its fruit":

① 苹果是苹果树的**果实**。An apple is the fruit of apple tree.

"果实"还可有抽象意义,指劳动、工作、战斗后得到的收获。如"劳动果实"、"胜利果实"等 ◇ 果实 also has an abstract sense, meaning "the result of labour, work or fight", e. g. 劳动果实(fruits of work/labor), 胜利果实(fruits of achievements), etc. For example:

② 这个研究课题,经过几年才取得成功,胜利**果实**确实来之不易啊! The subjects succeeded at last after dozens of years' efforts. How hard the success is!

"成果"指工作、事业的成绩、收获 ◇ 成果 means "the achievement of work or undertaking":

③ 他们近年在太阳能的开发和利用上很有**成果**。They have been making great progress in solar energy these years.

④ 由于双方意见严重分歧,会谈没有取得什么**成果**。No result achieved in the talks for there was a big difference of the two parties.

虽然都指工作的收获,但"果实"的比喻性较强,常说"劳动果实"、"胜利果实"等。而"成果"

主要是客观评价，常说“有成果”、“没有成果”、“取得了成果”、“丰硕的成果”等。所以例②与例③④不能换用 ◇ Though both indicate the achievement of work，果实 is more figurative and can be used in 劳动果实（fruits of work/labor），胜利果实（fruits of achievements），etc. 成果 mainly indicates the objective evaluation, e. g. 有成果（be fruitful），没有成果（achieved no fruit），取得了成果（achieved fruits），丰硕的成果（be fruitful），etc. So 果实 in example ② is not interchangeable with 成果 in examples ③④.

▶［结果 jiéguǒ—成果 chéngguǒ—后果 hòuguǒ］

过（动）guò 过度（动）guòdù 过分（副）guòfèn

Ⓔ exceed/exceed/excessive

“过”的义项很多，这里只比较“过”的“超过”义与“过度”、“过分”的区别 ◇ 过 has many meanings. Here we just analyze the difference between its meaning of exceeding and 过度 and 过分.

“过”表示超过一定的标准或限度，一般是客观的叙述。“过度”表示超过限度，主要用于身体、精神的承受，一般也是客观叙述。而“过分”表示超过分寸和本分，主要用于人的言谈举止，带有主观的评价色彩 ◇ 过 means "over a certain standard or limit" and is a generally objective statement. 过度 means "outstrip a limit" and is mainly applied to the endurance of the body or spirit, also in an objective statement. 过分 means "to outstrip proper limits or one's duty", usually applied to one's speech and deportment with the colour of subjective evaluation, e. g.:

① 这本词典内容很好，可惜字体**过**小。The dictionary is very nice, but it's a pity its typeface is too small.

② 钟挂得**过**高了，都看不清楚了。We cannot see the time clearly for the clock is hung too high.

③ 这两天他忙于工作，疲劳**过度**，需要好好休息一下。He is too tired for he has been working for two days and he needs a rest.

④ 一个人的精神，长时间处于**过度**兴奋状态，也是不正常的。It is abnormal for a man if he is too excited for a long time.

⑤ 你对她说话这么没礼貌，太**过分**了。You go too far, for you talk to her too rudely.

⑥ 科长严厉批评他工作不尽心，

并不**过分**。It's not too much for the sector head to severely blame his careless working.

以上例句三个词不能互换 ◇ In the examples above the three words are not interchangeable.

但在口语中,有时"太过"、"太过了"表示过分,这时与"过分"的肯定式有共同点,可互换 ◇ But in colloquial speech, sometimes 太过, 太过了 mean 过分. In this case, they are interchangeable:

⑦ 父母对他的迁就太**过**(/**过分**)了。Their parents went too far, for they gave in to him.

另外,像"谦虚"等既属于精神也属于言谈举止的词语,"过分"和"过度"都可以 ◇ Besides, with words such as 谦虚 which indicate spirit as well as behaviour, either 过分 or 过度 can be used:

⑧ **过分**(/**过度**)谦虚,反而不自然。Over-modesty is unnatural instead.

这时"过分"的主观评价色彩自然更浓些 ◇ Here the subjective evaluation of 过分 is even stronger.

至于"饮酒过度"等,虽然也有分寸问题,但因其属于身体的承受度,不属于言谈举止,所以不宜用"过分"。如果用"过",应说"饮酒过量" ◇ As to 饮酒过度, etc., which also concerns sense of propriety, since it is related to the physical endurance and not behaviour, 过分 is not suitable. If 过 is used, one ought to say 饮酒过量 (overdrink).

H

还 仍 仍然

(副) (副) (副)

hái réng réngrán

Ⓔ still/still/still, yet

◪ 我们已经比较了"更"、"更加"和"还",对"还"的各种义项都作了分析。现在再比较一下"还"、"仍"、"仍然"。关于"还"的用法不再重复。"仍"、"仍然"都较书面化,表示某种情况、状态继续不变或恢复原状 ◇ We have compared 更, 更加 and 还 and thoroughly analyzed their different usages. Now we are going to analyze 还, 仍, 仍然. The usages of 还 will not be repeated. 仍 and 仍然 are more literary and indicate that some state remains unchanged or resumes its original form:

① 夜**仍**(/**仍然**)是那么静,好像什么事也没有发生。The night is still as before, as if there is nothing happening.

② 企业走出困境,**仍**(/**仍然**)需要一定时间。It will still take some time for the enterprise to step out of its difficult position.

③ 他毕业后**仍**(/**仍然**)在原来的大学工作。He returned to his original university to work after his graduation.

④ 用完辞书请**仍**(/**仍然**)放回原处。Please return the reference book to its original place on the shelf after reading.

以上四句可换用"还",但较为口语化 ◇ In the four examples above, 还 can be used instead, but is more colloquial.

在音节上,"仍"多与单音节搭配,如例②可说"仍需一定时间" ◇ 仍 is mostly used in collocation with monosyllabic words, e. g. in example ② one can say 仍需一定时间.

"还"的有些义项(表示比较、补充等),不能用"仍"、"仍然" ◇ There are some other usages of 还 (indicating comparison, supplement, etc.) which cannot be replaced by 仍 or 仍然.

▶ [更 gèng—更加 gèngjiā—还 hái]
[仍 réng—仍然 réngrán—仍旧 réngjiù]

还是 (连) háishi　　或者 (连) huòzhě

Ⓔ or/or

◪ 这两个连词,都表示选择关系,“还是”用于询问或含有问题的叙述中,“或者”常用于叙述 ◇ Both conjunctions indicate "alternative relationship". 还是 is used in inquiry or a statement which contains inquiry. 或者 is often used in statements.

① 你去**还是**不去? Are you going to or not?

② 今天是星期二**还是**星期三? Is today Tuesday or Wednesday?

③ 阴天**还是**晴天都无所谓。It matters little whether it is fine or not.

④ 吃中餐**还是**吃西餐,你自己决定吧。It's up to you that we are to take Chinese food or Western food.

以上,例①②是单纯的询问,用“还是”。例③④也可用“或者” ◇ Examples ① and ② are pure inquiries, so 还是 is used. In examples ③ and ④ 或者 can be used instead.

⑤ 他准备五月**或者**六月出发。He is going to start either in May or June.

⑥ 大会工作语言,可以用汉语**或者**英语。The congress languages can be either in Chinese or English.

例⑤⑥是纯叙述,用“或者” ◇ Examples ⑤ and ⑥ are pure statements, so 或者 is used.

这两个词都可以连用:“还是……还是……”、“或者……或者”,前者常用于询问,后者常用于叙述 ◇ Both words can be repeated like 还是……还是……, 或者……或者. The former is used in inquiry and the latter in statement:

⑦ 你喝茶**还是**喝咖啡? **还是**喝饮料? Which would you prefer: tea, coffee or drinks?

⑧ 晚饭以后,他们**或者**散步**或者**听音乐。After supper, they either listen to music or go for a walk.

▶[或者 huòzhě—或 huò]

害怕 (动) hàipà　　怕 (动、副) pà

Ⓔ fear; be afraid of/ fear; be afraid of; most probably

◪ **1**. 动词“害怕”和“怕”都可表示有恐惧不安之感 ◇ Both 害怕 and 怕 mean "to be afraid of":

H

① 我今天是第一次学游泳，真有点儿**害怕**(/**怕**)。I was a bit afraid when I learnt swimming today for the first time.

② 到国外去闯闯吧，没有什么可**害怕**(/**怕**)的。Go abroad to have a try, for there's nothing scary.

以上二例可以互换。"怕"可直接表示惧怕，如"老鼠怕猫"，"害怕"较少这样用 ◇ In examples ① and ② either 害怕 or 怕 can be used. 怕 can be used directly to mean "actual fear", e. g. 老鼠怕猫(A rat is afraid of a cat). 害怕 is rarely so used.

动词"怕"还表示担心 ◇ 怕 as a verb also means "to worry":

③ 雨这么大，我**怕**他来不了。I'm afraid he will not come back for it is raining heavily.

④ 这个箱子很重，我**怕**拿不动。I'm afraid I cannot lift the box for it's too heavy.

一般的担心用"怕"，如果担心有较大的风险，也可用"害怕" ◇ 怕 is used for usual fear. If there is some risk, 害怕 can be used:

⑤ 飞机晚点了四个钟头还没消息，我**害怕**(/**怕**)会出事。I'm very worried that there is something wrong with the plane for it is late for four hours.

2. 副词"怕"表示估计，也多用于非一般的(或以为非一般的)情况。"害怕"不这样用 ◇ 怕 as an adverb indicates estimation, used in unusual (or supposed unusual) occasion. 害怕 cannot be so used.

① 这么晚了，他**怕**是不会来了。I'm afraid he won't come, for it's so late.

② 这本词典，**怕**得上百元吧！I guess the dictionary will cost you more than 100 *yuan*.

寒 (形) hán　寒冷 (形) hánlěng　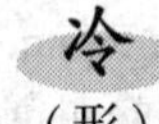 (形) lěng

Ⓔ cold/cold/cold

1. 表示气温低 Indicating low temperature:

"寒"、"寒冷"、"冷"三个词都可表示气温低。"冷"可以自由运用；"寒"多用于固定短语；"寒冷"也可自由运用，但较书面化。下边例①②"冷"和"寒冷"都可使用，但语体色彩有所不同；例③④只能用"寒" ◇ 寒、寒冷、冷 all indicate "low temperature". 冷 can be used freely; 寒 is mostly used in set phrases; 寒冷 can also be used freely, but is more literary. In examples ① and ② below, either 冷 or 寒 can be used, but with different styles. In examples ③ and ④ only 寒 can be used:

① 今年的冬天特别**冷**(/**寒冷**)。It's very cold this winter.
② 这么**冷**(/**寒冷**)的天气,你还要出门? Are you going outside in such a cold day?
③ 尽管是数九**寒**天,大家仍然喜欢到户外活动。Everyone likes going out even if it is in harsh winter.
④ 冬天要注意防**寒**保暖,以免感冒。Pay attention to keep warm in winter in case of catching.

2. 表示情绪、感情低落或不热情 ◇ Indicating " low or cold, indifferent attitude":

常用"冷冷"、"冷下来"、"不冷不热"、"心灰意冷"等。"寒"用得很少,限于"寒心"、"寒了心"(表示失望) ◇ Usually 冷冷 (coldly)、冷下来 (becomes cold)、不冷不热(neither cold nor hot)、心灰意冷(be disheartened) etc. are used. 寒 is seldom used by itself, but can be used in phrases 寒心(be bitterly disappointed)、寒了心(was bitterly disappointed) meaning disappointed:

① 她对小王一直是**冷冷**的。She is cold to Xiao Wang all the time.
② 小王约她吃晚饭,她**冷冷**地说:"对不起,我有事!"小王的心里一下子就凉了半截。Xiao Wang invited her for a dinner, but she just said coldly: I'm sorry, for I have other things to do. This made him very disappointed.
③ 她对小王简直是**冷若冰霜**,小王只能知难而退。She is very cold to Xiao Wang and he has no choice but to give up.
④ 小王的热情逐渐**冷下来**了。Xiao Wang's passion is fading.
⑤ 这事真让小王**寒心**。This made Xiao Wang upset.

"冷"还有生僻、寂静、不受欢迎等含义,但多用于词语中,如"冷僻"、"冷清"、"冷货"等 ◇ 冷 also means "rare, quiet, not well-received, etc", but it is usually a part of a word, for example: 冷僻(deserted), 冷清(desolate), 冷货(dull goods), etc.

▶ [冷 lěng—凉 liáng—凉快 liángkuai]

喊	叫	嚷
(动)	(动)	(动)
hǎn	jiào	rǎng

Ⓔ shout, yell/
shout, cry/
shout, yell

◪ 这里只比较这三个动词。另外,"叫"还是介词 ◇ Here we only compare the three as verbs. Besides, 叫 is also a preposition.

1. 表示发出大声,三个词都可

用,其中"嚷"的声音最大,"喊"次之,"叫"一般。"叫"可用于人和动物,其他两个词只用于人。如下列二例三个词都适用,但声音大小仍有不同 ◇ The three words all mean " to shout". 嚷 is the loudest, 喊 is next to it and 叫 is just ordinary. 叫 is applied to human beings and animals while the other two are applied to human beings only. All the three words can be used in examples ① and ② but with different degree of loudness:

① 孩子看见一个黑影,吓得**叫**(/**喊**/**嚷**)了起来。The child was frightened to cry when he saw a black figure.

② 不要**叫**(/**喊**/**嚷**),别人都睡觉了。Don't cry! For others are sleeping.

如果是动物,只用"叫" ◇ If it is an animal, only 叫 can be used:

③ 鸡**叫**了,天亮了。It is dawning and the cock is crowing.

④ 看看屋外狗**叫**什么呢? Go and see why the dog is barking outside.

⑤ 羊在咩咩地**叫**着。The goat is baaing.

至于"汽笛在叫"等,一般是拟人表达法 ◇ As to the phrase 汽笛在叫(steam whistle is whistling), it is personification.

2. 表示为了宣传等大声地喊简短的话,用"喊口号"、"喊话" ◇ To shout slogans loudly or shout propaganda to enemy troops across the frontline, 喊口号 or 喊话 is used:

① 大街上,欢庆的队伍**喊**着口号前进。The festival parade is matching shouting the slogan.

② 两军对垒,互相**喊**话劝降。The two armies are in conflict and they shout to their enemies to persuade them into surrendering.

3. 表示呼唤、招呼,一般用"叫",有些地区可用"喊" ◇ To call, greet, 叫 is used, but in certain regions 喊 is used, too:

① 妈妈**叫**(/**喊**)你呢! Mother is calling you!

② **叫**(/**喊**)大家一下,开会了。It's time for meeting. Go and tell them.

③ 听,小王在街对面**叫**(/**喊**)你呢! Listen, Xiao Wang is calling you on the other side of the street.

打电话用"叫通"、"叫不通",不用"喊" ◇ To make a phone call, 叫通 or 叫不通 is used, not 喊.

④ 电话怎么**叫不通**呢? Why can the telephone not get through?

4. 表示雇用,请服务行业提供服务,用"叫"(限于"叫菜、叫酒、叫车”等）◇ To order something for service, 叫 is used (only applied to 叫菜(order dishes), 叫酒(order wine)、叫车(hail a taxi), etc.):

① 小张，去**叫**一辆**车**，我们要赶紧送老人进医院。Xiao Zhang, hurry up and call for a taxi for we must send the old man to hospital at once.

② ——我已经**叫**了两个**菜**，够了吧？I have ordered two dishes, aren't they enough?
——再**叫**一瓶白酒！Please order a bottle of spirits.

③ 水龙头坏了，快**叫修理工**！There is something wrong with the tap; hurry to send for a repairman.

5. 表示称呼为……、名称是……，对于人的称呼，一般用“叫”，也可用“喊”（对他人不够客气）；对于事物的名称，只能用“叫”◇ To tell one's name or to address somebody, 叫 is used, 喊 can also be used (not very polite when applied to other people). Only 叫 is used for the name of something. e. g. :

① 我**叫**张大可。I'm Zhang Dake.

② 你就**叫**（/**喊**）我小张吧。Calling me Xiao Zhang is OK.

③ 土豆也**叫**马铃薯。Chinese Tudou (the potato) is also called Malingshu.

6. 表示（不好的事）宣扬出去，用“嚷”（如重叠为“嚷嚷”，则为 rāngrang）◇ To publicize something disgraceful, 嚷 is used (If reduplicated to 嚷嚷, it will be pronounced as "rāngrang"):

① 这事可千万别**嚷**出去！家丑不可外扬嘛。Just as the saying goes" Don't wash your dirty linen in public", so don't spread it.

② 注意保密，**嚷**出去对咱们没好处。Keep it secret, for it will do us no good if you make it public.

③ 一点儿小事，让她**嚷嚷**(rāngrang)得大家都知道了。She can make the trivial thing known.

7. 表示吵闹，一般用“嚷”（如重叠为“嚷嚷”，则为 rāngrang）◇ To make a lot of noise, 嚷 is used (If reduplicated into 嚷嚷 the pronunciation is "rāngrang"):

① 孩子们别**嚷**了，让我安静一会儿吧！Don't make noises, my children. Let me be quiet.

② 他们又是喝酒又是唱歌，**嚷**得邻居都提意见了。That they sang over drinks made their neighbors unhappy and complaining.

③ 别**嚷嚷**(rāngrang)了，大家都睡觉了。Be quiet, for all the others are sleeping now.

汉语 中文

(名) (名)

Hànyǔ Zhōngwén

Ⓔ Chinese language/Chinese

◪"汉语"指汉族的语言，即现代汉语的标准语普通话。"中文"指中国的语言文字，也特指汉族的语言文字 ◇ 汉语 means "the language of the Han nationality, i. e., *Putonghua*, the standard contemporary Chinese language". 中文 means "the Chinese language and script, in particular the language and script of the Han nationality".

① 他到中国来学**汉语**(/**中文**)。 He came to China to learn Chinese.

例①中，两个词都指汉族语言，所以可以互换。"中文"包括"语言文字"中的"文字"，但学习"汉语"也可包括文字，所以并不矛盾 ◇ In example ①, both words mean "the language of the Han nationality" and so are interchangeable. 中文 includes the written form of the language; to learn the Chinese language the learning of also includes the written form, hence there is no contradiction in between.

② 他在中文系学习现代**汉语**。 He is learning Modern Chinese in the Chinese Department.

例②中，"中文"指汉语言文学，"中文系"是大学汉语言、文学系的习惯说法。而"汉语系"则单指汉语言专业。这一类的"中文"、"汉语"不能换用 ◇ In example ②, 中文 means "the language and literature of the Han nationality". 中文系 is the customary name for the department of Chinese language and literature in a university. 汉语系 means the specialized studies of the Chinese language. Here, 中文 and 汉语 are not interchangeable.

好处 优点

(名) (名)

hǎochu yōudiǎn

Ⓔ advantage; merit/ strongpoint; merit

◪"好处"可以表示对人或事物有利的方面，"优点"则表示人的特长或事物的长处 ◇ 好处 is sth. that can help one succeed or to gain a desired result. 优点 means "the speciality or strong point which one possesses".

① 这种药酒对老人有**好处**。The drug is good to the old people.

② 勤勤恳恳是他的**优点**。Diligence is his merits.

"好处"是对"坏处"而言;"优点"是对"缺点"而言的 ◇ 好处 is the antonym of 坏处(disadvantage, harm); 优点 is the antonym of 缺点(weakness shortcomings):

③ 吸烟对你只有坏处,没有**好处**。Smoking does only harm to you, and does no good to you.

④ 与会者肯定了这部作品的**优点**,也指出了它的缺点。The meeting participants affirmed the works' good points, and meanwhile they also pointed out its weak points.

以上各句,两个词不能互换 ◇ In the examples above, the two words are not interchangeable.

但某事物的有利方面,有时也是该事物的长处,这时两个词可以换用 ◇ However, sth. that can help one to succeed is sometimes also its merit, so the two words are interchangeable:

⑤ 这种布料的**好处**(/**优点**)是结实耐用。The good of the cloth lies in that it is durable.

⑥ 住北房的**好处**(/**优点**)是冬暖夏凉。The good of the room facing south is in that it is warm in winter and cool in summer.

注意:可以互换的,常用例⑤⑥这样的句式(X 的好处/优点是 Y) ◇ Note: those which are interchangeable are usually expressed in sentence patterns of examples ⑤ and ⑥(the advantage /merit of X is Y).

另外,"好处"还可表示有利可图、利益、可享有的份额或事物 ◇ 好处 also means "gain or profit":

⑦ 他假公济私,一定捞了不少**好处**。He got a lot of illegal benefits from his abusing his power.

⑧ 你帮助公司推销商品,一定会有**好处**给你。You can get some commissions if you sell the products of the company.

这和"优点"没有共同之处 ◇ Such usages of 好处 have nothing in common with 优点.

好多 好些 许多

(形) (形) (形)

hǎoduō hǎoxiē xǔduō

Ⓔ a good many, numerous/ plenty, numerous/ plenty, numerous

◥ 这三个词都表示数量多、程度深。其中"许多"较书面化,并能按形容词的方式重叠(AABB式)。三个词都不能做谓语 ◇ The three words all indicate "large quantity, high degree". 许多 is more literary and can be reduplicated into 许许多多. None of the three can function as the predicate.

① 今天的晚会,来了**好多**(/**好些**/**许多**)贵客。(做定语,"好些"不能加"的")There are a lot of distinguished guests attending tonight's party. (as attributive, 好些 cannot take 的)

② 客人里边,**好多**(/**好些**/**许多**)都是我的老朋友。(做主语)Many of the guests are my old friends. (as the subject)

③ 这一类书籍,我已经买了**好多**(/**好些**/**许多**)。(做宾语)I bought a lot of books of this kind. (as the object)

④ 近来她瘦了**好些**(/**好多**/**许多**)。She has lost some weight recently.

以上四个词一般可换用,但"许多"较书面化 ◇ In the examples above, the four words are interchangeable, but 许多 is more literary.

因为只有"许多"能按 AABB 式重叠,下面的句子只能用"许多" ◇ Since only 许多 can be reduplicated into 许许多多, in example ⑤ only 许多 can be used:

⑤ 还有**许许多多**的知识,是我们不懂的。There are many new things for us to learn.

注意:"好多"有时是"好"+"多",可做谓语,如"客人好多呀" ◇ Note: 好多 sometimes is a phrase made up with adverb 好 + 多, and can function as the predicate, e.g. 客人好多呀!(There are so many guests!)

好看 (形) hǎokàn　**漂亮** (形) piàoliang

美 (形) měi　**美丽** (形) měilì

Ⓔ good looking; beautiful/ handsome/ pretty/beautiful

1. 这四个词都可表示使人产生美感的。但"好看"、"漂亮"是口语词;"美"有时是口语有时是书面语;"美丽"较正式和书面化。另外,除了上述基本意思,还各有一些义项。基本义项例如 ◇ All the four words mean "having the qualities that give pleasure to the senses". 好看, 漂亮 are colloquial; 美 is both colloquial and literary; 美丽 is formal and literary. Moreover, besides the basic meaning, each has some other meanings and usages. The basic meanings are as follows:

① 这儿的风景真**好看**(/**漂亮**/**美**/**美丽**)! The scenery here is really beautiful.

② 她长得很**好看**(/**漂亮**/**美**/**美

丽)。She is good-looking / beautiful / pretty.

以上两句,四个词均可以用,主要涉及人、风景、花木、艺术品等。但其语体色彩仍略有不同 ◇ In examples ① and ②, all four words can be used, mainly applied to human beings, landscapes, plants, works of art, etc. As far as the style is concerned, however, there is still a difference.

2. 由于"美丽"具有书面色彩,所以有些书面语的句子宜用"美丽" ◇ Since 美丽 is literary, it is used in written language:

① 牛郎织女的故事是一个**美丽**的传说。The Cowherd and the Weaving Maid is a moving story.

② 青春是**美丽**的。Youth is beautiful.

"美"由于音节的关系,如用于例①②应加"很"。其他两个词不能使用 ◇ Since 美 is monosyllabic, if used in examples ① and ②, it must be preceded by 很. The other two words cannot be used.

3. "好看"虽然也表示"使人产生美感的",但只限于眼睛能看到的、可以诉诸观感的。因此,我们不能说"好看的乐曲",但可以说"美的乐曲" ◇ Though it also means "giving pleasure", 好看 is limited to visual sense. Therefore we cannot say 好看的乐曲, but 美的乐曲, e.g.:

① 这是一支很**美**的乐曲。This melody is pleasing.

② 这首诗的意境很**美**。The mood of the poem are beautiful.

"漂亮"由于另有限制(详见 4)也不宜在 2 的例①②中使用。"美丽"书面化,但"美丽动听的乐曲"还是可以的 ◇ Because of other limitations (see 4), 漂亮 cannot be used in examples ① and ② of 2 美丽 is literary, but one can say ① 美丽动听的乐曲 melodious tune.

"好看"还可表示体面、觉得脸上有光彩(常用"脸上"、"脸面上") ◇ 好看 can also mean "respectable, honored (often used with 脸上 or 脸面上)":

③ 学生获了奖,老师脸上也**好看**。A teacher will feel honored if his students got awards.

④ 送的礼物如果太轻,脸面上不**好看**。If our gift is not valuable, which will make us lose face.

其他三个词不能这样用 ◇ The other three words cannot be so used.

"要……的好看"表示使人难堪 ◇ 要……的好看 means "to make one awkward":

⑤ 我不会讲话,你非要我代表大家说话,这不是要我的**好看**嘛! I am poor at speech. I will be awkward if you ask me make a speech on behalf of you.

⑥ 谁要是要他的**好看**,他也不会让别人舒服。If somebody makes him faceless, he will revenge on him.

4.“漂亮”可以表示出色。它可以重叠,这个义项也常使用重叠式 ◇ 漂亮 can mean "outstanding". In this meaning, it is often reduplicated into 漂漂亮亮:

① 这件事他干得很**漂亮**。He did a good job about it.

② 风格高,球艺好,这场球他们队踢得**漂漂亮亮**。Their team won the match brilliantly by their good quality and skills.

③ 他们的普通话说得很**漂亮**。They can speech manderin fluently.

“漂亮”含有色彩美的意思,因此虽然也表示“使人产生美感的”,但多形容光彩照人的事物,而不用于歌曲等 ◇ 漂亮 also means "beautiful, handsome, and is applied to things beautiful to the eyes, but not to music, etc.":

④ 她今天打扮得真**漂亮**。She made up and looked beautiful today.

⑤ 节日的夜景,显得十分**漂亮**。The night scene of the festival is very splendid.

5.“美”用于书面也用于口语。较书面语(表示美学或美学的)的例子如 ◇ 美 is literary as well as colloquial. More literary (aesthetic) examples are:

① 看京剧,真是一种**美**的享受。It is really an enjoyment to see Peking Operas.

② 她所追求的是一种朴素的**美**。What she seeks for is a plain beauty.

其他三个词不能这样用 ◇ The other three words cannot be so used.

口语的例子,如例 3 中的例①。在口语中,“美”还可表示令人满意的 ◇ Example ① of 3 is a colloquial example. In spoken language, 美 can also mean "satisfactory":

③ 今天我一定要**美美**地吃一顿。I'd like to have a satisfactory dinner today.

④ 他们的日子过得很**美**。They lead a satisfactory life.

▶[美观 měiguān—美丽 měilì]

好像 似乎 仿佛

好像	似乎	仿佛
(动)	(副)	(动)
hǎoxiàng	sìhū	fǎngfú

Ⓔ seem; be like/
as if; seem/
seem; as if

1.“好像”作为动词,有“和……相像”的意思 ◇ As a verb,

好像 means "to be like".

① 乍一看，小王长得**好像**小张。Xiao Wang resembles Xiao Zhang at first sight.

② 从作风上看，他**好像**一个军人。He is like a soldier judging from his style.

"仿佛"也可以这样用，但比"好像"书面化，还可说"和……相仿佛" ◇ 仿佛 can also be so used, but is more literary. One can also say 和……相仿佛：

③ 妹妹的容貌和姐姐相**仿佛**。The little sister and her sister are alike in appearance.

以上，例①②"好像"、"仿佛"两个词可互换，但"仿佛"略为书面化。"似乎"没有以上用法 ◇ In examples ① and ② 仿佛 and 好像 are interchangeable, but 仿佛 is more literary. 似乎 cannot be so used.

注意："好像"、"仿佛"表示相像的用法较窄，不如"像"用得广泛，如"学谁像谁"，不能用"好像"和"仿佛" ◇ Note: 好像，仿佛 are not so often used to mean "like" as 像. For example, one can say 学谁像谁 (whoever he imitates, he looks like…), but neither 好像 nor 仿佛 can be so used.

2. 这三个词还有一个共同用法，表示不十分确切的了解或感觉，做状语 ◇ The three words have a common meaning " to seem to be", usually as an adverbial:

① 我没看清是谁，**好像**(/**似乎**/**仿佛**)是一个老太太。I could not see clearly, and it seemed to me she was an old lady.

三个词可互换，但"好像"最口语化，"似乎"次之，"仿佛"比较书面化 ◇ The three words are interchangeable, but 好像 is the most colloquial, next comes 似乎，仿佛 is most literary.

另外，"好像"、"仿佛"可以和"似的(shide)"呼应 ◇ Besides, 好像，仿佛 can be used in concert with 似的(be like …):

② 她**好像**(/**仿佛**)很悲伤似的。She seemed very sad.

"似乎"较少和"似的"呼应 ◇ 似乎 is not often used in this way.

3. 以上两种用法，都可以用于比喻 ◇ The two usages above can be used in analogy, e. g. :

① 他**好像**(/**仿佛**)一个大将军一样，总是对人发号施令。He always commands others and as if he were a great general.

② 谁跟他说话他都不理，**好像**(/**似乎**/**仿佛**)是一个聋子似的。He turned a deaf ear to nobody as if he were a deaf.

(动)　　(动)

hào　　ài

Ⓔ be fond of, love/love

◪ 请注意,"好"读 hào 而不是 hǎo ◇ Please note that 好 is pronounced in the fourth tone, not the third one.

"好"和"爱"都用于口语,都可表示 ◇ Both 好 and 爱 are colloquial and mean:

1. 喜爱(做某事) ◇ To be fond of(doing sth.):

① 她**好**(/**爱**)逛商店。She likes window-shopping.

② 老张**好**(/**爱**)下象棋。Lao Zhang likes playing chess.

③ 我不**爱**吃咸的。I don't like salty food.

有些属于习惯搭配,如"好学"、"好吃懒做"。但可以说"爱吃好的"、"不爱吃咸的"(例③)等。一般地说,用"好"常表示喜爱已成习惯。例③如说"她不好吃咸的",也是可以的 ◇ Some of them are idiomatic phrases, e. g. 好学(studious), 好吃懒做(gluttonous and lazy). But one can say 爱吃好的, 不爱吃咸的(e. g. ③), etc. Generally speaking, 好 indicates a habitual fondness. Example ③ can be said as 她不好吃咸的.

2. (某种情况)常常发生 ◇ Indicating(sth.) taking place very often:

① 这孩子**爱**(/**好**)哭。The child is apt to crying.

② 他冬天**爱**(/**好**)感冒。He is apt to catching a cold in winter.

③ 这种铁锅**爱**生锈。The inn pot is easy to rust.

一般地说,完全没有主观色彩的,如例③,不用"好" ◇ Generally speaking, if there is no sense of subjectivity at all, as in example ③, 好 is not used.

3. (动植物)具有某种习性 ◇ (Animals and plants) having a certain characteristic:

① 这种植物**爱**在背阴的地方生长。The plant likes growing in the shade.

② 这种动物**爱**扎堆儿。The animals like getting together.

例①也属于没有主观色彩的 ◇ There is no subjectivity in example ①.

► [爱 ài—喜欢 xǐhuan]
[爱好 àihào—喜欢 xǐhuan]

合适 适合 适宜

合适	适合	适宜
(形)	(动)	(形)
héshì	shìhé	shìyí

Ⓔ suitable/suit/suitable

◪ 这三个词都可表示符合一定的情况或要求 ◇ All three words mean "to be suitable to certain situation or demand".

1. 合适 适宜

都是形容词,但"合适"在口语中更常用 ◇ Both 合适 and 适宜 are adjectives, but 合适 is used more in colloquial language:

① 这双鞋正**合适**。The shoes suit me well.

② 我们找一个**合适**的时间聚一聚。We should meet at a proper time.

③ 描写人的外貌,用这个词不**合适**。This is unsuitable for a man's appearance.

以上"合适"用于具体或抽象事物,都可以,而且都很口语化。其中例①非常具体,不能用"适宜",例②③也可用"适宜" ◇ In the examples above 合适 is applied to both the concrete and the abstract and is very colloquial. The content of example ① is very concrete, so 适宜 cannot be used, while in examples ② and ③适宜 can be used instead.

"适宜"还有(事物的程度或性质)合人意的意思,可带"于";"合适"没有这种用法 ◇ 适宜 also means (the level or nature of sth.) "to be suitable to one's taste", and can take 于. 合适 cannot be so used.

④ 北京的秋天**适宜**旅游。It is pleasing to visit Beijing in autumn.

⑤ 这种减肥茶**适宜**于中老年人。The slimming tea is suitable for middle-aged and old people.

"合适"可带程度补语,"适宜"不能 ◇ 合适 can take a complement of degree, while 适宜 cannot:

⑥ 那件衣服**合适**极了。The dress suits perfectly.

⑦ 这份工作,对我再**合适**不过了。The job cannot be more suitable for me.

2. 适合

是动词,可带体词或谓词宾语,可带"于" ◇ 适合 is a verb. It can take nouns, measure words, numerals, pronouns, verbs, adjectives as its object, and can take 于:

① 这种装饰材料很**适合**你的房间。The decoration material suits your room well.

② 你的年龄不**适合**剧烈运动。Fierce exercises are unsuitable for you in this age.

③ 他太粗心,不**适合**做这种工作。He is unsuitable for the job for he is too careless.

④ 那种科普读物**适合**于初中一年级的学生。This kind of popular science books is designed for first-year students of junior high school.

合算 上算

(形、动) (形)

hésuàn shàngsuàn

Ⓔ worthwhile, reckon/ worthwhile

1. 动词"合算"表示考虑和计划 ◇ 合算, as a verb, means "to calculate and plan":

① 咱们得**合算**一下,这样做值不值得。Let's reckon whether it is worthy or not to do it.

② 这件事先别忙着决定,咱们再**合算合算**。Don't decide it hastily. Let's think over it.

H

2. "合算"和"上算"都是形容词,都表示因付出较少、效果较好而符合施事者的利益。有时"上算"含有"占便宜"的意味 ◇ 合算 and 上算 both are adjectives meaning "worth doing", indicating that one gains more than one pays. Sometimes, 上算 has a sense of gaining profit at other people's expense:

① 你这次去上海真**合算**,公事私事全办了。It is worthwhile for you to go to Shanghai this time for business as well as for your personal affairs.

② 买这种股票真不**上算**,赔了不少。The stocks are unworthy, for we lost much.

③ 这个人很精明,不**合算**的事从来不干。The man is very smart and he never does anything unworthwhile.

④ 买房比租房**上算**。Buying a house is more worthy than renting one.

以上例句中两个词可以互换 ◇ In the examples above 合算 and 上算 are interchangeable.

喉咙 嗓子

(名) (名)

hóulóng sǎngzi

Ⓔ throat/throat, voice

1. "喉咙"、"嗓子"这两个词都是咽部和喉部的统称,后者常用在口语中,前者较书面化。下列例句中,有时两个词可换用 ◇ Both 喉咙 and 嗓子 are common names for pharynx and throat. The latter is colloquial while the former is more literary. In the following examples, the two words are interchangeable:

① 他渴得**喉咙**(/**嗓子**)里直冒烟。His throat feels parched.

② 因为**喉咙**(/**嗓子**)痛,他去看了大夫。He had a sore throat, so he went to see a doctor.

③ 抽烟喝酒都对**喉咙**(/**嗓子**)有害。Smoking and drinking both do harm to your throat.

2. "嗓子"还表示嗓音;"喉咙"在一些固定短语(如下面例②)中也可以表示嗓音 ◇ 嗓子 also means "voice"; 喉咙, used in some fixed phrases(e. g. in example ② below) can mean the same thing. e. g. :

① 这位歌手的**嗓子**真好。The singer's voice is very good.
② 你高喉咙大**嗓子**地嚷什么? Why do you cry out?
③ 他的**嗓子**哑了。He has lost his voice.
④ 她有一副好**嗓子**。She has a good voice.

后悔 悔 悔改

(动) (动) (动)

hòuhuǐ huǐ huǐgǎi

Ⓔ regret, repent/
regret, repent/
regret and mend one's ways

1. "后悔"表示事后觉得做得不对而懊悔。"悔改"除了"后悔"还有改正错误的意思(因之所指的事也较大) ◇ 后悔 means "to feel unhappy because of one's mistake". 悔改 means "to regret and mend one's ways". e. g. :

① 他当初学了文科而没有学工科,现在有点儿**后悔**。He studies arts instead of science and he felt a bit regretful.
② 张先生做事果断,只要是他决定的事,从来都不**后悔**。Mr. Zhang is firm: he never regrets what he determines to do.
③ 这孩子原来不务正业,并有偷窃行为,现在已经**悔改**,走上了正路。The boy did unde-cent work every day and he stole things before. He has corrected his shortcomings and is a changed man.
④ 他已经对自己的错误表示了**悔改**之意。He has expressed his repentance and willingness to mend his ways.

以上例①②与③④两词不能互换 ◇ In examples ① ② and ③ ④ 后悔 and 悔改 are not interchangeable.

"悔改"是不及物的。"后悔"虽然也不能带单独的宾语,但可以带小句宾语 ◇ 悔改 is an intransitive verb. 后悔 cannot take a word as its object, but can take a clause as its object:

⑤ 我很**后悔**没有买那场歌舞晚会的票。It's a pity that I didn't buy the ticket for the dance-and-singing party.
⑥ 她**后悔**自己认错了人。She regretted her misjudging him.

2. "悔"的意思与"后悔"相似,但一方面较粘着化,不单用(如例①);另一方面又有一定的及物性,可带少数几个词单独做宾语(如例②) ◇ The meaning of 悔 is similar to that of 后悔 but cannot be used independently in most occasions (as in example ①). On the other hand, however, 悔 is sometimes transitive and can take a few objects of a single word (as in example ②):

① 小王对自己的错误已经有**悔**意了。Xiao Wang has a bit regretted for the mistakes he made.

② 你怎么**悔**棋？我们讲好了不能悔棋的。Why do you want to change your move? We agreed that we would not retract our incorrect move.

再如"无怨无悔"、"悔不当初"等 ◇ There are some set phrases such as 无怨无悔(no repentance at all), 悔不当初(regret having done sth. or not having sth.),etc.

忽然 突然

(副) (形)

hūrán tūrán

Ⓔ suddenly/suddenly

这两个词都表示事情发生得迅速而且意外，但"忽然"是副词，只做状语，"突然"是形容词，可做状语、定语、谓语、补语等。同时，"突然"含有的意外性多些，"忽然"在口语中用得更多些 ◇ Both words indicate that sth. happens quickly and unexpectedly. 忽然 is an adverb and can only function as an adverbial. 突然 is an adjective and can be an adverbial, attributive, predicate, complement, etc. Besides, 突然 means "more unexpectedly". 忽然 is used more in spoken language than 突然.

① 天**忽然**下起雨来。It rained suddenly.

② 大祸**突然**来临。The disaster befell suddenly.

③ 两车**突然**相撞，伤亡惨重。The two cars crashed suddenly and cause heavy casualties.

也可以用"忽然间"、"忽然之间"、"突然间"、"突然之间" ◇ One can also say 忽然间，忽然之间，突然间，突然之间.

以上①②③例，例①较口语化，用"忽然"，但如强调其意外性，也可用"突然"。例②③因有较大意外性，应用"突然" ◇ In the three examples above, example ① is rather colloquial, so 忽然 is used. If the unexpectedness is stressed, however, 突然 can be used instead. Examples ② and ③ concern some serious accidents, so 突然 ought to be used.

再如 ◇ e.g.:

④ 这是一次**突然**事件，让人猝不及防。（定语）It happened suddenly and unexpectedly. (attributive)

⑤ 对方对我们搞了**突然**袭击。（定语）Our rival attacked us beyond our expectation. (attributive)

⑥ 问题出现得很**突然**。（补语）

The problem emerged suddenly. (complement)

⑦ 这消息真**突然**。(谓语) The news is a surprise. (predicate)

胡乱 乱 随便

(副) (形) (形)

húluàn luàn suíbiàn

Ⓔ at random/
in disorder, in confusion/
casual, random

1. "胡乱"表示马马虎虎地、不经意地 ◇ 胡乱 means "careless, casual":

① 他起晚了,**胡乱**擦了把脸就赶去上班了。He got up too late, so he washed himself briefly and went to work.

② 天黑灯暗,他**胡乱**找了件衣服披上就走了。It was dark and the light was dim, so he put on a coat casually and left.

这些句子中的"胡乱"虽然口语化,但属于较"雅"的口语,来自古白话。以上两句也可用"随便",那才是真正的口语 ◇ 胡乱 in examples ① and ②, though colloquial, is rather refined as it originated from ancient vernacular. In examples ① and ②, 随便 can also be used, which is really colloquial.

"胡乱"还表示没有道理地、任意地 ◇ 胡乱 also means "unreasonable, willful":

③ 他话还没听完,就**胡乱**地批评了一通。He just heard part of it and began criticizing without reasons.

④ 你怎么**胡乱**骂人? Why do you swear others without reasons?

以上例③可说"随便批评(人)",例④也可换用"随便"。但意思没有"胡乱"重。"乱"也可说"乱批评人"、"乱骂人",意思接近 ◇ In example ③ one can also say 随便批评(人). In example ④胡乱 can also be replaced by 随便, but not as serious as 胡乱. One can also say 乱批评人, 乱骂人, with a similar meaning.

2. "乱"意思较多 ◇ 乱 has quite a few different meanings:

(1) 表示无条理,无规矩,无秩序,如 ◇ To mean "disorderly, confused, in a mess", e. g.:

① 这篇文章写得太**乱**。The article has a disorderly organization.

② 屋子里东西多,**乱**得很。The room was a mess for it was full of items.

(2) 表示心情、心绪不安宁,如 ◇ To mean "confused, perturbed", e. g.:

③ 我心里很**乱**,让我安静一下。I'm in a mess, so please let me be.

(3)表示使混乱 ◇ To mean "to create a disturbance", e. g. :

④ 这幅画虽然是赝品,但足以以假**乱**真。The picture is a fake, but it can create confusion.

⑤ 别让这些琐事打**乱**我们的工作程序。Don't make the trivials disturb our routines.

(4)表示任意,随意 ◇ To mean "willful, as one pleases", e. g. :

⑥ 你不要不懂装懂,**乱**说一气。You just comment unknowingly and pretend to know what you don't know.

⑦ 小摊儿上的东西不卫生,不要**乱**吃。Don't buy the food in the stalls outside for it is dirty.

⑧ 你刚到这个大城市,还不熟悉,别各处**乱**跑。Don't go everywhere, for you came to the city not long and are unfamiliar with it.

以上例⑥也可说"胡乱发表意见"或"随便发表意见"或"随便乱说"。例⑦可说"胡乱吃东西"或"随便吃东西"。例⑧可说"随便跑"或"随便乱跑";不能用"胡乱" ◇ Example ⑥ can be turned into 胡乱发表意见 or 随便发表意见 or 随便乱说. Example ⑦ can be turned into 胡乱吃东西 or 随便吃东西. Example ⑧ can be turned into 随便跑 or 随便乱跑. 胡乱 cannot be used here.

3."随便"有下列三个意思 ◇ 随便 has three different meanings:

(1)不论,任凭 ◇ To mean "no matter (how, what, where, etc.)", e. g. :

① **随便**什么电影,他都爱看。He likes a variety of films.

② **随便**中餐西餐都可以,我是客随主便。I'll take what you prefer whether it is Chinese food or Western food.

(2)不受限制和约束的 ◇ To mean "casual, random", e. g. :

③ 别客气,**随便**坐。Make yourself at home, and take your seat please.

④ 在大会上讲话不能太**随便**。You cannot deliver a casual speech at a meeting.

⑤ 老朋友见面**随便**闲谈起来。The old friends chatted as they met each other.

(3)任意,随意,马虎 ◇ To mean "arbitrary, as one pleases, careless", e. g.

⑥ 平时东西**随便**放,到用的时候什么都找不着。You cannot find it when needed, for you put it away casually.

此句也可说"胡乱放"或"乱放"。值得注意的是,"随便"和"乱"有时可同时出现 ◇ In example ⑥ 胡乱放 or 乱放 can be used instead. It is noteworthy that 随便 can be used together with 乱:

⑦ 这些材料不要**随便**乱动。Don't touch these materials without their owner's consent.

“随便”可以重叠为“随随便便” ◇ 随便 can be reduplicated into 随随便便:

⑧ 他这个人总是**随随便便**,什么事都不放在心上。He is a casual man and would not like to have a lot on his mind.

⑨ 这封信很重要,要好好考虑一下怎么写,**随随便便**可不行。It's not OK if you write the letter casually for it is very significant.

互相 相互

（副） （形）

hùxiāng xiānghù

Ⓔ mutually; each other/ mutually; each other

◪ 这两个词都表示两个或两个以上的人或事物之间彼此以同样态度对待对方,但“互相”是副词,只做状语,“相互”是形容词,可做状语和定语。另外,“相互”较为书面化 ◇ Both words mean "two or more people or things treat each other in the same way". 互相 is an adverb and can only function as an adverbial. 相互 is an adjective and can function either as an adverbial or as an attributive. 相互 is more literary.

① 姐弟俩都在镇上上中学,应该**互相**照顾。The sister and brother went to the middle school in the town and looked after each other.

② 夫妻间应该**相互**(/互相)体谅。Husband and wife should be understanding mutually.

例①,是口语中常用的句子,用“互相”。例②较为书面化,两个词都可以用,意思一样 ◇ Example ① is a very colloquial sentence, so 互相 is used; example ② is more literary, and either word can be used.

以下三例,是做定语,用“相互” ◇ In examples ③ and ④⑤, 相互 is an attributive:

③ 企业和顾客的**相互**关系,应该是彼此信赖。The relationship between the enterprise and its clients should be trusty.

④ 通过实验,同学们进一步了解了这两种物质的**相互**作用。The students further know the interaction between the two substances through the chemical test.

⑤ 随着中国加入世贸组织,中国与国际社会之间的**相互**交往会更加频繁。With China's entry into WTO, she will communicate with the world more frequently.

“相互”做定语,搭配较少 ◇ 相互 is rarely used as an attributive.

"相互"可与"间"、"之间"一起做定语或状语 ◇ 相互 can be used together with 间 or 之间 as an attributive or adverbial, e. g. :

⑥ 要处理好两个单位**相互**间的关系。We should handle the mutual relationship of the two units well.

⑦ 两个厂的产品**相互**之间竞争很激烈。There is a fierce competition between the products of the two factories.

"互相"是不能直接做定语的,我们不能说"互相关系"、"互相的感觉"等,可以说"互相合作的关系"、"互相信赖的感觉"等,"互相"在这里还是做状语 ◇ 互相 cannot be an attributive by itself. We cannot say 互相关系 or 互相的感觉, etc. , but we can say 互相合作的关系(the relationship of mutual cooperation)、互相信赖的感觉(sense of mutual reliability), etc. Here 互相 is still an adverbial. 同时,"互相"要与双音节或多音节词语搭配,不能与单音节词搭配("互"常与单音节搭配或构成四字语,如"互敬互让"、"互有伤亡"等) ◇ Besides, 互相 must be used with disyllabic or polysyllabic words and not with monosyllabic words. (互 is usually used with monosyllabic words to form four-character phrases, e. g. 互敬互让 yield to each other, 互有伤亡 the two sides at war suffered casualties, etc.)

花 用 费

花	用	费
(动)	(动)	(动)
huā	yòng	fèi

Ⓔ spend/use/spend

◪ 这三个动词都可表示耗用 ◇ The three verbs all mean "to spend, to use":

① 他**花**(/**用**/**费**)了不少时间学习电脑。He is willing to spent a lot of time studying computer.

这时三个词都可带"时间"这个宾语。"用时间"是一般的表述,"花时间"常有特意安排时间的含义,而"费时间"有时含被动或浪费意味 ◇ All the three words can take 时间 as their object. 用时间 is a general description of spending time; 花时间 indicates a special arrangement of time; 费时间 sometimes indicates an obligation to spend time on sth. or a waste of time.

② 在学习电脑方面,他真舍得**花**(/**用**)时间。He is ready to spend time studying computers.

例②就不能用"费",因为"费"含被动意味 ◇ In example ② 费 cannot be used because it suggests a sense of passivity.

另外,这三个词也都可以带"钱"

这种宾语 ◇ Besides, all the three words can have 钱 as their object:

③ 她**花**(/**用**)了300元买礼品。She spent three hundred *yuan* on the gifts.

④ 我觉得自己做衣服又**花**时间又费钱,而她却不以为然。I think it takes more time and money to make clothes by oneself, but she disagrees.

例③可用"花"或"用",而例④只能用"费",这里的"费"是"用得多"的意思 ◇ In example ③ either 花 or 用 can be used, but in example ④ only 费 can be used, which indicates the sense of "being wasteful".

"花心思"、"用心"、"费心",宾语差不多,但含义不一样。"花心思"褒贬义都可以,"用心"一般用于褒义。"费心"用于自身,含耗费精神的意思;用于他人,有请求的意思 ◇ The object of 花心思, 用心, 费心 is similar, but the implication is different. 花心思 can either be commendatory or derogatory, while 用心 is generally commendatory. 费心, if applied to oneself, means "to consume one's energy"; if applied to other people, it is a polite formula for request.

因为"费"含浪费、用得过多的意思,所以可说"费(汽)油"、"费工夫"、"费衣服"等,"花"和"用"没有这个意思 ◇ Since 费 implies "waste full, excessive consumption", we can say 费(汽)油 (be gas-consuming), 费工夫 (time-consuming), 费衣服 (wear out clothes quickly), etc. Neither 花 nor 用 has such a meaning.

▶[使 shǐ—使用 shǐyòng—用 yòng]

怀念 想念 思念

(动) (动) (动)

huáiniàn xiǎngniàn sīniàn

Ⓔ cherish the memory of; think of/

long to see again; think of/

think of; long for

这三个动词都表示对人、事、环境等的不能忘记。"怀念"侧重于对时间过去较久的、不易再现或已经逝去的人、事、地、情景的不能忘怀。"想念"则多指对尚健在的人、较易见到的具体的事、情境的不能忘记,但有时也可指对逝世的人的追忆。"思念"的词义在以上两个词之间,为书面语,用得较少。有时可互换,但侧重点有所不同 ◇ All the three verbs indicate the unforgettable memory of people, things, environments, etc. 怀念 stresses the memories of remote past or the dead. 想念 is applied to people alive or things that are available; it can also include the dead. 思念 has the same meaning as the other two, but is literary and not so commonly used. The three words are sometimes interchangeable, but have different stresses:

① 在老舍诞辰一百周年的纪念会上,与会者纷纷表示了对这位作家的深切**怀念**。The participants expressed their deep condolence in succession for Lao She in his 100th anniversary.

② 尽管旅居海外多年,但他仍然对祖国充满了深厚的**怀念**(/**思念**)之情。The old oversea Chinese has deep yearning for his motherland though he has been living abroad for many years.

③ 他写信告诉妈妈,他非常**想念**(/**思念**)爸爸、妈妈。He wrote his mother that he missed her and his father very much.

④ 这个情景引起了他对往事的**思念**。The scene reminded him of the past.

⑤ 他很**怀念**(/**想念**/**思念**)几位逝世的朋友。He missed his dead friends.

"怀念"侧重久远的追忆、"想念"侧重具体的追忆;"思念"也侧重具体的追忆,但较书面化 ◇ 怀念 stresses the recollection of things long ago. 想念 stresses the concrete memory. 思念 also stresses the concrete memory but is more literary. e. g. :

⑥ 久居国外,难免**思念**(/**想念**)家乡和亲人。It's hard not to miss one's native place and family if one lives abroad for a long time.

"思念"较书面化,"想念"较口语化 ◇ 思念 is literary while 想念 is colloquial.

又如 ◇ Another example:

⑦ 她的文章里充满了对童年生活的**怀念**(/**思念**)。Her article is full of nostalgia of childhood life.

"怀念"更抽象化 ◇ 怀念 is more abstract.

怀疑 疑心

(动) (动、名)

huáiyí yíxīn

Ⓔ doubt, suspect/ suspect; suspicion

"怀疑"和"疑心"作为动词,都有对人对事不太相信的意思,可互换使用 ◇ As verbs, both 怀疑 and 疑心 mean to "have doubt in a person or thing". They are interchangeable:

① 我一点儿也不**怀疑**(/**疑心**)他的真诚。I don't doubt his honesty at all.

② 她早就**怀疑**(/**疑心**)这封信不是他写的。She was suspicious early that the letter was not written by him.

但是,"怀疑"可用于被动句中,而"疑心"不可 ◇ 怀疑 can be used in the passive voice, but 疑心 cannot:

③ 他成了被**怀疑**的对象。He became the suspect.

"怀疑"可做介词"凭"等的宾语 ◇ 怀疑 can used as the objects of 凭, etc.:

④ 只凭**怀疑**不能给一个人定罪。It is reckless that convicting a person by mere suspicion.

"疑心"还是名词,"怀疑"不是 ◇ 疑心 is also a noun, but 怀疑 is not:

⑤ 这个人**疑心**太重,对什么人都不放心。The man is too suspicious to believe everyone.

⑥ 案发后,他的表现有些异常,因而别人对他起了**疑心**。He was doubted by others because of his abnormal behavior after the case.

还 (动) huán 回 (动) huí

Ⓔ return, go back/ return, go back

这两个动词都可表示返回原来的地方,"还"书面化,"回"口语化 ◇ Both words mean "to return to the original place". 还 is literary and 回 is colloquial.

① 他20年没有**还**乡了。He has not returned his native place for 20 years.

② 她下午6点下班,6点半就可以**回**到家。She left off work at 6 p. m, and arrived home at 6:30 p. m.

以上两句,例①"还乡"是书面化的词语,例②口语化,两句中的"还"和"回"不能互换。但"还乡"这种搭配较少。而"回国"、"回校"、"回家"等,是大量的(书面语也有"还家",现在用得较少)◇ In example ① 还乡 is a literary expression, while 回到家 in example ② is colloquial. 还 and 回 in these two sentences are not interchangeable. 还乡 is a rare collocation, but 回国, 回校, 回家, etc. are commonly used (In literary language, 还家 is said, but quite rare now).

这两个动词还可表示回报或反馈,如"还/回礼"、"还嘴","还价"等。在这种用法中,两个词有时可以互换,"还"略显书面化 ◇ This two verbs also mean "to requite or repay", such as 还/回礼 (send a present in return), 还嘴 (answer back/scold back), 还价 (counter-bid/counter-offer), etc. In this usage the two words are sometimes interchangeable, but 还 is more literary.

另外,两个词分别有其他一些义项。如:"还"可表示归还(物) ◇ Besides, the two words have their own usages respectively. For example, 还 means "to return sth.":

③ 我要去图书馆**还**书。I will go to the library to return the books.

④ 我欠你的钱下月可以**还**你。I will pay back your money next month.

"回"可表示答复,谢绝,掉转(身体)等 ◇ 回 means "to reply, to refuse or to turn round, etc.":

⑤ 我已经给他**回**了信。I have replied his letter.

⑥ 几个邀请都被他**回**了。He declined several invitations.

⑦ 他向前走了几步又**回**过头来望了望。He stepped forward a little and turned back.

这些义项,"还"、"回"是不能互换的 ◇ In these usages, 还 and 回 are not interchangeable.

换 (动) huàn　交换 (动) jiāohuàn

Ⓔ change/interchange

1. 这两个动词都可表示更换,"换"用于具体事物,较口语化;"交换"用于双方,除了用于具体事物,还可用于涉及双方的抽象事物 ◇ Both verbs mean "to change". 换 is applied to concrete things and is more colloquial. 交换 is applied to two parties, and besides concrete things, it can also be applied to abstract things.

① 比赛到二十分钟的时候,甲队要求**换**人。The team A requested to change a player after the match was going on 20 minutes.

② 你等我一下,我去**换**一件衣服。Just a moment. I'll change a coat.

③ 我从家里到学校要**换**两次车。I will change two buses from my home to my school.

例①②③这种具体事物,只能用"换" ◇ Examples ①②③all concern concrete things, so only 换 can be used.

④ 比赛进行到一半时,要**交换**场地。When the match came to its half, the two teams changed their courts.

⑤ 咱们俩**交换**一下礼物吧。Let's exchange our gifts.

例④⑤虽然也是具体事物,事关主客双方,可用"交换"。但因其宾语属于具体事物,也可用"换"。因为"换"是单音节词,较为口语化,常加"了"、"一下"等 ◇ Examples ④ and ⑤ also concern concrete things, but they involve two parties, so 交换 is used. Since the object is concrete, 换 can also be used. Yet because 换 is monosyllabic and colloquial, 了 or 一下 are often added:

⑥ 比赛到一半时,**换**了场地,比赛继续进行。When the match came to its half, the teams changed their courts and kept on their match.

⑦ 咱们俩**换**一下礼物吧! Let's exchange our gifts.

另外,"交换"可用于涉及双方的抽象事物,如"交换意见"、"交换秘密"、"交换看法",以及特殊的"交换俘虏"等;"换"不能这样用 ◇ Moreover, 交换 can be applied to abstract things, e. g. 交换意见(exchange ideas), 交换秘密(exchange mutual secrets), 交换看法(exchange opinions) and 交换俘虏(exchange captives) in particular. 换 cannot be so used. e. g. :

⑧ 针对这个问题,他们双方正在**交换**意见,估计很快就会作出决定。They are exchanging their view about the issue and they will make a decision very soon.

2. "换"还可以表示变换,兑换,"交换"不可以 ◇ 换 can also mean "alternate, exchange". 交换 has no such meaning:

① 话剧演到这里,**换**了场景。The setting was changed at this act.

② 他**换**了一个比较委婉的词语,使谈话得以继续下去。He changed his words to be more politely, and that enabled the conversation to resume.

③ 我到银行去**换**一下钱。I will go to bank to cash it.

3. "换"还可用于与时序有关的词语。如"换季"、"换代(产品)"、"换了人间"、"改朝换代"、"换届选举"等。"交换"不能这样用 ◇ 换 can be used with words of time, e. g. 换季(change garments according to the season), 换代(产品)(replace the older generations of products with new ones), 换了人间(change the environment), 改朝换代(dynastic changes), 换届选举(re-election), etc. 交换 cannot be so used.

回答 (动) huídá　答复 (动、名) dáfù

Ⓔ answer/reply

◪ 这两个词都表示对问题或要求的解释、回复等。"回答"是动词,"答复"既是动词又是名词 ◇ The two words mean "to reply to a question or request". 回答 is a verb. 答复 is both a verb and a noun.

“回答”较具体,“答复”有时有落实交代的含义 ◇ 回答 is concrete, while 答复 has the meaning of "putting into effect".

① 老师说:张兰,你**回答**下面这个问题。The teacher said: would you like to answer the following question, Zhang Lan?

② 对于考卷上的问题,他一一作了**回答**。He answered all the questions on the test paper.

以上两句,词意较具体,都是“有问有答”,所以应该用“回答”。例②“作了回答”,“回答”仍是动词 ◇ In the two sentences above, the meaning is concrete, so 回答 should be used. In example ②作了回答, 回答 is still a verb.

③ 对居民提出的问题,区政府及时作了**答复**。The block chief made replies to all the requests the residents asked.

④ 群众的每一封来信,有关单位都要给予**答复**。The department made a reply to every letter from the public.

⑤ 请他做报告的事,已经有了**答复**。He has made a reply to his report.

以上三句,词意含交代、落实义,所以应该用“答复” ◇ In the three sentences above, the meaning of "putting into effect" is implied, so 答复 should be used.

但有时词意较含混(具体抽象义都有)时,两个词可以互换 ◇ But sometimes the meaning is vague (both concrete and abstract) and the two words are interchangeable.

⑥ 对你们提出的要求,我们一定会给出一个满意的**答复**(/**回答**)。As for your request, We are likely to give you a satis factory reply.

另外,“答复”还是名词,如“一份答复”指具体的答复文件 ◇ Besides, 答复 is also a noun, e. g. 一份答复 means "a concrete reply document".

回头 等(一)会儿

(副)

huítóu děng (yī) huìr

Ⓔ in a moment/in a moment

◪“回头”是副词(另有动词“回”加宾语“头”,与此不同),“等(一)会儿”是短语 ◇ 回头 is an adverb (There is also a phrase made of the verb 回 and object 头 meaning "to turn one's head)". 等(一)会儿 is a phrase.

这两个词语都可表示稍过一会儿,都可做状语 ◇ Both 回头 and 等(一)会儿 mean "a moment later" and function as an adverbial:

① 咱们先谈到这里,**回头**(/**等(一)会儿**)再说吧! Let's

stop here, and we'll meet again soon.

② 你先忙你的事吧，**回头**(/**等(一)会儿**)我再找你。You can do your work first and I will talk to you later.

③ 赶紧把这几个错字改了吧，**回头**(/**等(一)会儿**)可能忘了。Correct these wrong words at once, or you will forget it soon.

以上例句，可互换 ◇ In examples ①② and ③ the two expressions are interchangeable.

"等(一)会儿"可以拆开，如"等了(一)会儿"。"回头"作为副词是不能拆开的，但容易与"回"(动)+"头"(名)混同 ◇ 等(一)会儿 can be separated by inserting a word, e. g. 等了(一)会儿. 回头 is an adverb and cannot be separated, but it may be confused with the phrase formed by the verb 回 and object 头. e. g. :

④ 他正忙着，所以**等了(一)会儿**，才去接电话。He was very busy, so he replied the phone after a while.

⑤ **回**过**头**来再看这件事，心里全明白了。You will understand it when you study it again.

例④"等了(一)会儿"，不是做状语而是做谓语；例⑤不是"回头"(副)，而是动词"回"+宾语"头" ◇ In example ④等了(一)会儿 is not the adverbial, but the predicate; while in example ⑤回头 is not an adverb, but a phrase made of the verb 回 and the object 头.

汇 寄

(动) (动)

huì jì

Ⓔ remit/post

"汇"、"寄"这两个动词都可表示邮寄，"汇"较书面化，宾语只能是"钱"、"款"，"寄"还可以用于"物" ◇ Both 汇 and 寄 mean "to send by post", 汇 is more literary and the object can only be 钱 or 款, while 寄 can also be applied to other things:

① 春节前，她给妈妈**汇**(/**寄**)了些钱。She remitted some money to his mother before the spring Festival.

② 你从银行**汇**的款，已经收到了。Your remitted money has been received.

③ 他买了几本书，**寄**给弟弟。He bought and posted some books to his little brother.

以上，用于"钱"(包括"货币"、"款项"等)时，两个词可通用(如例①)，用于"物"时，只能用"寄"(如例③)，"汇款"是习惯搭配(如例②) ◇ When applied to money (including 货币, 款项, etc.), the two words are inter-

H

changeable, as in example ①. When applied to other things, only 寄 can be used, as in example ③. 汇款 is a set phrase(as in example ②).

"寄"还表示寄托、依附等,多为固定格式 ◇ 寄 can also mean "to depend on" or "to entrust to the care of somebody, attach oneself to, etc". It is mostly used in set phrases:

④ 人类战胜各种疾病**寄**希望于科学。(表示寄托) Man hopes to cure diseases by sciences prosperous. (to entrust)

⑤ 她从小失去父母,**寄养**在亲戚家中,心中常有**寄人篱下**的感觉。(表示依附) She lost her parents since childhood and lived with her relatives and she has an inferior feeling of depending on others. (to attach oneself to)

H

会 能

(助动、动) (助动)

huì néng

Ⓔ know how to/ can, know how to

1. 两个词都是助动词,有时可互换 ◇ Both words are auxiliary verbs and interchangeable in many cases.

(1) 通过学习而掌握、熟悉(知识、技能等)多用"会" ◇ To master (knowledge, skill, etc.) through learning, 会 is used:

① 他**会**说英语。He can speak English.

② 我不**会**用电脑。I cannot use computers.

③ 你会不**会**弹钢琴? Can you play piano?

(2) 表示有能力有条件做某事,或达到一定标准,用"能" ◇ To have the ability to do sth. or to acquire certain efficiency, 能 is used:

④ 你**能**帮我计算一下这些数字吗? Can you sum up these figures for me?

⑤ 他病了,不**能**去了。He's ill and cannot go.

⑥ 一个小时之内,她**能**赶来吗? Can she come here in an hour?

1 中的例①"他会说英语",也可说"他能说英语",但多侧重于能力 ◇ In example ① of 1 他会说英语 can also be said as 他能说英语 which stresses the ability.

例②③如将"会"换成"能",意思就不同了,表示可能 ◇ In examples ② and ③, if 能 takes the place of 会, the concern will be possibility.

(3) 表示客观上有可能实现,可能性很大,用"会" ◇ To show great probability, 会 is used:

⑦ 看这天气,好像**会**下雨。It is going to rain.

⑧ 这么晚了,她不**会**来了。She is unlikely to come for it's so late.

⑨ 树上的果子熟了,自然**会**掉下来。When the fruit is ripe, it will automatically fall.

2.“会”也是动词,表示掌握、通晓(知识、技能等) ◇ 会 is also a verb meaning "to master, to know (knowledge, skill, etc.)":

① 她**会**法语。She can speak French.

② 老张**会**书法。Lao Zhang is adept at calligraphy.

③ 我一句汉语也不**会**。I cannot speak Chinese at all.

► [可以 kěyǐ—能 néng—能够 nénggòu]

会面 会谈 (动、名) 会晤 (动)

huì miàn huìtán huìwù

Ⓔ meet/talks/meet

◪ “会面”、“会谈”、“会晤”这三个词语都表示会见。但词性不同,“会面”是动宾词组;“会谈”是动词和名词;“会晤”是动词。“会谈”的施事者可以是国家、政府等,也可以是具体的人。“会面”、“会晤”的施事者必须是具体的人 ◇ 会面, 会谈 and 会晤 all mean "to meet", but they are of different parts of speech. 会面 is a verb-object phrase; 会谈 is both a verb and a noun; 会晤 is a verb. The subjects of 会谈 can be nations, governments, etc. and can also be people. The subjects of 会面 or 会晤 must be people.

由于“会面”是动宾短语,可以拆开说,下列用法只能用“会面” ◇ Since 会面 is a verb-object phrase and can be used separately, in the following examples only 会面 can be used:

① 这两位领导人只**会**过一次**面**。The two leaders met only once.

② 明年我们再**会会面**吧。Let's have a meet next year.

“会面”既可表示正式会见,又可表示一般的见面 ◇ 会面 can mean a formal meeting as well as an ordinary get-together:

③ 两国政府首脑又一次**会面**了。The heads of the two states met again.

④ 她和小张约定下午在老地方**会面**。She made an appointment with Xiao Zhang that they would meet at the same place this afternoon as before.

由于三个词语都可表示正式会见,并都可受定语修饰,下列三例三个词语可换用,但“会谈”侧重于商谈或谈判,“会晤”则是会面的意思,但都是词,不能拆开

用 ◇ Since all the three expressions can mean"a formal meeting" and can be qualified by an attributive, in the following three examples the three are interchangeable, but 会谈 stresses negotiation or discussion, while 会晤 means " to meet". 会谈 and 会晤 are words, not used separately.

⑤ 双方代表决定在北京**会面**(/**会谈/会晤**)。The delegates of the two parties planed to meet in Beijing.

⑥ **会面**(/**会谈/会晤**)时,双方畅所欲言,气氛融洽。The two parties spoke out freely and the atmosphere was harmonious when they met.

⑦ 这是一次亲切友好的**会面**(/**会谈/会晤**)。This is a friendly meeting / talk.

另外,"会谈"和"会晤"前面常加"进行"。这时"会谈"是名词宾语,"会晤"仍为动词做宾语 ◇ Besides, 进行 is often used in front of 会谈 and 会晤. In such a case, 会谈 is a noun used as the object of 进行 while 会晤 is a verb used as the object:

⑧ 合作双方的负责人进行了一系列**会谈**(/**会晤**)。The heads of each enterprise held a series of talks and meeting.

"会谈"的施事者常常不是个人而是集体 ◇ Often the agents of 会谈 are not individuals but nations, etc.:

⑨ 两国将在北京举行正式**会谈**。The two countries will hold an official talk in Beijing.

⑩ 两党**会谈**正在进行。The talks between the two parties are underway.

浑身 全身

(名) (名)

húnshēn quánshēn

Ⓔ from head to foot, all over/ from head to foot, all over

这两个名词都表示整个身体,异同之处是 ◇ Both words indicate the whole body, from top to toe. Their similarities and differences are as follows.

1. "全身"可以做主语和宾语,也可做定语和状语;"浑身"可做定语和状语,也可做主语,但不能做主语中的中心语(如不说"他的浑身"),不能做宾语 ◇ 全身 can function as the subject and the object, as well as the attributive and the adverbial. 浑身 can function as the attributive and the adverbial, and also as the subject; but it cannot be the headword of a subject(e. g. one cannot say 他的浑身), nor can it be the object.

2. "全身"用于对部位的客观叙

述，也可用于感觉和描写；“浑身”只用于感觉和描写。同时，后者比前者更为口语化 ◇ 全身 is used in objective statements of location, also in perception and description; 浑身 is only used in perception and description. The latter is more colloquial than the former.

3. “全身”除用于人和动植物，有时也可用于机身、船身等。“浑身”只用于人或动物 ◇ Besides human beings and animals and plants, 全身 can also be applied to the body of an airplane, a ship, etc. 浑身 can only be applied to human beings or animals. e. g. :

① 他照了一张**全身**像，又照了一张半身的。He took a whole-length picture and then took a half-length picture.

② 朋友的话像一股暖流传遍了他的**全身**。His friends' words warmed him.

③ 这次手术需要**全身**麻醉。The operation needs a general aesthesia.

以上三个例句都只能用“全身”不能用“浑身”，因为，例①③是部位上的客观叙述，区别于“半身”或“局部”；例②“全身”是做宾语。其他如“全身检查”、“全身性骨折”也不用“浑身” ◇ In examples ①②③ only 全身 can be used, not 浑身, because examples ① and ③ are just objective statements indicating 全身 as opposed to 半身 or 局部. In example ② 全身 is the object. In other phrases like 全身检查 (general physical check), 全身性骨折 (general fracture), etc. 浑身 cannot be used either.

④ 他感冒了，**全身**(/**浑身**)不舒服。He is not feeling well for he's got a cold.

⑤ 因为没带伞，他**全身**上下(/**浑身**上下)都被大雨淋湿了。He was wetted all over in the heavy rain because he did not take an umbrella.

⑥ 这艘巨轮的**全身**上下都涂上了耀眼的白色油漆。The huge ship is painted white brightly.

例④⑤也可用“全身”或“浑身” ◇ In examples ④ and ⑤ either 全身 or 浑身 can be used.

活 (动、形、副) huó　　生活 (名、动) shēnghuó

Ⓔ live; alive; living/life; live

1. 动词“活”表示有生命或处于生存状态，动词“生活”表示人的社会性生存 ◇ 活 as a verb means " to be alive or to be living", while 生活 means " to live one's life as a social being".

① 母亲移栽的花,已经**活**了。The flowers planted by mother are alive.

② 这鱼还**活**着呢。The fish is still alive.

③ **活**着就需要工作和娱乐。Our life needs work and entertainment.

以上,都是指生物或人处于生存状态,用"活" ◇ In examples ①② and ③ 活 means "to be living".

④ 最近**生活**得怎么样? How's your life been?

⑤ 他们俩已经一起**生活**了三十年,还是恩爱如初。They have been living together for 30 years and they still love each other deeply.

以上,指人的社会性的生存,用"生活" ◇ In examples ④ and ⑤,生活 means "the social life". 但"活"有时也指社会性的生存,与"生活"差不多 ◇ Sometimes 活 also means "social life", about the same as 生活:

⑥ 我最近**生活**(/**活**)得很不愉快。My recent life is quite unhappy.

2. 名词"生活"指生存活动或人类衣食住行等情况。如"政治生活"、"经济生活"、"艺术生活"等 ◇ 生活 as a noun means living or livelihood, e. g. 政治生活(political life),经济生活(economic life),艺术生活(arts life), etc. More examples:

① 他晚年的**生活**十分幸福。His late life is very happy.

② 这段**生活**对他来说是难以忘怀的。He cannot forget the time.

3. "活"也是形容词,表示有生命力的、灵活的、流动的、活生生的,等等 ◇ 活 is also an adjective meaning " vivid, lively, flowing, brisk, etc. ":

① 他把生意做**活**了。He makes his business run well.

② 这个人物写得很**活**。The character was depicted quite vividly.

③ 那条小溪,是**活**水,比较干净。The creek is very clean for its water is running.

4. 副词"活"还可表示简直、几乎完全(像)等 ◇ The adverb 活 can also mean "to be exactly, simply":

④ 他性格呆板,**活**像个木头人。He is dull and looks exactly like a woodenhead.

或者 (连) huòzhě　　或 (连) huò

Ⓔ or/or

这两个连词都表示选择关系或表示等同等,常用在叙述句中。"或"书面色彩较浓。口语中句子多用“或者” ◇ Both conjunctions indicate choice and are used in declarative sentences. 或 is more literary, and 或者 is colloquial:

1. 表示任选其一 ◇ 或 or 或者 means "to make a choice":

① 开会的时间定在明天上午**或者**下午都可以。Either tomorrow morning or afternoon will be OK for the meeting.

② 吃中餐**或者**西餐都行。Either Chinese food or Western food will be OK.

句中常有“都” ◇ There is often 都 in the sentence.

2. 表示以其中之后者为宜 ◇ 或 or 或者 indicates that the latter is a better choice:

① 这篇文章我老写不好，**或者**你来试试。I cannot write the article well. Would you like to have a try?

② 颐和园人太多，**或者**我们去圆明园吧！Since there are too many tourists in the Summer Palace, let's go to the Yuanmingyuan Garden instead.

3. 表示等同（名义或形式不同，实质相同）◇ 或 or 或者 indicates that the two are the same (the names or forms may be different, but in reality are the same):

① 毛竹，**或者**（/**或**）南竹，是一种优良的建筑材料。Bamboos also called the south bamboos are good construction materials.

② 叫她大嫂**或者**大姐都没关系。You can call her either sister-in-law or sister.

例①较书面化，可用“或” ◇ Example ① is more literary, so 或 can be used instead.

4. 如有“不管”、“不论”、“无论”，“或者”用在后边，表示包括两种情况。其中“无论”较书面化，可以用“或” ◇ If 不管，不论，无论 is used, 或者 comes before the latter to indicate what follows is included. 无论 is more literary, so 或 can go with it:

① 不管是京剧**或者**粤剧，她都会唱。She can sing either Peking Opera or Cantonese Opera.

② 无论大病**或**小病，都应及时治疗。No matter what disease you've got, you should go to see a doctor at once.

如果用“或者”、“或者是”，书面色彩略淡化 ◇ If 或者 or 或者是 is used, it is less literary.

5. 表示几种情况交替出现，或同时存在，“或”、“或者”用在动词短语前 ◇ To show that several situations take place alternately or simultaneously, 或 or 或者 is used in front of the verbal phrases:

① 晚饭后，我和朋友们**或**（/**或**

者)散步、**或**(/**或者**)闲谈,十分愉快。After supper,my friends and I either went for a walk or chatted,and we were very happy.

② 同学们毕业后**或者**(/**或**)在本地,**或者**(/**或**)去了外地,还有的留在本校当教师。After graduation,some of the students stayed in the city,some left it,and others stayed in their college as a teacher.

▶[还是 háishi—或者 huòzhě]

J

基本 根本

（形） （形、名）

jīběn gēnběn

Ⓔ basic, fundamental/ basic, fundamental; foundation, base

1. 这两个词都表示事物的重要部分或本源。但"根本"包含全部、彻底、从头至尾等意思，"基本"则指大部分，大体上。同时，词性有所不同。形容词的用例如 ◇ Both words can be used to indicate the most important part or source of sth. But 根本 means "completely, thoroughly, from beginning to end"; while 基本 means "roughly, on the whole". Besides, 基本 is an adjective, while 根本 can be used as an adjective as well as a noun. For instance, they are used as adjectives:

① 这个城市的能源问题已经**根本**解决了。The energy problem of this city has been completely solved.

② 这个城市的能源问题虽然**基本**解决了，但还有不少工作要做。Generally speaking, the energy problem of this city has been solved; however, there is still a lot to be done.

从以上二例可以看出，做状语时，"根本"是彻底、全部的意思，而"基本"是绝大部分。两个词做状语，都可以加"上"。"根本"还可以说"从根本上" ◇ From examples ① and ② we can see that, as an adverbial, 根本 means "thoroughly and completely", while 基本 means "mostly". When used as an adverbial, both words can take 上. 根本 can also be said as 从根本上.

"根本"做状语，还表示从来如此、自始至终，并多为否定式，"基本"没有这种用法 ◇ 根本, as an adverbial, also means "simply, from beginning to end, mostly in the negative". 基本 cannot be used in such a way:

③ 他**根本**没读过大学。He has never been at college.

④ 我**根本**就不赞成你这样做。I didn't approve you at all.

做定语时，"基本"表示最起码的，也是最必要的；"根本"的意思是主要的，具有前提性的，所以搭配也有差异 ◇ As an attributive, 基本 means "the minimal and the elementary", while 根本 means" the principle, prerequisite", therefore they are used in different collocations, e. g.

基本方法 basic way
基本思路 basic thinking
基本数字 basic numbers
基本资料 basic materials
基本参考书 basic reference books
基本队伍 basic personnel
根本出路 essential way out
根本命脉 essential fate

⑤ 这是学习本课程的**基本**参考书，必须认真阅读。You'd better read the book earnestly, for it is the main reference book of the course.

⑥ 改变经营思想，生产适销对路的产品，是我们这个厂的**根本**出路。The only way out for our factory is to change our managing idea and to produce products fulfilling the social needs.

有些词语，可以分别受两个词的修饰，如“方针”、“条件”、“原因”、“问题”等，但词义侧重点不同 ◇ Some words and phrases can be qualified by either word, e. g. 方针，条件，原因，问题，etc. but with different stress in meaning.

2. 名词“根本”，意思是事物不可缺少的最关键的东西 ◇ 根本，as a noun, means" the essential and the crux of sth. ", e. g. :

⑦ 水、肥、土壤，是农业的**根本**。The essentials for agriculture are water, fertilizer, and soil.

极 极端 极其

(副) (名、形) (副)

jí jíduān jíqí

Ⓔ extremely/
extreme, extremely/
extremely

1.“极”、“极端”、“极其”这三个词有共同点，都表示最高程度。但这限于三个词做状语时。“极”和“极其”是副词，只能做状语。而“极端”是形容词，也可做状语 ◇ 极，极端，极其 all mean" extremely" when they are used as adverbial. 极 and 极其 are adverbs and can only function as adverbials. 极端 is an adjective but can also function as adverbial. e. g. :

① 这种商品**极**(/**极其**)昂贵。This commodity is very expensive.

② 那里地处寒带，**极**(/**极其**)寒冷。The place is in cold zone and it is very cold there.

③ 他对工作**极**(/**极其**)不负责任。He is irresponsible for his job at all.

但这种三个词可互换的情况较

少。因为“极端”和“极其”多修饰双音节词。“极”一般多修饰单音节词 ◇ But they are seldom interchangeable, because 极端 and 极其 mostly qualify disyllabic words while 极 qualifies monosyllabic words:

④ 这篇文章**极**富特色。The article is unique.

⑤ 这些民工**极**能吃苦。These civilian workers are very industrious.

⑥ 这里地处热带，天气**极**热。The place is in tropical zone, and it is very hot.

以上三句，例④如用“极其”，常说“极其富有特色”。例⑤可换用“极其”。例⑥可说“极其炎热” ◇ In the examples above, if 极其 is used in example ④, one will say 极其富有特色. In example ⑤ 极其 can replace 极. In example ⑥ one can say 极其炎热.

2. 表示顶点（含贬义），做宾语，只能用名词“极端”，而且句中动词限于“走”、“陷入”、“陷于”等 ◇ To mean "extreme" (with derogatory sense) and used as an object, only 极端 can be used and the verbs are limited to 走, 陷入, 陷于, etc.:

① 哥哥一定要做流浪诗人，弟弟一定要当和尚，真是各**走**各的**极端**。The brother wants to be a minstrel, while the little brother wants to be a monk. They really go to extremes.

② 我们看问题要全面，不能**走极端**。We should take a balanced point of view — don't go to extremes.

3. 表示很高的程度（含贬义），做谓语，只能用形容词“极端” ◇ To mean "very high degree" (with derogatory sense) functioning as the predicate, only the adjective 极端 can be used:

① 他们这种做法太**极端**了！Their way is really in an extreme!

② 你怎么总是这么**极端**？难道不能温和一些吗？Why are you so radical? Why not be mild?

4. 表示很高的程度，做定语，只用“极端”，常带有非积极、非寻常的意义 ◇ To mean "very high degree", as an attributive, only 极端 is used, with a non-positive, extraordinary sense:

① 他是个**极端**的利己主义者，所以没有朋友。He is a complete individualist, so he has no friends.

② 她表现出的**极端**的热情，真让人受不了。Her enthusiasm is too much to be accepted.

③ 她这种**极端**兴奋的状态未必

利于比赛。Her extreme excitement does not necessarily do good to her match.

④ 这是一种**极端**情况,所以要采取极端措施。This is an extreme that should be dealt with by responding measures.

5. 表示很高的程度,修饰方位词及"少数"、"个别"等词语,只能用"极" ◇ To mean" a very high level", qualifying nouns of locality and the few words like 少数,个别,etc. ,only 极 is used:

① 那条河流地处这个省的**极**南部。The river flows in the southernmost part of the province.

② 这个城市在我国**极**北部。The city lies in the northernmost part of our country.

③ 只有**极**少数几个人同意这种观点。Only a few people agree with the view.

④ 这是一种**极**个别的情况,不能说明问题。This is a special case, which cannot indicate the whole.

这是副词"极"的特殊用法 ◇ This is a special usage of 极.

6. 表示很高的程度,做补语,只能用"极",并常加"了" ◇ To mean "a very high level", used as a complement, only 极 is used, and often with 了:

① 山里的秋天美**极**了。The mountainous area is very beautiful in autumn.

② 最近张先生忙**极**了。Mr. Zhang has been extremely busy recently.

▶[非常 fēicháng—极 jí—十分 shífēn]

即使 即便 就是

(连) (连) (连)

jíshǐ jíbiàn jiùshì

Ⓔ even if/even if/even if

这三个连词都表示退一步而言(假设的让步),用在前一分句,后一分句常有"也"、"还"等呼应(表示结果不受前面假设条件的影响)。"就是"(即"就是……也……")在口语中最常见;"即便"较书面化;"即使"书面、口语中都常用 ◇ All the three conjunctions mean" concession", and are used in the first clause; in the following clause there is usually 也 or 还, etc. to correspond (to show the result remains unchanged). 就是……也……is the most common in speech; 即便 is more literary; 即使 is used in either written or colloquial language.

① **即使(/就是/即便)**同意对方的要求,也应该提出条件。Even if you agree with the requirements of the other party, you should still propose your terms.

② 她**即使**(/**就是**/**即便**)原谅了你,你也会受到良心的谴责。Even if she forgives you, you will also feel guilty.

③ **即使**(/**就是**/**即便**)雨下得再大,也要按时出发。Even though it rains hard, we'll still start on time.

以上三句,三个词可互换,但语体色彩有所不同。同时,后一分句常有助动词。前后分句的谓语都可以是否定形式 ◇ In examples ①②③ the three words are interchangeable, but the style is different. There is usually an auxiliary verb in the following clause. The predicate of either clause can be in the negative:

④ **即使**(/**就是**/**即便**)赢不了,也不要灰心。Even if you lose it, don't lose your heart.

⑤ **即使**(/**就是**/**即便**)条件再好,我也不去。Even if the condition is very good, I will not go.

有时,"即便"和"即使"可用在后一分句,"就是"一般不能这样用 ◇ Sometimes 即便 or 即使 can be used in the second clause, but 就是 cannot:

⑥ 谁劝他他也不会听的,**即便**(/**即使**)是他的母亲。He turned a deaf ear to anyone even to his mother.

或在分句的后面加"的话",表示是假设让步条件 ◇ 的话 can be added at the end of a conditional clause to indicate the concession:

⑦ 我们应该按时出发,**即使**(/**即便**/**就是**)天气不好的话。Even it is not fine, we should still start on time.

这时可用"就是" ◇ With 的话 at the end, 就是 can also be used.

计划 规划

(动、名) (动、名)

jìhuà guīhuà

Ⓔ plan; program/plan; program

1. 名词"计划"是运作之前拟定的步骤、内容、程序等,名词"规划"是较长远的、规模较大的计划 ◇ The noun 计划 is a predetermined programme or scheme for making, doing or arranging sth. The noun 规划 means "a prolonged and large-scale plan". e. g. :

① 他这学期开学时定了一个学习**计划**。He made a learning plan at the beginning of this term.

② 学校最近制定了三年发展**规划**。Our school has carried out a three-year developing plan recently.

例①较具体,涉及面也较小,所

以用"计划"。例②较长远,规模较大,所以用"规划"。但因"计划"有时也指较长远的、大规模的,所以不能一概而论地说"计划"小、"规划"大。如中国的"发展国民经济的五年计划",规模可算大了,但习惯用"计划"而不用"规划" ◇ The content of example ① is more concrete and of a small scale, so 计划 is used. Example ② is concerned with something prolonged and of a large scale, so 规划 is used. Since 计划 sometimes can also mean" something prolonged and of a large scale", we cannot say that all 计划 are small and all 规划 are large. China's 发展国民经济的五年计划(Five-year Plan of National Economic Development) is undoubtedly of a large scale, but 计划 is still used customarily.

2. 动词"计划"是做计划的意思,动词"规划"表示做规划。另外,"计划"有时有打算、考虑的意思 ◇ The verb 计划 means" to make a plan"; the verb 规划 means" to make a layout or blueprint". Besides, 计划 sometimes means" to intend, to consider, etc". e. g. :

① 出国考察,要仔细**计划**一下行程。Please make a good plan about the itinerary of this overseas investigation.

② 他俩**计划**下半年结婚。They are going to get married after June.

③ 我们应该全面规划一下企业今后几年的发展道路。Our enterprise should work out a marketing development plan of the forthcoming years.

④ 我们要**规划**一下各种果树的种植面积。We'd better make a plan about the planting area of fruit trees.

例②就有打算、考虑的意思 ◇ In example ② 计划 means to intend, to consider.

继续 接着

(动) (副、连)

jìxù jiēzhe

Ⓔ continue/carry on; follow

◥ 这两个词都可表示不间断、延续,但词性不同 ◇ Both words indicate continuation, but they are of different parts of speech.

① 他病好以后,又**继续**(/**接着**)写他的论文。He resumed his thesis after he got over.

② 请你**继续**(/**接着**)讲下去。Go ahead, please.

以上二例,虽然"继续"是动词,"接着"是副词,但都是做状语,因此都可以用。但当"继续"做主要谓语时,不能用副词"接着"

替换 ◇ In examples ① and ②, 继续 is a verb and 接着 is an adverb, but they both function as the adverbial, so either can be used. When 继续 functions as the predicate, however, the adverb 接着 cannot replace it:

③ 大家要把他的事业**继续**下去。The unfinished research work should be continued.

而且,同是做状语,"继续"表示的不间断性更强,有些句子中也只能用"继续" ◇ In addition, though both function as the adverbial, 继续 denotes a stronger sense of continuity. In some sentences, only 继续 can be used, e.g.:

④ 他毫不松劲儿,**继续**做试验,终于有了结果。He kept on the experiment without any stopping, and as a result, he made some progress.

"接着"也是连词,表示前后的动作、行为或状态在时间上连结得很紧 ◇ 接着 is also a conjunction, referring to the following of states or actions:

⑤ 先听见脚步声,**接着**,就有人敲门。There's footstep followed by a knock.

⑥ 10月末,这里就会下雪,**接着**,就是漫长的冬天。It snowed at the end of October here, and then it was long harsh winter.

这与"继续"无共同点 ◇ This usage has nothing in common with 继续.

另外,"继续"偶尔可做宾语,但用得较少,较书面化 ◇ Besides, 继续 occasionally can be an object, but is rarely used in such away and is rather literary:

⑦ 这一事件是恐怖活动的继续。The event is the extension of terrorism activities.

▶[坚持 jiānchí—继续 jìxù]
[连续 liánxù—继续 jìxù]

家 家庭

(名、量、尾) (名)

jiā jiātíng

Ⓔ home; family/family

这两个词都可表示以婚姻和血统关系为基础的社会生活单位 ◇ Both words mean family:

① 这是一个幸福的**家庭**(/**家**)。This is a happy family.

但像例①这种两个词都可用的情况较少。"家"较通俗,口语化,"家庭"较正式,书面化 ◇ It is not common to find a case like example ① where either word can be used. 家 is colloquial, and 家庭 is more literary.

② 我**家**有四口人。There are four people in my family.

例②不宜用较正式的"家庭" ◇ 家庭, which is relatively formal, is

not suitable in example ②.

"家"还可表示住址、住地 ◇ 家 can also mean "address, residence":

③ 他**家**住在王府井大街。He lives in Wangfujing Street.

④ 现在她已经下班回**家**了。She leaves off work and goes home.

⑤ 现在她不在**家**。She is not at home now.

⑥ 我的左邻是王**家**,右邻是李**家**。The neighbor living on my left is the Wangs, and on the right is the Lis.

"家"有时还有比喻的意思,如"职工之家"(文娱活动场所)。以上例③④⑤不用"家庭"。但特指地址(如填写表格)时,用"家庭地址"。"家庭"还有些习惯搭配,如"家庭关系"、"家庭作业"、"和睦家庭"等 ◇ 家 sometimes is used figuratively, e. g. 职工之家(Workers' Home, a place for recreational activities). In examples ③④⑤, 家庭 is not used, but when the address is referred specifically (as when filling in a form), it is used, such as 家庭地址. There are also some customary collocations, e. g. 家庭关系(relationship between family members), 家庭作业(homework), 和睦家庭(harmonious family), etc.

"家"也是量词,用于人家、店铺、工厂等,如"住着两家人"、"一家饭馆"、"一家商店"、"两家工厂"等 ◇ 家 is also a measure word for household, store, factory, etc. e. g. 住着两家人(Here live two families), 一家饭馆(a restaurant), 一家商店(a store), 两家工厂(two factories), etc.

"家"还是词尾,指从事某种社会活动或精通某种知识技能,并有一定知名度的人,或有某种特征的人,如"作家"、"科学家"、"画家"、"探险家"等 ◇ 家 is also a suffix, meaning "a specialist", e. g. 作家(writer), 科学家(scientist), 画家(painter), 探险家(explorer), etc.

假如 如果 要是

(连) (连) (连)

jiǎrú rúguǒ yàoshi

Ⓔ if; in case/
if; in case/
if; in case

◪ 这三个词用法相同,只是"要是"在口语中最常用 ◇ The three words have the same usage, only 要是 is the most colloquial.

1. 表示假设的条件,后一分句常有"就"、"那么"等呼应。三个词一般可互换 ◇ Indicating a hypothesis, and in the second clause there is usually 就, 那么, etc. to correspond. The three words are generally interchangeable:

① **假如(/如果/要是)**下雨,运动会就顺延。If it rains, the sports meet will be put off.

② **假如(/如果/要是)**你同意,我们就一块儿干吧! If you agree, let's do it together.

有时可加"的话"、"的时候"(表示时间条件) ◇ Sometimes 的话 or 的时候(indicating the condition of time) can be added:

③ **要是(/如果/假如)**老人还在的话,该有 100 岁了。If the old man is still alive, he can be 100.

④ **要是(/如果/假如)**你有空儿的时候,请去看看她。If you are free, please go to see her.

2. 表示类比(如果 A 判断成立,与之类似的 B 判断也应成立);也用于比喻;有时可加"说"。三词可互换 ◇ Indicating analogy (if judgment A is tenable, the similar judgment B ought to be tenable, too). Sometimes 说 can be added. The three words are interchangeable.

① **假如(/如果/要是)**说食物是用来满足身体需求的,那么书籍就是用来满足精神需求的。If food can meet the need of your body, books will meet that of your spirit.

② **如果(/假如/要是)**说小学老师是园丁,那么医院的护士就是白衣天使。If we view the teachers in a primary school as gardeners, the nurses in a hospital as angels in white.

3. 表示让步,三个词可互换 ◇ Indicating concession; the three words are interchangeable:

① **假如(/如果/要是)**说他的伤能好,也将留下残疾。Even if his wound is well, he will be disabled.

② **假如(/如果/要是)**说我这篇东西还有可取之处,那就是罗列了一些可靠的资料。If there's something valuable in my article, I think it is a display of some reliable information.

4. 以上各种用法,在口语中三个词都可直接用在体词短语前(特别是"要是") ◇ In the above usages, the three words can all be used in front of nouns, pronouns, numerals and measure words (especially 要是):

① 这事亏得大家,**要是(/如果/假如)**我一个人,还真办不成。But for you, I would not have done it.

② 明天必须去吗? **要是(/如果/假如)**下雨呢? Must we go tomorrow? How can we do in case of rain?

▶[如 rú—如果 rúguǒ]
[若 ruò—如果 rúguǒ]

J

坚持 继续

(动) (动)

jiānchí jìxù

Ⓔ uphold, stick to/ continue, go on

◪ 这两个动词都可表示保持下去。但“继续”一般只是客观地保持不间断状态,而“坚持”含有主观努力和毅力。“坚持”还有坚决维护或维持的意思,可以带宾语 ◇ Both verbs mean" to continue". But 继续 means" to keep on continuity objectively", while 坚持 implies" subjective will power". 坚持 also implies" to uphold or maintain resolutely" and can take an object:

① 他这个人一向**坚持**原则。He adheres to principles all the time.

② 你不要**坚持**错误的意见了! Don't persist in your wrong idea.

以上两句,“坚持”主观性较强。“继续”也可带宾语,如“继续这一工作”,但叙述较客观 ◇ In examples ① and ② 坚持 implies a strong subjectivity. 继续 can also take an object, e. g. 继续这一工作(keep on the work), but it is an objective statement.

③ 这个工作,请大家**坚持**下去。Please stick to the work!

④ 这个工作,请大家**继续**(做)下去。Please keep on doing the work.

以上两句,如例③不用动词“做”,则两句一样。但例③表现的主观毅力的意义强,例④的客观性强。而且,一般而言,例④加“做”(或“干”等)更为常见。甚至可以说“继续坚持下去”,“继续”是状语,“坚持”是主要动词 ◇ In examples ③ and ④, if 做 is not used in example ④, the two sentences are the same, with example ③ expressing a stronger subjective will power and example ④ a stronger objectivity. Moreover, in example ④做(or 干, etc.) is usually used. One can even say 继续坚持下去, in which 继续 is the adverbial and 坚持 the main verb.

“坚持”可以带结果补语,如“坚持住”;还可以说“坚持到底”、“坚持到胜利”等。“继续”不能 ◇ 坚持 can take a complement of result, e. g. 坚持住(stick to), 坚持到底(stick to the end), 坚持到胜利(stick to it until victory), etc. 继续 cannot.

如果与其他动词搭配,如“坚持研究”、“坚持工作”、“继续研究”、“继续工作”等,都是可以的。但侧重主观努力与客观表述的差别依然存在 ◇ 坚持 and 继续 can be used with many other verbs, e. g. 坚持研究(keep on research), 坚持工作(keep on working), 继续研究(keep on researching), 继续工作(keep on working), etc., but the difference of stress on subjective effort and objectivity remains.

"继续"偶尔可做宾语,如"这一事件是恐怖活动的继续";"坚持"没有这种用法 ◇ 继续 occasionally can function as the object, e. g. 这一事件是恐怖活动的继续(This event is a continuation of terrorism); 坚持 cannot be so used.

► [继续 jìxù—接着 jiēzhe]

坚定 (形、动) jiāndìng　坚决 (形) jiānjué

Ⓔ firm; strengthen/ resolute, firm

◪ 这两个词都表示主观上不动摇、不犹疑 ◇ Both words mean "subjectively unwavering, staunch".

"坚定"侧重于大的方面,如政治路线、立场、观点、意志等 ◇ 坚定 is applied to serious matters, such as political line, standpoint, viewpoint, will, etc.:

① 他们**坚定**地执行科教兴国的路线。They firmly carry on the guideline of revitalizing a country by science and technologies.

② 她立志做好教师的**坚定**信念始终没有改变。Her firm ambition of being a good teacher is unchangeable.

③ 他虽然表示支持这个提案,但态度不够**坚定**。Though he expresses his support for the plan, he is not firm about it.

"坚决"侧重于具体的态度。上面例①③可换用"坚决" ◇ 坚决 stresses one's actual attitude. In examples ① and ③ 坚决 can replace 坚定. More examples:

④ 我们要**坚决**刹住行贿受贿的不正之风。We are determined to stop the corrupt practices of bribe and accepting bribes.

⑤ 既然知道这样做是错的,就要**坚决**改正。Since you know it's wrong, you'd better overcome it determinedly.

这种表示具体态度的句子,不用"坚定"。"坚决"多做状语,如例④⑤。但两个词都可做各种句子成分 ◇ Examples ④ and ⑤ relate to the actual attitude, so 坚定 is not used. 坚决 usually functions as the adverbial, as in examples ④ and ⑤. However, both words can function as other sentence elements.

另外,"坚定"还是动词,有使坚定、使不动摇的意思 ◇ Besides, 坚定 is also a verb meaning " to strengthen":

⑥ 在谈判中,我们应该**坚定**立场,据理力争。We should be firm and strive for the success in the negotiation.

⑦ 我们要**坚定**必胜的信心,不要泄气,否则这场球一定会输。We should strengthen the conviction that we are likely to win, and don't be discouraged, or we will lose the ball game.

J

艰难 (形) jiānnán　　困难 (名、形) kùnnan

Ⓔ difficult, arduous/ difficulty; difficult

◪ 形容词"艰难"和"困难"都表示事情的复杂、有阻力,或境遇的不顺、穷困等。但"艰难"所指的规模和程度上较"困难"更甚。有时"艰难"还指创业的难度很大 ◇ Both adjectives 艰难 and 困难 indicate "complication, resistance, predicament, poverty-stricken, etc". But the scale and degree of difficulties denoted by 艰难 surpass those of 困难. Sometimes 艰难 refers in particular to the great hardships in starting an undertaking.

名词"困难",与形容词意思相同,做主语或宾语,一般说"有困难"、"遇到了困难"、"克服困难"、"困难不小"等。而"艰难"常说"艰难困苦"、"艰难险阻"等 ◇ The noun 困难 has the same meaning of the adjective and can function as the subject or object of a sentence. We usually say 有困难 (have difficulty), 遇到了困难 (encountered difficulties), 克服困难 (overcome difficulties), 困难不小 (a big difficulty), etc. While 艰难 is usually found in phrases like 艰难困苦 (difficulties and hardships), 艰难险阻 (hardships and dangers), etc.

① 科学事业是一项十分**艰难**的事业,必须脚踏实地去干,没有捷径可走。The scientific work is full of hardships, and there is no shortcut in it, so we must work steadily and patiently.

② 他这个人很有韧性,任何**艰难**困苦都挡不住他。He is tenacious, and can overcome every hardship and difficulty.

③ 他在做作业的过程中遇到了一些**困难**,但都一一克服了。He had some difficulties in his homework, and he overcome them one by one.

④ 他是个善于克服**困难**的人。He can overcome difficulties with ease.

以上,两个词不能互换 ◇ In the sentences above, the two words are

not interchangeable.
当涉及“生活困苦”或“穷困”时，两个词都可以用，但“艰难”所指比“困难”更困苦或穷困 ◇ When talking about a hard life or a life suffering from financial problems, either word can be used, but 艰难 sounds more intensified than 困难.

⑤ 从前他们家的日子很**艰难**(/**困难**)。Their family had a hard time before.

涉及较大的事时，两个词也都可以使用，但难度上仍有不同 ◇ When applied to more serious events, either word will do, but there is still a difference in degree:

⑥ 他这个案子，进行得十分**艰难**(/**困难**)。The case he accepted is difficult to carry out.

▶[困难 kùnnan—难 nán]

监督 (动、名) jiāndū　监视 (动) jiānshì

Ⓔ supervise; supervision/ keep watch on

◥“监督”表示考察、察看、督促，如上级对下级、选民对代表、舆论对官员、人民对政府的监督。监督常是公开的。它可以做谓语，也可以做主语、宾语及定语 ◇ 监督 indicates " supervision, inspection, such as that of the superior to the subordinate, voters to the representatives, public opinion to officials, people to the government". 监督 is usually open. It can be the predicate and also the subject, object and attributive.

“监视”表示从旁密切注视并察看，如己方对敌方、警方对嫌疑犯，等等。监视常是隐秘的。除了状语，它也可以充当其他句子成分 ◇ 监视 means " to keep a close watch, e. g. on one's enemy, or the suspects by the police, etc". 监视 is mostly concealed. Besides being an adverbial, it can also function as other sentence elements.

“监督”的宾语可以是人或活动；“监视”的宾语是人或活动，以及处所等(如例④) ◇ The object of 监督 can be a person or action, while the object of 监视 can be a person, an action or a place (such as example ④).

“监督”的着眼点在促其向上(如例②);“监视”着眼于发现和防范违法的或不利于自己的活动等(如例③) ◇ The purpose of 监督 is to promote (such as example ②); while the purpose of 监视 is to discover and guard against activities illegal or harmful to oneself (such as example ③). e. g. :

① 人民代表有**监督**政府依法行政的责任。The people's delegates are responsible for supervising the government.

② 公务员应受到舆论的**监督**。The civil servants should be supervised by the public opinion.

③ 警方正在严密**监视**犯罪嫌疑人的活动。The police are keeping an eye on the suspects.

④ 犯罪嫌疑人的住所已经处于警方的严密**监视**之下。The suspect's house has been closely watched by policemen.

两个词不能互换 ◇ The two words are not interchangeable.

"监督"还可以做名词，是指专门做监督工作的人 ◇ 监督 is also a noun referring to the supervisor, e. g. :

⑤ 他是舞台**监督**。He is in charge of the stage.

J

将来 今后 以后

（名） （名） （名）

jiānglái jīnhòu yǐhòu

Ⓔ future/
from now on, in the future/
afterwards, later

◥ 这三个时间名词都表示某个时间之后的未来一段时间。"将来"和"今后"指现在之后，"以后"也可指过去某个时间之后。另外，三个词虽都可做主语、宾语，但"将来"这样用的时候，除表达较正式外，还能受定语修饰。"今后"较"以后"略显书面化 ◇ The three words of time all indicate a period of time after a certain moment. 将来 and 今后 indicate the time after the present moment, while 以后 can also indicate the time after a moment in the past. Moreover, all three words can function as the subject or object, but 将来 sounds more formal and can take an attributive. 今后 is more literary than 以后.

① 快毕业了，**将来**(/**今后**/**以后**)你打算做什么？You are going to finish your school, and what are you going to do in the future?

② 这件事**将来**(/**今后**/**以后**)会有什么变化，还很难说。It's difficult to predict what will happen to it in the future.

③ **将来**(/**今后**/**以后**)的生活，一定会更好。The future life is likely to be better.

以上三句，三个词可互换，但有所侧重："将来"较正式，"今后"较书面化 ◇ In the three examples above, the three words are interchangeable, but with different stress. 将来 is more formal, while 今后 is more literary.

有时"以后"表示过去某个时间之后 ◇ Sometimes 以后 indicates the time after a certain moment in the past:

④ 我十年前见过他一次，从那**以后**再没有见过他。I met him ten years ago, and from then on I have never met him.

⑤ 她结婚**以后**回过两次老家。She returned to her native place twice after her marriage.

其他两个词不能这样用 ◇ The other two words cannot be so used.

“将来”可受定语的修饰 ◇ 将来 can be modified by an attributive:

⑥ 我们一定会有一个美好的**将来**。（宾语）We are likely to have a brilliant future. (object)

⑦ 一个不可预料的**将来**在等待着她。（主语）An unforeseeable future is awaiting her. (subject)

其他两个词不能这样用 ◇ The other two words cannot be so used.

▶[未来 wèilái—将来 jiānglái]

讲 （动） jiǎng　　说 （动） shuō

Ⓔ speak/say

◥ 这两个动词都可表示用言语来表达。“说”较为随便；“讲”较为正式，常为成段的。如“讲故事”、“说闲话”等。再如下列二例，两个词可互换，但意思仍有侧重 ◇ Both verbs mean "to express with words". 说 is more casual and 讲 is more formal, e.g. 讲故事(tell a tale), 说闲话(gossip, make sarcastic or critical comments), etc. In the examples below, the two words are interchangeable but with different stress:

① 他对我**说**(/**讲**)：别忘了明天的事。She told me not to forget what to do tomorrow.

② 我不会唱歌，就**讲**(/**说**)个笑话吧。Since I can't sing, I'd like to tell a joke.

除了这个基本意义，两个词还可表示说明、解释 ◇ Besides this basic meaning, both words also mean "to explain":

③ 发生了误会，双方**讲**(/**说**)清楚了就行了。It will be OK if you two parties make clear about the misunderstanding.

④ 他详细地给我**讲了讲**(/**说了说**)这种电器的工作原理和使用方法。He introduced the structure of the electric appliance and how to use it in detail.

另外，两个词还各有一些不同的义项，如“讲”有论述、教授的意思，多用于教学 ◇ Moreover, each word has its own usages. For instance, 讲 means "to expound" and is often used in teaching:

⑤ 今天王老师要**讲**汉语的“把”

字句。Teacher Wang will give us a lesson on sentences with "把".

⑥ 明天**讲**第八课。We will learn lesson eight tomorrow.

"讲"还表示与对方商议并争取有利的结果 ◇ 讲 also means "to negotiate so as to get an advantageous result", e. g. :

⑦ 如果你有心买这几间房,你可以和房主**讲**价钱。You can bargain with the house owner if you want to buy it.

⑧ 赡养老人怎能**讲**条件? How can you raise terms about supporting the seniors.

"讲"还表示就某方面而言 ◇ 讲 also means" as far as sth. is concerned", e. g. :

⑨ **讲**体力,他不如你;**讲**技术,他比你强。He does not match you in terms of strength, but he is more skillful.

"讲"还表示提倡追求某种规范或辩论是非 ◇ 讲 also means" to lay emphasis on or pay special attention to", e. g. :

⑩ 从小就要养成**讲**卫生的好习惯。We should develop a good hygiene habit.

⑪ 朋友之间要**讲**信用。There should be credit between friends.

⑫ 企业要**讲**效益。The enterprise must strive for effect and benefit.

而"说"还可表示批评、责备 ◇ 说 sometimes means" to criticize or reproach":

⑬ 孩子惹了祸,被妈妈**说**了一顿。The child was criticized by his mother for his bad deed.

⑭ 因为连续几天迟到,他昨天挨**说**了。He was scolded yesterday because he was late successively for several times.

"说"还表示介绍婚姻对象,用于口语,如"说媒"、"说婆家"、"给他说个媳妇"等 ◇ 说 can also mean" to recommend somebody for marriage," e. g. 说媒 (act as matchmaker),说婆家(find a husband for her),给他说个媳妇(introduce a wife for him),etc.

这些,二词是不能互换的 ◇ In these examples 讲 and 说 are not interchangeable.

还有一点要注意的,在例①②③④中,中国北方人用"说"较多,南方人用"讲"较多 ◇ One should note that in examples ①②③④ northern Chinese use 说 more often, while the southerners use 讲 more often.

浇	浇灌
(动)	(动)
jiāo	jiāoguàn

Ⓔ water/water, irrigate

1. 表示液体(多呈线或条状)落到物体上用"浇",不用"浇灌" ◇ To water something,浇 is used,not 浇灌:

① 因为出去没带雨伞,他的全身都被**浇**透了。He was drenched in the downpour because he did not take his umbrella.

② 老人泡茶,喜欢把滚开的水**浇**到茶壶里。When making tea, the old man likes pouring the boiling water into the teapot.

③ 这道菜,最后还要**浇**上番茄汁。Finally, he will pour over the dish with tomato ketchup.

2. 表示灌溉 To mean"irrigate":用"浇"指一般的灌溉,用"浇灌"指较大面积、较大量的水的灌溉。下面例①②宜用"浇" ◇ 浇 means "to water". 浇灌 usually means "to irrigate, that is, a large area and a lot of water". In examples ① and ② below, 浇 ought to be used:

① 这种花每天要**浇**一遍水。The flower need watering every day.

② 后院那块菜地刚**浇**过水。The vegetable land in the back yard has just been watered.

③ 麦田经过**浇灌**,开始返青。The wheat becomes green after watered.

例③也可用"浇",但要改为"麦田浇了水,开始返青" ◇ In example ③,浇 can also be used;but the sentence must be changed into 麦田浇了水,开始返青.

3. 表示将液体往模具或一定的表面灌注,"混凝土"可用"浇灌","铅字"等用"浇" ◇ To mean"to pour liquid into a mould or surface". 浇灌 can be used for concrete;"浇"for type casting:

① 工人正在桥面上**浇灌**混凝土。The workers are pouring concrete on the bridge.

② 老式印刷用的铅字,是用铅水**浇**出来的。The type used before was molded with liquid lead.

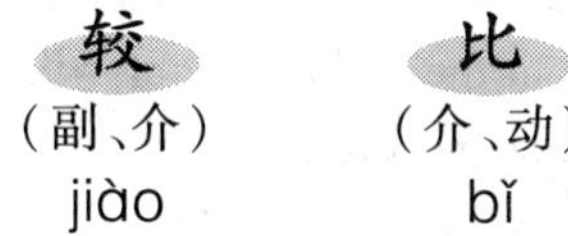

(副、介) jiào　　(介、动) bǐ

Ⓔ comparatively;than/than;compare

前面已经比较过"比"和"比较"。现在再比较一下"比"和"较"。关于"比",这里就不多举例了 ◇ 比 and 比较 have already been dealt with. Now we are going to compare 比 and 较, especially 较.

1."较"(副)表示具有一定程度,略显书面化,如"较便宜的报价"、"发现较早" ◇ The adverb 较 means "comparatively, quite", and is rather literary, e. g. 较便宜的报价(comparatively cheaper offer)，发现较早(earlier discovery)，and：

① 这间屋子**较**宽敞。Comparatively speaking, the room is spacious.

② 小王的性格**较**内向。Xiao Wang is a bit introvert.

③ 今天有太阳，没有风，**较**适于出行。It is sunny, windless and comparatively speaking, it is nice for going out.

"较"(副)和"比较"(副)基本相同，但更为书面化。在音节搭配上，"较"与"比较"区别不大 ◇ As an adverb，较 and 比较 are basically the same，while 较 is more literary. There is little difference in terms of the collocation of syllables between the two.

2. "较"(介)与"比"(介)用法一样，只是"较"也略显书面化 ◇ As a preposition，较 is the same with 比，only 较 is more literary：

① 老王**较(/比)**老李更有教学经验。Lao Wang has more teaching experience than Lao Li.

② 沈阳的冬天**较(/比)**北京冷多了。It is much colder in winter in Shenyang than that in Beijing.

③ 他今年的成绩**较(/比)**去年差。His marks of this year are lower than that of last year.

因为"较"更为书面化，可以用书面化的"较"+"之"，"之"代表比较参照的事物；另外，"较前"等也是书面化的说法 ◇ Since 较 is more literary，one can say 较之，with 之 introducing the thing compared. Besides，较前，etc. are also more literary expressions：

④ 工业**较**之农业有很大的可控制性。The industry is more controllable than agriculture.

⑤ 港人对目前经济预测**较**前乐观。The peaple of Hong Kong are optimistic about the economic forecast of the present time.

3. 至于"比"(动)，如"你们俩比一比"，与"较"不同。"较"也是动词，用法有限，如"较劲儿" ◇ As to the verb 比，e. g. in the sentence 你们俩比一比(You two have a competition.)，it is different from 较. 较 sometimes is also a verb，e. g. 较劲儿(have a contest) but less frequently used.

▶[比 bǐ—比较 bǐjiào]
[比 bǐ—比赛 bǐsài]

教室　课堂

(名)　(名)

jiàoshì　kètáng

Ⓔ classroom/classroom

◪ 这两个名词都表示教学单位中用作上课的较大房间。但"教室”具有实指性,“课堂”常含抽象泛指意义。“教室”的用法如下 ◇ Both nouns indicate a large room in a school where a class meets for a lesson. 教室 refers to the actual room, while 课堂 can be used figuratively. For example, the usage of 教室:

① 这是我们每天上课的**教室**。This is the classroom where we have a class every day.

② 请同学们到 101 **教室**去。Please go to Classroom 101.

又如“阶梯教室”、“听力教室”等,都是实指的。而“课堂”的用法与此不同 ◇ Even 阶梯教室 (lecture theatre), 听力教室 (Listening classroom), etc., all refer to actual rooms. But 课堂 is different, e. g.:

③ 这个房间已经很久没有用作**课堂**了,里面堆满了各种教学用具。The room has not been used for a classroom for a long time. Various teaching aids are put inside.

④ 今天的**课堂**作业是下边这些内容。Today's homework is as follows.

以上两句中的“课堂”都不是实指性的,甚至可说 ◇ 课堂 in the two examples above are not actual rooms. One can even say:

⑤ 社会是我们的大**课堂**。Society is our extensive class.

⑥ 做人,是人生**课堂**里最重要的一课。How to conduct oneself is the most important lesson in life class.

结实 坚固 牢固

结实	坚固	牢固
(形)	(形)	(形)
jiēshi	jiāngù	láogù

Ⓔ strong, durable/
solid, strong/
solid

这三个形容词都表示不易损坏,但“坚固”、“牢固”只用于事物,“结实”还可表示身体健壮。“结实”在口语中用得最多,可重叠;“牢固”较书面化,且多用于抽象事物 ◇ All the three adjectives mean" strong", but 坚固 and 牢固 are applied to things only and 结实 can also be applied to a person's health. Of the three 结实 is the most frequently used in colloquial language and can be reduplicated into 结结实实. 牢固 is more literary, mostly applied to abstract things.

1. 结实

① 老人的身体十分**结实**。The old man is very strong.

② 这个桌子做得可真**结实**。The table is very endurable.

③ 被捆得**结结实实**的,魔术师眨眼就解脱了。The magician

freed himself in an instant though he was tied tightly.

以上三句,例②也可换用"坚固",但不够口语化,例③如换用"牢固",则无重叠形式 ◇ In all the three examples above, 坚固 can be used instead in example ②, but is not very colloquial. If 牢固 is used in example ③, it cannot be reduplicated.

2. 坚固

① 这些家具**坚固**耐用。These furniture are sturdy and durable.

② 这顶帐篷不太**坚固**,晚上有大风,要加固一下。The tent is not fixed well. It is going to be windy, so please anchor it.

③ 那支球队严防死守,似乎形成了一个**坚固**的阵地,使对手无法突破。The defense of the team is tight, and it seems like an invincible front that the rivals cannot defeat.

以上例①也可用"结实"。例②也可用"牢固" ◇ In example ① above, 结实 can also be used instead. In example ② 牢固 can be used instead.

3. 牢固

① 两国结成了**牢固**的友谊。There is solid friendship between these two countrys.

② 他们之间已经形成了**牢固**的同盟关系。They have firm alliance.

③ 经过多次复习,这些生词他已经记得很**牢固**了。He can remember these new words well after repeating a lot of times.

以上三句都用于抽象事物,不能用其他两个词。但2中的例②也可用"牢固",即"牢固"有时也可用于具体的物 ◇ All the three examples above are about abstract things and so neither of the other two words can be used. But in example ② of 2, 牢固 can be used, that means, 牢固 can sometimes be applied to concrete things.

揭露 揭发

(动) jiēlù　(动) jiēfā

Ⓔ expose; uncover/ expose; bring to light

◪ 这两个动词都表示使隐蔽的事物公开出来或显露出来,但"揭露"是中性的(既可使积极的事物显露,如"揭露事物的本质",也可使消极的事物暴露,如"揭露阴谋"),"揭发"则用于使坏人坏事公之于世 ◇ Both words mean" to expose, to uncover", but 揭露 is neutral(either applied to a good thing, e. g. 揭露事物的本质(to expose the essence of sth.),or a bad thing,e. g. 揭露阴谋(to expose an intrigue)). 揭发 is applied to bad things only.

① 这篇文章**揭露**了一些惊人的事实。The article reveals some surprising facts.

② 我们要敢于**揭露**工作中的矛盾和问题。We should boldly expose the contradictions and problems in our work.

以上两句都不能用"揭发" ◇ In neither of the two examples can 揭发 be used instead.

③ 气愤的群众纷纷**揭发**检举他的贪污行为。The public angrily revealed his embezzlement.

上句则不能用"揭露" ◇ 揭露 cannot be used in example ③.

但在涉及较轻微的消极事物时,两个词可以互换 ◇ When something trifling and negative is concerned, the two verbs are interchangeable:

④ 这件不太光彩的事,最终还是被**揭露**(/**揭发**)出来了。The disgraceful thing is exposed to the public at last.

⑤ 对坏人坏事一定要**揭发**(/**揭露**)。The evil persons and things must be exposed.

但意思上仍有区别,用"揭露"侧重将隐蔽的事物显露出来。用"揭发"侧重将(别人隐瞒的)错误、罪行等公开 ◇ But there is still a difference in meaning. 揭露 stresses the exposure of something hidden, while 揭发 stresses publicizing some mistakes or crimes concealed by someone.

节省 (动) jiéshěng　节约 (动) jiéyuē

Ⓔ economize, use sparingly/ economize, save

这两个词都表示少耗费或不耗费人力、物力等,"节约"多用于较大的事 ◇ Both words mean" to use manpower, material resources sparingly", but 节约 is mostly applied to greater things.

① 这孩子把**节省**下来的零用钱捐给了灾区。The child donated his savings to the disaster area.

② 她过日子非常**节省**。She lives a thrifty life.

③ 使用这种操作方法,可以**节省**时间。This operating method can save a lot of time.

以上例句,由于所指多为具体的事,宜用"节省"。但为了强调或突出其意义,如例②③,也可换用"节约" ◇ In examples ①②③, since all are applied to concrete things, it is better to use 节省, but in order to emphasize the significance, 节约 can also be used instead in examples ② and ③.

"节约"有一些习惯搭配,如"增产节约"、"勤俭节约"。"节约"还可做状语(如例⑤) ◇ 节约 is used in some set phrases, e. g. 增产节约(increase production and practice economy),勤俭节约(be diligent and thrifty). 节约 can also function as an adverbial, as in example ⑤:

④ 这个工厂正在大搞增产**节约**。The factory is implementing the practice of economically increasing production.

⑤ **节约**办企业是他们的原则。One of their business principles is to be economical in business.

这两个词虽是动词,但具有一定的描写性,可受程度副词修饰,如例② ◇ The two words are verbs, but they are descriptive, so they can be modified by adverbs of degree as in example ②.

结果 后果 成果

(名、连) (名) (名)

jiéguǒ hòuguǒ chéngguǒ

Ⓔ result; as a result/ consequence/ achievement, result

1. "结果"、"后果"、"成果"都是名词,都表示事物发展到一定阶段的最后状态。区别是"结果"是中性的,"后果"是消极的,"成果"是积极的 ◇ 结果,后果 and 成果 are all nouns indicating the outcome of development. The difference is that 结果 is neutral, 后果 is negative, and 成果 is positive. e. g. :

① 比赛时的辉煌战绩,是他们平时刻苦训练的**结果**。Outstanding achievements are the results of long years practice.

② 那件事情的**结果**并不让人满意。Its result is out of our satisfaction.

③ 你这样做一定会失败,如果你不听劝阻,一意孤行,**后果**由你自己负责。You are likely to fail if you persist in doing so. If you turn a deaf ear to our persuasion, you will be responsible for the bad consequences.

④ 他们的科研项目,已经取得了初步的**成果**。Their research project has made certain progress.

以上例①②都用"结果",但①是积极的,②是消极的,这是因为"结果"是中性词。例③"后果"是消极的。例④"成果"是积极的。由于"结果"是中性词,例④也可说"取得了一定的结果",但例③只能用"后果" ◇ 结果 is used both in examples ① and ②, but in example ① it is positive, while in example ② it is negative, because 结果 is a neutral word. In example ③ 后果 is negative and in example ④ 成果 is positive. Since 结果 is neutral, example ④ can also be said as 取得了一定的结果, but in example ③ only 后果 can be used.

2. 连词“结果”联系两个分句,前面是事情的经过,后面用“结果”引出发展的结局;这个结局可以是顺接的也可以是反接的,可以是积极的也可以是消极的,如 ◇ The conjunction 结果 connects two clauses; the former relates to the process of the event, and the latter, introduced by 结果, relates to the result. The result may comply with the event or may be the converse of it, that is, it may be positive or negative. e. g. :

① 经过讨价还价,**结果**以八折成交。After bargaining, we made a deal at a 8-discount in the end.

② 你说早起叫我,**结果**还是我起来叫你。You said you would get up to call me earlier, but as a result, it is I who got up to call you.

③ 这小子早就说他要考北京大学,**结果**他还真考上了。The guy claimed earlier that he would register for the entrance, examination to Peking University. As a result, he was admitted.

④ 我去图书馆找了好几次你提到的那些资料,**结果**都是空手而归。I went to the library for several times searching for the materials you mentioned, but my efforts were all in vain.

▶[果实 guǒshí—成果 chéngguǒ]

竭力 尽力

竭力 (副) jiélì　　尽力 jìn lì

Ⓔ do one's utmost/ do one's best

◥ 这两个词语都表示用了全部的力量(心力或最大的努力)。但“竭力”是副词,“尽力”是动宾短语。另外,“竭力”更书面化一些。在修饰非正面形式(否定或消极形式)时,也多用“竭力” ◇ Both the word and the phrase mean "do all one can", but 竭力 is an adverb and 尽力 is a verb-object phrase. Besides, 竭力 is more literary. When applied to non-positive things(negative or passive), 竭力 is used more.

① 这件工作,我一定**竭力**(/**尽力**)完成。I will do my utmost to finish the work.

② 他**竭力**表示反对,但还是没能阻止决议通过。He exerted his

J

every effort to disapprove the proposal; however, he cannot prevent it from being adopted.

③ 对这个方案,一些人尽力支持,另一些人却**竭力**阻挠。As for the plan, some did their utmost to be for it, while some against it.

例①两个词可以互换,但"竭力"书面色彩略重。例②中"竭力"修饰的是"表示反对",是非正面形式。例③中正面用"尽力",反面用"竭力" ◇ In example ①, the two words are interchangeable, but 竭力 is more literary. In example ② what 竭力 qualifies is 表示反对, a non-positive expression. In example ③, the positive effort is qualified by 尽力, while the negative effort, by 竭力.

④ 我已经**尽了全力**去做。I have exerted every effort to do it.

⑤ 他虽然没有考好,但他已经**尽了力**。Though he failed, he has made every effort to do it.

以上两句,动词和宾语拆开,用"尽力" ◇ In examples ④ and ⑤, the verb and object are used separately, so 尽力 is used.

另外,"竭力"还可用于四字短语"尽心竭力" ◇ Besides, 竭力 can be used in the four word set phrase 尽心竭力:

⑥ 父母**尽心竭力**地培养和教育他们兄弟俩。Their parents did their best to bring up and educate them.

仅 (副) jǐn　　仅仅 (副) jǐnjǐn

Ⓔ only/only

这两个副词都表示限制范围或数量。"仅"更书面化一些;"仅仅"略显强调化 ◇ These two adverbs indicate limit of scope or quantity. 仅 is more literary and 仅仅 is more emphatic.

1. 限制范围 ◇ To limit the scope:

① 这**仅(/仅仅)**是猜测,不能作为证据。This is only guesswork, and it is unreliable.

② 看他们俩那亲密的样子,好像不**仅(/仅仅)**是一般的同学。Their intimacy shows they are not the common classmates.

③ 这本书我**仅(/仅仅)**看了开头。I read only the beginning of the book.

以上两个词可互换,但"仅"略显书面化,"仅仅"略显强调 ◇ In the examples above, the two words are interchangeable, but 仅 is more literary and 仅仅 is more emphatic.

2. 限制数量 ◇ To limit the quantity:

① 她离家**仅(/仅仅)**一天时间,家里就出了事。She left home only one day, and you see there was something wrong with her family.

② 我**仅**(/**仅仅**)见过她一次。I met her only once.

③ 这个工程**仅**(/**仅仅**)用半年就完工了。The project was completed in only half a year.

"仅"和"仅仅"在音节搭配上区别不明显 ◇ In collocation of syllables, there is no obvious difference between 仅 and 仅仅.

注:"仅仅"比"只"更显强调 ◇ Note: 仅仅 is also more emphatic than 只.

劲儿 劲头儿

(名) (名)

jìnr jìntóur

Ⓔ strength, energy/ strength, energy

1. 表示力量,"劲儿"、"劲头儿"两个词都可以用。以下各例,两个词常可换用 ◇ To mean "strength", either 劲儿 or 劲头儿 usually will do. In the following examples, the two words are interchangeable:

① 他年轻力壮,手上的**劲儿**(/**劲头儿**)很大。(体力) He is young and vigorous, and his hands have strength. (strength)

② 这头牛**劲儿**(/**劲头儿**)真大。(兽力) The bull is really strong. (animal strength)

③ 拖拉机的**劲儿**(/**劲头儿**)可不小,能拉好多东西呢。(机械力) The tractor is so powerful that it pulls a lot of weight. (mechanical force)

如果充当动词"用"、"使"等的宾语,则多用"劲儿" ◇ When functioning as the object of 用, 使, etc. usually 劲儿 is used. e. g. :

④ 他用**劲儿**推开了沉重的大门。He pushed the heavy gate with efforts.

⑤ 箱子很重,抬的时候,你们两个人得使点儿**劲儿**! The box is very heavy, so you'd better exert some efforts to lift it up.

2. 表示情绪、精神、神态等,尤其是在比较固定的搭配中,常用"劲儿",如"冲劲儿"、"倔劲儿"、"钻劲儿"、"傻劲儿"等。如用"劲头儿",则常需加"的",前面多为非单音节词,如"倔强的劲头儿"、"欢喜的劲头儿"、"兴高采烈的劲头儿"等 ◇ To indicate sentiments, spirit, air, expression, etc. 劲儿 is usually used, esp. in some set phrases, e. g. 冲劲儿(vigour), 倔劲儿(bluntness), 钻劲儿(spirit of studying intensively), 傻劲儿(folly, foolishness), etc. If 劲头儿 is used, there is usually a non-monosyllabic word in front, e. g. 倔强的劲头儿(tenacity), 欢喜的劲头儿(high spirits),

兴高采烈的劲头儿(with joy and expedition),etc. e. g.:

① 他有一股子倔**劲儿**。He is a man of tenacity.

② 瞧你那坏**劲儿**,总是捉弄人! You are too tricky and always like playing tricks on others.

③ 她有一种不出成果不罢休的**劲头儿**。She is determined to get good results.

前边不加定语,"劲头儿"也可以表示积极的情绪、兴趣 ◇ Without an attributive,劲头儿 can also mean" positive mood and interest":

④ 他们做试验很有**劲头儿**! They take great interests in doing experiment.

⑤ 说起歌星来,这几个人**劲头儿**十足。When it comes to singers,they showed great interests in them.

有时"劲儿"不加定语也可表示积极情绪,常与"上来"搭配,表示有了积极的情绪 ◇ Sometimes 劲儿 without an attributive can also mean " a positive sentiment" and often takes 上来:

⑥ 在领导的表扬和鼓励下,小王的**劲儿**(/**劲头儿**)逐渐上来了。With the praise and encouragement of the leaders,Xiao Wang gradually cheered up.

"上劲儿"、"来劲儿"也有类似用法 ◇ 上劲儿 or 来劲儿 has a similar usage:

⑦ 听了领导的表扬,小王工作得更**上劲儿**了。Xiao Wang worked harder than before at his leader's praise.

⑧ 他们越干越**来劲儿**,连吃饭都忘了。They become more and more interested in it and even forget their meals.

经常 (形) jīngcháng　常常 (副) chángcháng　常 (副) cháng

Ⓔ frequent/often/often

◪ 这三个词都可表示重复发生(间隔较短)、时常。但词性不同:"经常"是形容词,可做定语、状语等。"常常"、"常"两个词都是副词,只做状语。另外,"经常"较正式,所表示的"重复发生",也常指在较大的时间段落之内,有规律性和一贯性;"常"和"常常"则指动作频率高,屡次发生,并不涉及是否成规律,常用于一般情况,也更为口语化 ◇ All the three words indicate frequency (with very short intervals). 经常 is an adjective and can function as attributives, adverbials, etc. 常常 and 常 are adverbs and only function as adverbials.

Besides, 经常 is formal, and the repetition happens in a rather long period of time and is regular and consistent. 常 and 常常 mean" high frequency which may not be regular";they are applied to ordinary situations and are more colloquial.

至于"常"也是形容词(表示一般、普通),如"常理"、"常人","常时",不在比较范围 ◇ 常 is also an adjective (meaning ordinary, common), e. g. 常理(common sense),常人(average people),常时(usual time/usually) which is not involved in the comparison here.

① 他**经常**(/**常常**/**常**)去图书馆看书。He often goes to the library to study.

这种表达一般性内容的句子,三个词都可以用,但"经常"较正式 ◇ In such sentences of ordinary content, all three words can be used, with 经常 being more formal.

② 对布置下的工作应当**经常**督促检查。We should/must supervise and accelerate fulfilment of the assignments.

③ 在小区内**经常**可以看到园林工人忙碌的身影。In the community, we often see figures of gardeners working around busily.

以上两句,所指内容较为正式,时间段落也较长,用"经常"为宜。另外"经常"也可做定语 ◇ The two examples above involve a rather formal content as well as a rather long period of time, therefore 经常 is more suitable. Besides, 经常 can also function as an attributive:

④ 干这种工作,出差是**经常**的事。The work involves in frequent trips.

"常"和"常常"音节虽有不同,搭配上的区别不大 ◇ 常 and 常常 are of different number of syllables but they are similar in terms of collocations:

"常"多与单音节搭配,但也不限于单音节,这两个词否定式都是"不常" ◇ 常 is mostly collocated with monosyllabic words but is not limited to monosyllables. The negative of these two words is 不常.

形容词"经常"还有一个意义,表示平常、日常,常做定语 ◇ The adjective 经常 has another meaning" ordinary, daily" . It often functions as an attributive:

⑤ 我们研究所的**经常**工作是研究"饮用水"的课题。The routines in our institute are studying the drinking water.

⑥ 这笔**经常**办公费用是不能省的。This part of the running expense cannot be saved.

"经常"做谓语,常纳入"是……的"框架,加"很"等 ◇ 经常 as the predicate is often put in the frame of 是……的, along with 很, etc.:

J

⑦ 发生这种事**是很经常的**。This kind of thing is a common occurrence.

“经常”还可构成“经常性”、“经常化”等短语，如：“经常性的讨论”、“交流学习经验已经经常化了” ◇ 经常 can be used in such phrases as 经常性，经常化，etc. e. g. 经常性的讨论(regular discussion)，交流学习经验已经经常化了(Exchange of studying experience has become a regular practice).

▶[常常 chángcháng—常常 cháng]

[往往 wǎngwǎng—常常 chángcháng]

惊奇 (形) jīngqí　　惊异 (形) jīngyì

Ⓔ surprised, amazed/ surprised, amazed

这两个词都表示感觉奇怪。“惊异”更为书面化 ◇ Both words mean " to be surprised". 惊异 is more literary.

① 这个演员表演的魔术“大变活人”真让人**惊奇**(/**惊异**)。We are amazed at the magician's performance of" turning out a living person".

② 这完全是我意料之中的事，我并不**惊奇**(/**惊异**)。I am not surprised at all, for it is not out of my expectation.

③ 听了哥哥讲的探险故事，弟弟用**惊奇**(/**惊异**)的目光望着哥哥问：“真有这事吗？”After having heard his brother's adventurous story, the little brother looked at his brother with wonder and asked: Is it real?

④ 她**惊奇**(/**惊异**)得目瞪口呆。She was dumbfounded.

以上各句，两个词可互换，但“惊异”更为书面化 ◇ In the examples above, the two words are interchangeable, but 惊异 is more literary.

“惊异”也可加“于”，书面色彩较重 ◇ 于 can be added to 惊异，making it even more literary:

⑤ 他**惊异于**这本历史书材料如此丰富。He was amazed at the diverse history materials.

⑥ 大家**惊异于**这位学者竟能熟练地使用多种语言。We are amazed at the scholar's good command of a lot of foreign languages.

“惊奇”较少加“于” ◇ 于 is rarely added to 惊奇.

精细 (形) jīngxì　　精致 (形) jīngzhì

Ⓔ meticulous, fine/

exquisite, fine

◥ 这两个形容词,“精细”表示精密细致,另外,“精细”还可以形容人,表示细心、精明。“精致”表示精巧细致,多形容物 ◇ The adjective 精细 means" meticulous". It can also be used to describe a person who is sagacious and careful. 精致 means" ingenious and meticulous" and is mostly used to describe things.

① 这件工艺品制作得十分**精细**(/**精致**)。The art craft is made exquisitely.

② 小客厅里古色古香,布置得十分**精致**。The small living room is decorated exquisitely and in good taste.

③ 这部作品**精细**地描写了中国历史上惟一的一位女皇帝武则天的性格特征。The work depicts fully the character of Wu Zetian, the only empress in the Chinese history.

例①是说工艺品的,两个词可以互换,因为含义较宽 ◇ Example ① is about a handicraft article and the two words are interchangeable, since the meaning is rather comprehensive.

例②是说客厅布置,侧重于精巧,用“精致” ◇ Example ② is about the decoration of the drawing room with the stress put on ingenuity, so 精致 is used.

例③是说小说中的描写,也是状物,侧重精密,用“精细”。注意,这里不是说武则天精细,而是说小说的描写精细 ◇ Example ③ is a description in a novel, a description of something with the stress put on the accuracy, so 精细 is used. Note that 精细 is not applied to Wu Zetian, but to the description concerning her in the novel.

④ 他为人十分**精细**,什么事都瞒不过他。He is very circumspect. Nothing can escape his notice.

例④是形容人的性格的,用“精细” ◇ Example ④ depicts someone's character, so 精细 is used.

竟 (副) jìng　　竟然 (副) jìngrán

Ⓔ to one's surprise, unexpectedly/
to one's surprise, unexpectedly

◥ 1. 表示超乎估计。“竟”比“竟然”更为书面化 ◇ Indicating exceeding estimation. 竟 is more literary than 竟然.

① 三十多岁的大男人,说着说着,**竟**(/**竟然**)流出了眼泪。The over-thirty-year-old man talked and talked, and to my surprise, he was in tears.

② 想不到,几年不见,**竟**(/**竟然**)认不出她了。To my surprise, I cannot recognize her after several years.

③ 书上说这里夏天少雨,结果今年夏天**竟**(/**竟然**)连降大雨。It is said that there will be a little rainfall this summer here, but to our surprise, it rained heavily and continually.

J

2. 表示终于、以至于,多用"竟" ◇ To mean"at last, in the end, to such an extent", 竟 is mostly used:

① 没想到他家的日子一天不如一天,最后**竟**连女儿都退了学。His family's life became harder and harder unexpectedly, and at last his daughter dropped out of her school.

② 老人先是大口地喘气,后来**竟**没了声音。The old man first gasped and then he was silent.

③ 大雪连着下了三天,**竟**把门都封了。It snowed heavily for three days and the snow blocked the road in the end.

以上三句也可用"竟然",但不如"竟"的意思重 ◇ In the three examples above 竟然 can be used instead, but is less forceful than 竟.

具备 (动) jùbèi　具有 (动) jùyǒu

Ⓔ possess, be provided with/possess, have

◥"具有"表示"有",宾语多为抽象的"意义"、"风格"、"气质"、"水平"、"水准"、"作用"等,而且经常要带宾语。"具备"也表示"有",但包含"齐备"的意味,多涉及"条件"、"能力"等 ◇ 具有 means "to have", and the object is usually something abstract such as 意义(meaning), 风格(style), 气质(temperament), 水平(level), 水准(standard), 作用(effect), etc., which in many cases is a must. 具备 also means "to have", but contains the meaning of completeness and the object is usually 条件(condition), 能力(ability), etc.

当宾语为"条件"、"能力"以及与之相关的"水平"、"水准"、"气质"、"资质"、"本领"等时,两个词可互换,但"具备"侧重于"全部都有" ◇ When the object is 条件, 能力 or something related to it, such as 水平, 水准, 气质, 资质(aptitude), 本领(skill, ability), etc., the two words are interchangeable, but 具备 stresses to have all that is needed:

① 你已**具有**(/**具备**)报考音乐学院的条件。You have been qualified for the conservatory of music.

② 他**具有**(/**具备**)担负那项工作的各种能力。He is eligible for the job.

③ 她**具有**(/**具备**)编剧所需的艺术水准。She is qualified for a play writer in terms of artistic talents.

下列宾语为“意义”等的句子,只能用“具有” ◇ In the following examples with words like 意义 as the object,only 具有 can be used:

④ 这次会议**具有**很重要的历史意义。The conference is of great historical significance.

⑤ 这道程序**具有**什么作用? What's the use of the program?

⑥ 权力和地位对他**具有**极强的诱惑力。Power and social status are very attractive for him.

“具有”和“具备”都可受“不”的修饰 ◇ Both 具有 and 具备 can be qualified by 不:

⑦ 我还不**具有**(/**具备**)做同声传译的水平和资格。I am not qualified for simultaneous translator yet.

但“具备”可受“没有”和“不大”的修饰,“具有”不能 ◇ But 具备 can be qualified by 没有 and 不大,while 具有 cannot:

⑧ 他还**没有具备**参加大赛的条件。He is not qualified for an international game.

⑨ 这方面的知识我**不大具备**。I am not very knowledgeable about this area.

剧烈 激烈

(形) jùliè　　(形) jīliè

Ⓔ violent,severe/fierce,violent

◥ 这两个词都可表示厉害、猛烈 ◇ Both words mean" to be fierce, violent".

1. 用于身体伤痛时,用“剧烈”不用“激烈” ◇ When applied to injury or wound,剧烈 and not 激烈 is used:

① 脚扭伤了,他感到一阵阵**剧烈**的疼痛。He sprained his ankel and felt attacks of gnawing pain again and again.

② 忍着**剧烈**的腰痛,他下了床。He got off the bed with his acute waist pain.

2. 用于思想、言论、情绪等,用“激烈”不用“剧烈” ◇ When applied to thought,speech,sentiments, etc. 激烈 and not 剧烈 is used:

① 他的发言言辞很**激烈**。His speech is fierce.

② 小伙子,情绪不要太**激烈**,慢慢说。Don't be excited,young

man. Please speak slowly.

③ 这里刚刚发生过一场**激烈**的辩论。There was a heated debate just now here.

3. 用于竞赛、竞争等,多用"激烈" ◇ When applied to competition, etc. 激烈 is usually used:

① 双方球员你争我夺,打得十分**激烈**。The two football teams are having a fierce match.

② 在市场上,这些商家竞争得很**激烈**。The businesses compete bitterly for the markets.

4. 用于思想起伏,两个词都可以用 ◇ When applied to undulation of thoughts, either word will do:

① 他经过**激烈**(/**剧烈**)的思想斗争,最后下了决心。He made up his mind after his intense thought.

② 究竟应该怎么办?他的内心经历了痛苦而**激烈**(/**剧烈**)的斗争。How could he do? He went through a hard thought.

5. 用于跳动、摇动、变动,用"剧烈" ◇ When qualifying beat, shake, change, 剧烈 is used:

① 他的心脏**剧烈**地跳动着。His heart beats quickly.

② 汽车在山路上行走,车身晃动得很**剧烈**。The cart rocked violently while driving on the mountain road.

③ 最近一百年来,中国社会经历了**剧烈**的变动。The Chinese seciety has undergone a series of great changes in the last century.

6. 用于变革、冲突,两个词都可以用 ◇ When applied to transformation, conflict, either word will do:

① 国内手机市场一个更加**剧烈**的变革时代即将来临。A more dramatic change time of domestic markets of mobile phone is imminent.

② 各种政治力量进行了**激烈**的交锋。Intense confrontations took place among various political forces.

前一句多用"剧烈",后一句多用"激烈" ◇ In example ①剧烈 is usually used, while in example ② 激烈 is usually used.

K

开动 发动

(动) (动)

kāidòng fādòng

Ⓔ start, set in motion/ start, launch

1. 这两个动词都可表示使机器运转 ◇ Both verbs mean" to set a machine in motion" :

① 印刷机**开动**(/**发动**)起来了。The printing press started.

"开动"侧重于开始运作;"发动"侧重于通过点火等过程进行运作 ◇ 开动 stresses " to start motion", while 发动 stresses " the process of operation through ignition".

② 天寒地冻,汽车好容易才**发动**起来。It was not easy to start the car for it was freezing.

例②属于第二义,用"发动" ◇ Example ② is of the second meaning, so 发动 is used.

作为使机器运转的引申义,"开始"还可以表示运用思想等,例如在口语中可以说 ◇ 开动 can be used figuratively to mean" using one's brain, etc. " For instance, in colloquial speech one can say:

③ 大家要积极**开动**脑筋想办法。Everyone is racking his or her brain to find a way.

2. "开动"还可表示队伍开拔或车辆开行 ◇ 开动 can also mean" to be on the move of the troop or traffic" :

① 队伍休息了一会儿就**开动**了。The troops were on the move again after a short rest.

② 火车**开动**了。The train has started.

3. "发动"可表示一方主动开始战争行动 ◇ 发动 can mean" to start a war" , e. g. :

① 侵略者**发动**了战争。The invaders launched the war.

"发动"还可表示使人员展开行动(一般为较大行动) ◇ 发动 can also mean" to mobilize people to engage in a campaign (usually of a big scale)" :

② 县里**发动**了大批民工抗洪抢险。The county government mobilizes a body of civilian workers to fight against the floods.

③ 厂长**发动**青年工人在厂房周围植树。The director of the factory called up young workers to plant trees around the factory compound.

K

开始 开头

（动、名） （名）

kāishǐ kāitóu

Ⓔ begin; start/start

1. 名词"开始"和"开头"都表示事物发展最初的阶段，但意思各有侧重："开始"只是一般的初始阶段，"开头"还表示一个明显过程的开端。"开头"更为口语化 ◇ 开始 and 开头 as noun both mean "the initial stage of development", but have different stresses: 开始 is just a beginning stage, while 开头 means "the beginning of an obvious process". 开头 is more colloquial.

① 好的**开始**是成功的一半。A good beginning is half done.

② 故事的**开头**还挺有意思，后来就不行了。The beginning of the story is interesting, but the rest is not so.

例①不宜用"开头"。例②如用"开始"，应说"开始的时候"或"开始的部分"等 ◇ It is not suitable to use 开头 in example ①. If 开始 is used in example ②, one ought to say 开始的时候 or 开始的部分, etc.

2. "开始"也是动词，表示从头起或从某一点起。"开头"也是动宾短语，表示从头起始，较口语化 ◇ 开始 is also a verb, meaning "to start from the beginning or from a certain point". 开头 is also a verb-object phrase, meaning "to start from the beginning", which is very colloquial.

下面看动词"开始"和动宾短语"开头"的比较 ◇ Following is a comparison of the verb 开始 and the verb-object phrase 开头:

① 现在**开始**上课。Now class begins.

② 大会**开始**了。Now the meeting begins.

以上例①②都不能用"开头" ◇ 开头 cannot be used either in example ① or example ②.

③ 这场讨论刚**开了个头**。This is just the beginning of the discussion.

④ 我不知道这篇文章怎么**开头**好。I don't know how to begin the article.

以上例③④也不能用"开始"。因为，"开始"只表示一般的从头起始，而"开头"强调如何使一个过程的最初阶段运作起来。特别是，这里"开了个头"比较特殊 ◇ 开始 cannot be used in examples ③ and ④, since 开始 only means "to start from the beginning", but 开头 stresses "how a process begins from the very beginning". Especially, here 开了个头 is rather special.

但在下列句子中,“开始”、“开头”都可以用 ◇ But in examples ⑤ and ⑥, either 开始 or 开头 will do:

⑤ 这学期刚**开始**(/**开头**),还有三个多月呢。This is just the beginning of the term, and there are over three months left.

⑥ 他讲的故事才**开始**(/**开头**),你慢慢听吧! He just starts telling his story, and you'd better follow it with patience.

以上例⑤⑥二者可换用。因为这时有一个较明显的过程(如学期、讲故事),“开始”和“开头”都可表示这个过程的启动。但“开头”这方面的意义更为明显 ◇ In examples ⑤ and ⑥ the two expressions are interchangeable, as there is obviously a process(学期 and 讲故事). Either word can mean "the start of the process", but 开头 is more obvious in this aspect.

▶[起初 qǐchū—开始 kāishǐ]

看法 (名) kànfǎ　意见 (名) yìjiàn

Ⓔ view/opinion

1. “看法”、“意见”两个词都表示对客观事物所持的一些想法、见解,但“看法”不一定很具体,而“意见”多针对具体的对象 ◇ Both 看法 and 意见 mean " one's opinion and views concerning something", but 看法 may not be very concrete, while 意见 is directed against a concrete target. e. g. :

① 大家可以谈谈自己的**看法**(/**意见**)。You can tell us your views.

② 我的**看法**(/**意见**)不一定对,只供你参考。My opinion is not necessary to be correct, so it only offers some references.

以上①②两例因泛泛而言,没有说出具体对象,“看法”、“意见”均可用 ◇ Examples ① and ② only talk in generalities, so both 看法 and 意见 will do.

③ 我的**意见**是这篇文章写得不够深刻。In my opinion, the article lacks profoundness.

④ 我同意老王的**意见**,咱们明天休息一天,后天再接着干。I agree with Lao Wang, that is, we will take a rest tomorrow and keep on working the day after tomorrow.

③④两例,均针对具体的对象,用“意见” ◇ Examples ③ and ④ are aimed at very concrete objects, so 意见 is used.

2. “意见”有时含有贬义,特别是在某些短语中 ◇ 意见 sometimes has a derogatory sense, especially in some set phrases, e. g. :

① 半夜里吵吵闹闹的，邻居会**有意见**的。（“有意见”表示不满）The neighbors will be opposed to your night's noise.
（有意见 means" to have complaints about"）

② 他们俩不知为什么事**闹意见**了。（“闹意见”表示不团结）They are somehow in conflict.
（闹意见 means" to have conflicts"）

③ 你对别人太苛刻了，大家对你的**意见很大**。（“意见很大”表示很不满意）You are too hard on others, so they have a lot of complaints about you.
（意见很大 means" quite dissatisfied with sb. "）

3.“有看法”是指对某人某事不满意，有不同的意见 ◇ 有看法 means" to disapprove of something or somebody", e. g. :

① 她对小王这样处理问题**有看法**。She disapproved Xiao Wang's handling things this way.

② 对这个人我**有些看法**，所以平时很少跟他接触。I dislike him a little and keep in little touch with him.

考试 （动、名） kǎoshì　　考 （动） kǎo

Ⓔ examine; examination/ examine, test

◪ 动词“考试”指学校或其他单位通过一定方式考查应试者的知识或技能，而“入学考试”、“数学考试”等正式名称中的“考试”就是其名词形式。“考”也可表示动词“考试”的意思，但“考”较口语化。“考”还泛指生活中一般的提出难题让人回答 ◇ The verb 考试 means" that a school or some other institution finds out the knowledge or skill of the examinee by a certain means"; 考试 in 入学考试（entrance examination），数学考试（maths examination），etc. is a noun. 考 has the same meaning as the verb 考试，but is more colloquial. 考 can also mean" to raise a difficult question for sb. to answer. "

① 今天我**考试**，得早点儿到校。Today I'll have a test, so I'd better go to school earlier.

② 我明天有**考试**，不能玩了。I cannot play now, for there will be a test tomorrow.

③ 他没有通过化学**考试**。He failed his chemistry test.

以上，例①“考试”是动词；例②③“考试”是名词，都不能用“考”。“考”经常带宾语、补语 ◇ In example ①考试 is a verb.

In examples ② and ③考试 is a noun, which cannot be replaced by 考. Besides, 考 always takes an object or complement:

④ 今天我们**考**数学。Today we'll have a math test.

⑤ 这次考试没**考**好。I didn't do a good job in this examination.

⑥ 不知道下次**考**得好**考**不好。I wonder whether I can do a good job or not in the next test.

"考"带宾语还可以构成"考托福"、"考执照"、"考本子"等,用得较广 ◇ 考 is widely used in many phrases, e. g. 考托福(take part in TOEFL), 考执照(sit exams in applying for a licence), 考本子(test for a driving license), etc.

"考"可以用于泛指 ◇ 考 is often used in a general sense, e. g. :

⑦ 我**考考**你,你知道电话是谁发明的吗? Let me ask you a question. Do you know who invented the telephone?

⑧ 他被学生**考**住了,觉得很尴尬。He felt embarrassed when he was baffled by a student.

当然,"考试"也可表示比喻性的泛指意义 ◇ 考试 can also be used figuratively, e. g. :

⑨ 参加这次商品交易会,能不能拿下较多的订单,对我们企业是一次**考试**。Whether we can get more orders at this fair, which is a test for our enterprise.

但"考试"的比喻性泛指义不如"考"的泛指义用得广泛 ◇ But the figurative usage of 考试 is not as wide as that of 考.

可能 也许

(助动、名) (副)

kěnéng yěxǔ

Ⓔ may; possibility/perhaps

A. 可能

1. 名词"可能"表示可以实现的属性、可能性,与"也许"无共同点 ◇ The noun 可能 means" the state or fact of being possible, which has nothing in common with 也许", e. g. :

① 他有**可能**进入政界。It's possible for him to go into the political life.

② 想几个月就成为作家,那是没有**可能**的。It is impossible to be a writer in a few months.

③ 在北京就业,是一种**可能**;另一种**可能**就是到外地工作。Taking up an occupation in Beijing is one possibility; another choice is to obtain employment in other places.

2. 助动词"可能"表示 ◇ The auxiliary verb 可能 means:

(1)大概、估计。这时与"也许"

有共同之处 ◇ probably, which is very similar to 也许, e. g. :

① 老王**可能**住在城外。Maybe Lao Wang does not live in the city.

② 天阴沉沉的,**可能**要下雪。It is overcast and it seems to snow.

③ 你**可能**不记得这件事了。Maybe you forget it.

以上例①②③可换用"也许"。"可能"较"也许"所指的或然率大些,但"可能"可受"不"、"很"等修饰,"也许"不能 ◇ In examples ①②③也许 can be used instead. 可能 is more probable than 也许, but 可能 can be modified by 不, 很, etc. while 也许 cannot, e. g. :

④ 他**不可能**住在城外。He can't live in the suburb.

⑤ 学校**很可能**会发给他奖学金。The school is likely to offer him the scholarship.

(2)表示最大的范围内。"也许"不能这样用 ◇ To mean " within the widest scope". 也许 cannot be so used:

⑥ 我们要团结一切**可能**团结的力量。We should unit with all the forces that can be united with.

⑦ 在上海,**可能**去的地方他都去玩了。He has been to every tourist spot that is reachable.

⑧ 我去求他,**可能**说的理由全说了,但是他仍然不同意。When I went to ask for him, I used up my words, but he still disproved it.

3. "可能"也是形容词,表示能成为事实的,如"在可能的范围内"、"在可能的条件下"、"惟一可能的选择"等 ◇ 可能 is also an adjective, meaning " possible", e. g. 在可能的范围内(within certain scope), 在可能的条件下(under certain possible conditions), 惟一可能的选择(the only possible choice), etc.

B. 也许(副)

表示不大肯定、估计。同"可能"(助动)1 的用法。但"也许"可与"能"直接搭配,"可能"不这样用 ◇ The adverb 也许 means " not very sure", which is the same as 可能 in 1. But 也许 can be used together with 能, while 可能 cannot:

① 他**也许**能按时到达。He maybe arrived on time.

② 今天**也许**能下雨。It is possible to rain today.

► [大概 dàgài—大约 dàyuē—也许 yěxǔ]
[恐怕 kǒngpà—也许 yěxǔ]

可以 (助动、形) kěyǐ　　能 (助动、形、名) néng

能够

（助动）

nénggòu

Ⓔ can; may; possible/can; possible; energy/can

1. 可以、能、能够（助动）

The usage of 可以，能，能够 as auxiliary verbs：

（1）表示有条件、有能力、有可能等，三个词一般可互换 ◇ All the three words mean "to be able to, to know how to and to be possible to"; they are interchangeable in many cases：

① 她**能**（/**可以**/**能够**）教英语。She is able to teach English.

② 这屋子**能**（/**可以**/**能够**）放两个沙发。The room is big enough to put two sofas.

③ 你**能**（/**可以**/**能够**）帮我修理一下电视机吗？Would you like to repair my TV?

但否定式多用"不能"，有时也用"不能够"，不用"不可以" ◇ But the negative is usually 不能 or 不能够，not 不可以：

④ 我没空儿，**不能**（/**能够**）参加聚会了。I cannot go to the party for I have no time.

（2）表示对不可控制的现象的推测，用"能"、"能够"，不用"可以" ◇ 能 and 能够 are used in conjecture of uncontrollable phenomena; 可以 is not used：

⑤ 物价也许还**能**（/**能够**）再降一些。The prices may lower a little.

⑥ 你看今天夜里风**能**（/**能够**）停吗？Do you think the wind will stop this evening?

⑦ 这棵小树还**能**（/**能够**）长。The young tree can grow.

（3）表示对主观因素可予控制的现象的推测，三个词一般都可用 ◇ All three words can be used in conjecture of phenomena controllable by subjective factors：

⑧ 飞机**能**（/**可以**/**能够**）准时到达。The plane can arrive on time.

⑨ 如果我们采取及时有力的措施，这场灾害是完全**可以**（/**能够**/**能**）避免的。If we take forceful measures in time, the disaster is completely avoidable.

（4）表示具有一定的用途，三个词都可以用 ◇ All three words can mean "to have certain usage"：

⑩ 大豆**能**（/**可以**/**能够**）榨油。Oil can be extracted out of the soybeans.

⑪ 这件衣服还**能**（/**可以**/**能够**）穿。The coat is wearable.

⑫ 这种蔬菜**能**（/**可以**/**能够**）生吃。You can eat the raw vegetable.

否定式用"不能"，有时也用"不能够"，一般不用"不可以" ◇

K

The negative form is 不能 or 不能够,not 不可以:

⑬ 这肉放得太久了,**不能**(/**能够**)吃了。The meat is not editable for it has been kept for a long time.

⑭ 电脑坏了,**不能**(/**能够**)用了。There is something wrong with the computer and it doesn't work now.

(5)表示允许、许可,一般用“可以”。表示自己被允许也可用其他两个词 ◇ 可以 is used to show permission. To show permission applied to oneself, the other two words can also be used:

⑮ 我**可以**(/**能**/**能够**)用这个电话吗? May I use the telephone?

⑯ 你**可以**使用这个浴室。You can take a bath in the bathroom.

⑰ 警察执行任务时**可以**带枪。Policemen may take guns when they are out to fulfil tasks.

否定式一般用“不能” ◇ The negative form is usually 不能.

(6)表示无妨、值得,用“可以”,不用其他两个词 ◇ 可以 also means" to be worth or worthwhile", but the other two words have no such meaning:

⑱ 这个电影**可以**看看。You can see the film.

⑲ 那本小说**可以**翻翻。You can have a read of that novel.

⑳ 这个机会**可以**试一试。You can try this chance.

否定式不用“不可以”,而用“不值得” ◇ The negative form is 不值得,not 不可以:

㉑ 这本小说没意思,**不值得**看。The novel is not interesting and not worth reading.

2. 可以、能(形) ◇ The usage of 可以 and 能 as adjectives

“可以”表示还好、过得去 ◇ 可以 means" tolerable":

① 他的英语还**可以**。His English is nice.

② 那支球队踢得还**可以**。The football team is good.

“……真可以”、“……太可以了”常表示不可忍受,用于令人不满的事情 ◇ ……真可以 and ……太可以了 mean" intolerable" and are applied to undesirable things only:

③ 这天气热得**真可以**,快打开空调吧! It is really hot. Please hurry to turn on the air conditioning.

④ 这屋子乱得**太可以**了。The room is really messy.

但这种用法只用于肯定式 ◇ This usage is never in the negative.

“能”表示有能力的,多用于固定词语,如“能人”、“能干”、“能者” ◇ 能 means" capable", mostly used in set phrases like 能人

K

(man of ability),能干(talented),能者(the able one). e. g. :

⑤ 这件工作就由你做吧! **能者**多劳嘛! You'd better take on the job! Able person should do more!

⑥ 这个人可真**能干**! 见什么人说什么话。The man is really smart, who can talk whatever suitable.

3. 能(名)

表示能源,如电能、风能等 ◇ The noun 能 means "energy", e. g. 电能(electrical energy),风能(wind energy). The other examples like:

① 电器产品必须节**能**。It is necessary that the electric appliances save energy.

② 燃料、水力、风力等都可产生**能**。Energy can be generated from fuel, water, and wind.

▶[会 huì—能 néng]

肯 愿意 情愿

(助动) kěn　(动) yuànyì　(动) qíngyuàn

Ⓔ agree, consent/ be willing to/ be willing to

这三个词都可表示主观上乐意,因而有共同点 ◇ All the three words mean "to be willing", so they are quite similar:

① 小张**肯**(/**愿意**/**情愿**)帮我做这件事。Xiao Zhang is willing to help me do it well.

② 她不**肯**(/**愿意**/**情愿**)去找他。She is unwilling to ask for him.

但也有所侧重,侧重之点见下面谈的不同之处 ◇ However, they have different stresses.

三个词的不同之处是 ◇ The differences of the three words are as follows:

1. "肯"不仅口头上,而且实际行动上一定有所表示,但有时内心不一定完全乐意 ◇ 肯 means "to agree not only verbally, but also in practice". But sometimes it may not be totally voluntary.

① 这孩子好动,一会儿也不**肯**安静。The child is active and cannot keep calm for a moment.

② 他做事肯动脑筋。He likes using his head at work.

③ 我请他来给我们做报告,他不**肯**,跟他谈了半天,他才答应了。I invited him to deliver a lecture for us, but he was unwilling. After I persuaded him for a long time, he agreed at last.

这个意义有时可用"愿意",上面例①②也可换用"愿意",但意思没有"肯"重。"情愿"不能这样

用 ◇ 愿意 can also be used in examples ①②, but not as forceful as 肯. 情愿 cannot be so used.

"肯"是助动词,后边常有动词谓语或形容词谓语。但有时也可单用 ◇ 肯 is an auxiliary verb and is usually followed by a verb or an adjective, but it can also be used by itself:

④ ——让他道歉,他**肯**答应吗? Is he reluctant to promise apologizing?

——他肯。Sure.

有时也可用"愿意" ◇ 愿意 can also be used here sometimes.

K

2."愿意"还可表示希望发生某种状况,可受程度副词修饰 ◇ 愿意 can also express a strong desire for sth. and can be modified by adverbs of degree.

① 我**愿意**清净几天。I want to be alone these days.

② 她十分**愿意**私下解决这件事。She is willing to solve it in private.

这时也可用"情愿"。但"情愿"侧重于表示甘心的,从内心深处的。"情愿"一般不受程度副词修饰(有时受"不大"修饰) ◇ 情愿 can also be used here, but 情愿 stresses the willing. 情愿 is generally not modified by any adverb of degree (with the exception of 不大).

3."情愿"除了表示甘心的、从内心深处的,还可表示宁可、宁愿(后边常有转折) ◇ Besides willingness, 情愿 can also mean "would rather (often followed by a transition)":

① 我**情愿**赔钱,也不想放弃权利。I would rather pay for it than give up my rights.

② 他**情愿**不结婚,也不打算娶她。He would rather be single than marry her.

其他两个词都没有这种意思。另外,"情愿"还可构成"心甘情愿"、"两相情愿"等四字语 ◇ Neither of the other two words has this meaning. Besides, 情愿 can also be used in set phrases such as 心甘情愿 (be most willing to), 两相情愿 (both parties being willing).

恐怕 也许

(副) kǒngpà　(副) yěxǔ

Ⓔ probably/probably, perhaps

"恐怕"和"也许"都是副词,都有表示估计的意思,但还是有区别的 ◇ Both 恐怕 and 也许 are adverbs and both indicate estimation, but there is still some difference between the two.

1. 表示估计、揣测,"恐怕"、"也许"一般可以互换 ◇ To mean

"conjecture", 恐怕 and 也许 are interchangeable:

① 他离开这里以后，**恐怕**(/**也许**)不会再来了。He probably didn't return after he left here.

② 写这么几个字，**恐怕**(/**也许**)连两分钟都用不了。I think it will take less than two minutes to write such few words.

③ 他**恐怕**(/**也许**)明天才能来。He perhaps will come here tomorrow.

2. 表示估计，带有担心的成分，多用"恐怕" ◇ If there is anxiety besides estimation, 恐怕 is usually used:

① 天**恐怕**要下雨。I'm afraid it's going to rain.

② 用这些钱买家具，**恐怕**不一定够。I'm afraid the money is not enough for furniture.

③ 他的病**恐怕**很难治好。I'm afraid it's not easy to cure him.

3. 表示不很肯定的估计，用"也许" ◇ If the estimation is not very definite, 也许 is used:

① **也许**他妹妹来，他不来。His sister may come, but he may not.

② 现在出发**也许**能赶上火车。If we start now, maybe we can catch the train.

③ **也许**咱们还有机会再见面。We maybe have a chance to meet again.

4. 表示一种委婉的肯定，用"也许" ◇ 也许 is used to show a tactful affirmation:

① **也许**这些材料对你写论文有帮助。These materials may be useful for your paper.

② 这样处理，**也许**大家意见少些。Such a resolution can lessen the dissatisfaction.

③ 你跟他熟，你去说**也许**更好些。Since you are familiar to him it may be better if you tell him.

5. "也许"能独立成句，而"恐怕"不能 ◇ 也许 can be used independently, while 恐怕 cannot, e.g.:

——你今天不回来了吧？Are you not going to come back today?

——**也许**。你们不要等我。Maybe. So please don't wait for me.

6. "也许……也许……"不能用"恐怕"代替 ◇ 也许……也许……cannot be replaced by 恐怕:

① **也许**今天**也许**明天，我会打电话给他的。I will call him either today or tomorrow.

② **也许**因为天气不好，**也许**因为时间太紧，反正他决定不去旅行了。He said he wouldn't go on a tour because of either bad weather or urgent time.

▶[可能 kěnéng—也许 yěxǔ]

K

[大概 dàgài—大约 dàyuē—也许 yěxǔ]

夸 (动) kuā　夸奖 (动) kuājiǎng

Ⓔ praise, commend/ praise, compliment

◪ 我们比较过"称赞"和"赞美"。"夸"和"夸奖"意思与它们相同,但更口语化,并且多用于人 ◇ We have already compared 称赞 and 赞美. 夸 and 夸奖 mean" the same as the two but are more colloquial and mostly applied to human beings":

① 他们都**夸**(/**夸奖**)这孩子聪明伶俐。They all complimented the child's cuteness.

② 别**夸**(/**夸奖**)我了,我都不好意思了。Don't praise me any more, I feel embarrassed.

以上这种口语化的,涉及人及人的具体行为素质的句子,两个词都可以用。但"夸"有一些习惯搭配,如"夸海口"、"夸夸其谈"、"夸大其词"。同时,"夸奖"可做"受到"的宾语(这与"称赞、赞美"相同),但"夸"不能 ◇ Examples ① and ② are colloquial sentences relating to people's behaviour and quality, in which either word can be used. But 夸 is also used in some set phrases, e. g. 夸海口(brag about), 夸夸其谈(indulge in exaggeration), 夸大其词(make an overstatement in speaking or writing). 夸奖, on the other hand, can function as the object of 受到 (which is the same as 称赞 and 赞美), but 夸 cannot.

③ 这个学生很优秀,受到了校长的**夸奖**。The excellent student was praised by his principal.

"夸"和"夸奖"有时也可涉及人的不平凡事迹 ◇ 夸 and 夸奖 can also be applied to extraordinary deeds:

④ 人人都**夸**(/**夸奖**)他们的英雄行为。They was praised for their heroic deeds.

款待 (动) kuǎndài　招待 (动) zhāodài

Ⓔ entertain, treat cordially/ entertain, serve

◪ 这两个动词都表示对宾客或顾客给以照顾。"款待"含有亲切热情优厚地招待的意思,而"招待"则指一般的照顾 ◇ Both verbs mean" to give food and drink to one's guests". 款待 implies cordiality while 招待 is just entertaining.

① 他家的规矩是,一般客人来了,茶水**招待**;至亲好友来了,则要**款待**一番。Their family rule of treating guests is as follows: a common guest will be served with tea; a close friend or relative will be cordially treated.

例①中出现了这两个词,区别是很清楚的 ◇ The difference between the two words is very clear in example ①.

② 国务院新闻办公室今天举行记者**招待会**。A press conference will be held today by the News office of the State Council.

③ 老王到上海出差,住在某机关的**招待所**。Lao Wang was on business in Shanghai and stayed in the official hotel.

"记者招待会"、"招待所"经常结合使用,都含有一般照顾茶水或食宿的意思 ◇ 记者招待会(press conference) and 招待所(guest house) are common terms which imply providing food and drink or board and lodging.

④ 该国元首来我国访问,受到我国政府的热情**款待**。The state head of that country paid an official visit to our country and was greeted with a cordial treat of our government.

例④因属于贵宾访问,用"款待" ◇ Example ④ concerns a visit of an honored guest, so 款待 is used.

况且 何况

(连) (连)

kuàngqiě hékuàng

Ⓔ moreover, besides/let alone

这两个连词都表示追加理由。"何况"可以直接带短语或体词,"况且"不能。"何况"还可以用反问形式 ◇ Both conjunctions introduce additional cause. 何况 can introduce a phrase or a noun, pronoun, numeral or measure word, but 况且 cannot. 何况 can also be used in a rhetorical question.

① 天气很好,**况且**(/**何况**)又有空儿,出去走走吧! It's fine; moreover, you are free. Let's go out for a walk.

② 她年纪大了,**况且**(/**何况**)腿脚又不好,所以不大出门。She is old and walks with difficulty, so she does not go out often.

③ 连成绩好的学生都听不懂,**何况**是成绩差的学生? The good students cannot understand it, let alone the slow ones.

④ 坐在前面都看不清,**何况**坐在后面? I cannot see clearly in the front of the classroom, let alone at the back.

K

以上例①②二词可换用。例③④因用于反问形式，只能用“何况” ◇ In examples ① and ②, the two words are interchangeable. Examples ③ and ④ are rhetorical questions, so only 何况 can be used.

“又”可用于二词之后（如例①②），“又”如用在前边，只能用在“何况”之前 ◇ 又 can be used after both words (as in examples ① and ②), but if used in the front, it can only precede 何况：

⑤ 大人都答不出这个问题，又**何况**是孩子？ The grownups don't know the answer to the question, let alone children.

⑥ 房子不错，又**何况**不太贵，你就买了吧。The house is nice and not expensive, so you'd better buy it.

K

困难 难

（形、名） （形）

kùnnan nán

Ⓔ difficult; difficulty/difficult

这两个词都表示（行为或事情）费事费力、阻碍多。“困难”还有生活穷困的意思。两个词的词性有所不同。作为形容词的基本义，有时可以互换 ◇ Both words mean "(an action or thing) needing great effort". 困难 also means poverty-stricken. 困难 is a noun as well as an adjective while 难 is just an adjective. As an adjective, the two words are interchangeable:

① 这道题，做起来很**困难**（/**难**）。It's difficult to solve the question.

但“困难”在语感上比“难”的难度更大。有时“困难”侧重主观感受，“难”侧重客观叙述 ◇ However, 困难 sounds more difficult than 难. Sometimes 困难 stresses the subjective feeling while 难 stresses narration.

“难”可直接做状语。“困难”做状语，常加程度副词和“地” ◇ 难 can be an adverbial by itself, while 困难, as an adverbial, often takes an adverb of degree and the particle 地：

② 下雨以后，这条山路很**难**走。It's difficult to walk on the mountain road after rain.

③ 这次考试比较**难**通过。It's not easy to pass the examination.

④ 他十分**困难**地过了关。He went through at last.

做定语时，单音节的“难”与后面的词搭配较紧时，可不加“的”，如“难题”、“难事”、“难词”。“困难”常加“的”，如“困难的局面”，搭配较紧时也可不加“的”，如“困难户”、“困难时期” ◇ As an attributive, the monosyllabic 难 usually does not take the particle 的, e. g. 难题(difficult question/a hard nut to crack), 难事(something difficult to be dealt with), 难词(difficult words). 困难 usually takes 的, e. g. 困难的局面, but some commonly-used set phrases, which combine closely, do not take 的, e. g. 困难户(family with financial difficulty, or family difficult to deal with), 困难时期(difficult period).

做补语时,"困难"常带"得"。"难"较少做补语,可不需要"得"(做结果补语) ◇ As a complement, 困难 usually takes the particle 得. 难 is rarely used as a complement, and if so used (as a resultative complement), 得 is unnecessary:

⑤ 他家的日子过得有些**困难**。His life is a bit hard.

⑥ 这道题出**难**了。The test question is too difficult.

做谓语时,除了例①,还可遇到两个词可互换的例子 ◇ As the predicate, the two words can be found interchangeable in more examples besides example ①:

⑦ 学习汉语并不**难**(/**困难**)。It's not difficult to learn Chinese.

但"困难"的意思更重(难度更大,有时侧重主观感受)。一般说,由于音节关系,"难"需加程度副词等,"困难"可以不加 ◇ But 困难 sounds more serious (with the stress on subjective impression sometimes). Owing to syllabic reasons, 难 needs to take an adverb of degree, while 困难 does not:

⑧ 这位老人走路**困难**。The old man walks with difficulty.

例⑧不能用"难"。从中也可以看出,由于老人腿脚不利索这种主观条件或感受,用"困难"不用"难"。而一般的客观叙述(如例①⑦)二词可互换 ◇ 难 cannot be used in example ⑧. It can be seen that, because of the subjective factor of old age, 困难 and not 难 is used. However, in the objective narration (e. g. in examples ① and ⑦) the two words are interchangeable.

"难"虽然是形容词,可以加补语后再带宾语 ◇ Though an adjective, 难 can take a complement followed by an object:

⑨ 艰苦的环境**难不倒我们**。We are never afraid of hard conditions.

⑩ 这些数学题**难住了我**。The math question confused me.

(也可用"把"字句:这些数学题把我难住了 ◇ The sentence with 把 can also be used: 这些数学题把我难住了.)

K

重叠后可直接带宾语，但较为口语化 ◇ 难 can be reduplicated and takes an object, and this kind of usage is very colloquial:

⑪ 你提这样的问题是不是想**难难我**? Do you mean to baffle me with such a question?

"困难"也是名词，表示阻碍多的事情等 ◇ 困难 is also a noun, meaning" sth. difficult":

⑫ 这么一点儿**困难**，怕什么? There's nothing to be worried as to such a little difficulty.

⑬ 在生活中，他确实遇到了一些**困难**。He did encounter some difficulties in life.

这与"难"作为形容词充当宾语等(如"不怕难")，是不同的 ◇ 困难 as a noun is different from the adjective 难 used as the object (e.g. 不怕难).

▶[艰难 jiānnán—困难 kùnnán]

K

L

劳驾 请

(动)

láo jià qǐng

Ⓔ please/please

"劳驾"是动宾短语,用于客套话,表示有礼貌。原来只用于北京地区,现在已逐渐被普通话所接受。有时,它与敬辞"请"的用法接近 ◇ 劳驾 is a verb-object phrase used in polite greetings. Originally used only in Peking dialect, it has gradually been adopted by mandarin speakers. Sometimes it has the same usage as 请:

① **劳驾(/请)**让让路! Excuse me, please make way for me!

② **劳驾(/请)**给我一杯咖啡。Excuse me, would you like to give me a cup of coffee?

但在"请您务必光临"这种较正式的措辞,不宜用"劳驾"。在句法上,常说"劳您驾"或"劳驾你……" ◇ But in more formal polite expressions like 请您务必光临 (You are cordially invited to come), 劳驾 is not used. Syntactically, one usually says: 劳您驾 or 劳驾你…….

有时,"劳驾"与"请"在句中可以同时出现 ◇ Sometimes both 劳驾 and 请 can be used in a sentence:

③ **劳你驾**,请帮我把这封信寄出去。Would you like to post the letter for me?

另外,"请"还有请求、邀请、聘请等意义,如"请人装修房屋"、"请客吃饭"、"请老师教课"等,"劳驾"不能这样用 ◇ Besides, 请 also means "to invite, to ask someone to do something", etc. e. g. 请人装修房屋 (ask sb. to refurbish the house), 请客吃饭 (treat sb. to dinner), 请老师教课 (ask sb. to give lectures) etc. 劳驾 cannot be so used.

老 总

(副) (副)

lǎo zǒng

Ⓔ always/always

1. 副词"老"和"总"都可表示某一状态持续不变或某一动作不断重复 ◇ Both adverbs 老 and 总 indicate "an unchanged situation or continuous repetition":

① 我怎么**老**(/总)记不住这个字的读音? Why do I always forget the word's pronunciation?
② 你别**老**(/总)玩儿了,该看看书了。Don't play all the time. It's high time you read.
③ 我感冒了,**老**(/总)咳嗽。I've got a cold and I kept on coughing.
④ 这些松树一年四季**老**(/总)那么绿。The pine trees are evergreen.

2. 副词"老"和"总"都可表示一直、经常 ◇ The adverbs 老 and 总 both mean" always, all along":
① 别**老**(/总)让家里人操心。Don't make your family worry about you all day long.
② 上学时他俩**老**(/总)在一起。They used to stay together at school.
③ 这点儿小事,你别**老**(/总)记在心上。Don't keep such a trivial on your mind all the time.
④ 他的房间里**老**(/总)那么干净、整齐。His room is always kept clean and tidy.

3. 副词"老"修饰少数几个单音节形容词,还表示程度高,是不能用"总"替代的 ◇ The adverb 老 is used to qualify a few monosyllabic adjectives to show the high degree, which cannot be replaced by 总:
① 他每天**老早**就起来,出去跑步。He gets up very early to jog every morning.
② **老长**的一根绳子让他给剪断了。(不说"老短") He cut a very long rope. (never 老短)
③ 他儿子已经长得**老高老高**了。(不说"老矮") His son is very tall now. (never 老矮)

4. 副词"总"有些用法也不能用"老"替代 ◇ The adverb 总 has some usages which cannot be replaced by 老 as well:
(1) 用于估计,表示较低的设想 ◇ Used in estimation to show a low assumption:
① 100 元不够,150 元**总**够了吧! If 100 Yuan is not enough, I think 150 Yuan must be enough.
② 今天是星期日,他**总**该有时间了吧! Today is Sunday. He must be free.
③ 这样处理,他**总**会满意了。He must be satisfied with the solution.
(2) 指出事物最根本的一点,有"毕竟"的意思 ◇ To points out the most critical point, meaning "after all":
④ 他**总**学过两年医,在医学知识上比我强多了。He is superior

to me in medicine, for he learned it for two years after all.

⑤ 孩子**总**是孩子，哪能像大人那样懂事？A child is a child after all. How can you expect him to be as sensible as a grown-up?

⑥ 我们**总**是20年的朋友了，彼此很了解。We are friends for twenty years after all and therefore we know each other well.

⑦ 一个人的力量**总**是有限的。The strength of an individual is limited after all.

(3) 表示肯定，有把握的推断 ◇ To show assurance in estimation:

⑧ 这个问题**总**会解决的。The problem is likely to be solved.

⑨ 这件事**总**不能这样拖下去。This issue should not be put off this way.

⑩ 你要是这么不注意，身体**总**有一天会垮的。If you don't care about your health, you will collapse some day.

老师 先生

(名) (名)

lǎoshī xiānsheng

Ⓔ teacher/teacher

◣ "老师"和"先生"都可指教师。"老师"用得更为普通，从幼儿园到高等学府，对教师都可称"老师"（包括当面称呼）。"先生"较特殊，只用于某些高等学府，也可以当面称呼 ◇ Both 老师 and 先生 mean "teacher". 老师 is more common. From kindergarten to university, the teachers can all be addressed as 老师 (including address face to face). 先生 is a bit special, only used in universities and colleges; it can also be an address in sb.'s face.

"老师"还用于社会上对一些资历较深的文化人的称呼 ◇ 老师 is also used to address older and experienced intellectuals.

"先生"则用于社会上男性人士的称呼，一般指成年的白领工作者 ◇ 先生 is used to address a man, usually white-collar professional adult:

① 这是**老师**今天留的作业。This is today's homework.

② 王**老师**讲的文学史很受学生们的欢迎。The literature history course given by Mr. Wang is popular.

③ 李**老师**是戏剧界的前辈。Mr. Li is the father of theatrical circles.

④ **先生**，您想买什么？Can I help you, sir?

⑤ 这位李**先生**在一家贸易公司工作。This is Mr. Li and he works in a trade company.

"先生"还可用来称别人的丈夫或对人称自己的丈夫 ◇ 先生

can also be the address of someone else's husband or the address of one's own husband:

⑥ 你**先生**在哪儿工作? Where does your husband work?

⑦ 我**先生**姓王。My husband's surname is Wang.

类似 相似 近似

(形) (形) (形)

lèisì xiāngsì jìnsì

Ⓔ similar/similar/similar

◥ 这三个词都表示大致相像。其中"近似"较书面化,侧重于相同中有不同或接近于……。"类似"侧重于同类的,可类比的。"相似"侧重于形式内容相像 ◇ The three words mean" similar". 近似 is more literary, stressing difference in sameness or very close to. 类似 stresses being of the same sort, comparable. 相似 stresses similarity in form and content.

1. 做谓语 ◇ As the predicate:

① 这两个城市的布局**类似**(/**相似**/**近似**)。The layouts of the two cities are similar.

② 我的业余爱好和你**相似**(/**类似**/**近似**)。My hobby is similar to yours.

以上两句,三个词可互换 ◇ In exemples ① and ② the three words are interchangeable.

但如有补语,一般用"相似" ◇ If there follows a complement, 相似 is used:

③ 这姊妹俩的相貌**相似**极了。The two sisters are very alike in appearance.

如有程度副词等多用"相似"或"近似" ◇ If there is an adverb of degree, 相似 or 近似 is used:

④ 那两本书的笔调和风格十分**相似**(/**近似**)。The tones and styles of the two books are very similar.

"类似"可加"于",有时可省略,而"相似"不能这样用;"近似于"可带动词 ◇ 类似 can take 于, which can be omitted sometimes. 相似 cannot be so used. 近似于 can take a verb:

⑤ 这个故事**类似于**神话。The story is like a myth.

⑥ 写文章**类似于**建筑房子,要讲究层次和布局。That writing an article is like building a house is in that both of them have levels and layout.

2. 做定语 ◇ As the attributive:

有时三个词可互换 ◇ Sometimes the three words are interchangeable:

① 这些影片都有着**类似**(/**相似**/**近似**)的题材。The theme of these films is similar.

如有侧重,则不宜互换 ◇ If they have different stresses, they are not

interchangeable:

② 以后不能允许**类似**的事故发生。Such kind of thing should not happen any more.

③ 这姊妹俩**相似**的相貌,常常让人认错。It's easy to take the elder sister for the young one, for the two sisters are too alike in appearance.

④ 两个人运用不同的演算方法,得出了**近似**的数值。With different way of calculation, they came to approximate result.

▶[相似 xiāngsì—相像 xiāngxiàng—相同 xiāngtóng]

冷 凉 凉快

(形) (形) (形)

lěng liáng liángkuai

Ⓔ cold/cool/pleasantly cool

"冷"、"凉"、"凉快"这三个形容词,在表示较低的气温方面,是近义词;但各自还有其他一些义项 ◇ 冷,凉 and 凉快 are synonyms when indicating low temperature. But each has some different usages.

1. 表示气温低,"冷"最低;"凉快"较低,身体觉得舒适;"凉"也较低,但程度上比"冷"略差 ◇ To mean "low temperature", 冷 is the lowest; 凉快 is low, but very pleasant; 凉 is not as low as 冷. e. g.

① 哈尔滨地处中国北方,冬天很**冷**。It is cold in winter in Harbin, for it lies in the north China.

② 今天零下20度,**冷**得要命,别出去了。It's twenty degrees below zero today, and it's freezing, so don't go out.

③ 这里的秋天气候适中,感觉很**凉快**。It is cool here in autumn, for the temperature is moderate.

④ 屋子里很热,外面稍微**凉快**些。It's hot in the room, while it's cool outside.

⑤ 天气有点儿**凉**了,早晚要注意加减衣服。It's a bit cold, so wear more in the mornings and evenings.

以上三个词一般不能互换 ◇ In the examples above, the three words are not interchangeable.

但有时"冷"和"凉"都表示一般的温度较低,可互换 ◇ But sometimes 冷 and 凉 both mean "low temperature" and are interchangeable:

⑥ ——这是**凉**(/**冷**)水,加热以后再喝吧! This is cold water. Drink it after heated.

——不要紧,我习惯喝**凉**(/**冷**)一些的水。It doesn't matter, for I prefer cold water.

⑦ 屋子里有些**冷**(/**凉**),她加了件毛衣。It is a bit cold in the room, so she put on a sweater.

2. 表示缺少热情,用"冷"(有时需重叠) ◇ To mean " cold in manner",冷 is used (sometimes it needs to be reduplicated):

① 她似乎对客人并不大欢迎,只是**冷冷**地说了一句:有什么事? She did not seem to welcome the guest, for she only said dryly: what's up?

② 他对任何人都**冷**若冰霜。He treats everyone coldly.

③ 她对人总是一副**冷**面孔,使人不敢接近。She always treats others coldly, which makes her difficult to access.

L

3. 表示灰心失意、失望,一般用"凉"(或"凉了半截") ◇ To mean " discouraged, disappointed",凉(or 凉了半截)is used:

① 听到落榜的消息,她的心里**凉了半截**。Her heart sank at her failure in the entrance examination.

② 这么好的机会错过了,我一听,心都**凉**了。My heart sank when I heard the news that they missed such a golden opportunity.

以上用"凉"十分口语化。但有时也可用"冷",如例②,则口语色彩较淡化 ◇ 凉 is very colloquial in the examples above. But 冷 can also be used as in example ②, then it would not be so colloquial.

4. 表示(情绪、气氛等)冷静,一般用"冷" ◇ To indicate (mood, atmosphere, etc.) coolness,冷 is used:

① 一场争论过后,等了几天气氛才**冷**了下来。The atmosphere cooled off a few days later after the debate was over.

② 对方太激动了,我们不要忙,**冷一冷**再说。Take it easy, for the other party is too excited. We will discuss it when they calm down.

③ 这场纠纷应该**冷**处理,不要使矛盾激化。Don't intensify the contradiction and you should ignore the dispute now.

5. 表示温度较自然地降低,使冷却,普通话的口语中用"凉",有时可用"冷" ◇ " To lower temperature naturally, to cool down",凉 is used in colloquial speech . 冷 can also be used at times:

① 刚出锅的菜,**凉**了再吃吧! The newly cooked dish is hot. Don't take it until it is cold.

② 面都放**凉**了,你怎么还不吃啊? Why not take the noodles, for they cooled off now.

例①如用"冷",是方言(多见于南方)。例②也可用"冷",则口语色彩略淡 ◇ In southern dialects,冷 can be used in example ①. In example ②, if 冷 is used instead, it

would not be so colloquial.
“凉”也可读 liàng，是动词，表示主动使温度降低 ◇ 凉 is also pronounced "liàng", which is a verb meaning "to make something cool down".

③ 刚出锅的菜，**凉**(liàng)一下再吃吧！The newly cooked dish should be served after it cools off.

6. 表示生僻，用“冷”(限于文词等) ◇ To mean "uncommon, rarely-used", 冷 is used (esp. in writing, diction, etc.)

① 这是个**冷**字，一般很少用。This is a rarely used word.

② 今年高考的语文题，出得太**冷**太偏。The Chinese questions of College Entrance Examination are too strange for the candidates.

“冷”还有其他一些义项，如“放冷箭”，指乘人不备暗中射箭，比喻暗中害人 ◇ 冷 also has some other usages, e.g. 放冷箭, meaning "to make a sneak attack".

▶[寒 hán—寒冷 hánlěng—冷 lěng]

里 (名) lǐ　　里边 (名) lǐbiān

里面 (名) lǐmiàn　　里头 (名) lǐtou

Ⓔ in/inside, in/inside, in/inside, in

◪ 这四个名词都表示在一定的空间、时间以内。“里”是粘着词，其他三个是自由词。“里”用得最多。“里面”略为书面化。“里头”更为口语化 ◇ All the four nouns mean "within a certain space or time". 里 is an agglutinative word and the other three are free words. 里 is the most commonly used, 里面 is a bit literary, and 里头 is the most colloquial.

① 大厅**里**(/**里边**/**里面**/**里头**)灯火通明。The hall is brightly-lit.

② 这笔钱，我们一定要在一个月**里**(/**里边**/**里面**/**里头**)还给对方。We should pay the money back in a month.

以上两句，用在表示处所或时间的名词后面四个词可以通用 ◇ In examples ① and ②, used after nouns of place or time, the four words are interchangeable.

③ 小树林外面我都扫过了，你再到**里边**(/**里面**/**里头**)扫一扫。I have swept the ground outside the grove. Please sweep that inside it.

④ 冰箱**里边**(/**里面**/**里头**)有什

么喝的吗? Is there anything to drink in the fridge?

例③不能用"里",因为"里"是粘着词。例④也不能用"里"因为"里边"等独立做主语,这里可能指冰箱、酒柜、厨房等处的"里边",说话人和听话人都已经知道的地方 ◇ In example ③ 里 cannot be used, because it is an agglutinative word. In ④ 里边, etc. function independently as the subject, indicating 里边 of the refrigerator, cupboard, kitchen, etc. which the speaker already knows and 里 cannot be used.

有时,"里边"等表示某个部门、某种人物 ◇ Sometimes 里边, etc. indicate a certain unit, or personage:

⑤ 请他向**里边**(/**里面**/**里头**)捎个话。Please ask him to take a message to the superior.

⑥ **里边**(/**里面**/**里头**)说了,大家做事要小心。The superior told us that we should be careful.

例⑤⑥也不能用"里" ◇ In examples ⑤ and ⑥ 里 cannot be used.

但"这"或"那"可加"里"、"里边"等("这里"、"那里"已经成词) ◇ But 这 or 那 can take 里 or 里边, etc. (这里 and 那里 are already words):

⑦ 这**里**(/**里边**/**里面**/**里头**)一定有秘密! There must be secrets in it.

理解 (动) lǐjiě　了解 (动) liǎojiě

Ⓔ understand, comprehend / understand, know

"理解"、"了解"都是动词,都有"懂"、"知道"的意思 ◇ Both 理解 and 了解 are verbs meaning "to understand".

A. 理解

1. 指经过思索和推理过程而懂得其中的道理、用意等,并非只懂语言或文字表面的意思 ◇ To understand the truth, meaning, etc. not just by the superficial meaning of the words through thinking and reasoning.

① 他的话没全说出来,但是我**理解**(/**了解**)了。Though he only told me part of his words, but I see what he will say.

② 刚刚感觉到的东西不一定马上就能**理解**(/**了解**)。What has been learned is not likely to sink in.

③ 这篇文章学生们**理解**(/**了解**)得很深刻。Students have a good comprehension about the text.

以上各句中,"理解"可换用"了

解”，但只是侧重“明白”、“知道”的意思 ◇ In the examples above，理解 can be replaced by 了解，but the stress will be just to know.

2. 表示说话人认为某种情况的存在、产生等是合乎情理的，不奇怪，有时甚至暗含着同情的色彩 ◇ Indicating that the speaker considers the existence or origination of some situation is reasonable，not strange，and may even be sympathetic.

① 我完全**理解**你实验失败后的心情。I understand your feeling completely when you fail in your experiment.

② 大家都能**理解**你的苦衷。Every one can understand your difficulties.

③ 人与人之间要经常沟通，才能互相**理解**。If people want to know each other，they should communicate frequently.

以上各句中，如严格保持原句意义，“理解”不能换用“了解” ◇ In the examples above，if the meaning is" to be kept intact"，理解 cannot be replaced by 了解.

B. 了解

1. 表示明白，懂得（意思、内容等） ◇ Indicating that one understands (the meaning，content，etc.)：

① 我还不**了解**（/**理解**）这首古诗的意思。I cannot understand the ancient poem yet.

② 我们不但要**了解**（/**理解**）词义，还应掌握词的用法。We not only understand the meaning of a word，but also master its usage.

以上各句中“了解”可换成“理解”，但侧重思索、推理等过程 ◇ In examples ① and ②，了解 can be replaced by 理解，but the stress will be on inference and reasoning.

2. 表示知道（详细情况等） ◇ Indicating that one knows (details，etc.)：

① 你**了解**他们之间的关系吗？Do you know their relationship?

② 我们只是一般的同事，他的经历我并不**了解**。We are just average colleages，and I don't know his experiences.

③ 我不**了解**情况，没有发言权。I have no idea about it，so I have no right to say.

以上各句“了解”不能用“理解”代替 ◇ In the examples above，了解 cannot be replaced by 理解.

3. 表示通过调查、询问等而知道 ◇ Indicating that one gets to know something through investigation or inquiry：

① 老师要**了解**学生课外的学习

情况。A teacher should know something about his students' learning after class.

② 我们应该**了解**一下，大家有哪些想法。We should know everyone's opinions.

③ 政府已经派人去**了解**事件发生的原因了。Someone has been sent to investigate the cause of the accident.

以上各句"了解"也不能用"理解"代替 ◇ In the examples above, 了解 cannot be replaced by 理解 either.

L

力 力量 力气

（名） （名） （名）

lì lìliang lìqi

Ⓔ force, strength/
physical strength/
physical strength

1. 表示人或动物的体力，"力"、"力量"、"力气"三个词都可用。但"力"是半粘着词，常用于固定词组或附着于其他词语之后 ◇ To mean "the physical strength of a human being or an animal", 力, 力量 and 力气 can all be used. But 力 is a semi-agglutinative word often used in set phrases or attached to other words:

① 这个人**力**大无比。The man is powerful.

② 你干活儿怎么不肯用**力**呢？Why not exert your efforts at work?

③ 锻炼了一段时间之后，我的**臂力**和**腿力**明显增强。My arms and legs become stronger after some training.

④ **兽力**车不许进入城市中心。The animal-drawn vehicles are not permitted to go to the city center.

"力量"和"力气"则常独立运用，基本上可以换用 ◇ 力量 and 力气 are used independently and are basically interchangeable:

⑤ 那个摔跤手**力量**(/**力气**)真大。The wrestler is really strong.

⑥ 我们两个人使尽了全身的**力量**(/**力气**)，也没能推倒他。We two exerted our every effort to push him, but he was motionless.

⑦ 这匹老马，还有**力气**(/**力量**)拉车吗？Is the old horse strong enough to pull the cart?

2. 表示能力，用"力"或"力量"。但"力"是半粘着的，"力量"是独立运用的 ◇ To mean "ability", 力 or 力量 is used. But 力 is a semi-agglutinative word while 力量 can be used independently:

① 你的理由没有**说服力**。Your reason is unconvincing.

② **火力**、**水力**都可以发电。Fire

and water can generate electricity.

③ 他已经无**力**还债。He is unable to pay his debt.

④ 团结是**力量**,知识也是**力量**。Unity is strength, and so is knowledge.

⑤ 他们还有**力量**重新振兴这个企业。They are capable of thriving the business again.

3. 物理学中的“力”指改变物体运动状态的作用 ◇ In physics, 力 means"force":

① 这座桥梁的毁坏,是几种**力**相互作用的结果。The bridge is destroyed by the combination of forces.

② 在一般的物理学课本中,**力**的方向通常用箭头表示。The direction of force is indicated by an arrow in average physics books.

4. 在固定句式中,表示尽力地,用“力” ◇ In some set phrases,力 is used to mean"with full strength":

① 这些战士**力挽狂澜**,保证了大坝的安全,也保护了人民和财产。The soldiers do their utmost to combat the floods. As a result, the dam was safe, and, thus, they made the people and their property safe.

② 我们一定要**力争上游**,为国家培养更多的人才。We should strive to run the school well and cultivate more talents for our country.

历来　从来　向来

(副、名)　(副)　(副)

lìlái　cónglái　xiànglái

Ⓔ always, all along/ always, all along/ always, all along

◣“历来”、“从来”和“向来”都有“从过去到现在”的意思。“历来”多用于书面语及肯定句中(如例①②③④),语气也较正式;“从来”和“向来”则多用于口语中(如例⑤⑥⑦⑧),“从来”常用于否定句中(如例⑥⑦⑧ ⑪⑫⑬),“向来”否定句和肯定句都很常见(如例⑤⑥⑦⑧⑨⑩) ◇ 历来,从来 and 向来 all mean" all along". 历来 is usually used in literary language and affirmative sentences(as in examples ①②③and ④) and sounds very formal. 从来 and 向来 are more colloquial (as in examples ⑤⑥⑦ and ⑧); 从来 is often used in negative sentences (as in examples ⑥⑦⑧ ⑪⑫⑬) while 向来 is often used in both affirmative and negative sentences (as in examples ⑤⑥⑦⑧⑨ and ⑩):

① 中国政府**历来**主张,国家不分

大小，一律平等。The unchanging advocacy of Chinese government is that every country, big or small alike, is equal.

② 中华民族**历来**有勤俭节约的好传统。The Chinese nation has cherished the fine tradition of thrifty through the ages.

③ 景德镇的瓷器**历来**享有国际声誉。The Jingdezhen china is world-famous for a very long time.

④ 四川盆地的物产**历来**十分丰富。The Sichuan Basin is rich in its produces through the ages.

例③④多用"历来"，有时也可用"从来"，语气较重些。而能用"从来"的句子基本可以用"向来" ◇ In examples ③ and ④, 历来 is mostly used, but sometimes 从来 can also be used, which sounds more emphatic. All the sentences with 从来 can be replaced by 向来：

⑤ 她家**从来**(/**向来**)都很干净。Her house is always kept clean and tidy.

⑥ 我**从来**(/**向来**)不吃辣的。I never taste spicy food.

⑦ 他**从来**(/**向来**)没有早睡早起的习惯。He never gets up and goes to bed early.

⑧ 小王上课**从来**(/**向来**)不迟到。Xiao Wang has never been late for his class.

但"向来"可以修饰双音节动词、形容词，"从来"一般不可以 ◇ 向来 can qualify disyllabic verbs and adjectives, but 从来 cannot：

⑨ 小王对工作**向来**认真。Xiao Wang is always conscientious about his work.

⑩ 上级的决定，他**向来**服从。He always obey the superior's orders.

"从来"、"历来"可以和"过"一起使用，"向来"一般不可以 ◇ 从来 and 历来 can collocate with 过, but 向来 usually cannot：

⑪ 他是你的什么人？我**从来**没见过。Who is he? I have never met him.

⑫ 他**从来**没有像今天这样认真过。He has never been so serious as today.

⑬ 公司的经济状况**从来**(/**历来**)没有这么好过。The company has never been in such a good economical condition.

"历来"还可以做定语 ◇ 历来 is also a noun and can function as an attributive：

⑭ 这是他**历来**的习惯。This is his usual habit.

⑮ 一身布衣裤，这是他**历来**的装束。He was often dressed in cotton clothes.

立刻 (副) lìkè　　立即 (副) lìjí

Ⓔ at once, immediately/

at once, immediately

◪ “立刻”和“立即”都是副词，都表示某一动作、行为刚结束，另一动作、行为紧接着在较短的时间内发生 ◇ Both 立刻 and 立即 are adverbs meaning that just when an action is over, another action appears in a very short time.

1. “立刻”表示一个动作或情况很快就要发生，或表示一个动作或情况的出现紧跟另一动作或情况，强调时间短 ◇ 立刻 indicates that an action or situation is to appear very soon or that an action or situation appears closely after another action or situation with the stress on shortness of time：

① 大家**立刻**集合。Please gather at once.

② 天太热了，动一动**立刻**就满身大汗。It's so hot that we will sweat all over as soon as we take a move.

③ 收到他们的信后，我**立刻**写了回信。I replied as soon as I heard from them.

④ 他一按电钮，机器**立刻**开始运转。The machine started the moment he pressed the button.

“立刻”较为口语化，例②全句也较为口语化，所以用“立刻”不用“立即”。例①③④也可用“立即”。例④如用“立即”，“开始”可省略 ◇ 立刻 is more colloquial. Example② is a colloquial sentence, so 立刻 and not 立即 is used. In examples ①③ and ④ 立即 can also be used instead. If 立即 is used in example ④, 开始 may be omitted.

2. “立即”表示立刻就，就在说话的当时，强调没有时间间隔，多用于书面语 ◇ 立即 means" the instant when, at the very moment of speaking", with the stress on no intermission. It is used mostly in written language：

① 听到呼叫，他**立即**跑下楼去。He ran downstairs immediately he heard the call.

② 大家**立即**行动起来，不要耽搁时间。Please take action at once. Don't delay.

③ 接到电话，我**立即**赶到了出事现场。I hurried to the accident spot as soon as I received the phone.

以上例①②③也可用“立刻”，但口语色彩较浓 ◇ In examples ①②③ 立刻 can be used instead but it would be more colloquial.

► [顿时 dùnshí—立刻 lìkè]
[马上 mǎshàng —立刻 lìkè]

连忙 (副) liánmáng 赶忙 (副) gǎnmáng

Ⓔ promptly; at once/ promptly; hastily

◪"连忙"和"赶忙"都是副词，用法相同，表示加快行动。只用于客观叙述，不能用于祈使句或表示未然的句子 ◇ Both 连忙 and 赶忙 are adverbs and have the same usage. They are used only in narration and not in imperative sentences or sentences relating to future events.

① 见到有人来，他**连忙**(/**赶忙**)过去招呼。He hurried to greet the guest as soon as he saw him.

② 听见叫声，我**连忙**(/**赶忙**)回过头去。I turned back the moment I heard the call.

③ 他知道自己做得不对，**连忙**(/**赶忙**)向大家道歉。As soon as he knew it was his fault, he made an apology.

④ 下课后，他**连忙**(/**赶忙**)到图书馆去借参考书。He went to the library to borrow the reference book as soon as the class was over.

⑤ 老人一上车，好几个人**连忙**(/**赶忙**)起来让座。There were some people standing up to offer their seats to the old man as soon as he got on the bus.

有时"连忙"略为书面化一些，如例⑥这样的风格较为正式的句子，以用"连忙"为好 ◇ Sometimes 连忙 sounds more literary, so in a more formal sentence like ⑥, it is better to use 连忙:

⑥ 接到上级指示，各个单位**连忙**行动了起来。The work unit took action as soon as they got the order from their superior.

▶ [赶快 gǎnkuài—赶忙 gǎnmáng]

连续 (副) liánxù　继续 (动) jìxù

Ⓔ continuously; successively/ continue

◪"连续"、"继续"都有接连不断的意思，但词性不同 ◇ 连续 and 继续 both mean "ceaselessly", but they are of different parts of speech.

1. "连续"是副词，表示接连不断，一个接一个地 ◇ 连续 is an adverb meaning "successively, one after another":

① 我们已经**连续**工作了四个小时，该休息一下了。We kept on working for four hours, and we should take a rest now.

② 他已经**连续**几年在工地上过春节了。He spent several successive Spring Festivals on the construction site.

③ 试验**连续**失败，得好好总结一下经验了。The experiments failed in succession, and it's time to draw a lesson from them.

2. "继续"是动词，表示(活动等)不停止，延长下去 ◇ 继续 is a verb, meaning "something (action, etc.) does not stop, but keeps going on":

① 他站起来活动了一下，又坐下来**继续**写文章。He got up and moved about and then sat down to resume his writing.

② 老人未完成的事业将由后人**继续**下去。The old man's unfinished cause is carried on by his successors.

③ 这个会议还没开完，明天**继续**开。The meeting is not over and it will be resumed tomorrow.

▶[继续 jìxù—接着 jiēzhe]
[坚持 jiānchí—继续 jìxù]

亮 明亮

(形、动、名) (形)
liàng míngliàng

Ⓔ bright; shine, reveal; light/bright

1. 形容词"亮"和"明亮"都形容光线充足或由于发光体照射而光线好 ◇ The adjectives 亮 and 明亮 both mean "there is plenty of light or something giving out light strongly":

① 室内灯光很**亮**(/**明亮**)。The room is brightly-lit.

② 这里不够**亮**(/**明亮**)，看书对眼睛不好。The dim light here will do harm to your eyes.

③ 我们在又**亮**(/**明亮**)又宽敞的教室里上课。We are having lessons in a bright and spacious classroom.

④ **明亮**的月光照在窗户上。The bright moonlight is shining on the window.

做定语时多用"明亮"，常带"的"，如例④。"亮"做补语或定语时，由于音节的关系前边常加"很"或"亮"变为重叠形式"亮亮"。如例④可说"亮亮的月光照在窗户上" ◇ When used as an attributive, 明亮 is mostly used and usually with 的, as in exemple ④. When used as a complement or attributive, 亮 is usually preceded by 很, or is reduplicated into 亮亮. e. g., in example ④ one can say 亮亮的月光照在窗户上.

2. 形容发亮的、有光泽的，多用"亮" ◇ To describe something shiny, 亮 is mostly used:

① 皮鞋擦得很**亮**。The leather shoes are shiny.

② 这种漆涂在木器上，**亮**得很。The paint is shining in carpentry.

③ 姑娘的一双眼睛又黑又**亮**。 The girl has black and shining eyes.

例③也常用"明亮",一般做定语:"姑娘有一双明亮的眼睛" ◇ In example ③ 明亮 is also often used, usually as an attributive: 姑娘有一双明亮的眼睛.

例①②不用"明亮" ◇ In examples ① and ②, however, 明亮 is not used.

3. 表示明白、清楚,多用"亮",不用"明亮" ◇ To mean" know something clearly", 亮 is mostly used, not 明亮:

① 对这件事,大家心明眼**亮**。 We are clear about it.

② 你这么一说,我心里**亮**多了。 I'm enlightened at your words.

4. "亮"还有响亮的意思 ◇ 亮 also means" loud and clear":

① 这孩子嗓子真**亮**。 The boy's voice is clear and loud.

② 他唱歌很有感情,但声音不够**亮**。 He can sing with passion, but his voice is not sonorous.

这个义项"亮"不能用"明亮"代替 ◇ To mean" this", 亮 cannot be replaced by 明亮.

5. "亮"还是动词,而"明亮"只是形容词 ◇ 亮 is also a verb, but 明亮 is only an adjective:

(1) 表示显现出光来 ◇ Meaning "to give out light":

① 晚上街上的灯全**亮**了。 The street lamps are all lit at nights.

② 天还没**亮**,人们就起来了。 Though it was dark, people got up.

③ 屋里**亮**着灯,肯定有人。 There is light in the room, so there must be someone in it.

(2) 表示公开出来;显露出来 Meaning" to make public":

④ 大家纷纷**亮**出自己的观点。 Everyone expressed his or her views.

⑤ 他的真实想法还没**亮**出来。 He didn't tell us his true ideas.

⑥ 他终于**亮**出了本来面目。 He showed his color at last.

以上各例不用"明亮" ◇ In examples 明亮 is not used.

6. "亮"还是名词,指光线、灯火照明物等 ◇ 亮 is also a noun meaning " light, fire, illuminator etc".

① 山洞里黑极了,一点**亮儿**都没有。(指光线) It's pitch-black in the cave, and there is no light at all. (light)

② 屋子里一片漆黑,快拿个**亮儿**来。(指照明物) The room is too dark, so hurry to light an illuminator. (illuminator)

这里"亮"一般儿化为"亮儿" ◇ Here ,亮 is usually retroflexed as 亮儿.

▶[光 guāng—亮 liàng]

谅解 原谅

(动) (动)

liàngjiě yuánliàng

Ⓔ understand, make allowance for/forgive

◥ 这两个词都可表示容忍缺点、意见、误解等。但"谅解"还有达成默契、一致的意思,"谅解"侧重于对缺点错误不加怪罪,一般是对他人的。"原谅"还可以针对自己 ◇ Both words mean "to put up with defects, complaints, misunderstandings, etc". But 谅解 also means "to have tacit understanding or agreement". 谅解 stresses not blaming defects or mistakes and is usually applied to other people. 原谅 can be applied to oneself as well as others.

① 双方经过商谈,取得了**谅解**,协调了步骤。The two parties forgave each other and coordinated their steps after a talk.

② 希望大家互相**谅解**,搞好团结。I hope you will unite well and understand each other.

以上两句用"谅解",不用"原谅" ◇ In examples ①② 谅解 is used and not 原谅.

③ 他犯了不可**原谅**的过失。He made an unforgivable mistake.

④ 他已经道了歉,对方也**原谅**了他。He apologized and was forgiven.

⑤ 不能轻易**原谅**自己的疏忽。Don't simply forgive your ignorance.

以上三句用"原谅",不用"谅解" ◇ In examples ③④⑤ 原谅 is used and not 谅解.

但有时词意较宽泛、模糊时,两个词可互换,而又各有侧重 ◇ But when the meaning is somewhat blurred, the two words are interchangeable with different stresses.

⑥ 他对朋友们说了一些请求**原谅**(/**谅解**)的话。He told his friends that he hoped they would forgive him.

聊 谈 谈天

(动) (动)

liáo tán tán tiān

Ⓔ chat, talk/ talk, chat/ chat, talk

◥ 1. 表示说话,"谈"用于正式的或随便的场合都可以,"聊"则是随便的。如下面的例子,涉及严肃的问题,宜用"谈" ◇ To mean "talk", 谈 can be applied in an occasion either formal or casual, whereas 聊 must be casual. The following examples concern serious matters, so 谈 is used:

① 两国领导人在**谈**到对方的领土争端问题时,都表示将以和平的方式解决。When it came to their territorial disputes, the leaders of two countries expressed that this should be solved peacefully.

② 小张在工作中出了问题,经理要他到办公室**谈话**。There's something wrong with Xiao Zhang's work, so he was asked to have a talk with his manager.

③ ——你有什么为难的事,就跟哥哥**谈**吧! If you have some difficulties, please tell me.

——我现在还不想**谈**。I'm afraid I'm not ready to talk about it now.

④ 双方在研究如何合作的问题时,**谈**得很不愉快。The two parties had an unpleasant talk about their cooperation.

注意:只能说"谈话",不能说"聊话" ◇ Note: One can only say 谈话, not 聊话.

下面的例子,涉及非严肃的话题,两个词都可以用 ◇ The following examples concern informal topics, so either word can be used:

⑤ 喝酒时,两个朋友**谈**(/**聊**)得很投合。The two friends talked very congenially over their drinking.

⑥ 小张,咱们随便**谈一谈**(/**聊一聊**)吧! Xiao Zhang, let's have a chat.

"谈天"是动宾词组,表示闲谈。也可以说"聊天",还可以说"聊大天" ◇ 谈天 is a verb-object phrase, meaning " to chat ". One can also say 聊天, and even 聊大天:

⑦ 星期日,他到朋友家**谈**(/**聊**)了一会儿**天**。He went to his friend and they had a chat on Sunday.

⑧ 别整天**聊大天**,多读读书好不好? Don't chat all day long. Why not read more?

2. "谈"还表示言论、话语,多用于固定词组,如"美谈"、"趣谈"、"奇谈"。也可做报章杂志的栏目名称或题目,如《自由谈》、《一夕谈》、《一席谈》、《古今谈》 ◇ 谈 also means" discussion, talk", which can be used in set phrases, e. g. 美谈 (story passed on with approval), 趣谈(funny story), 奇谈(strange tale). It is also used in the title of a column of newspapers or magazines, e. g.《自由谈》(On Freedom),《一夕谈》(A Day's Talk),《一席谈》(On Conversation),《古今谈》(On History). e. g.

① 鲁迅曾写过一篇讨论汉字问题的文章:《门外**文谈**》。Lu Xun once wrote an article about

Chinese characters——*Menwai Wentan*.

② 《饮茶**古今谈**》是本期这个杂志的一个专栏。On Tea History is a column in this issue of the magazine.

3. "谈"还可组成一些比较固定的词组,表示进行有关婚恋的活动,如"谈对象"、"谈恋爱"等 ◇ 谈 can form some set phrases about activities concerning love and marriage, e. g. 谈对象(be in love),谈恋爱(be in love), etc. e. g.:

① 他们俩正在**谈恋爱**。They are in love now.

② 她**对象谈**好了没有? Has she met her Mr. Right?

③ 哼,他一年**谈**了好几个**对象**! He changed several girl friends a year!

另 (形、副) lìng　　另外 (形、副) lìngwài

Ⓔ other, another/another, moreover

1. 形容词"另"和"另外"都表示前面说的范围以外的,一般用于数量短语前 ◇ The adjectives 另 and 另外 mean "what is not included in the aforementioned and are usually used before a numeral-measure word phrase".

① 这本书不太好,我借给你**另**(/**另外**)一本吧。This book is not good, so I will lend you another one.

② 这条路不好走,咱们走**另**(/**另外**)一条路吧! This road is difficult for us, so let's take another one.

③ 这件衣服如果不合适可以试试**另**(/**另外**)一件。If you are dissatisfied with this coat, you can try on another one.

④ 他们三个人明天下午走,**另**(/**另外**)几个人后天走。They three will leave on tomorrow afternoon, and others the day after tomorrow.

以上各句中"另"和"另外"可以互换,但"另"后不能加"的","另外"后可以加"的"。如例④可说"他们三个人明天下午走,另外的几个人后天走" ◇ In the examples above 另 and 另外 are interchangeable, but no 的 can be used after 另, while 另外 can take 的. e. g., in examples ④ one can say 他们三个人明天下午走,另外的几个人后天走.

2. 副词"另"、"另外"相同处是 ◇ The adverbs 另 and 另外 sometimes are the same:

(1) 表示前面说的范围以外,二词可以互换 ◇ When indicating

what is not included in the aforementioned, the two words are interchangeable:

① 这事我办不了,你**另**(/**另外**)请别人吧! It's beyond me, so please ask others to do it.

② 房间太小,得**另**(/**另外**)找一间大些的。The room is too small, for we need a bigger one.

③ 他要演唱这支歌,我只好**另**(/**另外**)选一支。He wanted to sing the song. I had no choice but to choose another one.

(2)有"单独"和"重新"的意思,可互换 ◇ When meaning "alone" or "anew", the two are interchangeable:

④ 她不吃鱼,我给她**另**(/**另外**)做了些菜。She doesn't like fish, so I cooked her other dishes.

⑤ 我的账**另**(/**另外**)算,不跟他们的在一起。Don't mix my bills with theirs.

⑥ 这篇文章写得不好,得**另**(/**另外**)写。The article is not good, so please rewrite it.

⑦ 如果这几天你没时间的话,咱们**另**(/**另外**)找时间吧。If you are busy these days, we can put it off.

3."另外"还是连词,有"此外"的意思 ◇ 另外 is also a conjunction, meaning "in addition":

① 他学英语,**另外**还学法语。Besides English, he learned French.

② 我买了一些电子读物,**另外**又买了两张电影光盘。Besides some electronic-books, he bought two film VCDs.

"另"不能这样用 ◇ 另 cannot be so used.

留 (动) liú　　遗留 (动) yíliú

Ⓔ leave/leave over

1."留"和"遗留"都是动词,都有过去留下来的事、物继续存在的意思,使用时可互换(但"留"比"遗留"更为口语化) ◇ Both 留 and 遗留 are verbs meaning "to leave or leave over something". They are interchangeable (but 留 is more colloquial than 遗留):

① 这都是李经理在任时**留**(/**遗留**)下来的问题。These problems are left over by Manager Li when he was in power.

② 中华几千年的历史**留**(/**遗留**)下了许多宝贵的文化遗产。The over-thousand-year history of China bestowed many valuable culture heritages on us.

③ 他父亲死时给他**留**(/**遗留**)的财产已被他挥霍光了。He spent lavishly all the wealth left by his father.

2. "留"还有"停在某地","保存"和"收"的意思,而"遗留"没有这些意思,所以不可互换使用 ◇ 留 also means " to remain at some place, to keep"; 遗留 has no such meanings, so the two are not interchangeable:

④ 我们班的学生毕业后**留**北京工作的不多。There are only a few students living and working in Beijing after their graduation.

⑤ 给你原件,我**留**一份复印件就行了。Here is the original, and I will keep one of its copies.

⑥ 我只**留**下这本诗集,其余的你都拿回去吧。I only keep the poetry anthology and you can take the others.

L

M

马上 立刻

(副) (副)

mǎshàng lìkè

Ⓔ at once;immediately/at once

◥ 这两个副词都表示很快(发生),时间间隔很短。"马上"在口语中更常用 ◇ Both adverbs mean "something happen very quickly". 马上 is more colloquial:

① 我**马上**(/**立刻**)去买票。I will buy tickets at once.

② 车**马上**(/**立刻**)就要到站了! The train is to pull in.

二词可互换 ◇ The two words are interchangeable.

有时"马上"含最近的、将来的意思 ◇ Sometimes 马上 means "in the nearest future":

③ 她已经考上了大学,**马上**就要去报到了。She has been admitted by a university, and is about to register there.

④ 这个城市的面貌**马上**就会发生很大的变化。The city will change greatly soon.

这个意思不能用于"立刻" ◇ 立刻 cannot be so used.

▶[立刻 lìkè—立即 lìjí]

买 购 购买

(动) (动) (动)

mǎi gòu gòumǎi

Ⓔ to buy;to purchase/to purchase/to purchase

◥ 这三个词都表示用货币交换商品或实物。区别是,"买"是最常用的口语词,"购"和"购买"带有一定书面色彩。另外,"买"和"购"是单音节的,与后面的词语在音节搭配上较自由,但因"购"较书面化,搭配又受到一定限制。"购买"是双音节词,多与双音节或多音节词语搭配。同时,与各自的反义词也要求对称 ◇ All the three words mean "to obtain something by paying money". The difference is:买 is the most colloquial;购 and 购买 are literary. Besides,买 and 购 are monosyllabic and therefore more free in collocation with other words. But since 购 is literary, its collocation is somewhat limited. 购买 is disyllabic and mostly collocates with disyllabic or multi-syllabic words. Moreover, each word must be used symmetrically with its antonym. e. g. :

① 昨天我**买**了一本书。I bought a book yesterday.

② 这双鞋**买**得挺合算。The pair of shoes is a bargain.

③ 香港是**购**物的理想城市。Hong Kong is a shopping paradise.

④ 这里的市场**购**销两旺。The markets thrives both in its supply and demands.

⑤ 他**购买**了不少国债。He bought a lot of national bonds.

⑥ 这家进出口公司,不仅从国外**购买**机器,还向国外销售制成品。The import & export company purchases spare parts of machines from foreign markets and then sell their finished products overseas.

"买"的反义词是"卖","购"、"购买"的反义词分别是"销"和"销售" ◇ The antonym of 买 is 卖;the antonyms of 购 and 购买 are 销 and 销售.

以上的例句,例①②因口语化和一般化,用"买",不能用"购"或"购买"。例③④因较书面化和习惯搭配,用"购"而不能用"买"或"购买"。例⑤可用"买"替换,这是因为"买"的适用性强;但不能用"购"(比较:"购—物""购买—公债")。例⑥则因"购买"与"销售"对称,不能用"买"或"购" ◇ In the above examples,① and ② are colloquial,so 买 is used and not 购 or 购买;③ and ④ are literary and contain set phrases,so 购 is used not 买 or 购买. In example⑤买 can be used instead because it is very applicable, but 购 cannot be used (compare: 购—物,购买—公债). In example ⑥,购买 and 销售 are symmetrical, so 买 and 购 cannot be used instead.

"购"还可以组成词组,如"急购"、"求购"、"函购"、"邮购"等,用于广告性语言 ◇ 购 can also form set phrases,e. g. 急购(urgent buying),求购(need buying),函购(buying by mail),邮购(buying by post),etc.,which can be found in advertising language.

忙 (形) máng　　急忙 (形) jímáng

Ⓔ busy;hurry/
in haste;hurriedly

1."忙"表示没有空闲时间,事情多 ◇ 忙 means "very much occupied or having a lot to do":

① 我这两天很**忙**。I have been busy these days.

② 他是个大**忙**人,难得有一点儿空闲。He is very busy,and he is not free often.

③ 妈妈正**忙**着给女儿织一件毛衣。The mother is busy knitting a sweater for her daughter.

"忙"也可表示急迫不停地 ◇ 忙

M

can also mean" urgent, pressing" :

④ 你最近**忙**什么呢? What have you been doing recently?

以上不能用"急忙" ◇ In the examples above, 急忙 cannot be used.

2. "急忙"多表示内心紧张或着急而加快动作,可重叠为"急急忙忙"。"急忙"是非谓形容词,但重叠式"急急忙忙"可用"是……的"做谓语(例④) ◇ 急忙 usually means" to be keyed up and hasten in action", and can be reduplicated into 急急忙忙. 急忙 can be used as an attributive or adverbial but not as a predicate. But 急急忙忙 used in the pattern of 是……的 can function as a predicate (example ④):

① 听见孩子哭,妈妈**急忙**跑去看。The mother hurried to see what happened to her child when she heard his cry.

② 他看了一下表,**急急忙忙**上班去了。He glanced at his watch and went to work hurriedly.

③ 见前边有人,他**急忙**刹住了车。When he saw a person in front of his car, he stopped the brake hurriedly.

④ 他干事总是这么**急急忙忙**的。He is always in haste.

例①②③可换用"忙",这里"忙"表示急迫不停。例④不能用"忙" ◇ Examples ①②③ can use 忙 instead, meaning " to hasten". Example ④ cannot use 忙.

美观 美丽

(形) (形)

měiguān měilì

Ⓔ pleasing to the eye/beautiful

◪ 我们已经比较过"美"、"美丽"、"漂亮"、"好看",现在再比较一下"美观"、"美丽" ◇ We have already compared 美, 美丽, 漂亮, 好看. Now we are going to compare 美观 and 美丽.

这两个词都是表示使人产生美感的。但"美观"多从形式着眼,用于物不用于人;"美丽"则可用于人、事、物 ◇ Both words indicate that sth. arouses a person's aesthetic feeling. 美观 stresses the form and is applied to things and not human being, while. 美丽 can be applied to human beings as well as things.

① 她长得很**美丽**。She is good-looking.

② 这是一个**美丽**动人的民间传说。This is an attractive and moving folklore.

③ 花坛被装点得十分**美丽**。The flower garden is decorated beautifully.

以上例①用"美丽",虽然不如用

"好看"、"漂亮"口语化,也是常用的。例①②都不能用"美观"。"美丽动人"是习惯搭配。例③因指物的外表,可换用"美观" ◇ In example ①,美丽 is used, though not as colloquial as 好看 or 漂亮,yet is not unusual. In examples ① and ②,美观 cannot be used. 美丽动人 is a set phrase. In example③, since it refers to the exterior, 美观 can be used instead.

④ 房间布置得**美观**大方。The room is artistically decorated.

⑤ 这个布景不太**美观**,有点儿俗气。The scenery setting is not beautiful,but a bit in poor taste.

以上例④⑤用"美观",不用"美丽"。除了因为这是用于物,还因为"美观大方"是习惯搭配 ◇ In examples ④ and ⑤,美观 is used instead of 美丽,not only because it is applied to a thing, but also because 美观大方 is a habitual collocation.

►[好看 hǎokàn—漂亮 piàoliang—美 měi—美丽 měilì]

猛 (形) měng　　猛烈 (形) měngliè

Ⓔ fierce; violent/fierce; violent

这两个词都表示发生得突然、力量大、有气势等 ◇ Both words mean"something happening abrupty and with momentum".

做定语时,"猛"可搭配的词语较少,如"猛虎"、"猛兽";"猛烈"搭配较多,如"猛烈的风雨"、"猛烈的炮火"、"猛烈的洪水"、"猛烈的攻势"等 ◇ As an attributive,猛 can qualify relatively few words,e. g. 猛虎(a fierce tiger), 猛兽(beast of prey); 猛烈(fierce, violent) are used more freely,e. g. 猛烈的风雨(violent storm),猛烈的炮火(fierce gunfire),猛烈的洪水(violent attack/fighting),猛烈的攻势(fierce offensive),etc.

做状语时,"猛"可修饰单音节词,也可加"地"修饰非单音节词语,多为具体动作 ◇ As an adverbial,猛 can qualify monosyllabic words and,with 地,polysyllabic words denoting specific actions:

① 他一阵**猛**跑,转眼就到了山边。He ran quickly and came to the foot of the mountain in an instant.

② 豹子**猛**地一转身,向人们扑来。The leopard turned around abruptly and sprang onto the people.

"猛烈"多修饰非单音节词语,多为非具体动作 ◇ 猛烈 usually qualifies non-monosyllabic words denoting abstract actions:

③ 大火**猛烈**地燃烧着。The fire burnt briskly.

④ 湖水**猛烈**上涨。The lake was fiercely rising.

做补语时,多加“得”,“猛烈”较“猛”更抽象 ◇ As a complement, 得 is added, and 猛烈 is more abstract than 猛:

⑤ 客队攻得很**猛**。The visiting team fought violently.

⑥ 山火燃烧得越来越**猛烈**。The mountain fire got fiercer and fiercer.

做谓语时,两个词用法接近,但“猛烈”可不加程度副词,“猛”常加“很” ◇ As the predicate, the two words are similar, but 猛烈 can do without adverbs of degree, while 猛 is often qualified by 很:

⑦ 主队的攻势很**猛**(/**猛烈**)。The host team fought violently.

⑧ 炮火很**猛**(/**猛烈**)。The shellfire was heavy.

M

免得 (连) miǎnde　省得 (连) shěngde

Ⓔ so as not to/so as not to

◥ 这两个连词都表示前面所说的行为目的,是避免后面情况的发生;前后用两个分句,连词用在后一分句中。“省得”更口语化一些 ◇ Both conjunctions indicate what goes before aims to avoid what follows. There must be two clauses and the conjunction is used in the second clause. 省得 is more colloquial.

① 别吃得太多,**免得**(/**省得**)发胖。Don't eat too much in case you put on some weight.

② 把闹钟上好,**免得**(/**省得**)明天早晨起不来。Please set the clock in case that you cannot get up in time.

③ 你要仔细向他解释解释,**免得**(/**省得**)引起误会。You'd better explain this to him in detail to avoid his misunderstanding.

以上数例两个词可互换 ◇ The two words are interchangeable in the examples above.

但有时后一分句中,情况如果不发生,是省时省钱省力的,多用“省得” ◇ If what mentioned in the second clause does not happen, time or money or strength will be saved, 省得 is usually preferred:

④ 我顺便替你买来吧,**省得**你再去了。I'll buy it for you in case that you go to buy it.

⑤ 这些家具将就用吧,别扔了,**省得**再多花钱。Please make do with the furniture and don't throw them away so that you can save some money.

渺小 微小

(形) (形)

miǎoxiǎo wēixiǎo

Ⓔ tiny, insignificant/ tiny, infinitely small

◪ "渺小"、"微小"这两个词都表示极小。"渺小"多用于抽象意义。"微小"多用于具体意义,有时也用于较抽象的差别、幅度方面 ◇ Both 渺小 and 微小 mean" extremely small". 渺小 is mostly used in an abstract meaning. 微小 is applied to concrete things, but sometimes also to abstract difference or range.

1. "渺小"有时含贬义 ◇ 渺小 sometimes has a derogatory sense:

① 这出话剧既歌颂了英雄人物的伟大,也描写了苟且偷生之辈的**渺小**和卑微。In this play, the great hero was eulogized, while the insignificant who seeks ease and comfort at others' expense was criticized.

但"渺小"并不是典型的贬义词,而是经常表示弱小,微不足道 ◇ But 渺小 is not a typical derogatory term, but just means" small and weak, insignificant":

② 在大自然的力量面前,个人的力量显得十分**渺小**。Man looks insignificant before the nature.

③ 跟那位英雄人物相比,我自己是多么**渺小**啊! Compared with the hero, how insignificant I am!

2. "微小"不含贬义,多用于具体的形体方面 ◇ 微小 has no derogatory meaning and is mostly applied to the shape of concrete things:

① 细胞的形体非常**微小**。A cell is very tiny.

② 这种零件的体积十分**微小**。The spare part is very small.

或用于差别 ◇ Or to difference:

③ 这两种机器的作用大体相同,只有一些**微小**的差别。The two kinds of machine function in a similar way, there is only a little differences between them.

或用于幅度 ◇ Or to scope :

④ 他最近的进步虽然**微小**,还是值得鼓励的。Though he has made a little progress in his study recently, he deserves the encouragement.

⑤ 他虽然撤走了他的资金,但数量不大,对整个企业的影响是**微小**的。Though he withdrew his capital, this has an insignificant effect on the enterprise, for the capital is not much.

以上,不能用"渺小" ◇ In the examples above, 渺小 cannot be used instead.

有时这两个词在句中与“巨大”等对比时，可以互换；但“渺小”仍侧重于微不足道，“微小”仍侧重于细小 ◇ Sometimes when used in contrast with 巨大 etc., the two words are interchangeable; but 渺小 still stresses insignificance in the abstract sense, and 微小, smallness in the concrete sense, as in the following example:

⑥ 个人的作用是**渺小**(/**微小**)的，集体的作用才是巨大的。The strength of a collective is great, whereas that of an individual is tiny.

M

敏捷 (形) mǐnjié　敏锐 (形) mǐnruì

Ⓔ quick, nimble/sharp, acute

◪“敏捷”、“敏锐”这两个形容词都表示人、动物或某些机器的反应灵敏、迅速 ◇ Both 敏捷 and 敏锐 mean" the reaction of a person, animal", is sensitive or machine.

1.“敏捷”，侧重于灵敏迅速，多用于动作行为 ◇ 敏捷, with the stress on being nimble and quick, is mostly applied to action and behavior:

① 这孩子动作**敏捷**，一下子就跳过了障碍。The child was agile and jumped over the obstacles quickly.

② 这只小狗**敏捷**地将主人抛出的东西衔住。The little dog nimbly got the object thrown by its owner.

③ 练武功的人，一般都身手**敏捷**。Most of Chinese-Gongfu practicers are nimble.

2.“敏锐”，侧重于灵敏锐利，多用于感官、感觉 ◇ 敏锐, with the stress on being nimble and acute, is mostly applied to sense organ or perception:

① 这位记者具有**敏锐**的观察力。The report has acute insight.

② 你感觉太不**敏锐**了，人家夸你，你还不知道。You are too insensitive for you even don't know when you are praised.

③ 雷达兵练就了一双**敏锐**的眼睛。The radarman has sharp eyes.

但在同时修饰灵敏迅速和锐利的事物中，有时这两个词可以互换，不过在意义上有倾斜 ◇ When applied to things both nimble and sharp, the two words are interchangeable, but with different stress:

④ 他在辩论中思维**敏捷**(/**敏锐**)，举止从容，发挥得很好。His mind is nimble and he performed well and calmly in the debate.

⑤ 他反应**敏捷**(/**敏锐**),应变能力很强。He is nimble and very adaptable.

明明 明

(副) (副)

míngmíng míng

Ⓔ obviously/obviously

◪ 这两个关联副词的用法是,在一个分句中用它们强调一事实的真实性,另一分句指出似乎与真实性相对的情况 ◇ Both are conjunctive adverbs used in one clause to stress the truth of a fact, whereas the other clause points out a situation which appears to be opposite to the fact:

① 她**明明**(/**明**)知道这件事,但是故意装糊涂。She knew it obviously, but she pretended to be silly.

② 这里**明明**有人证物证,你还敢抵赖? There are evidence and witnesses. How can you deny?

③ 这台洗衣机**明明**是好的,你怎么能说它是坏的呢? Obviously the washing machine is in good condition. How could you say it doesn't work.

以上只有例①二词可互换,因为“明”一般只用于“知”、“知道”之前 ◇ Only in example ① are the two words interchangeable, because 明 usually appears only before 知 and 知道.

“明明”还可以用在反问句中,加强确认的语气,隐含“虽然表面上不是如此”或“虽然有人怀疑其真实性”等意味。“明”不能这样用 ◇ 明明 can also be used in a rhetorical question to emphasize the assertion, implying "although it may not be so seemingly" or "although sb. may doubt the truth". 明 cannot be so used:

④ 一定让他这么做,不是**明明**逼他犯错误吗? If you must have him do so, you just force him to make mistakes.

⑤ 我不是**明明**说过我不知道嘛!你怎么还问? I have definitely told you I don't know. Why do you still ask me?

目标 目的

(名) (名)

mùbiāo mùdì

Ⓔ target/aim

◪ **1**. 表示射击、追踪、寻找等的具体对象,用“目标” ◇ 目标 is the target of shooting or trailing:

① 在靶场上,他举枪瞄准了**目标**。In the target field, he raised his gun and aimed at the target.

② 队长通过对讲机通知队员:**目标**已经出现,大家要缩小包围

圈。The team leader informed his team through his walker-talker that the target was in view and they should narrow the ring of encirclement.

③ 雷达兵在显示屏上发现了**目标**。The radarman found the target on the screen.

④ 小王已经有了恋爱**目标**,不过还不知道人家肯不肯呢。Xiao Wang has fallen in love with a girl;however,he has no idea about whether the girl is willing or not.

2. 表示想要到达的地点,多用"目的地" ◇ 目的 is used to mean" destination" ; it can also be said as 目的地:

① 这次骑自行车旅游,我们沿江而行,**目的地**是武汉。We will go on a trip by bike along the river and our destination is Wuhan.

② ——你今天去哪儿啊? Where are you going today?

——还没有具体**目的地**。I have no idea about it.

3. 表示追求的境地、意图,较具体多用"目标";较抽象多用"目的"。但具体、抽象只是相对而言,并不是绝对的 ◇ To mean "the aim of one's attempt", 目标 is used for something concrete, and 目的 is used for something abstract. But concrete and abstract are only relative, not absolute:

① 他俩的奋斗**目标**是在五年之内买一套房子。They will both strive for buying their flat in five years.

② 我现在的学习**目标**就是考上北京大学。My learning goal is to be a student in Beijing University.

③ 我们的**目标**(/**目的**)一定能够实现。Our goal can certainly be attained.

④ 为人民服务是他的生活**目的**。His life goal is to serve the people.

⑤ 这次来的**目的**是做生意。That he came here this time is for his business.

如果对追求的境地、境界、意图,加以褒贬(通过加定语等),多用"目的" ◇ If the aim is to be evaluated (with an attributive), 目的 is used:

⑥ 建设好国家是这位政治家的人生理念和崇高**目的**。The noble political goal of the statesman is to make his country more prosperous.

⑦ 那个家伙怀着不可告人的**目的**,接近老实忠厚的张大妈。The man with a mean motive approached to Grandma Zhang, an honest woman.

⑧ 你把享乐作为人生的最终**目的**,我不赞成! I disapprove your life goal of hedonism.

"目标"也是可以修饰的,但一般为判断而不是褒贬,如"正确目标"、"错误目标"等 ◇ 目标 can also be qualified,but it shows judgment rather than evaluation, such as 正确目标,错误目标,etc.

目光 视线

(名) mùguāng (名) shìxiàn

Ⓔ eye-sight/line of sight; view

"目光"指眼神,如"目光炯炯" ◇ 目光 means "eye-sight", e. g. 目光炯炯(sparkling eyes) and:

① 法官那威严的**目光**,使受审者不由得低下了头。The judge's awe-inspiring look made the accused look down.

② 他的**目光**有些忧郁。There is some melancholy in his look.

"视线"不能这样用 ◇ 视线 cannot be so used.

"目光"还指见识,如"目光如豆" ◇ 目光 can also mean "experience and knowledge", e. g. 目光如豆(of little experience and knowledge), and:

③ 这位企业家**目光**远大。The entrepreneur is far-sighted.

④ 像他这种**目光**短浅的人,怎么能做大事? How could those short-sighted guys like him accomplish great tasks?

"视线"也不能这样用 ◇ 视线 cannot be so used either.

"目光"和"视线"都可指眼睛和物体之间的假想的直线 ◇ 目光 and 视线 can both indicate an imagined straight line between the eye and the object looked at:

⑤ 她的**目光**(/**视线**)移向远处。She turned and looked far.

但"挡住……视线"、"遮住……视线",少用"目光" ◇ But in phrases like 挡住……视线 or 遮住……视线,meaning "block the eye- sight", 目光 is rarely used.

"视线"还可比喻注意力,多用于"转移视线" ◇ 视线 can also be used metaphorically to mean "attention", mostly in 转移视线(divert one's attention).

N

年纪 年龄 岁

（名） （名） （量）

niánjì niánlíng suì

Ⓔ age/age/year (of age)

◪“年纪”、“年龄”、“岁”这三个词都表示生存的年数，但词性不同 ◇ 年纪，年龄 and 岁 all mean" age" but they are of different parts of speech.

1.“年纪”和“年龄”都是名词。“年纪”只用于人（或用于拟人事物）。“年龄”则可用于人、动植物、天体等 ◇ 年纪 and 年龄 are both nouns. 年纪 is only applied to human beings (or personified things). 年龄 can be applied to human beings, animals, plants and celestial bodies. e. g. :

① 这个人的**年纪**（/**年龄**）大约在三十（岁）左右。The man is about 30 years old.

② 树的**年龄**可以从年轮中看出。The tree age can be told from its growth rings.

③ 地球的**年龄**已达四十亿年。The earth has existed for 40 billion years.

如果说“地球的年纪”，则是拟人说法 ◇ The usage of 地球的年纪 is personification.

当面询问人的岁数时，用“多大年纪”较客气；“几岁”、“十几岁”可用于孩子；“年龄有多大”等较一般化 ◇ To ask somebody's age face to face，多大年纪 is more polite；几岁，十几岁 can be used for children；年龄有多大 is a general usage. e. g. :

④ 老先生，您多大**年纪**了？How old are you, sir?

⑤ 小朋友你几**岁**了？How old are you, boy?

⑥ 请问，您的**年龄**？Your age?

“年纪”可说“年纪轻”、“年纪不小”、“年纪不大”。“年龄”可说“年龄不小了”“年龄不大”等 ◇ With 年纪，one can say 年纪轻，年纪不小，年纪不大. If 年龄 is used, one can only say 年龄不小了，年龄不大，etc.

2.“岁”是量词，但较特殊，后边不能直接带名词，可认为是名量词。适用范围包括人、动植物 ◇ 岁 is a measure word, but rather unusual. It can take no nouns after it and may be considered as a measure word for nouns. It can be applied to human beings, animals and plants. e. g. :

① 这孩子刚五**岁**。The child is exactly five years old.

② 那棵老树据说已经有两百多**岁**了。It is said that the old tree is over 200 years.

③ 这只猫三**岁**半了。The cat is three and a half years old.

年轻 年青

（形） （形）

niánqīng niánqīng

Ⓔ young/young

这两个词现在常常混用。细分起来，有以下区别："年青"是指绝对年龄，"年轻"是指相对年龄。"年青"指青少年年龄段，即十几岁到二十几岁这一阶段。"青"给人以"青树绿叶"的感觉，即正处在蓬勃生长、充满朝气的感觉。（引自宋玉柱先生观点）◇ These two words are often interchangeable. Their differences lie in that: 年青 refers to an absolute age, while 年轻 refers to a relative age. 年青 indicates the age group of teenagers and those in their twenties, and 青 Rao a sense of " young tree with green leaves"—be in vigorous growth and full of youthful vitality. (From Mr. Song Yuzhu). e. g. :

① **年青**人，让你的青春更美丽吧。Young man, wish your youth more splendid!

② 我想起了**年青**时唱的一首歌。It remind me of a song I used to sing when I was young.

"年轻"表示相对年龄，年纪不大人的可以比较，年纪大的人也可以比较 ◇ 年轻 indicates a relative age, and can be used in comparision in age for the younger or the older.

③ 老王的孩子 15 岁，老张的孩子 18 岁，老王的孩子比老张的孩子**年轻**3 岁。Lao Wang's child is 15, while Lao Zhang's child is 18. Lao Wang's is 3 years younger than Lao Zhang's.

④ 老王 60 岁，老张 65 岁，老王比老张**年轻**5 岁。Lao Wang is 60, while Lao Zhang is 65. Lao Wang is 5 years younger than Lao Zhang.

⑤ 他是这个国家最**年轻**的总统。He is the youngest president of the country.

宁可 宁肯 宁愿

（连） （连） （连）

nìngkě nìngkěn nìngyuàn

Ⓔ would rather/
would rather/
would rather

这三个连词，表示经过比较得

N

失后选择一个方面（有时所选择的方面也不是很满意的）。有时用在前一分句，与后一分句的“也不”呼应；有时用在后一分句，与前一分句的“与其”呼应 ◇ All the three conjunctions mean "more willingly (sometimes the choice may not be very satisfactory either)". They may be used in the first clause in concert with 也不 in the second clause, or used in the second clause in concert with 与其 in the first clause.

① 他**宁可**（/**宁肯**/**宁愿**）骑车去，也不愿在路上堵三个小时（车）。He would rather go by bike than be in a traffic jam for three hours.

② 与其我去给大家增加负担，**宁可**（/**宁肯**/**宁愿**）你去。I would rather do it by myself than make you do more.

例①这种句式，可以颠倒次序 ◇ In example ①, the two clauses can be reversed.

③ 他可不愿意在路上堵三个小时（车），**宁可**（/**宁肯**/**宁愿**）骑车去。He would rather go by bike than be in a traffic jam for three hours.

有时，比较得失中舍弃的一个方面不明显或无须说出，则单说所选择的一个方面 ◇ Sometimes, when the side given up is very obvious or unnecessary to tell clearly, only the choice is told:

④ 我们**宁可**（/**宁肯**）早点儿出发才保险。We'd rather start earlier so as to be punctual.

⑤ **宁可**（/**宁肯**）少吃一点儿的好。I would rather eat less.

这时常有“（才）保险”“的好”等，放在句后。这样的句式，多不用“宁愿” ◇ Here there is usually（才）保险，的好 etc. at the end of the sentence. In this case, 宁愿 is not used usually.

“宁愿”还多少保留着“宁可愿意”的意味，所以少数情况下可以做主要谓语 ◇ 宁愿 more or less retains the meaning of 宁可愿意 and, therefore, can function as the predicate:

⑥ 我**宁愿**客队胜利。I would rather the visiting team had won.

⑦ 我**宁愿**他当领导。I prefer that he is our leader.

这种用法也隐含着两方面的比较选择，如例⑥是主队、客队（而且说话人可能是本城人），例⑦是其他人与“他”。如用“宁可”、“宁肯”，应加“让”：“……让客队胜利”，“……让他当领导” ◇ The usages above also insinuate a choice after comparison, of 主队 and 客队 in examples ⑥ and of 他 and 其他人 in example ⑦. If 宁可 or 宁肯 is used, 让 must be added: ……让客队胜利, ……让他当领导.

O

偶尔 偶然

(副) (形)

ǒu'ěr ǒurán

Ⓔ by chance; occasionally/accidental; fortuitous

这两个词都可表示很不经常，很少(发生)。但"偶尔"是副词，只做状语，而且不受其他词语修饰。"偶然"是形容词，可做状语、定语、补语、谓语等 ◇ Both words mean "rarely, seldom". 偶尔 is an adverb which only functions as an adverbial and cannot be modified by other words. 偶然 is an adjective and can function as adverbial, attributive, complement and predicate, etc.

"偶然"做定语，如"偶然的机会"、"偶然的现象"、"偶然事件"等 ◇ 偶然 functions as the attributive, e. g. 偶然的机会(fortuitous chance), 偶然的现象(fortuitous phenomenon), 偶然事件(accident), etc.

"偶然"做谓语 ◇ 偶然 functions as the predicate, e. g.

① 这件事的发生很**偶然**。This happened by chance.

② 他的落选，有些**偶然**。His failure in the election is a bit out of our expectation.

"偶然"做补语 ◇ 偶然 functions as the complement:

③ 甲队虽然胜了，但胜得有点儿**偶然**。Though Team A won, it won by chance.

以上，都不能用"偶尔" ◇ 偶尔 cannot be used in the examples above.

做状语时，两个词都可以用。主要是在表示"很不经常"、"间或"时 ◇ As attributives, both words will do, meaning "very rarely or occasionally":

④ 他不是专业作家，只是**偶尔**(/**偶然**)写些小文章。He was not a writer, and he wrote some essays only occasionally.

⑤ 她不常去书店，**偶尔**(/**偶然**)去转转，也不买什么书。She didn't go to the bookstore often, If she occasionally went there, she bought nothing.

但"偶然"还可表示事理上出乎预料、不大可能发生(而竟发生)的，"偶尔"不能这样用 ◇ 偶然 can also mean "unexpectedly or unlikely", whereas 偶尔 cannot:

⑥ 昨天在街上**偶然**发现了这种最

新式的钓具,他就买了一个。He happened to see the new-style fishing tools yesterday in the street and bought one.

⑦ 大家都以为他在美国呢,谁知有人竟在街头**偶然**遇见了他。He was supposed to live in the United States and he was come across in the street yesterday.

另外,“偶然”还可在四字语如“事出偶然”中做宾语;组成“偶然性”等词语。这也是“偶尔”没有的用法 ◇ Besides,偶然 can form phrases of four characters such as 事出偶然(happen by chance) or words like 偶然性, while 偶尔 cannot.

O

P

盼望 (动) pànwàng　希望 (动、名) xīwàng

Ⓔ long for/hope

◥ 动词“盼望”和“希望”都有心里想达到某种目的，或者希望出现某种情况的意思 ◇ The verbs 盼望 and 希望 both mean"to wish to reach a certain aim or wish a certain situation to appear".

1. 动词“盼望”表示殷切地期望(人、物、事等快些到来)，宾语多为主谓结构、动词性结构，也可以是名词或名词性结构 ◇ The verb 盼望 means"to long for somebody or something eagerly";the object is usually a subject-predicate construction, a verbal construction, a noun or a nominal construction.

① 他**盼望**着那一幸福时刻的到来。He is looking forward to the coming of the happy moment.

② 孩子们都**盼望**(过)新年。All the children are looking forward to New Year.

③ 他**盼望**家人早日团聚。He is looking forward to the family reunion.

④ 我总**盼望**能跟他见一面。I'm always looking forward to meeting him.

⑤ 父母**盼望**着儿子学成归来的那一天。The parents are looking forward to their child's return when he finishes his school.

以上各句①②⑤不用“希望”。例③④如用“希望”，意思较淡化 ◇ In examples ①②⑤, 希望 is not used. In examples ③ and ④, if 希望 is used, the wish would not be not so eager.

2. 动词“希望”，表示希望达到某种目的或出现某种情况，宾语是主谓结构或动词性结构，但不能是名词或名词性结构 ◇ The verb 希望 means"to wish to reach a certain aim or wish a certain situation to appear". The object is a subject-predicate construction or a verbal construction, but not a noun, nor a nominal construction:

① **希望**你坚持下去，把实验完成。I hope you will hold on your experiments until it completes.

② **希望**我们以后能保持联系。I hope we will keep in touch with each other in future.

P

③ 大家都**希望**你能留下来。We all hope you will stay with us.

④ 我**希望**将来能考上北京大学。I hope I will be a student of Beijing University.

动词"希望"比"盼望"用得广，但"盼望"程度更深，心情更殷切。另外，"希望"可用于句首（主语"我"或"我们"可省略），如例①②；可用于别人也可用于自身，如例④。"盼望"较少这种用法 ◇ The verb 希望 is more widely used than 盼望，but 盼望 expresses a higher degree and is more ardent. Besides，希望 can be used at the beginning of a sentence（with the subject 我 or 我们 omitted），as in examples ① and ②，and can be applied to other people or to oneself as in example ④. 盼望 is fewer in such usage.

P

3."希望"还是名词，"盼望"只是动词 ◇ 希望 is also a noun，while 盼望 is only a verb.

(1) 表示心里希望达到的某种目的、出现的某种情况；或希望所寄托的对象 ◇ Indicating the aim one hopes to attain, the appearance of a certain situation or the target of one's hope：

① 他们的**希望**没有落空。Their hope came true.

② 我们的**希望**终于实现了。Our dream came true at last.

③ 青年是国家的**希望**。The youth is the future of the country.

(2) 表示正面或负面的可能性（多与"有"、"没有"搭配）◇ Indicating the positive or negative possibility（usually used with 有 or 没有）：

④ 这次谈判有**希望**成功。The talk is probable to be successful.

⑤ 学校的发展是大有**希望**的。The development prospect of our school is promising.

⑥ 她康复的**希望**不大。There is little hope of her recovery.

跑（动）pǎo　跑步（动宾）pǎobù

Ⓔ run/run，jog

◪ 这两个词都可表示（人）迅速前进。但"跑"是动词；"跑步"是动宾词组，而且专指体育或军事训练中按一定姿势迅速前进。只有在限定的场合，两个词可以互换 ◇ Both words mean "to move forward quickly". However，跑 is a verb；跑步 is a verb-object phrase and a special term used in physical training or military drills. Only in a specified situation are the two words interchangeable：

① 体育课上老师让同学们在操

场上**跑**(/**跑步**)。In the class the PE teacher asked his students to jog around the playground.

下列句子中两个词不能互换 ◇ The two words are not interchangeable in the following sentences:

② 他在操场上**跑**了三圈。He ran three cycles along the playground.

③ 这孩子**跑**得很快。The child runs very fast.

④ **跑步**对身体有益。Jogging is good to your health.

例③如须用"跑步",应说"跑步跑得很快" ◇ If 跑步 is used in example ③, one must say 跑步跑得很快.

另外,"跑"还有其他义项 ◇ Besides, 跑 has some other meanings:

1. 表示动物迅速前行,如:"这马跑得真快" ◇ 跑 can mean "the running of an animal", e. g. 这马跑得真快(The horse runs fast. 或 How fast the horse runs!).

2. 表示(人或动物)逃走 ◇ 跑 can mean (a human being or animal) "to run away or flee":

⑤ 他为了躲债,**跑**到外地去了。He left his home in order to evade his debt.

⑥ 那只狐狸**跑**了。The fox ran away.

3. 表示为事务或物品奔走,如"跑买卖"、"跑单帮"、"跑运输"、"跑批件"、"跑材料"等 ◇ 跑 can also mean" to rush about for some business or goods", e. g. 跑买卖(be a commercial traveller),跑单帮(travel around trading on one's own),跑运输(do transportation business),跑批件(run for an official, written reply),跑材料(run about collecting material),etc.

4. 表示物体(油、气等)外溢,如"跑电"、"跑水" ◇ 跑 means "overflow, spill, leak (of oil, gas, etc.)", e. g. 跑电(leakage of electricity)跑水(leakage of water).

5. 表示物体因外力离开了应该在的位置,或用于比喻 ◇ 跑 means "to be swept away from its proper place by external force". It may be used figuratively:

⑦ 风把帽子刮**跑**了。The hat blew off.

⑧ 别让到手的东西**跑**了。Don't let your catches go.

6. 表示非一般地(不是逃跑)到某处 ◇ 跑 means "to get to some place in an unusual way (but not flee or escape)":

⑨ 毕业以后,他就**跑**到大西北去了。He went to work in the northwest China after his graduation.

P

⑩ 他一有空儿就往歌舞厅**跑**。He will go to dance hall if only he is free.

这都是"跑步"没有的义项 ◇ 跑步 has no such meanings.

培养 （动） péiyǎng　培育 （动） péiyù

Ⓔ foster; train; culture/cultivate; breed

◥ 这两个动词都可用于花草等，有给予适宜条件，使合理繁殖的意思。用于人时，都有哺育、教育的意思；"培养"侧重于长期的教育、训练，"培育"侧重于抚育使成长。用于事物时，"培养"可说"培养……作风"、"培养……习惯"等 ◇ Both verbs can be applied to plants, meaning" to breed or cultivate". When applied to human beings, they mean" to foster, to educate". 培养 stresses education and training in the long run while 培育 stresses"bringing up". When applied to things, 培养 is usually said of a style of work, habit, etc.

① 园艺工作者正在**培育**(/**培养**)一种新的菊花品种。The horticulturist is cultivating a new species of chrysanthemum.

例①两个词可互换。但在其他用法中各有一些不同的习惯搭配，如"培养细菌"、"培育树苗"等一般不能互换 ◇ In example ① the two words are interchangeable. But in other usages each has some customary collocations, such as 培养细菌(culturing of bacteria), 培育树苗(grow sapling), etc. which are not interchangeable.

② 教师的责任是**培育**(/**培养**)人才。The teacher's duty is to create talents.

例②也可互换，再如"培养(/培育)骨干、干部、科学家、新人"等也可互换。但"培养接班人"、"培育英才"等，也是习惯搭配 ◇ In example ② the two words are also interchangeable, and so are 培养(/培育)骨干、干部、科学家、新人 (cultivate key members/cadre scientists/new talents) etc. But each word also has its customary collocations, such as 培养接班人(cultivate successor), 培育英才 (cultivate elite), etc.

③ 他自幼失去双亲，是叔父把他**培养**起来的。(侧重于教育) His parents died in his early childhood, and it was his uncle who cultivated him. (the stress is on education)

④ 他自幼多病，全靠母亲辛勤**培育**，才长大成人。(侧重于抚育) He was sickly since his childhood and it was his mother

P

who brought him up painstakingly. (the stress is on breeding)

以上例③④各有侧重,不宜互换 ◇ In examples ③④ each has a different stress and are not interchangeable.

⑤ 这所大学的优良传统,**培养**了师生严谨的学风。The university has fine traditions, which develop the good learning habits of its students.

例⑤多用"培养"。但在用于事物时,"培育"可说"培育市场",是"培养"没有的用法 ◇ In example ⑤ 培养 is usually used. When 培育 is applied to things, one can say 培育市场(develop markets), but 培养 cannot be used instead.

佩服 钦佩

(动) (动)

pèifu qīnpèi

Ⓔ admire; think highly of/admire; esteem

这两个动词都表示感到别人有特长而心服、敬重。"钦佩"意思更重,使用时更客气,或用于优秀的人及重大行为。另外,"佩服"可用于自己(把自己作为客体看待) ◇ Both words mean "to admire sb.'s strong point". 钦佩 sounds more forceful and polite, so it can be applied to outstanding people or deeds. Besides, 佩服 can be applied to oneself (treating oneself as an object).

① 小张为人正直勇敢,我很**佩服**(/**钦佩**)。I admires Xiao Zhang's integrity and bravery very much.

② 你的篮球打得那么好,**佩服**,**佩服**。I admire you very much for your excellent skills of playing basketball.

以上例①涉及"为人正直勇敢"这个较高的标准,也可换用"钦佩" 例②只涉及"篮球打得那么好",不宜用"钦佩" ◇ 为人正直勇敢 in example ① is a very high praise, so 佩服 can also be replaced by 钦佩, whereas example ② just refers to a good player, so 钦佩 cannot be used.

③ 他这种华而不实的作风,让人实在不敢**佩服**。It's difficult for us to admire his superficial cleverness.

例③"实在不敢佩服"是不赞同、看不起的委婉说法,不能换用"钦佩" ◇ In example ③, 实在不敢佩服 is a tactful way to show disdain; it cannot be replaced by 钦佩.

④ 我们对你排除万难的抗洪精神,表示**钦佩**。We express our admiration for your tenacious anti-floods actions.

例④涉及重大人事,用"钦佩" ◇ Example ④ refers to distinguished

P

deeds, so 钦佩 is used.

另外,"佩服"可用于自己(有时带有诙谐意味) ◇ Besides, 佩服 can be applied to oneself to show humor:

⑤ 我能说出那样的话? 连我自己都要**佩服**我当时的勇气了。Can I say that? I will have to admire my courage at that time.

偏偏 (副) piānpiān　　偏 (副) piān

Ⓔ deliberately; alone/ deliberately

◪ 这两个副词都用于表示转折的分句中,是关联副词 ◇ Both words are adverbs of connection used in the second clause of a complex sentence.

P

1. 表示客观事件的发生或客观状况与愿望正相反 ◇ They indicate that the happening of something or some situation is opposite to what one expects:

① 他正要出门,电话**偏偏**(/**偏**)响了。The moment he was going out, the telephone rang.

② 本来这个会 20 分钟就能开完,**偏偏**大家却说个没完,结果开了一个钟头。The meeting had been intended to last for 20 minutes; however, everyone talked constantly, as a result, it lasted for an hour.

以上例①两个词可互换。例②"偏偏"用在主语前,"偏"不能这样用。如改为"大家却偏偏(/偏)说个没完",可互换 ◇ In example ① the two words are interchangeable. In example ② 偏偏 is placed in front of the subject, where 偏 cannot. If example ② is turned into 大家却偏偏说个没完, 偏 can replace 偏偏.

2. 表示主观上故意跟客观相违反 ◇ Both words indicate that the subject acts deliberately against the objective situation:

③ 不让带那些违禁品,他们**偏偏**(/**偏**)要带。They are not permitted to take the contraband, but they just do the opposite.

④ 天气这么冷,**偏偏**你们穿得这么少,不感冒才怪呢! It's very cold. But you dress that little, you're likely to get a cold.

以上例③二词可互换。例④不能用"偏",因"偏"不能用在主语前。如改为"你们偏偏(/偏)穿得这么少",则可互换 ◇ In example ③, the two words are interchangeable. In example ④, however, 偏 cannot be used because 偏 cannot be placed in front of the subject. If example ④ is turned into 你们偏偏穿得这么少, 偏 can replace

偏偏.

3. 表示单单、独独,多用“偏偏” ◇ To indicate the meaning of "alone",only 偏偏 can be used:

⑤ 大家都同意,**偏偏**他一个人不同意。Everyone agreed with it, but he disagreed.

⑥ 这么多新鲜水果,可我爱吃的菠萝**偏偏**没有。There is a lot of fruit. However,there isn't my favorite pineapple.

贫　穷　贫穷

(形)　(形)　(形)

pín　qióng　pínqióng

Ⓔ poor;impoverished/ poor;impoverished/ impoverished

◪“贫”指缺少钱物(生活、生产资料)等,多组成双音节词语,如“贫民”、“贫农”,也见于四字语,如“贫病交加”、“一贫如洗”。还表示缺少,如“贫血”、“贫油” ◇ 贫 means "poor" and mostly form disyllabic words or phrases,e. g. 贫民(paupers),贫农(poor peasant). It is also found in four word phrases,e. g. 贫病交加(suffer from both poverty and sickness),一贫如洗(penniless). 贫 also means "to be lacking in",e. g. 贫血(anaemia),贫油(oil poor).

“穷”也指缺少钱物,较“贫”更能独立运用,如“穷人”、“穷日子”、“由穷变富” ◇ 穷 also means "poor" and can be used more independently than 贫,e. g. 穷人(the poor),穷日子(days of poverty),由穷变富(turn from poor to rich). More:

① 他小时候家里很**穷**,还当过童工。His family was poor when he was a child,and he worked as a child laborer then.

② 实行改革开放政策以后,这个**穷**村子逐渐富起来了。Along with the implement action of reform and opening up policy,the poor village is becoming rich gradually.

“贫穷”的意思与“穷”相同,但较书面化,多用于较抽象、正式的场合 ◇ 贫穷 has the same meaning as 穷 but is more literary and used in abstract or formal situation,e. g.

③ 经过几年的奋斗,这个县已经改变了**贫穷**落后的面貌。The county has changed its poverty after a few years' efforts.

“贫”与“富”相对,“穷”和“富”、“阔”相对 ◇ The opposite of 贫 is 富;the opposite of 穷 is 富 or 阔.

平凡　平常

(形)　(形)

píngfán　píngcháng

P

Ⓔ ordinary; common/ ordinary; common

◪ 这两个词都表示常见的、一般的、普通的。但"平常"可用于人、事、物,"平凡"多用于人或人所处涉及的领域,如"岗位"、"劳动"、"世界"、"工作"等。"平凡"主要是相对于"伟大"而言,有评价的色彩;"平常"主要是相对于"特殊"而言的。二者都可重叠使用 ◇ Both words mean "ordinary or common", but 平常 can be applied to human beings, things and matters while 平凡 is mainly applied to human beings. 平凡, opposite to 伟大 has a sense of or the work fields such as " post ", " work ", "world", " work ", " evaluation "; whereas 平常 is the opposite of 特殊. Both words can be reduplicated.

① 我爸爸是个**平凡**(/**平常**)的人。My father is an average person.

② 退休后,这位将军过着**平常**(/**平凡**)的生活。The general led an ordinary life after his retirement.

以上两句二词都可用,但侧重不同。如"平凡的人"多指无辉煌业绩、老老实实的人,"平常的人"多指与众人无区别的人 ◇ In examples ① and ② either word can be used but the stress is different. 平凡的人 means " a common person without any outstanding achievement". 平常的人 means "an ordinary person just like anyone else".

可说"伟大出于平凡",不用"平常"。"平常"可说"平平常常,一点儿也不特殊" ◇ We can say 伟大出于平凡 (The great is out of the ordinary.) in which 平常 is not used. 平常 can be reduplicated: 平平常常,一点儿也不特殊. More:

③ 他**平凡**地度过了一生。He led an ordinary life.

以上例③用"平凡"或"平平凡凡","平常"如做状语,必须重叠为状态形容词 ◇ In example ③ 平凡 or 平平凡凡 can be used, but 平常 cannot. If used as an adverbial, 平常 must be reduplicated:

④ 他**平平常常**地度过了一生。He led an ordinary life.

但在用于人以外的事物时,一般用"平常" ◇ When applied to things other than people, 平常 is used instead of 平凡, e. g. :

⑤ 这个电影很**平常**。The movie is common.

⑥ 这是一顿很**平常**的饭菜。This is not a special meal.

⑦ 这个城市的建筑太**平常**了。The buildings in this city are too common.

"平常"还指平时 ◇ 平常 also means " usually or ordinarily" :

⑧ 大赛前,他和**平常**一样,一点

儿也不紧张。As usual, he was not nervous before the important game.

普通（形）pǔtōng　一般（形）yībān

Ⓔ common, general/general

1. "普通"和"一般"都有平常的、常见的、没什么特殊的意思 ◇ Both 普通 and 一般 mean "ordinary with nothing unusual", e. g. :

① 他穿了一身很**普通**（/**一般**）的衣服。He wore ordinarily.

② 我不过是个**普通**（/**一般**）工人。I am only an average worker.

③ 这种纸很**普通**（/**一般**），到处都买得到。The paper is common, and you can buy it anywhere.

如指人的社会地位很平常，多用"普通" ◇ When referring to ordinary social status of a person, 普通 is mostly used, e. g. :

④ 不论是工厂的工人还是学校的教师，都是**普通**劳动者。Either a factory worker or a teacher is a common worker.

⑤ 校长以**普通**会员的身份参加了学校的工会会员大会。As its ordinary member, the president attended the trade union meeting.

⑥ 他出生在**普通**人家，没有什么地位和声誉。He was born in an ordinary family and he has no status and prestige.

2. "一般"还指质量或水平等不高不低，属大多数情况，"普通"没有这个意思 ◇ 一般 also indicates an ordinary quality which is neither very high nor very low. 普通 has no such meaning, e. g. :

① 他的学习成绩**一般**。He was an average student.

② 这种手机质量**一般**，比不上那些名牌。The mobile phone is ordinary, and it is not as good as those of famous brands.

③ 他的研究成果很不**一般**。His research result is not ordinary.

3. "一般"还有一样、同样的意思，"普通"没有这个意思 ◇ 一般 also means "the same". 普通 has no such meaning:

① 两个人的英语水平**一般**高。Their English is nearly the same.

② 小船像飞**一般**向前驶去。The boat is speeding forward.

③ 屋子里书堆得像小山**一般**。The pile of books in the room is like a hill.

4. "一般"还有"在多数情况下"的意思，"普通"没有这个意思 ◇ 一般 also means "usually, as a rule", while 普通 has no such

meaning, e. g. :

① 这里的商店**一般**晚上8点停止营业。The shop here usually closes at eight p. m.

② 周末他**一般**都和家人一起出去。He usually goes out with his family at weekends.

③ **一般**都是我去他家，他很少来我这里。I usually went to his place, and he seldom came to mine.

5. "普通"可以重叠(AABB式) ◇ 普通 can be replicated (AABB), e. g. :

① 他是个**普普通通**的人。He is a very common person.

② 一件**普普通通**的小事，别看得那么严重。Don't take the ordinary thing seriously.

"一般"不能重叠 ◇ 一般 cannot be reduplicated.

Q

起初 开始

（名） （动、名）
qǐchū kāishǐ

Ⓔ in the beginning; at first/ begin, start; beginning

1. "起初"是名词，表示事物的初始阶段，多与以后或现在对举。"开始"是动词，也是名词，名词用法与"起初"近似 ◇ 起初 is a noun meaning " the beginning stage", often in contrast to 以后 or 现在. 开始 is a verb as well as a noun. As a noun, its usage is similar to that of 起初:

① **起初**（/**开始**）他对法语不感兴趣，后来因为工作需要才慢慢地学了起来。He was not interested in French in the beginning, but later he began to pick it up because his work can't do without it.

② 现在你后悔了，**起初**（/**开始**）你怎么不听我劝呢？Now you regret. Why not follow my advice in the beginning?

以上二句，两个词可互换 ◇ In examples ① and ②, the two words are interchangeable.

但名词"开始"可受定语修饰（定语后一般加"的"），"起初"不能 ◇ The noun 开始, however, can be modified by an attributive (usually followed by 的), while 起初 cannot:

③ 从学期的**开始**，他就抓紧时间，学好各门课程。At the beginning of this term, he made the best of his time to study all his courses hard.

④ 在一年的**开始**，我们应该有一个年度计划。At the beginning of a year, we'd better make a one-year plan.

⑤ 你换了工作，这是一个新的**开始**，应该有新的面貌。Since you changed your job, I think it is a new start and you should change you, too.

"起初"和"开始"都可修饰名词，如"起初（/开始）的时候"、"起初（/开始）的安排"等 ◇ Both 起初 and 开始 can modify a noun, e. g. 起初（/开始）的时候 (in the beginning)，起初（/开始）的安排 (former/initial arrangement), etc.

2. 动词"开始"，如下列各例，不能用"起初" ◇ The verb 开始

cannot be replaced by 起初, as in the following examples:

⑥ 寒假结束了,新学期从今天就**开始**了。The winter holidays are over, and today's the beginning of the second semester.

⑦ 他一**开始**就喜欢上这个地方了。He liked the place in the very beginning.

⑧ 人来齐了,我们**开始**座谈吧! Since everyone is here, let's start discussing now.

⑨ 现在**开始**讲新课。Today we'll learn a new lesson.

▶[开始 kāishǐ—开头 kāitóu]

气愤 生气 发火儿

(形)

qìfèn shēng qì fā huǒr

Ⓔ indignant; furious/ get angry/get angry

◥"气愤"是形容词,"生气"和"发火儿"是动宾词组。这三个词语都表示愤怒,"气愤"、"生气"有时不一定表现出来,而"发火儿"一般都表现出来,如吵嚷、骂人等。"气愤"还较书面化。三个词因词性不同,用法也不同 ◇ 气愤 is an adjective while 生气 and 发火儿 are verb-object phrases. All the three indicate indignation: 气愤 and 生气 may not be showed sometimes, but 发火儿 is usually revealed, by quarrel or curse, for example. Besides, 气愤 is more literary. Since the three words are of different parts of speech, their usages are also different.

① 因为受到不公平的对待,他**气愤**极了。He was furious at being treated unfairly.

以上例①,"气愤"可带"极了"、"至极"等补语,其他两个词一般不这样用("生气"在口语中偶尔可带补语)。但"气愤"和"生气"可加状语,有时可互换 ◇ In example ①, 气愤 can take 极了, 至极 as its complement, but the other two phrases cannot be so used (生气 in colloquial speech may take a complement occasionally). 气愤 and 生气 can take an adverbial and the two are interchangeable sometimes:

② 这件事使他十分**气愤**(/**生气**)。He was angry / furious at it.

以上例②"气愤"除较"生气"略显书面化以外,"愤怒"的程度也略强 ◇ In example ②, besides being more literary, 气愤 is also fiercer than 生气.

"发火儿"则是词义最强的◇ 发火儿 is the fiercest of the three.

③ 处长为这事都**发火儿**了。The section chief was angry at his men's mistakes in their work.

例③用"发火儿",不宜用其他两个词 ◇ In example ③ 发火儿 is used and the other two are not suitable.

另外,"生气"和"发火儿"可插入不同的成分 ◇ Besides, 生气 and 发火儿 can be inserted into different elements:

生了一天的气 get angry for a whole day

生了大气 flare up

生闷气 sulk about

生闲气 get angry about trifles

生谁的气 be angry with sb.

发了大火儿 flare up

发了半天火儿 in a bad temper for a while

勤劳 勤奋

(形) (形)

qínláo qínfèn

Ⓔ diligent; hardworking/ diligent; industrious

◪ 这两个词都表示刻苦努力,"勤劳"主要指一般行为(生活、劳动、从事某事业等),"勤奋"主要指学习、研究、工作等 ◇ Both words mean "hardworking". 勤劳 is applied to daily life, labour, undertaking, etc. and 勤奋 is mainly applied to study, research, and work.

以下前两句用"勤劳",后两句用"勤奋",不能互换 ◇ In the following examples, 勤劳 is used in examples ① and ② and 勤奋 in examples ③ and ④. They are not interchangeable:

① 这些农民非常**勤劳**,庄稼活儿和副业都搞得不错。The farmers are very industrious, and they did a good job both in farming and sideline.

② **勤劳**勇敢是我们崇尚的美德。Hardworking and bravery are the traditional virtues we advocate.

③ 这孩子**勤奋**好学,成绩不错。The boy is diligent in his studies, and has got excellent marks.

④ 职工们都很**勤奋**,公司的业务也蒸蒸日上。Our business prospers for all the staff in our company is very industrious.

但在针对性较模糊时,两个词可互换 ◇ Yet when the referent is vague, the two words are interchangeable:

⑤ 在异乡谋生,**勤劳**(/**勤奋**)是生存的条件。You cannot make a living abroad if you are not hardworking.

轻视 看不起

(动)

qīngshì kàn bu qǐ

Ⓔ look down on; underestimate/ look down upon; disdain

◥这两个词语都有不重视、小看的意思。"轻视"较"看不起"显得书面化，并可做"受到"、"遭受"等动词的宾语。"看不起"较口语化，不能做宾语。以下例①②一般用"轻视"，不用"看不起"。例③二词都可用 ◇ Both words mean " to disdain, to slight". 轻视 is more literary than 看不起 and can function as the object of verbs like 受到，遭受 etc. 看不起 is more colloquial and cannot function as the object. In examples ① and ② 轻视 is used and not 看不起. In example③, either word can be used:

① 这工作很重要，不能**轻视**。The job is of importance, so take it seriously.

② 由于出身贫寒，他经常受到某些人的**轻视**。He is often looked down upon by some people because of his poor family background.

③ 你不能**看不起**(/**轻视**) 自己，因为自信是成功的前提。You should not look down upon yourself for confidence is the key to success.

在正面表示对人的态度时，"看不起"有时含有"觉得…不如自己"、"羞与为伍"的意思，一般不宜用"轻视" ◇ When applied to one's attitude, 看不起 means "to 觉得……不如自己 deem someone as below oneself and 羞与为伍 feel ashamed to be in his company"; in this sense 轻视 is not used.

④ 对残疾人，我们不应该**看不起**他们，而应该尊重他们，帮助他们。We shouldn't look down upon the disabled, but respect and help them.

⑤ 他一贯是只说不做，同学们都**看不起**他。He was disdained by his classmates for his usual empty talks without any deed.

情况 (名) qíngkuàng　情形 (名) qíngxíng

Ⓔ circumstances; situation/state of affairs; condition

◥这两个词都表示事物或事情呈现的面貌。用"情形"时，所指事物较具体。而"情况"的词义较宽，还指事物的变化(包括突变)、动静等，既指具体事情也指抽象的事情，并特指军事上的局势变化等 ◇ Both words mean "the state of affairs". 情形 is more concrete and 情况 is more widely applied, from the change of things (including sudden change) to something astir, from concrete things to abstract ones and especially the change of military situation, etc.

① 家长想向学校了解一下孩子的学习**情况**(/**情形**)。The parents want to know something about their child's performance in school.

② 如何办理，到时候看**情况**(/**情形**)再说吧。As to how to deal with it, we will have to wait and see.

以上例①②这种一般内容的句子，二词可互换 ◇ In sentences of general contents of examples ① and ②, the two words are interchangeable.

“情况”的使用更频繁，被定语修饰时，因搭配紧凑，常不需加“的”，如“学习情况”、“工作情况”、“健康情况”等。用“情形”，则常需加“的” ◇ 情况 is used very frequently and needs no 的 when it takes an attributive, e. g. 学习情况(study)，工作情况(work)，健康情况(health) etc., where as 情形 usually takes 的 in similar situations.

“情况”有时不需要加定语，就含有比较特殊的意思，如下列二例用“情况”而不用“情形” ◇ 情况 sometimes indicates a special case without an attributive. In example ③ and ④, 情况 is used, but not 情形:

③ 你到那里先熟悉一下**情况**。Please go there to be familiar with the situation.

④ 这两天市场上有什么**情况**吗? How've things been going in the market?

如果用“情形”，常须说“熟悉一下当地的情形”、“有什么值得注意的情形”等。可以说“谈情况”，却不说“谈情形”。至于特定的“思想情况”、“天气情况”、“生活情况”等，含有“思想表现”、“天气变化”、“生活好坏”等意义。这都不能简单地换用“情形”。而指军事变化的“情况”，也可不用定语，就包括特殊的“变化”等意义 ◇ If 情形 is used, one needs to say 熟悉一下当地的情形(be familiar with the local environment)，有什么值得注意的情形(something worth noticing) etc. One says 谈情况, but not 谈情形. As to 思想情况(thinking)，天气情况(weather)，生活情况(life) etc., they imply 思想表现(thoughts)，天气变化(weather changes)，生活好坏(life quality) etc. and cannot be replaced by 情形. When referring to military situation, 情况 can imply a special" change" without an attributive. e. g.:

⑤ 军官问哨兵:你那里有**情况**吗? The officer asked a guard: how've things been going there?

由于“情况”较“情形”的含义宽泛，所以，“情况”可受一些形容词的直接修饰，而“情形”一般不能。如可说“新情况”、“好情况”等 ◇ Since the meaning of 情况 is more extensive than 情形，it can be modified by adjectives while 情形 cannot. For instance, one can say 新情况（new situation），好情况（good news），etc.

“在……情况（/情形）下”，也有所不同。如果定语是“这种”、“那种”、“一般”、“特殊”等，两个词可互换 ◇ With the pattern 在……情况（/情形）下，the two words are interchangeable if the attributive is 这种（this），那种（that），一般（general, common），特殊（specific, special），etc. e. g.：

⑥ 在这种**情况**（/**情形**）下，两个人只好分手。In this situation, they cannot but separate.

⑦ 在一般**情况**（/**情形**）下，学游泳并不需要很长时间。In a normal case, it will not take you a long time to learn swimming.

如果定语是“危急”、“紧急”、“非常”等，只能用“情况”，不能用“情形” ◇ If the attributive is 危急，紧急，非常 etc.，only 情况 can be used and not 情形，e. g.：

⑧ 在**紧急**情况下，指挥塔命令飞行员跳伞。In emergency, the cupolas gave them orders of jumping from their parachute.

区别（动、名）qūbié　分别（动、名）fēnbié

Ⓔ distinguish; difference/ distinguish; difference

1. 动词“区别”和“分别”的意思都是对两个或两个以上的相近事物进行比较，辨别其中不同之处；或表示划分。如做谓语的例子 ◇ Both verbs 区别 and 分别 mean "to compare two or more things to find the difference between them". The following are examples with the two verbs as predicates:

① 你能**区别**（/**分别**）这两个词的意思吗？Can you tell the difference between the two words' meanings?

② 我**区别**（/**分别**）不出这两种草有什么不同。I cannot tell the difference between the two species of grass.

③ 他一下子就**区别**（/**分别**）出了这几种工艺品的产地。He identified the origin places of these crafts in an instant.

④ 对待他们的错误，应根据具体情形**分别**（/**区别**）对待。We should deal with their mistakes respectively according to their nature.

动词“区别”和“分别”一般可以

互换，但“区别”经常用于经过比较或研究，找出事物的不同情况（有时可加“加以”等）；“分别”则较一般 ◇ The verbs 区别 and 分别 are usually interchangeable, but 区别 always means" to find out the difference after study or comparison (sometimes 加以 can be added)" ;分别 is more general.

⑤ 继承古代的文学遗产，一定要**区别**精华与糟粕。When inheriting the ancient literature heritages, it is necessary for us to distinguish their essence and dross.

⑥ 这两种事物的性质，我们一定要区别开。We must distinguish the natures of the two things.

⑦ 对初犯和惯偷一定要加以区别。We must distinguish first offenders and habitual thieves.

例⑤⑥⑦句用“区别”，因为要通过分析、研究的过程，不用“分别” ◇ In examples⑤⑥⑦ 区别 is used, since a process of analysis and study is needed. 分别 is not used.

2. 动词“分别”和“区别”做状语时意思有所不同 ◇ When 分别 and 区别 are used as an adverbial, they have different meanings.

(1)“分别”表示一个一个地，分开进行 ◇ 分别 means "one by one":

① 老师**分别**找小张和小李谈了话。The teacher had a word with Xiao Zhang and Xiao Li respectively.

② 对他们提出的几个问题要**分别**进行处理。Their questions should be solved respectively.

(2)“分别”有“各自”的意思 ◇ 分别 means "each, respective":

③ 毕业后，同学们**分别**走上了自己的工作岗位。After graduation, the students worked at their own work.

④ 这次足球比赛，一班和二班**分别**获得冠军和亚军。Class One and Class Two won the first and second place of the football match respectively.

(3)“区别”做状语是表示用不同的态度、方法去解决或处理事物。常用的搭配如“区别对待”、“区别处理” ◇ 区别 as an adverbial means" to solve a problem or do something with a different attitude or method". Collocations like. 区别对待 (treat respectively), 区别处理 (handle respectively) are commonly used:

⑤ 这两个问题性质不同，应**区别**对待。The two problems differ in nature, so they should be handled in different way.

⑥ 小王和小李所犯的错误轻重不同，要**区别**处理。The mistakes made by Xiao Li and Xiao Wang are different, so they should be dealt with differently.

3. 动词“分别”还有离别、分离的意思,而“区别”无此义 ◇ The verb 分别 also means "to depart, to be separated", while 区别 has no such meaning:

① 我们**分别**了两年了。We parted for two years.

② 自从**分别**以后,他们没有联系过。After their departure, there was no contact between them.

4. “区别”和“分别”还是名词,指相近的两个或两个以上的事物的不同之处,一般可互换 ◇ 区别 and 分别 are also nouns meaning "difference" and are interchangeable:

① 我看不出这几支笔有什么**区别**(/**分别**)。I cannot identify the differences among the pens.

② 我觉得这两句话的意思没有**区别**(/**分别**)。I think there's no difference between the meanings of the two sentences.

③ 新旧操作方法**区别**(/**分别**)很大。There are a lot of differences between the new operation and the old one.

当表示完全不同或有较大不同的事物时,特别是再加定语时,多用“区别” ◇ When applied to entirely or greatly different things, especially when there is an attributive, 区别 is preferred:

④ 这两本书的论点有根本的**区别**。The arguments of the two books are radically different.

缺乏 (动) quēfá　　缺少 (动) quēshǎo

Ⓔ lack, be short of/
lack, be short of

1. 动词“缺乏”和“缺少”都可表示(某事物)应该或有或需要有,而实际上不足或没有。当不明显表示为有而不足,或是完全没有时,二者均可用(带宾语) ◇ The verbs 缺乏 and 缺少 both mean" to lack or to be short of something which one ought to have, but actually does not have enough or not have at all". When it is not clear whether it is complete lack or not enough, either word will do (with an object). e. g. :

① 他从小**缺乏**(/**缺少**)教育,不懂礼貌。He is impolite for he was lack of schooling since childhood.

② 他双眼通红,一看就是**缺乏**(/**缺少**)睡眠。We can see that he lacks sleep from his red eyes.

③ 我刚工作,**缺乏**(/**缺少**)经验。I'm a green hand, and I am lack of work experience.

④ 这项工作进行得很慢,主要是

因为**缺乏**(/**缺少**)人手。The progress of the work is very slow mainly due to the insufficiency of hands.

⑤ 他对学习**缺乏**(/**缺少**)信心。He has no confidence in his study.

⑥ 由于**缺乏**(/**缺少**)阳光,所以这些花长得不好。The flowers do not grow very well for they want sunlight.

2. 当要明确表示(某具体事物)应该有而没有或用具体数字表示所缺数量时,只能用"缺少"(带宾语) ◇ When it is necessary to indicate definitely the lack of something or the definite quantity which is short of, only 缺少 can be used (with an object), e. g. :

① 老教授**缺少**一个助手。The old professor wants an assistant.

② 这个房间**缺少**两张书桌。The room needs two desks.

"缺乏"不能这样用 ◇ 缺乏 cannot be used in the last two examples.

3. "不可缺少"常一起用,形成固定短语,不能说"不可缺乏" ◇ 不可缺少(indispensable) is a set phrase, and one cannot say 不可缺乏. e. g. :

① 妇女是国家建设中一支**不可缺少**的力量。Women are an indispensable force in our country's construction.

② 阳光、空气和水是我们生存所**不可缺少**的。Sunlight, air and water are essential to our living.

4. "缺乏"还可不带宾语,单独做谓语,"缺少"不能这样用 ◇ 缺乏 can function as the predicate without an object, but 缺少 cannot.

① 我们这里业务干部很**缺乏**。We lack business cadres badly.

② 经过化验得知,这种土壤中的钾元素很**缺乏**。From the test we know the soil is lacking for potash fertilizer.

确实 真实 实在

(形) (形) (形)

quèshí zhēnshí shízài

Ⓔ true, reliable/
real, true/
in fact, real

1. "确实"表示的确如此,"实在"也有近似的意义(做状语) ◇ 确实 means " really so". 实在 also has a similar meaning (as an adverbial):

① 今年夏天**确实**(/**实在**)热。It was really hot this summer.

② 你穿这身衣服**确实**(/**实在**)不好看。You looks very ugly

Q

in this dress.

但当“确实”做定语、谓语等，表示（信息、情况）真实可信时，不能用“实在” ◇ But when 确实, used as an attributive, predicate, etc., mean " (information, situation) reliable", it cannot be replaced by 实在.

③ 这是个**确实**的消息。This is reliable/certain news.

④ 这只是传说，不怎么**确实**。This is just uncertain news.

“确实”还可以重叠使用，如“这消息确确实实” ◇ 确实 can be reduplicated, e.g. 这消息确确实实.

2.“实在”还表示人品、才能的不虚假，多做谓语、定语，也可重叠。其他两个词不能这样用 ◇ 实在 also means "honest, dependable" and is mostly used as the predicate or attributive and can also be reduplicated. The other two words cannot be so used:

① 这个人表里如一，非常**实在**。The man's words accord with his deeds and he is very honest.

② 他的学识是**实实在在**的，没有一点儿虚假。His learning is undoubted.

③ 那小伙子是个特别**实在**的人。The young man is very honest.

“实在”还表示“其实”，含有并不一定如此的意思，做状语。其他两个词也不能这样用 ◇ 实在 also means 其实 (in fact), implying that it may not be so, used as an adverbial. The other two words cannot be so used.

④ 他吹得厉害，**实在**并不怎么样。He talked his head off, but in fact there was nothing special.

3.“真实”则表示与客观事实相符合，较为书面化 ◇ 真实, indicating something conforming to the fact, is more literary:

① 这是一段**真实**的历史。This is a real history.

② 他的话**真实**可靠。His words are trustworthy.

③ 我们还不了解**真实**的情况。We haven't known the truth yet.

例②③也可用“确实”，但意思不如“真实”重 ◇ In examples ② and ③ 确实 can also be used but with less stress.

“真实”较少做状语。但在叙述艺术作品或历史著作等时可用 ◇ 真实 seldom functions as an adverbial, but may be so used in relating an artistic work or historical writing.

④ 这部小说**真实**地再现了当年的艰苦岁月。The novel vividly makes the hard life at that time reappear.

▶[扎实 zhāshi—实在 shízài]

R

然后 以后

（副） （名）

ránhòu yǐhòu

Ⓔ then, afterwards/ after, afterwards

"然后"是可以表示联系的副词,可用于复句 ◇ 然后 is an adverb of conjunction and can be used in a complex sentence:

① 咱们先学习一小时,**然后**再讨论。Let's first learn it for an hour, and then discuss it.

② 他昨天上午先去买东西,**然后**才来我家吃饭的。After he finished his shopping on yesterday's morning, he came to my place for dinner.

以上两句,例①用于未来,例②用于过去 ◇ Example ① is applied to future and example ② to the past.

"以后"也可用于连接分句 ◇ 以后 can be followed by a clause:

③ 毕业以后,他到一家公司工作。He works in a company after graduating.

"以后"是时间名词,并可与前面的动词、短语和小句紧密结合,如"吃饭以后"、"从那以后""战争结束以后"等。"然后"之间不能这样用。例②"去买东西"和"然后"之间须有停顿,而"以后"可说"买东西以后",无须停顿 ◇ 以后 is a noun of time and can form a phrase with a verb or phrase, e. g. 吃饭以后(after dinner), 毕业以后(after graduation), 从那以后(since then), etc. 然后 cannot be so used. In example ② there is a pause between 去买东西 and 然后. If 以后 is used, it follows 买东西 without a pause.

"以后"可做定语、状语、主语、宾语,状语例已见例③ ◇ 以后 can function as an attributive, adverbial, subject and object. As an adverbial, it is shown in ③. Following are more examples:

④ **以后**的日子会越来越好的。(定语)The future life will be better and better. (attributive)

⑤ **以后**他再也没来过。(主语) Afterwards, he has never been here. (subject)

⑥ 环保项目,不但要为当前服务,还要多为**以后**考虑。(宾语) The environment project should not be only for the present, but also for the future. (object)

"然后"都不能这样用。例⑤的"以后"也可解释为状语,但也不能换用"然后"。"然后"前面,一般另有分句(如例①②)◇ 然后 cannot be used in these cases. 以后 in example ⑤ can also be seen as an adverbial but cannot be replaced by 然后. There is usually a clause in front of 然后(as in example ① and ②).

燃烧 烧

(动) (动)

ránshāo shāo

Ⓔ burn/ burn

1. 表示东西达到燃点而着火。"烧"较口语化,"燃烧"较书面化,同时"燃烧"表示的火势也较剧烈 ◇ 燃烧 and 烧 both mean "to burn". 烧 is colloquial while 燃烧 is literary, indicating a bigger fire. e. g.:

① 灶里的火**烧**得很旺。The fire in the oven is burning briskly.

② 孩子,别玩火,小心**烧**着手。Don't play with fire, boy, or you'll burn your hand.

③ 别**烧**落叶,会污染空气的。Don't burn the fallen leaves, for that will pollute the air.

④ 大火燃**烧**起来,映红了半个天空。The big fire burnt and shone the sky.

例①如用"燃烧",则显得书面色彩较浓 ◇ In example ①, if 燃烧 is used instead, it will be more literary. 这两个词都是及物动词,但"烧"带宾语的例子更多 ◇ Both can be used as transitive verbs, but 烧 is more often with an object.

2. 表示烹饪方法,用"烧" ◇ 烧 also means "to cook":

① 她今天**烧**了几个好菜。She cooked several delicious dishes today.

② 饭**烧**好了吗? Is the dinner ready?

③ 这盘红**烧**鲤鱼是王师傅的拿手好菜。Chef Wang is good at the dish of carp braised in brown sauce.

一般说来,例①②中的"烧",较多用于南方;北方用"做",但近年来,用"烧"的也多起来了。"烧菜"、"烧饭"是"做"的意思,但"烧"并不都等于"做"。"烧"还是一种特殊的烹饪方法,是将食物原料蒸或炒后,加汤汁用火焖透,如例③ ◇ 烧 in example ① and ② is used in South China, while in North China 做 is used, though 烧 is now used by more people. However, 烧菜 and 烧饭 mean "to cook", but 烧 is not always the same as 做. It is also a special way of cooking, that is, to steam or stir-fry the food first and then put in water and seasoning to simmer, as in example ③.

3. 表示体温因不正常而升高或表示比平常体温高的体温,用“烧” ◇ 烧 also means "fever":

① 他病了,**烧**得很厉害。He was ill and got a high fever.

② 吃了药,孩子已经退**烧**了。The child's fever was gone after he took the medicine.

③ 发**烧**可不能大意,最好去医院看看。Mind you, if you have got a fever, you'd better go to the doctor.

4. 表示加热或用化学方式等使物体变化;也指施肥过多或不当,影响植物正常生长,用“烧” ◇ 烧 means "to heat or change something by using certain chemical method." It also means "to kill the plant by over fertilizing". e. g. :

① 这个窑是**烧**砖的。This is a brick kiln.

② 做试验时,不小心,衣服被药水**烧**了一个洞。Because of his carelessness, his clothes was burnt a hole by the chemical liquid while he was doing an experiment.

③ 肥料上多了,花被**烧**死了。The flower was dead because of too much fertilizer.

5. 比喻情绪等激化高涨或爆发,多用“燃烧” ◇ 燃烧 is often used metaphorically to describe the intensification of emotion:

① 他心中的怒火几乎要**燃烧**起来。He nearly flew into a rage.

② 他的工作热情像一团**燃烧**的火。His enthusiasm for work is like a burning fire.

（名） rénjiā　　（代） rénjia

Ⓔ family, household/ another person

这两个词词性不同,用法也不同,不能互换。但由于汉字相同,读音相同(只是“家”的声调不同),容易混淆,因此进行比较 ◇ The two words are of different parts of speech and have different usages, and so are not interchangeable. However, they are made up with the same characters and have the same pronunciation and so are easily confused. Hence it is necessary to make a comparison of the two.

1. **人家**(rénjiā)(名)

(1) 指住户 ◇ Indicating "household":

① 村南有一户**人家**。There is a family living in the south of the village.

② 百里之内都是沙漠,根本没有**人家**。There is no one living

R

in the desert of about one hundred square *li*.

(2)指家庭 ◇ Indicating "family":

③ 她生在有钱**人家**,从小没受过苦。She was born in a rich family and never lived a hard life.

④ 不少商业**人家**的子女,长大后都继承父母的事业。Quite a lot of children from business families inherited their parents' business after they grew up.

⑤ 他们家生活非常简朴,是个勤俭**人家**。His family leads a plain and thrifty life.

(3)指女子未嫁前的丈夫家 ◇ Indicating" the family of a girl's betrothed":

⑥ 她的大女儿已经有了**人家**了。Her eldest daughter has been engaged.

⑦ 姑娘长大了,不愁找不到**人家**。Even the ugliest lid can find its own pot.

2. 人家(rénjia)(代)

(1)指自己或某人以外的人,别人 ◇ Indicating "another person, other people, excluding oneself":

① **人家**的东西,不要乱动。Don't touch the things without their owner's consent.

② **人家**都能去,我为什么不能? Everyone can go. And why not I?

③ 不能总听**人家**的,得有自己的看法。You should have your own views and don't follow others all the time.

(2)指谈话双方都知道的第三者 ◇ Indicating "a third person known by both sides engaged in talking":

④ 快把这些书给**人家**送回去吧! Please return these books at once.

⑤ 是你不对,还不向**人家**道歉? It's all your fault, why not make an apology immediately?

⑥ **人家**过去可帮助过咱们。He helped us before.

⑦ 现在**人家**有名了,看不起我们了。(带有不满或讽刺的感情色彩) Now he's famous and looks down upon us. (with a sense of dissatisfaction or irony)

(3)"人家"后边可带指人的名词同位语 ◇ 人家 can take an apposition of a person's name:

⑧ **人家**小李多好啊,待人热情、诚恳。How kind is that Xiao Li, sincere and enthusiastic.

⑨ 看**人家**小王多会说话。You know, Xiao Wang has a sweet mouth.

⑩ 咱们怎么能跟**人家**赵明比,人家是博士呀! (带有不满或讽刺的感情色彩) How can we be compared with Zhao Ming? He's a doctor after all.

忍耐 (动) rěnnài　忍受 (动) rěnshòu

Ⓔ endure, tolerate, bear/ endure, tolerate, bear

◣ 这两个词都有抑制自己的意思，但“忍耐”侧重于把不如意的感觉等抑制住不外露；“忍受”侧重于把痛苦等承受下来 ◇ Both words mean "to restrain oneself". 忍耐 stresses "to restrain one's unhappy feelings"; 忍受 stresses "the endurance of the pain":

① 即使这个单位不好，你也应该**忍耐**一段时间，不要刚来就想走。Though the work condition is not good in this work unit, you'd better stay here some time. Don't resign at once.

② 小王对小张早就有意见，只是一直**忍耐**着没有说。Xiao Wang was dissatisfied with Xiao Zhang, but he bit his tongue.

③ 我不能想像母亲**忍受**了多少艰难困苦才把我养育成人。I can't imagine how many hardships my mother has endured to bring me up.

但在表示较具体的不如意的境遇、感受时，两个词可互换 ◇ But the two words are interchangeable in expressing the actual undesirable lot:

④ 他的话如此刻薄，我实在**忍受**(/**忍耐**)不下去了。His caustic remarks was beyond my endurance.

⑤ 他**忍耐**(/**忍受**)不住寂寞，常常出去跳舞。He used to go dancing for he was afraid of loneness.

认得 (动) rènde　　认识 (动、名) rènshi

Ⓔ know, recognize/ know, recognize; understanding

◣ 1. 动词“认得”和“认识”都有能确定或分辨某人、某事物是这个而不是别的的意思 ◇ The verbs 认得 and 认识 both mean "to know or to be able to recognize". e. g.:

① 这个人我不**认得**(/**认识**)。The man is a stranger to me.

② 你**认得**(/**认识**)这个字吗？Do you know the word?

③ 这里的变化太大了，我都不**认得**(/**认识**)了。I cannot recognize the place for it has changed greatly.

2. 动词“认识”还有“了解”、“懂得”的意思，而“认得”没有这个意思 ◇ The verb 认识 also means "to understand", but 认得 has no such meaning. e. g.:

① 他已经**认识**到了他所犯错误的严重性。He realized the seriousness of his mistakes.

② 我**认识**到自己应负的责任。I come to know my responsibility.

R

这里的"认识"一般要经过观察、概括、分析、判断等过程，是不能用"认得"代替的 ◇ Here 认识 is to know through a process of observation, generalization, analysis and judgment and cannot be replaced by 认得.

3. 名词"认识"，指客观现实在人头脑中的反映，是一种思维活动的结果 ◇ The noun 认识 means "the reflection of the objective reality in the human brain, which is the result of thinking". e. g. :

① 我的**认识**是表面的，肤浅的，极不深刻。What I know is superficial and not profound.

② 人们对客观事物的**认识**要经过实践的检验。The knowledge about the real world should be tested by practice.

"认得"无此用法 ◇ 认得 has no such usage.

R

仍 仍然 仍旧

（副） （副） （副、形）

réng réngrán réngjiù

Ⓔ still, as before/
still, as before/
still, as before

1. 副词"仍"、"仍然"、"仍旧"都表示 ◇ The adverbs 仍, 仍然, 仍旧 all mean:

(1) 情况、事物等保持原样不变 ◇ A situation or thing, etc. remaining the same as before. e. g. :

① 几十年了，他**仍**(/**仍然**/**仍旧**)住在原来的地方。For decades, he still lives in the same place.

② 尽管遇到很多挫折，他**仍**(/**仍然**/**仍旧**)很乐观、很自信。Though he faced a lot of setbacks, he was still optimistic and self-confident.

③ 老房子里的家具**仍**(/**仍然**/**仍旧**)按原样摆放着。The furniture in the old house is displayed in its original order.

(2) 情况、事物等经过变动又恢复原状 ◇ A situation or thing, etc. being restored to its original state after some alterations, e. g. :

④ 手术后，他的病**仍**(/**仍然**/**仍旧**)不见好。He has shown no sign towards recovery, even after the operation.

⑤ 做完操的学生**仍**(/**仍然**/**仍旧**)回教室上课。Those who have finished doing the exercise, please go back and have classes in the classroom.

①②各例中三个词可互换，但"仍"多用于书面语，"仍旧"比"仍然"更口语化 ◇ In the examples ① and ② the three words are interchangeable, but 仍 is mostly used in literary language, and 仍旧 is more colloquial than 仍然.

2. 形容词"仍旧",表示照旧(多用于书刊),是书面语 ◇ The adjective 仍旧 means " as before (mostly used in books and periodicals) which is a literary expression":

① 这本书再版时,只是小标题略有改动,其他内容**仍旧**。The second edition of the book keeps the same except the changes of its subtitles.

② 文字改了一下,插图**仍旧**。The illustrations kept the same and only the text made a few changes.

▶ [还 hái—仍 réng—仍然 réngrán]

容许 (动) róngxǔ　允许 (动) yǔnxǔ

Ⓔ allow, permit, tolerate/ allow, permit

◣ 1. 表示许可。两个词都表示许可,但"允许"意思较轻,"容许"意思较重(多针对较严重行为) ◇ Both words mean " to allow", but 允许 is less forceful than 容许(mostly applied to grave behavior).

① 没有得到**允许**,你不能把这些资料拿走。You cannot take the materials away without any permission.

② 学校**允许**家住外地的同学在校住宿。The school permits the students living far from the school to live on campus.

③ 在关键时刻,绝不**容许**有丝毫的动摇或犹豫。Don't hesitate at all at critical time.

④ 允许公民有宗教信仰的自由。The law allows citizens to the freedom of religious belief.

但有时针对的问题的严重性可大可小时,两个词可互换 ◇ But sometimes the behaviour may be more or less serious, then the two words are interchangeable:

⑤ 他们提的要求太过分,如果**容许**(/**允许**)了,怎么得了? Their requirements are too much for us. How can things go if they are permitted?

⑥ 我们不能**容许**(/**允许**)类似的事件再次发生。We cannot have it alike happen any longer.

2. 表示或许、也许、容许(较书面化),只能用"容许" ◇ To mean " probable (more literary)", only 容许 is used:

① 这种特大洪水,百年**容许**一遇。This kind of severe flood is rare, but we should still be fully prepared for it.

② 这样的事情,30年以前,**容许**

R

有之，现在已没有了。Such kind of thing only happened 30 years ago, but it doesn't exist now.

如 如果

（连、动） （连）

rú rúguǒ

Ⓔ if, in case/if, in case

1. 连词"如"、"如果"表示的意思相同，但用法有所不同，"如"较"如果"略书面化些 ◇ The conjunctions 如 and 如果 have the same meaning, but their usages are different. 如 is more literary than 如果.

(1)表示假设或条件，用在复句的前一分句，后面常有"就"、"还"、"便"、"则""会"等与之呼应 ◇ To indicate " hypothesis or condition", they are used in the first clause of a complex sentence and there is often 就，还，便，则，会 etc. in the second clause to correspond. e. g. :

① **如(/如果)**不亲自去做，就不知道这工作有多难。If you don't do it by yourself, you'll never know how difficult it is!

② **如(/如果)**处理得当，问题很好解决。The problem will not be difficult to solve, if properly handled.

③ **如(/如果)**大家团结一致，便能战胜困难。If we unite, we are likely to overcome the difficulties.

④ **如(/如果)**发生这种情况，我们会诉诸法律。In this event, we would take the matter to court.

⑤ 事情**如(/如果)**已成定局，我们也没办法。What's done is done, so we have no other choice at all.

(2)表示类比。假定某一判断成立，则与之类比的另一判断也成立，重点在后一分句(后边常加"说"，特别是"如果"后边) ◇ To indicate " analogy". Suppose a judgment is tenable, then another analogous judgment is also tenable, with the stress on the second clause. (说 is usually added, especially after 如果):

⑥ **如(/如果)**说食物能满足人们身体的要求，那么，书籍就能满足人们精神的要求。If the food can satisfy the body, similarly, the books will satisfy the spirit.

⑦ 在他们家，**如(/如果)**说他是总经理，那么，他妻子就是董事长。In his family, if he is a commander, his wife will be a political commissar.

(3)"如果"常与"的话"呼应，而"如"不能 ◇ 如果 is often used

in concert with 的话, but 如 cannot:

⑧ **如果**遇到什么困难的话,就来找我。If you have some troubles, please come to me.

⑨ **如果**明天有空儿的话,我一定去找找那本书。If I am free tomorrow, I will be likely to go to the library.

2. 如(动)

(1)有符合,依照的意思 ◇ used as a verb, meaning "to tally with, according to":

① 这样就**如**了他的心愿了。He will be satisfied with this.

② 工程一定能**如**期完成。The project is likely to be completed on schedule.

(2)好像,好像……一样的意思 ◇ To mean "like, the same as":

③ 他几十年**如**一日辛勤地工作着。He has been working hard for decades.

④ 年轻人**如**早上升起的太阳,前途充满了光明和希望。The youth are like the rising sun, and their future is brilliant and promising.

(3)表示举例 ◇ To mean "for example":

⑤ 除了英语之外,学生们还可以选学其他外语,**如**俄语、法语、西班牙语、阿拉伯语等。Besides English, students are allowed to take other foreign language courses such as Russian, French, Spanish, and Arabian.

⑥ 他这次来中国去了不少地方,**如**上海、北京、南京、广州、福州等。This time he visited a lot of places in China such as Shanghai, Nanjing, Guangzhong, and Fuzhou.

▶[假如 jiǎrú—如果 rúguǒ—要是 yàoshi]

[若 ruò—如果 rúguǒ]

若 (连) ruò　　如果 (连) rúguǒ

Ⓔ if; in case/if; in case

◪ "若"书面色彩浓,用法与"如果"等基本一样 ◇ 若 is more literary and is basically used in the same way as 如果:

① **若**(/**如果**)你方同意,双方即可签字。If your party agree with it, the two parties can sign on it.

② 工程**若**(/**如果**)不立即开工,恐怕会耽误工期。If the project doesn't start at once, I'm afraid it will be delayed.

③ 天气**若**(/**如果**)有变化,运动会可以考虑延期举行。If the weather changes, the sports meet will be possible to be put off.

以上三句，两个词可以换用，但“若”的书面色彩更浓 ◇ In all the three examples above, the two words are interchangeable, but 若 is more literary.

另外，在四字语中用“若”不用“如果”，如“人若犯我，我必犯人”。也可用“如”，如“如泣如诉”、“如日中天” ◇ Besides, in four-character set phrases 若 is used and not 如果, e. g. 人若犯我，我必犯人(if we are attacked, we will certainly counterattack). 如 is also used, e. g. 如泣如诉(of music or singing querulous and plaintive), 如日中天(like the sun at high noon at the apex of one's power, career).

“若”也是副词，表示好像 ◇ 若 is also an adverb, meaning " to seem", e. g. :

④ 他惹了麻烦，还**若**无其事。He pretended that there was nothing happening though he has got into troubles.

⑤ 他坐在那里，一声不响，**若**有所思。He sat there silently, contemplating.

▶ [假如 jiǎrú—如果 rúguǒ—要是 yàoshi]
[如 rú—如果 rúguǒ]

R

S

色彩 颜色

(名) (名)

sècǎi yánsè

Ⓔ flavour, colour/colour

"色彩"、"颜色"这两个名词在意义或使用范围上有区别 ◇ 色彩 and 颜色 are different both in meaning and usage.

1. "色彩"多指各种配合在一起的颜色 ◇ 色彩 usually means "many colours in coordination":

① 节日的夜晚,天空的焰火和身着盛装的人们,**色彩**缤纷,交相辉映。On the festival night, the beautiful fireworks and people's colorful clothes enhanced each other's beauty.

② 这些绸缎的**色彩**十分绚丽。The colorful silk cloth is very gorgeous.

③ 这套房子的装饰,**色彩**有些单调。The decoration of the house is a bit dull.

2. "颜色"指具体的某一种色,如红、白、蓝 ◇ 颜色 usually means "a certain colour", such as red, white, blue, etc.:

① 我要买那双白**颜色**的皮鞋。I'd like to take the white leather shoes.

② 这种**颜色**不够鲜艳。The color is not bright enough.

③ 这张画的**颜色**有点儿发黄。The painting gradually becomes yellowish.

3. 两个词都可以用于比喻,"色彩"常比喻人的思想倾向或某种事物特有的情调,如"民族色彩"、"感情色彩"等。"颜色"指脸上现出的健康情况、面色;也指故意显示给人的厉害的脸色、态度,或面部表情(较书面化) ◇ Both words can be used metaphorically. 色彩 means "the tendency of one's thought or the unique appeal of something", such as 民族色彩 (national flavor), 感情色彩 (emotional flavor). 颜色 means the condition of one's health as shown by one's face, or a stern countenance, attitude, facial expression (rather literary):

① 这部电影具有浓厚的浪漫主义**色彩**。The film is very romantic.

② 这些工艺品具有鲜明的地方**色彩**。The art crafts have distinct local flavors.

③ 我看你的**颜色**不对，是不是生病了？You don't look well, I wonder whether you are ill or not.

④ 那家伙蛮横无礼，应该给他点儿**颜色**看看。The fellow is rude and we should teach him a lesson.

稍　稍微

（副）　（副）

shāo　shāowēi

Ⓔ a little, slightly/ a little, slightly

1.“稍”、“稍微”这两个副词都表示数量不多、程度不深或时间短暂。用在动词、形容词前做状语，被修饰的词或重叠或带表示少量的后置成分如“一”、“一点儿”、“一会儿”、“一下”等；若有宾语，则带表示少量的定语。“稍”较“稍微”略显得书面化一些 ◇ Both 稍 and 稍微 are adverbs meaning " slightly or a little". They function as adverbials qualifying verbs or adjectives. The qualified word either reduplicates or takes 一，一点儿，一会儿，一下，etc. If there is an object after it, it must take a small quantity of attributive. 稍 is a little more literary than 稍微. e. g. :

S

① 道理很简单，**稍**（/**稍微**）想想就明白了。Its reason is very simple and you can understand it if you have a thought.

② 汤盛得太满了，**稍**（/**稍微**）一碰就洒了。The soup in the bowl is too full and it will overflow out of it with a touch.

③ 咖啡里**稍**（/**稍微**）放一点儿糖就行了，不要太甜。Putting a little sugar into the coffee will do. Don't make it too sweet.

④ 我觉得这衣服的颜色**稍**（/**稍微**）红了点儿。In my view, the dress is a bit red.

⑤ 请**稍**（/**稍微**）等一下。Just a moment.

⑥ 面包需要**稍**（/**稍微**）烤一会儿再吃。Take the bread after it is baked for a while.

2.“稍”多修饰单音节动词、形容词，后面没有“一点儿”、“一些”、“一下”等 ◇ 稍 mostly qualifies monosyllabic verbs and adjectives and there is no 一点儿，一些，一下，etc. to follow. e. g. :

① 照片很快可以洗好，请**稍**等。Just a minute, the film will be developed very soon.

② 这个房间光线**稍**暗，但面积比较大。Though the room is a bit dim, it's bigger.

3.“稍”可用在少数单音节方位词前，后面有时可没有“一点儿”、“一些”等 ◇ 稍 can be used before a few monosyllabic nouns of locality and may not be followed by 一点儿,一些,etc. e. g. :

① 小王坐在最前面,**稍**后是小张和老李。Xiao Wang is seated in the front,and Xiao Zhang and Lao Li are not far from him.

② 宿舍楼**稍**东一点儿就有一个小卖部。Go a little further to the east of the dormitory building,you will find the Canteen.

①和②例中的“稍”都不能用“稍微”替换 ◇ In the examples ① and ② 稍 cannot be replaced by 稍微.

少女 女孩子

(名)

shàonǚ nǚ háizi

Ⓔ young girl/girl

◥ 这两个词语都表示未成年女子或年轻女子,都不能用于当面称呼。“少女”较书面化 ◇ Both words mean " young girl". Neither can be used as an address. 少女 is more literary. e. g. :

① 她在**少女**时代,已经对戏剧发生了兴趣。She showed interest in theater since her girlhood.

② 我不明白为什么男孩子能做,**女孩子**就不能? I wonder why boys are allowed to do and girls are not?

③ **女孩子**就是**女孩子**,动不动就哭。Girls are girls. They cry easily.

“女孩子”有时可表示女儿 ◇ 女孩子 sometimes refers to " daughter" :

④ 张大妈生了一个男孩子,一个**女孩子**。Grandma has a daughter and a son.

▶ [姑娘 gūniang—女孩子 nǚháizi]

深刻 深入

(形) (动、形)

shēnkè shēnrù

Ⓔ deep,profound/
penetrate into;thorough,deep-going

◥ 形容词“深刻”和“深入”都有透过外表达到内部的意思,但词性不同,“深入”是动词,又是形容词,“深刻”只是形容词,词义上也有不同 ◇ The adjectives 深刻 and 深入 both imply the meaning of "penetrating into sth. ",but they are of different parts of speech. 深入 is a verb and an adjective,while 深刻 is only an adjective. They are also different in meaning.

1. 深刻(形)(adj.)

(1)指达到事情或问题的本质,

S

不是表面的、粗浅的，多指达到很高的程度 ◇ 深刻 means "to get to the essence of something, not just the superficial understanding":

① 他对问题的分析十分**深刻**。He has a profound insight into problems.

② 这则寓言含有**深刻**的哲学道理。The fable has a deep philosophy.

③ 他对自己的错误有了一些认识，但认识得还不够**深刻**。He knew something about his mistakes, but that is still not enough.

④ 近十年来，这个城市发生了**深刻**的变化。The city changed greatly in the past ten years.

⑤ 鲁迅的作品**深刻**地揭露了封建社会吃人的本质。Lu Xun's works give a profound exposure to the cruel nature of the old society.

(2)指内心感受程度很深的 ◇ deeply affected:

⑥ 他生在音乐之家，家庭对他有**深刻**的影响。He was born in a musical family, by which he was influenced greatly.

⑦ 她的乐观主义精神给我留下了**深刻**的印象。I am impressed deeply by his optimism.

⑧ 这次试验失败，对我们是一次**深刻**的教训。The test failure is a bitter experience for me.

2. 深入(形)(adj.)

意思是透彻的、透过外表达到事物本质的 ◇ Meaning "penetrating; thorough; get to the essence of sth.":

① 他对古代汉语语法有**深入**的研究。He made an incisive research on ancient Chinese grammar.

② 我们要对情况进行**深入**的了解和分析，才能下结论。The conclusion can only be drawn after a thorough investigation and analysis.

③ 大家对这个方案**深入**、细致地进行了讨论。We made a in-depth and detailed discussion about the plan.

形容词"深刻"和"深入"一般是不能互换的，"深刻"一般修饰"感受"、"印象"、"认识"等词语，而"深入"一般修饰"了解"、"研究"、"调查"、"分析"等词语 ◇ The adjectives 深刻 and 深入 are not interchangeable. 深刻 is used to qualify 感受(experience), 印象(impression), 认识(knowledge), etc. while 深入 qualifies 了解, 研究, 调查, 分析, etc.

3. 深入(动)(v.)

意思是达到事物内部 ◇ Meaning "to penetrate into; enter deeply into":

① 作家要**深入**生活才能写出好

的作品。It's necessary for a writer to get into the real world to write good works.

② 领导要**深入**到群众中去，进行调查研究。Leaders should go into the mass to make an investigation.

另外，"深入人心"是固定搭配，指符合人们的愿望，大家都愿意接受，是对精神、思想、理论、口号、政策等抽象事物而言 ◇ Besides, 深入人心 is a set phrase, meaning "entirely accord with the wish of the masses and be willingly accepted by them". The phrase is applied to abstract things like spirit, thought, theory, slogan, policy, etc.:

③ 这项新的税收政策**深入人心**。The new tax policy has won the support of the people.

甚至　甚至于

(副、连)　(连)

shènzhì　shènzhìyú

Ⓔ even/go so far as to, even

1. 甚至(副)

用于引出一种极端性质的例证，说明某种情况达到很高程度 ◇ 甚至 is used to introduce an extreme example to show the high degree something has reached:

① 他不是大学生，**甚至**连中学也没进过。He has not been at college, and even not at middle school.

②爷爷年纪大了，记忆力不好，**甚至**出去常忘了锁门。My Grandfather is old and has a bad memory, sometimes he even forgot to lock the door when leaving the house.

③ 他们俩脾气不和，有时**甚至**当着人就吵起来了。They two could not get along well, and sometimes they even had a quarrel before others.

2. 甚至(连)　甚至于(连)

用于连接并列的词语或分句，"甚至"或"甚至于"后边是最突出的事例，表示强调。两个词可互换。有时可加"连" ◇ Both are used to connect phrases or clauses. 甚至 or 甚至于 is followed by the most outstanding case to show emphasis. The two words are interchangeable. 连 can be added sometimes:

① 他的衣服、书包，**甚至**(/**甚至于**)连眼镜都湿了。His clothes, satchel as well as his spectacles were all wet.

② 为什么人到老年记忆力常会衰退**甚至**(/**甚至于**)完全丧失呢? Why do the old people usually begin to lose their memory or even lose it completely?

S

③ 他不喜欢猫，**甚至**还有点儿讨厌猫。He doesn't like a cat and he even a bit hate a cat.

失掉 遗失

（动） （动）

shīdiào yíshī

Ⓔ lose/lose

"失掉"与"失去"基本相同，多用于抽象事物。"遗失"与"丢失"基本相同，多用于具体事物 ◇ 失掉 and 失去 are basically the same, mostly applied to abstract things. 遗失 and 丢失 are basically the same, mostly applied to concrete things.

① 那个公司招聘业务员，他因为临时有事没有去应聘，**失掉**了一个好机会。Because there was something emergent to do, he didn't go to the recruiting of business staff of the company, and he missed a good chance.

② 经过几次失败，他几乎**失掉**了信心。After several failures, he almost lost his heart.

③ **遗失**贵重物品，应立即向有关方面报案。If the valuable things are missing, you should report it to the department involved.

④ 他把护照**遗失**在车上了，幸亏司机发现得及时，才没造成什么麻烦。He left his passport in the bus; fortunately, the bus driver found it in time, so it brought no trouble to him.

以上，例①②是用于抽象事物，用"失掉"。例③④是用于具体事物，用"遗失"。"遗失"略书面化，所以可用于正式场合 ◇ In examples ① and ② the things lost are abstract, so 失掉 is used. In examples ③ and ④ the things lost are concrete, so 遗失 is used. 遗失 is somewhat literary and can be used in a formal case.

⑤ 本债券**遗失**不补。The bonds have no missing procedures.

▶ [丢失 diūshī—丧失 sàngshī—失去 shīqù]

时候 时间

（名） （名）

shíhou shíjiān

Ⓔ time/time

"时候"表示时点或时段，"时间"表示由过去、现在、未来构成的系统，也可表示某个时点或时段。"时候"比"时间"口语化 ◇ 时候 indicates " either a point of time or a period of time". 时间 can refer either to a continuous quantity from the past, through the present and into the future or a point or a period of time. 时候 is more colloquial than 时间.

① 现在是什么**时候**(/**时间**)了?到三点了吗? What time is it? Is it three o'clock?

② 他在电脑上打这么一段字,用不了多少**时候**(/**时间**)。It took him only a few minutes to type this paragraph on the computer.

以上二句,两个词可互换 ◇ In examples ① and ② the two words are interchangeable.

但在相当书面的语句中,只能用"时间" ◇ But in more literary language only 时间 is used:

③ **时间**紧,任务重。Time is pressing and the task heavy.

④ 办公**时间**不准吸烟。Smoking is not allowed during office hours.

"时间"可做定语,构成"时间跨度"、"时间观念"等。"时候"不能 ◇ 时间 can function the concept of time as the attributive and make up phrases such as 时间跨度(span of time),时间观念(the concept of time),etc.;时候 cannot.

"时候"可受"这"或"那"的修饰,表示一个时点 ◇ 时候 can be qualified by 这 or 那 to show a point of time:

⑤ 就在那**时候**,警察出现了。Just at this moment, the policeman appeared.

或表示"在上述情况下" ◇ Or to show " under the above circumstances" :

⑥ 如果你遇到了相似的困难,这**时候**你怎么办呢? How will you do if you face the similar difficulties?

使 使用 用

(动) (动) (动)

shǐ shǐyòng yòng

Ⓔ use/use/use

1. 这三个动词都可表示以工具或其他事物为手段从事活动。"使"的宾语有限,较特殊。"使用"较抽象,多表示以人力、物力、资金等从事活动。"用"用得最普遍,既用于具体事物,也用于抽象事物 ◇ The three verbs all mean " to use some instruments or some other things as the means to do something" . The object of 使 is limited. 使用 is more abstract and mostly used to mean " be engaged in some activity with man power, material resources, capital, etc" . 用 is the most commonly used and can be applied to either concrete or abstract things.

① 做领导的一定要善于**用**人。Being a leader should know how to choose the right person for the right place.

② 做领导的要善于识别和**使用**各种人才。Leaders should know how to judge men and use men.

③ 上个月她**用**了不少钱买化妆品。She spent a lot of money on cosmetics last month.

④ 我们应该合理**使用**资金。We should make reasonable use of our capital.

以上四句,宾语是较抽象的“人”或“钱”,一般用“用”和“使用”。“用人”和“使用人才”的不同是由单双音节决定的。“用钱”和“使用资金”也是如此。再如“人力”、“物力”、“手段”、“语言”等较抽象的双音节宾语也多用“使用” ◇ In the four examples above, the object is the more abstract 人(human being) or 钱(money), so 用 or 使用 is generally used. The difference between 用人 and 使用人才 is decided by the collocation of monosyllabic or disyllabic words. The case with 用钱 and 使用资金 is the same. Relatively abstract disyllabic objects like 人力(man power), 物力(material resources), 手段(means), 语言(language) are mostly used with 使用.

“使用”的宾语虽然较为抽象,但也可用于“使用电脑”、“使用微波炉”、“使用集成电路”、“使用武器”等有科技含量的东西。这些也可以用“用” ◇ Though used mostly with abstract objects, 使用 can be applied to technological things such as 使用电脑(use computer), 使用微波炉(use microwave), 使用集成电路(use integrated circuit), 使用武器(use weapons), etc.

2. 带具体意义的宾语则多用“用”和“使” ◇ 用 and 使 are used to apply to concrete objects:

① 大家都喜欢**用**(/**使**)圆珠笔写字。All of us like writing with ball-pens.

② 这把铁锹特别好**用**(/**使**)。The spade is easy to use.

③ 这种新式熨斗我**用**(/**使**)不惯。I dislike the new-style iron.

④ 许多山区还**用**(/**使**)牛耕田。The bull is used to till the land in many mountaineous areas.

3. “使”的宾语较特殊,具体的如“使圆珠笔(写字)”,抽象的如“使劲”(相当于“用力”),都是口语中常见的,主要用于北方。“使”的宾语是有限的,没有“用”普遍。如可说“用汽车运输”,不能说“使汽车运输”,等等 ◇ The objects of 使 are rather unusual, with concrete things such as 使圆珠笔(写字)(write), abstract things such as 使劲(meaning 用力(exert oneself)), all are very common in colloquial language, mostly in north China. The objects of 使 are limited, and not as general as 用. For instance, one can say 用汽车运输(transport by bus), but not 使汽车运输, etc.

"使"还表示致使,相当于"让"、"叫",但比"让"、"叫"正式、书面化 ◇ 使 also means "to make, to cause", which is equivalent to 让, 叫 but more literary and formal.

① 谦虚**使**人进步。Modesty helps one go forward.

② 这件事**使**她很高兴。This made her happy.

4. "用"还表示吃、喝(敬辞),如"请用点心"、"请用茶" ◇ 用 can also mean "to eat or to drink, as a polite expression", e. g. 请用点心(here's the pastry), 请用茶(here's the tea).

▶[花 huā—用 yòng—费 fèi]

事 (名) shì　　事情 (名) shìqing

Ⓔ thing/thing

1. 指生活和社会中的活动、现象等 ◇ Indicating "activities, phenomena, etc., in life and society":

① 报纸上登了什么**事情**(/**事**)? What's in the newspaper?

② 今天大家没什么**事**(/**事情**),出去玩玩吧! We are free today, so let's go out and enjoy ourselves.

这时,较正式、较大的用"事情"(也可说"大事") ◇ Here, 事情 is used for more formal, important things (one can also say 大事).

2. 指事故 ◇ Indicating "accident":

① 小王开车出**事**了! Xiao Wang had a traffic accident while driving.

② 操纵机器应该十分小心,不要出**事**。You should be careful while operating the machine and ensure its safety.

也可说"出事情" ◇ One can also say 出事情.

3. 指工作、职业 ◇ Indicating "job, profession":

① 快毕业了,她正在找**事**。She will graduate from her school soon, and she is looking for a job.

② 现在孩子大了,她准备找点儿**事**(/**事情**)做。Now her children are old enough, and she wants to look for a job.

常说"找事"、"找事情"、"谋事" ◇ To look for a job, one often says 找事, 找事情, 谋事.

4. 指责任、关系等 ◇ Indicating "responsibility, relation, etc.":

① 这次出了差错,是我的**事**。The accident is my fault.

② 他不在场,不关他的**事**(/**事**

S

情)。He had nothing to do with it, for he was absent then.

③ 出了一点儿小差错,没**事**儿。It's OK, for there is only a small mistake.

口语中较多用"事" ◇ In colloquial language, 事 is mostly used.

"事"可以重叠,如"事事如意"、"事事不顺心"、"你别事事都靠父母"等,常做状语,表示每一件事。"事情"不能这样用。"事"还可做动词,是古代汉语的遗留,表示从事等,如"不事生产"等 ◇ 事 can be reduplicated, to function as adverbials e.g. 事事如意(everything is as one wishes), 事事不顺心(everything is not as one wishes), 你别事事都靠父母(Don't rely on your parents completely), etc. meaning "every single thing". 事情 has no such usage. 事 in classical Chinese is a verb meaning "be engaged in", which is still used in this meaning now, e.g. 不事生产(lead an idle life), etc.

四字语多用"事",不用"事情",除上述各例外,再如"一事当前"、"万事如意"、"事无巨细"等 ◇ In four character phrases, 事 is mostly used, not 事情. Besides those mentioned above, more examples are 一事当前(have something to do), 万事如意(Everything is as one wishes), 事无巨细(all matters, big and small), etc.

由于"事情"在古代汉语中有"事的情形、过程"的意思,所以当"事情"与过程等有关时,可独立运用,而"事"不能如此 ◇ Since 事情 in classical Chinese has the meaning of "process", it can be used independently when it concerns process, but 事 cannot:

① **事情**不是那个样子。Things didn't happen in that way.

② **事情**是这样发生的。It happened this way.

③ 这就是**事情**的全部真相。This is the truth about it.

④ 请讲一讲这件**事情**的来龙去脉。Tell me all about it.

当不涉及过程时,可说 ◇ When it does not relate to process, one can say:

⑤ **事情**(/**事**)妥了! It is settled.

⑥ **事情**(/**事**)没办成。It is unsettled.

收拾 修理

(动) (动)

shōushi xiūlǐ

Ⓔ put in order, repair, teach a lesson/repair

1."收拾"的词义较宽,可表示整理、整顿、教训、消灭及使损坏物恢复原状或功能等。"修理"也可表示使损坏物恢复原状或功能,还可表示修剪(树木)等 ◇ 收拾 has several meanings: to put in order, rectify, teach sb. a lesson, wipe out, repair etc. 修理 also means "to repair, or to prune (trees), etc".

所以,在两个词的近似点上可以互换 ◇ Therefore, they are interchangeable sometimes:

① 椅子腿断了,你去**收拾**(/**修理**)一下吧。The legs of the chair are broken. Would you like to repair it?

但这个义项,"修理"可用于机器等结构复杂物体,"收拾"只用于结构简单的物体 ◇ To mean "repair", 修理 can be applied to more complicated structure like a machine, while 收拾 is only applied to things of a simple structure:

② 他把电视机**修理**好了。He repaired the TV set.

③ 他把椅子腿**收拾**(/**修理**)好了。He repaired the chair's leg.

2. "收拾"还可表示整理、整顿、教训、消灭等 ◇ 收拾 can also mean "to put in order, to teach sb. a lesson, or to wipe out, etc.":

① 她正在**收拾**屋子。(整理) She is putting the room in order. (to put in order)

② 留下几个人**收拾**局面。(整顿) Several of them will be left to put it in order. (to put in order)

③ 我早晚要**收拾**那小子。(教训) I will teach the evil guy a lesson some time. (to teach a lesson)

④ 恶势力被警方**收拾**了。(消灭) The evil force was wiped out by policemen. (to wipe out)

3. "修理"表示修剪。另外,"修理"也可表示教训、惩治等,比"收拾"更为口语化 ◇ 修理 means "prune". Besides, it can also mean "to teach a lesson or punish". It is more colloquial than 收拾. e. g.:

① 他正在**修理**树篱。He is repairing the hedge.

② 他被人**修理**了一顿。He was beat.

舒服 舒适

(形) (形)

shūfu shūshì

Ⓔ comfortable/comfortable

"舒服"、"舒适"这两个形容词都有轻松愉快的意思。但"舒服"多侧重于身体或精神上的感受,而"舒适"则多形容环境或和身体有关的居住、生活方面的感受,另外"舒服"在口语中用得更多些 ◇ Both 舒服 and 舒适 mean "comfortable, pleasant". 舒服

stresses physical or spiritual feeling, while 舒适 is applied to the environment or housing conditions. Besides, 舒服 is used more in colloquial language.

1. 身体或精神上感到轻松愉快，一般用“舒服”，“舒服”可重叠（AABB 式）◇ 舒服 is usually used to describe a physical or spiritual comfort and pleasure. It can be reduplicated into 舒舒服服：

① 昨天晚上睡得真**舒服**。He had a sound sleep last night.

② 他工作顺利，家庭和美，经济条件又好，生活得**舒舒服服**的。He has a good job, ahappy family and nice income, which make him cozy.

③ 运动之后，洗个热水澡，**舒服**极了。Taking a hot bath after exercise is really good.

④ 衣服小了点儿，穿起来不太**舒服**。The coat is a bit tight and it is very uncomfortable.

2. 能使人感到轻松愉快，两个词都可以用 ◇ Both words can be used to describe sth. that can bring people a relaxed and pleasant feeling：

① 这间房又大又亮，生活起居很**舒服**(/**舒适**)。The room is big and bright, and it is comfortable to live in.

② 那套沙发坐着特别**舒服**(/**舒适**)。The sofa sits comfortably.

③ 让老人在**舒服**(/**舒适**)的环境里安度晚年。The old man spent his late life with ease.

3. 指人的身体健康状况，用“舒服”◇ When referring to health, 舒服 is used, e. g.：

① 我最近不太**舒服**。I'm not feeling well these days.

② 你脸色不好，有什么地方不**舒服**吗？You look sick. What's the matter with you?

③ 吃过药，**舒服**些了吗？Are you feeling well after taking the medicine?

率领（动） shuàilǐng　带领（动） dàilǐng

Ⓔ lead, head/lead, guide

◪ “率领”、“带领”这两个动词都有领导、引导(人做某事)的意思，但意义范围有所区别 ◇ Both 率领 and 带领 mean "to lead and guide somebody or some people to do something", but their scopes of meaning are not the same.

1. “率领”指领导或指挥(一些人进行集体活动)，语意较正式、庄重 ◇ 率领 means "to lead or direct (some people in some collective activity)". The tone is formal and solemn, e. g.：

① 在这位将军的**率领**下，这支队伍南征北战，立下了战功。The army fought in a lot of places and won a lot of wars under the leadership of the general.

② 代表团将由外交部长**率领**于下周五出访美国。The delegation , under the lead of the Minister of Foreling Affairs will visit America next Friday.

2.“带领”有两个意思 ◇ 带领 has two meanings:

(1) 在前面引导带路，后面的人跟着 ◇ To be a guide in front to show the way followed by people:

① 去找小王，他会**带领**你去有关部门办手续的。Come to Xiao Wang and he'll take you to the department concerned for your formalities.

② 研究室主任**带领**我去见校长。The research section chief took me to meet the principal.

“率领”无此义，因此以上各例，不能换成“率领” ◇ 率领 has no such meaning, so in examples ① and ② above 率领 cannot be used instead.

(2) 领导、指挥或照管(一些人进行集体活动) ◇ To lead or look after (some people in some collective activity):

③ 爸爸**带领**孩子们去野外游玩。The father took his children to go on a field trip.

④ 这支队伍由团长亲自**带领**。The army was under the leadership of the regimental commander.

“带领”(2)中例④可换成“率领”。由于“率领”语意较庄重，因此“带领”(2)中的例③这种语意一般的句子，不能换用“率领”。而“率领”中的各例，可换成“带领”，只是语意没有“率领”庄重 ◇ In example ④ of 带领(2) ，率领 can be used instead. Since the tone of 率领 is rather solemn, in sentences like example ③ 率领 cannot be used; however, in all the examples of 率领，带领 can be used, only the tone will not be as solemn.

▶[带动 dàidòng—带领 dàilǐng]

睡 睡觉

(动)

shuì　　shuì jiào

Ⓔ sleep/sleep

◪“睡”、“睡觉”都表示睡眠。“睡”是动词，“睡觉”是动宾短语 ◇ Both words mean "sleep". 睡 is a verb, while 睡觉 is a verb-object phrase.

① 早**睡**早起，身体好。Early to bed and early to rise is good for

S

your health.

② 他今天一直**睡**到上午10点才起来。He didn't get up this morning until 10 o'clock.

以上用“睡”,不用“睡觉”。特别是这里“睡”与“起”对照,或加补语“到”,只能用“睡” ◇ To show ordinary sleep as in examples above,睡 is used,not 睡觉. 睡 is especially used here in contrast with 起,or with the complement of 到,so only 睡 can be used.

“睡觉”的“觉”是宾语,但含有量词的意味 ◇ 觉 in 睡觉 is the object but with the sense of a measure word:

③ 他太累了,躺在地板上就**睡**了一觉。He was too tired and slept on the floor.

④ 祝你**睡**一个好觉。I hope you have a sound sleep.

⑤ **睡**了一大觉起来,头脑很清爽。You will feel fresh after a sound sleep.

两个词语都可以加“着”(zháo),“睡着”,表示入睡 ◇ Both words can take 着(zháo), meaning "asleep":

⑥ 她刚躺下就**睡着**了。She fell asleep as soon as she went to bed.

⑦ 他翻来复去,怎么也**睡不着**。He tossed all night long.

⑧ 他半天也没**睡着**。After a long time, he couldn't go to sleep yet.

⑨ 我总是失眠,如果能一躺下就**睡着觉**就好了。I'm always sleepless. If only I could go to sleep!

⑩ 最近怎么老**睡不着觉**呢? Why not be able to go to sleep recently?

以上,例⑨⑩中因为是特别强调入睡,用“睡着(zháo)觉” ◇ 睡着(zháo)觉 is used in examples ⑨ and ⑩ above because falling asleep is specially emphasized.

但在并不强调什么的时候,两个词间或可以互换 ◇ If nothing is stressed ,the two words are interchangeable sometimes:

⑪ 他已经**睡**(/**睡觉**)了,你明天再来吧。He's asleep. Please come here tomorrow.

例⑪ 也可说“睡下了” ◇ In example one can also say 睡下了.

▶[睡眠 shuìmián—睡觉 shuì jiào]

睡眠 睡觉

(名)

shuìmián　　shuì jiào

Ⓔ sleep/sleep

◪ 我们已经比较过“睡”和“睡觉”,现在再比较一下“睡眠”和“睡觉” ◇ We have already compared 睡 and 睡觉. Now we are

going to compare 睡眠 and 睡觉.
"睡眠"是名词,有书面语意味;"睡觉"是动宾短语,是口语中常用的 ◇ 睡眠 is a noun and is more literary; 睡觉 is a verb-object phrase which is very colloquial:

① 人每天应该保证八小时的充足**睡眠**。Everyone should sleep at least eight hours a day.

② 吃大红枣有利于**睡眠**。Red dates are good to your sleep.

③ 他最近**睡觉**总睡不大好。He has been unable to have a good sleep recently.

④ 昨天累了,夜里**睡**了一大**觉**,今天起得也比较晚。I got up late today for I had a long sleep due to yesterday's weariness.

以上例①②用"睡眠",例②如换用"睡觉",词性就不一样了。例③④用"睡觉",不用"睡眠" ◇ In examples ①② above 睡眠 is used; if 睡觉 is used instead in example ②, it is no longer a noun but a phrase. In examples ③ and ④, only 睡觉 can be used, not 睡眠.

▶[睡 shuì—睡觉 shuìjiào]

顺便 (副) shùnbiàn　顺手 (副、形) shùnshǒu

Ⓔ incidentally/incidentally; smooth, without difficulty

1. "顺便"(副)、"顺手"(副)都有趁做某事的方便(做另一件事)的意思 ◇ Both 顺便 and 顺手 mean " while one does something, one does something else at the same time", e. g.:

① 你去邮局,请**顺便**(/**顺手**)替我寄一封信。Please post a letter for me if you go to the post office.

② 洗衣服的时候,她**顺便**(/**顺手**)把窗帘也洗了。She washed the curtain while she did washing.

③ 你出去的时候**顺便**(/**顺手**)把门关上。Please shut the door when you leave the house.

④ 你要是去他家,**顺便**把这本书给他带去。Please take the book to him if you go to his place.

⑤ 星期日想去西山玩玩,**顺便**看一个住在那里的朋友。I will drop in a friend there if I go to visit Xishan on Sunday.

"顺手"一般指轻易地一伸手(做某事),一般为用手做的事。因此例④⑤用"顺便",不用"顺手" ◇ 顺手 means " to stretch one's hand easily (to do something, usually with hand)", so in examples ④ and ⑤顺便 is used, not 顺手. e. g.:

⑥ 我**顺手**从书架上拿下一本杂

S

志来翻看。I took a book from the shelf and read.

⑦ 吃完橘子,**顺手**把皮拿出去扔了。After finishing the orange, please throw its peel away.

2. "顺手"(形)有(做事)顺利,没有遇到障碍的意思,多做谓语。"顺便"无此义 ◇ The adjective 顺手 means " without a hitch and usually functions as a predicate". 顺便 has no such meaning. e. g. :

① 事情办得很**顺手**,没费什么劲儿。(谓语)It was handled easily without much effort. (predicate)

② 最近工作不**顺手**,心里压力很大。(谓语)The job was done with some difficulties. (predicate)

③ 他最近遇到了一件不大**顺手**的事儿。(定语)He faced difficulties recently. (attributive)

S

说明 解释

(动、名) (动)

shuōmíng jiěshì

Ⓔ explain, illustrate; explanation/
explain, interpret

◪ "说明"、"解释"这两个词都可以表示说明白、分析乃至阐明。但"说明"是一般地说清楚,说明白,"解释"有时还有针对疑难乃至辩白的含意。另外,词性也有所不同 ◇ Both 说明 and 解释 indicate " to explain, analyze and clarify". 说明 means" just to explain clearly", while 解释 sometimes means" to explain a knotty problem or even to defend oneself". Besides, they are of different parts of speech .

1. **说明**(动) **解释**(动)

① 来访者**说明**来意后,被让进客厅。The visitor explained his intention and was asked to come into the sitting room.

② 他用几句话就**说明**了这个哲学问题。He made the philosophical problem clear with a few words.

③ 这只是一个误会,**解释**一下就行了。This is a misunderstanding. A little explanation will clear it up.

④ 她怎么也**解释**不明白她这样做的用意。She cannot understand her intention of doing so.

以上四句,两个词不能互换。其中"说明来意"、"说明问题"、"解释误会"、"解释明白"都是较固定的搭配("解释来意"虽然也可以,但要用于较特殊费唇舌的语境) ◇ In the four examples above, the two words are not interchangeable. 说明来意,说明问题,解释误会,解释明白 are all somewhat set phrases.(解释来意 can also be said,but is used in rather difficult cases)

两个词可以同时出现,如“这种解释很能说明问题” ◇ Both words can be used at the same time,such as 这种解释很能说明问题(the explanation can prove a lot).

因为“说明”的“明”与“解释明白、解释清楚”的“明白、清楚”词义近似,所以,“说明”与“解释明白”等中的“解释”不能互换 ◇ Since 明 in 说明 and 明白,清楚 in 解释明白,解释清楚 are very similar in meaning,说明 and 解释 in 解释明白 are not interchangeable.

当词义限于一般的分析明白时,两个词可互换 ◇ When the meaning is only a clear general analysis, the two words are interchangeable:

⑤ 请老师**说明**(/**解释**)一下这句话的意思。Please tell us the meaning of the sentence, sir.

⑥ 为什么用这样的方法,请你加以**说明**(/**解释**)。Please tell us the reason why the method was employed.

“加以”、“予以”、“作”等,可用在这两个词的前面 ◇ 加以,予以,作 etc. can be used in front of the two words.

2.“说明”(动)还有证明、证实的意思 ◇ 说明 as a verb also means "to prove or confirm":

① 调查结果充分**说明**了这一问题的严重性。The investigation result showed us fully the seriousness of the problem.

② 结果充分**说明**了饮食合理搭配的重要性。The results show clearly that balanced diet is very important.

“解释”不能这样用 ◇ 解释 has no such usages .

3.“说明”(名),表示说明性的文字材料等 ◇ 说明 as a noun means" directions, manual, or captions, synopsis" , e. g. :

① 一般商品都应该附有使用**说明**。The manual is attached to the goods.

② 图片下附有**说明**。There is a caption under the picture.

“解释”也可以做主语、宾语,但没有“说明”(名)的含义 ◇ 解释 can also function as subject or object, but does not have the meaning of 说明 as noun:

① 这种**解释**是入情入理的。(主语)The explanation is reasonable. (subject)

② 他不听我的**解释**,依旧认为我是故意不帮助他。(宾语)He didn't follow my explanation

S

and he thought I didn't help him advertently. (object)

思想 想法

（名） （名）

sīxiǎng xiǎngfa

Ⓔ thought/opinion

"思想"、"想法"这两个名词都指思维活动的结果，但"思想"是指客观存在反映在人的意识中经过思维活动而产生的结果，较抽象和书面化。而"想法"是指人经过思索所得的结果，较具体、口语化 ◇ Both 思想 and 想法 are the result of thinking. However, 思想 is the objective reality reflected in human consciousness as the result produced through thinking. It is more abstract and literary. 想法 is the result of thinking which is more concrete and colloquial. e. g. :

① 她的**思想**很进步。She is progressive.

② 父亲头脑中还有不少封建**思想**。There are still some feudal remnants in my father's mind.

以上例①②，不用"想法" ◇ In examples ① and ②，想法 is not used.

③ 关于到哪儿旅游，我有个**想法**。I have an idea about where to go on a tour.

④ 在书里加一些插图，这个**想法**很好。It's a good idea putting some illustrations in the book.

以上例③④也不用"思想" ◇ In examples ③ and ④，思想 is also not used.

"思想"有时也指较具体的思路，所以有时可以与"想法"互换 ◇ 思想 can also mean " some concrete thoughts", so sometimes it is interchangeable with 想法：

⑤ 你这种前怕狼后怕虎的**思想**（/**想法**）不对头！Your hesitation is not good.

"想法"有时指某种意见 ◇ 想法 sometimes means " a certain opinion" :

⑥ 关于这个计划，大家还有什么**想法**？Do you have something to say about the plan?

⑦ 有什么**想法**都可以提。Whatever you have in mind, you may tell us.

死 死亡 逝世

（动、形） （动） （动）

sǐ sǐwáng shìshì

Ⓔ die; inflexible/die/die

1. "死"、"死亡"、"逝世"这三个词都表示生命终结、失去生命。但"逝世"只用于人，较庄重、尊敬；"死"一般可用于人、生物；"死亡"较正式，一般用于人

或与人有关的事物 ◇ 死，死亡 and 逝世 all mean " the end of life". 逝世 is only applied to human beings, being more formal and reverential. 死 can be applied to both human beings and animals. 死亡 is very formal and is applied to human beings and things related to human beings.

① 今天是中国著名作家老舍先生**逝世**四十周年纪念日。Today is the 40th anniversary of the death of Lao She, a very famous writer in China.

② 唐代伟大诗人杜甫生于公元712年，**死**于公元770年。Du Fu, the poet of the Tang Dynasty, was born in 712 AD, and died in 770 AD.

③ 我们家的小狗**死**了。My lovely puppy died.

④ 经法医鉴定，这个人属于正常**死亡**。The court doctor proved the man died naturally.

⑤ 这一段陡坡非常危险，登山者称之为"**死亡**"地带。The hill slope is very dangerous; therefore, the climbers call it "dead belt".

从以上例句可以看出，"逝世"较尊敬，例①宜用"逝世"；如用"死"则显得不够尊重。例②因"生、死"是一般而言，所以可用"死"。例③是对于非人类的"狗"而言，应用"死"。例④⑤或用于法律，或用于比喻，都较正式，用"死亡" ◇ From the examples above one can see 逝世 is more reverential, so it ought to be used in example ①, where it would be improper to use 死. In example ② it means 生 and 死 in general, so 死 can be used . In example ③ 死 ought to be used as here the subject is a dog. In examples ④ and ⑤ 死亡 is used as the first is legal language and the second is a metaphor. Both are rather formal.

2. 死(形)

(1)表示固定、不能更改、不灵活、死板 ◇ Meaning " rigid, stiff" :

① 这条水沟里的水是**死**水，不干净。The water in the small ditch is not running, so it's very dirty.

② 你这个人考虑问题怎么这么**死**啊？一点儿灵活性都没有。Why is you so inflexible? There's no flexibility in it.

③ 我们学校的学生宿舍晚上10点熄灯，这是一条**死**规矩，不能更改。Turning off lights at 10 pm is a rigid rule, and nobody is permitted to break it.

④ 时间已经定**死**了，下个月15日动身。The time is settled, that it, we'll start on the fifteenth day of next month.

⑤ 你别把话说**死**,不然就没有缓和的余地。Do not speak so affirmatively; otherwise, you would leave no leeway for yourself.

(2)表示不能通行的 ◇ Meaning "no thoroughfare":

⑥ 这是一条**死**胡同。This is a blind alley.

⑦ 这个后门多年不用,已经堵**死**了。The back gate has not been used for many years and was blocked.

(3)表示程度深,达到极点的。做补语、状语 ◇ Indicating very high degree, the limit, used as the complement or adverbial:

⑧ 他今天丢了钱又摔坏了眼镜,可把他气**死**了。Today he lost his money and broke his glasses, which made him very angry.

⑨ 我考上大学了,我妈都要高兴**死**了。My mother is very glad that I'm admitted by a university.

S

⑩ 今年的夏天热**死**了! It is extremely hot this summer.

⑪ 我**死**追**死**赶才赶上了他。I caught up with him with great efforts.

⑫ 这箱子**死**沉**死**沉的,都装了些什么? The box is too heavy. What's in it?

⑬ 你干吗**死**跟着我? Why follow me all the time?

虽 虽然 虽说

(连) (连) (连)

suī suīrán suīshuō

Ⓔ though, although/although/although

◪ "虽"、"虽然"、"虽说"这三个连词都表示让步关系,先承认某种事实,后一分句常有"可是"、"但是"、"却"等呼应,说出与前一分句相反或相对的主要意思。"虽"较书面化,"虽说"较口语化,"虽然"一般均可用。"虽"一般用于主语后,其他两个词在主语前或后均可 ◇ All the three conjunctions 虽,虽然,虽说 mean "although" (in spite of the fact) to show concession, and the clause that follows usually takes 可是,但是,却 in correspondence to the main clause. 虽 is more literary, 虽说 is more colloquial, 虽然 is general. 虽 is usually used after the subject, whereas the other two can be used either before or after the subject:

① 他**虽**不大同意,可是不敢明说出来。He dare not express that he only partly agree.

② 天气**虽**已转暖,早晚还比较凉。It becomes warmer, but it's still cold in the mornings and at nights.

③ 这孩子**虽然**小，但却很懂事。Young as he is, the child is very sensible.

④ **虽然**他的声音不高，但在远处也能听见。Though his voice is not high, he can be heard in the distance.

⑤ 这衣服**虽说**不太漂亮，可是保暖性能很好。The coat keeps warm rather than look pretty.

⑥ **虽说**新年快到了，他却没有一点过年的心情。Though the New Year is drawing, he was not in the mood of it.

以上6句，④ ⑥不能用“虽”，① ② ③ ⑤三个词可互换 ◇ In the above examples, 虽 cannot be used in examples ④ ⑥, yet the three words are interchangeable in examples ① ② ③ ⑤.

有时“虽然”等在后一分句出现，有补充说明的作用 ◇ Sometimes when 虽然 etc. are used in the second clause to introduce, it functions as a supplementary explanation:

⑦ 丈夫发现妻子的性格有些不一样，**虽然**(/**虽**/**虽说**)只是一些细微的变化。The husband found a bit change in his wife's character, though it was subtle.

⑧ 张老板的生意今年赚钱了，**虽然**(/**虽**/**虽说**)赚得不太多。Mr. Zhang made money in his business though he made only a little.

▶[虽然 suīrán—固然 gùrán]

虽然 (连) suīrán　　固然 (连) gùrán

Ⓔ although, in spite of the fact/no doubt is it true

◪ 这两个连词都表示转折。“虽然”表示承认甲事实，下文引出乙，乙与甲在意义上相反；“固然”表示承认甲事实，下文引出乙，乙与甲在意义上可能相反，也可能不相反。如果甲与乙相反，一般用“虽然”，也可以用“固然” ◇ The two conjunctions mean "although" to show "concession". 虽然 means "admitting that A is a fact"; thus the main clause introduces B. The meanings of A and B are apposite. 固然 means admitting that A is afact, the main clause introduces B. However, the meanings of A and B may be apposite or not. If A is apposed to B, 虽然 is generally used, but 固然 can be used as well in this case.

① **虽然**(/**固然**)现在生活好了，但是也不能浪费。Though we lead a good life now, we shouldn't waste anything.

② 气温**虽然**(/**固然**)低，却并不

S

冷。Though the temperature is low,it's not cold.

注意:例①②中"虽然""固然"可以互换,这限于承认甲作为一种让步对乙是有意义的,否则只能用"虽然",不能用"固然"。下面例③如用"固然"是无意义的 ◇ Note:虽然 and 固然 in examples ①② are interchangeable, but this limits to the case in which the concession of A is meaningful to B, otherwise, only 虽然 is used inslead of 固然 In the following example③,固然 is meaningless.

③ 这种商品**虽然**很贵,可是质量并不好。Though the goods are expensive,its quality is not good.

如果甲与乙不相反,乙只是甲的引申或补充,则只能用"固然" ◇ If A is not opposed to B, and B is the extension or supplement, only 固然 can be used.

④ 气温**固然**不高,也不必穿得太多。Though the temperature is not high, it's not necessary to wear too much.

⑤ **固然**这种商品很贵,可是质量是很好的。Though the goods are expensive, its quality is fine.

也就是说,如例④甲事是"气温不高",如果是与意义上相反的,应该是"穿得多些",但乙事是"不必穿得太多",意义上并不相反 ◇ That is to say, in example ④, A is 气温不高, if it is apposed to B, B should means 穿得多些; however, B is 不必穿得太多 which is not contrary to A.

"虽然"和"固然"都可用于从句主语的前或后,主句中都常有"但是"、"可是"、"却"、"而"等与之呼应 ◇ 虽然 and 固然 can be both used before or after the subject of the subordinate clause. The main clause usually has 但是, 可是, 却, 而 etc. to correspond.

▶[虽 suī—虽然 suīrán—虽说 suīshuō]

损害 (动) sǔnhài　损坏 (动) sǔnhuài

Ⓔ harm, damage/ damage, spoil

◪"损害"、"损坏"这两个动词都表示使之有所损失或破坏。不同之处是:"损害"用于抽象事物,"损坏"用于具体事物 ◇ Both 损害 and 损坏 are verbs meaning damage. The difference is 损害 is applied to abstract things, while 损坏 is applied to concrete things.

1. 损害

① 这件丑闻,**损害**了这位先生的名誉。The scandal spoiled the man's reputation.

S

② 我们不能做**损害**公众利益的事。We cannot do something harmful to the good of the public.

③ 过度饮酒严重**损害**了他的身体健康。His excessive drinking spoilt his health.

以上三句,都用于抽象事物。"健康"也较抽象(相对于"头部"、"手脚"、"心脏"等具体事物而言)。但偶尔可见"损害了肝脏"等说法 ◇ Examples ①②③ are all about abstract things. 健康 is also more abstract (compared with 头部 (head), 手脚 (hands and feet), 心脏 (heart), etc.) . But occasionally one also sees 损害了肝脏, etc.

2. 损坏

① **损坏**公物要赔偿。If you damaged the public property, you should pay for it.

② 这座古庙保存得很好,**损坏**的地方都得到了及时的修缮。The old temple keeps in good condition and the damaged parts have been repaired in time.

以上两句,用于具体事物。但应注意,"损坏"较书面化,一般指整体的损失;口语中具体的东西一般用"弄坏"、"破坏"等(如"别把电视弄坏了") ◇ Examples ① ② are all applied to concrete things, but 损坏 is more literary, usually applied to loss as a whole; as to the concrete things in colloquial language, 弄坏, 破坏 are used (e. g. 别把电视弄坏了 (Don't damage the TV set)).

S

T

讨厌 (动) tǎoyàn　嫌 (动) xián

Ⓔ dislike, loathe/loathe, dislike

◣"讨厌"和"嫌"都有"不喜欢"、"不满意"、"厌恶"的意思，"讨厌"的意思较重，"嫌"的意思较轻 ◇ Both 讨厌 and 嫌 mean "dislike and loathe". The meaning of 讨厌 is stronger than that of 嫌.

"讨厌"和"嫌"都可带代词宾语 ◇ Both words 讨厌 and 嫌 can take a pronoun as object：

① 你要**讨厌**(/**嫌**)我，我马上就走。If you dislike me, I'll go right away.

② 我们从来也没**讨厌**(/**嫌**)过你。We never hate you.

"讨厌"可带名词宾语，"嫌"一般不能 ◇ 讨厌 can take a noun object ,while 嫌 usually cannot.

③ 大家都**讨厌**只会说大话的人。Everyone dislikes the boaster.

④ 我们都**讨厌**吹吹拍拍的不良作风。We all hate the bad style of flattering.

"嫌"后可带形容词或动词宾语；"讨厌"不可以 ◇ 嫌 can take an adjective or verb as object; while 讨厌 cannot：

⑤ 他每月挣 5000 块，还**嫌**少。He thought he earned not enough though he got 5000 *yuan* every month.

⑥ 她很有耐心，从来不**嫌**麻烦。She's patient.

⑦ 给您添个孙子，到时候您可别**嫌**闹。I will give birth to a grandson for you, and then you won't tell me he's noisy.

"讨厌"可以和"很"、"真"、"非常"、"极了"一起使用，"嫌"不可以 ◇ 讨厌 can be used together with 很，真，非常，极了，while 嫌 cannot：

⑧ 这种潮湿的天气很**讨厌**。I hate the humid weather.

⑨ 我非常**讨厌**春天的风沙。I dislike the wind and sand in spring.

⑩ 这个人说话啰啰唆唆，真**讨厌**。He's a nuisance, for he is always garrulous.

⑪ 对这种满嘴假话的人，我**讨厌**极了。I hate a liar very much.

"讨厌"和"嫌"都可带兼语句；但"嫌"意思较轻，"讨厌"意思较重，所以下列四句两个词一般不能互换 ◇ Both 讨厌 and 嫌

can be followed by a pivotal sentence; the meaning of 嫌 is less serious than 讨厌, so in the following four examples the two words are usually not interchangeable:

⑫ 我**嫌**这儿的冬天太冷。I dislike here for it is cold in winter.

⑬ 她**嫌**裙子太肥。She dislikes her loose skirt.

⑭ 他**讨厌**小李总打扰他。He dislikes Xiao Li's disturbing him.

⑮ 我**讨厌**有些人在公共场所大声说话。I hate those who talk in a high voice in public.

▶ [厌恶 yànwù—讨厌 tǎoyàn]

特殊 (形) tèshū　　特别 (形、副) tèbié

Ⓔ special, peculiar/ special; particularly

◪ 形容词"特殊"、"特别"都表示不同于平常的。但用法不完全一样 ◇ Both adjectives 特殊 and 特别 mean" not the same as the ordinary", but their usages are somewhat different.

1. 特殊(形)

指不同于同类人、事物或平常情况的,跟"一般"相对 ◇ The adjective 特殊 means" different from the ordinary person, thing or situation", it is contrary to 一般. e. g. :

① 他的情况有些**特殊**,我们应该慎重考虑一下。So we should be careful about him.

② 如果没有**特殊**情况,我一定会去的。If there's nothing specific, I'll go there definitely.

③ 这里自然条件很不好,也没有**特殊**的物质待遇。There is neither good natural condition nor special material condition.

④ 他从小生长在农村,对农村有着**特殊**的感情。He has specific feelings for the countryside for he was brought up there.

"特殊"主要用在名词前做定语,如例②③④,有时也可做谓语,如例① ◇ 特殊 is mainly used before a noun as an attributive, as in examples②and③④. Sometimes it can also function as the predicate, as in example①.

以上各例,也可换用"特别",但换用"特别"后语意略重。例②的"特殊情况"是习惯搭配,换用"特别"还应加"的" ◇ In the examples above, 特别 can be used instead, but if 特别 is used, the meaning is stronger. 特殊情况 in example②is an idiomatic expression, and if 特别 is used instead, 的 must be added.

"特殊"还可与"性"结合,构成名词,"特别"不能 ◇ 特殊 can

also take 性 to become a noun, but 特别 cannot.

2. 特别(形)

有与众不同、不普通的意思 ◇ The adjective 特别 means" different from the ordinary, not common", e.g.:

① 我觉得她这件衣服的颜色很**特别**,又像蓝又像绿。I think the color of the dress is specific, for it is between the blue and the green.

② 我没有什么**特别**(/**特殊**)的要求,只是想有个看书的地方。I have no special requirement, and what I want is only a reading room.

③ 我看不出这只花瓶有什么**特别**(/**特殊**)的地方,怎么那么贵? Why is the vase so expensive? I cannot see there's anything specific in it.

以上例②③可换成"特殊",侧重于与众不同的。例①则因"颜色"与"特别"搭配较习惯,不可换用"特殊"("特殊的颜色"常指抽象意义) ◇ In examples ② and ③ above, 特殊 can be used to stress being different from the ordinary. In example ①, since 颜色 is usually used with 特别, it cannot be replaced by 特殊. (特殊的颜色 often has abstract meaning). 有时"特殊"较抽象,"特别"较具体,如"特殊性格"、"特别通行证"。再如"特殊气味",意思较抽象,"特别的气味"较具体 ◇ Sometimes 特殊 is more abstract and 特别 is more concrete, e.g. 特殊性格(speical character), 特别通行证(special pass). 特殊气味(special odor) is more abstract, while 特别的气味 is more concrete.

3. 特别(副)

(1) 表示程度高,格外,非常,一般常用在形容词或描写性的词语前做状语 ◇ As an adverb indicating high degree, exceptional, 特别 is usually used before an adjective or descriptive phrase to function as an adverbial:

① 这些日子我**特别**忙,没时间去看他。I didn't go to see him these days for I have been very busy.

② 她对人**特别**热情,谁有困难就帮助谁。She's warm-hearted and is ready to help anyone in need.

③ 他对问题分析得**特别**深刻。He has an incisive insight into problems.

④ 他**特别**能吃苦。He's very hard-working.

⑤ 他的生活**特别**有规律。He leads a very regular life.

(2) 表示特地,专为某事,着重 ◇ Meaning " specially, for one

particular purpose":

⑥ 这是**特别**为他做的面条。This noodle is especially cooked for him.

⑦ 经理**特别**邀请他参加会议。The manager specially asked him to take part in the meeting.

⑧ 临走时,母亲**特别**嘱咐他别忘了带钱。As he was to start, his mother specially asked him not to forget to take some money.

⑨ 工作中不应该**特别**强调客观困难,主要靠主观努力。You should not lay stress on objective difficulties at work; all is up to your subjective efforts.

(3) 表示强调或进一层的意思,常与"是"连用 ◇ when expressing " emphasis or go forward further", often used with 是, e. g. :

⑩ 他喜欢体育运动,**特别是**游泳。He likes sports, especially swimming.

⑪ 这里非常安静,**特别是**晚上,几乎没有一点儿声音。It is very still here, especially at night and it is nearly soundless at all.

⑫ 祖母非常疼爱她的孙子孙女们,**特别是**最小的孙女。The grandmother loves her grandchildren very much, especially the youngest granddaughter.

⑬ 那里的风景很美,**特别是**春天,满山遍野都是花。The scenery there is beautiful, and especially in spring, there are flowers all over.

副词"特别"与形容词"特殊"在用法上无共同之处 ◇ Adverb 特别 and adjective 特殊 are entirely different in usage.

体会 心得

(动、名) tǐhuì　(名) xīndé

Ⓔ know from experience; experience, understanding. / what one has learned from work, study, etc.

"体会"、"心得"都有通过体验,领会、认识、理解的意思。但词性不同,"体会"是动词、名词,"心得"只是名词 ◇ 体会 and 心得 both mean" to learn from experience" but 体会 is both a verb and a noun, while 心得 is just a noun.

1. 体会(动)

表示通过亲身经历或思考,对事物有所感受、理解和认识 ◇ As a verb, 体会 means" through personal experience or deep thinking one has deep understanding and cognition", e. g. :

① 没有做过教师的,很难**体会**教师的辛苦与快乐。It's difficult for those who are not a teacher to know the painstaking and happiness as a teacher.

② 通过一段时间的学习，他深深**体会**到学习外语一定要多听多说。He felt deeply that how important listening and speaking practice is for a foreign language learner.

③ 这首诗需要仔细**体会**才会理解它的深刻含义。You cannot understand the profound meaning of the poem until you savor it in detail.

④ 我到农村的时间不长，对那里的生活**体会**不深。I'm not in the countryside for a long time, so I just get a superficial experience about it.

2. 体会(名)

是指所体会到的内容 ◇ As a noun 体会 is what one understands and realizes:

① 我要谈的不是什么经验，只是工作中的一些**体会**。What I want to say is not experience, but something I learned from my work.

② 他写了一篇参加夏令营活动的**体会**。He wrote down his experience about his Summer Camp life.

3. 心得(名)

指通过工作、学习等活动体验或领会到的知识、认识等 ◇ 心得 as a noun means"the knowledge and cognition one gets through work, study",etc.:

① 这是我平时看哲学书籍后写的一些读书**心得**。This is some reading experience about the philosophy books that I usually read.

② 他的学习**心得**对我很有启发。I got great enlightenment in his learning experience.

名词"体会"、"心得"有时可互换 ◇ As nouns, 体会 and 心得 sometimes are interchangeable, e. g.:

③ 我谈谈学习中的一些**体会**(/**心得**)。I'll try to say something about my learning experience.

但侧重点不同，"体会"的对象多是心理、感情或语言文字中的精神实质，而"心得"侧重通过学习能领会到的知识、思想认识等。所以"读书心得"、"学习心得"搭配比较固定 ◇ They, however, have different stresses. 体会 is usually applied to thought or sentiment while 心得 is knowledge and understanding, so we usually say 读书心得(reading experience) or 学习心得(learnig experience).

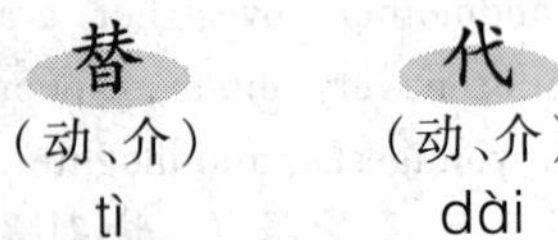

替 (动、介) tì　代 (动、介) dài

Ⓔ take the place of, replace; for/ take the place of, replace; for

◥ "替"、"代"都是动词和介词，都有替换的意思，但具体用法有区别 ◇ Both 替 and 代 are verbs and prepositions meaning "to take place of", but they have different usages.

1. 动词"替"的意思是以甲换乙，起乙的作用 ◇ The verb 替 means "A takes the place of B and functions as B":

① 王老师今天不能来上课，我来**替**他。I'll take the place of Mr. Wang today, for he's ill and cannot come to give you lessons.

② 这个手术，非王大夫不可，别人不能**替**。Only Dr. Wang can perform this operation.

③ 8号队员腿部受伤，教练让5号队员把他**替**了下来。Player No. 8 got an injury in his leg, so the coach asked player No. 5 to take the place of him.

2. 动词"代"的意思同动词"替"，多指以甲物换乙物，起乙物的作用 ◇ The verb 代 has the same meaning as 替 it usually refers that A replaces B, and A is the substitute as B.

① 我给李老师**代**过课。I took the place of Mr. Li for his lessons once.

② 让我们以茶**代**酒，为了友谊干杯。In place of wine let's drink tea to toast to our friendship.

③ 我**代**(/**替**)老王值夜班。I am on night shift in place of Lao Wang.

从以上三例可看出，动词"代"可用于人或事物，而且多用于事物，而动词"替"一般用于人。个别搭配，如"代班"、"替班"都可以，但这种情况是比较少的 ◇ From examples ① ② and ③, one can see the verb 代 can be applied both to human beings and things, and mostly to things, while 替 is applied to human beings. There are some rare cases when both can be used, such as 代班(take over sb.), 替班(take the place of shift for sb.).

另外，"代"可以直接放在动词前，如"代办"、"代买"、"代卖"、"代写"等构成固定搭配，"替"不能这样用 ◇ Besides, 代 can be placed right before the verb, such as 代办, 代买, 代卖, 代写, etc. to form relatively fixed collocations. 替 has no such usage:

④ 这个小商店**代**卖邮票。The small shop sells stamps.

⑤ 老王不在家，他的事由小张**代**办。Lao Wang is out, so Xiao Li take over him.

⑥ 这封信是母亲找别人**代**写的。Mother asked someone to write the letter.

这里"代"有受人委托，代表他人做

某事的意思。“代”还有暂时替别人担任某职务的意思 ◇ Here 代 means"to be entrusted and do something for another person". 代 also means"to assume the office of somebody else",e. g. :

⑦ 经理不在时,由副经理**代**经理。When the manager was absent, the vice manager took over.

3. 介词“替”和名词、代词组成介宾词组做状语,表示动作行为的对象 ◇ The preposition 替 and a noun or pronoun make up a preposition-object phrase functioning as an adverbial to point out the object of the behaviour.

(1) 引出关心、服务的对象 ◇ Introducing the object of one's concern:

① 这家报纸总**替**那个新产品做宣传。There's always advertisments of that new product in the newspaper.

② 他做事前总是先**替**别人着想。Whatever he does, he always thinks about the interests of others first.

③ 不要**替**弟弟担心,这事他会处理好的。Don't worry about our brother,for he is likely to handle it well.

(2) 指出代替的对象 ◇ Introducing the object of substitution:

④ 小王**替**主任开会。Xiao Wang took the place of the director to attend a meeting.

⑤ 这篇文章我**替**你写。I'll write the article for you.

4. 介词“代”和名词、代词组成介宾词组做状语,指出动作行为所代替的对象。3 中(2)的④⑤例均可用“代”替换(用“代”比用“替”较正式,“替”偏重于口语) ◇ The preposition 代 and a noun or pronoun make up a preposition-object phrase functioning as an adverbial, to point out the object of substitution. In examples ④ ⑤ of (2) in 3, all can be replaced with 代, but 替 is more colloquial than 代:

① 请你**代**(/**替**)我向小王问候。Please send my best regards to Xiao Wang.

② 这些文件都是秘书**代**(/**替**)他整理。It is the secretary who sorted out the files for him.

添 (动) tiān　　加 (动) jiā

Ⓔ add, increase/add, increase

“添”和“加”都是动词,都有增多的意思,但“加”的义项比“添”多,应用范围广 ◇ Both 添 and 加 are verbs meaning " to increase", but 加 has more usages than 添.

1. 添

“添”指在已有的之外，增加同类的，多用于人或具体事物 ◇ 添 means "to add more to what is already there" and is mostly applied to human beings or concrete things:

① 锅里还要再**添**(/**加**)点儿水。Please add some water to the pot.

② 房间里又**添**(/**加**)了两件新家具。Two more pieces of furniture are put to the room.

③ 他们家又**添**(/**加**)了一口人。Their family has another member.

“添麻烦”、“添乱”是习惯搭配 ◇ 添麻烦，添乱 are idiomatic phrases:

④ 有个问题请教您，给您**添麻烦**了。Sorry to bother you, for I have a question to ask you.

⑤ 大家正在准备明天的考试呢，哪有时间讨论你的文章？别**添乱**了。Don't disturb us, for we are all preparing for tomorrow's examination. How can we have time to discuss your article?

上面例①②③中“添”可以换成“加”，而④⑤不行 ◇ In examples①②③above, 加 can be used to replace 添, but not in examples ④and⑤.

2. 加

(1)“加”比“添”用得更为广泛，表示在已有的基础上增多或扩大、提高 ◇ 加 has more usages than 添. It can mean" to increase, enlarge, raise", e. g. :

① 你们还要不要再**加**(/**添**)碗饭？Would you like another bowl of rice?

② 这件衣服的腰身瘦了，要**加**肥3公分。The waist part of the dress is too tight, and it needs 3 more centimeters.

③ 工程速度能不能再**加**快一些？Can you fasten the project more?

以上例①可换成“添”，因是在原有基础上增多，其他各例表示扩大或提高的不能用“添”替代 ◇ In example ①加 can be replaced by 添, because it means " to become larger in amount", while in examples ② and ③ it means " to enlarge or raise" and cannot be replaced by 添.

(2) 把原来没有的增加上去，“添”没有这个意思 ◇ 加 can refer to adding what was not there originally. 添 has no such meaning. e. g. :

④ 在信的最后，我又**加**了两句话。I added two more lines at the end of the letter.

⑤ 这篇古文不好懂，得**加**注释。The ancient Chinese article is difficult to understand. Please give it some interpretation.

⑥ 衣服领子上**加**了个花边。A frill was added to the collar of the dress.

(3) 把两个或两个以上的数或东西合在一起,"添"不能这样用 ◇ 加 has the meaning of "putting together two or more numbers or things". 添 cannot be so used:

⑦ **二加二**等于四。Two and two is four.

⑧ 这两个数相**加**是多少? How much is the sum of the two numbers?

⑨ 聪明**加**勤奋,使他的事业获得了成功。Intelligence and diligence contribute to his success.

听见 (动) tīngjiàn 听说 (动) tīngshuō

Ⓔ hear/be told

1. "听见"是动补结构,表示耳朵接收到声音。可以拆开("听得见"、"听不见") ◇ 听见 is a verb-complement phrase, which can be inserted other elements. For instance, we can say 听得见 or 听不见 (" can hear" or " cannot hear"):

① 我**听见**敲门声。I heard knocking.

② ——你**听得见**外面的雨声吗? Can you hear the rain outside?

——雨很小,**听不见**。I cannot hear for it is very light.

③ 老人耳朵不好,细微的声音**听不大见**。The old man cannot hear the subtle sound for he is a bit deaf.

以上三句,不能用"听说" ◇ In the three sentences above, 听说 cannot be used.

2. "听说"也是动补结构,意思是听见别人说,也就是别人告诉自己。可以说"听人说" ◇ 听说 is also a verb-complement phrase, meaning "to be told by someone". We can say 听人说:

① **听说**今天有一个参观团要来学校。I heard there was a group coming to visit our school.

② 他**听人说**张老师病了。He was told that Mr. Zhang was ill.

③ **听说**的事情有时并不可靠,眼见为实。Gossips are not reliable, for seeing is believing.

④ ——这事你**听说**了吗? Did you know it?

——**听说**了。Yes.

以上四句不能用"听见" ◇ In the four sentences above, 听见 cannot be used.

下面两句,意思一样,但分别用两个词时,语法要求不同 ◇ The following two sentences have the same meaning, but with two different words they have different structures:

⑤ 他**听见**一个消息,股票要涨。He got a piece of news that the stocks prices were going to rise.

⑥ 他**听说**股票要涨。He learned that the stocks prices were going to rise.

同样 一样

(形、连) (形)

tóngyàng yīyàng

Ⓔ same; similarly/ same, identical

形容词"同样"、"一样"都有相同、没有差别的意思。但用法不同 ◇ The adjectives 同样 and 一样 both mean " the same", but their usages are different.

1. "同样"是非谓形容词,可以做定语、状语,不能做谓语,不能受程度副词修饰。做定语时,后面常带"的",做状语时,一般不带"地" ◇ 同样 is an adjective which can only function as an attributive, adverbial, but not as predicate and cannot be modified by adverbs of degree. As an attributive it usually takes 的, whereas as an adverbial it does not take 地. e. g. :

① 他们两个人有**同样**的性格,同样的生活习惯。They both have the same nature and life habit.

② 运动员们都穿着**同样**的运动服。All the players dress alike.

③ **同样**的教学方法也适用于其他有类似问题的学生。The same method can also be applied for other students with similar problems.

④ 学习和锻炼身体**同样**重要。Learning is as important as physical exercise.

⑤ 这两个学生的英语**同样**好。The two students both excel at English.

⑥ 生产速度和产品质量**同样**都要提高。Production speed and product quality should both be improved.

以上各例中"同样"均可换成"一样" ◇ In all the examples above, 同样 can be replaced by 一样.

2. "同样"还是连词,放在分句或句子之间,表示跟前面说的相同,后面有停顿,可加"的" ◇ 同样 is also a conjunction, used between clauses or sentences to indicate what follows is the same as what goes before. There is a pause to follow and 的 can be added. e. g. :

① 他工作非常认真、负责,**同样**,在生活上也是一丝不苟。He is conscientious and responsible for his work as well as for his life.

T

② 去年他是10月来北京的,**同样**,今年还是10月来。He came to Beijing in October last year, and so will he this year.

③ 他身体好了,**同样**的,精神面貌也发生了变化。He is healthy now, and similarly he takes on a new look.

④ 工作上要注意效率,**同样**,学习上也要注意学习效果。Attention should be paid to work efficiency as well as learning efficiency.

"一样"没有以上用法 ◇ 一样 has no similar usages.

3. 形容词"一样"可做定语、谓语、状语,可受副词等修饰,做定语时,后面一般带"的" ◇ 一样 is an adjective and can function as attributive, predicate, adverbial and can be modified by adverbs, etc. As an attributive, it usually takes 的. e. g. :

① **一样**的学校,**一样**的老师,为什么你的学习成绩不如小明呢? You and Xiaoming are in the same school and have the same teachers. Why do you study worse than him?

② 你来他来都**一样**。It is the same for either you or him to come.

③ 他们两个人的性格完全不**一样**。They differ completely in characters.

④ 这台电视和那台电视的图像**一样**清晰。The pictures this TV and that TV are all clear.

⑤ 今天和昨天**一样**冷。It is as cold as it was yesterday.

以上各例中①④⑤"一样"均可用"同样"替换。②③两句,"一样"做谓语,不能用"同样"替换 ◇ In examples ①④ and ⑤ 一样 can be replaced by 同样. In examples②and③, however, 一样 functions as the predicates and cannot be replaced by 同样.

4. 形容词"一样"还有依然、照旧的意思,多做状语 ◇ 一样 as an adjective also means " as before" and mostly functions as the adverbial, e. g. :

① 音乐的声音那么响,可他**一样**看书、写字,丝毫不受影响。The loud sound of music has no influence on him and he still reads and writes.

② 这笔虽说旧了点儿,但**一样**(/**同样**)可以写出好字。Though the pen is a bit old, it can write well.

③ 理工科的学生也**一样**(/**同样**)需要了解一点文史知识。Science students also need learn something about humanities.

如果后边有"能"、"可以"等助动词,"一样"可以换成"同样",

如上例②③,而例①则不能 ◇ If followed by such auxiliary verbs as 能,可以,etc.,一样 can be replaced by 同样,as in examples ② and ③,but not in example ①.

5.形容词"一样"常常与"跟"、"像"、"好像"、"当做"等配合使用,表示情况相似,或用于比喻,"同样"不能这样用 ◇ 一样 as an adjective is often used with 跟,像,好像,当做,etc. to show similar situation,or as a metaphor. 同样 cannot be so used,e. g.:

① 几年不见,他的样子还跟过去**一样**。He has not changed in his appearance at all for several years.

② 我跟您**一样**,都是教师。You and I are both teachers.

③ 她像她的母亲**一样**勤劳。She is as industrious as her mother.

④ 楼里安静极了,好像里面没有人**一样**。The building is still, as if there is no soul in it.

⑤ 我把他当做我的兄弟**一样**看待。I treat him as my brother.

⑥ 他对人像火**一样**地热情。He is too warm-hearted to others.

W

万万 (副) wànwàn　千万 (副) qiānwàn

Ⓔ be sure to/be sure to

◪“万万”和“千万”都有一定、无论如何的意思。“万万”的语气比“千万”重。“万万”多用在否定式中，几乎不用在肯定句中，但“千万”不受这个限制。“千万”多用在命令句（祈使句）中而不用在陈述句中，但“万万”不受这个限制 ◇ Both 万万 and 千万 mean "to be sure to do something at any rate". 万万 is stronger than 千万. 万万 is mostly used in negative sentences and almost never in a positive one. The usage of 千万 is not so limited. 千万 mostly appears in imperative sentences and not in a declarative one. 万万 is not so limited in usage.

“万万”用在“不”、“没有”、“不可”、“不能”等前面，表示特别强调否定。当“万万”用在命令式中时可以换用“千万”，如例①②，其他例句不能互换 ◇ When 万万 is used in front of 不，没有，不可，不能，etc.，it especially stresses the negation. 万万 in an imperative sentence can be replaced by 千万，as in examples① and②. In other examples they are not interchangeable：

① 手术的时候，**万万**（/**千万**）不可粗心大意啊。While performing an operation，don't be careless.

② 明天就要考试了，你今晚**万万**（/**千万**）不能再熬夜了。Please don't stay up tonight for you will have an examination tomorrow.

③ 我**万万**没有想到，背地里说我坏话的人竟是他。I never expected him to speak ill of me in secret.

④ 你**千万**要注意身体，按时服药。Beware of your health and take the medicine on time.

⑤ 这个电话号码，你**千万**要记住。You must learn the telephone number by heart.

往往 (副) wǎngwǎng　常常 (副) chángcháng

Ⓔ often/often

◪“往往”和“常常”都是副词，

都表示某种情况经常出现，但在具体用法上有区别 ◇ 往往 and 常常 are both adverbs meaning frequently, but they are different in usage.

1. 往往

表示在一定条件下，大多数情况总是这样的，不受否定词修饰 ◇ 往往 indicates that most cases are like this under a certain condition. It cannot be modified by a negative word. e. g. :

① 他星期六上午**往往**去图书馆，你可以去那里找他。You can find him in the library for he usually went there on Saturday morning.

② 他一忙起来，**往往**连饭都忘了吃。He usually forgot his meals if he was busy.

③ 我说话时**往往**考虑得不够，让人不高兴。I often make others unhappy by my inconsiderate words.

④ 在人们争论的时候，他**往往**保持沉默。He always kept silent over others' argument.

2. 常常

(1) 表示某种情况发生不止一次，而且相隔时间不久 ◇ 常常 indicates that something happens repeatedly and with short intervals, e. g. :

① 我**常常**回忆起小时候的一些事情。I often recalled what happened in my childhood.

② 老师**常常**给学生讲一些做人的道理。The teacher usually told his students about how to be a man.

③ 下午四点钟以后，他**常常**出去散步。He often went for a walk after 4 pm.

以上例③中的"常常"可以换为"往往"，因为前边有条件（下午四点钟后）。其他句子不能用"往往"替换 ◇ In example③, 常常 can be replaced by 往往, because there is a condition(下午四点钟以后). In examples①and②, 常常 cannot be replaced by 往往.

"常常"可以用否定词修饰，这时"常常"可简化为"常" ◇ 常常 can be modified by a negative word; in this case 常常 can be simplified into 常, e. g. :

④ 他搬家以后，就不**常**来我家了。He did not came to my place often since he moved.

⑤ 我不**常**看电影，电视倒是每天都看的。I do not go to cinema often, but I watch TV every day.

这个义项的"常常"可用于未发生的事情上，"常常"可简化为"常"，"往往"不能这样用 ◇ 常常 of this meaning can be applied to things that have not taken place, and can be simplified to 常. But 往往 has no such usage:

⑥ 以后我会**常常**去阅览室看书。From now on, I will go to the reading room to study frequently.

⑦ 希望你有空儿的时候**常**来玩。I hope you will see us frequently if you are free.

(2)"常常"的意思同"往往",即表示在某种条件下,大多数情况总是这样的。(1)中①~④句的"往往"均可用"常常"替换 ◇ 常常 means the same as 往往, i. e. under a certain condition, most cases are like this. In examples①~④ of (1), 往往 can all be replaced by 常常. examples:

⑧ 闲下来的时候,他**常常**(/**往往**)听音乐。He usually listens to music when he is free.

⑨ 遇到事情,他**常常**(/**往往**)很不冷静。He usually cannot keep calm when facing problems.

▶[常 cháng—常常 chángcháng]
[经常 jīngcháng—常常 chángcháng—常 cháng]

为 (动、介) wèi　为了 (动、介) wèile

Ⓔ for the sake of/ for the sake of, for

1. 为(动)　**为了**(动)

表示原因、目的;"为了"强调的意味更浓 ◇ Both mean "because of, for the purpose of"; 为了 is more emphatic:

① 母亲这样辛劳,完全是**为**(/**为了**)儿子。The mother is very painstaking for the sake of her son.

② ——你当演员,**为**(/**为了**)什么呀? Why do you want to be an actor?
——**为**(/**为了**)艺术。Just for the sake of arts.

③ 她呀,这样做完全是**为**(/**为了**)钱。Her doing so is completely for the sake of money.

有时"为"表示"对"、"向",是古代汉语的遗留,只用于"不足为外人道" ◇ Sometimes 为 means 对, 向, which is left over by classical Chinese and is found only in the phrase 不足为外人道(not worthy of saying to other people).

2. 为(介)　**为了**(介)

(1)引出动作、行为的对象、目的或原因 ◇ Introducing the target, aim or reason of a behaviour or an action:

① 我们的宗旨是**为**人民服务。To serve people is our mission.

② **为**(/**为了**)写毕业论文他四处搜集资料。He is collecting some materials everywhere for his thesis.

③ **为**(/**为了**)以后的生活着想,你应该多储蓄些。For the future life,you should save more.

以上,除了常用搭配(如"为人民服务"),两个词可互换,"为了"更显强调。为了强调目的,有时可加"起见" ◇ With the exception of some set phrases (such as 为人民服务(serve people)), the two words are interchangeable, with 为了 more emphatic. To stress the aim, sometimes 起见 is added:

④ **为**(/**为了**)慎重起见,请再核对一下数字。Please check the figures again for the sake of prudence.

⑤ 司机**为**(/**为了**)安全起见,要我一定系好安全带。The driver asked to wear the seatbelt for the sake of safety.

(2)"为……而……"较书面化,有时也可用"为了……而……" ◇ 为……而……is more literary; one can also say 为了……而……:

⑥ 我们**为**世界和平而奋斗。We are struggling for the world peace.

⑦ 他是**为**(/**为了**)人民利益而献身的。He lost his life for the sake of the people.

⑧ 我们是**为了**(/**为**)活着而吃饭,不是**为了**(/**为**)吃饭而活着。We eat to live;not live to eat.

未来 将来

(名) (名)

wèilái jiānglái

Ⓔ future/future

"未来"、"将来"这两个词都指将要到来的时间,是时间名词 ◇ Both 未来 and 将来 mean" the future". They are nouns of time.

1."未来"意思是就要到来的时间,可指时间近的,也可指时间较远的,可与时间词连用 ◇ 未来 means" time in the future". It may indicate near future or distant future, and can be used together with nouns of time:

① **未来**三天之内将会有一场中雨。There will be a moderate rain within three forthcoming days.

② **未来**的岁月你打算怎样度过? How are you going to spend your rest life?

例②也可换用"将来" ◇ In example ② 将来 can be used instead.

2."未来"还着重指现在以后的时间 ◇ 未来 also stresses time in the future:

① 展望**未来**,我们充满信心。We are filled with hope when looking forward to the future.

② **未来**是属于年青一代的。The future is yours, young men.

③ 我们寄希望于**未来**。We have hopes for the future.

④ 他向往着**未来**幸福美好的生活。He is looking forward to the happy bright future.

例③也可换用“将来”(较少用) ◇ In example ③ 将来 can be used instead (but rather rare).

3. “将来”主要区别于“过去”、“现在”,可做状语 ◇ 将来 is used mainly to differentiate from 过去(past) and 现在(present). It can function as an adverbial:

① **将来**你想干什么? What are you going to do when you grow up?

② **将来**,我大学毕业了,要到西北去工作。I'm going to work in the northwest China after my graduation.

③ 你要学会一门技术,**将来**会有用的。It will be useful to learn a skill.

④ 不久的**将来**我就要回到妈妈身边了。I will return to my mother in the near future.

以上各例是“未来”不能替换的。例④“不久的将来”做状语 ◇ In the examples above 未来 cannot be used instead. In example ④不久的将来 is an adverbial.

下面的例⑤可用“未来”,指现在以后的时间 ◇ In example ⑤ 未来 can be used, referring to the time in the future.

⑤ 我们不能只顾现在,还要考虑**将来**(/**未来**)。Our attention should be paid to the future, not just the present.

“将来”做状语时,可在句首,也可放在句中,例②也可说成 ◇ 将来 as an adverbial can be placed at the beginning of the sentence or in the middle example ②, as in example ⑥:

⑥ 我**将来**毕业了,要到西北去工作。I'm going to work in the northwest China after my graduation.

▶[将来 jiānglái—今后 jīnhòu—以后 yǐhòu]

稳 (形、动) wěn　　稳定 (形、动) wěndìng

Ⓔ steady; to become steady/steady; stabilize, calm

◪“稳”和“稳定”都是形容词、动词,但意义和用法上有区别 ◇ Both 稳 and 稳定 are adjectives and verbs, but they are different in meaning and usage.

1. 稳(形)

(1) 表示固定不动,不摇动 ◇ 稳, as an adjective, means" stead-

y, not shaking";

① 把椅子放**稳**了再坐。Sit on the chair after it is fixed.

② 冰面太滑，站**稳**了，别摔着。Hold on your feet please, for the ice is slippery.

③ 他开车开得很**稳**。He drives very smoothly.

以上不能换用“稳定” ◇ In the examples above, 稳定 cannot be used instead.

(2) 表示没有波动，平静（多指思想情绪、立场等）◇ Meaning "not undulating, steady (in mood, standpoint, etc.)":

④ 小王的情绪有些不**稳**。Xiao Wang is unrest.

⑤ 他的立场很**稳**，从没动摇或改变过。His stand is firm and never hesitant.

以上例④可换用“稳定” ◇ In example④, 稳定 can replace 稳.

(3) 表示可靠，（言语、行动）沉着，有分寸 ◇ Meaning "reliable, (of words, behavior) cool-headed, proper":

⑥ 这个人办事很**稳**。The man is reliable.

⑦ 这件事，他处理得不够**稳**。He handled it in a hurry.

以上不能换用“稳定” ◇ In examples ⑥ and ⑦, 稳定 cannot be used instead.

2. 稳（动）

表示使稳固安定，一般后面带补语“住” ◇ 稳, as a verb, means "to stabilize", usually takes the complement 住:

① 先把他的情绪**稳住**，再慢慢谈问题。First please keep him calm, and then you can talk over the issues with him.

② 在强手面前，要先**稳住**阵脚，再伺机反攻。Faced with a strong opponent, we have to hold our position first and counterattack when opportunities arose.

例②可换用“稳定” ◇ In example ② 稳定 can be used instead.

3. 稳定（形）

(1) 表示安定、没有波动或变动，多用于人的情绪、思想，以及某些容易变化的事物，如时局、生活、工作、物价等 ◇ 稳定, as an adj., means "steady without fluctuation or change"; it is mostly applied to a person's mood, thought and some changeable things, such as political situation, life, work, prices. e. g.:

① 这些年，他的生活一直非常**稳定**。He led a stable life these years.

② 他的病情**稳定**了，正慢慢向好的方面发展。His illness is under control and becomes better.

③ 物价**稳定**，人心才会**稳定**。The stable prices make people

assured.

④ 你一定要有一个比较**稳定**的工作。It's better for you to look for a regular job.

4. 稳定(动)

表示使稳定,后面一般可带补语"下来",这时不再带宾语,不能用"稳"替换 ◇ 稳定, as a verb, means "to stabilize"; it usually takes the complement 下来 but with no object. In this case it cannot be replaced by 稳:

① 新市长一上任,第一件事就是**稳定**物价。The first thing for the new mayor is to stabilize the prices.

② 在情况发生变化时,一定要设法**稳定**大家的情绪。When things changed, it's necessary to keep people calm.

③ 等我的工作**稳定**下来,就给你写信。After I found a job, I'll write you.

误会 误解

(动、名) wùhuì　　(动、名) wùjiě

Ⓔ misunderstand; misunderstanding/ misconstrue, misunderstand; misunderstanding

◪ "误会"、"误解"都是动词和名词,都表示对事物了解或理解发生错误。但"误会"多指对别人的言行理解、领会错了。而"误解"指对别人的言行理解得不符合实际,错了。与"误会"不同的是,"误解"可用于对语言、文字方面(如书籍、文章等)的理解错误 ◇ Both 误会 and 误解 are verbs as well as nouns meaning "to misunderstand". 误会 usually means "to misunderstand a person's words or behaviour". 误解 means " that one's comprehension of words or behaviour does not conform to the reality and is wrong". The difference is that 误解 can be applied to language and writing (such as books, articles, etc.).

1. 动词"误会"、"误解",表示了解或理解错了 ◇ The verb 误会 or 误解 means "to misunderstand":

① 你**误会**(/**误解**)他的意思了。You misunderstand him.

② 我并不是不愿帮你,你**误会**(/**误解**)了。You misunderstand me, for I will help you.

③ 我要把事情的经过说清楚,免得别人**误会**(/**误解**)。I'd like to tell the truth about it in detail so as not to be misunderstood.

④ 这段话写得不全面,容易让人**误解**。The passage is likely to be misunderstood for it is not all-round.

以上例④是指语言、文字方面

的,一般用“误解”,如用“误会”也可以,则侧重与人有关的言行 ◇ Example ④above is about language and writing, so 误解 is used. If 误会 is used, the stress will be something about a person.

2. 名词“误会”、“误解”,指不正确的理解。“误会”着重于对人的言行方面;“误解”除了对人的言行外,还可用于语言、文字方面 ◇ The nouns 误会 and 误解 mean " misunderstanding". 误会 stresses the misunderstanding of the words and behaviour of a person;误解 can also be about language and writing besides words and behaviour. e. g. :

① 我得找他谈谈,以消除**误会**(/**误解**)。I didn't explain it to him well, so I had to talk about it with him.

② 这纯属**误解**(/**误会**),请您别在意。This is sheer misunderstand, please do not take it seriously.

③ 这个句子,容易使人产生**误解**,得改一改。The sentence is apt to misunderstanding, so make a little change about it.

以上例①②“误会”、“误解”均可用。而例③是指对语言、文字方面的理解错误,一般用“误解” ◇ In examples ① and ② above, either 误会 or 误解 can be used. Example ③ is about the misunderstanding of language and writing, so 误解 is mostly used.

X

吸收 吸取

（动） （动）

xīshōu xīqǔ

Ⓔ absorb, assimilate/ absorb, draw, assimilate

◪"吸收"、"吸取"这两个动词都有从外部收进、取得有益的物质的意思。但使用范围不同，"吸收"的宾语多是具体的人或事物，而"吸取"的宾语多为抽象的事物 ◇ Both 吸收 and 吸取 mean"to assimilate useful things", but they are applied to different scopes. The objects of 吸收 are mostly people or concrete things, while the objects of 吸取 are mostly abstract things.

1. 吸收

(1)指某物体把外部物质吸进去 ◇ Meaning " to absorb what is outside":

① 粉笔把洒在课桌上的墨水全**吸收**了。The chalk took in all the spilt ink on the table.

② 植物从土壤中**吸收**水分。The plant takes in water from the soil.

③ 一个人如果肠胃不好，就不能很好地从食物中**吸收**营养物质。One cannot take in the nutrition well if there is some troubles with his stomach.

以上各例，除例③外，其他都不能换用"吸取" ◇ 吸取 cannot be used in the examples above except ③.

(2)（组织或团体）接受、接纳（成员） ◇ Meaning "(organization or group) to accept (members)":

④ 中国作家协会又**吸收**了几个新会员。The China writer association admitted a few members.

⑤ 他是京剧俱乐部最近**吸收**的新成员。He joined the Peking Opera Club recently.

在例④和例⑤中，"吸收"不能换作"吸取" ◇ In examples ④ and ⑤ 吸取 cannot be used instead .

2. 吸取

表示吸收、采纳的意思，宾语多为"经验"、"教训"、"智慧"、"力量"、"知识"等 ◇ 吸取 means "to absorb or adapt". The object is mostly 经验(experience), 教训(lesson), 智慧(wisdom), 力量

(strength), 知识(knowledge), etc. e. g.:

① 我们要听王老师的课,并与她座谈,以**吸取**她的教学经验。We came to Mr. Wang's class, talked to him and learned his teaching experience.

② 孩子们从这些科学杂志中**吸取**了不少知识。Children learned a lot from these scientific magazines.

③ 他们失败的教训,大家应该**吸取**。Everyone should draw lessons from their failure.

"吸取"的宾语有时可用于具体事物,如"通过食物吸取营养"。但更多的是用于抽象事物。以上各例不能换用"吸收" ◇ 吸取 can have a concrete thing as its object such as 通过食物吸取营养, but it is mostly applied to abstract things. In the examples above, 吸收 cannot be used instead.

喜欢 喜爱

(动) (动)

xǐhuan xǐ'ài

Ⓔ like, be fond of/ like, be fond of

◪ "喜欢"、"喜爱"这两个动词都表示对人或事物产生好感或有兴趣。"喜欢"除用于人的心理活动,还可用于动植物的习性。"喜爱"只指人的心理活动,不能用于动物、花木等,也较书面化 ◇ Both 喜欢 and 喜爱 mean "to be fond of or to be interested in a person or thing". Besides being applied to human psychology, 喜欢 can be applied to animals and plants. 喜爱 can only be applied to human psychology and is more literary; it cannot be applied to plants and animals.

① 她很**喜欢**小孩子。She likes children very much.

② 我**喜欢**旅游。I like traveling.

③ 这种花**喜欢**阴凉。The flower grows well in the shade.

④ 熊猫**喜欢**吃竹叶。Pandas live on bamboo.

以上例①②也可换用"喜爱",但书面色彩略重。例③④表示花木、动物的习性,不能用"喜爱" ◇ In examples ① and ② above 喜爱 can be used instead, but with a literary colour. Examples ③ and ④ are about the characteristics of plants and animals, so 喜爱 cannot be used.

"喜爱"可说"受到……喜爱" ◇ 喜爱 can be said as 受到……喜爱:

⑤ 这种商品,普遍受到消费者的**喜爱**。The commodity is popular among consumers.

另外,两个词可说"惹人喜爱(/喜欢)",特别是前者 ◇ Besides,

both words can form the phrase 惹人爱(/喜欢), especially the former:

⑥ 盛开的牡丹,特别**惹人喜爱**。The peony in bloom is charming.

▶[爱 ài—喜欢 xǐhuan]
[爱好 àihào—喜欢 xǐhuan]

细心 仔细

(形) (形)

xìxīn zǐxì

Ⓔ careful, attentive/ careful, attentive

"细心"、"仔细"都是形容词,都可表示做事用心、周到细密,但词义的侧重点不同,义项也不同 ◇ 细心 and 仔细 are both adjectives meaning "attentive and meticulous", but they have different stresses and usages.

1. 细心

形容用心细密,连小的地方都能注意到。不能重叠 ◇ 细心 means "so attentive that attention reaches even small places". 细心 cannot be reduplicated:

① 当医生一定要**细心**,千万不能疏忽大意。As a doctor, you must be careful.

② 他是个**细心**人,小事也不会忽略。He is careful and he cannot neglect the trivial.

③ 这个人胆子大,而且很**细心**,工作很有成绩。The man is bold and careful and he made great achievements in his work.

④ 奶奶年老体弱,需要**细心**照顾。The granny is old and weak and she needs careful cares.

以上例③可以换用"仔细" ◇ In example ③细心 can be replaced by 仔细.

2. 仔细

(1)意思同"细心",但多用于人对处理事务、工作的态度。可重叠(AABB 式) ◇ The meaning of 仔细 is the same as 细心, but it is mostly applied to a person's attitude to business and work. It can be reduplicated (in the pattern of AABB):

① 他做事有计划,而且很**仔细**。He is planned and careful.

② 账目要记得**仔细**点儿,可不能出问题。You should keep a detailed account and you're not permitted to make mistakes in it.

③ 我又**仔细**地找了一遍,还是没找到那枝钢笔。I looked for it again carefully, but found nothing.

④ 他**仔仔细细**地看了这篇报告,改动了一些地方。He read the report thoroughly and carefully and arouse doubt about it.

有时用"仔细"时也可换用"细心",但侧重点不同,例②如用"细心",则侧重考虑周密,连很小的地方都注意到 ◇ Sometimes 仔细 can be replaced by 细心 but with different stress. In example② if 细心 is used, the stress is on being attentive and meticulous.

(2)表示(提醒人)小心、注意。不能用"细心" ◇ To remind someone to be careful and attentive 仔细 can be used, but not 细心:

⑤ 搬箱子时**仔细**点儿,别把里边的玻璃杯打碎了。While lifting the box, be careful and don't break the glass in it.

⑥ 说话小点儿声,**仔细**让人听见。Please speak in a low voice so as not to be heard.

(3)指(生活)节俭。不能用"细心" ◇ 仔细 can means "frugal", but 细心 do not have such usage:

⑦ 妈妈过日子一向很**仔细**。Mother is always frugal.

⑧ 用钱**仔细**点儿,别大手大脚的。Don't be wasteful with your money.

▶[仔细 zǐxì—细致 xìzhì]

显然 (形) xiǎnrán　显著 (形) xiǎnzhù

Ⓔ obvious, evident/remarkable, outstanding

◪ 形容词"显然"、"显著"都有显露出来,使人看明白,了解清楚的意思,但在具体词义和用法上还是有区别的 ◇ Adjectives 显然 and 显著 both mean "very clear, easy to be understood, but they are still different in meaning and usage".

1. "显然"表示使别人很容易看清楚或感觉到。最常见的是做状语,一般不做定语、补语,偶尔做谓语,一般要用"是……的"结构 ◇ 显然 means "very easy to make a person see or feel clearly". It usually functions as an adverbial, but not as an attributive or complement. It occasionally functions as a predicate with the pattern 是……的, e. g. :

① 他脸色苍白,两眼发红,**显然**夜里没有睡好。Obviously he didn't have a good sleep at night for he looked pale and had red eyes.

② 他**显然**没办完事,不然,他早回来了。It's clear that he hasn't finished it or he would come back a long time ago.

③ 小李**显然**误解了老张的意思。It's clear that Xiao Li misunderstood Lao Zhang.

④ 南方和北方的气候**显然**不同。It's clear that the climate of the

south is different from that of the north.

⑤ **显然**,他并不知道昨天这里发生的事情。Obviously he didn't know what happened here yesterday.

⑥ 文章中的一些语法错误是很**显然**的。The grammatical mistakes in the article are clear.

以上各例中"显然"不能用"显著"替换 ◇ In the examples above,显著 cannot replace 显然.

2."显著"表示非常清楚地显露出来,而且很突出,多含褒义,常做谓语、定语、状语 ◇ 显著 means " very prominent and obvious" and is usually commendatory. It mostly functions as the predicate, attributive, and adverbial. e. g. :

① 两年来,这个城市的变化十分**显著**。The city has changed greatly for the two years.

② 这里冬天冷,夏天热,大陆性气候特点十分**显著**。The continent climate is typical here, that is, it's cold in winter and hot in summer.

③ 这个学生最近有了**显著**的进步。The student has made marked progress recently.

④ 人们的生活水平**显著**地提高了。People's living standards are improved noticeably.

以上各例,"显著"不能用"显然"替换 ◇ In the examples above,显著 cannot be replaced by 显然.

相似 相像 相同

相似 (形) xiāngsì

相像 (形) xiāngxiàng

相同 (形) xiāngtóng

Ⓔ be similar/resembling, be similar/identical, the same

1.形容词"相似"、"相像"都指彼此有相同或共同的地方。"相似"可用于事物,也可用于人;"相像"多用于人。"相似"较书面化 ◇ The adjectives 相似 and 相像 both mean " to be similar or have something in common". 相似 can be applied to things as well as people. 相像 is mostly applied to people. 相似 is more literary. e. g. :

① 这两座建筑物的布局非常**相似**。(用于事物) The layouts of the two buildings are similar. (applied to things)

② 这本小说的故事情节和那本小说有很多**相似**的地方。(用于事物)The novel has many similar plots as that one. (applied to things)

③ 这两个民族的生活习惯完全

不同,几乎没有什么**相似**之处。(用于事物) The lifestyles of the two nations are completely different. (applied to things)

④ 她的言谈举止跟她母亲十分**相像**(/**相似**)。(用于人) Her behavior is very similar to her mother. (applied to people)

2. 形容词"相同"表示彼此一致或一样,没有区别 ◇ The adjective 相同 means "to be identical, or the same, with no difference":

① 咱们星期日再聚会一次,时间、地点和上次**相同**。Let's get together on Sunday again and the time and the place are the same as the last one.

② 这几个人有着**相同**的兴趣和爱好。They have similar interests and hobbies.

③ 几封信笔迹**相同**,肯定是一个人写的。The handwriting of these letters is the same, and it must be written by one person.

④ 这两个问题的性质**相同**,可以放在一起讨论。We can discuss the two problems together, for their natures are the same.

以上各例不能换用"相似"或"相像" ◇ In the examples above, neither 相似 nor 相像 can replace 相同.

▶[类似 lèisì—相似 xiāngsì—近似 jìnsì]

相信 (动) xiāngxìn　信 (动) xìn

Ⓔ believe in, have faith in/ believe

◥"相信"、"信"这两个动词都表示认为确实或正确而不怀疑。后者较为口语化。两个词虽都是及物动词,但"相信"可带小句宾语;"信"的肯定式一般只能有条件地带简单的体词宾语,"信"的否定式"不信"则可带小句宾语 ◇ Both 相信 and 信 mean "to believe something to be true without doubt", with the latter being more colloquial. Both are transitive verbs, but 相信 can take a clause as the object, while 信 under certain condition can take a noun, measure word, pronoun, or numeral as its object. Its negative form 不信 can take a clause as its object.

① 我认为他很可靠,也很**相信**他。I think he's trustworthy, so I trust him.

② 我们**相信**这几个问题都能按时解决。I believe these problems are likely to be solved on time.

以上二句,例②宾语为小句,只能用"相信"。例①宾语虽为代词,但在这里也不宜用"信"。

"信"带宾语,常常是在十分口语化的语境中 ◇ In the above examples, the object in example ② is a clause, so only 相信 can be used here. In example ①, though the object is a pronoun, 信 is not as good as 相信. It is usually in very colloquial language that 信 takes an object:

③ 他是我的好兄弟,我绝对**信**他! He's my good brother, and I trust him completely.

④ 我**信**这话。/我**信**他的话。I believe the words. /I believe his words.

例③④也可用"相信" ◇ In examples ③ and ④相信 can also be used instead.

而"不信"的句法功能则较全面,从某种意义上说,这是双音化造成的结果 ◇ 不信 can be used very freely. This, to some extent, is because it is disyllabic:

⑤ 我就**不信**这事办不成! We don't believe we cannot do it.

⑥ 他根本**不信**这个人说的话! He didn't trust the man at all.

例⑤⑥也可用"不相信" ◇ In examples ⑤ and ⑥, 不相信 can be used instead.

"信"还表示信奉,如"信佛"、"信教"。书面语(古代汉语的遗留)中还可表示随意、听凭,多见于四字语,如"信口雌黄"、"闲庭信步"等 ◇ 信 can also mean "to profess faith in", e. g. : 信佛 (believe in Buddhism), 信教. In literary language, 信 can also mean" at will or at random, mostly in some four-character phrases, such as 信口雌黄 (make irresponsible remarks), 闲庭信步 (stroll in a quiet, tranquil courtyard).

► [信任 xìnrèn—相信 xiāngxìn]

响亮	**响**
(形)	(形、动)
xiǎngliàng	xiǎng

Ⓔ loud and clear/
loud and clear; to make a sound

1. 响亮(形)　**响**(形)

两个词都有"声音大"的意思,都可以做谓语和补语。"响亮"有时含褒义,"响"是中性词。由于"响亮"是双音节,"响"是单音节,所以替换极受限制 ◇ The adjectives 响亮 and 响 both mean" loud" and can both function as the predicate and complement. 响亮 sometimes is commendatory, whereas 响 is mutual. Since 响亮 is disyllabic and 响 is monosyllabic, they are not interchangeable in most cases:

① 她咬字不太清楚,可嗓门倒挺**响亮**(/**响**)。She cannot speak

clearly, but her voice is sonorous.

② 他叫得**响亮**(/**响**)极了,可就是没有实际行动。His words are much taller than his action.

③ 电话里她的声音**响亮**而又动听。Her voice was excited and sonorous on the phone.

④ 这架钢琴的声音非常**响亮**。The piano strikes loudly.

⑤ 除夕之夜的鞭炮声太**响**了。The sound of fireworks on the Eve of the New Year was very loud.

⑥ 你们说话别太**响**了,有人在上课呢。Please talk in a lower voice for there are classes.

以上例①②由于无明显褒义,音节上也允许,所以两个词可互换。例③④含褒义,用"响亮"。例⑤⑥含贬义,不用"响亮"而用"响"。"响亮"在句中还可以直接做定语和状语 ◇ In examples ① and ② above, the two words are interchangeable since there is no obvious commendation and no syllabic requirement. Examples ③ and ④ are commendatory in the meaning, so 响亮 is used. By contrast examples, ⑤ and ⑥ are derogatory, so 响亮 is not used. 响亮 can also function as the attributive and adverbial:

⑦ **响亮**的号声回荡在田野上。The sonorous bugle call lingered over the field.

⑧ 当老师问大家能不能按时完成任务时,同学们**响亮**地回答"能"。When the teather asked us whether we can finish our task in time, we all answered "yes" loudly and clearly.

"响"不能做状语,做定语则需要加"很"等副词 ◇ 响 cannot be an adverbial, and as an attributive it must take 很, etc.:

⑨ 远处传来一阵很**响**的枪声。A fit of loud shooting came in the distance.

⑩ 有没有不太**响**的鞭炮? Are there any fireworks which are not loud?

"响"做补语还可比喻事情成功或开始 ◇ 响 as a complement can mean " the initial success or the beginning of something":

⑪ 这位歌手的这支歌一下子唱**响**了。The song by the singer became popular overnight.

⑫ 这种冰箱的牌子已经叫**响**了。The brand of this refrigerator becomes famous now.

还常说"战斗打响了","打响"已成词 ◇ It is very common to say 战斗打响了 (the combat has begun). 打响 is already a word.

2. 响(动)

(1)发出声音的意思,有时是抽象意义 ◇ 响, as a verd, means

"making a sound". Sometimes it has an abstract meaning:

① 钟声**响**了。The bell goes.

② 这种家用电器的牌子已经**响**遍全国。The brand of the electric appliance becomes famous all over the country.

(2) 使发出声音 ◇ Causing something (like gun, gong etc. to make a sound), e. g.:

③ 那边**响**爆竹,是怎么回事? There's a shot outside. What's up?

④ **响**锣了,戏开演了。The play began as soon as the gong was beat.

想念 惦记

(动) (动)

xiǎngniàn diànjì

Ⓔ long to see again/ keep thinking about

"想念"、"惦记"这两个动词,共同点是都有思念的意思。不同点是:"想念"的对象既可以是个人,也可以是集体、祖国、环境等;"惦记"的对象是个人或较多的人。另外,"惦记"还含有对亲人可能出事故的担心的意思 ◇ The two words 想念 and 惦记 share the common meaning of thinking about. They are different in that, while the object of 想念 can be a person or a collective, motherland, environment, etc., the object of 惦记 is a person or some people. Besides, 惦记 also means "worrying about the dear ones that may have misfortune".

① 在海外留学的人,每逢年节,都分外**想念**亲人和祖国。Those studying abroad miss their family and country on festivals in particular.

② 儿子有哮喘病,一个人出门在外,我非常**惦记**他。I worried about my son when he left home for he got asthma.

以上两句,"想念"和"惦记"不能互换 ◇ In examples ① and ② 想念 and 惦记 cannot be exchanged.

③ 母亲很**想念**(/**惦记**)远行的儿子。The mother missed her son who lived away from her.

④ 她时时**想念**(/**惦记**)着在外地工作的丈夫。She missed her husband working in other place all the time.

③④两句,则可以互换。因为都是表示对亲人的思念。但意思上可以有所侧重:"想念"侧重于一般的思念;"惦记"含有担心的意味 ◇ In examples ③ and ④, the two words can be exchanged because they both mean "thinking about dear ones", but the stress may be different. 想念 stresses thinking about, while 惦记 has the implication of worrying about.

晓得 知道

（动） （动）

xiǎode zhīdào

Ⓔ know/know

◪“晓得”、“知道”这两个动词是指对某人、某事的存在有所了解，或对某个事实或道理有所认识。“晓得”有方言色彩（多用于南方），不能带补语 ◇ Both 晓得 and 知道 mean " to know". 晓得 is a dialect word (used mostly in South China) which cannot take a complement. e. g. :

① 看样子我就**知道**（/**晓得**）他不高兴了。I know he is unhappy from his looks.

② 今天晚上有音乐会，你**知道**（/**晓得**）吗？ Do you know there is a concert tonight?

③ 我**知道**（/**晓得**）那个穿蓝上衣的是小王的哥哥。I know the person in blue jacket is Xiao Wang's brother.

④ 这个道理我**知道**得很清楚。I know it clearly.

⑤ 我**知道**（/**晓得**）这个字该怎么写。I know how to write the word.

⑥ 你**知道**（/**晓得**）他是做什么工作的吗？ Do you know his occupation?

⑦ 你**知道**（/**晓得**）不**知道**（/**晓得**）这里不能放自行车？ Do you know NO PARKING here?

上面的句子除例④外，均可由“晓得”替换，但地域色彩略有不同 ◇ In the examples above, with the exception of ④ , 知道 can all be replaced by 晓得, but the local flavor will be stronger.

协助 帮助

（动） （动）

xiézhù bāngzhù

Ⓔ assist, help/help

◪ **1**. “协助”和“帮助”都是动词。都有“支援”的意思，都可重叠为 ABAB 式。“协助”多指在工作中下级对上级的配合、辅助，并多指具体事物 ◇ Both 协助 and 帮助 are verbs meaning " to support" and both can be reduplicated into ABAB form. 协助 mostly means " the support from the lower level to the upper level in work", and usually refers to actual things, e. g. :

① 院长派小刘**协助**（/**帮助**）王教授校对文稿。The dean sent Xiao Wang to help Professor Wang in proofreading the manuscripts.

② 公安局在居民委员会的**协助**（/**帮助**）下终于抓到了那名

罪犯。The policemen caught the criminal with the help of the neighborhood committee.

③ 这个任务很艰巨,他经验不多,你务必要多**协助协助**(/**帮助帮助**)他。You must offer him some help for the task is too difficult for him and meanwhile he lacks work experience.

用"协助"时,有时不是下级对上级的辅助,可以是同级的相助,或上级对下级的辅助。以上各例,"协助"也可换成"帮助",但配合、辅助的意义就淡化了 ◇ 协助 sometimes does not mean" help from the lower level, but at the same level or the upper level". In the above example, 协助 can be replaced by 帮助; however, its meaning of " cooperation or assistance is weakened".

2. "帮助"一般指替别人出力、出主意,在精神、物质方面援助别人,可指具体事物也可指抽象事物。"帮助"可说"得到……帮助",并可组成"大有帮助"等短语 ◇ 帮助 means " to do something or think of a way for somebody to help him, either in concrete things or spiritual matter "帮助 can be used as 得到……帮助, it can make phrases as 大有帮助:

① 在事业上,他得到了朋友们的**帮助**。He got help from his friends with his work.

② 坚持阅读对提高书面语言的水平一定会大有**帮助**。It will be useful if you keep the habit of reading.

③ 他学习有困难,请老师**帮助帮助**他吧。Please ask the teacher to help him for he has some troubles in learning.

▶ [辅导 fǔdǎo—帮助 bāngzhù]

[援助 yuánzhù—帮助 bāngzhù]

信任 相信

(动) (动)

xìnrèn xiāngxìn

Ⓔ trust, have confidence in/ believe in, be convinced of

1. "信任"和"相信"都是动词,都有不怀疑的意思。"信任"是因为相信而觉得放心,"相信"则是认为正确而没有疑虑。使用对象也有所不同,"信任"一般是对人、对组织;"相信"除了可适用于人、组织,还可用于思想、行为、能力等 ◇ Both 信任 and 相信 are verbs meaning " to have no doubt". 信任 indicates" that one trusts feels at ease because one believes in somebody". 相信 means" that one thinks something

is right and so has no doubt". The two are applied to different objects. The object of 信任 is a person or an organization; the object of 相信, besides persons and organizations, can also be thought, behaviour, capability, etc.:

① 她工作认真又负责任,大家都很**信任**她。She is conscientious, so she is reliable.

② 张先生做财会工作,一丝不苟,公司上上下下都觉得他是可以**信任**的。Mr. Zhang is an accountant and he is conscientious, so all the staff in the company trust him.

③ 大家都**相信**他有能力完成这个任务。Everyone believes that he is able to finish the job.

④ 妈妈**相信**孩子说的话是真的。The mother believed what the child said.

以上例①也可换用"相信",但"觉得放心"的意思就淡化了。其他各句不能换用 ◇ In example ① above, 信任 can be replaced by 相信, but the meaning of " feeling at ease will be reduced". In all the other examples, 信任 and 相信 cannot be interchanged.

2."信任"还是名词 ◇ 信任 is also a noun, e.g.:

① 厂长以实际行动赢得了员工的**信任**。The director won his staff 's trust by his action.

② 他说:"得到大家的**信任**,我觉得心情很舒畅。" He said: "I feel pleased that I'm trusted."

▶[相信 xiāngxìn—信 xìn]

兴奋 (形、动) xīngfèn　　**高兴** (形、动) gāoxìng

Ⓔ excited/

delighted, be willing to

"兴奋"和"高兴"都是形容词和动词,都与情绪激动有关;可做谓语、定语、状语等,可带补语,也可受程度副词修饰。但使用范围、对象有区别 ◇ Both 兴奋 and 高兴 are adjectives and verbs related to sentiments. They can function as the predicate, attributive, adverbial, etc. They can also take a complement or be qualified by adverbs of degree. But they have different usages and referents.

1. 兴奋

(1)形容词"兴奋",表示(精神、情绪)振作、激动(因高兴或紧张引起的),不能重叠 ◇ The adjective 兴奋 means "to bestir oneself because of happiness or nervousness". It cannot be reduplicated:

① 收到大学录取通知书那天,他**兴奋**极了,一夜没睡着。He was too excited to go to sleep the whole night on receiving his college admission notice.

② 学生们怀着**兴奋**的心情参加了毕业典礼。The students attended the graduation ceremony with excitement.

③ 辩论会后,人们还在**兴奋**地谈论着。People kept on talking the debate excitedly after it was over.

④ 老朋友见面,真是**兴奋**极了。The old friends were too excited when they met and talked about their past.

(2)动词"兴奋",表示使兴奋,可重叠(ABAB 式) ◇ The verb 兴奋 means "to bestir and can be reduplicated (in the pattern of ABAB)":

⑤ 这种药可以**兴奋**神经。The drug can stimulate the nerve.

⑥ 工作太累了,喝点儿酒让大脑**兴奋兴奋**。The work was too boring, so I drank some wine to refresh myself.

2. 高兴

(1)形容词"高兴",表示人的心理活动,因快乐而激动,可以重叠(AABB 式) ◇ The adjective 高兴 means "happy and excited". It can be reduplicated (in the pattern of AABB):

① 你的病好得这么快,真让人**高兴**。I am glad that you get over so quickly.

② 这是件**高兴**的事,得赶快告诉他。It's good news, and it's better to tell him immediately.

③ 收到他的来信,我非常**高兴**。I'm glad to hear from him.

④ 试验还没最后完成,别**高兴**得太早了。Don't be glad too early, for the experiment has not been finished yet.

⑤ 他**高高兴兴**地接受了我们的邀请。He accepted our invitation gladly.

例③可换用"兴奋"(形),表示激动的程度更高些 ◇ In example ③ 高兴 can be replaced by 兴奋, which is even more agitated.

(2)动词"高兴"有喜欢、愿意(做某事)的意思,动词"兴奋"没有这个意思 ◇ 高兴, used as a verb, means "to be willing to (do something)". 兴奋 as a verb has no such meaning:

⑥ 你如果**高兴**这样做,就这样做吧! If you are glad to do it this way, so be it.

⑦ 我不**高兴**这么晚去别人家里。I don't like to go to see others so late.

"不高兴"有情绪低落的意思 ◇ 不高兴 means "in low spirits":

⑧ 我没陪他去图书馆,他**不高兴**

了。He was unhappy for I didn't go to the library with him.

⑨ 为一点儿小事别**不高兴**。Don't be unhappy over a trivial.

动词"高兴"可以重叠(ABAB式)◇ The verb 高兴 can be reduplicated (in the pattern of ABAB):

⑩ 母亲节那天,我要送妈妈一件礼物,让她**高兴高兴**。I will give my mother a gift on Mother's day and make her happy.

形容词"兴奋"的例句中①④也可换成"高兴",但侧重程度不同。动词"兴奋",是不能用"高兴"替换的 ◇ In examples ① and④ of 兴奋 as an adjective, 高兴 can be used instead, but the stress is different. 兴奋 as a verb cannot be replaced by 高兴.

形式 形状

(名) (名)

xíngshì xíngzhuàng

Ⓔ form, shape/ form, appearance

◥ 名词"形式"、"形状"都表示事物的某种形态、样子,但词义和使用范围不同。"形式"指事物的外观、结构,表现事物的方式、手段等,可用于具体或抽象事物。而"形状"指事物外表的样子,用于具体事物。下列各例中"形式"和"形状"是不能互换的 ◇ Both 形式 and 形状 mean "the appearance of something", but they have different meanings and usages. 形式 means " the form, shape, construction, the way to manifest, etc". It can be applied to both concrete and abstract things. 形状 means" the appearance" and is applied to concrete things. 形式 and 形状 in the following examples are not interchangeable:

① 我们想采用座谈会的**形式**来征求各方面的意见。We held an informal discussion and got views from different people in it.

② 诗人通过诗歌的**形式**抒发对祖国的爱。The poet expressed his love for his country through his poems.

③ 这两个人都比较自私,只不过表现**形式**不同罢了。The two persons are both selfish, but they showed it in different ways.

④ 一部好的文学作品要做到内容和**形式**的协调统一。The content and the form of a good literature work should match each other.

⑤ 这些石头的**形状**各异,有的圆,有的方,有的像鱼,还有的像鸟。The shapes of these stones are different: some of them are round, some square, some like

a fish, and others like a bird.

⑥ 这个钟的**形状**很别致。The shape of the clock is exquisite.

⑦ 这两种产品的**形状**差不多。The two products look quite similar.

凶 凶恶

(形、名) (形)

xiōng xiōng'è

Ⓔ fierce; ferocity, murder/ fierce, ferocious

"凶"和"凶恶"都是形容词。两个词都有行为、相貌可怖、丑陋的意思。但"凶"还有"杀害人的"、"不幸的"、"程度深"等意思 ◇ Both 凶 and 凶恶 are adjectives meaning " fierce". 凶 also means " murder, unfortunate, very severely, etc. " e. g. :

① 那位经理对职员的态度**凶**(/**凶恶**)得很。The manager treated his staff badly.

② 这个老头儿的样子非常**凶**(/**凶恶**)。The old man looks vicious.

③ 两口子近来为赡养老人的事吵得很**凶**。The couple quarreled badly about supporting their parents recently.

例①②中的"凶"和"凶恶"可互换使用,但例③则不可互换。因例③"凶"表示程度深 ◇ 凶 and 凶恶 are interchangeable in examples ① and ②, but not in example ③ because in example ③凶 means "to a high degree".

"凶"还是名词,表示不幸的事、伤害或杀害行为,多用于固定词组中 ◇ 凶 is also a noun, meaning "misfortune, injury or murder", and is mostly used in set phrases:

④ 这位刑侦人员智勇双全,常能逢**凶**化吉。The scout man is intelligent and brave, and he is often able to defeat the dangers successfully.

⑤ 飞机失事了,我估计他也是**凶**多吉少。The plane crashed, and I'm afraid he must be very dangerous.

⑥ 暴徒企图行**凶**,但未得逞。The rabble attempted to kill the man, but he failed.

修正 改正

(动) (动)

xiūzhèng gǎizhèng

Ⓔ revise, amend/correct

1. "修正"和"改正"都是动词,都有消除偏差和错误,把不正确的、不合理的变为正确的和完善的意思,但"修正"较"改正"正式些 ◇ Both 修正 and 改正 are verbs, meaning " to eliminate deviations and mistakes, and

turn the incorrect or the irrational to the correct and perfect". 修正 is more formal than 改正.

"修正"和"改正"有时可互换 ◇ 修正 and 改正 are sometimes interchangeable:

① 他把大会发言提纲中的不妥之处一一**修正**(/**改正**)了。He revised the inappropriate parts in the meeting speech draft one by one.

② 文章中的这个定义还要**修正**(/**改正**)一下。The definition in the article should be revised.

2. "改正"还可用于其他具体事物 ◇ 改正 can also be applied to concrete things, e.g.:

① 老师要求学生把作文中的错别字**改正**过来。The teacher asked his students to correct the wrong words in their writing.

② 经过家人的帮助,孩子终于**改正**了说谎话的坏毛病。The child broke his lying habit with his family's help.

"改正"的宾语多是具体的事物,如上面例①虽然也涉及文章中的缺点,仍很具体,所以用"改正"而不用"修正" ◇ The object of 改正 is mostly a concrete thing, as in example ①.

例②中提到的"毛病",也有具体所指,所以用"改正" ◇ In example ② 毛病 is also a concrete thing, so 改正 is used.

▶[改正 gǎizhèng—纠正 jiūzhèng]

寻 寻找 找

寻	寻找	找
(动)	(动)	(动)
xún	xúnzhǎo	zhǎo

Ⓔ to look for, seek/
to look for, seek/
to look for, seek

"寻"、"寻找"和"找"都是动词,都有为要见到或得到一定的人或事物去尽力的意思。三个词的宾语都可以是具体的丢失的人或物等。"寻找"、"找"的宾语可以是具体的事物,也可以是抽象的事物。"寻"、"寻找"常用于书面语,"找"的口语色彩较浓 ◇ 寻, 寻找 and 找 are all verbs meaning "to try to find or get certain people or things". The objects of the three words can all be concrete lost things or persons. The objects of 寻找 and 找 can be concrete things as well as abstract things. 寻 and 寻找 are usually used in literary language, while 找 is rather colloquial:

① 小王去年走失的孩子今年还没**寻**(/**寻找**/**找**)到。Xiao Wang haven't found his child who lost last year.

② 他正在**寻**(/**寻找**/找)他的存折。He is looking for his bankbook.

③ 工厂正在为他们的新产品**寻**(**寻找**/**找**)出路。The factory is trying to seek a new way out for their new products.

④ **寻**人启事贴在左边,**寻**物启事贴在右边。The lost person notice is put on the left, while the lost property one on the right.

⑤ 我要**找**个清静的地方休息几天。I'd like to have a good rest for some days in a quiet place.

⑥ 下午我去**找**个朋友。I went to see one of my friends this afternoon.

⑦ 为了**寻找**真理,他奋斗了一生。He strived for his whole life to seek truth.

以上例①②③中,"寻"、"寻找"和"找"三个词都可以用,只是"找"更口语化。例④中的"寻人启事"是约定俗成的固定搭配,不用"找"和"寻找"。例⑤⑥是口语中的日常用语,一般用"找"。例⑦宾语是抽象事物,用"寻找" ◇ In examples ① ② and ③ above, 寻, 寻找 and 找 can all be used, only that 找 is the most colloquial. 寻人启事 is an idiomatic phrase where 找 and 寻找 are not used. ⑤ and ⑥ mean "to get something or to see somebody", so 找 is used. The object in example ⑦ is an abstract thing and so 寻找 is used.

"找"可以重叠 ◇ 找 can be reduplicated, e. g. :

⑧ 大家**找找**这台机器出问题的原因是什么。Please find the reason why the machine cannot function.

另外,"找"还有把多余的钱退还的意思,"寻"、"寻找"没有这个意思 ◇ Besides, 找 also means "to return the extra money". 寻 or 寻找 has no such meaning. e. g. :

⑨ 多余的 3 角钱,不用**找**了。Please keep the rest three *jiao*.

⑩ 我给他 5 块钱,他**找**给我 4 角 5 分。I gave him five *yuan* and he returned me 45 *fen*.

询问　　问

(动)　　(动)

xúnwèn　　wèn

Ⓔ inquire, ask about/inquire

1. "询问"和"问"都是动词。有征求意见和打听的意思。"询问"多用于书面语,而"问"则多用于口语 ◇ Both 询问 and 问 are verbs meaning "to solicit opinions or to ask about". 询问 is used in literary language, while 问 is more colloquial. e. g. :

① 许多留学生给招生办公室打电话,**询问**(/**问**)怎样报名。

Many foreign students phoned to the admission office to inquire how to register.

② 主任**询问**(/**问**)我们对新教材的看法。The director asked our views about the new teaching materials.

③ 外国记者**询问**(/**问**)这位中国官员,如何估计东南亚金融危机对中国的影响。The foreign reporter asked the Chinese official how to predict the influence of the Southeast Asia on China.

2."问"还有提出问题请解答,以及慰问、审讯、干预等意思 ◇ 问 also means "to raise a question, to express one's solicitude, to interrogate, to intervene, etc.":

① 老师**问**学生什么是补语。The teacher asked his students what is complement.

② 请代我向其他同学**问**好。Please send my best regards to the other students.

③ 对别人的冷暖,他从来不闻不**问**。He shows indifference to others' life all the time.

在1的例①②③中"询问"和"问"都有打听、征求意见的意思,所以可以互换使用;在2的各例中,"问"表示要求解答、慰问等意思,不可用"询问"替换 ◇ In examples ①②③ of 1 询问 and 问 both mean "to inquire about or to solicit opinions", so they are interchangeable. In the examples of 2, however, 问 means "to raise a question or to express one's solicitude etc.", so it cannot be replaced by 询问.

迅速 (形) xùnsù　快 (形、副) kuài

Ⓔ quick, swift/quick; quickly

1. 迅速(形)　**快**(形)

两个词都有速度高的意思,"迅速"为书面语,"快"多用于口语 ◇ As an adjective both words mean "speedy". 迅速 is literary while 快 is colloquial.

(1) 表示速度快,"迅速"和"快"都可做谓语(可带补语)、状语、定语、补语 ◇ To mean "speedy", both 迅速 and 快 can function as the predicate (with a complement sometimes), adverbial, attributive, complement, e. g.:

① 他们行动很**迅速**(/**快**),接到命令,马上就出发了。They took action quickly. They started as soon as they got the order.

② 他办事**迅速**(/**快**)得很,您尽管放心。Rest assured for he handles things quickly.

③ 工程进展得十分**迅速**(/**快**)。The progress of the project is quick.

④ 这座城市建设得相当**迅速**(/**快**)。The city's construction is at a quick speed.

做状语和定语时,"快"前常加程度副词"很"等 ◇ As an adverbial or attributive, 快 is often qualified by the adverb of degree 很, etc.:

⑤ 洪水刚退,交通**迅速**(/**很快**)恢复了。The traffic was normal as soon as the floods receded.

⑥ 他的学习成绩**迅速**(/**很快**)赶上了大家。He caught up with other students quickly.

⑦ 我希望住房问题能**迅速**(/**很快**)解决。I hope the housing problem can be solved as soon as possible.

⑧ 引进先进技术后,生产有了**迅速**(/**很快**)的发展。The production developed quickly after introducing the advanced technology.

(2) 意思与"慢"相对时,侧重于省时间,用时短,一般用"快" ◇ When meaning " the opposite of" 慢, with the stress on time saving or short time, 快 is used:

⑨ 他跑得很**快**。He ran very quickly.

⑩ 小林做事比以前**快**多了。Xiao Li handles things much more quickly than before.

⑪ **快**车只有上午有,下午和晚上你只好坐慢车了。The express train is only in the morning; you have no choice but to take the slow train in the afternoon or at night.

以上三句中"快"不能用"迅速"替换 ◇ In the three examples above, 迅速 cannot replace 快.

(3) 形容词"快"表示锋利,"迅速"没有这个意思 ◇ The adjective 快 means " sharp". 迅速 has no such meaning. e. g.:

⑫ 这把刀真**快**。The knife is sharp.

⑬ 解决这种问题就要**快**刀斩乱麻。A problem of this nature requires a prompt and resolute solution.

(4) 形容词"快",表示直爽、痛快,"迅速"没有这些意思 ◇ The adjective 快 also means " forthright, straightforward". 迅速 has no such meaning, e. g.:

⑭ 姐姐心直口**快**,妹妹就含蓄多了。The sister is straightforward, while the little sister is reserved.

⑮ 小王快人**快**语,心里有什么就说什么。Xiao Wang is outspoken and straightforward.

(5) 形容词"快"表示高兴,不能用"迅速"替换 ◇ The adjective 快

also means "delighted", which cannot be replaced by 迅速. e. g. :

⑯ 听了她的话,我心中不**快**。I'm unhappy at her words.

⑰ 抓住了抢劫犯,人心大**快**。To the immense satisfaction of the people, the robber has been seized.

(6) 形容词"快"表示反应敏捷,"迅速"没有这个意思 ◇ The adjective 快 means "nimble", while 迅速 does not have this meaning. e. g. :

⑱ 这孩子从小脑子就**快**。The child has a quick mind since his birth.

⑲ 他手疾眼**快**,一下子把掉下的花瓶接住了。He is deft and catches the falling vase accurately.

2. 快(副)

(1) 赶快的意思 ◇ 快 as an adv., means "hurry up, make haste":

① **快**动手吧,时间怕来不及了。Hurry up! Or the time will be very tight.

② 你们**快**帮帮忙,我一个人支持不住了。Please hurry to help me for I cannot hold it.

(2) 将要的意思,表示短时间内要出现某种情况或接近某一时刻 ◇ Meaning "something is going to happen or it is close to a certain moment". e. g. :

③ 天**快**黑了,他们该回来了。It is drawing night, and they should be back now.

④ 复印纸**快**用完了。The copy paper is nearly out.

⑤ **快**12点了,我们去吃午饭吧。It's nearly 12 o'clock, and let's go and have lunch right away.

⑥ **快**到目的地了,我们休息一会儿吧。We are to get to the destination soon, so let's have a rest.

以上各句均不能用"迅速"代替 ◇ In all the examples above, 迅速 cannot replace 快.

Y

严厉 厉害

(形) (形)

yánlì lìhai

Ⓔ stern, severe/severe, fierce

◪"严厉"和"厉害"都是形容词。"厉害"有难以对付，难以忍受或剧烈、凶猛、程度深等意思。"严厉"有严肃而厉害的意思，但着重指对人的态度、手段不温和 ◇ Both 严厉 and 厉害 are adjectives. 厉害 has the meaning of "being hard to deal with, severe, fierce, of high degree, etc". 严厉 has the meaning of" stern and severe with the emphasis on one's attitude or measures taken". e. g. :

① 这位老师对学生十分**严厉**(/**厉害**)。The teacher is strict with his students.

② 父母**严厉**地批评了逃学的儿子。The parents severely criticized his child for his playing truant.

③ 昨天刚做完手术，刀口疼得**厉害**。He had an operation yesterday, and he felt an acute pain in his incision.

④ 西北风刮得很**厉害**。The northwest wind blows strongly.

⑤ 她这个人**厉害**(/**严厉**)得有些不近人情。She is too merciless, and seems unreasonable.

"严厉"常加"地"做状语，如例②，"厉害"常加"得"做补语，如例③④，或自身加带"得"的补语，如例⑤ ◇ 严厉 often takes 地 to function as an adverbial, as in example ②. 厉害 often takes 得 to function as a complement as in examples ③ and ④, or takes a complement with 得 as in example ⑤. 例①也可用"厉害"，语气较轻。例③④都不可互换 ◇ In example ①厉害 can replace 严厉 but with a less severe tone. In the examples ③④ the two words are not interchangeable .

严密 紧密

(形) (形)

yánmì jǐnmì

Ⓔ tight, close/
close together, inseparable

◪"严密"和"紧密"都是形容词，都有"事物连接得紧，没有间隙"的意思。"严密"表示严实，或指周到没有纰漏；"紧密"除指事物间的联系非常密切,不能分开外,还有连续不断的意思 ◇ Both 严密 and 紧密 are adjectives meaning" to be very close together with no gap". 严密 means "tight or thoughtful with no error", whereas 紧密 not only means "closeness between two things, but also continuity with no gap", e. g.:

① 瓶口封得很**严密**。The bottle is sealed tightly.

② 他的论文结构**严密**,水平很高。His thesis has a good organization and high quality.

③ 指挥官**严密**注视着前线的战况。The commander is keeping a close eye on the battle of the front.

④ 我们应该把在学校学习的理论知识与社会实践**紧密**地结合起来。We should have a close combination of what we learn from the books and social practice.

⑤ **紧密**的雨点儿打在人的脸上,有些疼痛。The dense rain falls on my face, which makes me painful.

⑥ 共同的理想把他们**紧密**地联系在一起了。The common ideal connects them close.

虽然"严密"和"紧密"的意思有共同点,但"严密"强调的是结合得没有空隙,"紧密"的意思则是十分密切,不可分隔,所以一般不能互换 ◇ Although 严密 and 紧密 are close in meaning, 严密 stresses closeness with no gap, while 紧密 means "very intimate and inseparable"; therefore, they are not interchangeable in most cases.

掩盖 遮盖

(动) (动)

yǎngài zhēgài

Ⓔ cover, conceal/ cover, overspread

1. "掩盖"和"遮盖"都是动词,当它们与较具体的事物合用时,是盖住物体,使不显露的意思 ◇ Both 掩盖 and 遮盖 are verbs. When used with concrete things, they both mean "to cover up":

① 新长出来的片片绿草,**掩盖**(/**遮盖**)了光秃秃的山丘。The bare hills are covered with the new grass.

② 被大雪**掩盖**(/**遮盖**)的大地变成了银色的世界。The snow-covered land became white completely.

2. "掩盖"和"遮盖"与抽象事物合用时,是"隐藏"或"隐瞒"的意思 ◇ When 掩盖 and 遮盖 are used with abstract things, they mean "to hide, to conceal":

① 谎言**掩盖**(/**遮盖**)不了事实。Lies cannot hide the truth.

② 这事你不要再**掩盖**(/**遮盖**)下去了,快告诉他吧! Don't keep it secret any longer. It's time to tell him.

用于非常具体的事物时,多用“遮盖” ◇ When applied to very concrete things, 遮盖 is used:

③ 下雨了,快拿塑料布把自行车**遮盖**一下。It's raining. Take a piece of plastic cloth to cover the bike right away.

1 中的例①②和 2 中的①②“掩盖”、“遮盖”均可互换使用,但“掩盖”的语感更强些。2 中例③“遮盖”不能用“掩盖”替换,因为“遮盖自行车”是一件非常具体的事,而“掩盖”多是与抽象的事物合用 ◇ In examples ①② of 1 and ①② of 2, the two words are interchangeable, but 掩盖 sounds more forceful. In example ③ of 2 遮盖 cannot be replaced by 掩盖 because 自行车 is a concrete thing, while 掩盖 is usually applied to abstract things.

另外,当“遮盖”作为不及物动词使用且有“隐藏”的意思时,可重叠为 AABB 式,而“掩盖”则不能 ◇ Besides, when 遮盖 is used as an intransitive verb with the meaning of hiding, it can be reduplicated into 遮遮盖盖, while 掩盖 cannot:

④ 他这个人做事总爱**遮遮盖盖**,似乎在做什么见不得人的事情。He always handle things overtly, as if he did something not respectable.

掩护 保护

(动) (动)

yǎnhù bǎohù

Ⓔ shield, cover/ protect, safeguard

“掩护”和“保护”都有尽力护卫,使不受伤害的意思,但在用法上有区别 ◇ Both 掩护 and 保护 mean "to protect against harm", but they are different in usage.

1.“掩护”主要指暗中采取遮掩的方式维护人员或部队的安全 ◇ 掩护 means " to protect people or troops in secret by shielding", e. g. :

① 你带伤员先走,我用机枪**掩护**你们。Take the wounded to a safe place first, and I will protect you with my gun.

② 一连撤退,二连**掩护**。Company One retreat, Company Two will cover them.

2.“保护”既可以是公开的,又可以是暗中的护卫 ◇ 保护 can be open protection, or protection in secret:

① 在敌机轰炸中,班长用身体**保护**(/**掩护**)了我。The squad leader shielded me with his body during the bombing.

Y

② 在二战中,法国抵抗运动组织**保护**(/**掩护**)了英国飞行员。The French Resistance Organization protected the British pilots in the Second World War.

上面例①②中如果用“掩护”替换“保护”,则特指用“遮盖”、“隐蔽”的方式使人员不受伤害 ◇ In examples ① and ②, if 掩护 is used to replace 保护, it means "to protect in secret".

“保护”的对象除了人以外,还可以是事物,这时不能用“掩护”替换 ◇ The object of 保护 can be things as well as human beings when the objects are things, it cannot be replaced by 掩护:

③ 国家要**保护**妇女儿童的合法权益。A country should safeguard the rightful rights of women and children.

④ 事故发生后,要注意**保护**现场。When an accident takes place, we must try to keep intact the scene.

⑤ **保护**文物是每个公民的责任。Preservation of cultural relics is every citizen's duty.

▶[爱护 àihù—保护 bǎohù]
[保护 bǎohù—维护 wéihù]
[保障 bǎozhàng—保护 bǎohù]

眼前 目前

(名) (名)

yǎnqián mùqián

Ⓔ before one's eyes, at present/at present, at the moment

“眼前”、“目前”都是名词,都表示当前、现在的意思,但具体用法和词义上还是有区别的 ◇ Both 眼前 and 目前 are nouns meaning "now", but they are different in usage and meaning:

1. 眼前

表示眼睛前面,跟前,多用于口语,可做主语、状语、宾语、定语等,一般是不能用“目前”替换的 ◇ Meaning "right before one's eyes", mostly used in colloquial language. It can function as the subject, adverbial, object, attributive, etc. Generally it cannot be replaced by 目前:

① 穿过树林,**眼前**是一片碧波荡漾的湖水。Boundless clear water came into our sights after crossing the forest.

② **眼前**发生的一切,都令人难以理解。All that is happening confuses us.

③ 先把**眼前**的活儿做完,再做别的。First finish the present job, and then do others.

2. 目前

指最近一段时间，含有现阶段的意思，多用于书面语或正式场合 ◇ Meaning " the recent period of time, now". It is mostly used in a formal occasion or in literary language. e. g. :

① **目前**的生产情况不太好，得开会研究一下。At present the production is not good, so we have to hold a meeting to discuss it.

② 到**目前**为止，双方还未达成任何协议。Up to the present moment, we haven't reached any agreement.

③ **目前**的形势对我们极为不利。The current situation is completely against us.

3. "眼前"和"目前"都可表示现在或说话的时候，较口语化，没有"现阶段"那么正式 ◇ Both 眼前 and 目前 mean " now". It is rather colloquial and is not as formal as 现阶段(present stage):

① 我**眼前**(/**目前**)还不太缺钱。At present, I need no money.

② **眼前**(/**目前**)的任务还不太重，下半年就要忙了。At present, I'm not too busy, but I will be busy in the late half year.

③ **眼前**(/**目前**)最紧迫的事是筹集资金。At present, the most urgent thing is to raise money.

▶ [当前 dāngqián—目前 mùqián]

厌恶 (动) yànwù　　**讨厌** (动) tǎoyàn

Ⓔ dislike/loathe, dislike

"厌恶"和"讨厌"都是动词。都是不喜欢，让人心烦的意思 ◇ Both 厌恶 and 讨厌 are verbs meaning " to dislike, to loathe".

1. "厌恶"有对人对事不喜欢、很反感的意思，可达到憎恨的程度，且多用于书面 ◇ 厌恶 means " to disgust, to detest, even hate, and is mostly used in literary language, " e. g. :

① 一些干部用公款吃喝，令群众**厌恶**。The public hates the cadres' spending the public funds extremely.

② 消费者最**厌恶**那些不讲道德只知赚钱的不法商贩。The consumer hates those illegal businessmen who make money without morals.

2. "讨厌"反感的语气较轻，主要表示不喜欢和令人心烦 ◇ 讨厌 is less serious and mainly means " dislike and be disturbed" :

① 我**讨厌**这里的冬天，又寒冷又干燥。I hate the winter here

for it's cold and dry.

② 大家都**讨厌**那种只会吹吹拍拍的人。Everyone dislikes a flatterer.

③ 我的胃病一到冬天就犯，真**讨厌**！It's nuisance. I have a stomachache as soon as the winter comes.

如果将1中例①②的“厌恶”换成“讨厌”，则反感语气较轻。如将2中例②的“讨厌”换成“厌恶”，反感语气较重。2中例①③不可换成“厌恶” ◇ If 厌恶 in examples ① and ② of 1 is replaced by 讨厌, the tone would sound less serious. If 讨厌 in example ② of 2 is replaced by 厌恶, it would sound more serious. In examples ① and ③ of 2 厌恶 cannot be used.

▶[讨厌 tǎoyàn—嫌 xián]

样 (量) yàng　种 (量) zhǒng

Ⓔ kind/sort

◪ 量词“样”和“种”都用于表示事物的种类。“样”可做很多事物的量词，多是侧重于表面、形式的区别，可儿化，也可重叠（表示每一样）；“种”指根据事物本身的性质、特点等分成的门类，可重叠（表示每一种）◇ The measure words 样 and 种 are used to show the different sorts of things. 样 can function as the measure word of many things and the stress is on the outside appearance; it can take the retroflex ending "-er" and be reduplicated (meaning each kind). 种 means "classification according to the nature or character of things"; it can also be reduplicated (meaning each sort). e. g. :

① 我给你看**一样**(**儿**)(/**种**)东西，你肯定没见过。I will show you an item, and I'm sure you have never seen it.

② 今天晚饭有几**样**(**儿**)(/**种**)菜？How many dishes are there for the supper tonight?

③ 这些艺术品我**样样**都喜欢。I like every one of the art crafts.

④ 唱歌、跳舞、打乒乓球，她**样样**都行。She is good at singing, dancing and playing Ping-Pong.

⑤ 这**种**苹果甜，那**种**苹果酸。This kind of apple is sour, and that one is sweet.

⑥ 我有好几**种**信封，你要哪一**种**？I have a few kinds of envelopes, which one do you prefer?

⑦ 姐妹二人一起长大，但却有两**种**截然不同的命运。The two sisters have different fates though they grew up together.

⑧ 这**种**处理问题的方法比较妥当。The handling way is reliable.

⑨ 由于**种种**原因,他没有参加那次的学术讨论会。He didn't attend the academic symposium because of a variety of reasons.

如侧重与别的事物有所区别时,"样"、"种"都可用,如例①②。例⑥的"好几种信封"也可用"好几样信封",但意思不同,"好几种信封"是指有平信信封、航空信信封等,侧重于性质、作用;而"好几样信封"是指信封有白色的、黄色的,大的、小的等,侧重于表面形式。例⑤的"这种"、"那种"如改为"这样"、"那样",意思不同。"这样"、"那样"可理解为"这种样子"、"那种样子",而且后边多带"的",再如:"这样的台灯我以前没见过",强调台灯的外观。例⑦⑧是抽象事物,用"种" ◇ To stress the difference from other things, both 样 and 种 can be used, as in examples ① and ②. 好几种信封 in example ⑥ can be replaced by 好几样信封, but they are different in meaning: 好几种信封 means "that there are envelops for ordinary mail, for air mail, etc." with the stress on nature and usage; 好几样信封 means "that the envelops come in white, yellow, big, small", etc. with the stress on outside appearance. If 这种, 那种 in example ⑤ are changed to 这样, 那样, the meaning is also changed. 这样 and 那样 can be understood as 这种样子 and 那种样子 usually followed by 的. Another example: 这样的台灯我以前没见过(I have never seen a table lamp like this), with a stress on the appearance. Examples ⑦ and ⑧ are about abstract things and 种 is used.

一道 (副) yīdào 一块儿 (副、名) yīkuàir 一起 (副、名) yīqǐ 一同 (副) yītóng

Ⓔ together/together/together/together

1. 副词"一道"、"一块儿"、"一起"、"一同"表示两个或更多的人或物同时同地(做某事或受到同样的处置),前面常有"跟"和"同"组成介宾词组。"一道"有南方方言色彩,"一同"多用于书面语,"一块儿"、"一起"常用于口语,而"一块儿"口语中用得最多 ◇ The adverbs 一道, 一块儿, 一起, 一同 all mean" two or more people or things (do something or be treated in the same way)". There is usually 跟 or 同 in front to form a preposition and object phrase. 一道 is a southern expression. 一同 is literary. 一块儿 and 一起 are colloquial. 一块儿 is mostly used in spoken language. e. g. :

① 咱们**一道**(/**一块儿**/**一起**/**一同**)收拾一下房间吧。Let's put the room in order.

② 夏天我总是跟姐姐**一块儿**(/**一道**/**一起**/一同)去游泳。I always go swimming with my sister in summer.

③ 小王同老李**一起**(/**一道**/**一块儿**/**一同**)去上海了。Xiao Wang and Lao Li have gone to Shanghai together.

④ 你不认识路,最好找个人和你**一同**(/**一道**/**一块儿**/**一起**)去。You don't know how to get there, so you'd better ask somebody to go with you.

⑤ 这几个问题今天要**一起**(/**一道**/**一块儿**/**一同**)讨论。These issues will be discussed together today.

⑥ 等你把信写完,和我们**一块儿**(/**一道**/**一起**/**一同**)寄。Please post your and my letters together after you finished it.

⑦ 请把录音机跟磁带**一起**(/**一道**/**一块儿**/**一同**)给我带来。Please bring the recorder and the tape together to me.

以上各句四个词都可用,只是语体色彩不同而已 ◇ In all the examples above, any of the four words can be used, but with different local flavour.

2. 名词"一块儿"、"一起"表示同一个处所。常用于"在"、"到"等词之后 ◇ The noun 一块儿 or 一起 indicates the same place and is usually used after the words 在 or 到. e. g. :

① 这几个女孩子总在**一块儿**(/**一起**)玩。The girls always play together.

② 别把这几本杂志放到**一块儿**(/**一起**)。Don't put the magazines in the same place.

③ 我和老李早就认识,我们在**一起**(/**一块儿**)工作过。I knew Lao Li for a long time, for we were once colleagues.

④ 我们旅行时遇到**一起**(/**一块儿**)了。We met in a tour.

⑤ 他们兄弟二人在**一块儿**(/**一起**)住。The two brothers live together.

以上各句不能用"一道"、"一同" ◇ In the examples above, neither 一道 nor 一同 can be used.

注意:有时"一道"是"一"+"道",如:"口袋漏了,米洒了一道" ◇ Note: Sometimes 一道 is 一 plus 道, e. g. 口袋漏了,米洒了一道(The sack split and the rice is scattered along the road).

一点儿 一些

（量） （量）

yīdiǎnr yīxiē

Ⓔ a little, a bit/a few, a little

◪ "一点儿"、"一些"两个词都表示少量、些微，可用于具体、抽象事物。可用于名词前，形容词、动词后。"一些"较书面化。两个词的"一"都可省略 ◇ Both 一点儿 and 一些 mean "a little quantity" and can be applied to concrete as well as abstract things. They can be used before nouns or after adjectives and verbs. 一些 is more literary. 一 can be omitted in both words.

① 妈妈，给我**一点儿**（/**一些**）钱。Mum, please give me a little / some money.

② 我买了**一点儿**（/**一些**）日用品。I bought a few / some necessities.

③ 工作中，他积累了**一点儿**（/**一些**）经验。A few years later, he had got a little / some work experience.

④ 这双鞋小了**一点儿**（/**一些**），还有大**一点儿**（/**一些**）的吗？This pair of shoes is a bit tight. Do you have a bigger one?

⑤ 快**一点儿**（/**一些**）走。Hurry up.

⑥ 动作轻**一点儿**（/**一些**）。Please do it slightly.

⑦ 小树苗长大了**一点儿**（/**一些**）。The sapling grows a little.

⑧ 水洒出去了**一点儿**（/**一些**）。The water spilt a little.

以上例①②具体，例③抽象。用在名词前做定语（例①②③）◇ Examples ①② are concrete, and ③ is abstract. 一点儿 or 一些 is used in front of a noun as an attributive (such as examples ①②③).

用在形容词后做补语可表示比较（例④⑤⑥）。在动词后做宾语，表示动作幅度小（例⑦⑧）◇ When used after an adjective as the complement, both words can indicate comparison (like examples ④⑤⑥). When used after a verb as the object, they indicate small range (like examples ⑦⑧).

"一点儿"可重叠为"一点（儿）点（儿）"，表示数量更少；"一些"不能重叠 ◇ 一点儿 can be reduplicated into 一点（儿）点（儿） to show an even smaller quantity; 一些 cannot be reduplicated:

⑨ 汤里只放了**一点儿点儿**盐。There is only little salt in the soup.

▶ [有（一）点儿 yǒu (yī) diǎnr—（一）点儿 yīdiǎnr]

一面……一面……

（副）

yīmiàn …… yīmiàn ……

一边……一边……

（副）

yībiān …… yībiān ……

Ⓔ at the same time, simultaneously/
at the same time, simultaneously

◪ "一面……一面……"和"一边……一边……"都是关联性副词，位于动词前，表示前一个动作进行的过程中开始做后一个动作。这两个关联词都能连接表示具体事物或行为的成分 ◇ 一面……一面……and 一边……一边……are conjunctive adverbs placed in front of the verbs to indicate two actions taking place at the same time. Both conjunctions can connect elements indicating concrete things or actions:

① 学生们**一面**(/**一边**)听，**一面**(/**一边**)做笔记。The students took notes while they are having a lesson.

② 他**一边(/一面)打手机，一边**(/**一面**)向外走。He went out while he was phoning with his cell phone.

"一面……一面……"还可以连接抽象的或较宏观的事物成分，"一边……一边……"较少用 ◇ 一面……一面……can also connect elements of abstract or objective things, but 一边……一边……rarely used so:

③ 他**一面**体验生活，**一面**创作。He lives and learns from real life as well as creates works.

④ 我们**一面**发展经济**一面**治理污染。We develop the economy; meanwhile we also tackle the pollution.

"一边……一边……"在实际运用中，常将"一"省略，词意不变，但文字更简练，而"一面……一面……"则不可 ◇ The 一 in 一边……一边……is often omitted without changing the meaning, but 一面……一面……cannot:

⑤ 他们(**一**)**边**走(**一**)**边**说。They talked while they were walking.

当"一边……一边……"中的"一"省略时，还可连接两个以上的动作 ◇ When the 一 in 一边……一边……is omitted, more than two actions can be connected:

⑥ 大家边复印，**边**装订，**边**打包，配合得非常默契。They copied, bound, and packed, and they cooperated well.

一再 屡屡

(副) (副)

yīzài lǚlǚ

Ⓔ time and again, repeatedly/ time and again, repeatedly

◪ "一再"和"屡屡"都有同样的事情不止发生一次的意思,通常可互换使用,但侧重点不同,"一再"特指行为的重要性和严重性,语气较重,而"屡屡"则主要指动作的次数多 ◇ 一再 and 屡屡 both mean "repeatedly", and are usually interchangeable, but they have different stresses. 一再 stresses the importance and seriousness of the behaviour, while 屡屡 stresses the frequency. e. g. :

① 由于今天心情不好,他做事情**一再**(/**屡屡**)出错。He made mistakes again and again because of his bad mood.

② 一些商贩法制观念淡漠,**一再**(/**屡屡**)偷税漏税。Some businessmen have few legal sense, and they evaded taxes again and again.

③ 为什么这种事件**一再**发生? Why such things happen over and over?

④ 公司领导**一再**强调要建立科学的管理流程。The company leaders stressed time and time again that scientific managing flow should be established.

在例③④中,由于特指动作的重要性,宜用"一再" ◇ In examples ③ and ④, since importance of the action is stressed, 一再 is used and cannot be replaced by 屡屡.

需要注意的是,"一再"和"屡屡"都是用于人的主观行为。如果是客观叙述,例如"下雨",不能用"屡屡",用"一再"也是不规范的,应说"经常下雨"等 ◇ It is worth noting that 一再 and 屡屡 are both applied to man's subjective action. For example, we cannot use 屡屡 to modify 下雨, so does 一再, but we say 经常下雨(it rains often).

依旧 照旧 依然

(副) (副) (副)

yījiù zhàojiù yīrán

Ⓔ as before/ as before/ still, as before

◪ 这三个词都是副词,均有"与原来一样"的意思 ◇ All the three words are adverbs meaning "same as before".

"依旧"和"照旧"主要指事情经过变化,仍然维持原状,可互换使用,但"照旧"口语性较强 ◇ 依旧 and 照旧 mean "after a certain change in circumstances the thing remains unchanged". The two words are interchangeable, but 照旧 is colloquial:

① 处理完父亲的丧事，他**依旧**（/**照旧**）回到外地工作。After handling his father's funeral service, he left and went to work.

② 出院后，老李每天**依旧**（/**照旧**）工作到很晚。After his recovery from a serious illness, Lao Li worked into late night every day as before.

但是当“照旧”特指按老规矩、老样子行事时，则不可被“依旧”替换 ◇ But when 照旧 means "as before, as of old", it cannot be replaced by 依旧:

③ 教学计划**照旧**进行。The teaching plan was carried on as schedule.

④ 今天的课你**照旧**上。You will give a lesson as usual.

当“依旧”和“依然”都特指事物继续保持不变时，可互换使用 ◇ When 依旧 and 依然 mean "the state keeps on as before", the two are interchangeable:

⑤ 二十年不见了，他**依旧**（/**依然**）保持着俭朴的生活作风。We have not seen each other for twenty years, but he keeps the plain and thrifty living as before.

⑥ 如今十几年过去了，故乡在我心中，**依旧**（/**依然**）是那么美丽迷人。My native place is as beautiful and charming as it was over ten years ago.

“依然”多用于书面语，所以常出现在下列习惯搭配中，表示人、事情、景物等没有变化，不可用“依旧”替换 ◇ 依然 is mostly used in literary language and so often appears in the following set phrases to show no change. 依旧 cannot replace it:

⑦ 母校的景物**依然**如故。My school keeps the same as it was.

⑧ 任凭妻子如何苦口婆心地劝说，他**依然**如故，每天照喝不误。Despite his wife's repeated admonitions, he remained unrepentant and drank everyday.

依靠 靠

（动、名） （动、介）

yīkào kào

Ⓔ rely, depend; support, backing/
depend

◪ “依靠”、“靠”都有凭借、仰仗的意思。“依靠”、“靠”除为动词外，还分别是名词和介词。两个词的具体意义也有区别 ◇ Both 依靠 and 靠 mean "to depend". Besides being a verb, 依靠

is also a noun and 靠 is also a preposition. The meanings of the two words are also different.

1. 依靠

(1)"依靠"(动):表示仰仗、借助(一定的人、事物或力量,有时可能是自身的力量),达到一定的目的 ◇ 依靠,as a verb,means " to depend on (certain person, thing or strength, or sometimes one's own strength) to reach a certain aim". e. g. :

① 这次订货会开得如此成功,完全**依靠**(/**靠**)各位的努力。The success of the promotional meeting is your efforts.

② 不能只**依靠**(/**靠**)别人,得自己想办法才行。Don't just depend on others. You should solve it by yourself.

③ 他在医学上取得显著成就,就是**依靠**(/**靠**)他的自信和勤奋。His outstanding success on medicine depends on his self-confidence and diligence.

④ 在荒漠中辨别方向只能**依靠**(/**靠**)指南针。They told directions only by compass in the vast desert.

⑤ 在科学研究方面,这些年轻人是我们可以**依靠**的力量。The youth are dependable in scientific research.

以上各例除⑤不能用"靠"外,其他各句均可用"靠"替换,意思不变。"依靠"可做定语,如"依靠的力量"、"依靠对象"等,而"靠"由于是单音节词,一般不做定语,"靠垫"、"靠枕"等都已成词 ◇ In the examples above, with the exception of ⑤, all the other 依靠 can be replaced by 靠 without changing the meaning. 依靠 can function as an attributive, e. g. 依靠的力量,依靠对象, etc. ; while 靠, being monosyllabic, usually does not function as attributive. 靠垫 and 靠枕 (both mean " cushion for leaning on") are already words.

(2)"依靠"(名):指可以倚仗或依赖的人或事物 ◇ 依靠,as a noun, means " support, backing, a person or thing one can depend on":

⑥ 老人已经70多岁,由于生活没有**依靠**,住进了敬老院。The old man is over 70. Because there is nobody supporting him, he moved to the nursing home.

⑦ 回到了自己的祖国,他才觉得真正有了**依靠**。He returned to his country and felt assured.

⑧ 这片竹林是他一家生活的**依靠**。His family lives off the bamboo forest.

2. 靠(动)

(1) 同"依靠"(动)(1) ◇ 靠,

Y

as a verb, is the same as 依靠(as a verb)(1):

① 村民们现在所以能富起来,**靠**(/**依靠**)的是科学种田。The villagers of this village becomes rich by scientific cultivation.

② 他有今天的成绩完全**靠**(/**依靠**)自身的努力。He gained his success by his own efforts.

③ 我真是没有能力去做,这事全**靠**(/**依靠**)你了。I am unable to do it, so finishing it depends you completely.

④ 要发展农业必须兴修水利,只**靠**天是不行的。We must undertake water conservancy projects if we want to develop agriculture. And it's impossible to depend only on the natural force.

以上例①②③可用"依靠"替换。例④由于习惯用法及音节关系,一般不用"依靠" ◇ In examples ①② and ③ above, 靠 can be replaced by 依靠, whereas in example ④靠天 is an idiomatic phrase and 依靠 is not used.

(2)(人或动物)坐着或站着时,凭借别的人或物支持身体 ◇ (Of human being or animal) lean against another person or thing when sitting or standing. e. g.:

⑤ 他坐在那里,**靠**着椅背睡着了。He sat there sleeping on the chair.

⑥ 孩子**靠**着妈妈的腿坐着。The child sat against his mother's legs.

⑦ 别**靠**墙,上边有油漆。Keep off the wet paint on the wall.

⑧ 小猫正在**靠**着墙晒太阳。The cat is bathing in the sunshine against the wall.

(3)(物体)凭借其他东西支持而立住 ◇ (Of a thing) lean against other things. e. g.:

⑨ 他把手杖**靠**在桌边。Please put your walking stick against the table.

⑩ 梯子**靠**墙放着。The ladder is standing against the wall.

⑪ 这张桌子不稳,得**靠**墙放才行。The table is not stable, so put it against the window.

(4) 挨近的意思 ◇ Be near to. e. g.:

⑫ 船**靠**岸后,乘客陆续下来了。When the boat landed, the passengers get off one by one.

⑬ 他家**靠**着一条小河。He lives by a small river.

⑭ 书架**靠**墙,桌子靠窗户。The bookshelf is by the cabinet, and the table is by the window.

"靠"(动)(2)(3)(4)义项中各例均不能用"依靠"代替 ◇ In the usage of (2)(3)(4) above, no 靠 can be replaced by 依靠.

3. 靠(介)

表示动作、行为的依赖,凭借。

构成介宾结构做状语 ◇ As a preposition, 靠 means " to be dependent on and forms a preposition-object phrase functioning as an adverbial" :

① 他祖父**靠**手工艺起家。His grandfather started his business by handcraft.

② 过去全村人**靠**这一眼井浇地。The whole village used to water the land by the only well.

③ 一家人**靠**他的工资生活。His family lives on his wages.

例③也可用"依靠","依靠"是动词,意思较实(不是介宾结构做状语,是连动句) ◇ In example ③ above, 依靠 can be used instead ,but it is a verb. Then the senetence will become a sentence with verbal expressions in series and not one with a preposition-object adverbial.

以至 以致

(连) (连)

yǐzhì yǐzhì

Ⓔ to such an extent as to/ so that, as a result, consequently

◪"以至"和"以致"都是连词,位于后一分句的开头,表示结果。"以至"可与"于"连用,意义不变。"以至"前边强调事情进行的状况,引出的结果可好可坏;而"以致"前边强调事情的原因,引出的结果多是不好或不如意的 ◇ Both 以至 and 以致 are conjunctions, used at the beginning of the second clause to introduce the result. 以至 can take 于 with no change in meaning. The clause before 以至 stresses the stage of a situation and the result that follows can be either good or bad. However, what comes before 以致 stresses the cause and the following result is usually something bad:

① 事态的发展如此之快,**以至**许多人都感到意外。Things have been developing so fast that many people are amazed.

② 他汉语说得那么好,**以至**大家都误以为他是中国人。He speaks Chinese so well that he is taken for a Chinese.

③ 这个学生平时学习不努力,**以致**没能考上大学。The student did not study so hard that he failed in his college entrance examination.

④ 机器突然出了问题,**以致**今天的生产任务没有完成。The machine can not work suddenly, that they did not finish the production.

"以至"还有"直到"乃至的意思,表示程度、数量、范围、时间上的延伸,可以连接词和词组;"以致"没有这个意思 ◇ 以至

Y

also means " up to" , indicating" the extension of degree, quantity, scope, time, etc". It can connect words and phrases. 以致 has no such meaning:

⑤ 这个单位每年用于员工培训的费用要几十万**以至**几百万。The work unit spent thousands of *yuan* or even millions of *yuan* training their staff annually.

⑥ 除了自家的事以外，亲友家的，**以至**邻居家的事，没有她不关心的。Besides her family, she cares for her relatives and even her neighbors.

异常　　非常

（形、副）　（形、副）

yìcháng　　fēicháng

Ⓔ unusual, abnormal; very/ extraordinary, unusual; very

1. 形容词“异常”、“非常”都指不同于寻常的，特殊的。“非常”只做定语，而且与后面的名词结合紧密，它所修饰的名词有限，只有“时期”、“事件”、“措施”、“会议”、“事故”等，用“非常”时更强调的是特殊性。“异常”可做定语、谓语。形容词“异常”和“非常”在以下各句中不能互换 ◇ The adjectives 异常 and 非常 both mean" unusual, extraordinary". 非常 only functions as attributives and it is very closely connected with the nouns it modifies, which are limited to 时期(period), 事件 (event), 措施 (measure/ step), 会议(meeting), 事故(accident), etc. 非常 stresses particularity. 异常 can function as the attributive or predicate. 异常 and 非常 in the following examples are not interchangeable. e. g. :

① 病人有什么**异常**情况马上找大夫。If there's something wrong with the patient, come to the doctor at once.

② 最近他的表现有些**异常**，常常一句话不说，不停地抽烟，不知是怎么回事。I don't know why he behaved differently recently, such as being silent and constantly smoking.

③ 今年气候**异常**，该冷的时候不冷，该热的时候不热。The climate is abnormal this year: it is not as cold and hot as usual.

④ 在紧急情况下，召开了一次**非常**会议。They held a meeting in emergency.

⑤ 非常时期，国家采取一些**非常**措施也是可以理解的。It is understandable that some extraordinary measures are taken during the time of emergency.

2. 副词“异常”、“非常”，表示程度极高。“异常”比“非常”语意更重些，是书面语 ◇ Adverb 异

常 and 非常 indicate " very high degree". 异常 sounds more forceful than 非常 and it is literary. e. g. :

① 那棵小松树表现了**异常**(/**非常**)旺盛的生命力。The small pine is very thriving.

② 这件事发生后,她表现得**异常**(/**非常**)不安,总怕别人对她有误解。She is particularly upset after the event, worrying about others' misunder standing all the times.

③ 他的心情**异常**(/**非常**)激动。He's very excited.

④ 灯光**非常**暗,看不清眼前的景象。The light is too dim to see the scene before his eyes.

⑤ 房间**非常**小,放不下这么多东西。The room is too small to hold these items.

⑥ 那里的景色**非常**美。The scenery there is very beautiful.

⑦ 市场上热闹**异常**(/**非常**)。The market is usually exciting and noisy.

以上例①②③"异常"、"非常"可以互换。④⑤⑥修饰单音节形容词,一般用"非常",很少用"异常"。例⑥可说"异常之美"。例⑦"异常"放在双音节形容词后做补语,"非常"偶尔也可这样用 ◇ In examples ① ② and ③ above, 异常 and 非常 are interchangeable. In examples ④ ⑤ and ⑥, however, 非常 and rarely 异常 is used since monosyllabic adjectives are modified. In examples ⑥, one can say 异常之美. In ⑦ 异常 is placed after the adjective as the complement. 非常 can occasionally be so used, too. e. g. :

⑧ 我**非常**不愿意麻烦别人。I'm very reluctant to bother others.

⑨ 大家都**非常**想看那个话剧。Everyone wants to see the play very much.

⑩ 他**非常**不会讨好别人。He is not good at flattering others.

以上例⑧⑨⑩是修饰助动词(或副词+助动词),用"非常"不用"异常" ◇ In examples ⑧ ⑨ and ⑩ above, it is auxiliary verbs (or adverb + auxiliary verb) that are modified, so 非常 is used, not 异常.

另外,副词"非常"还可重叠,"异常"不能重叠 ◇ Besides, adverb 非常 can be reduplicated, while 异常 cannot. e. g. :

⑪ 当时的情景**非常非常**感人。The scene was very moving at that time.

► [非常 fēicháng—极 jí—十分 shífēn]

抑制 (动) yìzhì　控制 (动) kòngzhì

Ⓔ restrain, check/ control, dominate

◥ "抑制"主要指将内心的情感压下去,"控制"则表示掌握住使之不超出范围 ◇ 抑制 mainly means "to restrain one's sentiment", while 控制 means " to control something within a certain scope".

1. 做谓语时,"抑制"的对象常是表示内心活动的词语,如"痛苦"、"愤怒"、"喜悦"等;"控制"的对象可以是具体的人或事,有时也用于内心活动,如例⑥补语都可以用"住" ◇ As a predicate, the object of 抑制 can be a word or phrase expressing one's emotion, e. g. 痛苦(agony), 愤怒(outrage), 喜悦(delight), etc., whereas the object of 控制 can be a person or thing, and sometimes emotion, as in example ⑥. 住 can be used as the complement of the two:

① 看到这些腐败现象,他简直**抑制**不住心中的怒火。He cannot restrain his anger at these corruptions.

② 人们无法**抑制**悲痛的心情,失声痛哭起来。People cannot help weeping sorrowfully.

③ 大夫们已经**抑制**住了他的病情发展。The doctors have arrested his disease.

④ 妻子**控制**着家中的财权,丈夫连和朋友们一起吃饭的钱都没有。She is in charge of her family's income, and his husband nearly have no money to have a dinner with his friends.

⑤ 他把每月的开支都**控制**在1000元以内。He limits his monthly expenditure within 1000 *yuan*.

当"控制"的对象是抽象事物时,可被"抑制"替换 ◇ When the object of 控制 is something abstract, it can be replaced by 抑制:

⑥ 他用理智**控制**(/**抑制**)了感情,断绝了与她的来往。He will overcome his feelings and he broke off with her.

"控制"在口语中可重叠为ABAB式,"抑制"不可以 ◇ 控制 in everyday speech can be reduplicated as ABAB;抑制 cannot:

⑦ 你花钱太大手大脚,应当**控制控制**了。You spend money lavishly, and you should restrain yourself about it.

2. 做定语时,"抑制"和"控制"常与"难以"、"不可"、"不住"等搭配使用,要带"的","控制"可直接做定语,一般不带"的" ◇ As an attributive, 抑制 and 控制 are

often used in collocation with 难以,不可,不住,etc. and usually的 is necessary. 控制 can be an attributive without 的:

① 同学们的脸上都浮现着**难以抑制**的喜悦。The students looked uncontrollably happy.

② 局势已发展到**难以控制**的地步。The situation is out of control now.

③ 他很有**控制**能力。He is controllable.

④ 他绝不会放弃对公司的**控制**权。He will never give up the control of his company.

3. 做宾语时,"抑制"、"控制"都可以与"失去"、"得到"等动词搭配使用。"控制"应用的范围较广 ◇ As an object, 抑制 and 控制 often collocates with verbs like 失去(lose), 得到(gain/get), etc. 控制 is applied to a wider scope than 抑制:

① 病人体内的癌细胞已经**得到抑制**(/**控制**)。The cancer cells in the patient have been arrested.

② 超前消费的欲望已**受到抑制**。His desire of excessive consumption is under control.

③ 小船突然**失去控制**,在河心横了过来。The ship was uncontrollable suddenly and changed its direction in the middle of the river.

④ 太湖的水污染状况已基本**得到控制**。The water pollution in Tai Lake is basically under control.

⑤ 他能**摆脱**黑社会的**控制**吗? Can he get rid of the control of criminal syndicate?

⑥ 疯涨的物价已**受到了控制**。The crazily rising prices are under control now.

另外,"抑制"还是医学用语,特指阻止大脑皮层的兴奋 ◇ Besides, 抑制 is also a medical term meaning "inhibition":

⑦ 睡眠就是大脑皮层全部处于**抑制**状态时的生理现象。Sleep is the phenomenon in which the pallium is all restrained.

因此 因而 所以

因此	因而	所以
(连)	(连)	(连)
yīncǐ	yīn'ér	suǒyǐ

Ⓔ therefore, hence/ thus, as a result/ so, therefore

"因此"、"因而"、"所以"这三个连词都表示因果关系,但用法上有区别 ◇ 因此, 因而 and 所以 are conjunctions used to introduce result. They are different in usage.

1. "因此"有"因为这个……"的

意思，用在复句的第二分句前，也可放在句与句、段与段之间，引进结果，后面常有停顿，前面可有“由于”与之呼应，但不能与“因为”呼应 ◇ 因此 means "because of this"; it is used at the beginning of the second clause, or between sentences or paragraphs, to introduce the result and there is often a pause after it. What goes before it may be reasons introduced by 由于, but not by 因为:

① 由于连日大雨，**因此**河水猛涨。The river is swollen roughly because of the continuous rain.

② 他干什么事都不能坚持到底，**因此**，十几年来，工作上没什么成绩。He achieved nothing in his work for decades because he cannot keep on anything.

③ 潜水不仅需要较高的技术，还要有勇气和毅力才行。**因此**，像我这样胆小的人是不能学潜水的。Diving needs higher skills, courage and fortitude; therefore, it's impossible for me, a coward, to learn diving.

④ 他从小就喜欢音乐，而且有一定的基础，应该得到很好的培养。**因此**，我一直鼓励他报考音乐学院。He likes music since his childhood, and he has some basic musical knowledge, so he should be cultivated well. Thus I encourage him to attend the conservatory of music.

“因此”也可以放在第二分句的谓语前，起同样作用 ◇ 因此 can also be placed before the predicate of the second clause, e. g. :

⑤ 他的话引得大家都笑了，室内的气氛**因此**轻松了很多。What he said made everyone laugh, and consequently the atmosphere in the room lightened up a lot.

⑥ 今日清晨有大雾，交通也**因此**受到了影响。The traffic was influenced by the morning's heavy fog.

2. “因而”基本上同“因此”，连接复句中的两个分句，一般不连接句子、段落，后面不停顿，前面可有“由于”与之呼应，但不能与“因为”呼应。“因此”中例①⑤⑥可用“因而”代替，其他各句不能 ◇ 因而 is basically the same as 因此. It connects two clauses of a complex sentence, but not sentences or paragraphs, and there is no pause after it. The first clause can have 由于 to correspond with it, but not 因为. In examples ① ⑤ ⑥ above, 因而 can replace 因此, but not in other examples. e. g. :

① 他平时经常参与群众活动，**因而**最了解群众的意见和要求。He usually keeps in close touch with the mass and pays attention to their views. Thus he knows their proposals, and hopes most.

② 由于这种病早期的症状不太明显，**因而**往往被人忽视。The disease is usually neglected because its early symptom is not noticeable.

③ 他有两个星期的假期，**因而**可以好好地休息休息。He has two weeks off, so he can take a good rest.

以上三句均可用“因此”代替。“因此”、“因而”虽可互换，但侧重点有时不同，“因此”往往侧重于引出结果，“因而”往往侧重于推导，表示前事是后事凭借的条件 ◇ In the three examples above 因此 can replace 因而. Though 因此 and 因而 can be used interchangeably, the stress is different. 因此 often stresses the result, while 因而 often stresses the sense of inference expressing the former is the prerequisite of the latter.

3. “所以”用于复句的第二分句前，引进结果，前一分句多用“因为”说明原因，这是与“因此”、“因而”不同的。另外“所以”句中的原因和结果可同放在一个主语之后 ◇ 所以 is used at the beginning of the second clause of a complex sentence to introduce the result. 因为 is often used in the first clause to introduce the reason, and this is how it is different from 因此 and 因而. Besides, both the cause and the result can be placed after the same subject:

① 我因为病了，**所以**今天没去上班。I didn't go to work today for I'm not feeling well.

② 由于工作地点离家很远，**所以**他只有休息日才回家。He worked far away from his home, so it was only on holidays that he could go home.

③ 他因为从小生活优裕，**所以**缺乏吃苦耐劳的精神。He lacks industriousness owing to his early rich life.

以上例②也可换用“因此”或“因而”，但较“所以”在语感上正式一些。另外，“所以”还有以下用法 ◇ In example ② above, 因此 or 因而 can be used instead, but it would sound more formal than with 所以. In addition, 所以 also has the following usages:

(1) 有时为了突出前一分句是产生某种结果的原因，可将表示原因的前一分句中的“因为”、“由于”省去，后一分句用“是……(之)所以……的原因”的形式，是书面语，“因此”、“因而”没有这种用法 ◇ Sometimes, to highlight the point that the first clause is the cause of a certain result, 因为 or 由于 in the first clause may be omitted, and the second clause is put in the pattern

是……(之)所以……的原因. This is literary language and neither 因此 nor 因而 has such a usage:

① 明确的目标和正确的理论指导,是他的事业(之)**所以**能取得成功的重要原因。The important point of his career success is that he has clear goal and right theory to guide him.

② 内容贴近生活,真实反映民众的喜、怒、哀、乐,是这部小说(之)**所以**受到读者欢迎的原因。The reason why the novel is popular is that it is close to the reality,and represents the public's emotions such as pleasure,anger, sorrow,and joy.

(2) 为了突出强调原因或理由等,前一分句常用"(之)所以……"的形式,表示结果,后一分句用"(是)因为(由于)……"的形式表示原因。用于书面语。"因此"、"因而"也没有这种用法 ◇ In order to highlight the cause or reason,(之)所以……is often used in the first clause to show the result,and(是)因为(由于)……is used in the second clause to indicate the cause or reason. This is literary language and neither 因此,nor 因而 has this usage. e. g. :

③ 这种电冰箱(之)**所以**畅销全国,(是)因为它的价钱合理,而且质量有保证。The reason why the refrigerator sells well is that its price is reasonable and its quality is assured.

④ 他(之)**所以**能这样快地把企业发展起来,除了勤奋外,主要(是)由于信息灵通。The reason why his business develops so quickly is that he is well informed besides his industriousness.

⑤ 王大夫(之)**所以**要到边远地区工作,是因为那里更需要医生。The reason why Dr. Wang went to work in the rural region is that the region needs doctors much badly.

以上①~⑤例中,"所以"均不能用"因此"、"因而"替换 ◇ In examples ①~⑤,所以 cannot be replaced by 因此 or 因而.

(3)"所以"有时还可以单说,表示原因就在这里,后面常加"呀",用于口语,为承接上面的话 ◇ 所以 sometimes can be used by itself to indicate that this is the reason and is usually said as 所以呀! which is colloquial:

⑥ ——这个时间出门常遇到塞车。If you drive out at this time,you'll be in a traffic jam.

——**所以呀!** 我总是要提前出来。Therefore, I usually start ahead of this time.

⑦ ——这种布很薄,颜色也比较浅。The cloth is very thin and

its color is very light.

——**所以呀！**做夏天的衣服正合适。So it is suitable for summer clothes.

“因此”、“因而”没有这种用法 ◇ Neither 因此 nor 因而 has this usage.

▶[于是 yúshì—所以 suǒyǐ]

应 应当 应该

(助动、动) (助动) (助动)

yīng yīngdāng yīnggāi

Ⓔ ought to, should/ ought to, should/ ought to, should

1.“应”、“应当”、“应该”都表示从情理上讲，当然是这样。“应该”、“应当”多用于口语，也可用于书面语，而“应”只用于书面语。三个词的否定用“不” ◇ 应，应当 and 应该 all mean "to have the moral duty to do something". 应该 and 应当 are colloquial and can also be used in literary language, but 应 is used in literary language only. All the three words are negated by 不. e.g.:

① 大家都**应**(**应当**/**应该**)遵守纪律。Everyone should obey disciplines.

② 这篇文章**应**(**应当**/**应该**)分三段来写。The article should be written in three paragraphs.

③ 遇事**应**(**应当**/**应该**)镇静，万万不可慌张。Don't be panic when in trouble.

④ 你不**应**(**应当**/**应该**)这样性急，多考虑一下再决定。You shouldn't be too hot-tempered, and you'd better think about it before making a decision.

⑤ 我们**不应**(**应当**/**应该**)把责任推给他一个人。We ought not to make him take on all the blames.

⑥ 你是技术员，技术方面的事**应当**(/**应该**)你管。You ought to be in charge of all concerning technology for you are a technician.

⑦ 这份报告**应当**(/**应该**)他写。He should finish the report.

例①~⑤三词可以互换，只是语体色彩不同 ◇ In examples ①~⑤ the three words are interchangeable, but with different colour.

例⑥⑦“应当(/应该)”后边是小句，不能用“应”。这种小句一般限于简短的，如果较长，常加“由”，如“会议应当(/应该)由校长亲自主持”，这时也可用“应” ◇ In examples ⑥ and ⑦, 应当(/应该) is followed by a clause, and 应 cannot be used instead. Such clauses are limited to short ones. If they are long, 由 is usually added, e.g. 会议应当(/

应该)由校长亲自主持(The meeting should be chaired by our Principal), and 应 can also be used in such a case.

2.“应当”、“应该”可以单独回答问题,“应”不能 ◇ 应当 or 应该 can be an answer by itself, but 应 cannot:

① ——对老人不**应该**(/**应当**)尊敬吗? Don't we respect the old people?
——**应该**(/**应当**)! **应该**(/**应当**)! Of course.

② ——自己的事**应该**(/**应当**)不**应该**(/**应当**)自己做? Don't you approve DIY?
——**应该**(/应当)! Sure.

3.“应当”、“应该”还表示根据情理推测,情况必然是这样。“应”不能这样用 ◇ 应当 or 应该 also shows that the situation is reasonable to be so. 应 cannot be so used. e. g. :

① 我想这时候他**应该**(/**应当**)到上海了。I think he must be in Shanghai now.

② 他听到这个消息**应该**(/**应当**)高兴的。He must be happy at the news.

③ 那里的条件**应该**(/**应当**)不会像你想像的那么糟糕吧! The conditions there should not be as bad as what you imagine.

4.在一些四字语中,只用“应”而不能用“应当”或“应该”。如“应有尽有”、“理应如此”等 ◇ In some four character phrases, only 应 is used and not 应当 or 应该, e. g. 应有尽有(have everything that one expects to find),理应如此(ought to be like this),etc.

5.“应”还是实义动词,有答应、许诺、应允的意思,“应当”、“应该”只是助动词 ◇ 应 is also an ordinary verb meaning " to answer, to promise, or to comply with", while 应当,应该 are just auxiliary verbs, e. g. :

① 我叫了半天门,没有人**应**。I called for a long time, but there was no response.

② 你**应**了他们的条件,就不能反悔。If you promised them, you should not be regretful.

▶[该 gāi—应该 yīnggāi]

应付 (动) yìngfù　　对付 (动) duìfù

Ⓔ cope with, deal with/ cope with, deal with

1.当“应付”和“对付”表示设法对待、处理,且对象是事物时,可互换使用 ◇ When 应付 and 对付 mean " to treat, to deal with", and the object is a thing, the two words are interchangeable:

① 他经验丰富，应变能力强，叫他去**应付**(/**对付**)那复杂的局面吧。Send him to cope with the complicated situation for he is experienced and quick-minded.

② 这点儿困难，他完全能**应付**(/**对付**)得了。He is able to cope with such a few difficulties.

③ 他刚上任，还不曾**应付**(/**对付**)过这样的场面。He has just come into power and has never experienced such occasion.

2. 当对象是人时，"应付"特指被动地应酬别人(有时有敷衍了事的意思)，而"对付"则是采取一定的方法、措施主动地处置别人的意思，两个词不可互换 ◇ When the object is a person, 应付 means"to cope with passively (sometimes just perfunctorily)", but 对付 is "to deal with on one's own initiative", and the two are not interchangeable:

① 如果你答应了人家，就不能抱着**应付**的态度。If you promised their requirements, you shouldn't be perfunctory.

② 面对这种不讲理的顾客，经理不得不出面**应付**。Such an unreasonable customer, the manager have to come out and deal with him.

③ 我们必须采取有力措施来**对付**目前的干旱。We nust take effective measures to relieve the severe drought.

④ 这个人太坏了，看我怎么**对付**他。Look, I will cope with the cunning man.

3. "应付"和"对付"都还有"将就"、凑合的意思。在下面例①中可以互换 ◇ 应付 and 对付 both have the meaning of "making do with". The two are interchangeable in example ①:

① 这件大衣还不算太薄，今年冬天可以**应付**(/**对付**)过去。You can get by this winter with the coat for it is not too thin.

表示"将就"时，"对付(着)"可做状语，"应付"不能做状语，所以下面两例只能用"对付" ◇ When meaning " to make do with", 对付(着) can function as an adverbial, but 应付 cannot. So in the following two examples, only 对付 can be used:

② 这双鞋虽然有些旧了，但擦一擦油还可以**对付**着穿。Though the shoes are a bit worn, you can make do by polishing them.

③ 这家旅店条件不太好，您**对付**着住一夜吧。Though the hotel is not good, you'd better make do with it tonight.

"应付"还可以组成四字语"应付自如"等，"对付"不能 ◇ 应付

Y

can be used in some four-character set phrases, e. g. 应付自如(deal with skilfully), etc., but 对付 cannot:

④ 她非常聪明能干,什么事都能**应付自如**。She is intelligent and capable, and she can handle everything successfully.

用途 用处

(名) (名)

yòngtú yòngchu

Ⓔ use, application, purpose/use, application, purpose

"用途"和"用处"都表示应用的范围,但"用途"多用于书面语,且一般只用于物,而"用处"多用于口语,可用于物也可用于人 ◇ 用途 and 用处 both mean "the scope of use", but 用途 is mostly used in literary language and applied to things only, whereas 用处 is mostly used in colloquial speech and applied to both things and human beings.

当用于物时,可互换使用,但语体风格不同 When applied to things, the two words are interchangeable but with different styles:

① 木材的**用途**(/**用处**)很广。Wood is widely used.

② 塑料的**用途**(/**用处**)是多种多样的。Plastic is widely used.

③ 这种植物有两种**用途**(/**用处**),既可以作蔬菜,又可以作药材。The plant can be used as vegetables as well as herbs.

当用于人时,只能用"用处",并常简化为"用"。"有用的人"是赞美一个人有作为、能干,能做对别人、对社会有用的事 ◇ When applied to human beings, only 用处 can be used, and it is usually simplified into 用. 有用的人(able man) is used to praise a person who is capable and can do things useful to other people or the society:

④ 他从小就下决心要做一个对国家、对社会有**用**(/**用处**)的人。As a child he made up his mind to be a useful man to his country.

⑤ 这个人真没**用**(/**用处**)! 遇到困难总是束手无策。The man is really a good-for-nothing! He does not know what to do when in troubles.

由于 因为

(连、介) (连、介)

yóuyú yīnwèi

Ⓔ owing to, as a result of/because, for, on account of

1. 连词"由于"、"因为"表示原因,常用在表示因果关系复句

的前一分句里，在后一分句可有"才"、"所以"与其呼应，"由于"还可有"因此"、"因而"与其呼应 ◇ The conjunctions 由于 and 因为 indicate "reason" and are usually used in the first clause of a complex sentence. There is often 才 or 所以 in the main clause to echo with it; 由于 can also have 因此 or 因而 to echo with it. eg.:

① **由于**(/**因为**)科学技术发展了，人们的生产和生活才有了很大的改变。Our production and life have improved greatly because of the development of science and technology.

② **由于**(/**因为**)还没找到房子，所以他暂时住在朋友家。He stays with his friend at present for he has not rented a room.

③ **由于**大家的看法不一致，因此工作计划没有通过。The work plan was not adopted because our disagreement.

④ **由于**文章内容过于简单，因而我又补充了一些材料。I added a little to the article for it's too simple.

以上例①②"由于"、"因为"均可用。例③④后一分句有"因此"、"因而"，前一分句不能用"因为" ◇ In the examples ① and ② above, either 由于 or 因为 can be used. In the examples ③ and ④, however, 因为 cannot be used in the first clause as there is 因此 or 因而 in the second clause.

有时前一分句先说明结果，连词"因为"放在后一分句补充说明原因 ◇ Sometimes, the first clause shows the result and the conjunction 因为 is used in the second clause to explain the reason:

⑤ 这两个问题不能放在一起讨论，**因为**性质不同。The two problems shouldn't be discussed together for they are different in nature.

"(之)所以……是因为……"这种形式，只能用"因为"，不能用"由于" ◇ (之)所以……是因为…… is a form in which 由于 cannot be use:

⑥ 这孩子之所以惧怕父亲，是**因为**父亲太严厉了。The reason why the child is afraid of his father is that his father is very stern.

2. 介词"由于"、"因为"表示原因或理由，与后面的词语构成介宾结构做状语，可放在主语前，也可放在主语后 ◇ The prepositions 由于 and 因为 indicate reason and form a preposition-object structure with the following word or phrase to function as an adverbial. It can be placed either before or after the subject,e. g.:

① **由于**(/**因为**)时间的关系,今天先讨论到这儿吧。That's all for our discussion today for there is less time left.

② 他的身体**由于**(/**因为**)长期生病,已经非常衰弱了。He's very weak for he's been ill for a long time.

③ 他们会**由于**(/**因为**)你不来而失望的。They will be disappointed at your not coming.

④ **由于**(/**因为**)老师的耐心教导,他很快就跟上其他同学了。Thanks to patient teaching on the part of the teacher be soon caught up with other students.

⑤ **由于**(/**因为**)浇水太多的原因,叶子变黄了。The flower leaves become yellow because of being over-watered.

以上例①②③④⑤二词可换用 ◇ In the examples ①②③④⑤ either of the two words can be used.

有趣 有意思

(形)

yǒuqù yǒu yìsi

Ⓔ interesting/interesting

1. 表示引人入胜(使人喜爱或觉得好奇),"有趣"、"有意思"都可以用 ◇ To show something arousing one's interest, either 有趣 and 有意思 can be used:

① 他说的这个笑话真**有趣**(/**有意思**)。His joke is funny.

② 冬天到游泳馆去游泳,很**有趣**(/**有意思**)。It's fun to swim in swimming natatorium in winter.

③ 这是个**有趣**(/**有意思**)的传说。The legend is very interesting.

"有意思"可拆开使用 ◇ 有意思 can be split:

④ 这种笑话**有**什么**意思**呢? 我笑不出来。What fun in the joke? I cannot feel.

2. 表示有较深刻的意义或寓义,用"有意思" ◇ To show a rather deep meaning or implied meaning, 有意思 is used:

① 他的时事报告很**有意思**,发人深省。His report on current affairs is very interesting and thought-provoking.

② 这本书理论和实践并重,很**有意思**。The book is very though-provoking for it stresses on both theory and practice.

3. 表示有意于、有志于,用"有意思" ◇ To mean" one is inclined to",有意思 is used:

① 小王**有意思**学学电脑。Xiao Wang is inclined to learn computer.

② 我**有意思**深造一下。I am inclined to study further.
③ 她对服装设计**有**点儿**意思**。She is a bit inclined to learn dress designing.

4. 表示钟情于……、产生爱意，用"有意思" ◇ To mean " one take a fancy to",有意思 is used：
① 她对小王**有**点儿**意思**，小王对她也有那么一点儿意思。She seems to fall into love with Xiao Wang, and Xiao Wang seems to fall into love with her, too.
② 她对你**有意思**，你没看出来吗？Don't you see that she has shown fondness for you?

有时 (副) yǒushí　　时时 (副) shíshí

Ⓔ sometimes/often, constantly

"有时"、"时时"都是副词，但表示的意义不同，一般不能互换 ◇ Both 有时 and 时时 are adverbs, but they are different in meaning and are not interchangeable.

1. 有时

表示有时候，有一部分时间……◇ 有时 means "sometimes, a part of the time", e. g. :
① 这个影剧院**有时**也有歌舞表演。Sometimes there are dance and song performances at the cinema.
② 他经常在学校的图书馆借书，但**有时**也去国家图书馆。He often goes to the school library to borrow books and sometimes he goes to the national library as well.
③ 最近天气不好，**有时**下雨，**有时**刮大风。The weather is not good recently for sometimes it was rainy, and sometimes it was windy.

2. 时时

(1) 表示相隔时间不久，行为、动作、情况等重复发生，有"常常"的意思 ◇ 时时 means "frequently, behaviour, action or things taking place repeatedly", with short intervals, similar to the meaning of 常常, e. g. :
① 他**时时**写信把家乡的情况告诉我。He often wrote me something about our hometown.
② 她的身影**时时**浮现在我的眼前。She haunted in my mind.
③ 这个画廊**时时**举办一些画展，吸引了不少参观者。The gallery often held some arts shows which attracted a lot of visitors.

(2) 表示动作、行为、情况等在短时间内不规则重复，有"不时"的意思 ◇ Indicating that an action, behaviour or situation repeats irregu-

larly in a short time. it means 不时, e. g. :

④ 零零星星的雪花，**时时**飘落在我身上。The scattered snowfall fell on me from time to time.

⑤ 他在路上走着，**时时**向四周张望，像是在寻找什么。He was walking on the street, looking about from time to time, and seemed to be looking for something.

⑥ 花丛中**时时**飞起一些蝴蝶和蜜蜂。Some butterflies and bees flew out from the flowers from time to time.

(3) 表示某种动作、行为、情况一直延续不断，有每时每刻的意思 ◇ Indicating that an action, behaviour or situation lasts for a long time, at every moment. e. g. :

⑦ 前辈的教导，要永远铭刻在心，**时时**不忘。I will never forget my seniors' education and will keep it in mind forever.

⑧ 记住有人在远方**时时**关心着你。There is somebody far away who cares about you all the time.

⑨ 他**时时**处处为集体利益着想。The benefits of the collective are always on his mind.

有(一)点儿 (副)

yǒu(yī)diǎnr

(一)点儿 (量)

(yī)diǎnr

一点儿 (副)

yīdiǎnr

Ⓔ a little/a little/a low degree

◪ "有(一)点儿"、"(一)点儿"都表示少量、稍微。但"有(一)点儿"是副词，"(一)点儿"是量词，"一点儿"也是副词 ◇ Both 有(一)点儿 and (一)点儿 mean "a little", but 有(一)点儿 is an adverb while (一)点儿 is a measure word, and 一点儿 is an adverb also:

1. 副词"有(一)点儿"，表示程度不高，多用于消极的或不如意的事。放在动词性或形容词性词语前做状语 ◇ The adverb 有(一)点儿 mean "a low degree", mostly applied to negative or undesirable things. It is used as an adverbial in front of a verb or adjective or a phrase of similar function:

① 他没借着那本小说，**有(一)点儿**失望。He's a little disappointed for he didn't get that novel.

② 这棵花的叶子**有(一)点儿**发黄，少浇些水吧。Please water the flower less, for its leaves become a little yellowish.

③ 刚开始说汉语，**有(一)点儿**紧

张，现在好多了。I was a bit nervous when I first spoke Chinese, but now I'm feeling better.

如表示某种变化，没有消极或不如意的意思 ◇ If it shows a certain change, it has no negative or undesirable sense:

④ 他上大学以后，性格**有（一）点儿**变了。He changed a little in his character after he was at college.

⑤ 经过教育，这孩子似乎**有（一）点儿**醒悟了。The child seemed to be a bit reasonable after being persuaded, and he associated with the idle less.

注意："有（一）点儿"后面如是名词性词语，这时"有（一）点儿"不是副词，而是"有"+量词"（一）点儿"。如下例⑥⑦ ◇ Note: If 有（一）点儿 is followed by a noun or phrase of similar function, it is not an adverb but a phrase of 有 plus a measure word（一）点儿, as in examples ⑥ and ⑦:

⑥ 我看他**有（一）点儿**后悔的意思。I can see he is a bit regretful.

⑦ 做这种小生意只**有（一）点儿**利润。Only a bit profit can be made from the small business.

2. 量词"（一）点儿"，表示不定量的少量 ◇ The measure word（一）点儿 implies an indefinite small quantity:

(1) 用于名词前，表示少量 ◇ Used before a noun to mean "a little":

① 再给我**（一）点儿**时间就可以做完这些事。Given a little more time, I can finish it.

② 这么**（一）点儿**饭，哪够两个人吃啊？So little food is not enough for two persons, isn't it?

③ 壶里**（一）点儿**水也没有。There is no water in the kettle at all.

(2) 用于形容词后，表示程度变化不大或差别不太大 ◇ Used before an adjective to indicate a slight change or difference:

④ 今天似乎比前几天冷**（一）点儿**。It's a little colder today than those days.

⑤ 这件大衣短了**（一）点儿**。The coat is a little shorter than that one.

⑥ 快**（一）点儿**，要上课了。Hurry! It's nearly the time for class.

(3) 用于某些动词后，表示程度、数量增加或减少的幅度不大 ◇ Used after certain verbs to show a slight increase or decrease in degree or quantity:

⑦ 今年的房价似乎降了**（一）点儿**。It seems to me that the price of commercial housing has fallen a little this year.

⑧ 两个月不见,小明好像又长高了(一)**点儿**。It seems that Xiao Ming is a little taller than he was a month ago.

⑨ 汤里恐怕还得加(一)**点儿**盐。I am afraid I'd better add a little more salt in the soup.

3. 副词"一点儿",用于否定式前,表示完全否定,这时"一"不能省略 ◇ The adverb 一点儿 used in front of a negative form indicates a complete negation and 一 is absolute necessary:

① 你这样做**一点儿**不错。You are definitely right if you do it this way.

② 声音太小,他说什么,我**一点儿**也没听见。I didn't catch anything he said for his voice was too low.

③ 那里的东西**一点儿**都不贵。The goods there are not expensive at all.

④ 我对他**一点儿**也不了解,怎么介绍? I know nothing about him, so how can I introduce him to you?

⑤ 这消息他**一点儿**都没透露过。He never told the news to anybody.

副词"一点儿"可以重叠,多放在动词前做状语,"一"不能省略 ◇ The adverb 一点儿 can be reduplicated and mostly functions as an adverbial before a verb. 一 cannot be omitted:

① 这活儿不急,你**一点儿一点儿**地干吧! The job is not urgent;take it easy to do it bit by bit.

② 这些资料都是我**一点儿一点儿**地收集的。I collected these materials bit by bit.

▶[一点儿 yīdiǎnr——些 yīxiē]

有意 (动) yǒuyì　　存心 (动) cúnxīn

Ⓔ be inclined, deliberately/ intentionally, deliberately

1. "有意"和"存心"都有故意的意思,但"存心"的语意更重些,有时微含贬义。在句中做状语,可互换使用,但语气轻重不同 ◇ Both 有意 and 存心 mean deliberately, but 存心 sounds more severely and sometimes with a derogatory sense. When used as an adverbial they are interchangeable, but with different severity:

① 小李是**有意**(/**存心**)跟老张作对。Xiao Li is deliberately opposed to Lao Zhang.

② 他不是**存心**(/**有意**)不借给你词典,他真的没有。He wasn't deliberate not to lend

you his dictionary, but he has no one indeed.

③ 这句话他是**存心**(/**有意**)说给我听的。He said this to me deliberately.

④ 她**存心**(/**有意**)跟我过不去。She deliberately made things difficult for me.

2. "有意"还有打算做某事的意思,"存心"没有这种意思 ◇ 有意 also means " to intend to do something"; 存心 has no such meaning:

① 我**有意**帮她一把,又怕她误解。I intend to help her, but I'm afraid I'll be misunderstood by her.

② 我**有意**去海边度假,但妻子不同意。I was inclined to have holidays on the seashore, but my wife disagreed.

③ 他**有意**去英国留学。He intended to study in Britain.

"有意"可用于"是……的"结构,"存心"一般不这样用 ◇ 有意 can be used in the pattern of 是……的;存心 is not so used:

④ 她这样做不是**有意**的。She didn't deliberately do it this way.

► [故意 gùyì—有意 yǒuyì]

于是 所以

(连) (连)

yúshì suǒyǐ

Ⓔ hence, consequently/ therefore, so

◪ "于是"、"所以"都是连词,都用于复句,但用法不同 ◇ Both 于是 and 所以 are conjunctions used in a complex sentence, but they are different in usage.

1. "于是"连接分句或句子,表示两件事前后紧接,而后一事往往是由前一事引起的,"于是"可放在后一分句或后边句子的开头,也可放在句子当中 ◇ 于是 connects clauses or sentences, indicating that the two events are closely connected and the latter is usually caused by the former. 于是 can be placed in front of the second clause or sentence, or within the clause:

① 几个人都不肯放弃自己的意见,**于是**引起了一场争论。They were reluctant to give up their own ideas, which brought about a dispute.

② 大家都热情地支持他,鼓励他,**于是**,他决定再去试试。He decided to have a try, for everyone supported and encouraged him enthusiastically.

③ 他好像对这道题不太理解，我**于是**给他解释了一下。It seemed that he was unable to understand the question;so I explained it to him.

“于是”也可以说成“于是乎”，较书面化或诙谐 ◇ 于是 can also be said as 于是乎 which is more literary or humorous:

④ 我们都喜欢吃面条，**于是乎**就去了那家有名的面馆。We all like noodles, so we went to the famous noodle restaurant.

2.“所以”用于表示因果关系的复句中，连接两个或两个以上分句，常和前面的“因为”、“由于”相呼应 ◇ 所以 is used in the complex sentence of cause and effect to connect two or more clauses, usually echoing to 因为 or 由于 that appears ahead:

① 我考试前认真复习了，**所以**成绩还可以。I got good marks in the examination for I made a thorough revision before it.

② 因为他今天不在家，**所以**，你打电话到他家也找不着他。You cannot reach him even you phone his place for he's out today.

③ 由于天降大雨，**所以**运动会改期了。The date of the sports meet was put off because of the heavy rain.

也可以把原因或理由放在后面讲，带“所以”的分句提前，这时，“所以”可说成“(之)所以” ◇ It is also possible to defer the cause or reason and put the clause with 所以 ahead, then 所以 can also be said as(之)所以:

④ 他(**之**)**所以**能将公司办起来，是因为有朋友们的大力支持。The reason why he was able to set up the business is that he got help from his friends.

一般说来，“于是”、“所以”是不能互换的 ◇ Usually 于是 and 所以 are not interchangeable.

▶ [因此 yīncǐ—因而 yīn'ér—所以 suǒyǐ]

愚蠢　傻

(形)　(形)

yúchǔn　shǎ

Ⓔ stupid, muddle-headed/stupid

◪ “愚蠢”和“傻”都有“不聪明”和“笨”的意思。“愚蠢”多用于书面语，“傻”多用于口语。由于语体色彩不同，音节不同，所以用法上也有所不同 ◇ 愚蠢 and 傻 both mean "not clever, stupid". 愚蠢 is mostly used in literary language and 傻 is colloquial. Besides, 愚蠢 is disyllabic and 傻 is monosyllabic, therefore they are of-

ten different in usages.

1. 做定语时,“愚蠢”后一般加“的”,“傻”前一般还要加“很”等,如“愚蠢的想法”、“很傻的想法”。在较固定的搭配中,有时“傻”后可不必加“的” ◇ As an attributive, 愚蠢 usually takes 的 after it and 傻 often takes 很, etc. before it, e.g. 愚蠢的想法, 很傻的想法. In some set phrases sometimes 傻 can do without 的:

愚蠢的姑娘——傻姑娘 foolish girl—simple-minded girl

愚蠢的事(儿)——傻事(儿) foolish thing—silly thing

愚蠢的主意——傻主意 foolish idea—silly idea

做状语时,固定搭配中,“傻”也可直接修饰动词,如:“傻等”、“傻干” ◇ As an adverbial, in some set phrases 傻 can also qualify the verb directly, e.g. 傻等, 傻干.

做谓语时,可互换使用,但语体色彩不同 ◇ As the predicate, the two are interchangeable, but of different styles:

① 你的对手并不**愚蠢**(/**傻**),比赛前你要做好充分准备。Your rival is not silly, so you'd better be well prepared before the competition.

② 你这样做可是太**愚蠢**(/**傻**)了。You are too silly if you do it this way.

③ 这个想法实在是**愚蠢**(/**傻**)到家了。The idea is really too silly.

“愚蠢”可用在“是……的”格式中,但“傻”前必须要加“非常”、“很”等才可以 ◇ 愚蠢 can be used in the form of 是……的, but 傻 must take 非常, 很, etc. before it to be used in such a pattern:

④ 你这样做是**愚蠢**的。It's stupid of you to do it this way.

⑤ 你这样做是非常**傻**的。It's very silly of you to do so.

做补语时也可互换,但语体色彩不同 ◇ As a complement, the two are interchangeable, but of different styles:

⑥ 他变得越来越**愚蠢**(/**傻**)了。He becomes more and more stupid.

2.“傻”还有不明事理、糊涂的意思 ◇ 傻 also means "muddle-headed":

① 人们都被眼前发生的事吓**傻**了。People were dumbfounded at the scene before them.

② 平时你挺明白的,今天怎么会**傻**成这样? You are usually clever. How can you be so silly today?

③ 谈价钱时,你可别犯**傻**。When bargaining, don't be stupid.

3.“傻”还出现在下列四字语中 ◇ 傻 is also used in the following four-character set phrases:

① 你别装疯卖**傻**了。Don't play the fool.

② 这孩子看着**傻**头**傻**脑的，实际上鬼得很。The kid seems to be clumsy and stupid, but actually he is quite smart.

"傻"还有一些固定用法，如"傻乎乎"、"傻呵呵"等 ◇ 傻 has some fixed usage, for example 傻乎乎(silly/not very clever), 傻呵呵(simple-minded), etc.

与 及 以及

(连) (连) (连)

yǔ jí yǐjí

Ⓔ and/and/as well as, and

1. "与"、"及"和"以及"是连词，用于连接并列的主语、宾语、定语、状语等，书面色彩浓 ◇ 与, 及 and 以及 are all conjunctions to connect juxtaposed subjects, objects, attributives, and adverbials. They have a rather literary flavour:

① 商品的品质**及**(/**以及**)价格，均一一标明。(连接主语) The quality and prices are tagged clearly. (connecting subjects)

② 交通部门正在检查运货车辆的载重情况**及**(/**以及**)安全装置。(连接宾语) The communication department is checking the load capacity of the load-carrying vehicles and their safety equipment. (connecting objects)

③ 这件事引起了老师**及**(/**以及**)同学的深切关注。(连接定语) The incident called the attention of teachers and students alike. (connecting attributives)

④ 这笔钱对你**及**(/**以及**)对她都很重要。(连接状语) The money is important to both you and her. (connecting adverbials)

"以及"比"及"更显书面化和正式。"以及"前常可停顿。如例①可说"商品的品质，以及价格，均一一标明。" ◇ 以及 is even more literary and formal than 及 and there is often a pause before 以及. For instance, in example ① one can say 商品的品质，以及价格，均一一标明.

2. 这三个词都不能连接句子，有时可以连接谓语中并列的动词、形容词 ◇ The three words cannot connect sentences. but they can connect common adverbials or auxiliary verbs, or common objects or complements, or verbs or adjectives in the predicates:

① 整个建筑，设计**与**(/**及**)装修都十分华丽。The design and its decoration of the building are both magnificent.

② 她感到极度的不安**与**(/**及**)

焦躁。She felt very unrest and worried.

以上例①也可用“以及”,但更为书面化。如果句中有几个并列成分,“及”或“以及”放在最后。例④“以及”连接双音节词“一切”,与音节也有关系 ◇ In example ① above,以及 can also be used instead and it is more literary. If there are several elements juxtaposed,及 or 以及 is placed before the last one. In example ④,以及 can be used to connect the disyllabic word 一切 because it is disyllabic itself:

③ 天然气可以制造肥料和人造石油**及**其他许多化工产品。Fertilizer, artificial gasoline and many chemicals can be made from the natural gas.

④ 他熟悉家乡的风土人情、山山水水,**以及**其他一切的一切。He is familiar with the customs, landscape, and others of his native place.

预先 事先

(副) (名)

yùxiān shìxiān

Ⓔ in advance, beforehand/ in advance, beforehand

◪ 二者的意思都是“在事情或行动发生或进行之前,在句中常做状语,常可互换使用 ◇ Both the two words mean" before an event or action happens" they are adverbials and interchangable".

① 你应该**预先**(/**事先**)告诉我要发言,我可以准备一下。You should inform me that I will deliver a speech in advance, so I can prepare it.

② 他知道那个地方爱下雨,所以**预先**(/**事先**)买了件雨衣。He knew it was rainy there, so he bought a raincoat in advance.

③ 你应该**预先**(/**事先**)打个招呼。You should have told us in advance.

④ 他**预先**(/**事先**)已做了一些调查。He conducted some survey in advance.

二者的区别在于:“预先”着重于事情发生前的有意识的准备,而“事先”则没有这种意思,所以,对于不能预知的事情,不能用“预先”替换“事先”,如例⑤⑥ ◇ The difference is in that 预先 stresses the conscious preparation before a thing happening, while 事先 has nosuch meaning. Therefore, as for unpredictable things, 预先 can not replace 事先, such as examples⑤⑥:

⑤ 那次地震非常偶然,**事先**毫无迹象。The earthquake took place beyond our expectation, for there's no sign at all before it.

⑥ 对这次东南亚金融危机,老百姓**事先**都毫无心理准备。All

the civilians didn't expected the South Asian financial crisis.

另外,"事先"是名词,还可以做定语,带"的";"预先"是副词,只能做状语 ◇ Besides,事先 is a noun and can be used as an attributive with 的,while 预先 is an adverb and can only be used as an adverbial.

⑦ 他**事先**的态度跟现在正好相反。His attitude is different from his previous one.

⑧ 这是**事先**的安排。This is prearranged.

遇到 遇见 碰见

(动) (动) (动)

yùdào yùjiàn pèngjiàn

Ⓔ meet,come across/

meet,come across/

meet,run into

这三个短语都是动补式。表示偶然相逢(指人等)或偶然遭遇(指事物)。"碰见"更为口语化 ◇ All the three are verb-complement phrases meaning" to come across a person or thing by chance". Of the three,碰见 is the most colloquial.

① 昨天在路上**遇到**(/**遇见**/**碰见**)一位多年不见的老同学。Yesterday he came across one of his old classmates whom he had not seen for ages.

② 以后你**遇到**(/**遇见**/**碰见**)这种好书,也替我买几本。If you come across this kind of good book,please buy me some.

以上,例①用于人,例②用于事物,三个词可互换 ◇ In example ① the object is a person and in example ② it is a thing. The three words are interchangeable.

宾语为"机会"、"机遇"、"危险"、"风险"、"挑战"、"运气"等时,"遇到"的搭配能力较强,其他两个词有时也可以 ◇ If the object is 机会(chance),机遇(opportunity),危险(danger),风险(risk),挑战(challenge),运气(luck),etc.,遇到 is the best choice,but the other two will also do sometimes:

③ **遇到**危险,要随机应变。When at risk,just do what seems best.

④ 以前从来没有**遇到**过这样的好机会。I have never had such a golden opportunity before.

⑤ **遇到**这种倒霉的事,真让人哭笑不得。This kind of bad luck really makes me funny and annoying.

援助 帮助

(动) (动)

yuánzhù bāngzhù

Ⓔ help, support/help, aid

◪"援助"和"帮助"都有给以支持的意思。"援助"多用于经济、军事等大的方面,表示在人力、物力或其他行动上为别人出力;而"帮助"则多用于日常生活、工作、学习等,表示为他人提供支持 ◇ Both 援助 and 帮助 mean support. 援助 is mostly applied to economic or military matters, while 帮助 is mostly applied to daily life, work, study, etc. e. g. :

① 我们要在力所能及的范围内对他们予以**援助**。We shall give them what we can afford.

② 国际红十字会**援助**了灾区人民大批药品和衣物。The International Red Cross aided the disaster-stricken areas a host of medicine and clothing.

③ 他在学习上经常**帮助**同学。He often helped his classmates with their study.

④ 我们有责任**帮助**那些生活上有困难的人。We are responsible for helping those in need.

"帮助"可以组成兼语句、连动句,"援助"较少组成这种句式 ◇ 帮助 can make up a pivotal sentence or sentence of multiple verbs. 援助 is rarely so used:

⑤ 我们要**帮助**他克服不爱学习的缺点。We should help him overcome his shortcomings, that is, disliking study.

⑥ 孩子要主动**帮助**父母做家务。Children should help their parents with housework.

"援助"可以做定语,"帮助"较少做定语,但可说"帮助的时候"、"帮助的方式"等 ◇ 援助 can function as an attributive while 帮助 is rarely so used, but one can say 帮助的时候(helping time), 帮助的方式(helping way), etc. :

⑦ 得知她出了车祸,大家都向她伸出了**援助**之手。Everyone helped her at the news that she was suffering a traffic incident.

⑧ 县政府已把各地送来的**援助**物资送到了灾民的手中。The county government has sent the aided materials to the victims.

⑨ **帮助**的方式可以多种多样。The help ways can be various.

► [辅导 fǔdǎo—帮助 bāngzhù]

[协助 xiézhù—帮助 bāngzhù]

缘故 原因

(名) (名)

yuángù yuányīn

Ⓔ cause, reason/cause, reason

1.“缘故”和“原因”都可以指造成某种结果或引起另一件事情发生的条件或根源。“缘故”较口语化,前边的定语指“条件或根源”;“原因”用于口语、书面语均可,定语可指“条件或根源”,也可指“某种结果或另一件事情”。当前边的定语表示“条件或根源”时,二者可互换使用 ◇ Both 缘故 and 原因 mean "the condition or origin of some happening". 缘故 is more colloquial and its attributive is "the condition or origin";原因 can be used in both colloquial and literary languages and its attributive can be the condition or origin, or a certain result or happening. When the attributive indicates the condition or origin, the two words are interchangeable:

① 大气污染的**原因**多种多样,目前本地区主要是粉尘污染。The air pollution is various. The pollution in the area is dust pollution.

② 由于政治、经济、文化的**原因**(/**缘故**),许多老年人与儿孙之间产生了代沟。There is a gap between the old generation and their offspring, because of the political, economic, and cultural differences.

“缘故”常用于下列句型中,“原因”有时也可以用于这种句型 ◇ 缘故 is often used in the following sentence patterns; 原因 sometimes can also be used in these patterns:

……是因为(是由于)……的缘故,……是……的缘故.

③ 可能**是**做了手术**的缘故**(/**原因**)吧,她的体力大不如从前了。She becomes weaker and weaker maybe due to her operation.

④ 他不爱去舞厅,**是因为**他受不了那震耳欲聋的噪音的**缘故**。That he did not go to the dancing hall is because he cannot stand the loud noise.

例④使用了“因为”,所以后面一般不用“原因” ◇ 原因 is not used in example ④ because 因为 is used.

“缘故”和“原因”都可以和“什么”连用,是“为什么”的意思 ◇ Both 缘故 and 原因 can be qualified by 什么, meaning "why":

⑤ 今天他一回家就发火,弄不清是**什么缘故**(/**原因**)。He somehow became angry as soon as he got home.

⑥ 他到现在也不来电话,不知是**什么缘故**(/**原因**)。I don't know why he doesn't phone me until now.

2.“缘故”还可以构成“无缘无故”等四字语,“原因”不可以 ◇ 缘故 can also make up four-character set

phrases like 无缘无故, but 原因 cannot:

① 你**无缘无故**地生什么气呀? Why are you angry without any reason?

② 他又**无缘无故**地迟到了。He was somehow late for the class again.

3. 当"原因"前的定语指"某种结果或另一事情"时,不可与"缘故"互换 ◇ When the attributive before 原因 indicates a certain result or another matter, it cannot be replaced by 缘故:

① 你应该好好找一下这次落榜的**原因**。You should draw lessons from the failure in the entrance examination.

② 交通事故的**原因**已查明,卡车的刹车失灵了。The cause of the traffic accident has been made clear, that is, the brake of the lorry did not function then.

"原因"常用于下列句型中:"……(的)原因是……"、"……是……的(一个)原因" ◇ 原因 is often used in the following patterns:……(的)原因是……,……是……的(一个)原因.

③ 造成人口爆炸的根本**原因**是没有及时采取计划生育的政策。The basic reason for population explosion is that the government did not carry out an immediate family planning.

④ 大量砍伐树木是造成水土流失的一个主要**原因**。The main cause of soil erosion is excessive felling.

"原因"可以说"第一个原因"、"原因之一"、"根本原因"、"主要原因"等,"缘故"不可以 ◇ 原因 can appear in such patterns as 第一个原因(first reason), 原因之一(one of the reasons), 根本原因(basic reason), 主要原因(main reason), etc. 缘故 cannot.

允许　准许

(动) yǔnxǔ　(动) zhǔnxǔ

Ⓔ permit, allow/permit, allow

"允许"、"准许"这两个动词,都表示同意别人的要求,应允、答应别人做某事。但"允许"应用范围较广,可用于人,也可用于客观条件。"准许"比较正式,一般用于上级对下级、长辈对晚辈等 ◇ Both 允许 and 准许 are verbs indicating "agreement to another person's request to do something". 允许 has a wider application to people as well as objective conditions. 准许 is more formal and is usually used by the higher level to the lower level or the senior to the junior. e. g. :

① 我不**允许**你用这种态度跟我说话。You are not permitted to talk to me this way.

② 这里不**允许**(/**准许**)吸烟。No smoking here.

③ 不经**允许**(/**准许**),阅览室的杂志、报纸不能携出室外。Don't take out the magazines, newspapers out of the reading room without permission.

④ 如果时间**允许**的话,我想路过天津时顺便看一个朋友。Time permitting, I'd like to drop in one of my friends by way of Tianjin.

⑤ 他想买辆汽车,不过现在的经济条件还不**允许**。He wants to buy a car; however, he hasn't enough money.

⑥ 你要快点儿作出决定,事情发展很快,不**允许**你再拖延了。You're not allowed to put it off, for it gets along rapidly, and you'd better decide it quickly.

⑦ 军事要地,一般人是不**准许**进入的。No admittance to the military bases.

⑧ 经过校长特别**准许**,他们今晚将在这里开讨论会。With the principal's permission, they are going to have a discussion here tonight.

以上例①没有限定"我"是上级或长辈,用"允许"即可。例②③二词都可用,如用"准许"更正式些。例④⑤⑥因是客观条件,只能用"允许","准许"没有这种用法。例⑦⑧比较严肃、正式,宜用"准许" ◇ In example ① above, it is unclear as to whether 我 is a superior, so 允许 is all right. In examples ② and ③, either word will do, but 准许 is more formal. In examples ④ ⑤ and ⑥, since it is objective condition, only 允许 can be used, while 准许 cannot. Examples ⑦ and ⑧ are serious and formal, so 准许 is used.

运 (动) yùn　　运输 (动、名) yùnshū

Ⓔ transport/transport

"运"、"运输"这两个词都表示用交通工具把较多的物从一地移到另一地,也可用于较多的人。"运输"较"运"更为正式,所载物资等较多,行进路线也较长 ◇ 运 and 运输 both mean "to transport large quantity of things from one place to another"; they can also be applied to human beings of a large number. 运输 is more formal than 运 and indicates the quantity is bigger and the distance is longer.

1. 用于物资 ◇ Applying to goods and materials:

① 小张把货**运**到了附近的仓库。Xiao Zhang carried the goods to the warehouse nearby.

② 老李用小车把肥料**运**到田间。Lao Li carried the fertilizer to the field with the wheelbarrow.

以上两句，路线较短，物资较少，宜用“运” ◇ In the two examples above，运 is suitable because of shorter route and smaller quantity of goods.

③ 这条铁路线起着**运输**大动脉的作用。This railway line functions as the transportation artery.

④ 我们一定要尽快把这些物资**运输**到灾区去。We must transport these materials to the disaster area as soon as possible.

以上两句，物资较多，路线较长，宜用“运输”。但例④在口语中也可换用“运”。例③“运输大动脉”，由于音节搭配的要求和较为正式，只能用“运输” ◇ In the two examples above，运输 is better because of the bigger quantity of the goods and longer route. However，in ④运 can also be used instead in colloquial language. In ③ only 运输 can be used in 运输大动脉，because of the syllabic collocation and formality.

“运输”也是名词，如“交通运输”、“铁路运输”、“公路运输”等 ◇ 运输 is also a noun，e. g.，交通运输（traffic and transportation），铁路运输（railway transportation），公路运输（highway transportation），etc..

2. 用于人员 ◇ Applying to human beings：

用于人员时，搭配较少 ◇ There are relatively few collocations when applied to human beings：

① 这些车辆是**运**兵车。The vehicles are for carrying soldiers.

② 政府已将大批物资及医护人员**运输**到地震灾区。The government has sent a body of goods and paramedics to the quake-stricken areas.

以上例 ①“运兵”是习惯搭配；例②在口语中也可换用“运” ◇ In example ①，运兵 is an idiomatic collocation；in example ② 运 can be used instead in colloquial language.

3. 其他 ◇ Other usages：

“运”还可表示使用，限于“运笔”；表示集中力气，限于“运气”、“运了一口气”等 ◇ 运 can also mean "to use"，which is limited to 运笔（wield the writing brush）and to concentrate one's strength，which is limited to 运气（direct one's strength，through concentration to a part of the body），运了一口气（an instance of such），etc.

运送 输送

(动) (动)

yùnsòng shūsòng

Ⓔ transport, convey/ transport, convey

◪"运送"、"输送"这两个词都可表示移送物资或人员 ◇ Both 运送 and 输送 mean "to transport or transfer goods, materials or personnel."

1. 用于物,一般用"运送" ◇ When applied to goods, usually 运送 is used:

① 交通部门及时把农用物资**运送**到了农村。The communication department has sent the agricultural goods to the countryside.

② 这批货物要在三天之内**运送**到客户手中。The goods should be delivered to the customers within three days.

③ 这种车是用来**运送**煤炭的。The truck is for coal transportation.

用"输送"时,一般指通过管道或特定的路线 ◇ 输送 usually means "transport through pipes or specific route":

④ 电网把电流**输送**到各地。The electricity networks carry the electricity to every place.

⑤ 我们要想办法把药液**输送**到患者体内。We must find a way to infuse the liquid drug into the patient's body.

⑥ 公司通过网络配送的方式把鲜奶及时**输送**到城市的各个角落。The company transports in time the fresh milk to every corner of the city through its network.

例⑥也可换用"运送"。但用"输送"时更侧重其目的性和特定的路线网络等 ◇ In example ⑥运送 can replace 输送, but 输送 stresses the destination and the specific network of route.

2. 用于人,表示移送较多的人员,"输送"还可用于抽象意义 ◇ When applied to people, it means "to transport a large number of people". 输送 can also be used in abstract meaning. e. g.:

① 在寒暑假期间,**输送**学生是铁路部门的一项重要任务。To transport students during the winter and the summer vacations is an important task of the railway department.

② 为城市建设**输送**新鲜血液是本校的办学宗旨。To provide new talents to the city construction is the primary mission of our school.

③ 建校40年来,我们学校已向社会**输送**了大批高层次的外语人才。Since its construction 40 years ago, our university has provided the society with large numbers of advanced foreign language talents.

Z

咱们 (代) zánmen　我们 (代) wǒmen

Ⓔ we, us/we, us

◥ "咱们"、"我们"这两个代词都表示复数第一人称。但"我们"一般指对话双方中的己方；"咱们"指对话双方 ◇ Both 咱们 and 我们 mean "we" or "us". However, 我们 usually indicates the talking side in a conversation, while 咱们 indicates both sides.

① **我们**坐桌子这边，你们坐那边。We sit on this side; you on that side.

② **我们**的意见请你们认真考虑。Please take our suggestions into earnest consideration.

③ **咱们**一块儿干吧，我一个人干不了。Let's do it together, for I cannot finish it by myself.

④ 这个方案还有些问题，**咱们**一起再研究一下吧。There's something wrong with the plan, so let's discuss it again.

但在口语中，"我们"有时也可包括对方。如例④"咱们"也可换用"我们" ◇ But in colloquialism 我们 can also include the opposite side as in example ④, where 我们 can replace 咱们.

"我们"口语中也可指"我" ◇ In colloquial, 我们 sometimes means 我.

⑤ **我们**家离这儿很远。I live far away from here.

⑥ 在**我们**国家，妇女结了婚照样出来工作。In my country, married women continue working as they do before marriage.

暂时 (形) zànshí　一时 (形、名) yīshí

Ⓔ for the time being/
for a short while, momentary; moment

◥ "暂时"、"一时"都有时间短的意思，都是非谓形容词。但"一时"除形容词外，还是名词。虽然同是形容词，义项和用法也有所不同 ◇ Both 暂时 and 一时 mean "a short time" and both are adjectives which cannot function as the predicate of a sentence. Besides being an adjective, 一时 is also a noun. Though 暂时 and 一时 are both adjectives, their meaning and usage are not the same.

1. 暂时(形)

表示只是在短时间之内的,做定语、状语,如做谓语时,要放在"是……的"之中 ◇ 暂时 as adj. ,indicates within a short time. It can function as an attributive or adverbial. It cannot function as the predicate of a sentence unless it is used in the phrase 是暂时的(temporary):

① 这个新措施**暂时**(/**一时**)还不能实行。The new measure cannot be carried out at present.

② 服用这种药后有些口渴,这是**暂时**的现象,很快就会消失。You will feel a little thirsty after taking the medicine; that side effect is temporary and will disappear soon.

③ 因线路发生故障,这个地区**暂时**停电。There is temporary power failure here for there's something wrong with the electricity circuit.

④ 他们**暂时**在这里住几天,很快就搬走。They stayed here temporarily, and they would move very soon.

⑤ 这工作是**暂时**的,干完我就走。This is a temporary job, and I will leave here as soon as I finish it.

以上例①"暂时"可换成"一时",因后面为否定形式(详见下),其他各例不能用"一时"替换 ◇ In example ① above,暂时 can be replaced by 一时(the detailed explanation will come next), because it is followed by a negative phrase(the detailed explanation will come next). In all the other examples,暂时 cannot be so replaced.

2. 一时(形)

(1)也表示只是在短时间内,有时较"暂时"表示的时间段略长,常用于否定形式或带有否定意思的句子,做状语 ◇ 一时 as an adj. also indicates within a short time, but seems longer than the time indicated by 暂时. It is mostly used in a negative sentence or a sentence with negative sense, and functions as an adverbial. e. g. :

① 这么厚的一本书,我**一时**(/**暂时**)看不完,下星期再还你。I cannot finish such a thick book at a time, so I will return it to you next week.

② 这里**一时**(/**暂时**)安排不了这么多人的工作。There are no enough vacancies for so many people at a time.

③ 这么复杂的问题,我**一时**很难回答出来。It's too difficult for me to answer the question for the moment.

有时也可做定语 ◇ Sometimes it

can function as an attributive:

④ 做事要扎扎实实,不能只凭**一时**的热情。You should work steadily and cannot rely on an instant's enthusiasm.

以上例①②也可换用"暂时" ◇ In examples ① and ② above 暂时 can be used instead.

(2)表示(某些情况、现象等)不是经常地,是偶然地(发生),做状语 ◇ 一时 indicates (some situations, phenomenon, etc. occur) irregularly, only accidentally, functioning as an adverbial:

⑤ 他**一时**高兴,给大家唱了一段京剧。He sang us an act of Peking Opera at a temporary pleasure.

⑥ 他**一时**来了兴致,约几个朋友去爬山了。He invited a few friends to go climbing on impulse.

以上例⑤⑥不能用"暂时"替换 ◇ In examples ⑤and ⑥above, 暂时 cannot replace 一时.

3. 一时(名)

(1) 表示短时间 ◇ 一时 as a noun indicates a short time:

① 今天我值班,**一时**也不敢离开。I'm on duty today, and I cannot leave the work for a short while.

② 休息一下吧,用功也不在这**一时**。Take a break, and I think diligence does not necessarily mean this moment.

③ 我看**一时**半会儿他是不会答复我们的。I think he will make no reply to us in a little while.

(2) 表示一个时期 ◇ Indicating a period of time:

④ 这种样式的高跟鞋曾经风行**一时**。The high-heeled shoes of this style were once in fashion.

⑤ **此一时,彼一时**,这次的事情怎么能跟上次相比呢? How can you compare it with last one? For time is different.

"此一时,彼一时"是成语 ◇ 此一时,彼一时 (Times have changed) is an idiom.

"一时……一时"表示不同的动作、状态等在某个短时间内交替进行或出现,"暂时"不能这样用 ◇ 一时……一时 indicates that different actions or situations take place alternatively in a short time. 暂时 has no such usage:

⑥ 病人的病情不稳定,**一时**好,**一时**坏。The patient's symptom is unstable, for it is now better and now worse.

⑦ 她**一时**哭**一时**笑,到底怎么回事? What's wrong with her? Now cry, now laugh.

⑧ 你**一时**这样说,**一时**那样说,哪个是真的? Which is correct? For you told us about it differently at different time.

赞美 赞扬

(动) (动)

zànměi zànyáng

Ⓔ praise/praise

◪"赞美"和"赞扬"都有称赞的意思。但"赞美"的对象一般是事物(如2例①②③);"赞扬"的对象多为人,有时也可以是事物,有口头表扬的意思(如3例①②) ◇ Both 赞美 and 赞扬 mean to praise. The object of 赞美 is mostly a thing (e.g. examples ①②③ of 2); the object of 赞扬 is usually a person, but may also be a thing sometimes, when it means "verbal praise (e.g. examples ①② of 3)".

1. 当对象是事物,但属于人的品德、毅力、行为、精神时,两个词可以互换(如例①②③④⑤) ◇ When the object is something that belongs to a person's moral character, willpower behavior, spirit, the two words are interchangeable (e.g. examples ①②③④⑤):

① 大家都**赞美**(/**赞扬**)小李的顽强毅力。Xiao Li's perseverance was widely praised.

② 厂里人都**赞美**(/**赞扬**)他尊老爱幼的良好品德。He was praised for his good virtue of respecting the old and cherishing the young by his factory staff.

③ 爱护公物的行为应受到人们的**赞美**(/**赞扬**)。Taking care of public property should be approved.

④ 他一心为公的精神值得**赞美**(/**赞扬**)。He should be praised for his dedication to the people.

⑤ 听到一句**赞美**(/**赞扬**)的话,他就不知道东西南北了。He was carried away at a compliment.

2. 当"赞美"的对象是事物(自然物、土地、艺术品等)时,不可用"赞扬"替换 ◇ When the object of 赞美 is something (of the natural world, land, work of art, etc.), it cannot be replaced by 赞扬:

① 我们放声高歌,**赞美**我们的祖国。We eulogize our motherland with our sonorous songs.

② 他用诗一般的语言**赞美**阔别多年的故乡。He eulogized his picturesque native place with his poem-like words that he hadn't return to for ages.

③ 站在"蒙娜丽莎"的画像前,大家情不自禁地**赞美**起来。We cannot help admiring before the painting *Mona Lisa*.

3. 当"赞扬"的对象是人时,不可与"赞美"互换使用 ◇ When the object of 赞扬 is a person, it is not interchangeable with 赞美:

① 大家都**赞扬**他是新时代的雷锋。He is praised as today's Lei Feng—a role model of good deeds in China.

② 李主任把小张**赞扬**了一番。Director Li praised Xiao Zhang today.

▶[称赞 chēngzàn—赞美 zànměi]

遭到 (动) zāodào 遭受 (动) zāoshòu 受到 (动) shòudào

Ⓔ meet with, suffer/ suffer, sustain/ suffer

"遭到"、"遭受"都指遇到不利、不幸或损害,宾语都是坏事或不如意的事;"受到"有遭受的意思,还有接受、得到的意思;宾语可以是坏事,也可以是好事。三者的宾语多为动词性的,个别是名词性的(如例④) ◇ The verbs 遭到 and 遭受 both mean "to suffer harm, misfortune or damage". Their objects are all things bad or undesirable. 受到, meaning "to suffer or to receive, to get"; its object may be something bad or good. The objects of all the three verbs are mostly verbal, and only a few are nominal (as in example ④).

① 部队在穿过封锁线时,**遭到**(/**遭受**/**受到**)敌人的拦截。The army was attacked by the enemy while crossing the block line area.

② 他过去曾经**遭到**(/**遭受**/**受到**)过不公平的待遇。He was once treated unfairly in the past.

③ 这里水土流失严重,年年**遭到**(/**遭受**/**受到**)洪水的威胁。The area was threatened by floods every year because its severe soil erosion.

④ 五年前,这里**遭到**(/**遭受**/**受到**)地震灾害。The area was hit by earthquake five years ago.

⑤ 无线电波**遭到**(/**遭受**/**受到**)雷电的干扰,声音不清楚。The electromagnetic waves are disturbed and the sound is not clearly.

⑥ 他的小说**遭到**(/**遭受**/**受到**)舆论的批评。His novel was criticized by the public.

⑦ 他们的试验**遭到**失败,还要从头做起。They failed in their experiment and they had to do it from the very scratch.

⑧ 他的提案**遭到**反对。His proposal was opposed.

以上例①~⑥"遭到"、"遭受"、"受到"可以互换,例⑧中"遭到反对"是习惯搭配,这是个别的,"遭受"、"受到"都不能这样用。用"遭到"或"遭受"时,后果往往更严重些。如例⑤一般说"无线电波受到干扰",除非强调问题的严重性,才用"遭到"、"遭受"。例⑦试验失败,用"遭到",用"遭受"、"受到"时往往强调外力的影响,而试验失败没有这个意思 ◇ In examples ①~⑥, 遭到,遭受,受到 are interchangeable. In example ⑧遭到反对 is an idiomatic expression which neither 遭受 nor 受到 can be so used. When 遭到 or 遭受 is used, the consequence is usually more serious, as in example ⑤ where one usually says 无线电波受到干扰,and 遭到 or 遭受 is not used unless one wants to stress the seriousness of the problem. In example ⑦ the experiment ended in failure, so 遭到 is used. If 遭受 or 受到 is used, it stresses the influence from a foreign force. However, the failure of experiment has no such meaning. More examples:

⑨ 刘教授的学术报告**受到**热烈欢迎。Professor Liu's academic report was popular.

⑩ 客人**受到**主人的热情招待。The guests were treated cordially by the host.

⑪ 他因学习成绩优秀,**受到**老师的表扬。He was praised for his good school performance.

⑫ 他从小**受到**良好的教育。He was well educated since a child.

以上例⑨~⑫有接受、得到的意思,宾语是褒义的,只能用"受到",不能用"遭到"、"遭受" ◇ In examples ⑨~⑫受到 means "to receive, to get", and the object is something desirable; therefore, only 受到 can be used, not 遭到 or 遭受.

怎么 (代) zěnme　怎么样 (代) zěnmeyàng　怎样 (代) zěnyàng

Ⓔ how, why/how/how

"怎样"较书面化,"怎么"、"怎么样"书面、口语都常用 ◇ 怎样 is more literary; 怎么, 怎么样 are used both in literary and colloquial language:

1. 用于询问方式,三个词可换用 ◇ To inquiry about the ways, the three words are interchangeable:

① 到王府井,我该**怎么**(/**怎么样**/**怎样**)走呢? How can I get to the Wangfujing Street?

② 你知道菠萝是**怎么**(/**怎么样**/

怎样)种植的吗? Do you know how the pineapple grows?

③ 请告诉我这种电脑**怎么**(/**怎么样**/**怎样**)用。How to operate the computer?

2. 用于询问原因,用"怎么" ◇ In asking for a reason,怎么 is used:

① 他**怎么**没来上课? Why did he not come to class?

② 小李今天**怎么**不高兴呢? Why is Xiao Li unhappy today?

③ 天**怎么**老不晴呢? Why is it always overcast?

3. 用于询问性质状态等,三个词可换用 ◇ To ask for the nature or state of something,the three words are interchangeable:

① 这是**怎么**回事? What's wrong with it?

② 你说一说,那是**怎么**(/**怎么样**/**怎样**)一本书呢? Please tell me what kind of book it is.

③ 你们都说那个学生很出色,她到底**怎么**(/**怎么样**/**怎样**)出色呢? You think the student is excellent. Tell me how she is.

以上三句,除了例①为常见搭配外,三个词可换用。但有时"怎么样"和"怎样"可加"的",如例②可说"怎么样(/怎样)的一本书"。例③也是如此 ◇ In the three examples above,with the exception of example ①, which is a set phrase,the three words are interchangeable. Sometimes 怎么样 and 怎样 can take 的;for example,example ② can be said as 怎么样(怎样)的一本书. It is the same case with example ③.

4. 用于虚指、任指,三个词可换用 ◇ When used to indicate nature,condition or manner in general, the three words are interchangeable:

① 我不觉得这个电影**怎么**(/**怎么样**/**怎样**)好。I don't think the film is very good.

② 客人一定要走,**怎么**(/**怎么样**/**怎样**)留也留不住。The guest was determined to go, so we could not keep him stay.

③ 他**怎么**(/**怎么样**/**怎样**)问,你就**怎么**(/**怎么样**/**怎样**)回答。You can answer him by his request.

5. 用于询问情况,做谓语、补语,用"怎么样"或"怎样";但加"了"后可用"怎么",限于表示情况的改变,做谓语 ◇ To ask about a situation,怎么样 or 怎样 is used as the predicate or complement. 怎么 can also be used sometimes when 了 is followed:

① 今天天气**怎么样**(/**怎样**)?(谓语) What's it like today? (predicate)

② 她唱得**怎么样**(/**怎样**)?(补语)How did you like her song?

Z

(complement)

③ 他的病**怎么样**(/**怎样**)了?(+"了") How's his illness? (+了)

④ 你怎么了?是不是不舒服?(+"了") What's wrong with you? Are you not feeling well? (+了)

"不怎么样"或"不怎样"可用于指代情况,表示不太好 ◇ 不怎么样 or 不怎样 can be used euphemistically to mean "not very good":

⑤ 我的汉语**不怎么样**。I cannot speak Chinese well.

⑥ 这个人工作态度**不怎么样**。The man's work is so-so.

增加 增长

(动) (动)

zēngjiā zēngzhǎng

Ⓔ increase, raise, add/ increase, rise, grow

◪ 动词"增加"、"增长"都有在原有基础上加多的意思。"增加"多侧重于数量上的加多,可用于具体事物或抽象事物,使用范围广;"增长"不仅表示数量上的加多,更侧重于程度上的提高,多用于抽象事物 ◇ The verbs 增加 and 增长 both mean "to become more on the original base". 增加, stressing the increase in quantity, is applied to concrete or abstract things and has a wide usage, whereas 增长 not only indicates the increase in quantity, but stresses the raise in level and is mostly applied to abstract things. e. g. :

① 车间里又**增加**了几台新机器。There are a few more new machines in the workshop.

② 这学期班上**增加**了两位新同学。There are two new comers in our class this term.

③ 你要控制饮食,体重不能再**增加**了。You should be on diet, for you cannot put on any weight.

④ 这个季度工业生产值又**增加**(/**增长**)了4个百分点。The industry production has increased 4 percent this season.

⑤ 工厂要**增加**产量,也要注意提高产品的质量。A factory should not only pay attention to increasing the output, but also improving the products' quality.

⑥ 小孙子的到来,给老人的生活**增加**了许多乐趣。The old man derived great pleasure from his grandson's coming.

⑦ 有问题尽量自己解决,别给人家**增加**麻烦。Don't trouble others. You'd better deal with the difficulty yourself.

以上各例中,只有例④的"增加"可以用"增长"替换。"增长"表示数量上的加多时,一般不用于具体的几个,而适用于百分之几或几倍

◇ In the examples above, only 增加 in example ④ can be replaced by 增长. When 增长 means "the increase in quantity", the actual number is not used, but the percentage or fold. e. g. :

⑧ 今年全市大专院校招收的新生,比去年**增长**(/**增加**)了30%。The enrollment of all the colleges in the city has increased 30 percent compared with that of last year.

⑨ 这个城市商品的出口量在逐年**增长**(/**增加**)。The goods export is increasing annually.

⑩ 在几年的工作实践中,他大大**增长**了才干。He has improved his abilities greatly these years.

⑪ 这些科学普及读物,对中、小学生知识的**增长**很有帮助。These scientific books are helpful for the students of primary and secondary schools.

⑫ 常常出去旅行参观可以**增长**见识。Traveling and visiting often can broaden your horizon.

增强 加强

(动) zēngqiáng (动) jiāqiáng

Ⓔ strengthen, enhance/strengthen, enhance

◥ "增强"和"加强"都有"使之更强"的意思。对象多为抽象事物。"增强"着重在质量上,表示在原有的基础上增进、加强,宾语多为名词(如例①②);"加强"着重增加事物的强度或功效,宾语多为动词(如例④⑤)

◇ Both 增强 and 加强 mean "to strengthen". The object is mostly abstract things. 增强 means "to enhance or strengthen the quality on the original base" and the object is usually a noun (e. g. ①②). 加强 stresses the increase of strength or effect, and the object is mostly a verb (e. g. ③④):

① 体育锻炼可以**增强**体质。Physical exercise can improve your health.

② 这次考试成绩不错,**增强**了他学习的信心。The nice performance in this examination gives him more confidence in learning.

③ 我们要在全国**加强**法制教育。Legal education should be strengthened all over the country.

④ 现在的中学生整天忙于学习,身体素质普遍下降,应**加强**体育锻炼。The middle-school student is in growing poor health for he has been studying all day long. It's time for him to do more physical exercise to improve his health.

当"加强"的宾语是名词时,常可以和"增强"互换使用 ◇ When the object of 加强 is a noun, it is often interchangeable with 增强：

加强（/**增强**）自觉性/纪律性 strengthen consciousness/discipline

加强（/**增强**）法制观念 enhance the awareness of law

当宾语是"团结"、"影响"、"建设"等这些兼为名词、动词时，"加强"也可以和"增强"互换使用 ◇ When the object is 团结，影响，建设，etc.，which are both nouns and verbs，加强 and 增强 are also interchangeable，e. g.：

加强（/**增强**）团结 strengthen unity

加强（/**增强**）影响 enhance influence

加强（/**增强**）建设 enhance construction

扎实 实在

（形） （形）

zhāshi shízài

Ⓔ steadfast，down-to-earth/steadfast，real

◪ "扎实"和"实在"都可指工作、学习、做学问踏实、不浮躁，可互换使用 ◇ Both 扎实 and 实在 mean "down-to-earth，not impetuous in work or study" and are interchangeable：

① 无论工作还是学习，他都非常**扎实**（/**实在**）。Whether study or life，he is devoted.

② 李教授的文学功底很**扎实**（/**实在**）。Professor Li has a good mastery of literature.

"扎实"常重叠为 AABB 式，"实在"有时也可以重叠 ◇ 扎实 is often reduplicated into 扎扎实实，while 实在 is not so often used：

③ 你先**扎扎实实**地学一年英语再开始工作。You'd better start to work after one-year steady English learning.

④ 有了**扎扎实实**的工作作风，才能使教学和科研水平不断提高。Only a down-to-earth way can ensure the constant improvement of your ability in teaching and scientific research.

⑤ 他做什么事情都**实实在在**的。He works in a down-to-earth way.

"扎实"在口语中还有情绪安定的意思，"实在"没有这个意思 ◇ 扎实 in colloquial language also means "to be at ease"，while 实在 has no such meaning：

⑥ 女儿走后一直没有消息，妈妈心里总不**扎实**。The mother couldn't feel at ease after her daughter's leaving.

"扎实"还有结实的意思，"实在"没有这个意思 ◇ 扎实 also means "sturdy"，but 实在 has no such meaning：

⑦ 这包行李捆得很**扎实**。The package was packed tightly.

▶［确实 quèshí—真实 zhēnshí—实在 shízài］

占领 （动） zhànlǐng　占有 （动） zhànyǒu

Ⓔ occupy, capture/own, possess

◪“占领”指用武力或其他强有力的方法占据“领土”或“领域”等，通常用于军事、政治和商业方面 ◇ 占领 means "to occupy land or territory with military or other force". It is usually used in military, political or commercial aspect:

① **占领**别国的领土是侵略行为。Occupying the territory of other's countries is aggression.

② 1945 年 5 月 2 日，苏军**占领**柏林。In May 2, 1945, the USSR army occupied Berlin.

③ 我们一定要积极进取，努力开拓和**占领**新的科技领域。We are determined to keep on advancing and striving for a new scientific field.

④ 这个系列的产品**占领**了不少国内市场的份额。The series products have occupied a big part of market.

“占有”有拥有、居于和掌握的意思，宾语可以是人或事物，从具体到抽象，适用范围较广 ◇ 占有 means "to possess and own", and the object can be a person or a thing either concrete or abstract. It can be applied to a wide scope:

⑤ 王经理用卑鄙的手段**占有**了她。Manager Wang raped her in a mean way.

⑥ 他**占有**公司 10% 的股份。He has 10 percent shares of the company.

⑦ 这位诗人的作品在我国古代文学中**占有**一定的位置。The poet's poems occupied an important place in Chinese ancient poetry.

⑧ 日益壮大的个体经济在我国国民经济中**占有**重要的地位。The ever-enlarging individual businesses have occupied more and more important place in the whole country's economy.

⑨ 加工业在进出口贸易中**占有**相当大的比例。The manufacturing trade accounts for quite a little part in the total of import and export.

⑩ 机电、服装、水海产品在这个省出口商品中仍**占有**很大优势。Mechanic products, costume, and seafood accounts for a large part in the export commodity of this province.

⑪ 多年的教学实践使她得以**占有**许多宝贵的第一手资料。Many years' teaching enabled

her to have a lot of valuable research materials.

“占领”虽然可以说“占领市场”，但不能与“率”搭配；但“占有”可以，如“市场占有率” ◇ Although one can say 占领市场(dominate the market)，占领 cannot be used with 率(rate). But one can say 占有率，e.g. 市场占有率(market share)：

⑫ 如今，这个品牌的胶卷市场**占有率**已达到了35%。At present, this brand of film has occupied 35 percent of the market.

障碍 (动、名) zhàng'ài　妨碍 (动) fáng'ài

Ⓔ hinder, obstruct/ hamper, obstruct

动词“障碍”和“妨碍”都指造成一定的阻碍，使事物不能顺利进行 ◇ The verbs 障碍 and 妨碍 both mean "to obstruct and cause hindrance to progress".

1.“妨碍”的对象可以是交通、工作、进步、学习、团结、发展等，但“障碍”不能以这些为对象 ◇ The object of 妨碍 can be communication, work, progress, study, unity, development, etc., but these cannot be the object of 障碍.

① 这些违章建筑**妨碍**交通，必须马上拆除。These illegal building must be pulled down at once for they made traffic difficult.

② 柜子放在这里**妨碍**别人走路。The cupboard is in the way.

③ 计划经济体制**妨碍**了经济的发展。Planned economy hindered the development of our economy.

④ 我们在这里说话，会不会**妨碍**你学习？Would we disturb you if we speak here?

⑤ 你这样做会**妨碍**大家的团结。His doing so will have influence on our unity.

2.“障碍”的对象只能是“眼睛”、“视线”等，可以和“妨碍”互换使用 ◇ The object of 障碍 can only be 眼睛，视线，etc.，障碍 and 妨碍 are interchangeable：

① 这排高大的楼房**障碍**(/**妨碍**)了我们的视线。The tall building obstructs our view.

② 名利**障碍**(/**妨碍**)了他的眼睛，使他变得鼠目寸光。The fame screens his view and makes him shortsighted.

3.“障碍”还是名词，指阻挡前进的事物，“妨碍”不是名词 ◇ 障碍 is also a noun meaning "obstacle or barrier", but 妨碍 is not a noun：

① 为了加快国有企业的体制改

Z

革，必须消除各种思想**障碍**。In order to fasten the reform of state-owned enterprises, we must eliminate the wrong ideas.

② 要想使事业成功，我们就要排除前进道路上的一切**障碍**。To make our business successful, we must remove all the obstacles in our way.

③ 继母与孩子之间总是隔着一层难以消除的**障碍**。There is an irremovable obstacle between the stepmother and the child.

这么 这样

（代） （代）

zhème zhèyàng

Ⓔ so, such/so, such, like this

1. 指代程度，多用“这么” ◇ When indicating degree, 这么 is used:

① 这东西**这么**贵，我不买了。I cannot afford to buy such expensive goods.

② 弟弟已经有桌子**这么**高了。The little brother is as tall as the table.

③ 教室里怎么**这么**吵？Why is it so noisy in the classroom?

有时也可用“这样”，但“这么”更口语化一些 ◇ 这样 can also be used instead, but it is not so colloquial as 这么.

2. 指代方式，两个词都可以用，“这么”更为口语化，有时可加“一” ◇ When indicating way or manner, either will do. 这么 is more colloquial, and 一 can be added sometimes:

① 这个汉字应该**这么**（/**这样**）写吗？Is the Chinese character written this way?

② 大家**这么**（/**这样**）一挤，挤倒了一个人。Your pushing this way made a person fall to the floor.

③ **这么**（/**这样**）干太慢，要换一种方法。Doing this way is too slow, and we'd better change another way to do it.

有时可用“动词 + 这么 + 动量词” ◇ Sometimes the phrase "verb + 这么 + verbal measure word" is used:

④ 这首歌我只练习过**这么**两遍，还唱不好呢。I only practised the song twice, and I cannot sing it.

3. 指代性质、状态（不直接修饰形容词），用“这样” ◇ When indicating nature or state (but not qualify the adjective directly), 这样 is used:

① **这样**的好书我很喜欢。I like such good books.

② 我没见过**这样**的大雪。I have ever seen such heavy snow.

③ 他原来是**这样**一种人。He's such a man!

4. 指代动作或情况,用“这样” ◇ To indicate " action or situation" ,这样 is used:

① 只有**这样**,才能学好汉语。(“这样”表示使用某种学习方法等)Only in this way, you can learn Chinese well. (这样 means" to use a certain study method)"

② 老师重新讲了一遍,又举了几个例子,**这样**我才懂了。I didn't understand it until the teacher told me again and gave me some examples.

③ 你向她道歉了?对,你应该**这样**!Did you apologize to her? ——You are right if you do this way.

真 (形、副) zhēn　真正 (形) zhēnzhèng

Ⓔ real; really/real

“真”、“真正”这两个词都表示真实、不假。都是非谓形容词,如“真人真事”、“真的情况”,“真正的东北人参”、“真正的人”等。两个词的区别是:“真正”除了表示“真实”,还有名实相符等意义。如“真人真事”只是就不虚假而言,“真正的人”还有人格高尚的含义。“真(的)房子”只就不是假布景等而言,“真正的房子”还指够标准,等等。同时,两个词音节不同,“真”可直接修饰单音节名词,“真正”不能。但“真的东北人参”和“真正的东北人参”并无区别 ◇ 真 and 真正 both mean " real, not false", and are so-called non-predicate adjectives (adjectives which, unlike most adjectives, cannot function as the predicate of a sentence), e. g. 真人真事(real people and real events),真的情况(fact),真正的东北人参(genuine ginseng of northeastern China),真正的好人(a true good man), etc. The difference between the two words is that, besides being real, 真正 also has the meaning of being worthy of the name and reality. 真人真事 only means " real story or real persons and events", while 真正的人 means " noble-minded person". 真(的)房子 only means " it is not a false setting", whereas 真正的房子 means " a house up to a certain standard". Besides, 真 can qualify a monosyllabic noun, but 真正 cannot. However, 真的东北人参(real northeastern ginseng) and 真正的东北人参(real northeastern ginseng) are exactly the same.

“真”还可出现于四字语中,如“真心诚意”、“真知灼见”、“去伪存真"等 ◇ 真 is often used in four-character set phrases, such as 真心诚意(genuinely and sincerely),真知灼见(real knowledge and deep insight),去伪存真(eliminate the false and retain the true),etc.

形容词"真"还表示真切、清楚确实,常做补语 ◇ The adjective 真 also means "clear,vivid" and often functions as a complement:

① 这么小的字,你看得**真**吗? Can you see clearly the small writing?

② 这位播音员,字音咬得很**真**。The announcer speaks clearly.

"真正"不能这样用 ◇ 真正 cannot be so used.

"真"又是副词,表示的确;形容词"真正"也可做状语,表示的确或非虚假。"真正"略显强调 ◇ 真 is also an adverb meaning "really". The adjective 真正 can also function as an adverbial meaning really. 真正 is more emphatic:

③ 他**真**(/**真正**)够朋友! He's a good friend indeed.

④ 我**真**(/**真正**)佩服他! I admire him very much.

⑤ 他们俩**真**(/**真正**)合不来。They two can't get along well indeed.

在一些口语短句中,用"真"(副) ◇ In some colloquial phrases 真(adverb) is used:

⑥ **真**贵! How expensive it is!

⑦ **真**好吃! How delicious it is!

⑧ 你**真**没摔着吗? Wasn't you hurt?

这时较少用"真正"。而在书面化的词句中,常用"真正",如:"真正如实地记述了历史"、"真正实现了自我"、"真正开辟了新纪元"等等 ◇ 真正 is rarely used here. But in some literary phrases, 真正 is used,e. g. 真正如实地记述了历史(narrate the history accurately),真正实现了自我(have actually realized oneself),真正开辟了新纪元(have actually begun the new era),etc.

正在 正 在

(副) (副) (副)

zhèngzài zhèng zài

Ⓔ in process of ,in course of/ in process of/ in process of

1. 表示动作在进行中,"正在"、"正"、"在"三个词都可以用 ◇ To show that some action is in progress, 正在, 正, 在 can all be used:

① 妈妈**正在**(/**正**/**在**)忙着做晚饭。Mother is preparing supper.

② 他**正在**(/**正**/**在**)读大学。He's at college now.

③ 中国**正在**(/**正**/**在**)走向现代

化。China is marching to the modernization.

2. 处于相对静止的状态，用"正" ◇ To mean "in a quiet, motionless state", 正 is used:

① 午夜，村子里人**正**睡得香。At midnight, the villagers were sleeping soundly.

② 月亮下去了，北斗星**正**横挂在天空。The Big Dipper was shining over the sky as the moon set down.

③ 国家的经济**正**处于调整期。The country's economy is in the course of adapting.

3. 表示就是这个而不是别的，用"正" ◇ To mean "just this one and not any other", 正 is used:

① 我找的**正**是这本书。It is the very book that I'm looking for.

② **正**因为饿极了，才不应该一下子吃得很多。You shouldn't eat too much at a time just because of excessive hunger.

③ 你说到服装，这**正**是我感兴趣的话题。When it comes to the costume, that's the very thing I'm interested in.

4. 表示正好，用"正" ◇ To mean "happen to be" 正 is used:

① 我赶到会场，小王也**正**进门。When I got to the meeting, I saw Xiao Wang was coming in too.

② 钱币**正**掉在地上的一个小洞里。The coin fell into a very hole in the ground.

③ 我们这里**正**缺一个秘书，你来吧。We need a secretary here, so come to us.

5. 表示一个动作进行时，另一动作发生，用"正"或"正在" ◇ To show that while an action is in progress, another happens, 正 or 正在 is used:

① 他们**正**(/**正在**)说着话，走进一个人来。A man came in as they were talking.

② 我**正**(/**正在**)着急的时候，小王来了。Xiao Wang came in when I was in need.

③ 工人们**正**(/**正在**)施工，忽然传来一声巨响。A sudden explosion came when the construction was under way on the site.

如果一个动作将要开始时发生另一动作，用"正要"，不用"正在" ◇ If an action is just about to happen when another happens, 正要 and not 正在 is used:

④ 她**正要**打电话找小王，小王推门进来了。Xiao Wang came in just as she was to phone him.

⑤ 我**正要**去买书，他就把书送来了。He sent me the books just as I was to buy them.

6. 表示动作持续不断，三个词都可以用；有时有"着"或"呢"出

现 ◇ To show that an action is going on continuously, any of the three can be used; sometimes 着 or 呢 is also used:

① 姑娘**正**(/**在**/**正在**)等着小王。The girl is waiting for Xiao Wang.

② 这里的农民**正**(/**在**/**正在**)播种呢。The farmers here are sowing.

注意:这三个副词,"正"和"正在"没有否定形式;"在"可说"不在"(多用于双重否定)或"没在" ◇ Note: Of the three adverbs, 正 and 正在 have no negative forms; the negative form of 在 is 不在(especially used in double negatives) or 没在:

① 这里没有一个人**不在**为绿化尽力。Everyone here is exerting his or her efforts to the afforestation.

② 他**没在**看书,在看电视呢。He is not reading, but watching TV.

支持 (动) zhīchí　支援 (动) zhīyuán

Ⓔ support, sustain/ support, assist

◪ 动词"支持"、"支援"都表示通过实际行动对别人给予帮助,但在具体意义和用法上又有不同 ◇ The verbs 支持 and 支援 both mean "to help others with actual support", but their meanings and usages are not without difference.

1. 支持

(1) 表示支撑、勉强维持 ◇ 支持 means "to support, barely sustain":

① 这个木头架子**支持**不住这么重的箱子。The wood frame cannot support such heavy box.

② 他一个人**支持**这个家很不容易。It is not easy for him to support his family.

③ 只靠打营养针,病人是**支持**不了多久的。The patient cannot last long if relying on the nutrition shot.

④ 再**支持**一两天,很快就有人来接替你们了。There's somebody who will come here to take the place of you if you can be here one or two days.

⑤ 两天两夜没休息,我怕要**支持**不住了。I am afraid I cannot continue for I have no rest for two days and two nights straight.

(2)表示精神、道义上的维护和赞同,有时也包括物质上的援助(如下面例⑨),但一般不直接带表示具体物质的词做宾语,不说"他支持了500元"、"为了帮他建房,我支持他一些砖瓦”等 ◇ Indicating"to support morally",and may include material help sometimes(as in example ⑨ below),but generally does not take a concrete material word as the object. For instance one does not say 他支持了500元;为了帮他建房,我支持他一些砖瓦,etc.

⑥ 你的想法很不错,大胆地干吧,我们**支持**你。Go ahead and I will support you for your idea is nice.

⑦ 在工作上两个人互相**支持**,互相帮助。They two support and help each other with their work.

⑧ 这个建议非常好,我坚决**支持**。I'm determined to support the suggestion for it is very nice.

⑨ 我上大学的时候,大哥常常写信并寄钱来,给我很大的**支持**。When I was at college,I often received letters and money from my eldest brother,which encouraged me greatly.

⑩ 在会上你如投一张赞成票,就是对我们工程计划的大力**支持**。If you vote us at the meeting,that means you are in approval of our project plan.

以上① ~ ⑩例不能用“支援”替换 ◇ In examples ① ~ ⑩above,支援 cannot replace 支持.

2. 支援

表示用人力、物力、财力等实际行动去帮助。一般不用于个人对个人 ◇ Indicating "help with manpower,material or financial resources,etc."and is usually not applied to individual assistance:

① 这个城市派出大批教师、干部**支援**经济落后地区。The city sent a lot of teachers and cadres to aid the backward regions.

② 市里拨款500万元**支援**山区教育事业。The city earmarked funds of 5,000,000 *yuan* to the education in the mountainous areas.

③ 你们如果盖新厂房,我们可以**支援**一些水泥。We can supply you some cements if you build new factory buildings.

④ 两个地区在经济上可以互相支援。The two regions support each other's economy.

以上各例不能用“支持”替换 ◇ In the examples above,支持 cannot be used instead.

3.“支持”、“支援”前加名词、代词等做定语,嵌入“在……下”中,构成介词结构,多做状语 ◇ With an attributive of noun,pronoun,etc. 支持,支援 can be inserted in the pattern 在……下 to form a prepositional structure that functions mostly as an adverbial:

① 在领导和同事们的**支持**下,他

的研究取得了阶段性的成果。His research has made successive progress with the support of his leaders and colleagues.

② 在他们的**支持**下,我们克服了不少困难。We overcome a lot of difficulties with their support.

③ 在当地群众的**支援**下,这座森林公园终于建成了。The forest park has been completed with the help of the locals.

只得 只好

(副) (副)

zhǐdé zhǐhǎo

Ⓔ be obliged to, have to/ be obliged to, have to

"只得"和"只好"都有"不得不"的意思,表示只能这样,没有别的选择。常可互换使用。用"只得"更强调不得已的色彩,语气重一些 ◇ Both 只得 and 只好 mean " to be obliged to because there is no other choice". The two are usually interchangeable, and 只得 is more emphatic:

① 这几天我很忙,参观的事**只好**(/**只得**)以后再说。I have been busy these days, so the visiting had to be put off later.

② 我想快点儿通知他,可他家没有电话,我**只好**(/**只得**)发了一封电报。I'd like to tell him as soon as possible; however, he had no telephone, and I had to send a telegraph to him.

③ 小张的妻子住院了,他**只好**(/**只得**)一个人带孩子。Xiao Zhang had no choice but to look after his child by himself for his wife was in hospital.

④ 别人都走不开,**只好**我一个人去。I had to go by myself for the others were busy.

"只好"可用于主语前或后,"只得"一般用于主语之后,如例⑤可说"我只得一个人去" ◇ 只好 can be placed either before or after the subject, while 只得 is usually used after the subject, e. g. example ⑤ can be said as 我只得一个人去.

只要 只有

(连) (连、副)

zhǐyào zhǐyǒu

Ⓔ so long as/ if only, have to, be forced to

连词"只要"、"只有"都用于表示连接条件的复句中,但所连接的条件不同,与其呼应的关联词也不同。另外,"只有"还是副词 ◇ Both 只要 and 只有 are conjunctions used to connect the condition and the main clause in a complex sentence, but the conditions they introduce and the connectives used in correspondingly are different. 只有 is also an adverb.

1. 连词“只要”，表示充足的条件，说话人认为要求不高，有这起码的条件就能产生所求的结果，用在复句中前一分句的主语前或后，常与“就”呼应 ◇ The conjunction 只要 introduces adequate condition. The speaker considers the requirement is not high, and with this minimum condition one can get the beseeched result. It is placed either before or after the subject of the first clause, and often corresponds with 就：

① **只要**用心，就一定能学会。If only you work hard, you will learn it.

② 我**只要**有时间，就去找你。I will come to you if I have time.

③ **只要**他肯努力，这件事一定能办好。As long as he works hard, he will do a good job about it.

④ **只要**你去，我就去，不管别人去不去。Whether or not others go, I will go there if you go.

2. 连词“只有”，表示必需的惟一的条件，说话人认为要求高，别的条件不行。用在复句的前一分句，常与“才”呼应 ◇ The conjunction 只有 indicates " the only necessary condition". The speaker thinks that the requirement is high and no other condition will do. It is used in the first clause of a complex sentence and often corresponds with 才：

① **只有**用心学才能学会。You can master it as long as you are devoted to it.

② **只有**在紧急的情况下，才允许用这笔钱。The money will only be spent in case of emergency.

③ 他**只有**在最冷的时候，才穿棉衣。He will put on padded coat in case of cold weather.

④ **只有**他的父母才知道他的性格特点。Only his parents know his temper.

⑤ 他忙得很，**只有**在吃饭的时候，才能找到他。You can find him only when he is having dinner for he's very busy.

3. 副词“只有”，表示这是惟一可能做的，没有别的办法，有“只好”的意思 ◇ The adverb 只有 indicates that this is the only way out and there is not other way; it has the meaning of 只好 (cannot but) :

① 没有别的路可走，**只有**走这条小路了。We have no other road to go but to take this path.

② 雨下得这么大，登山**只有**改期了。Climbing had to be put off for it rained so heavily.

③ 他总不来，我们**只有**先走了。We had no choice but to go first for he did not come after a long time.

以上①②③各例中，两个词不能互换 ◇ In all the examples in ①②③ above, the two words are not interchangeable.

指引 引导

（动） zhǐyǐn （动） yǐndǎo

Ⓔ guide, point the way/ guide, lead

◪"指引"和"引导"都有指出方向并带领前进的意思。但"指引"着重于指点，使用的范围仅限于指示道路、方向、路线等；而"引导"还可以表示带着某人做某事，并有启发、诱导的意思。在例①②③中，两个词可以互换 ◇ Both 指引 and 引导 mean" to point the way or to guide". 指引 stresses the sense of giving directions and 引导 means" to take sb. along to do sth. by enlightening and guiding". In examples ①②③, the two words are interchangeable. :

① 这项政策**指引**（/**引导**）农民走上了改革开放的幸福之路。The policy of opening up and reforms leads farmers to the happy life.

② 守林人**指引**（/**引导**）我们走出了原始森林。The forest keeper took us out of the primeval forest.

③ 在大会精神的**指引**（/**引导**）下，农民脱贫致富的步子迈得更大了。The farmers are taking greater steps to the rich life with the guideline of the congress.

在以下各例中，只能用"引导" ◇ In the following examples, only 引导 can be used:

④ 王校长**引导**大家去各个部门参观了一遍。The Principal Wang showed the visiting delegation around each section.

⑤ 导游在前面**引导**，游客们在后面紧跟。The tour guide was before the tourist group, and the tourist followed him close.

⑥ 教师要善于**引导**学生。A teacher should be good at enlightening students.

⑦ 在老师的**引导**下，我说出了自己的真实想法。The teacher induced me to speak out my opinions.

⑧ 经过经理的一番**引导**，大伙儿一下子都明白了。Everyone understands it at once with the manager's explanation.

忠诚 忠实

(形) (形)

zhōngchéng zhōngshí

Ⓔ loyal, faithful/true, faithful

"忠诚"和"忠实"都有"真心实意"的意思,"忠诚"着重指对国家、人民、事业、朋友尽心尽力;"忠实"则指老实可靠,没有二心 ◇ Both 忠诚 and 忠实 mean "genuine and sincere". 忠诚 stresses the sense of being faithful to the country, people, undertaking, friends; 忠实 stresses being faithful, reliable and whole-hearted.

① 他一贯**忠诚**老实。He is loyal and honest all the time.

② 司法机关应**忠诚**地履行国家和人民赋予它的权力。The legitimate department should enforce the power bestowed by the people loyally.

③ 在紧要关头,他表现得非常**忠诚**。He was very loyal at its crucial stage.

④ 我们校长对教育事业的**忠诚**是有目共睹的。Everyone knows that our principal is devoted to the education cause.

⑤ 他对妻子非常**忠实**。He is very loyal to his wife.

⑥ 他的祖父是**忠实**的佛教信徒。His grandfather is the faithful believer of the Buddhism.

另外,"忠实"还有"真实"的意思 ◇ Besides, 忠实 also means "true and real":

⑦ 这篇小说**忠实**地反映了90年代中国农村发生的巨大变化。The novel is an authentic account of the great changes taking place in the countryside in 1990s.

⑧ "鞠躬尽瘁,死而后已"正是这位老将军一生的**忠实**写照。The general's whole life indicated the spirit of "giving one's best till one's death, working with devotion".

"忠诚"和"忠实"都可以带由介词"于"引导的补语,例⑨不带"于"只是一个特例 ◇ Both 忠诚 and 忠实 can take a complement introduced by 于; example ⑨ is an exception:

⑨ 作为一名人民教师,我们要**忠诚**教育事业。As a teacher for the people, we should be devoted to the education cause.

⑩ 翻译作品必须**忠实于**原文,不可胡编乱造。A translation should be faithful to the original, but not free from the original.

以上,两个词不可互换。如将例③中的"忠诚"换成"忠实"虽然是可以的,但意思有所不同,前者指尽心尽力,后者指老实 ◇ In the two examples above, the two words are not interchangeable. If 忠诚 in example ③ is replaced by 忠实, the meaning is different, with the former meaning staunch, while the latter meaning loyal.

重要 (形) zhòngyào　要紧 (形) yàojǐn

Ⓔ important/important, urgent

◪ "重要"、"要紧"都是形容词，都表示人或事物的地位、作用突出，但使用范围和意义有区别 ◇ Both 重要 and 要紧 are adjectives meaning "to matter a lot", but they have different usages and meanings.

1. "重要"表示关系、作用或意义重大，影响深，用于人或事，可做定语、谓语 ◇ 重要, meaning "to have important bearing or influence", is applied to people or things, and can function as attributive or predicate, e. g. :

① 今天广播电台将播送**重要**新闻。The radio station will broadcast important news today.

② 这个地方，战略地位十分**重要**。The place has an important strategic position.

③ 这本参考书太**重要**了，我一定要买。The reference book is very important, so I must buy it.

④ 今天的大会将有**重要**领导人参加。There are important leaders to attend the meeting today.

"重要"可加"性"构成名词 ◇ 重要 can take 性 (suffix used to denote a category) to become a noun:

⑤ 应当充分认识环境保护的**重要性**。The importance of environmental protection should be fully realized.

以上各句不能换用"要紧" ◇ In all the examples above, 要紧 cannot replace 重要.

2. "要紧"表示重要、紧急、严重，做定语、谓语等 ◇ 要紧 means "important, urgent, serious" and functions as attributive, predicate, etc. e. g. :

① 他来电话说有**要紧**(/**重要**)的事找我。He phoned me that he had something important to talk over with me.

② 对你来说，现在最**要紧**(/**重要**)的是休息。As for you, the most important thing is to take a rest.

③ 哎呀，最**要紧**(/**重要**)的一样东西，我忘了买了。My goodness! I forget to buy the most important item.

④ 他的病**要紧**吗？Is his illness serious?

⑤ 别担心，不**要紧**，我可以自己回家。It doesn't matter, and

don't worry about me. I can go home by myself.

⑥ 机器上少了一颗螺丝钉,**要紧**不**要紧**呀? Does it matter that a screw in the machine is missing?

以上例①②③"要紧"可以用"重要"替换。但用"要紧"有时语意比"重要"重,有紧迫感。例④⑤⑥"要紧"表示严重,不能用"重要"替换 ◇ In the examples①②③above,要紧 can be replaced by 重要,but 要紧 sounds more serious than 重要 and implies a sense of urgency. In examples ④⑤⑥要紧 means" serious, critical", and cannot be replaced by 重要.

周围 (名) zhōuwéi　四周 (名) sìzhōu

Ⓔ all around/all around

◪ 名词"周围"、"四周"都表示围绕人或事物的空间,一般是较近的空间。都可用于具体事物 ◇ The nouns 周围 and 四周 both mean "the space around a person or a thing,usually the near space". Both can be applied to concrete things:

① 房子**四周**有围墙。There is a wall around the house.

② 那个地区,**周围**(/**四周**)都是山。There are mountains surrounding the area.

③ 雕像的**四周**(/**周围**)都是参观的学生。There are full of students around the statue.

以上例①用"周围"也是可以的,但因重复用"围"字,不如"四周"好。表示抽象意义时,一般用"周围" ◇ In example ① above 周围 can also be used, but there will be two 围,so it is better to use 四周. When indicating something abstract,周围 is generally used:

④ 领导者要关心**周围**群众的生活。A leader should care about the mass's life.

⑤ 大家都冷言冷语,使他觉得**周围**的气氛不对。Everyone's cold words made him feel something wrong.

逐步 (副) zhúbù　逐渐 (副) zhújiàn

Ⓔ step by step, progressively/gradual,by degrees

◪ 副词"逐步"、"逐渐"都表示事物的发展、变化缓慢,但二词的侧重点不同 ◇ The adverbs 逐步 and 逐渐 both indicate that the development or change of something is slow,but they have different stresses.

1.“逐步”表示事物的发展、变化,一步一步地慢慢进行,特别侧重有意识、有计划、有步骤地(进行),一般修饰动词或动词性词语 ◇ 逐步 indicates that the development or change is slow, step by step. It stresses the sense of something being done consciously according to a plan. It usually qualifies a verb or a verbal phrase:

① 调查研究工作在**逐步**(/**逐渐**)深入。The research work has been made further step by step.

② 国民的文化素质正在**逐步**(/**逐渐**)提高。The citizen's quality has been improved little by little.

③ 改革计划已开始**逐步**实行。The reform plan has been carried out gradually.

④ 我们要逐步降低生产成本,**逐步**提高产品质量。The production cost should be reduced gradually and the products quality should be improved gradually.

⑤ 问题要**逐步**解决,不可能一下子就有结果。The problem should be solved bit by bit, and cannot be solved at a time.

以上例①②也可用“逐渐”,但侧重点不同 ◇ In examples ① and ② above, 逐渐 can be used instead, but with different stress.

2.“逐渐”表示行为状态等缓慢、连续地发展、变化,有时含有符合自然过程的意思,可修饰动词、形容词及形容词性词语 ◇ 逐渐 indicates that a behavior or a state develops and changes gradually and continuously sometimes it implies the meaning of fitting natural process. It can qualify a verb, adjective or adjectival phrase:

① 他虽然是个南方人,但在北方工作多年,已经对这里的饮食、气候**逐渐**习惯了。He, a man from the south, has been working in the north for ages, and comes to get used to the food and climate.

② 他的学习成绩确实在**逐渐**提高。He has made steady progress in his study.

③ 天色**逐渐**暗下来了。It is darker and darker.

④ 她的脸**逐渐**变得苍白。Her face became paler and paler.

⑤ 太阳出来了,室内**逐渐**亮了起来。The room was brighter and brighter as the sun rose.

⑥ 这条新修的商业街**逐渐**热闹起来了。The newly-built trade street is more and more exciting and noisy.

以上各例除例②外,都不能用“逐步”;例②可换用“逐步”,侧重点不同 ◇ With the exception of example ②, 逐步 cannot be used in all the examples above. In example ②逐步 can replace 逐渐,but with a different stress.

主意 办法 措施

(名) (名) (名)

zhǔyi bànfǎ cuòshī

Ⓔ idea,plan/ method,measure/ measure

名词"主意"、"办法"、"措施"都可表示处理事情或解决问题的方法、程序。但"措施"较正式,用于较大的事情;"主意"还可表示主见、办法等,大事小事都可用 ◇ The nouns 主意,办法 and 措施 all mean "measure,method of dealing with business or solving problems". 措施 is more formal,and is applied to more serious problems; 主意 can also mean"one's own judgment,method,etc."and is applied to serious business as well as trifles.

① 这事我真不知道怎么办好,你给我出个**主意**吧。I don't know how to deal with it. Please tell me a way.

② 遇事一定要拿得定**主意**,不能左右摇摆。We should be firm when facing a difficulty and shouldn't be in two minds.

以上例①"出主意",是习惯搭配,是"想办法"、"想对策"的意思;例②"拿得定主意"表示有主见。其他两个词都不能这样用 ◇ In example ① above,出主意 is an idiomatic phrase meaning "to think of a way or countermeasure";in example ②拿得定主意 means"to have an idea of one's own". The other two words cannot be so used.

③ 我们要针对具体情况,制定可行的**措施**。A feasible measure should be carried out according to the facts.

④ 这些**措施**很不得力。These measure are not very effective.

以上例③"制定措施"是常用搭配;例④"措施(不)得力"也是常见的搭配。其他两词不能这样用 ◇ In example ③ above 制定措施 is a common phrase. In example ④措施(不)得力 is also a common phrase. The other two words have no such usages.

⑤ 他坚持那样做,大家也没**办法**。We have no way if he insists on doing so.

以上例⑤"没办法"表示无能为力,是口语中常用的,其他两个词不能这样用 ◇ In example ⑤ above,没办法 is a common colloquial phrase meaning cannot do anything. The other two words have no such usage.

在表示一般的处理事情、解决问题的程序、方法时,三个词可以通用 ◇ To mean "a general way

or procedure to deal with a matter or solve problems", the three words are interchangeable, e. g. :

⑥ 这是一个很好的**主意**(/**办法**/**措施**)。This is a good idea.

⑦ 这个**主意**(/**办法**/**措施**)很能解决实际问题。The idea is very effective and practical.

还要注意一些习惯搭配。如"好主意"、"好办法"、"好(的)措施",都可以。"坏主意"可以。"有主意、没主意"、"有办法、没办法"可以,"有措施"、"没措施",除特定语境,一般少用 ◇ There are some idiomatic phrases, such as 好主意(a good idea), 好办法(a good way), 好(的)措施(a good measure), 坏主意(an evil idea) is also a common phrase. 有主意(have an idea), 没主意(have no idea), 有办法(have a way), 没办法(have no way) are common, while 有措施(have a measure), 没措施(have no measure) are rarely used except in certain circumstances.

嘱咐 吩咐

(动) (动)

zhǔfù fēnfù

Ⓔ exhort, tell/instruct, tell

"嘱咐"和"吩咐"都有把自己的要求告诉对方,希望别人照办的意思(如例①②③)。"嘱咐"主要是要别人记住现在或以后该做什么(如例④⑤⑥),"吩咐"还有要求别人马上照办的意思(如例⑦⑧) ◇ Both 嘱咐 and 吩咐 mean" to tell sb. one's request and have him or her act accordingly (as in examples ①②③)". 嘱咐 stresses the senses of asking the person remember what to do (as in examples ④⑤⑥); 吩咐 also demands immediate execution (as in examples ⑦⑧):

① 妈妈**嘱咐**(/**吩咐**)了几句,就上班去了。The mother exhorted him a little and went to work.

② 我已经**嘱咐**(/**吩咐**)她好几次了,出去一定要锁门。I exhorted her many times that she must lock the door when she left.

③ 大夫**嘱咐**(/**吩咐**)家属给病人多喝水。The doctor told the relatives of the patient to give more water to the patient.

④ 他一次又一次地**嘱咐**孩子,千万要注意安全。He told the child again and again to be careful of security.

⑤ 妻子上班前**嘱咐**过他要按时吃药。His wife told him to take medicine on time before she went to work.

⑥ 妈妈**嘱咐**爸爸下了飞机马上给家里来电话。My mother told my father to phone home as soon as he boarded off the plane.

⑦ 有什么事您尽管**吩咐**。Please tell us if you want us to do something.

⑧ 经理**吩咐**司机在楼门口等他。The manager told the driver to wait for him at the building gate.

两个词都可以做主、宾语 ◇ Both words can function as the subject and the object:

⑨ 父母的**嘱咐**语重心长。Parents' word is meaningful.

⑩ 经理的**吩咐**，应该照办，别误了事。You should do according the manager's order and do not delay it.

⑪ 孩子牢牢记着母亲临终前的**嘱咐**。The child keeps his mother's last instructions in mind forever.

⑫ 听完队长的**吩咐**，大家分头执行。Everyone takes action after receiving the captain's order.

“嘱咐”还可以重叠为 ABAB 式，“吩咐”少用 ◇ 嘱咐 can be reduplicated into 嘱咐嘱咐，but 吩咐 is rarely so used:

⑬ 您得好好**嘱咐嘱咐**他，免得他再出去惹是生非。You'd better educate him lest he makes troubles.

著名 有名

（形） （形）

zhùmíng yǒumíng

Ⓔ famous, well-known/ famous, celebrated

◪“著名”、“有名”这两个形容词都表示有名声或名字为很多人知道，一般做定语和谓语。“著名”常用于书面语，含褒义；“有名”用于口语（并可做状语，如例⑤），除含褒义外，有时还可用于贬义 ◇ Both 著名 and 有名 are adjectives indicating that the name is known by a lot of people. Both can function as attributive and predicate. 著名 is literary with a laudatory sense. 有名 is colloquial (and can function as an adverbial, as in example ⑤, and besides the laudatory sense, it can also be used in a derogatory sense. e. g. :

① 齐白石是中国**著名**（/**有名**）的画家。Qi Baishi is a famous Chinese painter.

② 王大夫是这家医院**著名**（/**有名**）的外科专家。Dr. Wang is a famous surgeon expert of this area.

③ 杭州的龙井茶很**著名**（/**有名**）。The Dragon Well tea produced in Hangzhou is well-known.

④ 他好吃懒做是**有名**的。He is

Z

notorious for his laziness.

⑤ 他这个人**有名**的自私自利。He is notorious for his selfishness and greed.

例④⑤含贬义，又很口语化，不能用"著名" ◇ Examples ④ and ⑤ are both derogatory and very colloquial, therefore 著名 cannot be used.

转变 改变

（动） （动）

zhuǎnbiàn gǎibiàn

Ⓔ change, transform/change

◥ 动词"转变"、"改变"都有发生变化，和以前不一样的意思。但具体含义和使用范围有区别 ◇ Both verbs 转变 and 改变 mean "to have changed and be different from before", but they are different in actual meaning and usage.

1. "转变"表示由于外界的影响，一种情况变为另一种情况，指人的思想、立场、行动等，一般从坏向好的方面发展 ◇ 转变 indicates that a certain situation changes to another situation owing to outer influence; it is usually applied to a person's thought, stand, action, etc., generally turning from bad to good:

① 对犯错误的青少年要耐心地引导和教育，使他们的思想逐步**转变**过来。We should give patient guide and instructions to the teenagers who made mistakes, and help them change to good gradually.

② 一个人**转变**立场不是短时间可以做到的。Time cannot quickly make a person to change his stand.

③ 他积极地改正自己的缺点，人们对他的看法也逐渐**转变**了。He paid much attention to his shortcoming correction, and as a result people changed their attitudes toward him.

④ 他前一段时间灰心丧气、意志衰退，现在有了明显的**转变**。He was discouraged and had a weak will those days, he has changed obviously at present.

以上各例，也可用"改变"，但用"转变"一般突出了由坏变好的意思 ◇ In the examples above 改变 can be used instead, but 转变 highlights the turning from bad to good.

2. "改变"，使用范围比"转变"广泛，人为的主动因素有时也略强；可以表示思想、立场、观点等的变化，还可以用来表示面貌、状况、性格、态度、风气等的变化，可能是由好变坏，也可能是由坏变好，可用于具体事物或抽象事物 ◇ 改变 can be used in a wider scope than 转变 and involves more initiative. It can be applied to the change of thought, stand, viewpoint, etc. and also to the appearance, situation, character, attitude, trend, etc. It may be a change from good to bad, or vice versa, and it can be applied to concrete things as well as abstract things. e. g.

① 几年不见,他的性格有所**改变**。He has changed a little in his character since I met him several years ago.

② 他的看法**改变**了,不支持我们了。He changed his idea and did not support us any longer.

③ 这种坏风气非**改变**不可。The evil practice must be removed.

④ 要**改变**这个城市的交通状况,就得下大力气改造道路设施。Much efforts should be made to improve the road facilities if we want to change the traffic situation of the city.

⑤ 社会发展的总趋势是不可**改变**的。We cannot change the general trend of social development.

⑥ 她请理发师给她**改变**一下发型。She had her hairstyle changed.

⑦ 我想**改变**一下室内家具的摆法。I want to get the display of the furniture in the room changed.

以上各例一般均不用"转变"◇ In the examples above, 转变 is not used.

Z

状况 状态

(名) (名)

zhuàngkuàng zhuàngtài

Ⓔ condition, state of affairs/ condition, state of affairs

"状况"、"状态"这两个名词都表示事物所呈现出的某种情况或样子,但侧重点不同。"状况"侧重于事物呈现的具体情况、形势,如"身体状况"、"政治状况"、"生活状况"、"生产状况"等;而"状态"则侧重于人或事物表现的形态,如"固体状态"、"液体状态"、"心理状态"、"停滞状态"◇ Both 状况 and 状态 indicate the state of affairs, but the stress is different. 状况 stresses the actual state of affairs, e. g. 身体状况(health), 政治状况(political situation), 生活状况(life), 生产状况(production) etc. while 状态 stresses the state or the formation, e. g. 固体状态(the state of solid)、液体状态(the state of liquid)、心理状态(state of mind)、停滞状态(stagnation). e. g.:

① 他家的经济**状况**不错。The financial situation of his family is not too bad.

② 母亲的健康**状况**近来有所好转。My mother becomes more

and more healthy.

③ 老师应全面了解学生的学习**状况**,以便进行有针对性的教学。A teacher should know students globally so that he or she can teach them with an aim.

④ 那片小麦生长**状况**很好。The wheat grows well in that land.

⑤ 病人处于昏迷**状态**。The patient was in coma.

⑥ 他最近精神**状态**甚佳。He was in good mood recently.

⑦ 这种无政府**状态**应该改变了。It's time for the undisciplined behavior to change.

一般情况下,充当句子成分时"状况"、"状态"前多带定语 ◇ As a rule, when used in a sentence 状况、状态 usually takes attributives.

以上各例"状况"、"状态"是不能互换的 ◇ In all the examples above 状况、状态 are not interchangeable.

▶[情况 qíngkuàng—情形 qíngxíng]

准 (形、动、副) zhǔn　准确 (形) zhǔnquè

Ⓔ accurate; allow, permit; definitely/ accurate, precise

"准"、"准确"都是形容词。"准"较口语化,"准确"较书面化。"准"还是动词和副词。具体区别如下 ◇ Both 准 and 准确 are adjectives. 准 is more colloquial and 准确 is more literary. 准 is also a verb and adverb. Their differences in usage are as follows:

1. 形容词"准"、"准确"都有正确无误的意思。"准"往往侧重于没有差误,"准确"则侧重于行动结果完全符合实际或要求。"准"在句中常做谓语、补语;"准确"除做谓语、补语外,还可做定语、状语 ◇ The adjectives 准 and 准确 both mean "accurate". 准 stresses the sense of there being no mistake while 准确 stresses that the result of an action entirely coincides with reality or demand. 准 often functions as predicate and complement, while 准确, besides being a predicate and complement, can also function as attributive and adverbial. e. g. :

① 我的手表不**准**,每天要快两分钟左右。My watch cannot keep good time, and it's two minutes fast every day.

② 他打枪打得真**准**。He can shoot the target accurately.

③ 她英语的发音很**准**(/**准确**)。Her English pronunciation is standard.

④ 那个篮球运动员,投篮投得相当**准**(/**准确**)。The basketball

player can shoot accurately.

⑤ **准确**的发音，对学外语是很重要的。Accurate pronunciation is important to English learning.

⑥ 这个词**准确**的解释应该怎样？What's the exact meaning of the word?

⑦ 他**准确**地回答了那五个问题。He answered the five questions correctly.

以上例①②侧重于没有差误，而且又是习惯搭配，用"准"。例③④做谓语和补语，两个词可互换，侧重点略有不同。⑤⑥⑦中做定语或状语，用"准确"（与后边词语为多音节有关），"准"不能这样用 ◇ In examples ① and ② the stress is on no mistake and both are idiomatic expressions, so 准 is used. In examples ③ and ④, as predicate and complement, the two words are interchangeable with different stresses. In examples ⑤⑥ and ⑦, as attributive and adverbial, 准确 is used (because the following phrase is polysyllabic), and 准 cannot be so used.

形容词"准"，还可表示确定不变，"准确"无此义 ◇ The adjective 准 can also mean "ascertained or determined", while 准确 has no such meaning.

⑧ 时间已经定**准**了，不能再改了。Since we settled the time, it cannot be changed.

⑨ 他没有**准**主意，一会儿想这样，一会儿想那样。He's changeable, and now this way, now that way.

2. "准"还是动词，有允许、同意的意思，"准确"不能这样用 ◇ 准 is also a verb meaning "to allow, to permit". 准确 has no such meaning. e. g. :

① 我想请几天假，不知领导**准**不**准**。I want to ask a few days off, and I wonder whether I will be permitted.

② 领导**准**了你的假。You've got the permission from your superior for your holidays.

③ 这台精密仪器，不**准**随便乱动。You're not allowed to touch the precise device.

④ 妈妈不**准**她参加那个舞会，她很难过。Her mother did not allowed her to take part in that party so she was upset.

3. "准"也是副词，"准确"无此用法 ◇ 准 is also an adverb. 准确 has no such usage.

(1) 表示一种估计（说话人认为这种估计是有把握的）◇ To indicate "an estimation (the speaker is sure of his or her estimation)":

① 他这么晚还不回来，**准**是在外边吃饭了。He hasn't come back so late, and I think he must dine out.

② 你去求求他,他**准**答应。If you go to ask for him, he must be likely to promise you.

③ 下午他**准**会来找你的。He must be likely to come to you this afternoon.

(2) 表示肯定,确定不移 ◇ To indicate "certainty". e. g. :

④ 放心吧! 这本书三天之内**准**还给你。Be assured! I will return you the book in three days.

⑤ 他临走时说到了上海**准**给我们写信。As he was leaving he said he was likely to write us when arriving in Shanghai.

⑥ 这花十分娇嫩,如果不小心侍弄**准**活不了。The flower is very delicate, and it cannot survive if you don't grow it properly.

⑦ 现在出发**准**能赶上早上 9 点的那趟火车。If we start now, we can surely catch the 9 o'clock train.

准备 (动) zhǔnbèi　预备 (动) yùbèi

Ⓔ prepare/prepare

"准备"、"预备"这两个动词都表示打算,预先安排。有时两个词可互换 ◇ Both 准备 and 预备 mean "to plan or arrange beforehand". Sometimes the two words are interchangeable:

① 你**准备**(/**预备**)考哪个大学? Which university do you prefer?

② 主人已经为客人**准备**(/**预备**)好了房间。The host has prepared the room for the guests.

不同点在于 ◇ The differences are as follows:

1."准备"侧重于事先考虑的条件和目的性,"预备"侧重于程序性 ◇ 准备 stresses the conditions and purpose considered beforehand; 预备 stresses the procedure:

① 这件事我还没做好**准备**。I am not ready for it.

② 这只是个**预备**会议,正式会议将在两周后举行。This is only a preparatory meeting. The formal one will be held in two weeks.

再如一些口令:"预备——放"、"预备——开始"等,都强调程序、步骤。"不打无准备之仗"等强调目的性 ◇ Commands such as: 预备——放, 预备——开始, etc. all stress procedure and step. 不打无准备之仗(fight no war unprepared) stresses the aim.

2."准备"可做宾语,如 1 中例①的"做准备",再如"有准备"、"进行准备"等。"预备"不能这样搭配 ◇ 准备 can function as the object, as 做准备(make preparations) in example ① of 1 and

有准备(be well prepared),进行准备(be preparing), etc. 预备 cannot make up such phrases.

但"预备"可构成"预备会议"(1中例②)、"预备队"、"预备役"、"预备党员"、"预备性会谈"等固定短语。"准备"不能这样搭配 ◇ But 预备 can make up set phrases such as 预备会议(as in example ② of 1),预备队(reserve force),预备役(reserve duty),预备党员(probationary party member),预备性会谈(preparatory talks), etc. 准备 cannot make up such phrases.

而"准备"可说"思想准备"、"精神准备"等;"预备"不能这样用 ◇ And 准备 can make up phrases such as 思想准备(mental preparation),精神准备(spiritual preparation), etc. 预备 cannot be so used. e. g. :

① 他们为这次登山活动,已经做好了充分的物质和精神**准备**。They have been well prepared in material and spirits for the climbing.

② 学校一般在第一节课上课10分钟之前,先打**预备**铃。Generally speaking, the preparatory bell rings ten minutes before the beginning of the first class in the school.

由于"准备"词义较为丰富,"预备"词义较为单纯,所以,可说"准备得很充分"、"做了充分的准备"(例①)等,"预备"不能这样用 ◇ Since 准备 has rather rich meanings while the meaning of 预备 is simple, one usually says 准备得很充分(well-prepared),做了充分的准备(well-prepared)(as in example ①), etc. 预备 cannot be so used.

总之,凡是有这些不同点的,不能互换。表示一般的打算、事先安排,可以互换(如最前面的例①②) ◇ All in all, when there are such differences the two words are not interchangeable. When applied to general plan or preparation, they are interchangeable (as in examples ①and ②).

姿势 (名) zīshì　　姿态 (名) zītài

Ⓔ posture, gesture/ posture, gesture

"姿势"和"姿态"都可以表示体态,当它们都用于人并和神情有关时,可互换使用,如例①② ◇ 姿势 and 姿态 both indicate "posture". When they are applied to human beings and facial expression, the two are interchangeable, as in examples ①②:

① 乐队指挥的**姿势**(/**姿态**)优

美、大方,动作有节奏,有感情。The posture of the music band conductor is elegant with rhythm and passion.

② 画面上的少女**姿势**(/**姿态**)端庄美丽。The posture of the girls in the painting is very graceful and beautiful.

当只表示人的具体样子,与神情无关时,用"姿势",不用"姿态" ◇ When it indicates only the gesture regardless of the expression, 姿势 and not 姿态 is used:

③ 练太极拳时,每个**姿势**都要准确到位。Every posture should be correct while you practice Taiji.

④ 他摆好**姿势**和老师合影。He posted for a photograph with his teacher.

⑤ 老师要求学生坐的**姿势**要端正。The teacher asked the students to sit well.

有时"姿势"还可用于人以外的动物和植物 ◇ Sometimes, 姿势 can be applied to animals or plants instead of human beings:

⑥ 这盆花一点儿**姿势**没有,你来修剪一下吧。The flower in the pot is in no beautiful posture, so prone it.

⑦ 老猫伸了伸腰,摆出一付懒散的**姿势**。The old cat stretched out and was in a lazy posture.

"姿态"还有态度和气度的意思,"姿势"没有这个意思 ◇ 姿态 also means " manner and bearing", but 姿势 has no such meaning:

⑧ 你是领导,**姿态**要高一些嘛!You are the leader and you should be tolerant.

⑨ 他那高傲的**姿态**令人敬而远之。His arrogance makes him awesome.

⑩ 大家要以主人翁的**姿态**参加有关学校规划的讨论。Everyone joined the discussion on school's planning as its host.

仔细 (形) zǐxì　　细致 (形) xìzhì

Ⓔ careful/careful, meticulous

1. "仔细"、"细致"都表示做事用心、周到、细密,连小的地方也不放过 ◇ Both 仔细 and 细致 mean " considerate, with great care, even to the minute places". e. g. :

① 他非常**仔细**(/**细致**),当产品质量检查员很合适。He is very careful and suitable for a quality examiner.

② 我做事比较马虎,可不如姐姐**仔细**(/**细致**)。I am not as careful as my sister, for I'm careless.

③ 对病人的 X 光片,医生观察

Z

得很**仔细**(/**细致**)。The doctor examined the patient's X-film very carefully.

④ 这是个**仔细**(/**细致**)活儿,得有耐心才行。This is a delicate job, and you should be patient with it.

⑤ 她耳朵贴着窗户**仔细**地听着外面的动静。She put her ear to the window to listen to what happened outside.

⑥ 桌面上的斑痕很不明显,不**仔细**看,就看不出来。The black spot on the table is not very obvious, and you will not see it if you are careless.

以上例①②③④做谓语、补语、定语,"仔细"、"细致"都可用 ◇ In the examples ①②③ and ④ above, as predicate, complement and attributive, either 仔细 or 细致 can be used.

"细致"很少做状语,所以例⑤⑥用"仔细"。"仔细"可以重叠(AABB 式),多做状语(如例⑦),"细致"不能重叠 ◇ 细致 is rarely used as an adverbial, so in examples ⑤ and ⑥ 仔细 is used. 仔细 can be reduplicated into 仔仔细细, mostly used as adverbial (as in example ⑦). 细致 cannot be reduplicated.

⑦ 我做完后,又**仔仔细细**地检查了一遍,没有发现什么错误。After I finished it, I examined it carefully and found few mistakes in it.

2."仔细"还有提醒人小心、注意的意思,"细致"没有这个用法 ◇ 仔细 can also be used to remind a person to be careful, but 细致 cannot be so used. e. g. :

① 他的嘴快得很,这事让他知道了,**仔细**他传出去。He has a fast tongue; if he knows it, beware that he will spread it.

② 天黑路滑,开车**仔细**点儿。It's dark and slippery at night, so be careful at the wheel.

3."仔细"还指生活节俭,"细致"没有这个意思 ◇ 仔细 also means "frugal". 细致 has no such meaning. :

① 由于父母过日子非常**仔细**,所以孩子们也养成了勤俭节约的好习惯。Because the parents lived a frugal life, their children developed the good habit of thrift as well.

② 他们家用钱**仔细**,收入虽不多,生活上也没什么问题。Their family live a frugal life, though their income is not much, their life is not hard.

4."细致"还指物品的加工非常精致细密,连最小的地方都不马虎 ◇ 细致 also means "the workmanship of some objects is very exquisite and even so in the smallest details",e. g. :

① 这套西装的手工非常**细致**。The workmanship of the suit is very delicate.

② 这些工艺品加工**细致**,形状别致,很吸引人。The workmanship of these arts crafts is delicate and they are shaped dedicatedly and very attractive.

③ 作家对小说中几个主要人物的心理描写得十分**细致**。The writer gives a vivid account of the characters' mentality in the novel.

以上各例中"细致"都不能用"仔细"替换 ◇ In the examples above, 细致 cannot be replaced by 仔细.

5. 有时"细致"还指木材或布料的纹理细密,"仔细"没有这个意思 ◇ Sometimes 细致 also means "very fine in the grain of wood or cloth". 仔细 has no such meaning. :

① 这种木料纹理**细致**,适合做高级家具。The grain of the wood is fine and it is suitable for high-grade furniture.

② 那种布织得很**细致**。The cloth is woven very finely and close.

▶[细心 xìxīn—仔细 zǐxì]

钻研 (动) zuānyán　研究 (动) yánjiū

Ⓔ study intensively/ study, research

◪ 动词"钻研"、"研究"都有思索、探求的意思,但使用范围和语意轻重程度等有所不同,"钻研"不能重叠为 AABB 式,"研究"可以重叠为 ABAB 式 ◇ Both 钻研 and 研究 as verbs mean "to study or research",but they have different scope of usage and emphasis. 钻研 cannot be reduplicated AABB, while 研究 can be reduplicated into 研究研究.

1. 钻研

指深入研究,其对象为科学、技术、学问等 ◇ Meaning "to study intensively",the object of which is science, technique, learning, etc. :

① 他近年来,一直潜心**钻研**古代汉语的虚词用法,很有成绩。In recent years, he has been studying the usage of the formal words in Ancient Chinese, and has made great progress in it.

② 老王对这个专题,钻研得很细。For this subject, Lao Wang has made a careful study.

③ 他用心**钻研**业务,工作能力提高得很快。He is devoted to his job and he has made progress in his work quickly.

2. 研究

(1) 指(对事物的真象、性质、规

律等)进行探索 ◇ Meaning "research on (the truth, nature, rule, etc.)":

① 他专门**研究**现代汉语语法。He is dedicated to the study of Ancient Chinese grammar.

② 我对中国历史毫无**研究**,只知道一些常识性的东西。I made no special study about Chinese history and I only have a general knowledge of it.

③ 这个**研究**课题由他们三个人承担。They three are responsible for the subject research.

④ 他**研究**"了"的用法,已经两年了。He has been studying the usage of Chinese character 了 for two years.

(2) 指(对事情、问题等)进行商量、讨论 ◇ Meaning "to discuss, to talk over (matters, problems, etc.)":

⑤ 你们提的意见领导要**研究**以后才能答复。The leader will give you a reply after discussing your proposal.

⑥ 他提的建议我们应该好好**研究**一下。His suggestion should be discussed carefully.

⑦ 这个工作计划得**研究研究**再确定。The work plan should be decided after careful consideration.

以上例①~例⑦都不能用"钻研"替换 ◇ In the examples of ①~⑦ 研究 cannot be replaced by 钻研.

Z

最近 (名) zuìjìn　近来 (名) jìnlái

Ⓔ recently, lately/ lately, recently

◪"最近"、"近来"都是时间名词。"最近"指现在前后不久的时光(一两天至几个月、几年都可以),可以放在具体的约略时间之前,也可以单用 ◇ Both 最近 and 近来 are nouns of time. 最近 indicates the time around the present (a few days, months, even a few years). It can be placed before an approximate time, or used independently:

① **最近**两三天他就要到了。(指以后) He will arrive in a couple days. (within two or three days)

② **最近**几年这里没发生洪水。(指以前) There's been no flood here over the past few years. (in recent years)

③ **最近**他出差了,不在家。(指说话之前之后) He is not in for he has been on business recently. (recently)

"最近"单用时(如例③)表示的时间段较短 ◇ When used independently (as in example ③), 最近 indicates "a relatively short period of time".

"近来"则指过去不久的一段时间(至现在为止),常单用 ◇ 近来 indicates "the short period of time up to the present", and is usually used independently:

④ **近来**身体怎么样? How've you been feeling these days?

⑤ 我**近来**比较忙。I have been busy these days.

⑥ **近来**天气有些反常。It is a bit abnormal recently.

例④⑤⑥也可用"最近",但表示的时间段较短 ◇ In examples ④ ⑤and ⑥,最近 can be used instead, but indicates "a shorter period of time".

作 (动) zuò　　做 (动) zuò

Ⓔ happen, do/
do, make, produce, be

"作"常表示抽象的动作,"做"常表示具体的动作。但其间还有不少例外;近年来这两个词的用法也有一些变化 ◇ 作 often indicates abstract action, while 做 means "concrete action"; however, there are a few exceptions. In recent years, the meanings of the two words have changed a little.

1. 表示发生、发作、出现,用"作",如"枪声大作"、"雷雨大作"、"一鼓作气"、"作怪"等 ◇ To mean "to happen, to take place, to appear", 作 is used, e.g.:枪声大作(heavy fighting broke out), 雷雨大作(a fierce thunderstorm broke out),一鼓作气(press on to the finish without letup),作怪(stir up trouble), etc.

2. 两个词都可用于表示从事某种活动,后面的宾语是具体的名词时,宜用"做",如:"做生意"、"做"、"做事";包括一些新出现的词语,如"做头发"、"做节目" ◇ The two words can indicate doing something when their object is a concrete noun, "do" is OK. For example,做生意(do business)做事(work), which include some new meanings as 做头发(do hairstyle), 做节目(produce programs).

宾语是双音节动词或抽象名词时,宜用"作",如:"作调查"、"作分析"、"作出成绩"、"作出努力" ◇ If their object is disyllabic,作 is preferred. For example, 做调查(conduct a survey),做分析(analyze),做出成绩(make achievements),作出努力(make efforts).

3. 表示制造,多用"做",如:"做家具、做衣服" ◇ To mean "to manufacture", 做 is usually used, e.g.:做家具(make furniture),

Z

做衣服(make clothes).

4. 表示写作(或与写作有关),用“作”,如:“作文”、“作画”、“作曲”。有时也可用“做” ◇ To mean " to write, to compose", 作 is used, e. g. :作文(write a composition),作画(draw a painting),作曲(compose a piece of music).

5. 表示充当、担任,用“做”,如:“做老师的”、“做爸爸的”、“做官”、“做个好学生”、“做谓语”。近年也有用“作”的 ◇ To mean " to be or to act as", 做 is used, e. g. :做老师的(be a teacher),做爸爸的(be a father),做官(be an official),做个好学生(be a good student),做谓语(be predicate). Recently 作 is also used.

6. 表示当做、作为,用“作”,如:“拜他作老师”、“过期作废” ◇ To mean " to regard as", 作 is used, e. g. :拜他作老师(regard him as a teacher),过期作废(invalid after the expiry date).

7. 表示装出某种样子或制造出某种情况,用“作”,如:“弄虚作假”、“扭捏作态”、“装模作样” ◇ To mean "to pretend, to be affected", 作 is used, e. g. :弄虚作假(practise fraud),扭捏作态(hem and haw),装模作样(be affected).

8. 表示结成(某种关系),用“做”,如:“做朋友”、“做兄弟”、“做对头” ◇ To mean " to form (certain relationship)", 做 is used, e. g. :做朋友(be friends),做兄弟(be brothers),做对头(be enemy).

9. 表示做什么用时,用“做”,如:“做课本”、“做原料”、“拿他的信做证明”。也有用“作”的 ◇ To mean " to use as", 做 is used, e. g. : 做课本(take as a textbook),做原料(take as raw materials),拿他的信做证明(take his letter as a certificate). 作 can also be used.

“作”还可以放在双音节动词之前,表示进行,如:“作调查”、“作分析”,也可扩展为:“作深入的调查”、“作详尽的分析” ◇ 作 can be placed before a disyllabic verb to mean "to carry on", e. g. :作调查(conduct a survey),作分析(make analysis),作深入的调查(conduct in-depth investigation),作详尽的分析(make thorough analysis).

10. “作”在词语中表示创作的作品,如“大作”、“近作”、“拙作”等 ◇ 作 is also a word which means " created work", e. g. :大作(masterpiece),近作(recent works),拙作(hum poor works), etc.

▶[当 dāng—做 zuò]
[干 gàn—做 zuò—搞 gǎo]

Z